Organizational Paradigms of Global Business:

Fusion of Technology and Cultural Diversity

Alessandra Ricciardelli
University of Naples "Federico II", Italy

Maurizio Decastri
University of Rome Tor Vergata, Italy

A volume in the Advances in Business Strategy and Competitive Advantage (ABSCA) Book Series

IGI Global
PUBLISHER of TIMELY KNOWLEDGE

Published in the United States of America by
IGI Global
Business Science Reference (an imprint of IGI Global)
701 E. Chocolate Avenue
Hershey PA, USA 17033
Tel: 717-533-8845
Fax: 717-533-8661
E-mail: cust@igi-global.com
Web site: http://www.igi-global.com

Library of Congress Cataloging-in-Publication Data

CIP DATA PROCESSING

ISBN13: 9798369334829
EISBN13: 9798369334836
Isbn13Softcover: 9798369350249

This book is published in the IGI Global book series Advances in Business Strategy and Competitive Advantage (ABSCA) (ISSN: 2327-3429; eISSN: 2327-3437)

British Cataloguing in Publication Data
A Cataloguing in Publication record for this book is available from the British Library.

For electronic access to this publication, please contact: eresources@igi-global.com.

Advances in Business Strategy and Competitive Advantage (ABSCA) Book Series

Patricia Ordóñez de Pablos
Universidad de Oviedo, Spain

ISSN:2327-3429
EISSN:2327-3437

Mission

Business entities are constantly seeking new ways through which to gain advantage over their competitors and strengthen their position within the business environment. With competition at an all-time high due to technological advancements allowing for competition on a global scale, firms continue to seek new ways through which to improve and strengthen their business processes, procedures, and profitability.

The **Advances in Business Strategy and Competitive Advantage (ABSCA) Book Series** is a timely series responding to the high demand for state-of-the-art research on how business strategies are created, implemented and re-designed to meet the demands of globalized competitive markets. With a focus on local and global challenges, business opportunities and the needs of society, the **ABSCA** encourages scientific discourse on doing business and managing information technologies for the creation of sustainable competitive advantage.

Coverage

- Entrepreneurship & Innovation
- Strategic Management
- Value Creation
- Strategy Performance Management
- Economies of Scale
- International Business Strategy
- Tacit Knowledge
- Business Models
- Customer-Orientation Strategy
- Foreign Investment Decision Process

IGI Global is currently accepting manuscripts for publication within this series. To submit a proposal for a volume in this series, please contact our Acquisition Editors at acquisitions@igi-global.com or visit: https://www.igi-global.com/publish/.

The Advances in Business Strategy and Competitive Advantage (ABSCA) Book Series (ISSN 2327-3429) is published by IGI Global, 701 E. Chocolate Avenue, Hershey, PA 17033-1240, USA, www.igi-global.com. This series is composed of titles available for purchase individually; each title is edited to be contextually exclusive from any other title within the series. For pricing and ordering information please visit https://www.igi-global.com/book-series/advances-business-strategy-competitive-advantage/73672. Postmaster: Send all address changes to above address.

Titles in this Series

For a list of additional titles in this series, please visit:
www.igi-global.com/book-series/advances-business-strategy-competitive-advantage/73672

Building Organizational Resilience With Neuroleadership
Shefali Saluja (Chitkara Business School, Chitkara University, India) Jyoti Kukreja (Jagannath International Management School, India) and Sandhir Sharma (Chitkara Business School, Chitkara University, ndia)
Business Science Reference • © 2024 • 352pp • H/C (ISBN: 9798369317853) • US $275.00

Business Continuity Management and Resilience Theories, Models, and Processes
José Carlos Rouco (Universidade Lusófona, Portugal) and Paula Cristina Nunes Figueiredo (Universidade Lusofona, Porugal)
Business Science Reference • © 2024 • 333pp • H/C (ISBN: 9798369316580) • US $290.00

Applying Business Intelligence and Innovation to Entrepreneurship
Kannapat Kankaew (International College, Burapha University, Thailand) Parinya Nakpathom (International College, Burapha University, Thailand) Alhuda Chnitphattana (International College, Burapha University, Thailand) Krittipat Pitchayadejanant (International College, Burapha University, Thailand) and Siwaporn Kunnapapdeelert (Faculty of Logistics and Transportation Management, Panyapiwat Institute of Management, Thailand)
Business Science Reference • © 2024 • 346pp • H/C (ISBN: 9798369318461) • US $275.00

Fostering Innovation in Venture Capital and Startup Ecosystems
Renuka Sharma (Chitkara Business School, Chitkara University, Punjab, India) Kiran Mehta (Chitkara Business School, Chitkara University, Punjab, India) and Poshan Yu (Soochow University, China & Australian Studies Centre, Shanghai University, China)
Business Science Reference • © 2024 • 430pp • H/C (ISBN: 9798369313268) • US $270.00

Entrepreneurship and Creativity in the Metaverse
Shivani Inder (Chitkara Business School, Chitkara University, India) Byoung-chul Min (Chung-Ang University, South Korea) and Sandhir Sharma (Chitkara Business School, Chitkara University, India)
Business Science Reference • © 2024 • 301pp • H/C (ISBN: 9798369317341) • US $275.00

Reskilling the Workforce in the Labor Market The Country Cases
Oytun Meçik (Eskişehir Osmangazi University, Turkey)
Business Science Reference • © 2024 • 286pp • H/C (ISBN: 9798369336694) • US $295.00

IGI Global
PUBLISHER of TIMELY KNOWLEDGE

701 East Chocolate Avenue, Hershey, PA 17033, USA
Tel: 717-533-8845 x100 • Fax: 717-533-8661
E-Mail: cust@igi-global.com • www.igi-global.com

Table of Contents

Detailed Table of Contents

This chapter deals with diverse organisational models pivotal in global business landscapes. Beginning with fundamental frameworks, it explores renowned models. Shifting beyond the traditional geocentric models, the discussion advances into the heterarchy, emphasising flexibility and adaptive structures. It then scrutinises the transnational organisation, fostering global integration whilst preserving local responsiveness up until the investigation on the metanational organisation, emphasising interconnectedness and collaborative networks. The chapter additionally examines the strategies of emerging market multinationals and digital multinationals by illuminating innovative approaches in global business paradigms. It explains the dynamic evolution of organisational structures within international companies, reflecting the ever-changing demands and opportunities of the global marketplace. Throughout, this chapter offers insights into the dynamic evolution of organisational structures within international companies, reflecting the ever-changing demands of the global marketplace.

This chapter focuses on the topic of organisational structures and addresses its contents by dealing with two fundamental issues. The first one deals with different types of international structures found in the global business sphere. It also offers an in-depth analysis of how these structures accommodate diverse geographical footprints, cultural disparities, and operational complexities encountered in a globalised setting. The second one refers to the strategic decision-making process involved in selecting the appropriate international organisational structure. Factors such as market diversities, regulatory frameworks, cultural intricacies, and operational efficiencies are examined when selecting the optimal structure. This chapter explains the necessary nuanced trade-offs and considerations for aligning the chosen structure with the strategic international objectives of an organisation, emphasizing adaptability, responsiveness, and scalability as crucial determinants in this strategic selection process.

This chapter deals with the core of conflicts arising from the territorial control within a broader international context, encompassing two pivotal areas of analysis. The first paragraph explores the intricate dynamics between the territorial control and the host country. It examines historical, political, and socio-economic factors contributing to tensions, shedding light on the divergent interests and power struggles between these entities. A comprehensive understanding of the genesis of conflicts is provided by emphasising the complexities inherent in their relationship. The second paragraph focuses on the allocation of functional responsibilities, separating the delicate balance between centralisation and decentralisation within the territorial control. It suggests new strategies employed in distributing roles and powers by weighing advantages and challenges of both approaches. Overall, this chapter seeks to offer insights into the intricate decision-making processes for achieving an effective and harmonious balance between centralisation and decentralization.

This chapter explores the multifaceted realm of alliances within the international business landscape. It starts with an examination of international alliances and scrutinises how alliances serve as pivotal vehicles for global expansion. It also discusses the relationship between alliances and international companies, unravelling the dynamics underpinning successful collaborations globally. The chapter introduces a managerial reference model clarifying the rationale behind forming alliances by considering some strategic imperatives. It deals with challenges and complexities in cooperation strategies for international expansion, highlighting natural difficulties encountered in such endeavours. Further sections explore the system of international competencies necessary for building and forging effective alliances by explaining how alliances offer organisational alternatives and learning potentials. Lastly, it examines alliance strategies in the context of digitalisation and Industry 4.0, highlighting their evolving significance in a technologically advancing world.

This chapter addresses the challenges posed by cultural differences in a global context. It examines the multifaceted dimensions of cultural differences and their impact on international business environments. It also discusses individual factors affecting the process of adaptation whilst emphasising the role of socialisation. Moreover, it examines the adaptation process through the lens of the position profile, offering insights into the specific challenges and requisites for successful integration. It further analyses the dynamic relationship between national and corporate cultures whilst explaining how these intertwined forces shape organisational strategies, operations, and interactions on the international stage. By exploring the advantages and disadvantages of cultural differences, strategic approaches to mitigate conflicts are suggested. Ultimately, the chapter equips readers with practical insights, tools, and frameworks that are crucial for devising adaptive internationalisation strategies in an increasingly interconnected global environment.

The relationship between national culture and organisational theory has been a subject of deep interest within academic research. This chapter explores the diverse methodological approaches employed in studying such a critical connection, which contribute to understanding how national cultural values affect organisational behaviour, structures, and practices. These perspectives provide information about different cultural aspects, capturing subjective experiences and contextual nuances through ethnographic studies or interviews. Acknowledging the significance of different methodological perspectives is crucial for developing a holistic understanding of how national culture influences organisational theories and practices. By embracing this diversity, practitioners have a more holistic understanding of the interplay between national culture and organisational phenomena.

This chapter deals with the topic of dynamic relationship between culture and management, exploring varying perspectives from the culture-free thesis to the culture-bound outlook. It goes through the studies of Laurent and his Western management styles, Hofstede, and Trompenaars' multifaceted cultural dimensions. Additionally, it examines the GLOBE Study, which synthesized cross-cultural theories, and acknowledges contributions by Triandis, Schneider, Boisot, and Sorge. The chapter addresses the issue of freedom and limitations within cultural action, contemplating the implications in management practices. This comprehensive review not only addresses the methodological aspects but also encompasses the substantive content of culture in the realm of management, offering a multifaceted understanding of its impact, significance, and application within organisational frameworks.

This chapter explores the multifaceted landscape of governance policies within international human resources (HR). It suggests six pivotal dimensions that shape effective governance strategies in multinational corporations. Firstly, it examines the dynamics of inter-company relationships in knowledge creation and dissemination, emphasising collaborative mechanisms. Secondly, it analyses international assignment policies, evaluating their impact on talent retention and global mobility. Thirdly, it addresses the challenges stemming from cultural backgrounds of staff, highlighting strategies to navigate diverse cultural landscapes. Fourthly, it studies the management of international assignments and the criteria for selecting adept global managers. Fifthly, it investigates local staff reactions, emphasising the phenomenon of opposite ethnocentrism and strategies to mitigate its effects. Finally, it assesses the design of HR management systems tailored for global contexts.

Foreword

Multinationals are out on a limb. Again. Four decades ago, they were caught in a divided and unequal world that yearned for integration and convergence. Today, they are caught in a world that, while integrated, remains divided, albeit differently. In strange ways, both nature and culture won. One certainty emerges: it is imperative that we cease oversimplifying the complexity of our world for the sake of convenience.

International Management, specifically the general management of the multinational company as a multinational entity, is intricate and multifaceted. There is little intuitive, let alone instinctive, about it. Establish the local presence of a company in its first host country, and the company suddenly becomes a multinational. Small, perhaps. But requiring robust international management skills and organisational capabilities it does not yet possess. Increase the geographic scope of the multinational, and the challenge multiplies. The company might recruit managers with international experience, but they may lack sufficient knowledge about the company to develop the necessary organisational capabilities. Conversely, if the company relies on its existing managers, they might be inexperienced in managing operations abroad or understanding the required capabilities for a multinational. This is quite a conundrum. Picturing the company as a business is important but will not solve it, as the key lies in managing the development of the budding multinational organisation both locally and globally. This problem alone would be enough to celebrate the work of Alessandra Ricciardelli and Maurizio Decastri and motivate an interested scholar or a studious manager to read their book whose subtitle eloquently conveys its significance. But there is more to this book, directly related to the management of many large incumbent multinationals today. Let me start with a stylised account of their recent past.

For over three decades, starting around 1980, the premise was clear and persuasive. Globalisation was the integration of local markets into a worldwide market. This aggregation was expected to result in a simpler, borderless world where geography took a backseat. Business considerations were paramount, and multinationals, in general, could reap unprecedented benefits from global scaling. Multinational companies rationalised their offerings and operations for the sake of global efficiency and increased competitiveness. 'Global' became synonymous with sameness and centralisation. This approach meant discarding complicated structures and the intricacies of cross-border management. Gradually, the leadership suite of multinational companies had no room for executives in charge of geographies. A new generation of managers was trained in the belief that international business was, well, business. The academic articles and books that founded the field of International Management between the late 60s and the late 80s were slowly shelved. Even the motto 'think global, act local' got lost in the wind of 'one company'. Then, as if in a plot twist, globalisation evolved and shifted, unveiling a path towards a world that was unexpectedly more complex and uncertain.

Reducing countries to market segments and sources of supply efficiency proved to be misleading. Globalisation, after all, is not about markets encompassing the whole of the world, it is about realising that our world is a whole. It is not a simple, stable aggregation; it is a complex, dynamic integration. It is not about sameness: it is about interdependence, horizontal and vertical. 'Global' and 'local' are not opposites calling for some strategic trade-off; they are different levels of our world, mutually determinant, calling for multilevel management skills.

The local level of our world is made of places. A 'place' – say, a country – is a situated whole, made of the differentiated biophysical space in its location and all that there is in it, people included, as well as the interactions in it and with all that is around it, its past and future to be. Each place is unique and irreplicable. Each place contains the specific knowledge that characterises it, implicit and immobile. Local culture, to start with. Local polity, local arts, local customs, local skills, local preferences, and, principally, local ways of learning and producing such local knowledge over time – all shaped by, and shaping, the local environment, local people, and local history. Knowledge that the locals don't even know they know. All things physical in our world, us included, exist in some 'place'. (Even the global headquarters of a multinational is really a local unit somewhere, most often in the company's home country.)

We are local beings, existing and thriving at the local level of our world, a world that is naturally global. Pandemics or climate change uncover the global nature of our world. Globalisation binds us together irreversibly. This came as a surprise, promising and alarming at once. Our local societies, our countries, were never as interconnected and integrated as now. Digital technologies play a key role in that respect. However, the tensions between the local *us* and our global world, which we still tend to describe as tensions between *us* and *them*, remain intractable and pernicious at times. The resulting anxiety, particularly following the 2007-09 financial crisis and even more so after the Covid-19 pandemic, became fertile ground for the rise of nationalism, protectionist policies, and populism. International institutions may be dysfunctional or broken, but we are now in a divided world that is very different from the 60s or the 70s. It is divided and global. And more and more people everywhere recognise the global nature of major challenges that cannot be addressed with local solutions, such as protecting our natural environment or reducing the high level of inequality that now exists within countries in most parts of the world. The globalisation clock may be slow or shaky, but it cannot turn back.

Managing a multinational company as a multinational is now more complex and more puzzling than it ever was. But it is also more compelling. Observing the recent evolution of our globalising world, a few dynamic features are particularly noteworthy. Such an emerging global world disperses world-class knowledge, be it technical knowledge or market knowledge; it deepens international specialisation; highlights differences across and, especially, within countries; shapes complicated international structures, such as multifaceted networks of partnerships or ecosystems, some centripetal, other centrifugal; and it fosters local emergence and objective uncertainty everywhere. Therefore, the more global the world, the more the differences and boundaries across countries matter – not the other way around. Remarkably, such differences and boundaries across countries may limit the potential scale of a multinational company while affording it the possibility to break free from the limitations of its original geography. For example, a multinational may need to start from a geopolitical imperative and face the fact that being present and operating in a certain set of countries effectively means being excluded from the rest. Geography remains destiny. (This is not new in the history of international business, but it is *new* to a whole generation of international managers.) Still, at the same time, geography is no longer destiny. The global performance of a multinational is not necessarily dictated by its home country but rather by the choice of the geographic composition (or footprint) of the multinational organisation and its capability of drawing on geographic co-specialisation and strong complementarity to *create from the world* and benefit from metanational advantage.

Global integration at the multinational level, the process of selectively interconnecting its local units around the world, was long dependent on integrating local outputs, including the outputs of the strategic allies and other partners that made up the multinational's global business network. In our world today such global integration can rely on integrating managerial work around the world. This integration of managerial work between those in charge of the global level of the multinational and those in charge of its units at the local level is tantamount to having a global virtual team of general managers as the management structure of the multinational. 'Virtual teams' have been common in multinationals and in global supply chains for a couple of decades, but these were by and large functional teams with an operational scope. Virtual teamwork at the general management level is rare and enigmatic, yet the concept of a 'virtual headquarters' may emerge as a hallmark of 21st-century multinationals.

This is why multinationals are currently out on a limb. After three decades of perceiving globalisation as the aggregation of local markets at the world scale while reducing countries to global market segments and sources of global supply efficiency, there is a generation of multinational managers that was not prepared to effectively address the managerial challenges described above nor develop the organisational capabilities that companies now require to *go international* and *be global* in our complex and uncertain world.

In such a world there are no quick fixes or generic solutions, the only alternative is an exploratory approach to managing a multinational and its organisational capabilities. Such exploration must be grounded on the accumulated knowledge that exists about these matters. Much of this knowledge was produced and published by academics when multinationals were growing in a divided world between the 60s and the 80s. A great deal of such seemingly old research gained an unexpected significance today and must be revisited. Many other contributing pieces of research, capturing different aspects of globalisation and its effects, including the impact of digitalisation, have been published since the 90s. Discerning what to study amid the vast amount of accumulated knowledge in International Business and International Management, a requirement for any academic interested in studying internationalisation, or for any general manager wishing to shape the future of an incumbent multinational company, is a daunting task. That is where this book excels. It does not make the task easy, but it makes it feasible.

Ricciardelli and Decastri open the book with their main thesis, relating the complexity of the multinational with its four specific dimensions: multiculturalism, geographic dispersion, context, and knowledge workforce. It becomes clear that this book gives primacy to the organisational dimension of the multinational and never attempts to simplify what cannot be simplified. The authors aim at augmenting the ability of the reader to choose the path of their international endeavour and, with that in mind, carefully present and explain a large array of organisational models, starting with a model dating back to the 60s and ending with a model for the digital world. The reader will find a comprehensive review of the cultural dimensions of internationality and, finally, a selected set of subjects about managing people in an international context. The authors keep pointing the reader to the original sources they used, allowing for a deep examination of each matter if the reader so wishes.

Humanity, geography, and history are ever-present in this book. I wonder if that speaks to the Italian origin of the authors. I am glad if it does. Because that is the point: in international management, people, place, and time are of the essence!

José Santos
INSTEAD, France

José Santos *began an early academic career in the 1970s, transitioning to the managerial world a few years later. He spent two decades gaining experience in international business and management. In the mid-nineties, José returned to academia at INSEAD, where he has since focused most of his research and teaching on the management of multinational enterprises, with a particular emphasis on global integration and innovation. Over the years, he has also taught at MIT (2009-2014), Portuguese Catholic University, and occasionally at IEDC-Bled School of Management, Università Bocconi, Università di Bologna, and the University of Cambridge.*

Preface

The world is changing fast, much faster than we can imagine. In such a turbulent and discontinuous scenario, firms should extend their range of action to become fully global in terms of strategic business, market relations, financial policies, in adopting an innovative culture that is functional to the management of human resources. It is a process that, accelerated by the transformation of the first and second Industrial Revolution, has generated a unique global scenario where technological innovation, new organisational models and transformation of production processes have played a pivotal role.

Looking at the parabola of economic development it is possible to see that whilst rural and artisanal societies survived for millennia with structural features that tended to remain unchanged, the first industrial revolution (second half of the 18th century) led to considerable transformations and produced major upheavals in people's working and social lives.

It is today's society, since the 1960s, that has imprinted a sort of 'turbo' on the ongoing process of change, producing four different transformations in just forty years, starting with the late industrial society, which exploded with the 1973 oil shock and inaugurated the era of dissolving stabilisation. It is certainly a symbolic date that produces a historical 'transition' rather than a historical passage. A transition that concludes the axial age of the last period of modernity (1494-1973) and inaugurates the phase of post-modernity, in which a series of continuous crises of an economic, political-cultural and religious nature follow one another.

Since then, nothing has been the same as before, as in just a few decades several transformations have taken place, at any rate as defined by scholars: the service society (1980s), the information society (1990s) and the knowledge society (2000s), which open up unexplored and unpredictable spaces of cooperation and competition, or cooperative competition and competitive cooperation. These are transformations that only a few years ago were hardly imaginable in societies and organisations which tended to be closed, were considered impregnable and unsinkable, but above all perennial.

Instead, the global scenario characterising the second decade of the new millennium has a complex and multifaceted configuration, marked by many opportunities that are not easy to seize, but also by the presence of four particularly critical phenomena:

- the inability of firms, including multinationals, to cope with new competitive modes, which risk or even suffer bankruptcy;
- the development and strong growth of new economy sectors that, in a jobless growth logic (Hanusch, 2012) tend to influence the structure of the economic system;
- the involvement of public policy and of local and national public institutions in such a decline as they are still stuck in a Fordist logic of development and an essentially statist welfare system;

- the advance of the new BRICS countries (Brazil, Russia, India, China, and South Africa) in the club of industrialised countries and the passing of the baton, in the attempt to govern global processes moving from an arrangement based on G8 to a G20 countries confrontation.

THE CHALLENGES

Being global means preparing to face the challenge of complex tasks due to an innovative culture connected with the advent of the third industrial revolution and the continuous economic, social and cultural changes taking place in our societies. Such greater complexity is a direct consequence of the four specific dimensions of international firms: *multiculturalism, geographic dispersion, context, knowledge workforce.*

Multiculturalism refers to the recognition, acceptance, and promotion of diversity among employees from various cultural backgrounds. It entails creating an inclusive and respectful work environment that values the unique perspectives, experiences, and contributions of individuals from different ethnicities, races, religions, languages, and nationalities. Multiculturalism recognises that diversity brings a wealth of knowledge, creativity, and innovation to organisations. To put it simply, it is all about the distances one can 'stumble' when crossing the border of a country: political system, economic structure, climate and orography, standard of living, religion, values with respect to work, boss, wealth, nature, etc.; tax, legislative and social security systems; educational facilities, architecture and artefacts, history, and more.

One of the key aspects of multiculturalism is fostering an inclusive workplace culture that encourages open communication, collaboration, and mutual respect. By embracing diverse perspectives, firms can tap into a broader range of ideas and approaches, leading to better decision-making and problem-solving. Multiculturalism also helps firms build stronger relationships with diverse customer bases, as employees with different backgrounds can better understand and connect with customers from various cultures.

Furthermore, multiculturalism promotes equality and fairness within organisations. It aims to eliminate biases and discrimination based on cultural differences, creating equal opportunities for all employees to grow and succeed. This can be achieved through diversity training programmes, mentorship initiatives, and policies that ensure a level playing field for individuals from diverse backgrounds. Multiculturalism also contributes to employee satisfaction, engagement, and retention. When employees feel valued and respected for who they are, they are more likely to be motivated, loyal, and committed to their work. In a multicultural environment, individuals can learn from each other, expand their cultural knowledge, and develop a global mindset, fostering personal and professional growth.

Implementing multiculturalism within firms may require strategies such as diversifying recruitment efforts, promoting cultural awareness and sensitivity, and establishing affinity groups or employee resource networks. These initiatives can help create a supportive and inclusive environment where everyone feels comfortable and empowered to contribute their best. Embracing multiculturalism goes beyond merely acknowledging diversity. It involves actively promoting inclusivity, respect, and equality among employees of different cultural backgrounds. By doing so, organisations can harness the full potential of their diverse workforce, foster innovation and create a more harmonious and successful work environment.

Geographic dispersion, that is the physical distance that operating in an *international chessboard* entails: the 'simplifiers' reduce this to the problem of the efficiency of the information set-up; even if one admits that this is the only critical factor, it is worth remembering the considerable differences between information and communication.

Informing means transferring data from one subject to another; inherent in communicating, on the other hand, is the possibility of touching the strings of emotion and involving the subjective, non-rational aspects of the relationship.

Information systems convey coded data and symbols, whilst communication systems convey meaning. Data and symbols find their raison d'être in the information channel. Meaning, on the other hand, lies in people and, above all, in their cognitive structure.

The critical phase, therefore, lies when the encoded symbol (i.e. the word) comes into contact with the recipient's cognitive maps: the 'symbol-cognitive structure' relationship is the key to understanding the complexity resulting from geographic dispersion. In this sense, the origin and meaning of the term 'cognitive' are of fundamental importance: it seems to be descended from *gnomon*, an ancient Sumerian term for the sundial stylus used to measure the passage of time. The term 'gnomon' was later associated with calculating and measuring operations. Aristarchus employed it to determine the distance between the sun and moon. Eratosthenes used it to arrive at an approximate determination of the 'length' of the earth.

The surprising results coming from these uses led to the definition of a term of a magical connotation such as the Gnomes. In general, gnomic means rules of wisdom, heuristic principles, and mechanisms of knowledge. This leads directly to modern cognitive psychology and its studies on communication, symbolism, human understanding and interpretation of 'objective' phenomena.

Cognitive interpretations of human mind-reality relationship imply that the transcoding of symbols brings with it a remarkable power to mobilise intellectual and emotional energies, a power that drives one to go far beyond the apparent, that transforms communication processes into something magical, something enchanted. Thus, a banal word such as 'authority' can create different reactions in the cognitive structure of an Indian employee (something unquestionable to which all corporate behaviour can be referred) than in that of a Swedish researcher (a typical characteristic of a leader who knows how to help and give advice to collaborators). Here, magically, seemingly objective data is transformed into communication and emotional reactions. All this leads to the assertion that any kind of distance communication tool can in no way have the same value and effectiveness as vis-à-vis communication; or, rather, if it can greatly improve the efficiency of information transmission, it severely penalises communication as understood here and, even worse, transforms it into something quite different.

Returning to geographic dispersion, it is perhaps superfluous to recall how complex a simple selection process managed remotely can become. How to understand the real profile of the position? How to understand the preferences of the direct superior? How to know the practices of contact with the labour market? How to best accompany the selected person in the corporate world? And so on. Perhaps, at a superficial level, there are two solutions to this problem: the reduction of cultural distances by covering spatial distances, or the construction of cognitive maps that are aware of cultural differences (and thus 'trained' to discount their effects) and, at the same time, as homogeneous as possible in their underlying mechanisms. Of course, this is not easy.

The Context encapsulates the surrounding conditions, circumstances, and factors that firms think about when internationalising. The context embodies the rationale and the ecosystem within which technological advancements, market dynamics, organisational culture and the pursuit of agility and responsiveness to local markets or customer needs unfold. It signifies a departure from traditional hierarchical structures, enabling firms to adapt swiftly, foster innovation, and empower local teams to make informed decisions. Understanding the context is pivotal for firms going international and aiming to navigate the evolving landscape of global business environments effectively. Firms' strategists, as well as researchers, need to be cognizant of the fact that the context within emerging markets, for example, will be changing rapidly and disruptively. In the book Third World Multinationals, Louis T. Wells (2017:3) affirmed: *"I fear that many of us assume that the context is simply a given and thus we fail to be explicit about the significance of a specific setting to our findings. We fail to imagine changes that may be just around the corner. Yet, those changes have a profound impact on the phenomenon we are studying."* Well's statement emphasises the significance for research into the context dynamics of today's emerging markets such as emerging market multinationals, born global firms and digital multinationals.

At this stage, apart from high-profile examples of born-global firms such as Skype, Facebook and Google, it is worth noting how very successful born-global start-ups such as Spotify, Zoom, Meero, Deezer or Alibaba started their internationalisation within the typical two to three years of born-global firms to the extent of achieving the status of multinationals very quickly.

Understanding the contextual intricacies within emerging markets, therefore, is crucial for start-ups and firms as they navigate diverse regulatory frameworks, cultural nuances, and economic landscapes. Research into these dynamics enables a comprehensive understanding of how these firms strategically position themselves, adapt business models, and leverage unique contextual advantages within these markets (Williamson and Santos, 2021).

Additionally, the rise of digital and born-digital start-ups and firms in these contexts (Øyna and Alon, 2018; Monaghan et al., 2020) accentuates the importance of studying the interplay between technological advancements, market peculiarities, and corporate strategies.

Analysing the contextual dynamics surrounding these digital players unveils their innovative approaches, disruptive strategies, and the fusion of technology with local market needs. Researching these aspects sheds light on how these born global firms, that have quickly become multinationals, manoeuvre within the intricate fabric of emerging markets, offering insights crucial for academia, policymakers, and businesses aiming to thrive in these dynamic environments.

The ascent of digital firms has also produced profound implications that transcend traditional business paradigms given the strong reliance on data-driven insights. The inherent scalability of digital platforms facilitates rapid international expansion, yet requires a keen awareness of diverse regulatory landscapes and cultural nuances. They have revolutionised decision-making processes, fostering personalised approaches in consumer engagement and have reshaped workforce dynamics, necessitating specialised skill sets and a readiness to embrace evolving technologies. Ultimately, the emergence of digital firms catalyses a paradigm shift, compelling businesses to embrace agility, innovation, and a nuanced understanding of the dynamic global market.

Knowledge workforce refers to a new particular professional category, typical of innovative organisations inspired by the principles of learning organisation and with high-specialised skills. This new professional and organisational category identifies a phenomenon already analysed with particular attention by numerous scholars (Nonaka, Takeuchi, 1995; Drucker, 1987; 1996; Heller, 2000; Butera, 2008). Knowledge workers possess qualities or roles that are akin to those of managers, even though they might not hold formal hierarchical managerial positions. Hence, knowledge workers exhibit certain managerial-like qualities in their roles, such as the ability to manage their tasks, make decisions, and utilise their expertise effectively, even without formal hierarchical responsibilities. They are characterised by the intertwining of management skills, interpersonal skills and cooperation, with specialised technical-professional skills, provided in a team perspective. They represent 'a firm's most valuable assets', an organisational phenomenon first analysed by Nonaka (1995) and by Peter Drucker (1996), who elaborated the concept of the knowledge worker and defined it as the most important economic and organisational phenomenon of the 21st century. As is well known, Nonaka (1995) himself stated that:

"In an economy where the only certainty is uncertainty, the only sure source of competitive advantage is knowledge, and it always comes from the contribution of one's employees." In the Italian debate, an important role is played by several contributions by Butera, in particular the essay *Knowledge Working.* Work, Workers, Knowledge Society (2008), which collects the results of research conducted in France, Germany, Italy, the United Kingdom and the United States on the work of scientists, managers, professionals and higher technicians who have reached significant proportions of the working population in innovative firms. These figures work on intangible processes, whose immediate output is the production of new knowledge, i.e. they generate ideas through ideas. A professional identity is increasingly linked to the need to express oneself through creative work, to be able to highlight one's own system of values that guides organisational behaviour, in a logic of coincidence and sharing with those of the firm. In this new heuristic direction, as Strati (2008; 2010) points out, a particular attention to the cultural, aesthetic and relational dimension has asserted itself in organisational and management studies, configuring a new field of analysis and a new methodological awareness.

The understanding of life of traditional organisations, dominated by the logic-rational paradigm, is succeeded by a new qualitative approach that aims to analyse the personal and organisational strategies acted out, bringing into play the experience of the subjects in their working practice, in which the role of emotions, sensitivity, taste, imagination and passion are fundamental elements for understanding organisational action. From a methodological point of view, the aesthetic understanding of organisations can give an account of the deeper dynamics of organisational life, which significantly direct production processes and interpersonal relations. In this heuristic direction, Attila and Gherardi (2007), make it clear that in the new technological and organisational scenario, work is characterised precisely by its growing knowledge content, in which the knowledge required to complete a complex task is increasingly elaborated and 'enclosed' within professional communities of people, who share a particular knowledge and certain working practices. An interpretative paradigm that re-elaborates the tools and methodologies for studying organisations, work and the particular interactions between people, roles, structures, processes and values that are the subject of in-depth study in the new economic sociology.

SEARCHING FOR A SOLUTION

Considering the state of the art in today's global strategic management, and facing the dynamic nature of emerging markets, firms need to strategically redefine their profile. This needs to be done to the extent of redefining a new managerial paradigm that aims at improving efficiency in the use of resources, but above all, at affirming effective leadership focusing on the valorisation of people in a perspective of creating shared value and social inclusive governance (Lyu et al., 2022). Evolving to become international is thus a process that is by no means taken for granted, extremely significant, a difficult challenge that involves the entire firm in every aspect. However, it is all too easy to say that, to move effectively in such complexity, more attention must be paid to inter-organisational relations and communication, differentiation of management practices and philosophies, the development of appropriate adaptation and flexibility skills, and so on. More particularly, international firms need people; never before has the job been about people (Masini, 1970). People are entrusted with the task of managing relations between different cultural, economic, political and geographical systems; they are expected to be effective in communication processes; they are expected to adopt management styles and governance practices consistent with the specific characteristics of different nations; they are expected to be flexible and adaptable, and so on. Leveraging on Heller's definition (1980) about international management defined as 'management to the *nth* power' (due to the greater complexity of the operational sphere), it is possible to state that the international firm needs 'people to the nth power'.

By this, we do not so much mean a super-manager but rather a person who is complete in his human and professional aspects. A man or a woman that may be weak, but aware of his/her weaknesses and strengths, capable of impulses and strong emotions, bound by strong ethical and moral principles, which are realistic and balanced. In other words, a man or a woman that goes global, hence, towards maturity!

ORGANISATION OF THE BOOK

The book is organised into 10 chapters. A brief description of each of the chapters follows:

Chapter 1 identifies the diverse organisational models, from Perlmutter's framework to EPRG profiles, tracing the orientation towards the new global scenario. The chapter identifies existing organisational models by transcending geocentrism through heterarchies, transnational and metanational structures, emerging market multinationals up until the ascent of digital multinationals that mark pivotal shifts. It also identifies the importance of current organisational models that reflect an evolving paradigm in organisational dynamics, emphasising adaptability and global interconnectedness.

Chapter 2 presents the various international organisational structures by describing their types and functionalities. The authors navigate through the intricacies of organisational structures by considering factors like geographical dispersion, cultural nuances, and operational requirements as necessary criteria. By analysing the pros and cons of different models, the authors provide insights into selecting an optimal international organisational structure aligned with specific business objectives and global operational needs.

Chapter 3 deals with the core of conflicts arising from the territorial presidium, exploring its relationship with host countries and the roots of clashes. It examines the tension stemming from the allocation of functional responsibilities, assessing the balance between centralisation and decentralisation. The overall aim of the chapter is to illuminate the complexities and challenges pertaining to such a relationship by shedding light on potential resolutions for conflict mitigation.

Chapter 4 focuses on strategic alliances as a cornerstone of global business expansion, exploring their multifaceted roles. It analyses international alliances, their implications for internationalisation, and their significance for multinational enterprises. The authors present a managerial reference model, which suggest the rationale behind forging alliances, addressing inherent cooperation challenges. By examining alliance systems, processes, and learning potentials, this chapter describes the evolving landscape of alliances amidst digitalisation and Industry 4.0.

Chapter 5 examines the challenge of cultural disparities, unveiling the adaptation process to new territories and roles. The authors consider the modes, timing, and degrees of adaptation to novel responsibilities by contending that in order to accelerate processes of adaptations individual and social factors are crucial alongside the influence of culture within organisational frameworks.

Chapter 6 presents an analysis of national culture and organisational theory through various methodological perspectives. The authors present diverse approaches employed in understanding the intricate relationship between national culture and organisational frameworks. Through different methodological lenses, this chapter illuminates the complexities and nuances inherent in studying how national culture influences and interacts with organisational theories, offering a comprehensive view of this dynamic relationship.

Chapter 7 addresses the dynamic relationship between culture and management, tracing from culture-free assertions to culture-bound perspectives. Based on Laurent's examination of Western management disparities, Hofstede and Trompenaar' cultural dimensions, the comprehensive synthesis in the GLOBE Study as well as contributions by Triandis, Schneider, Boisot, and Sorge, the authors highlight the constraints and opportunities inherent in cultural dynamics.

Chapter 8 analyses governance policies within international human resources, exploring inter-firm knowledge sharing, international assignment policies, and challenges stemming from diverse cultural backgrounds. The authors review the most important issue such as the management of global assignments and selection of international managers whilst unravelling the complexities of opposite ethnocentrism. By this light, the authors evaluate an array of human resources management systems that are tailored to diverse global contexts and offer insights for effective international HR governance.

Chapter 9 deals with international human resource management systems by focusing on two pivotal aspects: the selection process, and training. The authors review the complexities of selecting global talent and consider the diverse cultural and professional attributes as a benefit for the organisation. Furthermore, the chapter examines the significance of comprehensive training programmes tailored to meet the diverse needs and challenges posed by international assignments, ensuring effective performance within multinational environments.

Chapter 10 discusses issues related to expatriates' adaptation process to local contexts and addresses the main challenges such as family discomfort during relocation and reintegration upon return and anxiety in unfamiliar environments. The authors contend that manage those challenges it is imperative to addressing ethical, personalised work relationships and sustainability issues. By navigating these facets, the chapter aims to enhance understanding and support for expatriates in their cultural transitions and professional roles.

Alessandra Ricciardelli
University of Naples "Federico II", Italy

Maurizio Decastri
University of Rome Tor Vergata, Italy

REFERENCES

Attila, B., & Gherardi, S. (2007). *Studiare le pratiche lavorative.* Il mulino.

Butera, F. (2008). *Knowledge Working. Lavoro, lavoratori, società della conoscenza.* Mondadori Università.

Drucker, P. F. (1974). *Management Tasks, Responsibilities and Practices.* Harper & Row.

Drucker, P. F. (1996). The shape of things to come. *Leader to Leader, 1996*(1), 12–18. doi:10.1002/ltl.40619960306

Hanush, M. (2012). *Jobless Growth? Okun's Law in East Asia.* World Bank. doi:10.1596/1813-9450-6156

Heller, F. (2000). *Managing democratic organizations*. Ashgate.

Heller, J. E. (1980). Criteria for Selecting an International Manager. *Personnel*, *57*(3), 47–55.

Lyu, B., Liao, X., & Yang, Y. (2022). Relationships between temporal leadership, transactive memory systems and Team Innovation Performance. *Psychology Research and Behavior Management*, *51*, 2543–2559. doi:10.2147/PRBM.S380989 PMID:36124335

Masini, C. (1970). *Lavoro e risparmio*. Utet, Torino. Monaghan, S., Tippmann, E., & Coviello, N. (2020). Born digitals: Thoughts on their internationalization and a research agenda. *Journal of International Business Studies*, *51*(1), 11–22. doi:10.1057/s41267-019-00290-0

Nonaka, I., & Takeuchi, H. (1995). *The Knowledge creating company*. Oxford University Press. doi:10.1093/oso/9780195092691.001.0001

Øyna, S., & Alon, I. (2018). A Review of Born Globals. *International Studies of Management & Organization*, *48*(2), 157–180. doi:10.1080/00208825.2018.1443737

Strati, A. (2008). *Estetica e organizzazione*. Mondadori Università.

Strati, A. (2010). *Che cos'è l'estetica organizzativa*. Carocci.

Wells, L. T. (2016). Third World Multinationals: A Retrospective. In The Challenge of BRIC Multinationals. In R. Van Tulder, A. Verbeke, J. Carneiro, & M. A. Gonzalez-Perez (Eds.), *Progress in International Business Research* (11th ed.). Emerald Group Publishing.

Williamson, P. J., & Santos, J. F. P. (2021). Emerging Economies: The Impact of Context on Global Strategic Management. In Strategic management: State of the field and its future (pp. 319-335). Oxford University Press.

Section 1
The Organisational Structures of International Companies

Chapter 1
The Organizational Structures of International Companies: The Basic Outline of Organizational Models

ABSTRACT

This chapter deals with diverse organisational models pivotal in global business landscapes. Beginning with fundamental frameworks, it explores renowned models. Shifting beyond the traditional geocentric models, the discussion advances into the heterarchy, emphasising flexibility and adaptive structures. It then scrutinises the transnational organisation, fostering global integration whilst preserving local responsiveness up until the investigation on the metanational organisation, emphasising interconnectedness and collaborative networks. The chapter additionally examines the strategies of emerging market multinationals and digital multinationals by illuminating innovative approaches in global business paradigms. It explains the dynamic evolution of organisational structures within international companies, reflecting the ever-changing demands and opportunities of the global marketplace. Throughout, this chapter offers insights into the dynamic evolution of organisational structures within international companies, reflecting the ever-changing demands of the global marketplace.

1. THE BASIC OUTLINE OF ORGANISATIONAL MODELS

Tackling the subject of international organisational structures is not easy because it requires the use of an analysis and design perspective that, unlike the case of domestic structures, must emphasise and sometimes privilege soft aspects (values, communication, informal organisation) over hard factors (structures, formal mechanisms, hierarchical roles, etc.). The models that will gradually be illustrated will propose this basic characteristic: not only will this be disconcerting to the reader accustomed to 'boxes' and hierarchical lines of authority, but the considerably greater difficulties that the implementation process presents will become apparent. As we have already seen, all this is the result of the basic characteristics that differentiate the domestic company from the international one. The main characteristics of the organisational set-ups of international companies are the different cultural origins of the

DOI: 10.4018/979-8-3693-3482-9.ch001

people who make up the personal organism and the economic entity (multiculturalism), the different socio-economic configurations of the geographical areas and countries in which the company operates (geographic dispersion), and new professional figures (knowledge workers).

Multiculturalism, geographic dispersion, context, and knowledge workers are four characteristics that impose on international companies' organisational design processes and organisational structures that allow these two characteristics to be reconciled with the indispensable need for corporate unity. For example, in order to achieve high levels of organisational effectiveness in the individual geographical areas in which they choose to operate, international companies must adapt their managerial practices to the specific needs of different national communities. On the other hand, the need for cultural integration and managerial homogeneity may be strong.

This means that, whilst the unity of the company requires homogeneity and linearity, the variety of cultural contexts imposes levels of differentiation that are sometimes considerable. If one accepts the thesis that people who become part of an organisational system bring a substantial cultural background with them and that the influence of national culture is persistent over time, one must address, consequently and preliminarily, the problem of the relationship between corporate culture and national cultures.

Different national cultures thus entail divergent basic assumptions about the nature of management and organisations; the different value systems translate, in turn, into contrasting managerial practices and reinforce the original concepts. Embracing this perspective, organisational design on an international level also becomes a 'cultural artefact' reflecting the interrelationships between corporate culture, local national cultures and the cultures of origin of the people working in the company. In this sense, the international company is the most significant expression of the divided company (Masini, 1970). In particular, being characterised by a high level of *horizontal and spatial* extension (Airoldi, 1989; Coda, 1965) it is defined by a high number of partial economic combinations according to market and geographic areas. It also presents a high number of physically and spatially separated operating units, engaged in governing the various partial economic combinations identified by markets and by extra-national geographic areas.

At the same time and with the same force, it is observed that the international company – being a company as such - is a unitary whole of operations and elements connected with a plurality of relationships (Masini, 1970; Airoldi, 1989). Particularly relevant are those relations of commonality and policies of uniformity (Airoldi, 1989): the results are produced with common, or partially common, processes and resources (i.e. economic governance and management processes are common to all partial combinations by geographic areas). Secondly, integration and coordination methods must guarantee a minimum level of standardisation and uniformity of products and production processes, as well as of management, organisation and detection mechanisms and instruments.

Extent and unity are the distinctive characteristics of the economic subject of the international company. However, even in the case in which the shareholders are of a single cultural and geographical origin, phenomena linked to the differentiation of cultures from which the human resources come from are to be observed with considerable attention. In other words, work is personal and is expressed by the employees. In the case of international companies, apart from being holders of institutional interests and members of the economic subject, are bearers of extremely different values, cultures, traditions. The economic subject of international companies should favour internal coexistence of cultural differences that becomes the primary condition for implementing the principles of unity, direction and command being prerogatives of the economic governing bodies (Masini, 1970; Airoldi, 1989).

The combined effect of multiculturalism, geographical and unity issues is the increased complexity that an international company has to deal with, both at the level of the composition of interests within the economic entity and at the level of economic governance, management and execution tasks.

As far as the first case is concerned, it is possible to make a list of problems connected with the choices of the institutional organisation and the definition of the composition of the representative bodies of the economic subject and the top management bodies. The second aspect, on the other hand, directly influences the choices of organisation: the organisational structure, as an elective instrument of composition and individual work tuning with the economic combinations of the company, bears the task of reconciling the demands of governing the cultural and geographical issues with the need to safeguard the unity of the company. This also implies:

- the utmost attention to intra-organisational relations and socialisation processes;
- the use of different approaches and management systems within the same corporate community;
- an extreme sensitivity to the development of conditions of flexibility and adaptability.

In this perspective, the value choices (almost ideological) connected to the 'structure-people' relationship (Airoldi, 1989) are of great importance for the international company. Favouring the structural approach (i.e. assuming that economic combinations determine organisational structure and that people must adapt to this) indirectly leads to the 'export' of tools and organisational culture in a widespread and homogeneous manner in all partial combinations by market or geographical area. On the contrary, if the opposite approach is favoured and attention to human resources is prevalent over the organisational structure (hence, use is made of a design process that starts with the people and their needs and values to which the corporate structure is then adapted), this leads to the use of a 'loose' organisational structure. The latter guarantees that local values and traditions are not overridden by the top management and that the respect, as well as defence, of the typical cultures of individual geographical areas represent factors for success and a lasting economic life.

A third way, that is more complex and sophisticated than the previous ones, implies the employment of people coming from all cultural and geographical areas in which the company operates without assigning any particular relevance to ethnicity and nationality of origin. This results in a global approach to international management and organisation policies in which the global corporate interest prevails over cultural origins.

1.1 The Perlmutter Model

The Perlmutter model represents a pioneering contribution to the theory of the internationalisation of business that, even today, is still a useful starting point for more advanced theories.

It was written in 1969 and its originality is mainly attributable to the particular type of approach the author uses to classify international companies; this model, in fact, proposes a typology of different cognitive orientations towards international activities. The classification is based on an attitudinal criterion: in order to understand the true level of involvement and commitment of the company abroad, it is necessary to penetrate the reality experienced by the company and analyse its orientation towards resources, people and values, both in the country of origin and in the host countries. This is an approach that gives deserved importance to the variable of 'culture' (understood in the broadest sense as a set of attitudes, values, orientations), but above all it is a model that focuses on the typical issue of companies operating across borders, namely multiculturalism. Perlmutter's classification allows three types of companies to be defined:

a. *Ethnocentric companies.* This type of company adopts the key-positions of the international units of *parent country nationals*, i.e. managers from the country of origin, also referred to as *expatriates.* The basic reason given for this choice is the guarantee of greater reliability that such provenance ensures. This approach is normally accompanied by a strongly centralised organisational set-up: authority is centralised at the parent company, communication is essentially in the form of orders and suggestions from the centre, and the standards and objectives of the planning and evaluation systems are drawn up by the central functions and passed on from there to the local units.

In companies adopting this policy, the top management being either in the headquarter or in its subsidiaries, is the bearer of a single value system (corporate culture and national culture of the home country) that is exported and spread internationally.

b. *Polycentric companies.* This category of companies uses *host country nationals* in foreign positions, i.e. managers coming to the host country where the subsidiary is located.

Facing difficulties in understanding the local culture, the parent companiy considers policies of engagement of local staff to be thus more effective. This policy assumes more widespread power, stronger subsidiaries' autonomy, a two-way communication with limited frequency between the centre and the periphery, and evaluation and control systems developed mostly locally and autonomously.

A particular version of polycentrism is *region-centrism*, i.e. the attitude of considering not a single country, rather a larger geographical area with a common history, traditions, and lifestyle as a homogeneous cultural environment. In such areas, *regional headquarters* are headed by local managers, referring to managers coming from one of the countries included in the region.

c. *Geocentric companies.* These tend to employ a mix of *parent country national, host country national* and *third country national* in top positions, i.e. people recruited from across the international system, regardless of ethnicity and nationality. The result is a global approach to international assignment, an integrated system, close cooperation between centre and periphery and a high volume of communication. In the extreme conception of geo-centrism, the international dimension as such disappears, in favour of a global and competitive arena.

Taking into account the summary description of the three types of international orientation, Perlmutter's classification scheme makes explicit reference to international human resource management and related issues of managing multiculturalism. The managers interviewed in the course of the research had in fact indicated the human factor as the best starting point to push the companies towards an increasingly integrated level of internationalisation. However, it is important to emphasise that the applicative scope of the model is not limited solely to this sphere, but extends to various dimensions such as, for example, the macrostructure, the degree of centralisation/decentralisation, operational systems, as well as the structures of individual functional areas.

1.2 The EPRG Profile

The extent and intensity with which the management of an international company manifests its ethnocentric, polycentric, region-centric or geocentric orientation can be represented by what Perlmutter calls the 'EPRG profile' (initials refers to the four orientations). The four models of internationalisation may be present with different levels of intensity in the same company: the meaning that top management attributes to the variable 'internationality', the behaviour of managers towards people, the policies for allocating resources domestically and abroad, market policies, etc., may reflect, to varying degrees, characteristics of geo-centrism, ethnocentrism, polycentrism or region-centrism. In this sense, it is never quite correct to say that a company is only ethnocentric or only geocentric.

The non-uniformity of cognitive orientation towards international operations is very frequently found at the level of different corporate functions and represents a further manifestation of multiculturalism within the same company. In some research, an attempt has been made to deepen the analysis of the international orientation of different corporate functions by applying the Perlmutter classification and finding fairly consistent results:

- *Marketing*: in marketing policy decisions, the polycentric orientation seems to be prevalent: in particular, there is a much stronger polycentric approach in pricing policies, customer service, market research and choice of distribution channels. In contrast, polycentrism is weaker in areas such as brand policies, product quality and sales administration (areas where a geocentric approach may prevail) (Wind et al., 1973). In general, the strong polycentrism in marketing decisions is determined by giving importance to align with local market needs.
- *Production*: operational decisions in the field of production appear to be even more localised and polycentric, although managers generally rate a region-centric or geocentric approach more positively.
- *Finance:* ethnocentrism and polycentrism seem to prevail, although managers in the function would prefer a more pronounced geo-centrism, especially for the definition of investment criteria and financial resource allocation policies.

The EPRG profile may also vary between products and geographic areas, and there may be no consensus within the company itself on the ideal form of internationalisation to adopt, or towards which to strive.

The factors that influence the internationalisation model are many and range from the background of top management, history of the company and past experiences. The fundamental element that determines the EPRG profile, however, is the role that stakeholders play: the basic choices regarding international policies are often attributable to the composition and interests expressed by the broader economic entity.

The EPRG profile can often be influenced, for example, by the government of the host country, the nationality mix of shareholders and local suppliers. The EPRG profile cannot, therefore, be considered static: it simply represents, in a fairly comprehensive manner, the level of internationality achieved by the company at the time in question.

1.3 The Evolutionary Path Towards Internationality

Perlmutter's classificatory scheme can also be read and interpreted in terms of an evolutionary path. The four types of orientation towards internationalisation can be associated with successive stages in the evolution of international operations, the sequence ethnocentrism-polycentrism-geo-centrism represents the typical path.

Any entrepreneurial activity, in fact, develops abroad gradually; the process of expansion usually begins on a national basis and then continues, with increasing levels of intensity, in an international sense; in parallel with this growth of involvement abroad, the philosophy and managerial attitude towards internationalisation changes too.

This evolutionary process does not exclude different routes (phase jumps or reverse processes). However, the EPRG route is considered as typical and normal, without excluding different sectoral characterisations (Porter, 1987, 1990).

The stages of the company's journey are not clearly and unambiguously identifiable as the transition from one stage to the next occurs gradually and it is sometimes the result of seemingly minor incremental changes.

The following paragraph will take a closer look at the dynamics of this development of the company towards internationality. A number of variables relating to the strategic dimension and, above all, to the organisational dimension will be taken into consideration. Analysing the evolution of these variables, in correspondence with the increase in involvement abroad, will allow us to trace more precisely the ethnocentric, polycentric or geocentric profile corresponding to each phase.

a. *Towards ethnocentrism.* Any entrepreneurial activity, started on a national basis, follows an initial development path mainly oriented towards the home country, with foreign business assuming marginal importance. This first phase (in which the company is predominantly engaged within national borders) is, in general, all the more relevant the larger the domestic market, the greater the potential opportunities that can be exploited on that market and the less knowledge of the international territory. Usually, the company projects itself towards the international dimension because it owns a domestic monopolistic advantage that can be fully exploited by expanding its sphere of action beyond its borders. This advantage may exist in a particularly prestigious brand name, given the possession of a particular know-how in a patent as proposed by Dunning's eclectic theory (1980) and the early contributions of Hymer (1970) and Kindleberg (1969), who extended the theory of differentiated oligopoly to international relations.

The company begins to develop an international expansion process gradually, moving from simple exports to more demanding forms of investment involving first the commercial aspect and then the production aspect. The development follows a concentric path, first targeting neighbouring areas (not only geographically, but also culturally), and then moving on to areas further away from the domestic market.

The preponderance of the centre (parent company) over the periphery (foreign units) is very evident in the strategy definition process, which is typically top-down; the same applies to the allocation of resources, which is centrally managed and controlled. The level of autonomy of the subsidiaries is, therefore, very low.

As far as the organisational structure is concerned, it is very difficult to identify a univocal or ideal structural scheme: the possible structural solutions are diverse and vary according to the structure adopted at national level. As will be seen below, the product and function dimensions take on prevailing importance over the geographical area dimension because the need to co-ordinate initial efforts towards internationalisation is little felt and the need to maintain the national competitive advantage prevails over any need for local flexibility.

At this stage, the practice of adopting an International Division can be considered a sophisticated solution: the activities concerning foreign markets are grouped and coordinated in one autonomous unit and the company manages to retain its predominant orientation towards domestic markets.

The lack of experience across borders and the lack of in-depth knowledge about people and situations outside the country leads management to behave in a highly ethnocentric manner and foreign managers are regarded as 'second-class' managers. Appraisal standards are designed for parent company personnel without taking into account that operating conditions in different countries may be so different that criteria specifically designed for different local situations are required. Such standardisation often creates demotivation and a sense of injustice among off-site staff who, having to govern local areas away from the central structures, feel discriminated against or even punished.

Control is predominantly very formalised and regulatory, which is reflected in the intensity and direction of information flowing almost exclusively from the parent company to local units; local units merely execute orders and operate according to standard regulations. The logic of 'if it works at home, it works abroad, too' prevails; the novelty and uncertainty of foreign operations make a hierarchical rather than a market or agreement-based form of governance feel safer.

The identification of the company refers to the country in which the headquarter is located: it is an American, Italian or French company depending on whether the head office is in America, Italy, France.

Adopting an ethnocentric orientation also entails costs: among the main disadvantages are the difficulties in strategic planning and staffing, the lack of responsiveness to local needs, the distance of reference markets, the cumbersome nature of information systems, the limited flexibility, and the poor utilisation of potential located in the periphery.

The assignment of *parent country nationals* in key positions abroad also brings about a strong homogenisation of the corporate culture, which flattens the typical values of the parent company and the country of origin. This uniformity, whilst it can be a positive factor with strong cohesion, is also a considerable obstacle to the exploitation of potential opportunities that would derive from a greater intercultural confrontation.

b. *Towards polycentrism.* As the company increasingly projects itself beyond national borders, foreign activities take on significant importance within the strategic project. The competitive strength of the company is no longer solely based on the exploitation of domestic advantage, but also relates to the realisation of economies of scale and scope and accumulated international experience.

In this second phase, the company is much more sensitive to different national realities and attaches significant weight to local environmental factors. The shift from a policy of global integration to a marked national responsiveness affects the role assumed by subsidiaries and the very relationship between the parent company and local units. The latter become more autonomous, broaden their sphere of competence and level of discretion, and are not limited to the execution of plans dictated by the centre, but engage in strategy formulation and decision-making regarding operations in their specific local markets. Although control over critical resources and core competencies remains centralised, the foreign unit actively participates in allocation processes.

Thus the polycentric company comes to assume a form very similar to that of a confederation: in essence, it takes the form of a loosely connected group of almost self-sufficient units and, in a certain sense, its degree of internationalisation is to be considered less than that of an ethnocentric company.

The form selected for the governance of transactions is not the hierarchy, as it was the case in the first phase, but the quasi-market (Barney and Ouchi, 1985); an obvious symptom of this set-up is the tendency to use internal transfer pricing systems based mainly on market prices and, to a lesser extent, on costs (Pilati, 1990). The control over local units is of a quantitative nature based on financial and income results and no longer on behaviour. In this perspective, top management regards a central financial control system as an effective coordinating factor of this set-up.

The organisational structure frequently takes on a divisional configuration by geographical areas, allowing a very *host-country* orientation and facilitating the realisation of a high level of *host-country* responsiveness.

As far as human resources management policies are concerned, an initial host-country component emerges, which then becomes more and more consistent over time. The management of the *parent company*, aware of the diversity of the national cultures in which it operates, considers the direct involvement of local people to be relevant and assigns them to the key-positions within the subsidiaries. Staff rotation between countries, for example, is very low and transfers from the subsidiary to the *parent company* are very unlikely. No local manager can seriously aspire to a position of responsibility at the centre.

Local top managers enjoy a high degree of autonomy in the management, evaluation and control of their employees; the definition of evaluation and control criteria takes place locally and the reward systems may have different articulations.

Each subsidiary is a national entity characterised by a high degree of autonomy; the need for communication is, therefore, limited and information flows have a reduced frequency both between the parent company and the subsidiaries, and between the subsidiaries themselves.

The most obvious costs of adopting a polycentric approach arise from the duplication of resources at a local level and the consequent foregoing of potential savings that could result from central coordination. Equally inefficient are innovation processes due to the scant attention given to the accumulation of experience developed at the local level.

If the company continues on its international growth path, enters new markets and intensifies its foreign investments, it may become relevant to coordinate homogeneous geographical areas comprising countries with similar traditions, history, lifestyles, and social models. The attitude of management may change towards the particular form of polycentrism – *region-centrism* – that assumes not the single country, but a supranational area as a homogeneous cultural environment.

Each of these areas corresponds to a regional headquarter in which local managers, i.e. from one of the countries belonging to the region, are usually placed in key positions.

The *region-centric orientation* entails advantages such as a better allocation of resources and the realisation of economies of scale at regional level, richer and more stimulating career paths, a more effective coordination of human resource management and control policies; the costs are the same as those outlined for polycentrism.

c. *Towards geo-centrism.* The transition from a polycentric to a geocentric perspective is very critical and challenging to achieve for two reasons. The first is internal resistance (it is very often perceived by *host country nationals* as a return to an ethnocentric government pervaded by home country management philosophies). The second refers to environmental conditions that are a precondition for it: in this phase, competition is no longer played out at the national level, but the territory is extended to the entire international economic system and the actions carried out by a subsidiary in one country directly affect the competitive situation of subsidiaries in other countries. The ultimate goal of the geocentric approach is to develop a global vision and attitude both at headquarters and in local units.

The global strategy is not motivated by the exploitation of a specific monopolistic advantage, nor even by the attractiveness of individual local markets, but by the increasing focus on the global market as the only possible route to survival.

The concept of geo-centrism entails a very intense level of collaboration between subsidiaries and the parent company. The subsidiaries are no longer satellites or semi-independent units, but parts of a cohesive set-up whose *focus* is oriented towards global objectives. Compared to the previous phase, their level of autonomy is reduced and their role is substantially altered: they must implement globally formulated strategies in a coordinated manner and at the same time be capable of responding to local competitive conditions in a timely manner.

The interdependence between the parties is reciprocal: flows of *know-how*, people, products, and financial resources follow complex and articulated paths; corporate strategy implies a simultaneous criticality of function, product and geographical area dimensions; organisational management requires an equally complex structure and operating systems.

On the other hand, as far as human resources are concerned, the geocentric perspective tends to focus on high-profile people regardless of their nationality. Problems relating to different local cultures and management models are no longer seen as an obstacle, but rather as an opportunity: confrontation is experienced as a source of stimulation and enrichment. In this sense, efforts are made to provide a real core of international managers willing to move anywhere in the world, forgetting their own origins; a mix of *parent country national, host country national* and *third country national* is thus used, without discrimination determined by ethnicity or national origin.

The need to combine a considerable local sensitiveness with strong integration on a global basis entails a double responsibility of management on local and global objectives.

If, on the one hand, the geocentric approach allows this simultaneous global and local focus, on the other hand it implies considerable costs in terms of socialisation processes, decision-making time, and governance of a rather fragmented power structure.

For these reasons, too, the geocentric perspective is not an obligatory point of arrival; although there seems to be consistent evidence of a necessary evolutionary movement from ethnocentrism, to polycentrism, to geo-centrism (Perlmutter, 1969), the decision to achieve geo-centrism, due to the complexity involved, requires careful and thorough evaluation. On the other hand, an ethnocentric logic sometimes hides itself behind an apparent global perspective. An example can be that of a US company that employs managers from all over the world and implements a sort of 'pushed acculturation' to the value system, styles and, in general, the culture of the country of origin. By doing this it tends to 'Americanise' everyone, imposing management procedures, managerial styles, ways of dressing, languages, symbols and attitudes typical of the parent company.

1.4 Moving Beyond Geo-Centrism: The Heterarchy

The evolution of competitive conditions in recent years has prompted companies and scholars to carefully consider the possibility of going beyond the vagueness and generality of the geocentric perspective in order to identify a way of being international that would be able to better govern the two opposing dimensions of globalisation and local flexibility. This has resulted in some extremely interesting proposals, but which — it is worth anticipating right now — only partially meet the aforementioned expectations of greater punctuality. They certainly offer prospects for growth and maturity around which the success and survival of many international companies or those in the process of internationalisation will be played out. The models on which attention will be focused are due to Hedlund (*the heterarchy*) and Bartlett and Ghoshal (*the transnational company*).

Hedlund's (1986) heterarchical model represents an evolved conception of international organisation and applies to companies with a rather high level of internationalisation. It arises from the strong criticism of the geocentric approach, which is too unbalanced on an assumption of the ineluctable disappearance of socio-political differences between the geographical areas of our globe.

The model of a heterarchical organisation developed by Hedlund is a form of geo-centrism that is not fully developed; this new model, which should represent a target-structure towards which international companies will tend in the future, entails the maximum geographical spread of activities and, at the same time, a very strong investment in non-hierarchical coordination mechanisms.

Suggesting a precise definition of the concept of heterarchy is not a simple task. Hedlund argues that heterarchy does not have a diametrically opposed meaning to the conventional hierarchy nor is it synonymous with polyarchy. To summarise, heterarchy is an organisation composed of many nodal ganglia with multiple and differentiated roles, in terms of functional responsibility, product and geographic area, coordinated with each other by means of those instruments that Galbraith (1975) indicates as useful for socialisation or that Etzioni (1968) places within the sphere of regulatory-type control.

Heterarchy means not only a new way of organising the company on an international basis (the changes at the level of organisational variables are indeed very substantial), but it also means a new attitude of the company towards its environment. Hedlund rejects the idea that it is the strategy that determines the structure. It argues that there is an inversion of priorities between the two variables. The 'hypermodern' international company, organised in a heterarchical form, defines, at first, its cultural and structural characteristics and later chooses the strategic options arising from the organisational set-up or even tries to define them by taking a proactive stance towards the environment.

In the international heterarchical company, strategy is not an element defined before the structure; instead, the opposite logic applies, according to which 'strategy follows structure' so that the structural choice itself becomes strategy (Vicari, 1991; Decastri, 2016).

The central and strategic objective of the heterarchical company is thus the active search for and exploitation of any opportunities that arise throughout the geographical system in which it operates. This logic of seeking and exploiting opportunities, seen in an extreme form, could make it impossible to classify the company within a certain sector and lead towards a reduction in the focus of the core business.

The heterarchical organisation allows the company to develop the ability to create opportunities; strategy is no longer simply an analysis of strengths and weaknesses and a consequent implementation of sequential plans aimed at achieving competitive advantages that bring success. Instead, the greatest emphasis is placed on learning, the pursuit of opportunities and action to change the environment. It is clear that, although possible limitations, this logic is a clear departure from the concept of strategy as calculated, premeditated thinking, divorced from the moment of implementation. In the heterarchical company, strategy is action (and vice versa) and the implementation phase assumes crucial importance. Actions take the form either of programmes to exploit certain given environmental and organisational conditions (in the short term) or of experimentation programmes aimed at modifying relations with the outside world.

Although these early indications were devoted to strategic aspects, most of the specific features of heterarchy refer to purely organisational aspects. The idea of heterarchy is intended to recall the concept of a non-hierarchically organised company, a kind of holographic organisation in which the entire system is reproduced in each individual part (Bodega, 1988). With due caution, the heterarchical model can be likened to precursor models such as Mintzberg's (1983) adhocracy.

In more detail, the specific characteristics of the heterarchical company are as follows:

1. The international heterarchical company is *made up of many integrated centres*: the competitive advantage does not reside in one country and the company must, therefore, be able to grasp the ideas of new products and processes that originate in various parts of the globe and that can subsequently be exploited on an international scale. Each node of this geographically dispersed network has core competences common to other geographical centres and its own specific skills. The latter are usually the result of local learning processes to which each unit is oriented within a precise geographical and cultural division of labour; there is thus a process of international specialisation, for example an American company may have its financial management in Brussels, its research centre in Sweden, its production units in the Far East, etc. Sometimes overlapping responsibilities may result, but this is not a problem as conflict is accepted as a source of confrontation and innovation. Multi-centralism thus becomes an advantage: a local unit can be, at the same time, a global coordinator for a product or function and a local node with regard to other activities.
2. Heterarchy implies a variety of geographically dispersed centres. The organisational principle that inspires the design of the structure is not unique, but involves the use of a *mix of dimensions: functions, products, geographical areas, customer types, trade*. This multidimensionality (Airoldi, 1980) is in the first instance governed by the macro-structure, but is in fact characteristic of all organisational variables.

Apparently, this set-up may lead to think of a somewhat forced evolution of the matrix configuration, whereas, in reality, the levels of efficiency and flexibility of a heterarchical set-up are much higher than those obtained with a 'simple' formal matrix structure.

The heterarchical structure, Hedlund argues, *is not a matrix*; the most relevant differences between the two organisational solutions are:

- heterarchy implies a co-ordination model that allows several dimensions to be governed in a flexible and variable manner where in the matrix all units are co-ordinated along the two dimensions assumed to be relevant;
- the matrix implies a very rigid degree of stability and equilibrium between the arms of the structure; the heterarchical solution allows the activation of thematic coordination processes that go beyond the matrix's *dirigiste* scheme;
- the matrix creates conflicts that are mostly referred and resolved at the top;
- in heterarchy, on the other hand, conflict resolution occurs through rationalisation and negotiation, on the basis of shared values and visions.

3. Each subsidiary takes on a strategic role: the strategy is not conceived from the centre but implemented in the peripheries, as it is the case in the ethnocentric model. Terminologies such as *mother house, country of origin, centre* no longer have any meaning. The concept that counts is that of a

node in the geographically widespread network. The strategy is decided, formulated and translated into actions in the various nodes in compliance with the overall strategic design.

4. Integration is achieved primarily through *normative-social control* (Etzioni, 1968). Soft organisational variables such as company culture and management style assume central importance and become critical elements. Bureaucratic control does not work because it causes excessive information and decreases in terms of motivation. Quantitative control is scarcely effective because it does not produce the necessary level of mutual trust and does not facilitate the formation of a unified and shared perspective that leads to sacrificing the local for the global and the short term for the long term. Regulatory-social control, on the other hand, encourages a wide dissemination of information at all levels and ensures a more effective integration between nodes through the sharing of underlying objectives and achieving greater awareness.
5. The distribution and knowledge of information *is not selective but pervasive.* Heterarchy can be considered a hologram, i.e. a system in which the information necessary to reproduce the entire organisation is contained in every part of it. Obviously, the complete application of this concept has objective limitations: it is certainly impossible for each individual to know all aspects of all operations in which the company is involved. However, widespread knowledge of strategies, the organisational set-up, the rules of the game, management systems and an understanding of the critical interdependencies between the various parts of the organisation is the goal that must be attempted and that, although difficult and costly, seems realistic. Information technology is a crucial driving force that can facilitate the company's transition towards a heterarchy. In this regard, Hangstrom's (1990) study on the effects that new information technologies have on the structure and management of the international company is interesting, a study in which he shows how these technologies allow for new configurations and redefinitions of activities in both a geographical and organisational sense.

Organisational culture plays a crucial role in the hologram creation process and acts as the primary unifying element of a heterarchical organisation. The fact of sharing certain conceptions of the company, ways of acting and reacting in relation to certain events, and attitudes in relations with other individuals makes it easier for information to be disseminated rapidly, but, above all, it makes the interpretation attributed to events both outside and inside the organisation more uniform. In this sense, management must work hard to foster the formation of a strong and cohesive organisational culture.

6. Each part of the *organisation is a thinking and acting element.* This typical feature of the heterarchical international company is complementary to the previous concept of the holographic organisation. The fact that each part of the organisation contains all the necessary information to reproduce the whole system as well as each peripheral entity plays a pivotal role (in an exquisitely geographical sense), all this implies that the activity of *thinking* is not the exclusive privilege of a single centre (the parent company). Rather, it takes place at every level and in every part of the organisation. This should not lead to attributing predominant importance to the cognitive phase: the ideas, the thoughts that take shape in the various parts of the organisation simultaneously guide action. Thought drives action. Action, in every part of the organisation, is seen as an experiment that steers thinking.
7. The heterarchical company presents *a high degree of flexibility in the choice of how transactions are governed.* The fact that a company's strategic strength is linked to its ability to identify, create

and exploit opportunities on a global scale implies that some situations can arise that are better managed through hierarchy and others that are more effectively governed through the market. The dry, optimising choice between hierarchy and market is abandoned to pave the way for an articulated set-up composed of a mix of mechanisms for governing transactions. This composite mix varies over time and one of the typical tasks of the management of a heterarchy is the continuous refinement of the economic-organisational set-up. However, it is useful to emphasise that the heterarchical company, always striving for dynamism and change, has a characteristically strong preference for outsourcing and alliances. On the other hand, as far as the degree of centralisation of decision-making is concerned, in line with the need to take advantage of opportunities that arise, it is necessary to grant a high level of discretion and autonomy to all organisational units, within the framework of strictly controlled general principles and policies.

This attitude may be perceived as a kind of disintegration for a company coming from an approach of strict global control and ethnocentric policies; for a company with a history of polycentrism it may, on the other hand, appear to be a tendency towards strong centralisation.

8. *Cooperative relationships with other companies and actors outside the organisation* are very frequent in the heterarchical company. The organisation assumes a network configuration that is open to collaborative relations with the outside world. The set of mutually interdependent and geographically dispersed centres constitutes the core of the company, held together by common strategies, norms, information and, above all, by a set of strongly shared values. Then, there is a *second periphery*, made up of external entities connected to this core by more or less close ties of cooperation. These actors, in turn, may be the centre of other systems. This set-up can be considered a kind of dual organisation that allows the company to effectively implement a multi-focal strategy (Perrone, 1990). The network of decentralised, but integrated centres constitutes the organisational/information infrastructure necessary to exploit globally the competitive advantages originating all over the world. The set of quasi-integrated satellites surrounding this network represents a usable channel of communication with the outside world that allows the company to come into contact with new stimuli and new ideas, increasing the level of flexibility of its responses (Vaccà and Zanfei, 1989; Turati, 1990).

Overall, the flexibility in the choice of forms of governance of transactions and, jointly, the continuous process of establishing and dissolving ties with external actors and institutions makes organisational boundaries very labile and variable over time.

1.4.1. Human Resource Management. With the analysis of the main organisational characteristics of the heterarchical multinational company, it is possible to assume that this new organisational form differs significantly from traditional structures in both approach and operating logic. The fact that the organisational structure is characterised by multidimensionality and flexibility means that it enables radical changes in managerial processes. One area that is particularly affected by these changes is human resource management. In the heterarchical company, the human resource becomes so critical that it is considered a real source of competitive advantage (Kogut, 1990). The nervous core system of the company is, in fact, formed by human resources: the relationship created between the employee and the organisation is highly idiosyncratic. The main causes of such a high idiosyncrasy are to be found in the specificity of the holographic code that characterises the company as well as in high investments in people that the company makes. As already considered, the holographic essence of heterarchy implies that each employee owns a large amount of information, including strategic information, concerning the company. Each employee also represents an important element of the communication network built within the company. The incomplete reproducibility of this network makes any attempt to use the information, controlled by the employee by another company, as unprofitable.

High idiosyncrasy makes it more convenient and efficient to resort to the internal labour market: the core of the heterarchy is in fact people with long experience in the company. However, this attitude should not be interpreted as a sign of rigidity or static human resources management. On the contrary, the prolonged permanence of people in the organisation facilitates the formation of a strong corporate culture and a collective information base that guarantee a wide possibility of horizontal and diagonal mobility and reduce the risks of system sclerotisation.

A further element of flexibility in human resources is the *resistance of a dual career system*. It was pointed out earlier how the organisational structure of the heterarchical company envisages a network core, consisting of the various interconnected and integrated centres and a periphery of satellite companies or institutions, linked to a greater or lesser extent to the central network by collaborative relationships.

A dual career substantiates possible movements that take place within the core network: from and to the periphery, with single units making up the shape of an extreme network.

The numerous international collaboration agreements, *joint ventures* and other forms of cooperation in which the company is engaged create a continuous flow of people in and out of the system; the employment relationships established in connection with these agreements appear more precarious in form, but are more intense and solid in substance.

The heterarchical organisational set-up could be interpreted as an effective solution for maintaining the necessary balance between stability and flexibility. The set of people at the core, with their solid experience in the company, constitute the organisation's memory and allow its identity to be maintained over time. The set of people who have more transitory ties with the company play a very important role as an interface with everything that lies outside and act as channels of communication to convey new ideas to the company. The most critical problem is maintaining the right balance between these two sets.

The heterarchical model is also characterised by a high turnover rate of staff. Frequent position shifts between different centres located in different parts of the world facilitate the building of a strong corporate culture, ensure better information sharing and stimulate learning. During the selection, leveraging on the company's ability to understand the individual's real propensity to travel becomes critical. Static employees, reluctant to travel, are a very serious problem for the heterarchical multinational company.

Heterarchy is a rather flat structure where hierarchy plays little importance. It follows that movements are not so much bottom-top as between the different centres. It is difficult to promote an employee by assigning him or her a higher position in the hierarchy. It is therefore necessary to develop a *central nervous system* that ensure staff rotation so to make employees perceive that mobility and rotation are rewarding mechanisms within a long-lasting and equal based relationship. The *profile of the ideal employee*, in the heterarchy, is characterised by the following features:

- a good capacity for strategic thinking and considerable managerial skills. Staff turnover, decentralisation and widespread communication of strategies are powerful tools in this respect;
- a global mindset;
- strong skills in communication processes and in quickly and effectively turning ideas into action;

- being able to combine elements in new ways: being innovative in the perception of external stimuli (Decastri, 1984);
- have a high propensity for risk and experimentation;
- have a positive attitude towards even very different cultures, a good command of different languages, be socially inclined;
- have considerable loyalty to the company, personal integrity and honesty: these last qualities, which might seem important requirements in any organisation, become highly critical in order to avoid heterarchy turning into organisational chaos.

1.4.2. The Relationship with the Environment. The previous paragraph has enabled us to understand in which ways the heterarchical formula is rooted in a completely different conception of the relations between environment, structure and strategy compared to the contingency paradigm (Leoni, 2013).

In particular, the environmental variable is conceived in a substantially different way: it is no longer viewed as a given and an unchangeable element of the company that constrains the choice of strategy and structure, but it is a chosen factor that is selected, created and shaped by the company (Weick, 1969).

The organisational structure becomes the primary variable that defines the sphere of action considered and the spaces for strategic action available (Vicari, 1991). The heterarchic company does not limit itself to seeking new and profitable opportunities; rather it attempts to create them by interacting with its selected environment. The typical analysis of the environment has always focused on competitors (Valdani, 1991). The environment of the heterarchic company is, instead, conceived in a broader sense and is made up of a multiplicity of relevant actors: competitors, suppliers, customers, public institutions, universities, etc. The company abandons its passive position and assumes an active role that enables it to exploit the synergetic potential with the environment in which it has chosen to operate.

Summarising the considerations made up to this point, it can be argued that heterarchy is an organisation based on *experimentation, research, and learning*.

Experimentation is not the exclusive responsibility of the research and development function; all the company's activities contain, to a greater or lesser degree, an experimentation component (Bodega, Decastri and Prina, 1992). A strong propensity for experimentation in multiple directions and systems resistance that make the company capable of learning from experience assume crucial importance and can become real strengths compared to competitors.

In the heterarchical model, the most relevant variables of the corporate structure cannot be found in the formal organisation, but are found in the culture, managerial systems and communication processes. The greatest emphasis on the organisation's soft variables is consistent with the trend towards the emergence of a new internationalisation model that is particularly effective in uncertain and complex environmental realities (Fabris and Garbellano, 1991).

Hedlund proposed his concept of the heterarchic company on the basis of some experiences of internationalisation found in Sweden, and it is with reference to these companies that the limited empirical evidence available manifests itself.

The companies presenting the greatest probability of evolution towards a heterarchical structure are those that are not very large and with an organisational structure composed of subsidiaries that already have a high level of autonomy and entrepreneurship. The sectors that Hedlund considers most suitable for heterarchical structures are those that present a fairly high degree of homogeneity of global demand, a fast rate of technological and market change, the presence of various technologies and significant economies of scale, even if not necessarily in the production area.

Against significant changes in the international sphere, the strong inertia to organisational change is a very difficult obstacle to overcome for many companies. This is very likely that the reality of the pure heterarchical model is very limited (Hedlund and Rolander, 1990). On the other hand, some symptoms of a slow and gradual shift of a part of the companies towards a heterarchical logic are already becoming apparent, although the interpretation is not unambiguous. In particular:

1. There is a geographical spread of certain organisational units that have always been considered central; a number of companies have set up financial centres in London and Brussels; research laboratories are sometimes located in a geographical area far away from the parent company, etc.
2. There has been a significant increase in the use of forms of collaboration with external players, thus moving companies towards a more networked logic.
3. Recent developments in the field of information technology constitute a driving force, albeit not a sufficient one, towards heterarchical organisation and the concept of holographic organisation; the most innovative computer technologies facilitate communication and guarantee widespread and direct access to all information from all nodes of the system (Hangstrom, 1990).

1.5 The Overcoming of Geo-Centrism: The Transnational Company

Through an in-depth field research, lasting several years and focusing on the clinical study of nine major companies operating in three different sectors (telecommunications, consumer electronics, and packaged branded products), the concept of a *transnational company* was developed (Bartlett and Ghoshal, 1989).

At first glance, the underlying idea does not differ substantially from Perlmutter's proposition of geo-centrism; in fact, the geocentric company seems to exhibit a similar orientation to the transnational organisational form. Similarly, there are similarities between the transnational model and the heterarchical company. However, it should be noted that the mentioned models also differ significantly at various levels of specificity.

Bartlett and Ghoshal argue for the need to abandon the traditional view of adapting uniquely to the environment and relying on a single source of competitive advantage for the company's fate. Product differentiation, cost leadership, or technological leadership, when considered individually, do not constitute the true competitive advantage of an international company. Instead, the transnational model is multidimensional in nature.

It places particular emphasis on *the opportunity to leverage its international dimension to access multiple sources of competitive advantage simultaneously*. Furthermore, it is highlighted that a couple of decades ago, it was possible to seek a correspondence between the environment, strategy, and structural arrangement; however, the complexity of certain environmental segments no longer allows for such a straightforward approach. In particular, the purely structural nature of organisational design has been challenged: changing the structure seemed like a clear path to undertake, a direct and concise message capable of reaching all members of the organisation. As emphasised by Airoldi (1980), the structure is indeed a key and powerful element, but, flexible as it may be, it cannot accompany a change that has little to do with being static.

In other words, strategic and organisational flexibility must be delineated, especially in an international context, through a delicate work of informal (as well as formal) articulation that flattens the expected change from the new organisational situation and enhances clarity in conveying the message of readjustment. Complementarity could, therefore, be the key term that indicates the synthesis of the approach described in examining the organisational instrumentation: structure, operating systems, power arrangement, and culture are levers that should not exclude each other but, on the contrary, can mutually reinforce each other.

International companies have thus been forced to redefine their structures and organisational processes. The reasons for success or failure in business cannot be solely attributed to the presence or absence of good abilities to take a proactive stance towards the environment and the market. The problem lies not so much in knowing *what to do* but encompasses the different *how to do*, the moments of implementing corporate policies, the ways to shape their image, and clarify the features and boundaries to be given to their interventions. The mass of resources, experiences, and skills often turns out to be enormous but not so easily manageable. Therefore, it is a matter of lacking organisational capacity: the point is not to add resources to the existing ones but to redesign the use of those already in place; to do this, one does not necessarily have to proceed through revising the organisational structure. Instead, attention must also be given to the logic followed in connecting the means and tools together. The aim is not so much to demonstrate the superiority of certain organisational levers over others, but to emphasise the change in the approach as a whole.

Above all, the myth of the inevitability of the homogenisation process of needs and products has shown signs of weakness. Despite the extraordinary evolution of communication and transportation means, and the resulting less profound differences in preferences and market structures among different nations, the same cannot be said for consumption habits and typical preferences of individual national cultures.

The experience of using 'universal' consumer goods, especially those with high functional redundancy, ultimately leads to an increasing demand for differentiation, meaning a greater appreciation of variety and variability, which the supply can indeed satisfy at increasing differential costs (Vaccà, 1989).

In many countries, attempts to accelerate the convergence of preferences have not had significant effects, mainly because there is a group of consumers who reject standardised products with standard design and performance and reassert their traditional preferences. This has provided more space for national producers or international companies capable of orchestrating a broad range of actions with attention to local realities.

1.5.1 Multinational, Global and Multi-Local Companies. At this point, it becomes appropriate to offer an explanation of the chosen terms to address the topic. The entire debate that has taken place over the years regarding the adjective to accompany the word 'company' when discussing internationalisation has not resulted in a unanimous outcome. Therefore, it has been decided to use a personal and subjective (and hopefully clear) approach and not provide detailed explanations for the chosen labels. After all, they are merely labels, symbols; what matters is that the substance is transparent and intelligible.

In this sense, an *international company* refers to a company that operates outside of it's national borders in any way. It is undoubtedly a broad and perhaps generic definition, but it serves as a useful 'umbrella' to introduce more specific definitions such as those offered for *multinational, global,* and *multi-local companies* (Daniels and Frost, 1991).

The *multi-local company* bases its strategic and organisational choices on its ability to be responsive to different national demands. It sees the lack of identity between social, cultural, and consumer situations as an opportunity to excel and simply adapts to them; its subsidiaries are managed as a diversified portfolio of activities.

The *global company* is characterised by its ability to achieve high levels of efficiency. Strategic as well as operational decision-making processes take place at the centre. The global market is considered in an integrated manner, not investigated separately in each of its parts, except at the expense of the standardisation of production processes.

The *multinational company* is distinguished, on the one hand, by a centralised power (though less than in the global model), and on the other hand, by a significant degree of autonomy granted to foreign subsidiaries (though less than in the multi-local company). The core of the company's strategy lies in its ability to transfer and leverage the knowledge developed at the headquarters whilst leaving room for subsidiaries to adapt what has been transmitted to foreign markets. Multinational companies usually develop new products in their home countries and then gradually spread innovation worldwide, first in countries that are close to the level of development reached in the home country. For example, in Europe for American multinational companies and subsequently in less technologically advanced countries (Vernon, 1966).

The proposed definitions clearly reference the typology identified by Daniels and Frost (1991). The transnational company has the potential to combine economies of scale and differentiation, making it the true challenge at the forefront of internationalisation.

Daniels and Frost effectively highlight the existence of the dilemmas of centralisation/decentralisation and standardisation/differentiation; from the resolution of these dichotomies, the concept of the transnational company emerges. Specifically:

a. *From geographic dominance to business dominance.* Transnationality is not an easy concept to grasp, as it is more about a way of conceiving business – *how to do* business – rather than a geographical concept – *where* to do business. Therefore, it becomes a priority to organise the business as a whole, rather than focusing on the organisation of functions or geographic areas.
b. *From the centralisation-decentralisation dilemma to 'everywhere'.* Transnationality can be defined as the ability to do business anywhere, regardless of whether functions are centralised or decentralised. Customers and business partners do not consider whether decisions are made centrally or not, just as they do not consider whether business knowledge is transferred along functional lines or geographic boundaries.
c. *From a synergistic logic to a dyadic logic.* This transition moves from the idea of the company as an organisation where the whole is equal to or greater than the sum of its parts to understanding that each individual part reflects its 'genetic code' and, therefore, allows us to see or understand the entire business.
d. *From hierarchical relationships to a trust-based network.* It is essential to place trust in the people who occupy coordination positions within the company's network to reduce the time and effort required to achieve desired results.
e. *From existence to building positive relationships.* Being transnational means more than merely being present on a continent or in a country; it involves ensuring that local customers recognise the company and attribute positive characteristics to it.
f. *From central control to connection.* The central management of the organisation plays the role of coordinating the different nodes of the company's network, as well as being the *authentic interpreter* of the meaning of messages, contributing to the defence and development of collective cultural codes.

1.5.2. The Organisational Model of a Transnational Company. The potential source of competitive advantage inherent in operating beyond national borders lies in the opportunity to engage with diverse realities and explore global markets. Such a company must develop a management capability that transcends national boundaries and benefits from exposure to a wider and diversified range of environmental stimuli: the broad range of consumer preferences and competitive behaviours, the variety of government demands, different sources of technology, and learning, etc. To realise the potential advantages derived from the complexity of the international environment, the management must build a sensitive and responsive organisation capable of effectively transferring acquired knowledge.

The transnational company is structured in a way that allows it to harmonise diverse strategic demands within a highly flexible organisational framework. Unlike the three traditional formulas seen in the previous paragraph, the transnational strategy is simultaneously focused on *local responsiveness, efficiency, innovation, and knowledge transfer objectives*. The key attributes of the transnational model and its fundamental operating principles are highlighted below, keeping in mind that transnational does not simply mean a new strategic approach or a specific ideal organisational form to strive for. At its core, being transational represents a *new managerial mindset.*

1. The organisational configuration of the transnational company takes the form of an *integrated network*, composed of geographically distributed, specialised units, coordinated through mutual adjustment (Thompson, 1967). The geographic dispersion of activities enables the capacity to respond to local needs and perceive stimuli wherever they arise, specialisation ensures a degree of efficiency, and mutual adjustment is necessary to foster a collaborative attitude among the parties in communication processes, problem-solving, and the realisation of global projects.

The connections between the centre and the periphery, as well as among peripheral units, are highly flexible to maximise the exploitation of their respective competencies and capabilities. This marks a departure from the mindset of control and embraces a network logic. Within this framework, the flows of information, resources, components, and personnel assume a critical dimension and significance.

2. *The roles and responsibilities of the various units that make up the network are differentiated and subject to change over time.* The transnational management abandons the practice of treating foreign subsidiaries uniformly, as it represents a significant obstacle to achieving the flexibility that the company needs. The tendency to create a discriminating organisation that assigns different tasks and responsibilities to various local units must be initiated in parallel with the change in the conception of the relationship between the centre and the periphery.

In the transnational model, there is a clear departure from the metaphor comparing the relationship between the headquarters and local units to a typical parent-child relationship (Franko, 1976). This interpretation often leads to prohibiting discriminatory treatment among different subsidiaries and assigning a higher hierarchical status to the headquarters compared to local units.

The transition is evident from a hierarchical control logic, which often leads to tense and even hostile relationships between the centre and subsidiaries, to a network logic where each part plays a specific role and is entrusted with the responsibility necessary to contribute to the overall strategic design of the company.

The differentiation of roles assigned to subsidiaries is not only possible but necessary; this way, the transnational company can leverage its geographically dispersed presence to engage in increasingly sophisticated competitive games, requiring national units to adopt different strategic attitudes within the global competitive arena.

Each local unit participates in the global strategy to benefit the overall company. Naturally, due to the differing strategic relevance of local markets and the varying levels of resources and capabilities possessed by subsidiaries, the importance of the role attributed to each unit varies. It is essential to assign the most appropriate role to each local organisation; the same applies to the headquarters: it may be the case that for specific activities, a market initially considered internal is no longer essential for the global strategy. In such cases, the headquarters must be willing to relinquish its role of leader (for those activities) and assign it to a foreign subsidiary better positioned for that purpose.

From the strategic perspective, it considers the weight given to national environments within the global strategy; concerning organisational importance, it refers to the level of physical-technical and economic resources and expertise held by the local unit (Bartlett and Ghoshal, 1989). Four role configurations that a subsidiary can assume emerge from this analysis.

- *Strategic Leaders.* This role is played by national organisations with significant local resources and capabilities situated in strategically important markets. The strategic leader acts as a partner to the headquarters in the development and implementation of broad initiatives. They must be able to identify weak signals early on and actively participate in analysing potential dangers and opportunities, as well as formulating appropriate responses.
- *Contributors.* The foreign units in this category have the ability to gain advantages from the local environment and leverage them in different territories within the global chessboard. In this case, it is crucial for management to maintain a balance between the resources held locally and the lack of external stimuli. There is a risk of creating excessive resources in less vital environments or pursuing unnecessary or even harmful local autonomy and differentiation paths for the company's global strategy. Instead, these resources need to be channelled into a common project that presents challenging and motivating problems for the people involved.
- *Executors.* This scenario involves subsidiaries possessing simple but sufficient competencies for their characteristic management and operating in a context that is not strategically important for the company. These units cannot significantly contribute to the company's strategic processes, nor do they control specific resources. They mostly add value and often ensure the company's commercial continuity and the development of resources intended to finance innovative efforts. Through this category of subsidiaries, economies of scale characteristic of the transnational company can be achieved.
- *Black Holes.* They are found in all those geographically strategic areas where the company likely has limited possibilities of obtaining significant market shares due to resource constraints, but where it is essential to maintain a strong presence, albeit symbolic. However, this does not mean that such a role is passively accepted by everyone: the black hole is not a strategically useful position in the medium term, and it is the task of its management to find a way to lead the subsidiary towards assuming a role of strategic leader, developing within the local unit those critical resources it lacks.

Overall, the principle of homogeneity is abandoned in favour of a logic of differentiation and to produce a higher degree of organisational flexibility.

3. On the other hand, the transnational company must develop *flexible coordination processes*. The geographic dispersion of activities and resources, the differentiation of roles and responsibilities assigned to various local units, and the intensity of flows of people, goods, and information across the organisation make strong coordination necessary.

The typical coordination mechanisms employed in transnational companies are three: centralisation, formalisation, and socialisation. The empirical reality investigated by Bartlett and Ghoshal revealed significant uniformity in the use of a particular coordination mechanism by companies with the same cultural *background:* Japanese companies tend to employ centralisation, American companies lean towards formalisation, whilst European ones are more inclined towards socialisation mechanisms.

In the transnational company, however, these three mechanisms must be developed together, assigning them different weights depending on the activity or part of the organisation that needs coordination. The principle of flexibility, pervasive in the transnational model, reappears once again. Some activities, functions, or areas may require more centralisation, whilst socialisation and formalisation might be more suitable mechanisms for other parts.

4. *Internal differentiation in roles and managerial processes* can lead to fragmentation and internal conflicts within the transnational company. Without a strong source of unification, the transnational company risks degenerating into organisational anarchy. To create a sense of unity, the company must strive to develop a *unified managerial mindset and a shared vision*. The process of building a unified and shared vision must adhere to three fundamental requirements:
    - The vision must be clearly articulated and communicated in a simple manner.
    - There must be continuity in the management's commitment to its realisation.
    - A high degree of coherence between the objectives of different parts of the organisation is necessary to ensure that the vision is shared by all.

Communication, continuity, and coherence form the basis of a strong and widespread culture. It is evident, therefore, how the management of human resources plays a highly critical role in activating personal commitment and involvement. In particular, three aspects of personnel policies are of particular importance:

- *Selection and Hiring:* The transnational company adopts an international hiring policy to tap into a broad pool of talent. They seek managers who are open to relocation, capable of seeing issues from a broader perspective, and willing to negotiate on matters of mutual interest.
- *Training and Development*: Training and development programmes are valuable tools for transmitting basic cultural norms, a shared vision, and common values.
- *Career Paths:* Designing spiral career paths across different functions, geographical units, and activities allows for cross-fertilisation of ideas, the development of shared experiences, and a broader vision.

5. The transnational company, to implement a multifocal strategy, must have a highly flexible organisational structure that values all relevant dimensions. To jointly address the strategic needs of global efficiency, local responsiveness, and innovation, the company requires a strong functional

management, effective regional management, and efficient business governance. The main effort lies in preventing any one dimension from dominating the company's perspectives and capabilities.

The transnational organisational model is characterised by *maintaining a dynamic balance between different perspectives.* Once again, this involves not just making structural changes but also acting at the level of processes and behaviours to facilitate the integration of diverse viewpoints. In particular, it is essential to ensure that all managerial groups have legitimacy, credibility, and influence, and that executives representing different perspectives have unrestricted access to all relevant corporate information.

The continuous pursuit of balance among different perspectives is a dynamic process that requires constant adjustments, which may seemingly lead to further internal tensions. However, ambiguity and continuous change are viewed as stimuli for innovation and creativity. The key lies in not exceeding the limit beyond which role ambiguity and shifting power dynamics, instead of fostering creative tension, lead to chaos.

6. The transnational organisation *is not a matrix.* The concept of organisational multidimensionality is often mentally associated with the matrix structure. Many companies respond to the increasing complexity of their environment and the resulting need for multifocal perspectives by introducing increasingly complex organisational formulas. The global matrix may seem like the most suitable form for such needs; the multiple information channels, overlapping responsibilities, dual *reporting channels*, etc. seem to guarantee the flexibility the company needs.

However, in reality, the apparent rationality of the matrix structure hides a strong difficulty in governing organisational processes, which becomes insurmountable even in the international context due to both physical and cultural distances. The transnational model proposes to approach the problem from a broader perspective: it is not just about finding a structural adaptation, but rather about *building the organisational capacity* to operate in an international environment. The transnational company has a new mentality, a new orientation towards foreign business that cannot be synthesised in a rigid structural concept. The transnational organisation, moreover, is formed gradually; it takes shape in a complex form with differentiated roles and responsibilities, but these roles are clearly defined and not subject to joint responsibility that creates tension and conflict in the matrix structure.

The goal of the transnational company is not to create a complicated matrix structure, but to forge a matrix in the minds of managers, encouraging them towards coordinated actions and the formulation of shared and focused decisions.

7. The transnational *company is characterised by a multitude of innovation and learning processes.* In the international environment, a company's ability to innovate is one of the key sources of competitive success. Traditionally, there are two types of innovation processes: the *central* innovation process and the *local* innovation process.

In the first case, typical of the global company organisational model, the company identifies an opportunity in its home country and, using centralised resources at the headquarters, develops a new product/process that is then utilised worldwide.

Conversely, in the local innovation process, it is the national subsidiary that uses its own capabilities to create an innovation that perfectly fits the needs of the local environment in which it operates; the multi-local company typically follows this approach to innovation.

The challenge lies in creating an organisation capable of simultaneously facilitating both types of processes: the transnational innovation process supports and integrates traditional local and central processes and utilises the connections between different units to leverage existing resources and capabilities, regardless of their location; the ultimate goal is to capitalise on every new opportunity, wherever it arises in the world.

8. The transnational company acts as a *dual network*. Those operating in the international arena encounter significant challenges in developing all the strategic capabilities (efficiency, responsiveness, innovation) required by the increasingly complex and interconnected competitive environment. One possible solution to acquire these multifocal capabilities in a timely manner compared to competitors is to connect with other companies that have complementary strategic competencies or positions. The transnational company, therefore, interacts with external actors, engaging in *cooperative agreements* to achieve a high level of strategic and organisational flexibility.

The transnational structure thus takes the form of a *dual network*, comprising an internal network and an external network. The internal network consists of all the integrated and interdependent units that make up the organisation (as mentioned in point 1), whilst the external network represents all the collaborative ties the company establishes with the external environment to rapidly acquire the strategic capabilities needed to compete successfully (Perrone, 1990).

9. The transnational company has its primary and *true factor of success in its management*. As seen, there is a strong risk of fragmentation and atomisation of the organisational structure; to limit the damage, it is necessary to set in motion a coordinated set of integration forces, without exaggerating in that direction. There are three main tasks that the management must ensure to prevent the company from being: too coordinated to be flexible, too dispersed to be competitive, and too complex to develop and exploit common learning processes. The three mechanisms useful for this purpose are:
    - Legitimising the different capabilities and perspectives present in the system.
    - Developing multiple and flexible coordination processes.
    - Building a shared vision and individual commitment.

Integration mechanisms and corporate culture are thus the cornerstones of managerial practices in the transnational company.

1.5.3 The Transition towards Transnationality. The transnational model has been conceived to manage complexity and change in an increasingly interconnected and demanding international environment (Galbraith, 1973). This organisational model, however, should be seen as an ideal destination that companies can strive for in order to ensure the strategic and organisational flexibility required to compete internationally. The transition from a one-dimensional formula (global, multinational, or multi-local) to a multifocal formula (transnational) is a gradual and particularly challenging process. It involves not only changes in the organisational structure but, above all, the *soft variables* of the organisation. The shift towards transnationality represents a significant challenge for the company's leadership: it requires shaping the managerial mindset and abandoning provincial habits that could hinder the formation of a truly global and broad vision. The main problem is that management is often reluctant to let go of established systems that may have contributed to past success, even though the external situation has changed and requires different responses. A central variable in this process is the ability to learn: the company must learn quickly from its experiences (and those of its competitors) to deepen its understanding of the operating environment (Vicari, 1991).

However, the specificity of the path towards transnationality is described for each company based on its managerial heritage that has formed and consolidated over time. This managerial heritage is represented by the specific characteristics of the company, its history, values, and culture that have developed over the years and manifest in a particular way of doing things, a certain organisational configuration, and a specific distribution of responsibilities (Bodega, 1996; Zamenopoulos and Alexiou, 2018).

The managerial heritage is simultaneously a positive element, as it is a source of specific skills on which the company must build a more articulated and complex capacity, and a negative element, as it can be a potential source of resistance to change. The role of the company's founder or a particularly strong and determined leader, the impact of the country's culture of origin, and relevant experiences accumulated in the past are some of the main forces that contribute significantly to creating typical norms and values.

The company must carefully evaluate its managerial heritage, making a clear effort to identify aspects that could hinder change and act as a source of rigidity. Through a careful and objective analysis of this heritage, the company can understand whether it potentially has the capacity to respond adequately to new external demands or, more ambitiously, to shape and influence environmental forces.

The change process should not begin with modifications to the formal organisational structure. The starting point should be an effort to change attitudes and mindsets of individuals, followed by the implementation of changes in processes and interpersonal relationships, and finally, the modification of the formal structure. In particular, company routines must be modified in the first instance.

Pettigrew (1986) studied organisations in terms of a longitudinal process, recognising that systems have continuity in the present and future relative to the past. In this way, he identified a sequence of 'social dramas' in the evolutionary process of a company, interspersed with periods of adaptation and routine. Routines punctuate each drama and, in this sense, form the backdrop against which it unfolds (Pettigrew, 1986).

Building on the concept of organisational routines, research by Becker (2004), Parmigiani and Howard-Grenville (2011), Pentland and Feldman (2005) explores their significance in understanding how companies adapt and evolve over time. They emphasise the importance of routines as stabilising forces that contribute to an organisation's ability to maintain continuity amidst environmental changes and uncertainties.

Moreover, Nelson and Winter (1982) also discuss organisational routines, using a Darwinian approach and focusing on the logic of population ecology (Grandori, 1984). This perspective has been further expanded upon by contemporary scholars who argue that organisational routines are a source of competitive advantage when effectively managed and aligned with the strategic goals of a company (Von Vorrel and Franco, 2017). According to these authors, the success of companies depends on:

a. The surrounding environment, which, however, is not directly knowable due to the limited nature of human rationality.
b. The subjective capacity of the company to survive and adapt.

Recent research by Howard and Grenwille (2016) deal with into the mechanisms through which routines develop and persist in organisations. They highlight that routines not only serve as a response to uncertainty but also act as mechanisms for organisational learning and knowledge creation. In this way, routines become a means of accumulating knowledge and experience over time, which contributes to their entrenchment.

Furthermore, the argument is that whilst routines can enhance organisational efficiency and stability, they can also lead to inertia and resistance to change if not properly adapted or updated. They emphasise the importance of continuous monitoring and evaluation of routines to ensure their relevance and effectiveness in dynamic and evolving environments.

In addition to these recent contributions, novel perspectives from scholars like Jerab and Tarek, (2023) emphasise the role of organisational culture and leadership in shaping routines. They contend that a strong organisational culture and effective leadership can facilitate the development of adaptive routines and foster a culture of continuous improvement and innovation. The literature suggests the identification of three functions performed by routines:

- they reduce uncertainty in decision-making in situations of interdependence among different parties, as they allow the development and stabilisation of highly probable expectations of reciprocal behaviour.
- They reduce internal conflict between divergent interests, as they replicate solutions that have been accepted through negotiation or tacitly.
- They form and preserve the 'memory' of organisational knowledge (Schein, 1984; Gagliardi, 1986; Nonaka and Takeuchi, 19951), as they transmit solutions that work and discard those that have led to difficulties and failures.

When the company realises that its routines are no longer effective, it initiates a process of search, which involves seeking new and effective ways to reduce uncertainty. Routines are seen as the genes of the organisational organism, and the concept of search is likened to biological mutation. Innovation occurs as a response to the environment; otherwise, inertia and a tendency to maintain the *status quo* dominate.

However, this perspective of organising relationships between the company and the environmental context, based on the stabilisation of routines, encounters increasing limitations in highly dynamic situations. Vaccà (1989) refers to phenomena characterised by a net increase in complexity, driven by three major transformations:

a. The development of increasingly specialised and differentiated scientific and technological potential... introducing increasing degrees of flexibility – and hence variety and variability – in production, design, decision-making processes, and product policies within the company.
b. The expansion of the global reference context.
c. The change in the nature of the relationships between demand and supply, both in the intermediate demand stage and, to some extent, in the final demand stage.

Recent research by Schotter, Mudambi, Doz and Gaur (2017) sheds light on the challenges organisations face in coping with highly dynamic and complex environments. They argue that traditional routines, whilst effective in stable contexts, may not be agile enough to adapt to rapidly changing conditions and emergent challenges. Moreover, the work of Awais, Khattak, Arfeen, Chaudhary and Syed (2023) highlights the importance of organisational flexibility and dynamic capabilities in such environments. They propose that organisations need to develop the ability to sense and respond to emerging opportunities and threats, effectively incorporating new information and learning from novel experiences (Awais et al. 2023).

Furthermore, Weber and Tarba (2014) emphasise the role of strategic agility, which involves the rapid adjustment of routines and strategies in response to changing circumstances. They suggest that organisations need to embrace a mindset of continuous adaptation and experimentation to thrive in highly dynamic situations.

In light of these recent contributions, it becomes evident that whilst routines play a crucial role in organisational stability and knowledge preservation, companies must also complement them with a strategic focus on flexibility, adaptability, and agility to navigate the complexities of highly dynamic environments.

Taking into account the aforementioned premises, it is appropriate to identify two different types of genes:

- Biological genes, so to speak, immutable conditions that can be defined as the profound conditions of existence of that particular company (Davis, 1987).
- A second type of genes, improperly called routines, which are no longer perceived as immutable or changeable with extreme difficulty, but instead can undergo changes without affecting the core of the company, its personality, and its original way of interpreting the environmental complexity.

It is on this second aspect that work is needed, using typical methods of cultural change (Brumana et al., 2014), to achieve a stable and sufficiently profound modification of the company's cultural profile and to relatively quickly approach the models of the heterarchical and transnational company.

1.6 The Metanational Organisation

The recently presented transnational business model implies a conception of the global company as an efficient network of subsidiaries, built to ensure penetration into global markets. This approach to global operations is gradually being surpassed due to the development and strengthening of the knowledge economy, which is introducing a new element of attention and challenge for businesses: learning from geography. The international dimension may no longer constitute a distinctive competitive advantage, as an efficient global network is now merely a prerequisite for competitiveness. Prioritising the competitive advantage of the nation one represents and a single geographical location can no longer represent the ultimate development of an industrial sector due to the geographic dispersion of knowledge.

The intensification of competition has thus generated a new competitive paradigm, within which a company's success is determined by its ability to identify and leverage widely distributed knowledge. Since knowledge with innovative potential is difficult to acquire and often requires even greater complexity in processing, it becomes evident that a company can plausibly identify a form of competitive advantage in its capacity to internalise and globally exploit such dispersed knowledge.

From these simple considerations arises the metanational company model proposed by Doz, Santos, and Williamson (2001). The term 'metanational' was chosen by the authors to indicate not the surpassing of national borders, but their annulment within the business network, as suggested by the Greek prefix 'meta', which, when translated, means beyond, not above (Doz, 2006). Metanational means *"seeing the world as a single reservoir of knowledge with pockets of technology, market skills, and capabilities"* (Doz, Santos, and Williamson, 2001, p. 5), which represent an untapped competitive potential.

The metanational company is thus characterised by a new approach to international markets: its success derives from the ability to perceive and mobilise dispersed knowledge to achieve exclusive competitive advantages. The innovations thus generated have an intrinsic global character, as they have been conceived through the synergistic application of knowledge from around the world. With a single product, the latent needs and desires of a wide variety of consumers are addressed, making every innovation immediately projectable on a global scale. *"By acquiring and integrating knowledge from dispersed geographical contexts, companies can generate a greater number of more valuable innovations at lower costs"* (Santos, Doz, Williamson, 2004, p. 31).

The realisation of such a competitive approach is made possible by acting on the basis of three different but complementary strategic perspectives: sensing, mobilising, and making new forms of available knowledge usable. The process of metanational innovation is structured as follows:

- *Sensing.* It is necessary for the company to identify and ensure adequate access to new competencies, innovative technologies, and knowledge related to recent trends in dominant markets. This implies being able to perceive complex knowledge in markets and translate it into forms that the company can understand and process. The success of this strategic approach lies in having perceptive capabilities that are more sensitive than those of ordinary companies, allowing the discovery and reworking of truly innovative knowledge.
- *Mobilising.* The metanational company must create international structures capable of conceiving pioneering products and processes by integrating capacities and opportunities emerging from global markets. These structures are called 'magnets' because they attract dispersed knowledge with high strategic potential necessary to activate innovative processes.
- *Operating*. The metanational company must optimise the dimensions and geographical configuration of its activities to achieve flexibility, efficiency, and financial rigor. When global learning processes generate innovations, it is important for these innovations to be engineered and produced in a way that ensures their profitability.

The metanational company must possess a broad range of knowledge and capabilities, which are realised in very diverse forms. These forms change based on the characteristics of the knowledge to be learned and exploited, as well as the type of business in which the company operates. Therefore, it is not possible to propose a single organisational model for the implementation of a metanational innovation system: the elements composing the process must be identified on a case-by-case basis, based on specific contingencies.

In a metanational organisation, the emphasis is not just on coordinating activities across borders but also on actively shaping the competitive landscape and industry dynamics in multiple countries. It goes beyond the transnational model by emphasising the company's ability to influence and reshape markets, regulations, and industry norms on a global scale. Key characteristics of a metanational organisation include:

1. Strategic agility and Global Vision
2. Co-creation of value
3. Strategic Flexibility

4. Dynamic governance
5. Innovation Ecosystems
6. Knowledge Sharing
7. Shared values and identity

1. *Strategic agility* and *Global Vision.* A metanational organisation stands apart with its distinct and far-reaching global vision, which serves as the guiding force behind its strategic decisions (Salomon, 2016). Unlike traditional companies that merely respond to external changes and market shifts, a metanational organisation takes a proactive approach in shaping the future of the industry and markets it operates in (Schotter et. al., 2017). The foundation of this global vision lies in its deep understanding of the interconnected and interdependent nature of the modern business landscape. At the heart of the metanational organisation's global vision is a comprehensive grasp of emerging trends, technological advancements, and evolving consumer preferences across diverse markets worldwide. Instead of limiting its focus to a single region or country, it extends its gaze to embrace the entire global ecosystem (Luu, 2023). This panoramic view enables the organisation to foresee potential disruptions, identify untapped opportunities, and anticipate market demands even before they fully materialise (Lioukas and Reuer, 2015).

By fostering a culture of foresight and innovation, the metanational organisation positions itself as a trailblazer in the industry (Zamenopoulos and Aloxiou, 2018). Rather than passively reacting to market shifts, it proactively anticipates changes and devises strategies to capitalise on emerging trends. This forward-looking mindset empowers the organisation to be at the forefront of technological advancements and market disruptions, ensuring its relevance and competitiveness in an ever-evolving world.

Moreover, the metanational organisation recognises the importance of collaboration and partnership on a global scale (Vieira, 2023). It actively seeks out alliances with industry leaders, start-ups, research institutions, and governmental bodies worldwide (Godiwalla, 2018). These strategic collaborations not only enrich the organisation's knowledge pool but also enable it to leverage the strengths and expertise of diverse partners (Rios et al., 2022). Through collective efforts and shared visions, these partnerships drive innovation, create synergies, and propel the organisation towards achieving its ambitious global goals (Ariño et al., 2005).

In essence, the global vision of a metanational organisation extends beyond immediate market success; it embodies a commitment to driving positive change and influencing the industry's trajectory (Lioukas and Reuer, 2015). By actively shaping the future of its sector, the organisation assumes a leadership role in the global marketplace, guiding industry standards, and setting benchmarks for sustainable growth and responsible practices. Embracing agility and adaptability, the metanational organisation continually reinvents itself to remain relevant and impactful in a rapidly changing world. It is this unwavering global vision that sets the metanational organisation apart, allowing it to thrive as a transformative force in the global economy (Allegretti et. al, 2021).

2. *Co-Creation of Value.* Metanational organisations co-create value with diverse stakeholders, including customers, suppliers, governments, and local communities. They engage in partnerships and collaborations to leverage the strengths and capabilities of various players in different countries. Metanational organisations excel in the art of co-creating value by actively engaging with a diverse range of stakeholders (Öberg and Lundberg, 2022). They recognise that value is not generated in isolation but emerges through dynamic interactions with customers, suppliers, governments, and local communities. Embracing a collaborative approach, these organisations forge strategic partnerships and alliances with key players worldwide to leverage their unique strengths and capabilities. By involving stakeholders from

various countries and cultures, metanational organisations tap into a wealth of knowledge, insights, and resources that fuel their innovative endeavours and market responsiveness. Customer co-creation is a core aspect of their strategy, as they involve customers in the design, development, and refinement of their products and services. By soliciting feedback and insights from customers across different markets, they gain a deeper understanding of diverse needs and preferences, allowing them to tailor their offerings more effectively. This customer-centric approach not only enhances the quality of their products but also fosters customer loyalty and brand advocacy. Furthermore, metanational organisations actively collaborate with suppliers to foster mutually beneficial relationships. They recognise that strong partnerships with suppliers are essential for ensuring a smooth and efficient supply chain, enabling them to meet market demands swiftly and cost-effectively. By engaging in open dialogue and sharing information, they build trust and transparency, fostering a collaborative ecosystem that drives value co-creation throughout the supply chain (Öberg and Lundberg, 2022). Moreover, metanational organisations are cognizant of the critical role that governments play in shaping business environments. They actively engage with governments to understand local regulations, policy changes, and emerging opportunities. This collaboration allows them to navigate complex regulatory landscapes and align their business strategies with broader societal and environmental goals. Lastly, these organisations recognise the importance of contributing positively to the communities in which they operate. By investing in social initiatives and sustainable practices, they create a positive impact and build strong relationships with local communities. This not only enhances their reputation and brand image but also leads to long-term, sustainable growth. In summary, metanational organisations embrace the philosophy of value co-creation, recognising that the collective efforts of diverse stakeholders lead to shared success and prosperity. Through strategic collaborations and partnerships, they leverage the strengths of global networks to achieve innovative solutions, enhanced customer experiences, and positive societal impact. By continuously nurturing these relationships and remaining responsive to changing dynamics, metanational organisations stand at the forefront of a new era of collaborative and sustainable business practices.

3. *Strategic Flexibility*. The metanational organisation is highly adaptive and flexible in responding to changing market conditions and opportunities. It can quickly reallocate resources and capabilities to exploit emerging trends or address new challenges. Strategic flexibility is a fundamental attribute of a metanational organisation, allowing it to thrive in the dynamic and competitive global business landscape. As an entity with a clear and ambitious global vision, the metanational organisation is not merely reactive to external changes but actively shapes the future of the industry and markets in which it operates (Doz and Prahalad, 1987). This proactive approach empowers the organisation to stay ahead of emerging trends and capitalise on new opportunities, leveraging its diverse and dynamic resource base (Prahalad and Ramaswamy, 2004). In response to changing market conditions and opportunities, the metanational organisation exhibits a remarkable level of adaptability and responsiveness. It possesses the ability to quickly reallocate resources and capabilities to seize emerging trends or address new challenges (Ohmae, 1989). This strategic flexibility enables the organisation to enter new markets, capitalise on emerging technologies, and meet the evolving needs of customers worldwide (Hitt et al., 2013). By continuously monitoring and analysing market developments, the metanational organisation can proactively adjust its strategies to maintain a competitive edge and sustain growth (Bartlett and Ghoshal, 1989). One of the key aspects of strategic flexibility is the organisation's capacity to form and manage strategic partnerships and collaborations (Luo and Shenkar, 2006). By engaging with diverse stakeholders such as customers, suppliers, governments, and local communities, the metanational organisation co-creates value (Doz and Prahalad, 1987). These partnerships enable the organisation to leverage the

strengths and capabilities of various players in different countries, enhancing its ability to respond to local market demands effectively (Bartlett and Ghoshal, 1989). This collaborative approach not only fosters innovation but also enhances the organisation's understanding of local markets, allowing it to tailor its products and services to meet the specific needs of customers worldwide (Luo and Shenkar, 2006). In conclusion, strategic flexibility is the driving force behind the metanational organisation's success in a rapidly changing global environment. The ability to quickly adapt, reallocate resources, and capitalise on emerging opportunities is essential for sustaining a competitive advantage and achieving long-term growth (Doz and Prahalad, 1987). By actively shaping the future of the industry and markets it operates in, the metanational organisation remains at the forefront of innovation and consistently meets the evolving demands of customers worldwide.

4. *Dynamic Governance.* Governance in a metanational organisation is dynamic and decentralised, with decision-making authority distributed across the organisation. It allows for agility and responsiveness to local market needs whilst maintaining a global perspective. Strategic flexibility is a critical characteristic of a metanational organisation, enabling it to thrive in a fast-paced and unpredictable global business environment. The metanational organisation's capacity for strategic flexibility empowers it to swiftly and effectively respond to evolving market conditions and capitalise on emerging opportunities. By maintaining a diverse and adaptable resource base, the organisation can readily reallocate its assets and capabilities to align with dynamic market demands. This agility allows the metanational organisation to seize new growth prospects, address unexpected challenges, and maintain a competitive advantage in multiple regions and industries. To achieve strategic flexibility, metanational organisations emphasise a decentralised decision-making process, empowering local units to respond promptly to market changes whilst maintaining alignment with the broader global vision. This localised approach enables the organisation to leverage regional insights, customer preferences, and market trends to make informed decisions. Additionally, metanational organisations invest in advanced data analytics and technology to gain real-time market insights, enabling proactive decision-making and resource optimisation. A strong commitment to fostering a culture of continuous learning, innovation, and adaptability further reinforces the metanational organisation's strategic flexibility, positioning it as a formidable player in today's ever-changing global marketplace.

5. *Innovation Ecosystems.* A metanational organisation nurtures innovation ecosystems that span multiple countries and cultures. It promotes a culture of creativity and experimentation, leveraging diverse perspectives to drive innovation (Öberg and Lundberg, 2022). Innovation ecosystems lie at the core of a metanational organisation's success, providing a fertile ground for cultivating ground-breaking ideas and driving transformative change. Embracing the power of collaboration and diversity, metanational organisations foster innovation ecosystems that transcend geographical boundaries and cultural barriers. By connecting with stakeholders from various countries, industries, and disciplines, these organisations create a rich tapestry of perspectives that fuels creative thinking and experimentation. To foster a culture of innovation, metanational organisations encourage employees to challenge the status quo, take calculated risks, and explore unconventional approaches to problem-solving (Chesbrough, 2003). They recognise that innovation can emerge from unexpected sources, and as such, they facilitate open communication and knowledge-sharing across their global network of subsidiaries, partners, and research institutions. This collaborative approach facilitates the cross-fertilisation of ideas and technologies, generating novel solutions and products that address diverse customer needs. Moreover, metanational organisations invest in research and development initiatives that transcend national borders, enabling access to specialised talent, cutting-edge technologies, and emerging market trends worldwide (Wadhwa et al., 2018). They

actively participate in innovation clusters, technology hubs, and entrepreneurial ecosystems, tapping into the vibrancy of start-ups and academia to stay at the forefront of industry advancements. To maintain their edge in the ever-evolving global landscape, metanational organisations continuously evolve their innovation ecosystems and adapt to the changing needs of customers and markets. They demonstrate a nimble approach to resource allocation, strategically investing in promising ventures and swiftly withdrawing support from projects with limited potential. In this way, metanational organisations strike a delicate balance between fostering long-term innovation initiatives and embracing the fast-paced, dynamic nature of global markets.

6. *Knowledge Sharing*. Information and knowledge sharing are integral to a metanational organisation's success. The company fosters a learning culture, encouraging the exchange of best practices and insights across its global network. Information and knowledge sharing play a pivotal role in the success of metanational organisations, fostering innovation, agility, and adaptability in an ever-evolving global landscape (Zamenopoulos and Alexiou, 2018). These organisations recognise that their competitive advantage lies not only in their access to diverse resources and capabilities but also in their ability to leverage collective intelligence across their global network (Gooderham et al, 2022). As such, they actively cultivate a learning culture that encourages the exchange of best practices and insights, creating a collaborative ecosystem where knowledge flows freely (Gupta and Govindarajah, 1990). Metanational organisations aspire to become:

- *learning organisations*, where knowledge creation, dissemination, and application are ingrained in the company's DNA (Pennington, 2022). Learning is not limited to individual employees but extends to teams, business units, and even partner organisations. Leaders in these organisations foster a culture of continuous improvement, where employees are encouraged to seek new knowledge, experiment with novel approaches, and learn from both successes and failures.
- *global knowledge hubs* (Beverly, 2015). These hubs serve as virtual or physical platforms where employees from different countries can connect, share experiences, and collaborate on projects. Virtual communication tools, online forums, and real-time collaboration platforms further enhance the accessibility and efficiency of knowledge sharing (Garro-Abarca et al., 2021).
- *Communities of practice* (CoPs) are an integral part of the knowledge-sharing ecosystem in metanational organisations (Nicolini et al., 2022). CoPs bring together individuals with shared interests, expertise, and goals, fostering organic knowledge exchange and problem-solving. These communities may be organised around specific functional areas, projects, or emerging industry trends, enabling cross-functional and cross-cultural collaboration (Zamenopoulos and Alexiou, 2018).
- *Places that put a strong emphasis on identifying and disseminating best practices across the organisation.* Through internal case studies, success stories, and lessons learned, employees are encouraged to adopt proven strategies, accelerating the diffusion of effective practices and avoiding redundant efforts (Santistevan and Josserand, 2019).
- *Organisers of regular learning events, workshops, and seminars are organised to promote knowledge sharing and skill development* (Gutterman, 2023). These events may involve internal and external subject matter experts, encouraging employees to stay updated on the latest industry trends, technologies, and best practices.
- Entities that *leverage technology to facilitate knowledge sharing across borders* (Rammal et. al, 2023). Intranets, collaboration platforms, and knowledge repositories allow employees to access

relevant information and expertise from anywhere in the world. Additionally, artificial intelligence and machine learning are increasingly used to capture and curate knowledge from diverse sources, making it easily accessible to employees.

- *Entities that recognise and reward knowledge sharing* behaviours (Gooderham et. al, 2022). Recognition programmes, performance incentives, and career development opportunities are designed to promote a culture of knowledge sharing and continuous learning.

Therefore, knowledge sharing is a key enabler of success in metanational organisations (Godiwalla, 2018). By fostering a learning culture, establishing global knowledge hubs, nurturing communities of practice, sharing best practices, organising learning events, leveraging technology, and providing recognition and incentives, these organisations create a collaborative ecosystem that accelerates innovation and adaptability. In an increasingly interconnected and dynamic global environment, metanational organisations understand that the collective intelligence of their global network is a strategic asset that drives sustainable growth and competitive advantage (Martínez-Peláez et al, 2023).

7. Shared Values and Identity. Despite its global presence, a metanational organisation maintains a strong shared set of values and a unified identity. This sense of purpose and belonging helps align employees and stakeholders towards common goals. In our globalised and diverse landscape, metanational organisations strive to build a cohesive and unified culture that transcends geographic boundaries and fosters a strong sense of shared values and identity (Andersson et al., 2015). For a metanational organisation to maintain a common purpose and sense of belonging among its employees and stakeholders, there is a need to ensure alignment towards common goals:

- *Core values and purpose.* At the heart of a metanational organisation lies a set of core values that define its fundamental beliefs, principles, and ethical standards (Rammal et al., 2023). These values serve as guiding principles, influencing decision-making and shaping the organisation's actions across all locations. They reflect the organisation's identity and form the basis for a shared sense of purpose that unites employees and stakeholders worldwide.
- *Cultural integration.* Metanational organisations proactively work towards integrating diverse cultures and perspectives to create a harmonious and inclusive environment (Syed and Tariq, 2017). Through cultural exchange programmes, cross-cultural training, and initiatives that celebrate diversity, the organisation seeks to foster mutual understanding and appreciation among its global workforce.
- *Leadership role modelling.* Leaders within a metanational organisation play a crucial role in exemplifying the shared values and identity (Buch, 2020). They serve as role models, consistently demonstrating the organisation's core values in their behaviour and decision-making. This leadership commitment reinforces the importance of shared values throughout the organisation.
- *Communication and transparency.* Effective communication is key to reinforcing shared values and identity in a metanational organisation (Evans et al., 1990). Regular communication channels, such as internal newsletters, town hall meetings, and video conferences, provide a platform for leaders to share updates on the organisation's progress and reaffirm core values.
- *Employee engagement.* Employee engagement initiatives are instrumental in instilling a sense of belonging and commitment to the organisation's shared values (Imanding et al., 2014). Recognising and rewarding employees who embody the core values and actively contribute to the organisation's success reinforces the importance of these values in daily operations.

- *Organisational rituals and traditions.* Metanational organisations establish meaningful rituals and traditions that unite employees across different locations (Ariño et al., 2005). These may include annual conferences, global team-building events, or commemorative activities that strengthen the organisation's shared identity.
- *Purpose-Driven Strategy.* It aligns its strategic objectives with its shared values and purpose (Durand and Ioannou, 2023). This purpose-driven strategy guides decision-making and resource allocation, ensuring that the organisation remains committed to its core values whilst pursuing its global ambitions.
- *Social responsibility.* Demonstrating a commitment to social responsibility and sustainability reinforces the organisation's shared values and identity (Von Borell and Franco, 2017). Engaging in initiatives that address global challenges, support local communities, and promote ethical business practices further strengthens the organisation's reputation and sense of purpose.

By upholding core values, fostering cultural integration, practising leadership role modelling, promoting effective communication, engaging employees, establishing meaningful rituals, aligning strategic objectives, and demonstrating social responsibility, these organisations create a strong sense of purpose and belonging that transcends geographical boundaries. This shared identity unites employees and stakeholders, driving a collective effort towards common goals and ensuring the organisation has enduring success on the global stage. In other words, the metanational organisation is not confined by national boundaries but transcends them, integrating global and local perspectives into a cohesive whole. It strives to create unique advantages by tapping into the diversity of markets, resources, and talents across different countries. However, building and managing a metanational organisation is no easy task. It requires visionary leadership, a deep understanding of local contexts, and an ability to navigate complex geopolitical and cultural landscapes. Nonetheless, for companies aiming to succeed in today's interconnected and fast-changing world, embracing the principles of the metanational organisation can provide a powerful strategic advantage.

Figure 1. The process of metanational innovation (Doz, Santos, and Williamson, 2001)

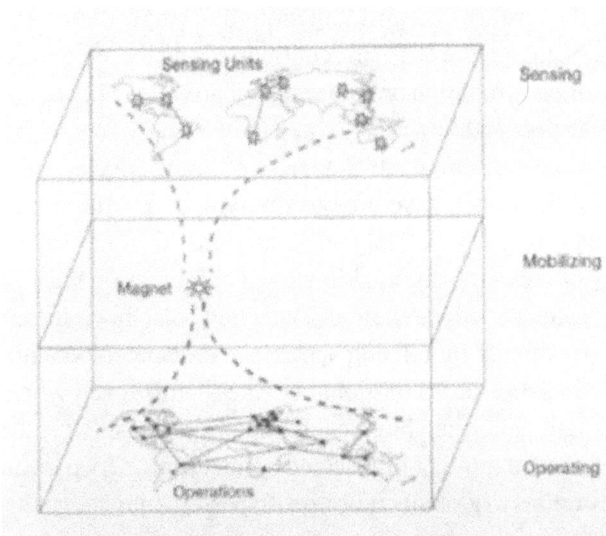

Table 1. Six capabilities that the metanational company must develop, interpreted through examples provided by the activities of the network's peripheries

To perceive new knowledge more quickly and effectively than the competition	**Predictive ability**: Making forecasts about the emergence of innovative pockets of technology and new consumer needs allows companies to anticipate evolving trends, gaining a competitive edge in terms of timing
	Access capability: The ability to capture technological innovations and emerging needs through a responsive network of relationships with customers, suppliers, distributors, universities, and research institutions ensures a gateway to access innovative knowledge relevant to business activities
To mobilize dispersed knowledge to achieve more creative innovative processes compared to competitors.	**Transfer capability**: An effective process must be established for creating "magnets" that can identify and globally transfer dispersed knowledge, in such a way that it can be incorporated into innovative problem-solving processes
	Fusion capability: Knowledge about technologies and consumer needs from various sourcesmust be fused into coherent innovations, overcoming the challenges arising from the existence of complex forms of knowledge
To make innovations productive more efficiently than the competition	**Transmission capability**: Once new solutions are conceived, it is necessary to transfer them in a usable form to the daily operations that make up the production chain
	Enhancement capability: Innovations must be distributed to global consumer segments or applications, and it is necessary to implement a global production chain that flexibly combines operational strength from geographically dispersed manufacturing sites, whether owned or by partners

(Adapted from Doz, Santos, and Williamson, 2001)

1.6.1 The Inadequacy of Traditional Frameworks in Relation to Metanational Competition: 'Square Pegs in Round Holes'. The creation of a metanational company necessitates a fundamental change in the very approach to business activity. For knowledge to act as a catalyst for innovation and consequently a source of competitive advantage for the company, a process of global integration must be initiated. This is only achievable through a discontinuous transformation: the logic of local autonomy, where different parts of the company operate as separate units, needs to be replaced with the logic of global cooperation, where the business network functions as a single entity. However, this discontinuous process can unfold gradually, taking the form of a continuous and incremental transformation that occurs independently at the level of each function or geographical area. This linear and progressive transformation appears to be more effective and less risky than a comprehensive and pervasive turnaround.

What has been said demonstrates how the challenge of knowledge cannot be overcome through the partial adaptation of more traditional structures to the new competitive paradigm. The conventional structures of multinational companies are designed to facilitate the one-way transfer of knowledge from the centre to the periphery of the company, enabling local combination with the efficiency derived from low-cost labour and raw materials. Since they are designed to achieve these objectives, multinational companies are incapable of globally mobilising specific and dispersed cognitive inputs.

The connections between subsidiaries or global business units, even when brought to high levels of complexity as in the transnational or heterarchical company, are insufficient to mobilise knowledge. It is necessary to establish a limited number of selected connections between sites, units, teams, partners, and specific customers. Attempts to globally mobilise dispersed knowledge through ICT tools also prove futile, as they do not allow for the transmission of complex forms of knowledge, nor do they capture the valuable spill overs that occur when individuals with different areas of expertise cooperate closely over a significant period of time.

Moreover, within traditional multinational companies, there is a strong attachment to the logic of globalisation or transnationalism, driven by cognitive and organisational patterns that are ingrained in the company's history of successes (and mistakes). Often, the management of international companies seems not to conceive that local adaptation can be a potential advantage for the company's globalisation or that the market in which it was founded may no longer represent the primary source of competitive strength.

Another limitation lies in the fact that peripheral subsidiaries, potential sources of new knowledge, are rarely valued. Learning capability and the availability of knowledge are not considered valid parameters for the distribution of resources and strategic responsibilities. The basic assumption is that the weight of a subsidiary in terms of profits or labour determines its strength within the organisation. Whilst transnational companies use a retrospective approach to evaluating different subsidiaries, metanational ones have a prospective vision linked to the need for continuous learning. The existence of the fundamental differences highlighted above renders attempts to adapt structures that were designed to strike a balance between local and global aspects in the face of changing knowledge-based competition futile. *"It would be like trying to fit a square peg into a round hole"* (Doz, Santos, and Williamson, 2001, p. 23).

First, it would not be feasible to effectively search for isolated pools of knowledge. Even if roles or structures were designated for this purpose, the emphasis would still be placed on maximising cost efficiency and searching for factors or suppliers that meet predetermined specifications, rather than seeking new forms of knowledge. Accessing these potential new sources of knowledge would be equally difficult, as local management is primarily responsible for implementing and adapting global strategy within a given market. Expanding this responsibility bi-directionally, with the task of localising new knowledge, would involve shifting the focus from the local environment to the global network, creating a strong contrast with the assumptions on which the structure was conceived.

Lastly, it would also be challenging to use classic organisational patterns to mobilise knowledge present in local markets. Global research and development centres, which could potentially be designated as metanational 'magnets', are configured as distributors of new technologies and products and would hardly be capable of receiving innovative flows of knowledge from regional branches.

As evidence that the transition to metanationality represents a considerable change for classic multinational companies, it is worth noting that pioneers of this approach were companies characterised by a (geographical) disadvantage compared to the competition. Competitive pressures forced them to seek knowledge elsewhere. In order for producers of mobile phones in Finland, guided missiles in Switzerland, pianos in Japan, personal computers in Taiwan, insurance in China, and business management software in Germany to be competitive on the global stage, they must necessarily respond to the limited technical competence of their home country. This can be done through extensive and differentiated research at geographical, industry, and sector levels, seeking knowledge capable of generating an exclusive advantage.

1.6.2 Exploiting the Potential of Dispersed Knowledge: Building a Metanational Organisation. The metanational approach to competition among companies requires the establishment of an organisational model that simultaneously addresses the needs for perception, mobilisation, and utilisation of new but dispersed knowledge. This results in a complex corporate configuration, equipped with dedicated units, within which a network of connections is created based on the strategic level in which they are positioned. As the ultimate goal is to achieve high sensitivity and integration, specific solutions must be devised each time based on the industry's characteristics, the company, and the forms of knowledge involved in the innovative process. The authors propose a series of organisational and managerial solutions, distinguishing between three phases of the process, to ensure maximum effectiveness: the sensing, the mobilising and the operating phases.

1. The Sensing phase. In order to activate an effective perceptual capacity, a company must first develop an awareness of the need for learning. The senior management must take on the task of identifying the main knowledge needs of the company and defining them in detail, directing research activities towards specific sources (customers, partners, objectives, etc.) in restricted geographical areas and in specific fields of investigation (technology, market knowledge, etc.), rather than wasting resources on costly random research. It is possible to predict where certain competencies can be found through the analysis of revealing dynamics of ongoing cognitive processes. For this purpose, observing the most innovative consumers, the so-called 'leap froggers', or places where different technologies converge is helpful.

The second step, knowledge access, is no less challenging. It is necessary to identify an access channel and also set up a local organisational presence for the collection and reprocessing of knowledge. Depending on whether the desired knowledge is simple and well-structured, or complex and context-bound, access can take the form of economical and rapid casual observation or as a long-term investment, costly and risky. Given the increasing strategic importance of complex knowledge, which is deeply rooted in the territory or only available in tacit form, it follows that another challenge for the metanational company is to simplify complex knowledge, codify it, make it explicit, and break it down into modules. In this process, a balance must be struck between informational needs and simplification needs, as there is a high risk that the result of these operations might be an unnecessary informative representation of real knowledge (Doz, 2006). Insiders, who constitute the access channels to knowledge from which the company can choose, are numerous and diverse. Choosing between customers, partners, and competitors, as well as venture capital funds, universities, research centres, or even strategic acquisitions, leads to different advantages and disadvantages each time. In particular, it is essential to consider that locals are better suited for this task than outsiders, as they can decipher the environment due to shared values and culture. It is also necessary to establish a local unit responsible for the knowledge acquisition process. This perceptual unit, or 'probe', may easily appear as a common operational structure (a laboratory, a production facility, a design or marketing centre), but it actually has an additional cognitive function. For a company to be sensitive, it must adopt a flat and non-rigid organisational structure, very different from that of the traditional multinational.

Strong integration ties between subsidiaries must give way to a free and flexible network of sensitive units that are, however, deeply rooted in the environment in which they operate. The staff of the local unit must consist of a wide variety of highly skilled specialists with intellectual curiosity, empathy with the local population, sensitivity to other places and cultures, tenacity, and a strong motivation for research and discovery. Only in this way can motivation and dedication to the cause be kept high, as well as the credibility of acquired knowledge. It is also important to establish performance evaluation systems consistent with the purpose of the structure. Indicators such as the number of innovations contributed by the unit, the percentage of technology absorbed from the local environment, or the estimated value of the innovative contribution of the probe unit must be used to create motivation and focus. However, evaluation must be long-term, in line with the temporal perspectives and complexity of the work performed.

2. The Mobilising Phase. Mobilising knowledge represents the key challenge of metanationality: merging different knowledge from various places to generate radical innovation. The organisation must therefore focus the knowledge mobilised from the cognitive network on a particular opportunity or a specific problem, studying the best timing and methods for transfer on a case-by-case basis. A key factor for the success of the process is the existence of awareness within the organisation regarding available knowledge and its positioning, in order to identify possible combinations and assess their strategic potential. To this end, it is also important to prepare a mapping of available dispersed knowledge: rather than analysing the placement of research, production, or sales structures, a metanational company must equip itself with a 'map of knowledge sources' to clearly identify the types and locations of its available knowledge. The mobilisation of knowledge is made possible through the use of the so-called 'magnets', activities or structures capable of collecting, processing, and reworking the knowledge available within the company's network. The magnet can consist of a customer, a leader in its sector, a global platform for product development, or a global activity. The choice among these possible solutions must be made through an evaluation of the level of knowledge achieved regarding latent consumer needs, and the number, as well as the potential impact, of innovations that can be obtained through a single process. If consumer knowledge is limited, the ideal magnet consists of a partnership with a leading customer, in order to identify the right research trajectory and avoid unsuccessful market products. If, on the other hand, customer needs are clear enough to ensure the correct focus of the innovative process, the establishment of a global design platform allows for greater efficiency in the mobilisation and reprocessing of knowledge. Finally, if the process itself takes on the role of innovator, as it generates a series of small innovations with limited individual impact, structuring a global activity to attract knowledge is advisable.

Table 2. How to mobilise knowledge within the metanational innovation process

Complexity of Market Knowledge	*High*	**Transferring technological knowledge to the location where market knowledge is held**	**Connecting and merging knowledge through personnel transfers and temporary co-location**
	Low	**Exchanging information**	**Transferring market knowledge to the location where technological knowledge is held**
		Low	*High*
		Complexity of technological knowledge	

(Source: own. Adapted from Doz, Santos, and Williamson, 2001)

At this point, it is necessary to outline the organisational and managerial archetypes that can ensure the proper functioning of the innovation process. The organisational structure of a magnet is extremely simple: it consists of a team of individuals dispersed across locations where knowledge is available, in proportion to its complexity and transfer difficulty. The vertical links of magnets, those with probes upstream and with operational structures downstream, are very strong. A solid connection of all phases of the innovation process is necessary to ensure its effectiveness and coherence.

The links with top management are also very strong; on the contrary, lateral connections between magnets either do not exist or are very weak, as each one is dedicated to a defined and specific innovative project. These structures are integrated into the global organisation of the company, unlike probes, for which a strong symbiosis with the local environment is required. The role of top management is significant, as they are responsible for setting up magnets and creating an organisational context that promotes mutual respect, discourages knowledge hoarding, and constitutes a robust communication infrastructure. Last but not least, top management is responsible for managing the life cycle of the magnet, whose duration can vary greatly depending on the activity it performs and the productivity it demonstrates.

The staff of these organisational units comprises a wide variety of individualities and expertise. There should be both magnet champions, individuals with strong entrepreneurial sensibilities responsible for promoting new initiatives and the original recombination of knowledge, and high-profile operational personnel capable of working in the multicultural environment resulting from the interdependence and overlap of different organisations. Personnel management must be particularly motivating and rewarding, attributing the right value to leadership demonstrated in the management of the process. Once again, this should be based on a long-term evaluation logic. To achieve such a result, remuneration should be linked to the value of the innovations produced and the rate of their global adoption.

3. The Operating Phase. In order for such a complex process to generate value for shareholders, it is necessary for metanational innovations to be rapidly integrated into the company's production chain. The production system and its relationships with other network units must be completely rethought so that they can ensure efficiency whilst also fostering vertical cooperation and the spread of a strong corporate culture. The operational organisation of a metanational company must naturally fulfil the typical functions of traditional multinational companies (production, sales, etc.), but it is based on very different assumptions. The operational structure is defined using the global distribution of knowledge as a criterion for localisation choices, thus ignoring geopolitical divisions. This is because local expertise should be leveraged to implement global advantages ('think locally, act globally'), not the other way around as theorised by Bartlett and Ghoshal. As such, the organisation is composed of production sites and associated personnel, rather than national subsidiaries. The individual units are interdependent and must be flexible and receptive to the incremental contributions that the network can provide. However, they must also maintain an empathetic relationship with the environment in which they are located, which has generated the operational skills underlying their advantage. This is to avoid disregarding new potential sources of development.

Operational activities may also exhibit different levels of international standardisation. The metanational logic requires the balance between global and local to be based on a contingent approach, rather than constantly seeking economies of scale and knowledge through centralisation of functions.

The risks arising from a metanational operational configuration are mainly related to the fact that tensions may arise between the needs for efficiency and stability and the destabilising force of the continuous flow of innovations. These tensions could undermine the effectiveness of knowledge transfer between different levels of the organisation. If such circumstances arise, top management has the responsibility to support the diffusion of innovations by attributing them greater strategic significance, demonstrating and signalling their value, increasing resources invested in a project, or adapting the organisational structure and processes to changing needs. It is also the responsibility of magnet structures to stimulate the transfer of the knowledge they have developed. They must select appropriate transmission vehicles and create a bidirectional and synchronised relationship with the receiving unit. Lastly, but no less important, investment in fostering trust and building a metanational culture is necessary. These are the fundamental bonds that unify all the different parts into a single network. It is essential to recognise that each local unit represents a potential source of advantage and to spread this message through geographically dispersed 'virtual teams'.

1.7 The Rise of Emerging Market Multinationals

In this paragraph, we deal with the distinct characteristics of emerging economies, aiming to *reconsider their definition* in the realm of strategic decision-making. Rather than relying solely on traditional metrics like GDP growth and developmental stages, this paragraph uses other alternatives defining aspects of emerging economies, concerning strategy formulation, stemming from their nonlinear, unpredictable, and fluctuating paths of economic progress, spanning extended periods. These economies exhibit complexity and dynamism, highlighting a stage of development where innovative interactions between market and non-market forces pervade the entire economic landscape. Consequently, the emergence of new systemic properties within these economies significantly influences the overall economic milieu. Given this portrayal, it could be argued that theories and practices of global strategic management might necessitate adjustments when operating within these less stable, dynamic emerging markets, differing from approaches effective in more established and steady developed markets.

The rise of emerging market multinationals (EMMs) represents, indeed, a significant shift in the global economic landscape (Santos, Doz and Williamson, 2004; Santos and Williamson, 2015; Williamson and Santos, 2021). Over the past few decades, EMMs have undergone a rapid expansion, transforming from regional players to global contenders (Cuervo-Cazurra et. al., 2018). Factors such as economic liberalisation, technological advancements, and globalisation have facilitated this ascension (Hoskisson et al., 2013). These companies, originating from emerging economies such as China, India, Brazil, for example, have capitalised on their homegrown advantages, including lower production costs, extensive market knowledge, and flexibility in adapting to local market nuances.

Moreover, EMMs have increasingly pursued internationalisation strategies, establishing a global footprint through mergers, acquisitions, and strategic alliances (Ramamurti and Singh, 2009). This rise underscores the evolving competitive landscape, challenging established Western multinationals whilst reshaping the dynamics of global business (Cuervo-Cazurra and Ramamurti, 2014).

Emerging economies are distinguished by several key factors that set them apart from developed economies. These distinguishing features have been extensively studied and highlighted in scholarly works. Firstly, emerging economies exhibit a characteristic of non-linear, unstable, and unpredictable economic development paths spanning across significant periods of time (Meyer and Grosse, 2019). This non-linearity contrasts starkly with the more stable and predictable growth trajectories typically observed in developed economies.

Secondly, emerging economies highlight a complex interplay between market and non-market forces, creating novel interactions that shape their economic landscapes. This complexity signifies a stage of development where unique systemic properties emerge, influencing the overall economic environment (Hoskisson et al., 2000; Meyer and Grosse, 2019). Emerging economies are characterised by their diversity across various dimensions, including natural resources, demographics, cultural disparities, technological advancements, and institutional infrastructure (Redding, 2005; Barkema et al., 2015). These diverse characteristics contribute to varying levels of technological sophistication and comparative advantages among emerging economies.

Lastly, the historical legacies of foreign influence, state intervention, institutional inefficiencies, and prolonged turbulence have significantly shaped the business landscape and societal structures within these economies (Austin, Dávila and Jones, 2017). These distinguishing features collectively delineate emerging economies from their developed counterparts and underscore the necessity for nuanced strategic approaches when operating within such dynamic and multifaceted environments.

Despite their differences, emerging markets outline distinctive characteristics, that are set below, that contribute to the challenges and opportunities in global strategic management.

1. *Complexity of emerging markets.* Emerging markets are characterised by dynamic and unpredictable transformations over time. These changes encompass various elements such as institutions, policies, technologies, industries, and market preferences. This dynamic nature leads to unforeseeable outcomes, posing challenges for companies in transferring their advantages to foreign markets and building competitive edges. The emergent nature of these markets involves systemic and irreversible changes that cannot be comprehended merely by aggregating individual behaviours, necessitating adaptive strategies that can influence markets and even affect entire countries (Santos and Williamson, 2015; Arthur, 2014).
2. *Economic complexity and technological capabilities.* As emerging economies progress, they diversify their technological capabilities, affecting their economic productivity. The concept of 'economic complexity' and metrics like the Economic Complexity Index (ECI) provide insights into countries' growth potential and future performance based on their technological capabilities. Understanding these indicators is crucial for companies to evaluate market potential, innovation opportunities, and differentiation strategies within specific emerging markets (Hidalgo and Hausmann, 2009; Cristelli et al., 2013).
3. *Dynamic capabilities for competitive advantage.* Rapid changes in emerging markets demand dynamic capabilities for companies to remain competitive. Differentiating between moderately dynamic and high-velocity markets, dynamic capabilities in high-velocity markets are characterised by uncertainty, unpredictability, and adaptive processes, necessitating managed selection strategies. Understanding and developing such capabilities become critical for companies to thrive in varying emerging market contexts (Teece, Pisano and Shuen, 1997; Eisenhardt and Martin, 2000). Additionally, emerging markets, particularly in digital spaces, exhibit faster rates of innovation, offering opportunities for breakthroughs in customer solutions and business models. Studying domestic companies in these markets and their innovative approaches is becoming crucial for future research in global strategic management.

Overall, emerging markets present unique challenges related to their complex and dynamic nature, technological advancements, and the need for adaptive strategies and dynamic capabilities. Understanding these distinct characteristics is vital for companies aiming to succeed in these diverse and rapidly evolving markets. The unconventional success of companies from emerging economies (EMNEs) in international markets, challenging traditional internationalisation theories. Despite lacking traditional intangible assets, EMNEs have effectively competed against established multinational companies (MNEs) in various industries like technology, consumer electronics, and e-commerce.

Researchers suggest that EMNEs have excelled due to their ability to create innovative business models, combining domestic cost advantages with strategic overseas investments to address capability gaps and exploit latecomer status in the global market (Zeng and Williamson, 2007; Williamson, 2015; Prahbu and Jain, 2015).

Moreover, EMNEs have leveraged their home market contexts, converting inherent advantages like cost and frugal innovation into competitive advantages in global markets. These advantages differ from those of established MNEs and encompass strategies such as managing uncertainty, tapping low-end market segments, adapting products for emerging markets, dealing with institutional weaknesses, and addressing market gaps. Notably, these EMNE-specific advantages cater to the needs of both emerging and developed economies seeking value-for-money products in today's markets.

Additionally, successful EMNEs, particularly in China, have exhibited dynamic capabilities enabling them to disrupt incumbents and continuously innovate, staying ahead in rapidly evolving markets (Santos, 2007; Wan, Williamson, and Yin, 2015). Despite this success, EMNEs face capability gaps whilst expanding internationally, which can be addressed through strategies like the 'springboard' model (Luo and Tung, 2007). However, integrating different internationalisation models and leveraging foreign assets effectively remain critical challenges for EMNEs, along with gaining legitimacy in host countries (Kostova and Zaheer, 1999) amidst country of origin effects and increased scrutiny on national security risks.

Large multinational companies (MNEs) from developed markets (DMNEs) possess advantages such as strong brand recognition, proprietary technologies, and expertise in cutting-edge innovation acquired from their home countries. These established DMNEs benefit from ties both within their multinational organisations and with the local environments where they operate. These connections allow them to learn from diverse markets and access research and development resources globally. However, despite their strengths, DMNEs face challenges when operating in emerging markets. They often struggle to utilise local advantages and integrate effectively into local contexts. Additionally, the rapidly changing and uncertain demands of emerging markets pose a significant challenge for DMNEs, as their core capabilities are primarily developed in stable and predictable home markets. This mismatch creates 'capability holes' leaving DMNEs ill-prepared to meet the demands of today's global markets (Ramamurti and Williamson, 2019)

Whilst DMNEs can achieve success in emerging markets, such instances are less common than often assumed. Active involvement in the development of emerging economies is crucial for DMNEs to succeed in these markets (Santos and Williamson, 2015). Further exploration of this active participation can enhance our understanding of how global strategic management can effectively address the challenges presented by emerging markets.

1.8 An Emerging Paradigm: Digital Multinationals

An emerging paradigm in the global business landscape of today's Fourth Industrial Revolution (Eden, 2018) is the rise of digital companies that very rapidly become multinationals, representing a transformative shift in the way companies operate and compete. Although digital companies, these are, firstly of all, born-global ones as they transcend traditional industry boundaries. Øyna and Alon's review (2018) likely explores the phenomenon of born-global and digitally conceived companies, investigating their characteristics, strategies, and the factors contributing to their rapid internationalisation. This article provides interesting insights into the significance of born-global multinationals born in the contemporary global business landscape as well as their impact on traditional models of internationalisation as they exhibit certain key features that enable them for a global reach. Nevertheless, it is important to point out that the term *born global* first appeared in the literature with Rennie in 1993 and Oviatt and McDougall in 1994.

Amongst this type of company, there is a strong focus on innovation, a highly internationalised management team, reliance on networks and partnerships, agility in adapting to diverse markets, leveraging on technology and on the role of digitalisation in their growth. Multinationals of this type are distinguished by their immediate or rapid expansion into global markets whose speed of internationalisation is measured as *"within three years of inception"* (Øyna and Alon, 2018; p. 162).

Adding on the global nature of these companies there is the fact that the core component of their business models is technology, which has enabled them to disrupt established industries by creating innovative solutions across various sectors. As argued, *"these are new international market makers (Exporting/Importing Start-Ups and Multinational Traders), Geographically Focused Start-Ups, and Global Start-Ups. Further, their focus is on international activity and strategy"* (Øyna and Alon, 2018; p. 166).

In an economy increasingly dominated by digital companies, it is important to understand the organisational impacts that these newly emerged multinationals produce and refer to:

1. Integration of *digital technologies into a company's core strategies* and operations in a successful manner. Unlike conventional companies, digital entities are characterised by their heavy reliance on digital technologies, data-driven decision-making, and agile operational frameworks whilst harnessing digital platforms, advanced analytics, artificial intelligence, cloud computing, and other emerging technologies to create novel products, services, and business models (Aksoi, 2023). They often prioritise customer-centric approaches, personalisation, and rapid innovation, thereby reshaping customer expectations and industry standards and offering personalised and user-focused solutions. This significantly influences consumer behaviour and sets new industry benchmarks.

As argued, the disruptive nature of digital technologies do "reinforce the centrifugal forces that favour dispersing the company's high knowledge activities" (Luo, 2022; p. 4), hence, digital multinationals pose significant challenges to established industries, regulatory frameworks, and traditional business models. Their ability to rapidly adapt to technological advancements and their agility in responding to market demands set them apart in the dynamic global marketplace (Welch and Welch, 2019).

2. Operating with *agile organisational structures* and flexible work processes which include flat hierarchies, rapid decision-making, and adaptable structures. Their global reach extends far beyond traditional borders, leveraging digital platforms to engage with a diverse array of markets, customers, and stakeholders across the globe (Stallkamp and Schotter, 2021; Stallkamp and Li, 2023). By building extensive digital ecosystems designed to enhance companies' technological prowess, expand market influence and drive innovation, they form collaborations, partnerships, and networks with smaller tech companies, startups, and innovative companies at a global scale (Iansiti and Lakhani, 2020).

However, navigating various regulatory landscapes, cultural diversities, and socio-economic differences across different markets is a critical aspect of the operational strategy for digital multinationals (Autio et al., 2021) who need, at the same time, to effectively managing ethical concerns related to data privacy, cybersecurity, and responsible use of technology (Chui, 2018).

3. Unique approaches to *talent acquisition, retention, and management*, with emphasis on talent diversity and, at the same time, foster a culture of innovation that provides valuable lessons for attracting and retaining talent in a competitive digital environment. These companies prioritise diverse talent pools with specialised digital skills, recognising the importance of assembling teams with varied backgrounds, experiences, and perspectives (Plekhanov et al., 2022). Emphasising talent diversity enables these organisations to harness a wide range of skills crucial for innovation and problem solving in a rapidly evolving digital environment (Tondolo and Bitencourt, 2014). In addition to

diversity, these companies cultivate cultures of innovation that encourage experimentation, creative thinking, and continuous learning (Edmondson, 2019).

They establish environments that empower employees to challenge norms, explore new ideas, and take calculated risks, fostering an atmosphere conducive to innovation and ideation (West, 2020). Digital multinationals often promote a 'fail-fast' culture that embraces learning from failures and views them as valuable opportunities for growth and improvement (Denning, 2019). This approach encourages employees to experiment, iterate, and innovate without the fear of repercussions for unsuccessful attempts. Moreover, these organisations provide a supportive infrastructure that enables employees to thrive in a digital environment. This includes offering opportunities for up-skilling and reskilling, providing access to cutting-edge technologies, fostering collaborative workspaces, and promoting a healthy work-life balance (Chui et al., 2018). By investing in employees' professional development and well-being, digital multinationals create an attractive environment for top talent seeking opportunities for growth, development, and meaningful contributions (Liang and Cao, 2021).

4. The emergence of digital multinationals that has *reshaped competition and challenged traditional business* models. The advent of digital multinationals signifies a new era in global business where technology serves as the cornerstone of innovation. This contemporary paradigm shift is evidenced by the rise of companies from developed market economies like Amazon, Microsoft, Apple Inc., Google (Alphabet Inc.), Facebook (Meta Platforms Inc.) or multinational companies coming from emerging economies like Alibaba Group, Tencent Holdings and ByteDance (known for TikTok) from China which leverage cutting-edge digital technologies to revolutionise industries and reshape global commerce. Multinationals mentioned above, that are only a few compared to worldwide numerous companies that have proliferated in the last few years, especially during the COVID-19 pandemic (Altman and Bastian, 2021) have been widely recognised as prominent digital multinationals that engage with global markets and audiences in real-time.

After considering the above premises about global digital companies and multinationals, one may argue what makes companies such as Amazon, Apple, Microsoft, Alibaba different from those such as Netflix, Spotify, TikTok, Tencent Holdings. Whilst all these companies operate within the technology or digital space, their core offerings business models and approaches to leveraging digital technologies vary, leading to differences in how they reach consumers and generate revenue. Understanding these distinctions is crucial, especially when these companies aim to expand internationally.

Hence, two types of companies emerge. The first type, such as Amazon, Apple, Microsoft, Alibaba, embody a category of multinationals that amalgamate digital services with physical products or services.

These companies initially established themselves in various sectors, including e-commerce, technology hardware, software development, and retail, utilising digital platforms to complement or enhance existing physical operations. Their approach involves integrating digital technologies into traditional business models, leveraging both online and offline channels to deliver goods or services to consumers. For instance, Amazon, whilst predominantly an e-commerce platform, blends digital shopping experiences with brick-and-mortar retail. Similarly, Apple merges digital hardware (such as iPhones and Macs) with retail stores, providing physical spaces for customer engagement and service support. These companies leverage their physical and digital presence to create an integrated customer experience, demonstrating a hybrid model that intertwines digital innovation with traditional business approaches.

Engaged in international business and global operations right from their inception or early stages, are the second type of companies, such as born-digital companies whose emergence have also influenced international business research (Birkinshaw, 2022). Given their reliance on digital technologies as the foundation of their business models, allowing them to be agile, innovative, data-driven, and globally oriented right from their inception, their main characteristic is that born-digital companies strive to minimise analogue components wherever possible, focusing on digital innovation and efficiency. They tend to possess an innovative business model so that their niche offerings are purely digital and digitally delivered. This is such a unique value proposition that enables them to compete effectively on a global scale from the outset. Born-digital companies and multinationals like Netflix and Spotify specialise in digital content delivery, offering streaming services for movies, music, and online entertainment without physical product lines. Similarly, social media platforms like TikTok and Tencent Holdings focus on providing digital content sharing and communication services through online platforms and applications, predominantly operating in the digital space. Born-digital multinationals are characterised by their foundation and growth within the digital ecosystem, leveraging technology, data-driven strategies, and online platforms to establish global reach and influence (Monaghan, et al, 2020). Their business models centre around digital content creation, distribution, and user engagement, showcasing a distinct reliance on digital platforms without extensive involvement in physical product lines or traditional physical infrastructure. To put it more simply, differences that matter are schematically reported below:

1. Nature of offerings:
    - Product-centric companies (Amazon, Apple, Microsoft, Alibaba): these companies often offer a mix of physical products, software, and digital services. They rely on manufacturing, retail, software development, and cloud computing, among other offerings.
    - Service-centric companies (Netflix, Spotify, TikTok, Tencent Holdings): these companies primarily provide digital services, entertainment content, social networking, or platforms accessible via the internet.
2. Revenue models:
    - Product-centric companies: revenue is derived from the sale of physical products (Amazon's retail sales), hardware (Apple's devices), software licensing (Microsoft), or a combination of these along with services.
    - Service-centric companies: revenue is typically generated through subscription models, digital advertising (in some cases), or micro-transactions within their platforms (Tencent's gaming revenue, for instance).
3. User Engagement and interaction:
    - Product-centric companies: focus on selling products that consumers directly use or consume.
    - Service-centric companies: prioritise user engagement within their digital platforms by offering content, social interactions, or entertainment experiences.

Regarding international expansion, these differences matter significantly:

1. Localisation and cultural relevance:
    - Product-centric companies: they may need to adapt physical products, services, and retail strategies to fit diverse international markets, considering cultural nuances, language, and preferences.

   - Service-centric companies: international expansion relies on content localisation, understanding regional tastes, and compliance with local regulations to ensure that digital services or content resonate with the local audience.
2. *Monetisation strategies*:
   - Product-centric companies: need to consider international logistics, supply chains, and pricing strategies for physical products and global distribution.
   - Service-centric companies: subscription models and digital content licensing might require different pricing strategies or adaptations based on the purchasing power and preferences of various international markets.
3. Regulatory compliance and data localisation:
   - Service-centric companies: face challenges related to data privacy laws, content censorship, and regulations concerning user data, which vary significantly across different countries. This affects how they operate and store data internationally.
   - Product-centric companies: whilst also impacted by regulations, their challenges might differ due to physical distribution, trade agreements, and manufacturing standards.

Understanding these distinctions is crucial, especially when these companies aim to expand internationally. Both categories of digital multinationals significantly affect organisational structures, cultures, approaches to innovation, global expansion strategies, and the overall competitive landscape. Digital multinationals often evolve into digitally mature organisations, whilst born-digital multinationals are inherently born and bred in the digital realm, shaping the future of business and industries in their wake (Monaghan et al., 2020).

The distinct organisational impacts of these digital multinationals underscore the evolving nature of modern business ecosystems and the strategic imperatives for companies aiming to thrive in an increasingly digital and interconnected world. Hence, these two types of companies, although both use digital technologies, are indeed different. Such difference matters for going international!

To conclude, the distinction between digital companies and their traditional counterparts holds far-reaching implications across various facets of business and global markets. Digital companies, inherently reliant on technological innovations, revolutionise the way products and services are delivered and consumed. As it has already been possible to grasp, the implications of these companies' emergence are multifaceted.

Firstly, their emphasis on data-driven decision-making and advanced analytics significantly alters the landscape of market insights and consumer behaviour understanding. This, in turn, prompts a shift in marketing strategies, focusing more on personalised and targeted approaches.

Moreover, the global reach and scalability inherent in digital business models allow for rapid international expansion, posing both opportunities and challenges. Whilst this facilitates borderless operations, it also demands an acute awareness of diverse regulatory environments, cultural sensitivities, and local market preferences. Furthermore, the rise of digital companies disrupts traditional industry structures, leading to increased competition and necessitating continuous innovation and agility to stay ahead in a fast-paced, tech-driven ecosystem.

The dynamic nature of digital companies also reshapes workforce dynamics, calling for specialised skill sets and an adaptable workforce comfortable with constant technological advancements. Additionally, the digital realm confronts issues related to cybersecurity, privacy concerns, and ethical considerations, underscoring the need for robust cybersecurity measures and responsible data handling practices.

Overall, the advent of digital companies permeates nearly every aspect of modern business, redefining norms, challenging existing paradigms, and fostering a relentless pursuit of innovation and adaptation in the global marketplace.

REFERENCES

Airoldi, G. (1980). *I sistemi operativi*. Giuffrè.

Airoldi, G., & Decastri, M. (1983). *Le funzioni di organizzazione in impresa*. Giuffrè.

Aksoy, C. (2023). Digital Business Ecosystems: An Environment of Collaboration, Innovation, and Value Creation in the Digital Age. *Journal of Business and Trade*, *4*(2), 156–180. doi:10.58767/joinbat.1358560

Allegretti, S., Seidenstricker, S., Fischer, H., & Arslan, S. (2021). Executing a business model change: Identifying key characteristics to succeed in volatile markets. *Leadership, Education, Personality. An Interdisciplinary Journal*, *3*(1), 1–13. doi:10.1365/s42681-021-00020-x

Altman, S., & Bastian, C. (2021). *DHL Global Connectedness Index 2021 Update. Globalization Shock and Recovery in the Covid-19 Crisis*. NYU Stern School of Business Centre for the Future of Management. DHL Initiative on Globalization.

Andersson, U., Gaur, A., Mudambi, R., & Persson, M. (2015). Unpacking inter unit knowledge transfer in multinational enterprises. *Global Strategy Journal*, *5*(3), 241–245. doi:10.1002/gsj.1100

Ariño, A., de la Torre, J., & Ring, P. (2005). Relational quality and inter-personal trust in strategic alliances. *European Management Review*, *2*(1), 15–27. doi:10.1057/palgrave.emr.1500026

Attila, B., & Gherardi, S. (2007). *Studiare le pratiche lavorative*. Il mulino.

Austin, G., Dávila, C., & Jones, G. (2017). Emerging Markets and the future of Business History. *Working Paper*, 18-012, Harvard Business School.

Autio, E., Mudambi, R., & Yoo, Y. (2021). Digitalization and globalization in a turbulent world: Centrifugal and centripetal forces. *Global Strategy Journal*, *11*(1), 3–16. doi:10.1002/gsj.1396

Awais, M., Ali, A., Khattak, M. S., Arfeen, M. I., Chaudhary, M. A. I., & Syed, A. (2023). Strategic Flexibility and Organisational Performance: Mediating Role of Innovation. *SAGE Open*, *13*(2). Advance online publication. doi:10.1177/21582440231181432

Barkema, H. G., Chen, X. P., George, G., Luo, Y., & Tsui, A. S. (2015). West Meets East: New Concepts and Theories. (2015). *Academy of Management Journal*, *58*(2), 460–479. https://ink.library.smu.edu.sg/lkcsb_research/4750. doi:10.5465/amj.2015.4021

Barney, B. J., & Ouchi, W. G. (1985). Costi delle informazioni e strutture economiche di governo delle transazioni. In R. C. D. Nacamulli & A. Rugiadini (Eds.), *Organizzazioni e Mercato*. Il Mulino.

Bartlett, C., & Ghoshal, S. (1990). The multinational corporation as an interorganisational network. *Academy of Management Review*, *15*(4), 603–625. doi:10.2307/258684

Bartlett, C. A. (1982). National Culture-Business Relations: United States and Japan Contrasted. *Management International Review*, 4–12.

Bartlett, C. A., Doz, Y., & Hedlund, G. (1990). *Managing the Global Company*. Routledge.

Bartlett, C. A., & Ghoshal, S. (1987). Managing Across Borders: New Organisational Responses. *MIT Sloan Management Review*, *29*(1), 43–54.

Bartlett, C. A., & Ghoshal, S. (1988). *International Transfer of Manager in Multinational Corporation*. Acta Universitatis Upsaliensis, Studia Oeconomiae Negotiorum. Lars Engwall and Jan Johanson.

Bartlett, C. A., & Ghoshal, S. (1989). *Management Globale. La soluzione transnazionale per la direzione d'impresa*. Etas Libri.

Becker, M. C. (2004). Organisational routines: A review of the literature. *Industrial and Corporate Change*, *13*(4), 643–678. doi:10.1093/icc/dth026

Beverly, S. Y. T., & Vinh, V. T. (2015). Global knowledge hubs: Introducing a new conceptual model. *International Journal of Knowledge-Based Development. Inderscience Enterprises Ltd*, *6*(2), 131–151. doi:10.1504/IJKBD.2015.071471

Birkinshaw, J. (1996). How Multinational Subsidiary Mandates Are Gained and Lost. *Journal of International Business Studies*, *27*(3), 467–495. doi:10.1057/palgrave.jibs.8490845

Birkinshaw, J. (2022). Move fast and break things: Reassessing IB research in the light of the digital revolution. *Global Strategy Journal*, *12*(4), 619–631. doi:10.1002/gsj.1427

Bodega, D. (1988). L'organizzazione si proietta in se stessa. *Sviluppo and Organizzazione,* 110.

Bodega, D. (1991). *Cultura and Organizzazione*. Este.

Bodega, D. (1996). *Organizzazione e cultura. Teoria e metodo della prospettiva culturale nell'organizzazione di azienda*. Guerini e Associati.

Bodega, D., Decastri, M., & Prina, G. (1992). *Innovazione, apprendimento e formazione: un'indagine empirica*. Franco Angeli.

Brumana, M., Decastri, M., Scarozza, D., & Za, S. (2014). A bibliometric study of the literature on technological innovation: an analysis of 60 international academic journals. In Management, Organisation and Control: Smart Practices and Effects (pp. 141-152). Springer International Publishing. doi:10.1007/978-3-319-07905-9_9

Buch, A. (2020). People and practices in organisational learning. *Forskning or Forandring*, *3*(1), 70–88. doi:10.23865/fof.v3.2103

Butera, F. (2008). *Knowledge Working. Lavoro, lavoratori, società della conoscenza*. Mondadori Università.

Chesbrough, H. (2003). *Open Innovation: The New Imperative for Creating and Profiting from Technology*. Harvard Business Press.

Chesbrough, H., Vanhaverbeke, W., & West, J. (2006). *Open Innovation: Researching a New Paradigm*. Oxford University Press. doi:10.1093/oso/9780199290727.001.0001

Chui, M., Manyika, J., & Miremadi, M. (2018). What Ceos Are. Mckinsey and Company.

Coda, V. (1965). *Le coordinazioni produttive. Introduzione al sistema delle rilevazioni d'impresa*. Giuffrè.

Cristelli, M., Gabrielli, A., Tacchella, A., Caldarelli, G., & Pietronero, L. (2013). Measuring the Intangibles: A Metrics for the Economic Complexity of Countries and Products. *PLoS One*, *8*(8), e70726. doi:10.1371/journal.pone.0070726 PMID:23940633

Cuervo-Cazurra, A., Ciravegna, L., Melgarejo, M., & Lopez, L. (2018). Home country uncertainty and the internationalization-performance relationship: Building an uncertainty management capability. *Journal of World Business*, *53*(2), 209–221. doi:10.1016/j.jwb.2017.11.002

Cuervo-Cazurra, A., & Genc, M. (2008). Transforming disadvantages into advantages: developing country MNEs in the least developed MNEs. *Journal of International Business Studies, 39*(6), 957-979. https://www.jstor.org/stable/25483316

Daniels, J. L., & Frost, N. C. (1991). The Global Frontier. Harper and Row.

Davis, S. M. (1971). *Comparative Management, Organisational and Cultural Perspective*. Prentice Hall.

Decastri, M. (1984). *Organizzazione e cultura dell'innovazione in impresa*. Giuffrè.

Decastri, M. (2016). *Indagine sulle trasformazioni indotte nel processo produttivo dalle nuove tecnologie e dall'innovazione in generale*. Editoriale Scientifica.

Decastri, M., Buonocore, F., Battini, S., & Gagliarducci, F. (2020). *Organisational Development in Public Administration: The ltalian Way*. Palgrave Mc Millan.

Denning, S. (2019). *Agile innovation: The revolutionary approach to accelerate success, inspire engagement, and ignite creativity*. John Wiley and Sons.

Doz, Y. (1986). *Strategie Management in Multinational Company*. Pergamon Press.

Doz, Y. (1987). Technology Partnerships between Larger and Smaller Companies: Some Critical Issues. *International Studies of Management & Organization*, *17*(4), 31–57. doi:10.1080/00208825.1987.11656466

Doz, Y. (2006). *Harnessing Global Knowledge for Metanational Innovation. Special Interview. Rieti Report, 066- 25*. Research Institute of Economy, Trade and Industry.

Doz, Y. (2011). Qualitative research for international business. *Journal of International Business Studies*, *42*(5), 582–590. https://www.jstor.org/stable/29789446. doi:10.1057/jibs.2011.18

Doz, Y., & Kosonen, M. (2010). Embedding Strategic Agility: A Leadership Agenda for Accelerating Business Model Renewal. *Long Range Planning, 43*(2–3), 370–382. . doi:10.1016/j.lrp.2009.07.006

Doz, Y., & Prahalad, C. K. (1981). An Approach to Strategic Control in MNCs. *Sloan Management Review*, *22*(4), 5.

Doz, Y., & Prahalad, C. K. (1986). Controlled Variety: A Challenge for Human Resource Management in the mnc. *Human Resource Management*, *25*(1), 55–71. doi:10.1002/hrm.3930250105

Doz, Y., & Prahalad, C. K. (1987). *The Multinational Mission. Balancing Local Demands and Global Vision*. The Free Press.

Doz, Y., Santos, J., & Williamson, P. (2001). From Global to Metanational How Companies Win in the Knowledge Economy. *Ubiquity*, *2001*(December), 2. Advance online publication. doi:10.1145/503351.503119

Doz, Y., Santos, J., & Williamson, P. (2004). Is Your Innovation Process Global? *MIT Sloan Management Review*, *45*(4), 31–37.

Doz, Y. M., & Prahalad, C. K. (1984). Patterns of Strategic Control within Multinational Corporation. *Journal of International Business Studies, 15*(2), 55-72.

Drucker, P. F. (1974). *Management Tasks, Responsibilities and Practices*. Harper & Row.

Drucker, P. F. (1996). The shape of things to come. *Leader to Leader*, *1996*(1), 12–18. doi:10.1002/ltl.40619960306

Dunning, J. H. (1980). Toward an Eclectic Theory of International Production: Some Empirical Tests. *Journal of International Business Studies*, *11*(1), 9–31. doi:10.1057/palgrave.jibs.8490593

Dunning, J. H. (1981). *International Production and the Multinational Enterprises*. George Allen and Unwin.

Dunning, J. H. (1988). The Eclectic Paradigm of International Production: A Restatement and Some Possible Extensions. *Journal of International Business Studies*, *19*(1), 1–31. doi:10.1057/palgrave.jibs.8490372

Durand, R., & Ioannou, I. (2023). *How Leaders Can Create a Purpose-Driven Culture*. Harward Business Review.

EdenL. (2018). The Fourth Industrial Revolution: Seven Lessons from the Past. In R. van Tulder, A. Verbeke & L. Piscitello (Eds.), *International Business in the Information and Digital Age, Progress in International Business Research, 13*. Emerald. https://ssrn.com/abstract=3244096

Edmondson, A. (2019). *The fearless organisation: Creating psychological safety in the workplace for learning, innovation, and growth*. John Wiley and Sons.

Eisenhardt, K. M., & Martin, J. A. (2000). Dynamic capabilities: What are they? *Strategic Management Journal*, *21*(10/11), 1105–1121. doi:10.1002/1097-0266(200010/11)21:10/11<1105::AID-SMJ133>3.0.CO;2-E

Etzioni, A. (1968). *The Active Society*. The Free Press.

Evans, P., Doz, Y., & Laurent, A. (1990). *Human Resource Management in International Companies. St.* Martin Press.

Fabris, A., & Garbellano, S. (1991). Modelli di internazionalizzazione delle imprese. *Sviluppo and Organizzazione, 124*.

Franko, L. G. (1976). *The European Multinational*. Greylock.

Gagliardi, P. (1986). *Le imprese come cultura*. Isedi.

Galbraith, J. R. (1897). *Designing Complex Organisation*. Addison Wesley.

Galbraith, J.R. (1975). La progettazione organizzativa: un'analisi dal punto di vista del trattamento delle informazioni. *Problemi di gestione,* 9.

Galbraith, J. R., & Kazanjian, R. K. (1986). Organizing to Implement Strategies of Diversity and Globalization: The Role of Matrix Design. *Human Resource Management*, *25*(1), 37–54. Advance online publication. doi:10.1002/hrm.3930250104

Garro-Abarca, V., Palos-Sanchez, P., & Aguayo-Camacho, M. (2021). Virtual teams in times of pandemic: Factors that influence performance. *Frontiers in Psychology*, *12*, 624637. Advance online publication. doi:10.3389/fpsyg.2021.624637 PMID:33679543

Godiwalla, Y. (2018). Strategic Management for Global Companies: A Conceptual Discussion. *International Journal of Social Science Studies*, *6*(40), 40. Advance online publication. doi:10.11114/ijsss.v6i11.3695

Gooderham, P. N., Pedersen, T., Madsen Sandvik, A., Dasí, A., Elter, F., & Hildrum, J. (2022). Contextualizing AMO Explanations of Knowledge Sharing in MNEs: The Role of Organisational and National Culture. *MIR. Management International Review*, *62*(6), 859–884. doi:10.1007/s11575-022-00483-0

Gupta, A., & Govindarajah, G. (1990). Knowledge Flows and the Structure of Control Within Multinational Corporations. *Academy of Management Review*, *16*(4), 768–792. doi:10.2307/258980

GuttermanA. (2023). *Human Resources Management*. doi:10.2139/ssrn.4549619

Hagstrom, P. (1990). New information systems and the changing structure of MNCs. In C. A. Bartlett, Y. Doz, & G. Hedlund (Eds.), *Managing the Global Company* (pp. 164–185). Routledge.

Hanush, M. (2012). *Jobless Growth? Okun's Law in East Asia*. World Bank. doi:10.1596/1813-9450-6156

Hedlund, G. (1986). The Hypermodem MNC - A Heterarchy? *Human Resource Management*, *25*(1), 9–35. doi:10.1002/hrm.3930250103

Hedlund, G., & Rolander, D. (1990). Actions in heterarchies: new approaches to managing the MN. In C. A. Bartlett, Y. Doz, & G. Hedlund (Eds.), *Managing the Global Company*. Routledge.

Hedlund, H. (1984). Organisation In-Between: The Evolution of the Mother-Daughter Structure of Managing Foreign Subsidiaries in Swedish mncs. *Journal of International Business Studies*, *15*(2), 109–123. doi:10.1057/palgrave.jibs.8490485

Hidalgo, C. A., Hausmann, R., & Dasgupta, P. S. (2009). The Building Blocks of Economic Complexity. *Proceedings of the National Academy of Sciences of the United States of America*, *106*(26), 10570–10575. doi:10.1073/pnas.0900943106 PMID:19549871

Hitt, M., Ireland, R., & Hoskisson, R. (2013). *Strategic Management: Competitiveness and Globalization* (10th ed.). Cengage Southwestern Publishing Co.

Hoskisson, R. E., Eden, L., Lau, C. M., & Wright, M. (2000). Strategy in emerging economies. *Academy of Management Journal, 43*(3), 249–267. doi:10.2307/1556394

Hymer, S. (1970). The Efficiency (Contradictions) of Multinational Corporations. *The American Economic Review, 60*(2), 441–448.

Iansiti, M., & Lakhani, K. R. (2020). *Competing in the Age of AI: Strategy and Leadership When Algorithms and Networks Run the World.* Harvard Business Review Press.

Imandin, L., Bisschoff, C., & Botha, C. (2014). A model to measure employee engagement. *Problems and Perspectives in Management, 12*, 520–532.

JerabD. A.MabroukT. (2023). *The Role of Leadership in Changing Organisational Culture.* doi:10.2139/ssrn.4574324

Jones, G. R. (1983). Psychological Orientation and the Process of Organisational Socialization: An Interactionist Perspective. *Academy of Management Review, 8*(3), 464–474. doi:10.2307/257835

Jones, G. R. (1986). Socialization Tactics, Self-efficacy, and Newcomers Adjustment to Organisations. *Academy of Management Journal, 29*(2), 262–279. doi:10.2307/256188

Jones, R. A., Jimmieson, N. L., & Griffiths, A. (2005). The impact of organisational culture and reshaping capabilities on change implementation success: The mediating role of readiness for change. *Journal of Management Studies, 42*(2), 361–386. doi:10.1111/j.1467-6486.2005.00500.x

Kindleberg, C. (1969). *American Business Abroad, Six Lectures on Direct Investments.* Yale University Press.

Kogut, B. (1990). International Sequential Advantages and Network Flexibility. In: *Managing the Global Company*. In C. Bartlett, Y. Doz, & G. Hedlund (Eds.), *Managing the Global Company* (pp. 47–68). Routledge.

Kostova, T., & Zaheer, S. (1999). Organisational Legitimacy under Conditions of Complexity: The Case of the Multinational Enterprise. *Academy of Management Review, 24*(1), 64–81. doi:10.2307/259037

Leoni, R. (2013). Organisation of Work Practices and Productivity. In A. Grandori (Ed.), *Handbook of Economic Organisation*. Edward Elgar.

Liang, F., & Cao, L. (2021). Linking Employee Resilience with Organisational Resilience: The Roles of Coping Mechanism and Managerial Resilience. *Psychology Research and Behavior Management, 14*, 1063–1075. doi:10.2147/PRBM.S318632 PMID:34321935

Lioukas, C. S., & Reuer, J. J. (2015). Isolating trust outcomes from exchange relationships: Social exchange and learning benefits of prior ties in alliances. *Academy of Management Journal, 58*(6), 1826–1847. doi:10.5465/amj.2011.0934

Luo, Y., & Shenkar, O. (2006). The multinational corporation as a multilingual community: Language and organisation in a global context. *Journal of International Business Studies*, *37*(3), 321–339. doi:10.1057/palgrave.jibs.8400197

Luo, Y., & Tung, R. L. (2007). International expansion of emerging market enterprises: A springboard perspective. *Journal of International Business Studies*, *38*(4), 481–498. doi:10.1057/palgrave.jibs.8400275

Luo, Y., & Tung, R. L. (2018). A general theory of springboard MNEs. *Journal of International Business Studies*, *49*(2), 129–152. doi:10.1057/s41267-017-0114-8

Luu, D. T. (2023). Internationalisation, knowledge intensity, adaptive culture and absorptive capacity: A strategic entrepreneurship enabling logic for export companies. *Journal of Small Business and Enterprise Development*, *30*(2), 390–418. doi:10.1108/JSBED-06-2022-0288

Lyu, B., Liao, X., & Yang, Y. (2022). Relationships between temporal leadership, transactive memory systems and Team Innovation Performance. *Psychology Research and Behavior Management*, *51*, 2543–2559. doi:10.2147/PRBM.S380989 PMID:36124335

Martínez-Peláez, R., Ochoa-Brust, A., Rivera, S., Félix, V. G., Ostos, R., Brito, H., Félix, R. A., & Mena, L. J. (2023). Role of Digital Transformation for Achieving Sustainability: Mediated Role of Stakeholders, Key Capabilities, and Technology. *Sustainability (Basel)*, *15*(14), 11221. doi:10.3390/su151411221

Masini, C. (1970). *Lavoro e risparmio*. Utet.

Meyer, K. E., & Grosse, R. (2019). Introduction to Managing in Emerging Markets. In Oxford Handbook of Management in Emerging Markets. Oxford University Press.

Mintzberg, H. (1980). *The Nature of Managerial Work*. Prentice Hall.

Mintzberg, H. (1983). *Structuring in Fives: Designing Effective Organisations*. Prentice Hall.

Monaghan, S., Tippmann, E., & Coviello, N. (2020). Born digitals: Thoughts on their internationalization and a research agenda. *Journal of International Business Studies*, *51*(1), 11–22. doi:10.1057/s41267-019-00290-0

Nelson, R., & Winter, S. (1982). *An Evolutionary Theory of Economic Change*. Beiknap Press.

Nicolini, D., Pyrko, I., Omidvar, O., & Spanellis, A. (2022). Understanding Communities of Practice: Taking Stock and Moving Forward. *The Academy of Management Annals*. Advance online publication. 16

Nonaka, I., & Takeuchi, H. (1995). *The Knowledge creating company*. Oxford University Press. doi:10.1093/oso/9780195092691.001.0001

Öberg, C., & Lundberg, H. (2022). Mechanisms of knowledge development in a knowledge ecosystem. *Journal of Knowledge Management*, *26*(11), 293–307. doi:10.1108/JKM-11-2021-0814

Ohmae, K. (1986). Becoming a Triad Power: The New Global Corporation. *International Marketing Review*, *3*(3), 7–20. doi:10.1108/eb008307

Øyna, S., & Alon, I. (2018). A Review of Born globals. *International Studies of Management & Organization*, *48*(2), 157–180. doi:10.1080/00208825.2018.1443737

Parmigiani, A., & Howard-Grenville, J. (2011). Routines revisited: Exploring the capabilities and practice perspectives. *The Academy of Management Annals*, *5*(1), 413–453. doi:10.5465/19416520.2011.589143

Pennington, M. W. (2002). The coming metanational era. *Strategy and Leadership*, *30*(4). Advance online publication. doi:10.1108/sl.2002.26130dae.003

Pentland, B. T., & Feldman, M. S. (2008). 13 issues in empirical field studies of organisational routines. In M. Becker (Ed.), *Handbook of organisational routines* (pp. 281–300). Edward Elgar. doi:10.4337/9781848442702.00021

Perlmutter, H. V. (1972). The Multinational Firm and the Future. *The Annals of the American Academy of Political and Social Science*, *404*(1), 139–152. Advance online publication. doi:10.1177/000271627240300113

Perlmutter, H. V., & Heenan, D. (1974). How Multinational Should Your Top Managers Be? *Harvard Business Review*, *52*(6), 121–132.

Perrone, V. (1990). *Le strutture organizzative d'impresa. Criteri e modelli di progettazione*. Egea.

Pettigrew, T. F. (1986). The intergroup contact hypothesis reconsidered. In M. Hewstone & R. Brown (Eds.), *Contact and conflict in intergroup encounters* (pp. 169–195). Basil Blackwell.

Plekhanov, D., Franke, H., & Netland, T. H. (2022). Digital transformation: A review and research agenda. *European Management Journal*. Advance online publication. doi:10.1016/j.emj.2022.09.007

Porter, M. E. (1987). *Competition in Global Industries*. Harvard Business School Press.

Porter, M. E. (1990). The Competitive Advantage of Nations. Macmillan. doi:10.1007/978-1-349-11336-1

Prabhu, J., & Jain, S. (2015). Innovation and entrepreneurship in India: Understanding Jugaad. *Asia Pacific Journal of Management*, *32*(4), 843–868. doi:10.1007/s10490-015-9445-9

Prahalad, C. K., & Doz, Y. (1981). Headquarter's Influence and Strategic Control in Multinational Corporation. *Sloan Management Review*, *23*(1), 15–29. http://search.epnet.com/login.aspx?direct=trueanddb=buhandan=4014035

Prahalad, C. K., & Doz, Y. (1987). *The Multinational Mission*. The Free Press.

Prahalad, C. K., & Ramaswamy, V. (2004). Co-Creation Experiences: The Next Practice in Value Creation. *Journal of Interactive Marketing*, *18*(3), 5–14. doi:10.1002/dir.20015

Ramamurti, R., & Singh, J. V. (2009). *Emerging multinationals in emerging markets*. Cambridge University Press. doi:10.1017/CBO9780511576485

Ramamurti, R., & Williamson, P. J. (2019). Rivalry between emerging-market MNEs and developed-country MNEs: Capability holes and the race to the future. *Business Horizons*, *62*(2), 157–169. doi:10.1016/j.bushor.2018.11.001

Rammal, H. G., Rose, E. L., & Ferreira, J. J. (2023). Managing cross-border knowledge transfer for innovation: An introduction to the special issue. *International Business Review, 32*(2), 102098. Advance online publication. doi:10.1016/j.ibusrev.2022.102098

Redding, G. (2005). The Thick Description and Comparison of Societal Systems of Capitalism. *Journal of International Business Studies, 36*(2), 123–155. doi:10.1057/palgrave.jibs.8400129

Rios, C. M., Erhardt, N. L., & Manev, I. M. (2022). Interfirm collaboration for knowledge resources interaction among small innovative companies. *Journal of Business Research, 153*, 206–215. doi:10.1016/j.jbusres.2022.08.024

Salomon, R. (2016). *Global Vision. How Companies Can Overcome the Pitfalls of Globalization*. Palgrave Macmillan.

Santistevan, D., & Josserand, E. (2019). Meta-Teams: Getting Global Work Done in MNEs. *Journal of Management, 45*(2), 510–539. doi:10.1177/0149206318793184

Santos, F., & Eisenhardt, K. (2005). Organisational Boundaries and Theories of Organisation. *Organization Science, 16*(5), 491–508. doi:10.1287/orsc.1050.0152

Santos, F. P., & Williamson, P. J. (2022). Discovering Strategy: Dealing With Uncertainty By Harnessing Serendipity. *Working Paper, 2*(22). Cambridge Judge Business School.

Santos, J. (2007). Strategy lessons from left field. *Harvard Business Review, 85*(4), 20–21.

Santos, J., Doz, Y., & Williamson, P. (2004). Is Your Innovation Process Global? *MIT Sloan Management Review, 45*(4), 31–37.

Santos, J. F., & Williamson, P. J. (2015). The new mission for multinationals. *MIT Sloan Management Review, 6*(4), 45–55.

Schein, E. H. (1985). *Organisation Culture and Leadership*. Jossey-Bass.

Schein, E. H. (1986). International Human Resource Management: New Directions, Perpetual Issues and Missing Opportunities. *Human Resource Management, 25*(1), 169–176. doi:10.1002/hrm.3930250112

Schotter, A. P. J., Mudambi, R., Doz, Y. L., & Gaur, A. (2017). Boundary spanning in global organisations. *Journal of Management Studies, 54*(4), 403–421. doi:10.1111/joms.12256

Stallkamp, M., Chen, L., & Li, S. (2023). Boots on the ground: Foreign direct investment by born digital firms. *Global Strategy Journal, 13*(4), 1–25. doi:10.1002/gsj.1474

Stallkamp, M., & Schotter, A. P. (2021). Platforms without borders? The international strategies of digital platform firms. *Global Strategy Journal, 11*(1), 58–80. doi:10.1002/gsj.1336

Syed, J., & Tariq, M. (2017). Global Diversity Management. In Oxford research Encyclopedia of business and management. Oxford University Press. https://doi.org/ doi:10.1093/acrefore/9780190224851.013.62

Teece, D. J., Pisano, G., & Shuen, A. (1997). Dynamic capabilities and strategic management. *Strategic Management Journal, 18*(7), 509–533. doi:10.1002/(SICI)1097-0266(199708)18:7<509::AID-SMJ882>3.0.CO;2-Z

Thompson, J. D. (1967). *Organisation in Action*. McGraw-Hill.

Tondolo, V., & Bitencourt, C. (2014). Understanding Dynamic Capabilities from Its Antecedents, Processes and Outcomes. *Brazilian Business Review, 11*(5), 122–144. doi:10.15728/bbr.2014.11.5.6

Turati, C. (1990). Economia ed organizzazione delle joint venture. EGEA.

Vaccà, S., & Zanfei, A. (1989). L'impresa globale come sistema aperto a rapporti di cooperazione. *Economia e Politica Industriale, 64*, 47–89.

Valdani, E. (1991). *Marketing globale*. Egea.

Vernon, R. (1966). International Trade and International Investment in the Product Cycle. *The Quarterly Journal of Economics, 80*(2), 190–207. doi:10.2307/1880689

Vicari. (1991). *L'impresa vivente*. Franco Angeli.

Vieira, E. S. (2023). The influence of research collaboration on citation impact: The countries in the European Innovation Scoreboard. *Scientometrics, 128*(6), 3555–3579. doi:10.1007/s11192-023-04715-4

Von Borell, D., & Franco, M. (2017). Trust-Building Mechanisms in a Coopetition Relationship: A Case Study Design. *The International Journal of Organizational Analysis, 25*(3), 378–394. Advance online publication. doi:10.1108/IJOA-04-2016-1012

Wadhwa, V., Aggarwal, R., & Holly, K. (2018). *The Immigrant Exodus: Why America Is Losing the Global Race to Capture Entrepreneurial Talent*. Wharton Digital Press.

Wan, F., Williamson, P., & Yin, E. (2015). Antecedents and implications of disruptive innovation: Evidence from China. *Technovation, 39-40*, 94–104. doi:10.1016/j.technovation.2014.05.012

Weber, Y., & Tarba, S. Y. (2014). Strategic Agility: A State of the Art: Introduction to the Special Section on Strategic Agility. *California Management Review, 56*(3), 5–12. doi:10.1525/cmr.2014.56.3.5

Weick, K. E. (1969). Social psychology in an era of social change. *The American Psychologist, 24*(11), 990–998. doi:10.1037/h0028881

Wells, L. T. (2016). Third World Multinationals: A Retrospective. In Progress in International Business Research. Emerald Group Publishing. doi:10.1108/S1745-886220160000011003

West, D. M. (2020). *Digital governance: New technologies for improving public service and participation*. Brookings Institution Press.

Williamson, P. J. (2015). The Competitive Advantages of Emerging Market Multinationals: A Re-assessment. *Critical Perspectives on International Business, 11*(3/4), 216–235. doi:10.1108/cpoib-02-2014-0008

Williamson, P. J., & Santos, J. F. P. (2021). Emerging Economies: The Impact of Context on Global Strategic Management. In I.M. Duhaime, M.A. Hitt, & Lyles, M. A. (Eds.), Strategic management: State of the field and its future (pp. 319-335). Oxford University Press.

Wind, Y., Douglas, S. P., & Perlmutter, H. V. (1973). Guidelines for Developing International Marketing Strategies. *Journal of Marketing. Journal of Marketing, 37*(2), 14–23. doi:10.1177/002224297303700205

Zamenopoulos, T., & Alexiou, K. (2018). Co-Design as Collaborative Research. *Open Research Online*. Connected Communities Foundation Series. University of Bristol/AHRC.

Zeng, M., & Williamson, P. J. (2007). *Dragons At Your Door: How Chinese Cost Innovation Is Disrupting Global Competition*. Harvard Business School Press.

ENDNOTES

1 Nonaka and Takeuchi (1995), who are known for their work on organisational knowledge creation and the concept of 'tacit knowledge' in the context of routines and organisational learning.

Chapter 2
Organizational Structures

ABSTRACT

This chapter focuses on the topic of organisational structures and addresses its contents by dealing with two fundamental issues. The first one deals with different types of international structures found in the global business sphere. It also offers an in-depth analysis of how these structures accommodate diverse geographical footprints, cultural disparities, and operational complexities encountered in a globalised setting. The second one refers to the strategic decision-making process involved in selecting the appropriate international organisational structure. Factors such as market diversities, regulatory frameworks, cultural intricacies, and operational efficiencies are examined when selecting the optimal structure. This chapter explains the necessary nuanced trade-offs and considerations for aligning the chosen structure with the strategic international objectives of an organisation, emphasizing adaptability, responsiveness, and scalability as crucial determinants in this strategic selection process.

2. ORGANISATIONAL STRUCTURES

As previously emphasised, the specific characteristics that distinguish international companies are the diverse cultural backgrounds of the individuals who compose the personnel and the economic subject (multiculturalism) and the different socio-economic configurations of the geographical areas and countries in which the company operates (geographic dispersion) (Salomon, 2016; Robert et al., 2022). Multiculturalism and geographic dispersion are two traits that impose organisational design processes on international companies, enabling the reconciliation of these two characteristics with the essential need for corporate unity.

In this sense, the international company is the most significant expression of the divided company (Masini, 1970). It is characterized, in particular, by a high level of horizontal and spatial extension (Airoldi, 1989; Coda, 1965). At the same time, it is observed that the international company - as a company - is a unified set of operations and elements (Masini, 1970; Airoldi, 1989; Allegretti et al., 2021).

The organisational structure is the main tool for managing these two contrasting forces: extension and unity.

DOI: 10.4018/979-8-3693-3482-9.ch002

The design of the formal structure is equivalent to the preparation of a framework that defines the type of links established between various organisational units. It represents the formal framework that delimits and guides the decision-making processes that concern the centre and the periphery of the organisation. In particular, from the examination of the most recurring structural typologies in international companies, some initial indications can be drawn regarding the localization of activities and decision-making responsibilities, and thus, in summary, the characteristics of centralization-decentralization.

The penetration of companies into multiple national states and, therefore, into a plurality of economic and social systems, subjects organisational structures to conditions quite different from those that characterize companies operating in a single national context. First and foremost, it can be stated that while for companies operating solely in the national market, the fundamental dimensions influencing the determination of the structural form may be no more than two, namely, product and functions (Lioukas and Reuer, 2015). In international companies, it is necessary to reconcile organisational choices with a third dimension, which is geographical localization.

Secondly, the structural design of an international company must satisfy two fundamental needs: on one hand, the need to adapt the organisation to various local situations and the tendency of some subsidiaries to become independent, leading to a push towards decentralization. On the other hand, the need to coordinate the entire company according to unified strategies. These needs represent two opposing forces that international companies often resolve in a non-uniform manner.

Once again, it is emphasised that the international company is characterized by the need for *unified governance* of horizontally and spatially *extensive* economic combinations. *Unity and extension* are the distinctive features from which to begin every logical path of organisational design for this type of company (Salomon, 2016).

This implies dedicating great attention to:

1. Defining the spaces of decision-making autonomy of partial economic combinations for each geographical area (local branches) in relation to the economic governing bodies (the central headquarters).
2. Identifying mechanisms of coordination and integration capable of bringing together into unity the articulation defined in point 1.

2.1 Types of International Organisational Structures

The organisational structures that can be employed by international companies, often adopted quite frequently - as will be seen later - along an evolutionary path, correspond to the following types:

a. Functional/Divisional structure with “widespread internationality”. In at least one of the company’s functions/divisions, there is a unit specifically dedicated to managing an extensive, albeit partial, international presence. This presence may either be limited to overseeing a foreign plant, sales unit, or research facility or involve coordinating all business activities directed towards foreign countries (a kind of International Sales Department).
b. Divisional structure with “centralized internationality”. Alongside product divisions, there is an international division with global responsibility for all foreign activities. This division oversees not only commercial outlets, as before, but also manufacturing, research, and any other operations conducted outside national borders.

c. Global functional structure or global product divisional structure. Each division is assigned the global responsibility for governing all business activities present in specific geographic areas or related to a product.
d. Global matrix structure. The typical two-dimensional structure has the governing bodies for products and geographic areas placed on its arms; each local unit falls along the hierarchical relationships identified by the two arms, thus encouraged to focus its attention on the two strategically relevant dimensions (Decastri, 2012).
e. Transnational Structure. A transnational structure is designed to create a highly integrated and interdependent network of operations across multiple countries. It aims to balance global coordination with local responsiveness (Salomon, 2016).
f. Virtual Structure. In a virtual structure, the company relies heavily on outsourcing and strategic alliances to carry out various functions. This allows for a lean and flexible organisation without significant physical presence in many locations (Riemer, 2012).
g. Network Structure. Similar to the virtual structure, a network structure emphasizes collaboration with external partners. The company forms networks of suppliers, distributors, and other stakeholders to create value together (Vuchkovski et al, 2023).
h. Holacracy. This is a relatively new concept that replaces traditional hierarchical structures with a more fluid and self-organizing system. It distributes authority and decision-making to self-managing teams (Bernstein et al., 2016).
i. Hybrid Structures. Companies often adopt hybrid structures, combining elements from various organisational types to suit their specific needs and unique challenges in the international business landscape (Battilana, 2018).

a. *Functional/Divisional structure with "widespread internationality"*. It represents the simplest organisational form that a company operating internationally can adopt and involves loosely binding and personal relationships between the headquarters and foreign activities. Typically found in companies in the initial stages of internationalization, during this period, managers of international units report directly to the CEO of the parent company, and supervision, control, and evaluation are conducted on a personal basis. The company may maintain this type of structure for a certain period of time; if the foreign units remain a rather limited and insignificant part of the system, there is no pressure to change the organisational setup. However, as foreign sales and operations grow, the international component of the company demands more time and attention. Continuing to rely on a widespread international structure risks causing significant communication difficulties.

b. *Divisional structure with centralized internationality.* In what can be considered the typical second stage of the strategic evolution of an international company, local activities remain the most important for the overall economy of the company. The top management still has limited experience in international operations, which are still in their early stages of development. However, it is precisely at this moment that the management begins to understand that significant synergistic advantages can be obtained by coordinating international activities and foreign subsidiaries. This coordination is achieved by centralizing decision-making power in an international division established within the central headquarters. This allows concentrating the limited internationalization experience available in a single unit, rather than dispersing it within the organisation. This structural type implies a clear distinction between national and foreign activities, although there is a considerable variety of solutions among organisations adopting this type of structure. Considering that the organisational structure of companies in the early stages of international expansion can take various forms, it can be stated that the international division can be integrated into different organisational structures, from functional to divisional. However, establishing an international division within a divisional structure seems more likely, as the latter has already developed management systems suitable for dealing with a variety of development alternatives in different markets.

The fundamental characteristic of the structure with centralized internationality, which impacts its ability to effectively coordinate international operations, is its capacity to coordinate foreign and domestic activities. In fact, the success of the international division heavily depends on the cooperation and assistance provided by the national product divisions. It requires a significant flow of information on technical developments, design innovations, etc., from the national divisions, without which it is destined to lose competitiveness. However, the rigid separation between domestic and foreign activities hinders the effective realization of such cooperation, mainly because product division managers are evaluated based on national-level results and thus have no incentive to collaborate.

Additionally, it may happen that national divisions form coalitions against excessive expansion of foreign activities: the transfer of production abroad, which involves its transfer under the control of the international division, usually concerns products with strong growth potential. As a result, the national divisions may lose particularly profitable product lines.

Furthermore, if international operations involve the transfer of products or semi-finished goods from national divisions to foreign subsidiaries, managers of the international division often face difficulties because they do not have sufficient control over transfer prices (Salomon, 2016).

Coordination through a structure with centralized internationality proves to be feasible to the extent that *multidimensionality* is limited, especially in terms of the number and diversity of product lines present abroad (Airoldi, 1980).

Regarding the *dimensional aspect*, the number and size of foreign subsidiaries are particularly important. The expansion of international activities generally implies an expansion of the international division itself. However, empirical research indicates that this division is maintained until it reaches a certain size threshold, specifically until its size surpasses that of the most significant national product division(s). In such cases, it can happen that national divisions, feeling threatened in their positions of power, form coalitions to challenge the foreign units. It can be inferred from the above that environmental and strategic variability must be rather limited or not exceed a certain limit, as otherwise, the international division's management would be unable to perform its coordinating role typically assigned to it. A high frequency of introducing new products once again requires intensive interactions between the international division and product divisions. On the other hand, frequent changes in the competitive and/or political climate demand a high level of local decision-making decentralization, as otherwise, it would overload the information management of the international division.

On the positive side, the international division is generally established to leverage synergistic advantages obtained by coordinating the activities of local units. For instance, if a transfer of goods and services occurs, tax liabilities can be modified through transfer pricing manoeuvres. Additionally, capital raising for subsidiaries can be achieved more efficiently through central control rather than relying on each subsidiary to seek funds in national financial markets. The activity of the international division is also particularly crucial when governing the integration between parts of the product manufactured domestically and other parts produced by foreign subsidiaries. However, overall, while the structure with centralized internationality appears suitable for achieving good coordination between the company's international activities, it seems less capable of managing interdependencies with national activities.

The natural evolution of a structure with centralized internationality is, therefore, towards a broader setup that allows embracing all the markets where the company operates, governing *products* on a global scale, and organizing *functional activities* to efficiently support all operational units. The aim is to better harmonize the three fundamental elements of the organisational structure of international companies: functions, geographical localization, and products.

As the size of the international division increases, the same forces that led to its development determine its progressive disappearance: the decisive turning point towards a global structure occurs when the top management realizes that the most relevant decisions must be made at central offices. This allows abandoning the artificial division between domestic and foreign activities and enables the diffusion of a *global and integrated perspective*.

c. Global functional structure or global product divisional structure.

I. The global functional structure. The adoption of this type of structure involves coordinating international activities based on functional dimensions and, at a second level, based on products or geographical areas. This setup typically applies to companies characterized by a single product line or relatively homogenous and standardized product lines and geographical areas, where maintaining specific professional expertise under strict control is particularly crucial. Centralization at the *headquarters* ensures that the company's strengths in functional activities are personally defended by top management. In this sense, it is the strategic apex that formulates and governs the strategic vision for the entire company. For this reason, this structure is suitable when all the information necessary for determining the strategy is already available at the centre, at the parent company, and when operational plans can be developed and managed on a global basis rather than based on the specific conditions of each geographical area or product.

However, this structure tends to operate functions separately, and the possibility of achieving cross-functional coordination is limited, as the exchange of information between functional units is not facilitated. For an international company, this means that the adoption of a global functional structure is preferable only when managing stable and homogeneous product lines and operating in an undifferentiated environment. This structure is not capable of handling high levels of *multidimensionality,* either in terms of the number of product lines or the diversification across geographical areas in which the company operates.

The *interdependence* that this structure allows to manage must be confined within the functions themselves: it is capable of achieving significant global integration of production, marketing, research activities, etc.

In terms of *variability*, a heavily centralized structure like this struggles to handle high levels of it successfully. The ability to respond to various situations at the local level necessitates a certain degree of decision-making decentralization at hierarchical levels closer to national realities.

II. Global Divisional Structure by products. When the strategy of an international company involves product line diversification, and the heterogeneity of these product lines is greater than that of the geographical areas where it operates, there is typically a need to manage the product dimension in a unified, coordinated, and prioritized manner. This entails assigning each division the responsibility to coordinate production, sales, research and development, design, and planning on a global scale. Each product division has considerable autonomy, given the specificity of pressures characterizing each product line. At the same time, central offices define *corporate-level* strategies and plans, which serve as boundaries within which individual divisions are expected to develop their specific strategies.

This structural solution also presents communication challenges, specifically between the central headquarters and foreign subsidiaries. When the international division, whose fundamental task was precisely to promote such communications, is removed, foreign subsidiaries are left to their own devices, subject to various and often conflicting pressures along the product dimension. In such circumstances, the foreign subsidiary may experience all the disadvantages of belonging to an international company (e.g., slow decision-making) without reaping any benefits. The coordination between different product divisions becomes very difficult, leading to conflicts in brand image or the failure to recognize local synergies. Sometimes, these difficulties are addressed by establishing *umbrella companies*, which, while maintaining the product-based structure, group all affiliates operating in a single country under one legal entity.

Choosing a global structure by products requires a strong heterogeneity in product lines coupled with limited differentiation in the markets where the company operates. Any significant diversity in this regard weakens the opportunity to manage products uniformly across different countries and achieve global economies of scale. Realizing these benefits is possible to the extent that products are substantially the same in all countries where the company has subsidiaries.

Studies on the organisational structures of international companies have generally found that this structural form is prevalent in companies operating in high research and development density sectors, characterized by high levels of technological and product innovation.

Companies adopting this structure typically operate by introducing new products first in domestic markets and then, when they are in the development phase, entering foreign markets. Consequently, their primary focus is on technology transfer to subsidiaries. At this level, the global structure by products enables the establishment of short and direct communication channels between different countries along the product dimension. The main weakness of this structure lies in the possibility of global product co-ordination failing to recognize significant differences between different countries in economic, political, and cultural aspects. This is often addressed by establishing regional offices responsible for seeking the most appropriate adaptations. However, it is worth noting that the capacity of this structure to tolerate high degrees of geographical heterogeneity is quite limited.

III. Global Divisional Structure by Geographical Areas. It may happen that the company's activities are quite extensive, complex, and sufficiently different between geographical areas, leading to opportunities for specialization, economies of scale, and synergies to manifest not at a global level but at a regional level. Typically, this occurs in companies operating with limited product lines, characterized by significant regional differentiation, and in the maturity phase. This allows standardizing the core of the products and seeking adaptations - mostly in terms of image - at the regional level. With this structure, international operations are grouped based on their geographical distribution, and for each geographical area, regional central offices are created, reporting to the central management for all sales, research, production, etc., activities carried out in the respective region. The main advantage of this structure is the decentralization of decision-making at the regional office level, meaning that decisions on matters such as product adaptations, distribution channels, and promotional policies can be made very close to the relevant markets.

However, the main difficulty encountered is the limited ability to reconcile the geographical orientation of management with the need to emphasize specific product lines. This becomes particularly challenging if the product lines are diversified and need to be marketed through different distribution channels. Furthermore, if a high level of product *know-how* needs to be developed in each geographical division, this structure requires duplicating efforts in technological development.

The application of products still in the development phase in the domestic market proves to be particularly challenging at the international level. In fact, many of the disadvantages of a product-based structure are the advantages of a geographical area-based structure, and vice versa (Phatak, 1983): the geographical area-based structure can achieve a good level of coordination at the regional level but shows some weakness in integrating product activities in subsidiaries belonging to different regional divisions. On the other hand, establishing central offices for different geographical areas allows for decentralized decision-making concerning local product policies and, consequently, a greater capacity to adapt them according to the specific needs of different global markets.

In this sense, the geographical area-based structure allows for successful management of interdependencies concerning marketing and production policies.

These interdependencies mainly arise in connection with the management of mature products, where a particular emphasis is placed on cost reduction activities. Mature products, indeed, largely address the same needs in different markets, and since they no longer rely on technological advantages, their only source of differentiation from competitors is price and external communication. Regional marketing policies can be easily developed within geographical area-based divisions.

Furthermore, as technology transfers between divisions are rarely necessary, communication difficulties between divisions do not have significant consequences, and cost reduction in production can be achieved through specialized policies at plants located in different countries. For example, the company can assemble semi-finished products from various countries in some subsidiaries or assign the complete production of a product to a single country. Integrating production on these bases requires assigning responsibility for strategic decisions to a higher hierarchical level than marketing policies, resulting in significant levels of centralization.

d. *The matrix structure.* As previously highlighted, the structural choices of international companies result from the conflict among three critical dimensions: functions, products, and geographical areas. When one of these dimensions emerges as a priority, it is placed at the top level of the macrostructure, while efforts are made to focus attention on the other dimensions by adopting them as criteria at lower levels. However, sometimes such solutions leave some significant coordination and focus problems unresolved. If traditional integration mechanisms (programs, meetings, committees, etc.) are not sufficient to handle the need for multidimensionality, more complex multifocal structures may be employed, including the matrix structure. This structure combines and overlaps two structural forms, allowing the company to manage its international activities through two relevant dimensions. This implies abandoning the principle of unity of command in favour of the so-called two-boss structure (Decastri, 2011).

Branch managers find themselves reporting to the headquarters along two hierarchical lines. While this ensures greater capacity to manage strategic conflicts, it also presents a potential source of conflicts associated with the dual nature of the objectives assigned to each unit. The fundamental problem of this type of structure is the situation of unstable power balance between different lines of authority, power that can be reallocated depending on the orientation required by the pursued strategy (Decastri, 2012). The smooth functioning of the matrix, therefore, requires extreme sensitivity towards power arrangements, which need to be adjusted to enable the implementation of certain strategies without causing asymmetries that lead to one-dimensional orientations. While studies from the 1970s showed a tendency for many multinational companies to adopt the matrix structure (Stopford & Wells, 1972), in the 1980s its usage seemed to decline. A study from 1984 revealed that most international companies had traditional organisational structures at the beginning of the 1980s. The reasons for this phenomenon, according to the authors, can be attributed to the excessive complexity of the matrix structure, which presents significant obstacles to decision-making processes, triggers power struggles, and generates anxiety among organisational members.

e. *Transnational structure.* It is a strategic organisational design that seeks to establish a highly interconnected and interdependent network of operations spanning multiple countries. It represents a response to the complexities and challenges of operating in a globalised business environment, where companies need to balance the benefits of global coordination and standardization with the necessity to be responsive to local market needs and conditions (Salomon, 2016). In this structure, a company aims to create a seamless flow of information, resources, and expertise across its various international units, allowing for efficient decision-making, resource allocation, and innovation on a global scale. The ultimate goal is to achieve synergies through collaboration and knowledge-sharing while still maintaining the ability to adapt and cater to diverse local market demands and preferences.

To implement the transnational structure successfully, companies foster a culture of open communication, trust, and cooperation among their international divisions. They embrace a multidimensional approach, where different units collaborate based on functional expertise, product lines, and geographical areas, enabling them to leverage the best practices and resources from different parts of the organisation (Salomon, 2016).

Furthermore, the transnational structure facilitates the integration of global strategies with local execution, as it empowers subsidiaries and regional offices to take more autonomous decisions that align with their specific market conditions and customer needs. This decentralized decision-making fosters a sense of ownership and accountability, enabling subsidiaries to respond swiftly to market changes and capitalize on emerging opportunities (Ismail et al., 2016).

Recent studies emphasize the growing importance of the transnational structure in today's global business landscape. With advancements in communication technology and increasing globalization of markets, multinational companies are seeking ways to optimize their operations and enhance their competitive advantage. Scholars have found that companies adopting a transnational structure outperform those with traditional hierarchical structures in terms of efficiency, innovation, and customer satisfaction (Salomon, 2016).

However, it is essential to recognize that implementing a transnational structure poses challenges related to organisational coordination, cultural differences, and conflicting priorities. Companies need to invest in effective cross-cultural training, communication tools, and shared performance metrics to overcome these hurdles and ensure that the metanational structure functions cohesively (Manzi et al., 2018).

This structure, therefore, represents a sophisticated approach to managing international operations, aiming to strike a delicate balance between global integration and local responsiveness. By fostering collaboration and knowledge exchange across borders, this organisational design enables companies to adapt swiftly to market dynamics while capitalizing on global synergies. As the global business landscape continues to evolve, the metanational structure is becoming increasingly relevant and instrumental in driving multinational companies' success (Kenworthy, 2008).

f. *Virtual Structure.* It represents an innovative organisational approach where companies heavily leverage outsourcing and strategic alliances to execute various functions, resulting in a lean and flexible organisation that operates without substantial physical presence in many locations (Riemer et al., 2012). In this model, companies focus on their core competencies and outsource non-core activities to external partners who specialize in those areas, enabling them to achieve greater efficiency and cost-effectiveness. Virtual structures capitalize on advancements in technology and communication, allowing for seamless coordination and collaboration with external partners, regardless of their geographical location. This approach empowers companies to access specialized skills and resources from a global pool of talent while maintaining a nimble and adaptable organisational structure.

Recent trends in the business landscape have demonstrated the growing importance of virtual structures. With the rise of digitalization and the proliferation of online platforms, companies have increasingly turned to virtual teams and external partners to meet specific business needs and remain competitive in dynamic markets (Garro-Abarca et al., 2021). Studies have shown that companies adopting virtual structures experience enhanced agility and cost savings compared to traditional hierarchical organisations. They can quickly assemble teams with diverse expertise from around the world to address specific projects and respond to market changes promptly. Additionally, virtual structures enable companies to enter new markets and expand their reach without incurring the overhead costs associated with establishing physical operations in different locations.

However, the virtual structure also poses challenges that require careful management. As companies rely heavily on external partners, effective communication, and collaboration become paramount to ensure a cohesive and unified organisational effort. Building trust and maintaining strong relationships with external partners are critical to achieve seamless integration and alignment of goals. Moreover, companies must address potential cultural and time zone differences to ensure effective teamwork and avoid miscommunications. Implementing robust communication tools and project management systems becomes essential to facilitate smooth interactions among team members and external partners.

The virtual structure represents a modern and efficient organisational model that leverages outsourcing and strategic alliances to create a lean and agile company. Embracing this approach allows businesses to concentrate on their core competencies while accessing specialized skills and resources globally. As companies continue to navigate an increasingly digital and interconnected world, virtual structures are likely to gain further prominence as a means to achieve competitiveness, adaptability, and cost-effectiveness in the ever-changing business landscape.

g. *Network Structure.* It is a contemporary organisational model that bears resemblance to the virtual structure, as it prioritizes collaboration with external partners to achieve strategic objectives and create value collectively (Andreassen, 2018). In this context, companies adopt a more interconnected and interdependent approach by forming extensive networks of suppliers, distributors, customers, and other stakeholders. These networks serve as the foundation for mutually beneficial relationships, allowing businesses to tap into a vast pool of expertise, resources, and capabilities beyond their internal capacities. As a result, the network structure enhances flexibility, responsiveness, and innovation by enabling the seamless exchange of information, ideas, and innovations among network members. The concept of forming such collaborative networks has gained traction in recent years, particularly in the dynamic and rapidly evolving business environment, where traditional hierarchical structures may struggle to keep pace with market demands and technological advancements. One of the primary advantages of the network structure lies in its ability to foster specialization and efficiency throughout the value chain. By strategically aligning with specialized suppliers and distribution partners, companies can focus on their core competencies while relying on others to handle peripheral tasks, thus optimizing resource allocation. For instance, a technology company may collaborate with a logistics partner to streamline its supply chain and reduce operational costs, allowing it to allocate more resources to research and development to stay ahead in the fiercely competitive market.

Moreover, the network structure also facilitates risk mitigation and resilience in the face of disruptions. Diversifying suppliers and partners across various regions and industries ensures that a single point of failure does not cripple the entire operation. In times of crisis, such as natural disasters or global pandemics, this decentralized approach can prove invaluable in maintaining continuity and meeting customer demands despite challenges.

However, it is essential to acknowledge that adopting a network structure is not without its challenges. Establishing and maintaining trust-based relationships with external partners demand careful coordination, communication, and conflict resolution. Additionally, managing data security and intellectual property concerns in collaborative environments necessitates robust safeguards to protect proprietary information while fostering an open and innovative atmosphere.

To sum up, the network structure represents a strategic organisational model that emphasizes collaborative efforts with external partners, promoting shared value creation and specialization across the business ecosystem. By forming extensive networks of suppliers, distributors, and other stakeholders, companies can capitalize on synergies, optimize resource allocation, and enhance their resilience in an ever-changing business landscape. While challenges exist, the potential benefits of the network structure make it an attractive option for businesses seeking to thrive in the dynamic and interconnected world of today.

h. *Holacracy.* Holacracy is a management philosophy and organisational structure that challenges the traditional top-down hierarchy found in most companies. It was introduced by Brian Robertson in 2007 and has gained traction in various industries, particularly among startups and progressive organisations seeking to foster a more agile and adaptive work environment. The core principles of Holacracy revolve around distributed authority, self-organisation, and dynamic role-based governance.

It is a relatively new organisational concept, has been gaining attention in recent years as a potential alternative to traditional hierarchical structures. This innovative approach replaces the conventional top-down management system with a more fluid and self-organizing framework, aiming to distribute authority and decision-making across self-managing teams (Robertson, 2015). In Holacracy, power is decentralized, and employees are encouraged to take on roles with specific accountabilities and the autonomy to make decisions within their domain (Obholzer & Roberts, 2016).

In this type of structure, decision-making authority is distributed across self-managing teams, called circles, which are responsible for specific domains or areas of the organisation's operations (Robertson, 2015). Each circle has its own set of roles, and employees are encouraged to take on these roles based on their skills and interests rather than being assigned by managers. These roles come with clear accountabilities and authorities, granting individuals the autonomy to make decisions within their purview. One of the fundamental tenets of Holacracy is the separation of role and soul. This means that decisions are made based on the specific roles individuals occupy within the organisation, rather than personal opinions or emotions. This depersonalized approach aims to promote objectivity and efficiency in decision-making.

Holacracy also emphasizes regular and structured governance meetings, such as "tactical" and "governance" meetings, to facilitate transparent discussions about roles, responsibilities, and any tensions or conflicts that arise in the organisation. These meetings provide a platform for employees to raise issues and suggest improvements, fostering a culture of continuous improvement and adaptability.

Proponents of Holacracy argue that this decentralized approach increases agility, promotes employee empowerment and engagement, and enables quicker responses to changing market conditions (Robertson, 2015). By removing traditional management layers and allowing employees to participate actively in decision-making, organisations aim to tap into the collective intelligence and creativity of their workforce (Obholzer & Roberts, 2016). Hence, this approach fosters a more agile and adaptable organisation, as it empowers individuals to respond swiftly to challenges and opportunities without waiting for approval from higher-ups. Such a shift in power dynamics has been seen as a way to increase employee engagement and job satisfaction, as team members have more ownership over their work.

However, implementing Holacracy is not without challenges, including the need for robust communication and conflict resolution mechanisms to ensure alignment and prevent chaos. Critics argue that it can lead to role confusion, a lack of accountability, and difficulties in aligning the organisation's overall vision and strategy (Sarfraz et al., 2020). Without clear guidelines and effective communication channels, Holacracy can devolve into chaos and create tension between teams and individuals (Kumar & Mukherjee, 2018).

Despite its promise and growing popularity as well its challenges, Holacracy continues to intrigue and inspire many organisations to experiment with alternative management structures. As the future of work evolves, this innovative approach to organisational design may continue to be a source of interest and exploration for companies seeking to stay agile and responsive in an ever-changing business landscape. Nevertheless, it is worth noting that Holacracy might not be suitable for every organisation or industry, and further research and real-world experimentation are necessary to assess its long-term effectiveness and sustainability (Kumar & Mukherjee, 2018). This structure represents a disruptive shift in organisational design, providing a fascinating glimpse into the future of work and management structures.

i. *Hybrid Structures.* They have become increasingly prevalent in the corporate world as companies strive to navigate the complexities of the international business landscape and adapt to the rapidly evolving market demands (Verbeke et al., 2018). Such organisational approaches involve a mix of elements from various organisational types, including functional, divisional, matrix, and network structures, among others, in order to create a flexible and responsive framework. By doing so, companies can effectively balance the advantages of different organisational forms while mitigating their inherent limitations (Buch, 2020). In the wake of globalization, companies have realized the importance of customizing their structures to meet the unique challenges posed by diverse markets and cultural environments (Jessop, 2005). For instance, a multinational company operating in different regions may choose to combine elements of a functional structure, where different departments focus on specialized tasks, with a divisional structure, allowing each region or division to have its own autonomous decision-making capabilities. This amalgamation enables efficient coordination of operations across different geographical locations, while empowering regional teams to respond quickly to local market dynamics and consumer preferences.

The matrix structure is another essential component often integrated into hybrid models, particularly when companies undertake complex projects or deal with multiple product lines that require cross-functional collaboration (Goold & Campbell, 2003). By incorporating both functional and project-based reporting lines, the matrix structure promotes seamless communication and enhances innovation through diverse perspectives. Companies find that this approach not only fosters a culture of teamwork and knowledge sharing but also increases overall organisational agility, enabling them to stay competitive in a fast-paced global marketplace.

Additionally, the network structure has gained prominence as companies expand their operations through partnerships, alliances, and outsourcing arrangements (Swaminathan & Moorman, 2009). Integrating the network structure into a hybrid organisation allows companies to tap into external expertise and resources, thereby optimizing efficiency and reducing costs. This flexible approach to collaboration fosters innovation and agility as companies can swiftly adapt to changes in market demands and industry trends.

The rise of hybrid structures is evident across various industries, from technology giants to pharmaceutical companies and financial institutions. For instance, companies in the tech sector, such as Google, have adopted a hybrid approach that combines functional departments with cross-functional project teams, allowing them to balance innovation with operational efficiency (Godiwalla, 2018). Similarly, pharmaceutical companies like Pfizer have embraced hybrid structures that enable them to align their R&D efforts with specific therapeutic areas while maintaining a centralized core for administrative functions (Robertson, 2015). Financial institutions have also explored hybrid structures to enhance customer-centricity by integrating network partnerships with traditional product-focused divisions.

The adoption of hybrid structures has emerged as a strategic imperative for companies seeking to thrive in the dynamic and complex international business landscape. By blending elements from various organisational types, companies can achieve a harmonious balance between specialization and flexibility, centralized control and localized autonomy, and internal collaboration and external partnerships. As global markets continue to evolve, the versatility and adaptability offered by hybrid structures will undoubtedly remain a crucial competitive advantage for companies across industries (Durmuş-Özdemir & Mecikoglu, 2016).

It is important to note that the choice of organisational structure depends on the company's global strategy, industry, size, and the complexity of its international operations. As companies evolve and expand their international presence, they may transition from one type of structure to another to effectively manage their global activities.

2.2 The Choice of the International Organisational Structure

The strategic and structural considerations described in this paragraph can be briefly represented in Stopford and Wells' model (1972), a model in which strategy is measured in terms of two fundamental dimensions: the percentage of foreign sales and the level of product line diversification. As a company increases its volume of international activities and product diversification crosses certain thresholds, this transition implies structural changes. In the region characterized by low levels of both variables, companies adopting global functional structures and centralized international structures are positioned. The expansion of international activities accompanied by limited product diversification leans toward the adoption of a geographic divisional structure. However, if diversification exceeds a certain level, opting for a product divisional structure becomes more favourable.

Originally, Stopford and Wells represented the top-right region with a question mark; however, this area is of great importance for international companies. There is indeed a tendency towards geographic expansion through diversified product lines, a strategy that requires equal priority to be given to both aspects. As a result, there is increasing interdependence between product divisions, geographic divisions, and functions, making it more challenging to identify semi-autonomous organisational units (Jessop, 2005).

In summary, the current strategies of international companies emphasize the importance of the geographic dimension to achieve local responsiveness, the product dimension for global integration, and the professional dimension to transfer knowledge across the globe. This leads to a trend towards two-dimensional and matrix structures and innovative arrangements such as heterarchy or transnational companies.

Unlike other areas of organisational design, the choice of structure in international companies is influenced by process variables: the stage of the international development process in which the decision is made and the accumulated experience regarding foreign operations are crucial factors in selecting the international organisational structure. In other words, while the fundamental approach of contingency theories remains, where the characteristics of the company's productive combinations underlie organisational decisions (Airoldi, 1989), the stage reached by the company in the process of acquiring and accumulating knowledge of the international territory (Bodega, Decastri & Prina, 1992) can substantially influence the organisational effectiveness of the aforementioned structures. This will lead to the following selection criterion: Historical phase - organisational structure.

The process of international learning and the evolution of connected organisational structures typically involve several stages as companies expand their operations globally. While the specific stages and terminologies may vary depending on different perspectives and sources, the following four stages are commonly observed:

1. *Domestic Operation.* At the initial stage, a company operates solely in its home country with a domestic focus. The organisational structure is typically designed to cater to the local market demands and does not consider international operations.
2. *Exporting and Internationalization.* In this stage, the company starts exporting its products or services to foreign markets. It may establish relationships with international distributors or agents. At this point, the organisational structure may remain primarily domestic-focused, with limited modifications to accommodate export activities.
3. *Multinational Operation.* As the company expands its international presence further, it begins to establish subsidiaries or branch offices in foreign countries. The organisational structure evolves to include international divisions or regions, allowing for more decentralized decision-making to address the specific needs of different markets. Each subsidiary may operate somewhat independently, and knowledge transfer between the headquarters and foreign units becomes essential.
4. *Global Integration.* At this advanced stage, the company aims for greater global integration and coordination. The organisational structure shifts towards more centralized decision-making and standardized processes to achieve economies of scale and scope. There is a stronger emphasis on knowledge sharing and strategic alignment across all international units to create a cohesive global entity.

It is important to note that these stages are not rigid or universally applicable to all companies. Some companies may go through additional intermediate stages or face unique challenges during their internationalization process. Furthermore, the process of international learning and organisational evolution is iterative, with companies continuously adapting their structures as they gain experience and encounter new opportunities and challenges in the international business landscape.

Considering the above premises, it is possible to identify, at least three stages of evolution in the process of international learning and the related organisational structure.

Although the specific categorization may vary depending on the source and context, nevertheless, there are several stages that companies tend to go through as they expand internationally and adapt their organisational structures to accommodate their global operations. The three stages provide a useful framework to understand this evolution. Let us explore each stage:

a. *Trial and Error.* In the initial stage of international expansion, companies often rely on trial and error to explore foreign markets and understand the complexities of doing business in different countries: foreign investment is limited and marginal, and knowledge of the international territory is scarce. They may adopt an ad-hoc approach, experimenting with various strategies and organisational structures to meet the challenges of international operations.

A classic example of this approach is the expansion of Honda, a world leader in the motorcycle industry, into the United States. Pascale and Athos (1981) recall the words of the vice president of sales: *"My first reaction once in the USA was: How could we be so foolish! ... To be honest, we didn't have any strategies ... We decided to start with very little; two of us slept on the floor, and we managed to find a warehouse in a run-down neighbourhood; the first year we were clueless. We knew nothing. It was 1958; not even six years later, half of the motorcycles sold in the USA were Honda's. The actors' lucidity on the structuring of relationships beyond borders is extremely limited at this stage. They proceed adaptively: they try one path, evaluate it afterward, rationalize the path taken, and start again. In summary, the unity of the company is not jeopardized by the almost random pursuit of spatial and geographical expansion"* (Pascale & Athos, 1981; p. 51).

This phase is characterized by a lack of a standardized approach and a heavy reliance on local autonomy, which can lead to inefficiencies and inconsistencies across different international units.

b. *Structuring*. This is the phase of discovery and legitimization of the internationalization process and the partial combinations established abroad. As companies gain more experience and knowledge about international markets, they move into the structuring stage. In this phase, organisations start to develop a more deliberate and systematic approach to managing their global operations. They begin to standardize certain processes and adopt more formalized organisational structures that allow for better coordination and integration across different international units. This may involve the creation of regional or divisional structures, functional departments with international responsibilities, or matrix arrangements to balance global and local demands. In this stage, companies become aware of the differences and difficulties involved in managing international activities, while the potential of foreign development becomes clearer, prompting the company to project itself more decisively towards this dimension. Difficulties and potentials create a context rich in ambiguity and anxiety: the organisational system - after the intense learning experience of the first phase - must proceed towards structuring the acquired knowledge, moving towards a process of centralization and subjecting international activities to strong governance by top management (Ribeiro et al., 2020).

Continuing in a trial-and-error approach can become risky (even for simple reasons of economies of scale). The fear that centrifugal forces may compromise the company's balance pushes towards a strong expectation of organisational transparency and central coordination. This effort towards structuring, regulation, and convergence results in the expression and formalization of the strategic role played by international operations: an international division responsible for governing foreign activities is incorporated into the organisational structure. This leads to greater coordination of efforts but also a substantial decrease in the autonomy of international positions. The process of consolidating the experience gained in the initial phase requires a drastic reduction in the discretion of the periphery and the forced involvement of top management (not because they know more, but because they need to learn and regulate) in all relevant international decisions. In other words, unity prevails over expansion (Andersson et al., 2015).

c. *Diffusion*. This stage is characterized by the widespread dissemination of best practices and successful strategies throughout the organisation. Companies leverage the knowledge gained from their international experiences and distribute it across various units to enhance overall organisational learning and performance. Knowledge sharing facilitates a more cohesive and unified approach to international operations leading to an increased efficiency and effectiveness in the global marketplace. This phase is characterized by the institutionalization of international presence. Foreign operations, that are initially carried out almost casually and driven by a few "explorers", then confined to a special unit considered as "reserve", become part of the entire company. This allows spreading across organisational units, returning under the responsibility of the bodies within which they were born, but this time, fully and strategically valued, no longer tolerated, distrusted, or kept at a distance.

The process culminates in the design of a highly sophisticated organisational structure that - through structure and operational systems - allows for the simultaneous management of the three dimensions that presumably characterize the company's strategy: functions, products, and geographical areas. While it cannot be asserted that there exists a specific structural form characteristic of this phase, it is common to find two-dimensional organisational structures by product and geographical area: the country/product intersection is the critical point where the needs for unity (the product dimension) and extension (the country dimension) converge. Moreover, the clear distinction between domestic and foreign economic combinations also falls away.

In this phase, companies tend to adopt hybrid structures that combine elements from various organisational types to effectively manage the complexity of their international operations (Barkema & Vermeulen, 2022). These hybrid organisational structures allow for the integration of global strategies while maintaining responsiveness to local market conditions (Lioukas & Reuer, 2015). The convergence of product and geographic dimensions in the organisation's design reflects the need to balance centralization and decentralization to achieve strategic goals efficiently in the global marketplace (Drogendijk & Slangen, 2006). As companies reach this stage of internationalization, they become more adept at navigating the complexities of operating in different markets and optimizing their global reach and effectiveness.

It is important to note that these stages are not necessarily linear, and companies may revisit or experience overlaps between them as they continue to evolve and adapt to changing international business dynamics. Additionally, some sources may identify additional stages or use different terminology, but the general idea remains consistent: companies' progress from an initial phase of trial and error to a more structured approach, culminating in the diffusion of knowledge and best practices throughout the organisation.

REFERENCES

Airoldi, G. (1980). *I sistemi operativi*. Giuffrè.

Allegretti, S., Seidenstricker, S., Fischer, H., & Arslan, S. (2021). Executing a business model change: Identifying key characteristics to succeed in volatile markets. *Leadership, Education, Personality. An Interdisciplinary Journal, 3*(1), 1–13. doi:10.1365/s42681-021-00020-x

Andersson, U., Gaur, A., Mudambi, R., & Persson, M. (2015). Unpacking inter unit knowledge transfer in multinational enterprises. *Global Strategy Journal, 5*(3), 241–245. doi:10.1002/gsj.1100

Andreassen, T. W., Lervik-Olsen, L., Snyder, H., Van Riel, A. C., Sweeney, J. C., & Van Vaerenbergh, Y. (2018). Business model innovation and value-creation: The triadic way. *Journal of Service Management, 29*(5), 883–906. doi:10.1108/JOSM-05-2018-0125

Barkema, H. G., Chen, X. P., George, G., Luo, Y., & Tsui, A. S. (2015). West Meets East: New Concepts and Theories. (2015). *Academy of Management Journal*, *58*(2), 460–479. doi:10.5465/amj.2015.4021

Battilana, J. (2018). Cracking the organisational challenge of pursuing joint social and financial goals: Social enterprise as a laboratory to understand hybrid organizing. *M@n@gement*, *21*(4), 1278–1305. doi:10.3917/mana.214.1278

Bodega, D., Decastri, M., & Prina, G. (1992). *Innovazione, apprendimento e formazione: un'indagine empirica*. Franco Angeli.

Buch, A. (2020). People and practices in organisational learning. *Forskning or Forandring*, *3*(1), 70–88. doi:10.23865/fof.v3.2103

Coda, V. (1965). *Le coordinazioni produttive. Introduzione al sistema delle rilevazioni d'impresa*. Giuffrè.

Decastri, M., Scravaglieri, S., Trotta, M., & Yamak, S. (2011). The value of work: an antidote against the neo-bureaucratic drift of public administration. In E. Borgonovi & R. Mussari (Eds.), *Collaborare e competere per un mercato responsabile e solidale*. Il Mulino.

Decastri, M., Tomasi, D., & Scravaglieri, S. (2012). Performance Management Systems as Driver of Public Administration lmprovement: a Dream? In A. D'Atri & D. Saccà (Eds.), Designing Organisational Systems. An interdisciplinary discourse (pp.245-267). Physica-Verlag, Springer.

Drogendijk, R., & Slangen, A. (2006). Hofstede, Schwartz, Or Managerial Perceptions? The Effects of Different Cultural Distance Measures on Establishment Mode Choices by Multinational Enterprises. *International Business Review*, *15*(4), 361–380. doi:10.1016/j.ibusrev.2006.05.003

Durmuş-Özdemir, E., & Mecikoglu, S. (2016). A Case Study on Performance Implications of Hybrid Strategy in Automotive Supplier Industry. *International Business Research*, *9*(6), 31. doi:10.5539/ibr.v9n6p31

Garro-Abarca, V., Palos-Sanchez, P., & Mariano, A. (2021). Virtual Teams in Times of Pandemic: Factors That Influence Performance. *Frontiers in Psychology*, *12*, 624637. doi:10.3389/fpsyg.2021.624637 PMID:33679543

Godiwalla, H. Y. (2018). Global Organisational Innovation Strategy. *International Journal of Social Science Studies*, *6*(8), 45–53. doi:10.11114/ijsss.v6i8.3477

Goold, M., & Campbell, A. (2003). Making Matrix Structures Work. Creating Clarity on Unit Roles and Responsibility. *European Management Journal*, *21*(3), 351–363. doi:10.1016/S0263-2373(03)00048-3

Ismail, M., Sobri, S. S., Zulkifly, N. A., Hamzah, S. R., & Yamato, E. (2016). Knowledge transfer between expatriates and host country nationals: Contribution of individual and social capital factors. *Organizations and Markets in Emerging Economies*, *7*(2), 65–87. doi:10.15388/omee.2016.7.2.14208

Jessop, B. (2005). Critical Realism and the Strategic-Relational Approach. *New Formations*, *2005*(56). https://api.semanticscholar.org/CorpusID:142627525

Kenworthy, T. (2008). Multidivisional vs Metanational Governance of The Multinational Enterprise. *Journal of International Business Studies*, *39*(6), 940–956. doi:10.1057/palgrave.jibs.8400344

Kumar, V., & Mukherjee, S. (2018). Holacracy – the future of organizing? The case of Zappos. *Human Resource Management International Digest*, *26*(7), 12–15. Advance online publication. doi:10.1108/HRMID-08-2018-0161

Lioukas, C. S., & Reuer, J. J. (2015). Isolating trust outcomes from exchange relationships: Social exchange and learning benefits of prior ties in alliances. *Academy of Management Journal*, *58*(6), 1826–1847. doi:10.5465/amj.2011.0934

Manzi, C., Coen, S., Regalia, C., Yévenes, A. M., Giuliani, C., & Vignoles, V. L. (2018). Being in the Social: A cross-cultural and cross-generational study on identity processes related to Facebook use. *Computers in Human Behavior*, *80*, 81–87. doi:10.1016/j.chb.2017.10.046

Masini, C. (1970). *Lavoro e risparmio*. Utet.

Obholzer, A., & Roberts, V. Z. (Eds.). (2019). The unconscious at work: A Tavistock approach to making sense of organisational life (2nd ed.). Routledge/Taylor & Francis Group. doi:10.4324/9781351104166

Pascale, R. T., & Athos, A. G. (1981). *The Art of Japanese Management: Applications for American Executives*. Wamer Books. doi:10.1016/0007-6813(81)90032-X

Ribeiro, M. T., Wu, T., Guestrin, C., & Singh, S. (2020). Beyond Accuracy: Behavioral Testing of NLP Models with CheckList. In D. Jurafsky, J. Chai, N. Schluter, & J. Tetreault (Eds.), *Proceedings of the 58th Annual Meeting of the Association for Computational Linguistics*, (pp. 4902–4912). Association for Computational Linguistics. 10.18653/v1/2020.acl-main.442

Riemer, K., & Vehring, N. (2012). Virtual or vague? A literature review exposing conceptual differences in defining virtual organisations in IS research. *Electronic Markets*, *22*(4), 267–282. doi:10.1007/s12525-012-0094-2

Robert, G., Locock, L., Williams, O., Cornwell, J., Donetto, S., & Goodrich, J. (2022). *Co-Producing and Co-Designing*. Cambridge University Press., doi:10.1017/9781009237024

Robertson, B. (2015). *Holacracy: The Revolutionary Management System that Abolishes Hierarchy*. Portfolio Penguin. Penguin Random House.

Salomon, R. (2016). *Global Vision. How Companies Can Overcome the Pitfalls of Globalization*. Palgrave Macmillan.

Sarfraz, M., He, B., & Shah, S. (2020). Elucidating the effectiveness of cognitive CEO on corporate environmental performance: The mediating role of corporate innovation. *Environmental Science and Pollution Research International*, *27*(36), 45938–45948. Advance online publication. doi:10.1007/s11356-020-10496-7 PMID:32808125

Stopford, J. M., & Wells, L. T. (1972). *Managing the Multinational Enterprise*. Basic Books.

Swaminathan, V., & Moorman, C. (2009). Marketing Alliances, Firm Networks, and Firm Value Creation. *Journal of Marketing*, *73*(5), 52–69. doi:10.1509/jmkg.73.5.52

Verbeke, A., Coeurderoy, R., & Matt, T. (2018). The future of international business research on corporate globalization that never was. *Journal of International Business Studies*, *49*(9), 1101–1112. doi:10.1057/s41267-018-0192-2

Vuchkovski, D., Zalaznik, M., Mitręga, M., & Pfajfar, G. (2023). A look at the future of work: The digital transformation of teams from conventional to virtual. *Journal of Business Research*, *163*, 113912. Advance online publication. doi:10.1016/j.jbusres.2023.113912

Chapter 3
At the Core of the Conflict:
Territorial Control

ABSTRACT

This chapter deals with the core of conflicts arising from the territorial control within a broader international context, encompassing two pivotal areas of analysis. The first paragraph explores the intricate dynamics between the territorial control and the host country. It examines historical, political, and socio-economic factors contributing to tensions, shedding light on the divergent interests and power struggles between these entities. A comprehensive understanding of the genesis of conflicts is provided by emphasising the complexities inherent in their relationship. The second paragraph focuses on the allocation of functional responsibilities, separating the delicate balance between centralisation and decentralisation within the territorial control. It suggests new strategies employed in distributing roles and powers by weighing advantages and challenges of both approaches. Overall, this chapter seeks to offer insights into the intricate decision-making processes for achieving an effective and harmonious balance between centralisation and decentralization.

3. AT THE CORE OF THE CONFLICT: TERRITORIAL CONTROL

Every choice made at the macro-structural level cannot ignore the definition of the role and function of the organisational entity (regardless of its formal name or hierarchical reporting) which oversees the territory or geographical area. The so-called 'foreign subsidiary' is, by definition, the focal point of all organisational tensions that characterise the international company: at this point, the two major forces guiding international decisions — as seen before — converge and *intersect in a structurally and physiologically conflicting manner.* These forces include the need for *unity* (resulting from the uniqueness of economic combinations, economic governance, and the corporate economic entity) and the need for *articulation* (related to the characteristics of multiculturalism and geographical dispersion of the international company) (Masini, 1970; Airoldi, 1989). In other words, the territorial control area is where the complexity that differentiates the domestic company from the international company is explicit and must be managed. It is a difference in *intensity* (considering that the domestic company may still have

DOI: 10.4018/979-8-3693-3482-9.ch003

to handle some intra-national socio-cultural differentiation) that, at higher levels, leads to a substantial diversity in the *quality* of the phenomenon to be managed.

Essentially, territorial control is responsible for maintaining the unity of the company processes whilst safeguarding the socio-economic and cultural specificities of the coordinated geographical area. The person in charge of this area finds themselves at the centre of the conflict mentioned above and must succeed in reconciling the homogeneity required by central entities with the flexibility demanded by local expectations.

This chapter emphasises the critical role of territorial control in balancing the global objectives of a multinational company with the need to adapt to diverse local markets. According to recent studies in international business management, companies have to strike a delicate balance between centralised control, for efficiency, and local responsiveness to remain competitive in the global marketplace (Bartlett and Ghoshal, 1989). Multinational companies often face challenges in managing cultural differences, regulatory environments, and customer preferences across various countries. Effective territorial control is crucial in ensuring smooth coordination of operations, knowledge sharing, and leveraging economies of scale whilst remaining sensitive to the unique demands of each local market (Hitt et al., 2013).

Moreover, advances in technology and communication have made it easier for multinational companies to connect and collaborate across different locations. However, these advancements have also increased the complexity of managing diverse and dispersed operations. As a result, territorial control plays a pivotal role in facilitating communication and coordination among different units whilst ensuring that the global strategy is implemented effectively at a local level (Verbeke et al., 2023). Additionally, recent research highlights the importance of empowering local managers with decision-making authority to respond to dynamic market conditions and capitalise on opportunities swiftly (Rugman and Verbeke, 2008). In this context, the role of the territorial control area has evolved to become more dynamic and strategic in fostering a balance between centralisation and localisation in international organisations.

3.1 The Relationships Between Territorial Control and the Host Country: At the Origin of the Conflict

The relationships between the company and the environment are one of the main concerns of managers (Rugiadini, 1979). The international environment, due to its high complexity, is the source of much of the management's worries in the international company. The characteristics of the host country can be completely alien to the company's managerial mentality and culture: traditional cultural maps (Brumana et al., 2014) and 'normal' collective mental programmes (Hofstede, 1980) often, if not rarely, fail to be applied to local social and economic realities. The territory appears threatening, unfamiliar and, at best, 'curiously different'. The dilemma that needs to be addressed is defined, on the one hand, by the desire for security, which pushes towards the unconditional implementation of decisions made at the central level and complete convergence, and on the other hand, by the need to have the requests for adaptation of decisions made at the company level accepted according to local specificities.

The task of territorial control management is to orchestrate and regulate these tensions, and to effectively address this responsibility, understanding their role is of primary importance, straddling the pressures towards homogeneity and rationalisation of the so-called 'hardware' of the company and the pressures towards flexibility demanded by the demographic, political, economic, socio-cultural peculiarities of the host country. The host country represents a unique set of forces that can be significantly different from the profile of the international company. The needs of the latter - which usually derive from another *unique set of forces* represented by the home country or the country where the *headquarters* are located — must be somehow subordinate to those of the host country or, at the very least, find solutions compatible with local needs.

In this context, a strategy and a consequent set of managerial approaches at the territorial control level can emerge that do not coincide with either the competitive strategies adopted in the international arena or the local expectations and contingencies. This creates a challenging task for the management of territorial control, as they need to navigate the complexities of balancing global strategies and local adaptations whilst maintaining overall organisational coherence (Demir and Angwin, 2021). Successful territorial control management requires a deep understanding of both the home country and the host country contexts and the ability to harmonise diverse demands to achieve organisational effectiveness on a global scale (Luo and Tung, 2018). As companies continue to expand internationally, this aspect of management becomes increasingly critical for sustained success in the global marketplace.

The ideal of a clear, coherent, and well-integrated global strategy is limited by powerful forces that push the multinational company towards a more ambiguous, less integrated strategy that caters to national differences. As coherence with national requirements can only be achieved at the expense of global coherence and clarity, tensions arise (Doz and Prahalad, 1981).

This observation about the tensions between global coherence and local adaptation remains relevant in today's international business landscape. In an increasingly interconnected world, multinational companies must navigate diverse cultural, economic, and regulatory contexts across different countries. Recent research highlights the importance of striking the right balance between global standardisation and local responsiveness to achieve competitive advantage (Hitt et al., 2013).

Globalisation has led to intensified competition and increased pressure on companies to cater to local preferences and needs whilst maintaining a coherent global brand image and strategy. To address this challenge, some companies adopt a transnational strategy, which emphasises simultaneous global integration and local responsiveness (Bartlett and Ghoshal, 1989). This approach allows firms to leverage economies of scale whilst also adapting to varying market conditions.

The tensions between global and local forces require multinational companies to develop strategic flexibility (Verbeke et al, 2018). This means continuously assessing the fit between their global strategies and local market conditions and being open to making necessary adjustments. Successful companies use dynamic capabilities to effectively respond to changing global and local contexts, allowing them to achieve both global coherence and local adaptation (Pan et al., 2021).

The tensions described by Doz and Prahalad (1981) continue to challenge multinational companies today. Striking the right balance between global coherence and local adaptation is crucial for sustainable success in a dynamic and complex international business environment (Luo, 2022). Companies that can effectively manage these tensions and develop strategies that integrate both global and local considerations are better positioned to thrive in the global marketplace. Without claiming to be exhaustive, below are some of the sources of tensions between the global needs of the international company and the interests of the host country, tensions that territorial control must face and manage:

a. Financial-economic balance of the host country. International companies are often at the centre of criticism from governments, especially in developing countries, as they can pose challenges and hinder national economic policies. The financial independence and economic strength typically associated with these types of companies allow them to act with a significant degree of independence from the decisions of local political bodies; this may lead to operational choices that contradict the economic and financial decisions of the host country. Inflation levels can be raised: Canada, for example, has accused international companies of making it more difficult to achieve joint economic growth and monetary stability due to continuous fluctuations in capital transfers (Jacoby, 1984). The results of national economic planning can become more uncertain due to the limited controllability of decisions made by international companies; for instance, increasing employee income can have negative effects on the balance of payments. Given the political significance of parameters such as the inflation rate and trade deficit, and the sense of helplessness that can arise from obstructing economic policy choices, it is easy to diagnose the level of pressure that converges on the top management of territorial control in times of difficulty.

The tensions between international companies and host governments over economic policies remain a pertinent issue in the global business landscape. Recent studies have highlighted the complex relationship between multinational companies and national governments, particularly in developing countries (Luo and Tung, 2018). As multinational companies operate across borders, their actions can have significant implications for the host country's economy, prompting increased scrutiny from local governments and policymakers.

Furthermore, the global interconnectedness of economies and financial markets has amplified the impact of multinational companies on host countries. The ease of capital movements and cross-border investments has led to increased concerns about the potential destabilising effects of international companies on national economic stability (Narula et al, 2021). Policymakers must balance the benefits of attracting foreign direct investment with the need to safeguard the country's economic sovereignty and stability. In response to these challenges, some host governments have implemented regulatory measures to exert greater control over the activities of international companies within their borders (Buckley and Casson, 1976). Striking a balance between facilitating foreign investments and protecting national economic interests requires thoughtful and proactive engagement between international companies and host governments.

The pressures faced by territorial control management to navigate these tensions are significant and underscore the need for effective communication, collaboration, and compliance with local regulations and policies (Henisz and Zelner, 2012). Companies that proactively address host country concerns and align their strategies with national economic goals are more likely to build positive relationships and contribute to sustainable economic development in the countries where they operate.

b. Development of key sectors of the host country's economy. International companies are also accused of hindering the development of local businesses, especially in high-tech sectors, where know-how is a critical success factor, and its protection through non-transfer and obstruction to autonomous national growth is strongly sought after by *headquarters* (Arrow, 1974). In summary, competitive advantage is preserved through the continuous evolution of processes and products, forcing local competitors into exhausting pursuits, or by maintaining prices and margins that do not allow the development of research initiatives capable of bridging the technological gap (Gabriel, 1977). In other cases, one may witness acquisitions or alliances of various kinds aimed at blocking potential local *know-how* development projects. Furthermore, through more attractive reward systems, international companies attract and retain the most qualified personnel, limiting the potential of national businesses and entrepreneurs.

On the other hand, always due to the inherent mechanism in information transfers, international companies represent the most useful means of spreading *know-how* (Teece, 2006): within corporate boundaries, under the watchful protection of the hierarchy, transactions involving knowledge become easier, and the international company can be the only context in which such transfer can be efficiently realised. The management of the territorial outpost once again finds itself torn between the company's needs for protection and exploitation of competitive advantage and the local expectations of contribution or, at the very least, non-interference in the technological development processes of key sectors of the national economy.

c. *Legal and Political Control.* There is a structural conflict that relates to the legal and political sphere and concerns the control of the international company. This is all originated from the different national sovereignty to which the headquarters and the territorial outpost refer. Both the corporate top management and the political governing bodies of the host country may feel empowered to lead and regulate the fundamental decisions of the territorial outpost, especially if they have some political implications (consider choices regarding the location of a commercial branch or a production plant). The desire to assert national law and jurisdiction within the boundaries and the need to have the rights arising from ownership respected can lead to conflicting outcomes in the management of the territorial outpost. Added to all this are the possible tensions arising from the fact that the government of the home country of the international company may use the territorial outpost as a vector of foreign policy. Amongst the many episodes that have come to light, it is enough to remember the 'collaboration' between the CIA and the Chilean subsidiary of ITT during the deposition of Salvador Allende (Blake and Walters, 1976). Lastly, it is important to note the multiple legal references to which the international company is subject: in the case of conflicts between legal systems, should the expatriate manager adhere to local laws or those of the home country?

A Canadian subsidiary of a US company, following the instructions of the parent company, which state the need to comply with the laws of the United States, clearly cannot favour Canadian interests and expand exports (Jacoby, 1984).

d. Employment of local personnel. Decisions regarding the composition of the workforce and the capital-labour mix are a source of further tensions, perhaps the most evident and public ones. Particularly in countries with high unemployment rates, the pressures for the international company to commit to increasing employment opportunities are evident and strong. This objective can be achieved through investments that create new job positions or by limiting the use of labour-replacing technology. The extent of expatriate utilisation, whilst being substantially relevant, is usually perceived as marginal since it is associated with high level positions and limited absolute values. However, this aspect can become problematic when there is a clear expectation for alignment with the *headquarters*' choices concerning *expatriates*. Once again, control over the decisions of the territorial outpost is at the centre of the conflict.

Another aspect of this dispute can be attributed to the host country's expectations of seeing a 'native' managerial class grow within the international company, capable of facing the challenges posed by international competition and thereby strengthening the country's economic system. In this case, the issue can be traced back to the typical characteristics of transactions involving the transfer of *know-how.*

e. Economic and Financial Control. A final opportunity for conflict holds particular relevance in an international context: it concerns international equity control and the consequent process of wealth distribution created by the company in the host country. Specifically, the problem revolves around the power of appointing economic governing bodies and the decisions they make regarding the allocation of profits to central financial entities or other subsidiaries and the size of investments to be made at the local level.

A strong position of equity control enhances the sense of security for the management of the international company and its territorial outpost, especially when the cultural distance with the host country creates and fuels high levels of anxiety. *"In fact, it seems important to be able to command one's own ship even if it is not possible to control the sea"* (Ronen, 1986; p.341). Control over seats on the subsidiary's Board of Directors appears to be the most radical solution. On the other hand, an equal emotional investment is made by the host country, which sees the possibility of intervening in the processes of defining the top managerial positions of the outpost operating within its borders as an effective tool for guiding the decisions of the international company. This has led to the expansion of formal constraints to which host country governments - especially, once again, in developing countries — subject the forms of entry into their markets: the evolution and diffusion of intermediate and often sophisticated organisational modalities, such as *licensing and joint ventures*, have followed (Turati, 1990).

From the control of economic governing bodies, the possibility of guiding choices regarding the allocation of profits arises. To maximise global profits, multinational companies frequently use transfer pricing and other strategies to show profits in countries with the lowest tax rates (Robock, 1974; Agliati and Beretta, 1990). In addition to tax-related issues, tensions arising from differences in temporal perspectives are highly relevant in this area: the multinational company may have an immediate need to derive *cash flow* from its subsidiary, whilst the host country expects a long-term commitment.

Crucial for the prevention and management of the conflict that has been outlined so far are the decisions regarding the structure of the territorial outpost and, in particular, the distribution of power between the centre and the periphery. These decisions materialise in choices related to the formal decision-making autonomy of the local management, the level of personal prestige of individuals selected to govern the territorial outpost, the functioning of operational systems for resource allocation, result control, and reward, as well as the criteria for personnel selection and dynamics (Airoldi, 1980).

In organisations, prevention and management of conflicts are crucial for maintaining a harmonious and productive work environment. Effective communication is at the core of conflict prevention, encouraging open dialogue and transparency among team members. Strong leadership plays a vital role, promoting fairness and collaboration, and setting a positive example for employees. Clearly defining roles and responsibilities helps minimise misunderstandings and disputes. Investing in conflict resolution skills through training programmes empowers employees to address disagreements constructively. Team building and fostering camaraderie create a supportive atmosphere, reducing the likelihood of conflicts arising. Mediation and facilitation services ensure impartial resolution when conflicts do occur. Implementing conflict management policies and promoting emotional intelligence further contribute to a conflict-resilient organisation. Embracing diversity and inclusion fosters mutual respect and understanding, reducing potential conflicts based on bias or discrimination. Continuous monitoring and feedback help identify potential sources of conflict, enabling proactive interventions. By embracing these approaches, organisations can foster a positive and collaborative culture, ensuring long-term success and employee well-being.

Equally important in this process is the cultural perspective: the conflict is, in its deep features, a conflict between cultures, and as such, it needs to be read and addressed accordingly.

3.2 The Allocation of Functional Responsibilities Between Centralisation and Decentralisation

The issue of delegation at a local level, or centralisation of functional decision-making authority in the parent company, cannot be considered as a choice that international companies universally and uniformly confront. Not only do the contingencies faced by different subsidiaries require treating each of them in a more or less differentiated manner, but also the opportunity to centralise/decentralise arises differently for each of the functional activities that the company performs.

Centralisation involves concentrating decision-making authority and control at the top level of these organisations, whilst decentralisation distributes decision-making power to lower levels and departments. Striking the right balance between these two approaches is vital for organisational effectiveness and adaptability in today's dynamic business landscape. Recent research by Ostrom et al. (2021) highlights the importance of decentralised decision-making in promoting innovation and responsiveness, especially in rapidly changing environments. On the other hand, studies by Jong et al. (2021) emphasise how centralised control can enhance coordination and efficiency in certain organisational contexts. Organisations need to carefully assess their unique requirements, taking into account factors such as the complexity of tasks, the need for coordination, and the pace of change, to determine the optimal allocation of functional responsibilities for sustained success. As previously observed, the issue of balance between centralisation and decentralisation is essentially connected, on one hand to the coordination needs that push towards a centralised management of geographically dispersed activities; on the other hand, to the necessity of adequately responding to different local requirements, which presents itself as the main drive towards the decision-making autonomy of branches.

The different functions within a given economic sector can respond differently to these pressures: for example, in the IT sector, it is common to find a significant centralisation of research and development activities, which allows for the optimisation of scarce resources such as human intellectual capabilities and protects know-how and related development processes. The production function, on the other hand, may be decentralised, whilst the need to have a considerable sensitivity to the different needs of national customers suggests a decentralised approach to marketing.

Below, we will analyse in greater depth the essential activities that form the basis of company operations and through which it is possible to build the entire framework of centralisation/decentralisation decisions; in particular, we will focus on marketing, with a distinct attention to distribution policies and promotional activities, production, and finally, research and development.

3.2.1 Marketing. Marketing is the activity that must take into account the specific needs of consumers to the greatest extent. In international companies, this has traditionally meant adopting tailored marketing policies for the different countries in which they operate and consequently assigning decision-making responsibilities at the local level. A research conducted by Aylemer (1970) in the late 1960s reveals that the responsibility for decisions concerning product design, advertising policies, retail prices, and distribution channels was mostly allocated at the subsidiary level, with only partial involvement from central management. Managers at the headquarters were not considered the main actors in this regard. In particular, there are specific factors that have driven companies to extensively delegate the definition of marketing strategies and related operational responsibilities. Considerations in this regard typically include:

a. *Differences in the physical environment* (e.g., climate and topography) have significant effects on the sales potential of many products and can result in variations in packaging. The topography influences population density, which in turn can strongly affect the distribution system.
b. *Differences in the stage of economic development.* Disparities in per capita incomes lead to certain products being considered luxurious in some countries, whilst in others, they are more common and relatively inexpensive. Varying income levels also determine price fluctuations from one country to another. Moreover, consumer-buying habits tend to vary with the economic development stage of the nation. Less developed economies typically rely on small retail stores in their distribution

systems, and consumers often make relatively small purchases each time, in contrast to more advanced countries.

c. *Cultural differences.* For instance, certain nations consume specific foods more than others due to historical, geographical, or religious reasons. Mediterranean European countries, for example, consume more wine than beer, whereas the opposite is true for Nordic populations.
d. Different levels of competition.
e. *Diversity in infrastructures.* Particularly relevant are the arrangement of the distribution systems, information channels to the public, and the advertising agency sector.

In essence, the choice of the appropriate degree of centralisation or decentralisation in marketing is linked to the possibility of standardising policies and operational decisions related to the fundamental variables of the *marketing mix*: product, price, advertising, and distribution policies. The real question, correctly posed, is not so much whether marketing should be standardised and therefore centralised, but rather which elements of the marketing strategy can or should be standardised, and to what extent.

Below, we analyse the factors that hinder or promote the standardisation of decisions concerning the individual elements of the *marketing mix*.

1. *Product policies.* To succeed in a market, the product must closely align with the needs of consumers. Often, a given product may have potential demand in a foreign market, but certain characteristics need to be adapted, such as design, performance, *packaging*, branding, etc. The question then arises of whether to adapt the product or maintain it standardised whilst modifying other elements of the *marketing mix.* The reasons that push towards product adaptation are essentially:
   - Local regulations that impose specific features on products.
   - Conditions of product use in the new market, which are often different from those in the original market.
   - Culture and traditions, which typically vary from one country to another, encompassing diversity in habits, tastes, and lifestyle of potential buyers (consider, for instance, the varying eating habits among different nations).

When these elements are critical for the success of a product in a particular market, it is more appropriate for headquarters to delegate to local managers the responsibility of identifying which product characteristics need to be modified to meet the specific needs of the local market. Of course, product adaptation is not always necessary; in some cases, it may not be advantageous. For example, when the product's origin is equivalent to a quality image or when it possesses significant advanced technological features.

In general, local management is tasked with identifying the need to modify the 'contour elements' of the product rather than its intrinsic characteristics. These decisions may concern aspects such as branding (a specific name might evoke unfavourable associations in certain countries) or *packaging.*

2. *Price policies.* The issue at hand is whether it is more advantageous to seek price policy uniformity across different markets or to develop different pricing strategies based on each market's specific conditions. In this regard, it can be argued that:

- Each market has different conditions concerning demand elasticity, entry barriers, per capita income, etc., making it quite challenging to apply the same pricing policy in different countries.
- If there are significant price differences between neighbouring countries, there is a risk of encouraging cross-border trade, especially in economically integrated areas.
- Price uniformity is preferable when the product is highly standardised or when cross-border movement is easy.

Even for pricing decisions, the role of local management is relevant, although general guidelines can be established by central functions.

3. *Distribution channels.* Although at first glance, the distribution structures in different countries may appear similar, in reality, there are multiple and often profound differences. In fact, among all the choices concerning the marketing mix, the selection of the distribution channel is the one that is least amenable to rigid principles. Precisely for this reason, these decisions, more than others related to the marketing mix, are addressed on a case-by-case basis and are largely left to the discretion of market-specific managers. In particular, the factors that push towards the development of tailored policies are:
    - *Structure of local distribution.* The choice of the distribution channel must be adapted to the specific characteristics of the local distribution system. These characteristics primarily concern the intermediaries themselves: different levels of efficiency within the same channel in various countries may lead to different distribution solutions. Secondly, it pertains to the local legislation regarding commercial distribution.
    - *Buying behaviour patterns.* For the same product, potential buying behaviour patterns vary from one market to another.
    - *Geographic distribution of demand.* Population density strongly influences the development of the distribution system. In countries with low population density, demand concentrates in a few geographic areas. Therefore, the choice of the distribution channel also depends on the distances between the main geographical areas of a country. In such cases, it may be preferable to have a network with at least one wholesaler for each of the main areas instead of relying on a single wholesaler.

In general, economic development reduces the differences between markets in different countries, and when considering more sophisticated forms of retail distribution, such as supermarkets or hypermarkets, the distribution structure in advanced industrialised countries is very similar. This may lead to reconsidering the possibility of achieving greater uniformity in the future in the formulation of distribution channel policies.

4. *Advertising Policies.* One of the most crucial issues in defining advertising campaigns for international companies is to develop a message that takes into account both market characteristics and the overall company policies. Giving greater weight to specific market characteristics may lead to significantly different message formulations from one market to another. The current general orientation for advertising in international markets is to maintain certain fundamental characteristics of the advertising strategy (typically the target audience, channels, and essential message content)

whilst adapting the advertising policy to the specific needs of the local market. Even beyond slogans, it is still very challenging to conceive a completely uniform advertising approach, particularly because:

- The so-called global consumers, whilst increasing, are still relatively few and limited to specific segments. Although certain needs and aspirations tend to spread relatively uniformly across different countries, the ultimate expression of these needs in terms of product purchase can vary significantly. Even highly standardised products, such as automobiles, may require diverse advertising messages.
- There are limited supranational communication channels. Communications are mostly transmitted through local information systems and cater to the different needs of various countries. For example, commercial television differs significantly from one nation to another.
- Different legislations apply. For instance, in some countries, comparing products with competitors is allowed, whilst in others, it is prohibited.

These multiple factors contribute to decentralising marketing decisions. However, over time, the evolution towards market globalisation will allow the adoption of more uniform marketing approaches. The intensification of contacts and exchanges between different nations and the progress in communications, on the one hand, contribute to a gradual homogenisation of consumer needs and, on the other hand, impose on companies the need to build a coherent and consistent image across national borders.

Furthermore, in certain sectors, international companies face final customers in the form of retail and wholesale chains operating in multiple nations, which puts pressure to move towards similar products, prices, and services in different markets.

The advantages derived from a certain degree of standardisation of marketing strategies, and therefore from a certain degree of centralisation of decisions related to it, are diverse: significant cost savings can be achieved, especially concerning product design, economies of scale in production, and economies of scope in research. Standardisation can also affect aspects of packaging and advertising. Concerning the latter, large multinational companies are increasingly employing advertising campaigns that are essentially the same worldwide.

3.2.2 Production. The decentralisation of production units poses particular and complex problems, not encountered in a company operating in a single market. These challenges arise from the heterogeneity of the international environment, which affects the possibility of standardising production and complicates the tasks of production and logistical coordination.

The establishment of production units abroad can be attributed to various motivations. Firstly, there are reasons related to the lower cost of labour in countries different from the home country, which remains a determining factor even today. For instance, many Western companies have set up production units in Asian countries. Secondly, in the past, high customs tariffs imposed by governments to promote domestic production made it more convenient to establish local production facilities. As a result, branch plants or miniature replicas emerged, indicating how these subsidiaries initially used production technologies imported from the parent company and adapted to a smaller scale, suitable for serving the local market. Over time, as these subsidiaries are required to expand their scope, they gain more discretion and the possibility to develop autonomous technologies and supply sources. As the subsidiary demonstrates the ability to generate profits, the tendency and willingness of the parent company to further decentralise decision-making responsibilities strengthen.

However, recent economic developments have threatened the feasibility of international operations following the branch plant model. One of the key factors contributing to its decline is the general lowering of customs barriers due to various GATT negotiations, which eliminated a significant portion of the protection necessary to compensate for the branch plant's relatively non-competitive cost structure. Moreover, technological changes in some sectors have rendered this mode of operation in international markets obsolete. Competitors adopting new technologies often offer alternative products at prices that cannot be matched by producers relying on the experience curve. Additionally, achieving competitive efficiency levels often requires a scale that cannot be reached in a single market for commercialisation.

The regaining of adequate levels of competitiveness can, indeed, be achieved through *international production specialisation* (Crookell, 1986; Birkinshaw and Morrison, 1996). This involves a reorientation of subsidiaries of international companies towards a more focused and specialised role.

By adopting a strategy of production specialisation, subsidiaries can concentrate on producing specific components, products, or services for the global supply chain, leveraging their unique capabilities and expertise. This approach allows them to benefit from economies of scale and scope, access to specialised skills and technologies, and the ability to respond more effectively to the demands of specific markets.

Specialisation also enables subsidiaries to focus on areas where they have a comparative advantage, optimising their production processes and reducing costs. As a result, they can become more competitive in their specific niche and contribute significantly to the overall success of the international company.

Moreover, international production specialisation facilitates collaboration and coordination between different subsidiaries within the global network. Each subsidiary can focus on its core competencies whilst benefiting from the expertise and resources available in other parts of the organisations.

Overall, the repositioning of subsidiaries towards specialised roles can enhance the efficiency and effectiveness of the entire international company, enabling it to navigate the complexities of the global market and regain competitiveness in a rapidly evolving business landscape.

Crookell (1986) suggested two approaches to rationalisation that are also relevant in the context of international business: 1) *International specialisation* and 2) *the world product mandate*. Both are valid strategies for rationalisation in international business. Each approach has its benefits and challenges, and the choice between them depends on various factors, such as the company's resources, target markets, competitive landscape, and customer preferences. Ultimately, companies need to carefully analyse their specific circumstances and goals to determine which approach aligns best with their overall business strategy.

a. *International specialisation.* The phenomenon of international specialisation occurs when the parent company assigns a subsidiary the responsibility of producing a specific product or component. The product design and technical specifications are decided by the central headquarters, and the subsidiary is not required to make any effort to export the product or component, as the parent company manages these aspects. In this way, instead of multi-product plants serving a single domestic market independently, specialised production centres are developed to supply the global market. Companies that choose this path aim to exploit the potential efficiency gains resulting from the economies of scale thus achieved (Bartlett and Ghoshal, 1989). However, there are significant counter-forces to this process of specialisation. Firstly, the interests of host governments, in their attempt to gain greater control over the economic environment, often limit the autonomy of subsidiaries (Rugman and Verbeke, 2004). Secondly, geographic distances, cultural differences, variability in local markets, and specific contingencies affecting individual subsidiaries make production integration challenging (Buckley and Casson, 1976). Additionally, it has been argued from various quarters that the 1990s could witness the decline of economies based on large volumes: companies are seeking economies in the diversity of products and production processes. In essence, a subsidiary subjected to the phenomenon of specialisation ends up having less autonomy compared to a branch plant; much of what it produces is intended for export. This elevates many decision-making responsibilities above the subsidiary's managers and reduces their discretion.

b. *World product mandate.* As mentioned earlier, host governments exert increasing influence on the decisions of international companies regarding the location of production and other activities. Specifically, governments request that subsidiaries located within their territory be entrusted with the so-called world product mandate. These mandates have been defined as agreements between the parent company of an international company and one of its subsidiaries to grant the latter the exclusive right to produce and market a specific product and, if circumstances allow, to carry out necessary research and development activities. As a result of such agreements, the subsidiary typically gains greater managerial autonomy and effectively becomes the international centre for a particular product (Bartlett and Ghoshal, 1989).

In contrast to the specialisation process, with the world product mandate, subsidiaries also take on the responsibility for product innovation and international marketing. As a result, world product mandates imply greater decision decentralisation and, consequently, a more active role for the subsidiaries in decision-making (Bartlett and Ghoshal, 1989). However, there are some drawbacks to the world product mandate solution. Firstly, the transformation of a subsidiary from a branch plant to a world product mandate implies a profound change in the organisational culture of the subsidiary. The management must shift from imitation to innovation, from the security of *parent* protection to the risks of global competition, and from importing to exporting. Additionally, the world product mandate may face challenges in terms of *parent* company capability. If the product is an innovation of the subsidiary, the *parent* company's marketing function may know little about the product or how to market it. In such cases, the subsidiary will have to define and adequately segment the market, select appropriate distribution channels, develop advertising and promotional policies to support the product, and ensure that sales forces are well-versed in the product's quality and post-sales support (Bartlett and Ghoshal, 1989).

The feasibility of adopting a world product mandate is also connected to the product's life cycle. In the early stages of a product, a flexible production structure is preferable, enabling ineffective products to be quickly and easily eliminated. This flexibility, however, is incompatible with the world product mandate. On the other hand, when the product is well-established, and the production process stabilises, it becomes appropriate and cost-effective to decentralise production to lower-cost locations. In such cases, granting a world product mandate can be a viable solution.

In practice, both forms of specialisation can coexist within the same company. Large subsidiaries of international companies tend to seek mandates for activities they already have sufficient experience in, whilst opting for different structures for other products (Rutenberg, 1986).

The choice between specialisation and mandates appears to be influenced by the product's life cycle and the organisational culture of the parent company. When the principle of innovation dominates, the company tends to reinforce mandates originating from the initiatives of subsidiaries. On the other hand, when the majority of products are mature, efficiency considerations prevail, control becomes more centralised, and rationalisation is more likely to take the form of specialisation (Bartlett and Ghoshal, 1989).

3.2.3 Research and Development. Research and development (R&D) activities often represent the path through which companies can ensure vitality and continuity over time. For this reason, and in general, such activities are closely controlled by top management; from examining what happens in reality, it emerges that most international companies place their research centres in their home countries and, therefore, in proximity to their headquarters. Indeed, the mere geographic dispersion of research centres does not necessarily imply complete decentralisation; the latter aspect actually depends on the mission assigned to the centres located abroad. However, it is widely believed that research conducted abroad is typically oriented towards the development of the final stages of innovation, rather than radical scientific discovery. In this regard, Behram and Fisher (1989), in a study of 106 foreign research centres, have highlighted how different market orientations of international companies lead to different roles being assigned to foreign research and development activities. The identified market orientations are as follows:

- *Toward the national market.* In these companies, foreign research centres have a rather limited role. Foreign subsidiaries serve as support for local operations, and the need to develop innovative processes abroad is therefore minimal.
- *Toward the markets of host countries.* In this case, the foreign location of research activities primarily aims to adapt products to the specificities of local markets. These companies are the most active in establishing research centres abroad; however, the mission assigned to them mostly involves development (or at most applied research). However, the decentralisation that characterises these companies makes foreign research centres quite autonomous in defining the final characteristics of products and in process developments.
- *Toward the global market.* The primary consideration guiding these companies in locating foreign research is the availability of specific skills or expertise locally and the opportunity to gain access to foreign scientific communities. These companies often assign their foreign laboratories objectives related to identifying new products and basic research quite frequently. In terms of decisional autonomy, such research centres are often assigned a specialised role within a centrally coordinated research programme.

Other interesting conclusions from Behrman and Fisher's research (1980) concern the management style of foreign research and development activities. The difference between companies that favour a form of centralised control and those that prefer greater decentralisation lies in the fact that the former tend to have more elaborate forms of *reporting, budgeting, and communication.* Furthermore, they demonstrate a greater ability to allocate resources on a global basis. On the other hand, more decentralised companies adopt more informal methods of coordination and control.

Although most observed companies had central research and development laboratories, the role of these labs in fostering the technical growth of the company was found to be a function of the power orientation. In more centralised companies, central research is usually decisive in carrying out programmes and projects of crucial importance for the company's strategy. Conversely, in more decentralised companies, central research plays more of an advisory role and is not directly involved in all ongoing projects; thus, it acts as a coordinator of the capabilities and perspectives of various semi-autonomous research units and focuses on long-term projects.

As has already been observed for productive activities, research and development also play different roles depending on the configuration that the international company intends to assign to its subsidiaries. We have already discussed the so-called miniature replicas: they perform certain functions (typically production-related) in a manner similar to the parent company, with the aim of serving the market of the country where they are located. Among the most negative aspects of such a configuration is the total lack of innovative capacity. The subsidiary is primarily tasked with making minor product or process adaptations; this does not mean that these subsidiaries are completely denied the possibility of developing scientific knowledge, but the subsidiary's objectives do not include autonomous development of know-how, and often it is unlikely that they have the capabilities to do so.

In subsidiaries that are subject to a process of international specialisation, there is no simple replication of central activities; each subsidiary has a distinct role, especially concerning production. However, the technological dependency is equally strong as in miniature replica subsidiaries, meaning that technology is transferred from the centre. Furthermore, since the primary objective is not the local market but the global one, there is no research aimed at product adaptation, whilst innovations concerning the process are likely to arise. Sometimes research laboratories are found alongside the production facilities of these subsidiaries; however, their research programmes are generally defined by the central research unit, and the results are automatically channelled back to the central laboratories to be assimilated and contribute to the development of future new products. The decentralised research units operate in a network of specialised independent units.

Lastly, in subsidiaries operating according to the World Product Mandate (WPM), there is a higher level of autonomy in both marketing and research and development. However, this does not mean that the subsidiary needs to develop all the research necessary to support the evolution of its product line since it can always leverage the basic research of the group. It is certain, though, that in this case, local operations are based on a higher technological level compared to the scenario of miniature replica or specialised subsidiaries, and the technology incorporated into the product is distinctive, even if derived from the group's basic research.

The level of autonomy that the research in a WPM subsidiary actually enjoys depends on the type of research conducted there. To the extent that basic research is carried out, it seems quite likely that it will be placed under strict control of the central research unit; therefore, despite the granting of a WPM appearing as a step towards decentralisation, there is often more centralised governance. This implies not only the willingness to maintain a high degree of control over distinctive know-how but above all the desire to perform a vital coordination function for dispersed and substantially autonomous research and development units.

REFERENCES

Agliati, M., & Beretta, S. (1990). *I sistemi amministrativi nei gruppi di imprese*. Egea.

Airoldi, G., Brunetti, G., & Coda, V. (1989). *Lezioni di economia aziendale*. Il Mulino.

Arrow, K. J. (1974). *The Limits of Organisations*. W.W. Norton.

Aylmer, R. J. (1970). Who Makes Marketing Decisions in the Multinational Finn? *Journal of Marketing*, *34*(4), 25–30. doi:10.1177/002224297003400405

Bartlett, C. A., & Ghoshal, S. (1986). Tap your subsidiaries for global reach. *Harvard Business Review*, *64*(6), 87–94. doi:10.5465/amr.1990.4310825

Bartlett, C. A., & Ghoshal, S. (1989). *Managing Across Borders: The Transnational Solution*. Harvard Business School Press.

Behrman, J. N., & Fisher, W. A. (1980). *Overseas R&D Activities of Transnational Companies*. Oelgeschlager. doi:10.1002/tie.5060220309

Birkinshaw, J. M., & Morrison, A. J. (1996). Configurations of strategy and structure in multinational subsidiaries. *Journal of International Business Studies*, *26*(4), 729–794. doi:10.1057/palgrave.jibs.8490818

Blake, P. H., & Walters, P. S. (1976). *The Politics of Global Economic Relations*. Prentice Hall. doi:10.1002/tie.5060180211

Brumana, M., Decastri, M., Scarozza, D., & Za, S. (2014). A bibliometric study of the literature on technological innovation: an analysis of 60 international academic journals. In Management, Organisations and Control: Smart Practices and Effects (pp. 141-152). Springer International Publishing. doi:10.1007/978-3-319-07905-9_9

Buckley, P., & Casson, M. (1976). *The future of the multinational enterprise*. Macmillan. doi:10.1007/978-1-349-02899-3

Crookell, H. H. (1986). Specialization and International Competitiveness. In H. Etemad & L. S. Dulude (Eds.), *Managing the Multinational Subsidiary* (pp. 102–111). Croom Helm.

Demir, R., & Angwin, D. (2021). Multidexterity: Combining Competing Business Models in Transforming Economies. *Management and Organization Review*, *17*(2), 282–313. doi:10.1017/mor.2020.56

Doz, Y., & Prahalad, C. K. (1986). Controlled Variety: A Challenge for Human Resource Management in the mnc. *Human Resource Management*, *25*(1), 55–71. doi:10.1002/hrm.3930250105

Gabriel, P. (1977). mncs in the Third World: Is Conflict Unavoidable? *Harvard Business Review*, *56*, 83–93.

Hitt, M., Ireland, R., & Hoskisson, R. (2013). *Strategic Management: Competitiveness and Globalization* (10th ed.). Cengage Southwestern Publishing Co.

Hofstede, G. (1980). *Culture's Consequences: International Differences in Work Related Values*. Sage. London.

Hofstede, G. (1980). Motivation, Leadership, and Organisations: Do American Theories Apply Abroad? *Organizational Dynamics*, *9*(1), 42–63. doi:10.1016/0090-2616(80)90013-3

Jacoby, N. H. (1984). The multinational corporation. In P. D. Grub, F. Ghadar, & D. Khambata (Eds.), *The multinational corporation in transition*. Darwin Press.

Jong, J., & Faerman, S. R. (2021). Centralization and Decentralization: Balancing Organisational and Employee Expectations. In A. Farazmand (Eds), Global Encyclopedia of Public Administration, Public Policy, and Governance. Springer. doi:10.1007/978-3-319-31816-5_4179-1

Luo, Y. (2022). New connectivity in the fragmented world. *Journal of International Business Studies*, *53*(5), 962–980. doi:10.1057/s41267-022-00530-w PMID:35634198

Luo, Y., & Tung, R. L. (2018). A general theory of springboard MNEs. *Journal of International Business Studies*, *49*(2), 129–152. doi:10.1057/s41267-017-0114-8

Luu, D. T. (2023). Internationalisation, knowledge intensity, adaptive culture and absorptive capacity: A strategic entrepreneurship enabling logic for export firms. *Journal of Small Business and Enterprise Development*, *30*(2), 390–418. doi:10.1108/JSBED-06-2022-0288

Masini, C. (1970). *Lavoro e risparmio*. Utet.

Narula, R., Verbeke, A., & Yuan, W. (2021). The theory of international business strategy. In K. Mellahi, K. Meyer, R. Narula, I. Surdu, & A. Verbeke (Eds.), The Oxford Handbook of International Business Strategy (pp. 11-36). Oxford University Press. doi:10.1093/oxfordhb/9780198868378.013.1

Ostrom, A. L., Parasuraman, A., Bowen, D. E., Patrício, L., Voss, C. A., & Lemon, K. N. (2021). Service research priorities in a rapidly changing world. *Journal of Service Research, 24*(2), 129–145. doi:10.1177/1094670515576315

Pan, Y., Verbeke, A., & Wenlong, Y. (2021). CEO Transformational Leadership and Corporate Entrepreneurship in China. *Management and Organization Review, 17*(1), 1–32. doi:10.1017/mor.2020.59

Robock, S. H. (1974). The Case of Home Country Controls over Multinational Firms. *The Columbia Journal of World Business, 9*, 75–79.

Robock, S. H., Simmons, K., & Zwick, J. (1977). *International business and multinational enterprise*. Irwin.

Ronen, S. (1986). Equity perception in multiple comparisons: A field study. *Human Relations, 39*(4), 333–346. doi:10.1177/001872678603900403

Rugiardini, A. (1979). *Organizzazione d'impresa*. Giuffrè.

Rugman, A. M., & Verbeke, A. (2008). A New Perspective on the Regional and Global Strategies of Multinational Services Firms. *MIR. Management International Review, 48*(4), 397–411. https://www.jstor.org/stable/40658272. doi:10.1007/s11575-008-0023-y

Teece, D. J. (2006). Reflections on the Hymer thesis and the multinational enterprise. *International Business Review, 15*(2), 124–139. doi:10.1016/j.ibusrev.2005.11.003

Verbeke, A., Coeurderoy, R., & Matt, T. (2018). The future of international business research on corporate globalization that never was. *Journal of International Business Studies, 49*(9), 1101–1112. doi:10.1057/s41267-018-0192-2

Chapter 4
Alliance Making as a Strategy

ABSTRACT

This chapter explores the multifaceted realm of alliances within the international business landscape. It starts with an examination of international alliances and scrutinises how alliances serve as pivotal vehicles for global expansion. It also discusses the relationship between alliances and international companies, unravelling the dynamics underpinning successful collaborations globally. The chapter introduces a managerial reference model clarifying the rationale behind forming alliances by considering some strategic imperatives. It deals with challenges and complexities in cooperation strategies for international expansion, highlighting natural difficulties encountered in such endeavours. Further sections explore the system of international competencies necessary for building and forging effective alliances by explaining how alliances offer organisational alternatives and learning potentials. Lastly, it examines alliance strategies in the context of digitalisation and Industry 4.0, highlighting their evolving significance in a technologically advancing world.

4. ALLIANCE MAKING AS A STRATEGY

In the dynamic and interconnected landscape of modern business, companies often find themselves facing complex challenges that demand innovative approaches. In this pursuit of growth, efficiency, and market expansion, strategic alliances have emerged as a compelling solution for organisations worldwide. The concept of forming alliances, partnerships, or collaborations with other entities has become an integral part of the strategic decision-making process for businesses across diverse industries. In the reign of Charles V, the sun never set. Behind those twilightless days stood a vast array of noble marriages, and familial ties among royal houses, which turned the Spanish emperor into the greatest multinational of his time. In Japan, daimyos (feudal lords) forged their alliances of war and peace through strategic marriages. Love was scarce, and a strong sense of business favoured the inclusion of American tycoons into society. With a daring claim, one could even assert that all of history is a long series of selected and excellent marriages. This custom did not fade with the emergence of the global village, nor did it remain unrelated to the history of companies. On the contrary, intercompany alliances continue to be one of the main entry tickets to many regions of the world. The right path to replicate the dream of Charles V.

DOI: 10.4018/979-8-3693-3482-9.ch004

To use a less allegorical form, and closer to the common language of managerial literature: the historical era we are going through, and the challenges it necessarily entails, are characterised by a frequent emphasis on the importance of internationalisation as an essential component of excellence. This assumption cuts across companies of different sizes, industries, countries of origin, technologies, and all other categories typically used to differentiate businesses. Each of them is faced with the challenge of international competition, whether it is competing with foreign entities entering their home country or accessing territorial contexts different from their usual environment.

This chapter examines the pivotal role that strategic alliances play in the contemporary business environment by exploring the fundamental principles, benefits, and potential risks associated with forming alliances, as well as the various forms these cooperative ventures can take. From joint ventures and cross-licensing agreements to equity partnerships and consortia, each type of alliance comes with its unique advantages and challenges. Throughout this chapter, we will examine the underlying motivations that drive companies to seek alliances, such as gaining access to new markets, leveraging complementary capabilities, and sharing resources and risks. Additionally, we will explore the critical factors that contribute to successful alliance formation and management, including effective communication, alignment of objectives, and trust building among partner organisations.

Whilst focusing deeper into the realm of alliances, we will also address the evolving nature of alliances in response to technological advancements and global economic shifts. The chapter will shed light on the influence of digitalisation and Industry 4.0 on alliance strategies, as well as the impact of geopolitical factors and changing trade dynamics on cross-border collaborations. Whilst strategic alliances hold immense potential for growth and competitiveness, they are not without their challenges. We will examine the common pitfalls and complexities that can arise during alliance implementation and discuss strategies to mitigate these risks effectively. By understanding the intricacies of alliance formation, management, and adaptation, companies can make informed decisions to harness the power of collaborations as a strategic tool for achieving their organisational objectives in an ever-changing global marketplace.

In this overall framework, alliances between companies, albeit underestimated by international business theory, emerge as a tool to achieve the general goal of an active presence in the international context. The following pages aim to provide a map of some warnings and potential managerial responses on this subject.

4.1. International Alliances and Alliances for Internationalisation

Together with qualities, culture, learning, globalisation, and a few others, *inter-company cooperation* constitutes one of the privileged watchwords in the development strategies of companies in the latest phase of their official history. This is true; however, it is not entirely accurate to attribute the paternity of this instrument solely to the last century. From a historical perspective, alliances in the 2000s trace back to more ancient contractual forms. As historians of this instrument recall, there is a contractual, and often philological, coincidence between solutions such as the 'Commenda' and the 'Colleganza' of the Maritime Republics, joint ventures, and the joint companies of London's 'Gentlemen Adventurers', as well as cooperative initiatives and the various East India Companies, formed to exploit overseas wealth (Link, 2021). Perhaps it is not entirely correct to attribute the sole explanation of internationalisation to all these cases, as in most of them, there was also the urgency to share the costs and common risks of joint ventures among different partners. However, the underlying idea of an instrument born to cross the boundaries of the known by cooperating remains captivating even in the present day. Nonetheless, it is precisely starting from the 1970s that alliances between companies have become a privileged ground for strategic development. Commencing with the ominous title with which two Harvard researchers (Hennah and Perlmutter, 1978) officially opened the phase of widespread cooperation, both managerial practice and theory have emphasised the usefulness of this instrument in achieving contemporary objectives of development flexibility and cost-effectiveness (Drucker, 1974; Harrigan, 1985; Contractor and Lorange, 1988). They have also highlighted the risks and difficulties inherent in mismanagement (Killing, 1983 and 1988; Turati, 1990). Moreover, they have emphasised its adaptability to different motivations, among which nationalisation, innovation, and internationalisation stand out (Gorbis and Yorke, 1985; Contractor and Lorange, 1988). From an observational standpoint of the phenomenon, four distinct historical phases can be identified:

a. The phase of enthusiasm opened by Hennah and Perlmutter's article and characterised by extensive efforts to assess the strategic benefits of alliances.
b. The phase of scepticism, marked by concerns over the high failure rate (7 out of 10) exhibited by alliances, especially in the form of equity joint ventures (Beamish, 1988; Killing, 1983).
c. The phase of design, characterised by the effort to identify the values of relative superiority of alliances compared to other modes of governing relationships (Williamson, 1981) and the correct parameters for the organisational and managerial design of the alliance (Harrigan, 1985; Lorange, 1987; Killing, 1988).
d. The phase of process, denoted by extreme attention to constructing the alliance as a sequence of interdependent stages of convergence/divergence of means and ends (Wilson, 1990).

Along with the historical phases already identified, recent developments have given rise to additional distinct phases in the evolution of inter-company cooperation.

e. The phase of digitalisation and technology-driven alliances. With the rapid advancement of digital technologies and Industry 4.0, companies have entered a new era of alliance formation. Strategic alliances now focus on leveraging digital capabilities, data analytics, artificial intelligence, and emerging technologies to drive innovation, enhance customer experiences, and gain a competitive edge in the digital economy. The integration of digital elements into alliance strategies has opened up new possibilities for cross-industry collaborations and the creation of platform ecosystems (Pushpananthan, and Elmquist, 2022).
f. The phase of sustainability-driven alliances. In response to growing environmental and societal challenges, sustainable development has become a central concern for companies. Alliances are now being formed with a strong emphasis on sustainability goals, such as reducing carbon emissions, promoting circular economy practices, and achieving social impact. These alliances are driven not only by economic considerations but also by the shared commitment to address pressing global issues (Mariani et al., 2022).
g. The phase of geopolitical shifts and international alliances. The changing geopolitical landscape and trade dynamics have influenced the nature of alliances in recent times. Companies are navigating complexities arising from trade wars, protectionist measures, and shifting alliances between nations. In this context, strategic alliances are being re-evaluated to adapt to changing geopolitical realities and to secure access to critical markets and resources (Vakulchuk et al., 2020).

h. The phase of crisis-driven alliances. The outbreak of global crises, such as the COVID-19 pandemic, has spurred the formation of alliances aimed at addressing immediate challenges and fostering resilience. Collaborations have been established to pool resources, share knowledge, and develop innovative solutions to mitigate the impacts of crises and ensure business continuity (Leach et al., 2021).

These additional phases reflect the dynamic and evolving nature of strategic alliances in response to contemporary challenges and opportunities. As companies continue to adapt to the rapidly changing business environment, strategic alliances will remain a critical instrument in their pursuit of growth, innovation, sustainability, and competitiveness on a global scale.

In this context, when addressing the phenomenon of alliances from the perspective of international motivation, it is first necessary to distinguish between two general categories of objectives. These are: (a) alliances aimed at establishing a territorially focused relationship, meaning the international development of the company in a narrow sense; (b) alliances that connect two entities of different nationalities, regardless of the territorial contribution of each. Alliances of the first type typically link a local company with another local company of different nationality (or a multinational absent in that reference system), with the purpose of facilitating the penetration of the second into the country of the first.

These alliances can properly be defined as *internationalisation alliances*. The international component of type (b) alliances is confined solely to the different territorial origin of the allies, and they are more accurately defined as *international alliances*. Naturally, even in this second case, the exchange between partners may involve an 'exchange' of territories, for example, through the incorporation of a partner's products into the distribution chain of the other. However, typically, this represents a secondary reason compared to integration of product range, streamlining, joint innovation, and mutual knowledge fertilisation. Initiatives of type (a) are more targeted towards overcoming more or less explicit institutional obstacles (in developing countries, in countries of the former Soviet bloc, etc.), accelerating the penetration process, reducing the structural costs of such action, and so on.

Despite differing in basic motivations, the two types of alliances come closer in the type of problems they face due to their 'international' connotation. They are similar in the nature of the 'framework of exchange' that imposes a complex transaction between companies of different nationalities, thus different cultures, and different organisational models.

4.2. Alliances and International Companies

For a large part of history, multinational companies have often followed a development path that minimised the use of alliances, preferring extreme solutions or strong integration in the form of international hierarchy (as seen with U.S. multinational companies since the 1950s) or relying heavily on exporting domestic products (as long pursued by Japanese companies) (Ohmae, 1987). Without expressing a value judgment on these alternatives, it can be observed that for a long time, companies viewed foreign markets as an opportunity to generate capacity saturation and risk diversification in the case of export strategies. Moreover, even when this option was gradually replaced by a genuine intention of more comprehensive internationalisation, there still prevailed managerial preferences, generally oriented towards favouring greater control over foreign activities and traditionally sceptical about the potential of cooperative tools.

There is an interesting argument regarding the low propensity of U.S. companies to form alliances that has been a subject of research and analysis in the field of international business. Historically, some studies have suggested that American companies tend to be cautious in engaging in cooperative ventures compared to companies from other regions (Gomes-Casseres, 1990; Contractor and Lorange, 1988). However, it is important to recognise that this perspective has evolved over time, and recent trends indicate a shift in attitudes and practices among U.S. companies.

One significant development is the increasing recognition of the value of strategic alliances in the rapidly changing global business landscape. As the world becomes more interconnected and complex, companies are realising the benefits of collaboration to access new markets, pool resources, and share risks (Aiyar et al., 2023). Many U.S. companies have actively sought alliances to gain a competitive advantage in international markets and to leverage complementary capabilities. In particular, the rise of digital technologies and the emergence of the platform economy have driven a new wave of cooperative approaches among businesses. Digital platforms have facilitated alliances and enabled companies to create ecosystems that foster innovation, expand customer reach, and drive growth (Priyono and Hidayat, 2024). Moreover, addressing global challenges, such as sustainability and climate change, has become a priority for businesses worldwide. Collaborative efforts through alliances are seen as instrumental in tackling these issues collectively and in a more impactful manner (Gulati et al., 2012).

Whilst historical hesitancy towards alliances may have existed, contemporary strategic considerations are encouraging US companies to embrace collaborative ventures as a means to navigate the complexities of the global economy and to capitalise on the opportunities that arise through cooperation. The same theory of internationalisation, developed to provide a rational explanation for the economic convenience of multinational companies' existence, has offered little room for the exploration of a transaction area in which the cooperative solution would be superior to the choice of organisational integration. Instead, it has primarily focused on comparing the latter with a market-based choice (Gomes-Casseres, 1990; Contractor and Lorange, 1988).

Recent research, however, has begun to shed more light on the benefits of cooperative strategies and alliances in the international business context. Scholars have recognised that strategic collaborations can offer distinct advantages over traditional hierarchical approaches to internationalisation. Cooperative arrangements allow companies to access new markets, share risks, and pool resources and expertise (Gulati, 2012). Moreover, the digital revolution and the emergence of platform ecosystems have created new opportunities for companies to form alliances and partnerships to leverage technology and innovation (Nambisan et al., 2019). This has given rise to a more dynamic and interconnected global business landscape, where cooperative ventures are seen as a means to drive growth and competitiveness. As the business environment becomes increasingly complex and uncertain, the idea of considering cooperative solutions is gaining traction. Researchers are exploring how companies can navigate challenges more effectively through collaboration and shared expertise.

On the other hand, the direct experience of companies has highlighted management's awareness of prudent management of their international presence. This has primarily meant not ignoring the peculiarities and unique nuances of different country systems. Instead, the necessity to grasp specific national opportunities, operate as insiders, and reduce the likelihood of high-risk international campaigns being rejected locally has led to the development of hybrid organisational solutions with a strong hierarchical integration but also decentralisation. These solutions are deeply rooted in the national or regional fabric whilst being part of a multinational model; this is the case of the multi-domestic company configuration (Bartlett and Ghoshal, 1990). In such companies, the local reference is considered a priority in the organisational design, especially concerning marketing efforts and image building. At the same time, each subsidiary emerges as an offshoot of the parent company, representing the overall company within the reference country. Whilst maintaining exchanges of resources and knowledge with other units in the multinational system, each subsidiary can be viewed as a *quasi-sovereign and quasi-autonomous organisation*.

If this is the established past of the history of companies, recent research, instead, has also emphasised the importance of understanding and adapting to specific country contexts for successful international business operations. Scholars have recognised that cultural, regulatory, and institutional differences across countries can significantly have an impact on the effectiveness of a company's international strategies (Xu et al., 2021). Therefore, companies are increasingly adopting hybrid organisational structures that balance centralisation and decentralisation to cater to local needs whilst maintaining global coordination (Meyer, 2018). In today's global business environment, multinational companies are facing a myriad of challenges, including geopolitical uncertainties, shifting consumer preferences, and technological disruptions. As a result, they are exploring innovative ways to align their strategies with the diverse characteristics of different countries to enhance competitiveness and mitigate risks (Cuervo-Cazurra et al., 2018).

This approach of tailoring organisational designs to specific country contexts is evident in the multi-domestic company configuration mentioned earlier. Multi-domestic companies prioritise the local context in their decision-making and resource allocation processes, allowing subsidiaries to have a certain level of autonomy in adapting to local market conditions (Bartlett and Ghoshal, 1990). However, they also foster collaboration and knowledge sharing among subsidiaries and headquarters to leverage the benefits of being part of a global network (Doz and Prahalad, 1986).

In light of the considerations presented in the preceding paragraph, still today, the overall trend does not seem to deviate significantly from companies' preference for the ideal of maximum institutional integration.

Although not recent, the study conducted in 1989 by the Japanese External Trade Organisation (JETRO) on 14 cases of successful penetration into Japan is still relevant as it allows understanding how companies behave vis-à-vis policies of control over the local subsidiaries. In the aforementioned study, nine interviewed companies expressed their generalised preference for policies of allowing authority or supervision over the subsidiary companies operating in a specific locality).

Recent studies in managerial literature have continued to highlight the prevalent scepticism among managers towards cooperative solutions (Zeng and Williamson, 2007). This sentiment is rooted in concerns over potential risks and challenges associated with forming alliances or partnerships with external entities. Managers often perceive cooperative ventures as entailing a loss of control, increased complexity in decision-making and potential conflicts of interest with partner organisations (Castañer and Oliveira, 2020). As a result, they may lean towards more traditional approaches, such as hierarchical integration or market-based strategies in order to maintain a sense of control and certainty in their international business operations (Luu, 2023).

However, recent research is also uncovering the potential benefits of collaborative approaches, suggesting that a careful evaluation of the specific context and strategic objectives is necessary to make informed decisions regarding cooperative strategies (Hutzschenreuter et al., 2021).

Recent research has indeed observed a growing trend of foreign activities conducted through structures that are not entirely 100% controlled by the parent company. This quantitative relevance responds to the existence of a series of factors that can lead companies away from the deeply rooted 'integrative' preference. Decastri (1984) provides a first index:

- Government interventions in destination countries aimed at modifying the institutional arrangement of international investment in favour of local presence (public or private);
- Characteristics of the legal and fiscal system and employment relations.

These factors represent inevitable constraints for companies intending to operate in those markets, leading to coercive cooperative choices. In addition to these factors, attention should be drawn to a second group of elements that, together with the obligatory ones, add a general condition of country risk. These elements include:

- characteristics of the workforce in terms of skill gaps (Decastri, 2020);
- the level of infrastructure development.

The degree of technological symmetry/asymmetry of the host country, which expresses the set of infrastructural discomfort, technological inadequacy, and educational and managerial deficiencies specific to the host country of the international expansion process, compared to the traditional context of reference for the company.

The country risk factor does not represent a strict constraint (i.e., it does not create obligatory conditions) for companies pursuing international development policies, but it rather proposes a series of evaluation elements on the forms of organisation thereof.

These elements should include both the expression of managerial preferences, the analysis of costs related to individual alternatives, and the strategic objectives pursued.

On one hand, it has often been emphasised that as the technological asymmetry, skills, and infrastructural support grow, the go-it-alone strategy could be considered the winning one, eliminating a series of market imperfections and accelerating the company's local development through autonomous production of a range of services complementary to its operations. If this was more likely to reflect circumstances of the past, today scholars have identified this phenomenon as a significant shift towards more collaborative and alliance-based strategies in international business (Zhao, 1999). Companies are increasingly engaging in various forms of alliances, joint ventures, and strategic alliances to access new markets, leverage on local expertise, and share risks and resources with partner companies (Schaan and Beamish, 1988).

One study found that multinational companies are increasingly forming alliances with local companies in foreign markets to capitalise on their market knowledge and distribution networks (Gammeltoft and Cuervo-Cazurra, 2021). Such cooperative arrangements allow companies to gain a competitive edge by combining their strengths and capabilities with those of their partners, leading to enhanced innovation and overall performance.

Additionally, the rise of digitalisation and Industry 4.0 technologies has accelerated the adoption of collaborative approaches. Companies are forming strategic alliances to access cutting-edge technologies, pool resources for research and development, and improve supply chain efficiency (Javaid, 2022). Whilst some companies may still exhibit caution towards cooperative strategies, recent evidence suggests that a growing number of companies are recognising the benefits of collaborative initiatives as a means to expand their global footprint, enhance competitiveness, and navigate the complexities of foreign markets (Barkema et al., 2019).

In the case of technological asymmetry, for instance, it has been emphasised that due to the inherent difficulty of knowledge transfer, it serves as an incentive for companies to opt for solitary foreign investment. Simultaneously, the fear of disseminating knowledge to benefit local competitors through training a low-skilled workforce also prompts integration. In this latter scenario, the local subsidiary (i.e., internal development) surpasses alliances for two reasons:

a. it prevents the dispersion of knowledge and competencies, which is required in negotiation with alliance partners;
b. by implementing a strict horizontal division of labour between expatriates (managers and technicians) and locals (workforce), it allows companies to capitalise on labour cost differentials without real knowledge transfer.

However, this approach may hinder future local development prospects and impede the timely understanding of the environment in which the company operates. Some critics argue that this strategy may be more tactical than strategic, as it sacrifices, for example, the benefits of knowledge spillover to third parties or international cross-fertilisation (Kijek and Kijek, 2019).

Recent studies have shown that the choice between fully controlled subsidiaries and collaborative ventures is influenced by various factors, including the maturity of the target market, the complexity of technology, and the level of tacit knowledge involved (Li et al., 2020). Additionally, the increasing emphasis on knowledge sharing and open innovation in global value chains has led companies to reconsider traditional hierarchical structures in favour of more flexible and cooperative arrangements (Smale and Suutari, 2011). Consequently, companies are exploring innovative ways to collaborate with external partners whilst safeguarding their strategic assets and intellectual property (Luo and Tung, 2018). It is evident that the decision to adopt cooperative strategies is not uniform across industries or companies, and careful consideration of contextual factors is essential in making such choices.

From another perspective, although company preference functions tend to favour strong control, in a more rational decision-making process, the challenge of guiding a local unit in different countries cannot be ignored. In certain cases, regardless of the coerciveness of the choice, the cultural, infrastructural, legal, and labour regulatory distance is such that the decision for a solitary initiative becomes impractical. In summary, the risk of losing control by the international company is counterbalanced by the difficulty it faces in understanding the local reality and integrating naturally with it. Otherwise, one could speak of a risk of cognitive opacity. This term refers to the ability of a company's management to grasp the true nature of the host country, its potential, and its limitations (Cuervo-Cazurra and Genc, 2008).

For all the reasons just mentioned, the use of cooperative tools is particularly evident, first and foremost, for countries whose legislation discourages or prohibits foreign investment without the support of a local partner. However, it can also be understood as a broader strategy, an alternative that is not residual or extreme within the models of managerial choice. Oman (1980) introduces the notion of 'new forms of foreign investment' in this regard, defining that vast and heterogeneous set of contractual agreements between companies that represents a sort of mediation between the extreme models of international expansion of companies: exporting vs. establishing a highly integrated international hierarchy. In a nutshell, Balcet (1989) propose to regroup these 'intermediate' forms of international expansion into three main groups:

1. Joint ventures.
2. International subcontracting;
3. International industrial cooperation.

1. Joint ventures. In the current business landscape, joint ventures continue to be a popular strategy for companies seeking to enter foreign markets whilst sharing risks and resources with local partners. However, there has been a shift towards more strategic and innovative joint ventures, with companies collaborating on research and development, technology transfer, and market access to drive mutual growth and competitiveness (Pauwels et al., 2020).

2. International subcontracting. With the rise of global value chains and increasing outsourcing practices, international subcontracting has become more sophisticated and diversified. Companies now engage in complex subcontracting networks, involving multiple partners across different countries, to optimise production efficiency and access specialised skills (Kano et al., 2020).

3. International industrial cooperation. The concept of international industrial cooperation has evolved to encompass various collaborative arrangements, including strategic alliances, partnerships, and consortia. In today's context, companies are forming cooperative networks to pool resources, expertise, and capabilities for large-scale projects, research initiatives, and innovation-driven endeavours (Sarpong et al., 2023).

The brief list provided by Balcet can easily be expanded and further explored. In fact, recent developments reflect the dynamic and adaptive nature of international business strategies, where companies seek innovative ways to navigate the complexities of global markets whilst maximising their competitive advantages through collaborative efforts. The ongoing digital transformation and Industry 4.0 trends have also influenced these forms of international expansion, fostering greater connectivity and cooperation among companies from different countries and industries (UNCTAD, 2021). However, it is important to accept the proposition that the instruments above should be considered as valid integration of the modes of international development typically studied

The way in which forms of intercompany cooperation can be combined with traditional modes of action of multinational companies is well expressed by Hedlund (1986). In defining the notion of a heterarchical company, he emphasises the urgency of adopting organisational polymorphism in governing international exchanges, following the coordinates suggested by the transaction cost economics. According to Hedlund, an efficient company is capable of separating choices of international organisation from simple managerial preferences for control. Instead, these choices are subordinated to evaluations of transaction quality, cost-effectiveness, characteristics of the host country system, and third-party preferences in governing the specific exchange. Hedlund's proposition is of considerable importance for understanding and prescribing the behaviour of companies engaged in a process of international expansion. In particular, it can be understood as a reaffirmation of the non-sub-optimality of hybrid forms compared to the 'pure' solutions traditionally proposed by neo-institutional literature (Williamson, 1975 and 1981).

Finally, for internationalisation phenomena, the importance of the spread of intermediate forms is not merely theoretical. The presence of entry barriers, hostile legislations, and conditions of instability in host countries are factors that recommend resorting to cooperative solutions regardless of absolute economic convenience assessments. This is evident from the magnitude of the phenomenon, its diffusion in different regions of the world, and the willingness of companies to use these approaches regardless of theoretical transactional conditions.

Recent developments in the global business landscape have further emphasised the practical significance of adopting cooperative solutions for internationalisation phenomena. With the increasing complexity of international markets and the rising tide of protectionist policies in some countries, entry barriers and hostile legislations have become more prevalent challenges for multinational companies. In such an environment, cooperative arrangements like joint ventures, strategic alliances, and international subcontracting offer viable alternatives to navigate through the complexities and uncertainties of foreign markets.

For instance, in the context of emerging markets, where legal and regulatory frameworks can be uncertain and dynamic, multinational companies often find it advantageous to collaborate with local partners to navigate the intricacies of doing business. These collaborative approaches not only provide access to local expertise and resources but also help in overcoming cultural barriers and building relationships with key stakeholders. In regions where there is a high level of political and economic volatility, cooperative solutions can serve as a means of risk diversification, enabling companies to share risks and responsibilities with their partners. Furthermore, the ongoing trends of globalisation and technological advancements have facilitated the dissemination of intermediate forms of internationalisation across different regions of the world. Companies have increasingly demonstrated a willingness to embrace cooperative strategies, recognising their potential to enhance competitiveness, expand market reach, and foster innovation through knowledge exchange and shared resources.

In conclusion, the adoption of cooperative solutions for internationalisation is not merely a theoretical concept but a pragmatic response to the challenges and opportunities presented in today has globalised business environment. The increasing prevalence of these arrangements and their positive impact on companies' international expansion efforts underscore their relevance and effectiveness in achieving strategic objectives in diverse markets.

4.3. Why Make Alliances: A Managerial Reference Model

Coactivity, country risk, and cognitive transparency risk represent, as seen, an incentive for forming alliances instead of merely exporting a managerial management model through paths of activity internalisation. On the other hand, the managerial preference for control constitutes a hindrance to the implementation of cooperative strategies. Starting from the first and often underestimating the second, managerial literature provides a rather analytical index of the motivations that could lead a company to adopt agreements in an internationalisation process. Indeed, alliances can:

- *Reduce* market entry costs, for example, by leveraging a share of an already operating distribution channel or sharing entry burdens with other international partners, as in the case of internationalisation consortia;
- *Expedite* market entry by avoiding preceding it with a phase of autarchic preparation of supporting infrastructure;
- Quickly *gain awareness* of specific local needs, which, although mediated, becomes more precise from the outset;
- *Develop* an institutional identity that is not hostile to the host country or perceived as foreign by the local market, for instance, gaining brand recognition and/or establishing bonds with buyers untainted by xenophobia;
- *Facilitate* the overcoming of all cultural barriers that tend to replicate the known organisational model of the multinational company in host realities through learning by imitating;
- *Obtain legitimate access* to local physical and intangible resources, as well documented in a reflection by JETRO.

When the risk is compared to several problems such as:

- high rent,
- increasing costs of seeing an operation through the early stages of its development due to the steep rise in property values,
- time necessary to develop market strategies and to localise management, than the benefits that a foreign company enjoys from utilising Japanese company's resources may outweigh the risk (Jetro, 1989, p. 23).

Advantages closely related to the international phenomenon, to which all those more general stimuli that determine the utility of proceeding cooperatively must be added:

- risk reduction (through portfolio diversification, dispersion and/or reduction of fixed costs, lower capital investment, quicker entry, and shorter payback period);
- economies of scale and/or rationalisation (lower average costs for larger volumes, lower costs by exploiting the comparative advantage of each partner);
- complementary technologies and patents (technological synergy, exchange of patents and territories);
- co-optation or blocking of competition (defensive joint ventures to reduce the number of competitors, offensive joint ventures to form hubs and/or reduce the market share of a third company);
- overcoming government barriers to trade or investments;
- initial international expansion;
- quasi-vertical integration (access to: materials, technology, labour, capital, distribution channels, permits; advantages from brand recognition, ties with key buyers, utilisation of existing fixed marketing structures) (Contractor and Lorange, 1988, p. 22).

Unlike coercive explanations, the motivations listed here do not necessarily require resorting to local partners, but rather to partners who are generally experienced in the issues of the host country's system or have already developed the necessary operational structures to initiate the new activity, or are institutionally recognised as an integral part of the reference economic system. This set of conditions also gives the alliance a higher value than that of a mere extreme alternative of entry, which is constantly sub-optimal to solutions of complete organisational integration or pure market approaches.

Primarily, alliances play a central role in reducing the uncertainty that generally accompanies new initiatives. Using the notion of familiarity, Roberts and Berry (1985) suggest adopting different development strategies based on the sensitivity that each company has to the specific local context. When the target markets are distant and unfamiliar compared to the knowledge accumulated by the company, the authors argue that internal development (international integration) is risky, especially the longer the process of assimilating knowledge. In the extreme case of complete unfamiliarity, Roberts and Berry emphasise the importance of intermediate forms or, if necessary, acquisitions for 'educational' purposes (educational acquisitions). Only in the opposite extreme case of maximum technical-commercial confidence do the authors suggest the go-it-alone strategy.

It is quite evident that the degree of familiarity is not absolute but rather varies in relation to the company's level of experience with a particular country or, more generally, with a specific regional area or territorial cluster. In the case of international expansion, uncertainty depends on a balanced percentage of objective conditions (expressed by country risk) and subjective conditions, identifiable in the inexperience and knowledge gaps of the management dealing with the internationalisation process (Eriksson et al., 2015).

In this sense, alliances between companies primarily aim to manage cultural obstacles.

Decastri expresses the concept: *"the search for products, markets, techniques, and organisational forms different from the current ones is made complex by limited familiarity with potential innovation"* (Decastri, 1984; p. 19). Resistance to innovation, the difficulty of operating in a new and unknown environment, represent significant incentives for adopting more cautious entry strategies. Decastri's explanation leverages confidence with market-technologies, but it could be extended to dimensions of confidence with various aspects of culture (national, managerial, lobbying, legislative, political, technological, etc.) and the infrastructure of the host country's system in the internationalisation process (Miller and Chang et al., 1978). For each company, it is possible, excluding political and legislative interferences, to establish a continuum of host country systems ranging from known to unknown, thereby transferring the notion of simple economic risk to a different level. The useful level for analysing managerial behaviour in this context becomes the one of subjective complexity, where increasing subjective complexity leads to higher generic risk in international operations.

From a theoretical perspective, this approach incorporates the reflections of the indeterminist school (March, 1978; Weick, 1979; Cohen et al., 1972) that emphasise the subjective reconstruction of the environment through processes of perception and learning. Taken to extreme conclusions, this approach forces a reflection on the absolute data of complexity and ambiguity of the environment, overlaying it with the organisation's interpretive capabilities, which are in turn influenced by the perceptions and preference functions of the actors operating within it. As a result, when faced with the same host country, two different companies will perceive and assess the risk differently based on their prior exposure to that country by their management. It is important to consider that certain countries indeed pose an inherently high investment risk, but the key point here is that there exists a variable level of risk proportional to each individual company's prior experience with that specific country.

Proposition 1. The propensity to adopt intermediate forms for governing international expansion processes increases as the foreign investor's management has less experience with a given host country (Roberts and Berry, 1985; Scott-Kennel and Enderwick, 2004).

Proposition 2. As the subjective complexity of a particular host country grows, the convenience for the company to adopt entry forms that leverage entities with greater awareness of that host country, typically local partners, also increases (Sanchez and Mckinley, 1995). Although the notion of subjective complexity can provide an initial explanation for the use of intermediate forms in international expansion processes, it alone does not fully predict managerial behaviour. Three variables can further contribute to explaining firm choices: cost, power, and culture. Concerning the first variable (cost), the choice between internal development, market-based strategies, or intermediate forms can be explained through the contribution of transaction cost economics (Williamson, 1975; 1981). Transaction costs represent the costs incurred by the company in governing a transaction, i.e., an exchange of goods and services between two technically separable units. They typically include: costs of monitoring the counterparty's behaviour, costs of defining performance, costs of distributing the outcome, costs of coordination and information processing, and costs of transferring knowledge. Managerial behaviour, in this perspective, is precisely explained by the performance of these cost factors, which, in turn, are generated by the nature of the analysed transactions (Rodríguez-Espíndola et al., 2022). The relevant dimensions of a transaction are:

- its *specificity*: a transaction is specific if the resources applied to it are not easily transferable to other exchanges, where the measure of resource specificity is given by the marginal utility of its alternative applications. Highly specific resources show a marginal disutility when transferred to another activity, indicating substantial inflexibility in their allocation (Kogut, 1990). Specificity, by creating a condition of difficult mutual substitutability of the transaction's parts, favours the emergence of evasive and opportunistic behaviours that result in an escalation of transaction control costs (Milgrom and Roberts, 1992).
- its *uncertainty*: a transaction is uncertain if it is not possible to predict all the conditions of its execution. This is determined by the limited rationality of individuals (Simon, 1948) in not having a complete view of all the consequences of their behaviours and by the emergence of information asymmetry, leading to imbalances in the control of information between the parties involved in the exchange (Eisenhardt, 1989; Zaheer, 1995).
- its *ambiguity* (measurability/controllability): a transaction is measurable/controllable if: (a) it is comparable to other similar transactions in the market, meaning it is not unique; (b) objective parameters exist to assess the contribution of actors (ex ante - behaviours - or ex post - results) (Eisenhardt, 1989; Williamson, 1985; Teece, 2014).

The managerial behaviour is explained by the evolution of these three dimensions, as they increase, the company finds it more advantageous to shift its choices from market solutions (e.g., dealers) towards strategies of internalising the international organisation (i.e., wholly-owned subsidiaries) (Anderson and Gatignon, 1986). In fact, as specificity, uncertainty, and ambiguity grow, the costs of controlling behaviours, detecting incentives, attributing results, transferring knowledge and information, etc., rise to the point of causing a sort of exchange paralysis (Williamson, 2016). In all these cases, the use of hierarchical forms reduces the risk of gridlock and helps contain the transaction governance costs (Hennart, 1988).

However, there is a wide area of exchanges where, whilst the market solution is not feasible, the evolution of the three transaction dimensions does not justify full internalisation. This is the so-called area of intermediate forms, i.e., organisational solutions where market and hierarchical mechanisms are hybridised, corresponding to a broad definition of inter-company alliances (Kogut, 1990). From this perspective, they present themselves as true forms of safeguarding, established by the parties to protect their interests in the exchange. Typical examples of safeguards are binding contracts, the establishment of joint structures, common ownership, cross-exchange of resources or knowledge or assets. The introduction of these safeguards meets the companies' need to oversee transactions that are more complex than what is allowed by market structures but not so difficult as to require organisational integration (Dyer and Singh, 1998).

Contractor and Lorange (1988) suggest a different analysis of the comparative costs between the various forms of international development, closer to the business language. The question that the two authors pose is: 'How should managers compare the go-it-alone options and inter-company cooperation?' (p. 19). The comparison between wholly owned local subsidiaries and alliances should be approached in terms of differential costs and revenues. In particular, the choice should result from the outcome of the following inequality:

$$Cij < (1-Si) \cdot Cj$$

Where

- *Cij* represents the cost of establishing an alliance between the home country, i.e., the investing company, and the host country, i.e., the target market.
- *Cj* represents the cost of a wholly owned local subsidiary (100% ownership).
- *Si* represents the share of cost savings that can be captured by the investing company through the alliance.

According to Contractor and Lorange (1988), if the cost of establishing an alliance (Cij) is less than the cost of a wholly owned local subsidiary (Cj) multiplied by the share of cost savings (1−si), then the alliance option is more economically favourable and should be pursued by the company. This approach highlights the importance of cost differentials in guiding the decision between different forms of international expansion (Luo, 2022).

Where incremental benefits are observable in terms of relatively higher returns and relatively lower costs, and incremental costs are observable in terms of relatively higher costs and relatively lower returns, applying both direct and indirect principles to all four categories. For instance, direct relative higher returns can be observed in the case of an international development process, such as partner market knowledge and accelerated cash flows. Indirect returns can include the completion of the product range, learning, and marginal innovation resulting from the exchange with the partner.

Contractor and Lorange's comparison model suggests some areas of relevant analysis for deciding between internal development and resorting to alliance forms. It is the task of managerial sensitivity to enrich the individual items with both methodological (how to measure) and strategic (relative weight) depth. Strategic importance, in fact, represents a discriminating factor of extreme relevance in an evaluation model of international development alternatives. Regardless of cost considerations, it is necessary to emphasise that not all transactions are equivalent from the focal organisation's perspective, which evaluates the alternatives and makes decisions. Instead, they vary in strategic importance. In a general assumption, the strategic importance of the transaction (in its two components: the object of exchange and the exchanging parties) is expressed in the desired control over the governance structure. Given this basic equivalence, the desire for control increases when:

$$Pdesired > Pacceptable + Cexchange$$

Where:

- *P desired* represents the desired level of control over the exchange.
- *P acceptable* represents the level of control that is acceptable in the absence of the alliance.
- *C exchange* represents the incremental cost of forming and maintaining the alliance.

That is when:

- the exchanged resources are close to the strategic core of the company (Gorbis and Yorke, 1985; Harrigan, 1985; Porter et al., 2000);
- the exchanged resources are characterised by a weak appropriability regime (Ouchi and Boulton, 1988)
- the exchanged resources are in the ascending phase of their life cycle (Gorbis and Yorke, 1985);

- potential partner companies are in a relation of potential competitiveness ex ante to the agreement's conclusion (Omahe, 1986).

The model suggests that a company's desire for control over the exchange (and thus the choice between internal development and alliance) depends on how much additional control it seeks beyond what is deemed acceptable in the absence of the alliance, considering the associated incremental costs. This decision-making process is strategic and can significantly influence the choice between different forms of international expansion (Luo and Peng, 1999).

It should be noted that this equivalence assumes an interpretation of control as *a physiological expression* of the management's need to oversee critical resources. However, this does not mean that the management can express an absolute, and sometimes pathological, preference for the exercise of control itself. For instance, the research by Santos and Eisenhardt (2005) observes that in determining their managerial preference functions, decision-makers introduce elements of absolute expansion of organisational boundaries or they seek to accumulate resources beyond the necessary operational needs alongside dimensions of profit and efficiency.

The notion of strategic importance can also be related to the concept of the company's 'living space', even in a territorial sense. For example, a study involving CEOs of medium-sized companies emphasised that 'the element of choice is the physical distance between the heart of the company - the home country - and all potential peripheral hubs' (Kotler and Gertner, 2002). Strategic importance, and therefore institutional, strategic, and organisational control, decrease as the distances increase.

Certainly, the strategic importance also arises from other factors. For example, the risk to reputation and/or image and the balance (survival or strengthening) of other critical relationships. When the alliance is formalised, each partner becomes then responsible for the other's behaviour, reputation, and strategies.

The combination of these considerations leads to the following assertion:

Proposition 3. Management's preference for integrated solutions increases with the growing strategic importance of the transaction or the system of transactions considered.

The third group of variables includes the psychological dimension of managerial behaviour. This refers both to the management's past experiences and to the external culture concerning cooperation. Past experiences with cooperation not only influence the willingness to cooperate but also the chosen modalities to do so. For instance, as positive experiences increase, there is usually a dilution of the desired/exercised level of control. Regarding the second dimension, it can be observed that the evolution of thought on the topic of cooperation has influenced the desirability of these business choices.

Proposition 4. The rationale behind managerial choices concerning cooperation is influenced by factors of personal and corporate experience, cultural and environmental conditioning, desired control, and the strategic importance of the exchanged resources.

4.4 Natural Difficulties in Cooperation Strategies for International Expansion

Entering and maintaining a position in a foreign country are made challenging by the presence of numerous obstacles. These challenges have been a subject of study in international business and management literature. Scholars have highlighted the significance of cultural, organisational, and institutional factors as key barriers to successful international expansion. A repertoire of alliances relates issues with protected countries is, for example, provided by a study conducted by the journal Dialogo on 61 Italian-Soviet joint ventures:

- *Bureaucratic barriers* (registration, import-export licenses, financing authorisations).
- *Institutional obstacles* (legal systems, government regulations, political stability, currency convertibility, interpretation of laws, gaps in joint venture legislation - lack of a unified text, discretion in the application of norms, legislative overlaps between local and national levels - clarity and fairness of the tax system for joint ventures) can create uncertainties for foreign businesses. The level of institutional development in a host country can affect market entry barriers, contract enforcement, property rights, and overall business operations (North, 1990).
- *Cultural barriers* (mind-set and language) or cultural differences are those between the home country and the foreign market can affect business practices, communication, and relationship building. Scholars like Hofstede (1985) and Trompenaars and Hampden-Turner (1997) have extensively researched cultural dimensions and their implications for international business operations.
- *Organisational obstacles* (ownership arrangements, areas of responsibility, personnel management models, degree of organisational formalisation, difficulty in assessing contributions, management styles, decision-making processes and work ethics) can vary significantly across different countries. Companies need to adapt their strategies and operations to the local organisational norms to succeed in foreign markets (Luo and Shenkar, 2006).

To overcome these obstacles, companies often engage in various forms of international alliances and partnerships, such as joint ventures and strategic alliances. Collaborating with local partners can help companies navigate cultural and institutional complexities and gain access to local market knowledge and resources (Contractor et al., 1988).

The literature on Italian-Soviet joint ventures highlights other managerial difficulties. Uckmar (2005) consider the most relevant diversities in functional areas such as marketing, production, labour relations, and personnel management, attributing to the Soviet system a character of originality that is challenging for external observers to grasp. Although these types of difficulties have been rapidly overcome by recent history and upheavals in the internal dynamics of the Commonwealth of Independent States, the nature of the issues raised can be considered of general value for international operations in so-called 'protected' countries.

To emphasise the generalisability of the phenomenon to other national cases, one can consider the example of China, highlighting the illustrative nature of the specific country system under consideration:

- currency, financial, and accounting difficulties due to the non-convertibility of the currency;
- profit repatriation, possible only for joint ventures oriented towards export and not for those established to meet domestic demand;
- the sourcing of raw materials and semi-finished products for the joint ventures, which are foreign to the centrally planned and controlled production system;
- the slowness and lack of constructiveness in dealing with local bureaucracy;
- the scarcity of local managerial resources and skilled labour;
- a mix of cultures within the alliance (Ratti, 1989).
- logistical difficulties and practical impediments for foreigners in China (e.g., obtaining an entry visa) that signal the challenges of conducting the future joint venture;
- the absence or limited development of a business code based on sound economic principles and uniformly applied;

- the complex and sequential decision-making process required to establish the joint venture, with bureaucratic approvals at each milestone often being so slow as to 'kill' the project;
- the excessively protective foreign exchange system that reduces the attractiveness of purely financial investments or those aimed exclusively at domestic production;
- the advantage of low labour costs is offset by unnecessary high costs imposed on the foreign partner;
- labour policies that are excessively rigid and discourage individual productivity and entrepreneurship in occupational mobility (Smith, 1987, pp. 19-21).

On the other hand, whilst alliances in protected countries are more easily interpretable in terms of difficulties and obstacles, more subtle challenges can arise from contact with other nations.

Pucik and Katz, (1990) examines the case of Japan, with a particular focus on human resource management issues. Pucik and Katz conduct their research through interviews with managers from 23 Western and Japanese joint ventures in Japan. The results that emerge are summarised in the following framework. The difficulties identified by Pucik and Katz are related to the peculiarities of the managerial system and human resource management practices. Amongst them:

- *The ethnocentric and ethno-organisational tendencies* of Japanese companies, which lead the Japanese parent company to view the joint venture as a part of their corporate family regardless of the actual share ownership. This leads to the expectation that the joint venture will subordinate its personnel policies to the needs of the parent company.
- *The external labour market* is very limited due to the general internal market strategies of leading Japanese companies.
- The *culture of human resource development* in Japanese companies heavily relies on internal seniority and on-the-job learning. The parent company, and consequently its personnel, may not prioritise the training of the joint venture's personnel. Instead, it may view the joint venture as a centre for training and development.
- In Japanese companies, it is presumed that *competitive Western methods linked to individual performance discourage cooperation within the company* (Pucik, 1983). Similarly, the approach to feedback on evaluations differs, favouring a less explicit scheme compared to the Western approach. This creates a dual evaluation system for employees from distinct corporate backgrounds.
- *Compensation levels* in Japan are influenced by age and seniority of individual employees (Guth and MacMillan, 1986). As the workforce transferred from the Japanese parent company is heavily skewed towards older employees, labour costs are substantially higher without a corresponding increase in productivity.

In more general terms, Geringer and Hebert (1989) and Dymsza (1988) suggested an additional index of friction zones in international alliances has been proposed by in their study on global strategic alliances.

- Misjudgement of the partner's local technological evaluation capabilities and, in general, the host country's evaluation system, leading to tensions in determining the pricing of transferred know-how.
- Misjudgement of the dominant financial orientation in the host country, resulting in repercussions on the reinvestment and risk strategy of the joint venture.

- Misjudgement of the competitive capabilities of the host country, leading to imbalances in competitive dynamics within the joint venture.
- Misjudgement of the available managerial capabilities in the host country, leading to conflicts in defining top positions within the alliance, management style, and preferred managerial models to facilitate cooperation.
- Misjudgement of dominant cultural characteristics (ethical, moral, etc.) in the host country, resulting in consequences for building trust.
- Misjudgement of the local management's evaluation capabilities, leading to repercussions on the transparency of cost and revenue attribution criteria between the parties.

The list compiled by Dymsza based on the analysis of numerous business cases reinforces the importance of extra-legal factors in the success of alliances. It highlights the need to establish a framework of competencies required to navigate this particular form of international expansion, which combines managerial skills, cooperation abilities, and international knowledge (legal, contractual, cultural, etc.).

4.5 The System of International Competencies for Alliances

To address the issue of the competencies required to ensure an acceptable level of functioning in an international alliance, it is necessary to consider that two dimensions of complexity coexist within it: the first is related to the international nature of the operation, and the second depends on its cooperative essence. Whilst reflecting on this point, it is important to emphasise that, to some extent, these two dimensions tend to converge. In other words, what drives international complexity is quite similar to what generates cooperative complexity. Turati (1990) highlights the overlap, using the international company as a metaphor for the alliance. The two terms share numerous elements in common. The organisation that exposes itself to new and unfamiliar environmental contexts must:

- make an effort of integration with local realities greater than usual (in the alliance, with the partner/partners);
- evaluate the optimal profiles of resources to be allocated and the combination of profiles and nationalities;
- manage the physical detachment of individuals assigned to the local branch, their exile syndrome, their mobility, and their return to more central positions;
- govern the balance of loyalty between local and central levels, favouring integration between global and local needs;
- confront tensions between management models of exportation and indigenous cultural patterns;
- promote integration among heterogeneous national components;
- develop models of human resource governance in an unstable equilibrium between the central structure and the periphery of the empire;
- reduce tensions between opposing xenophobia and opposing mental patterns of superiority;
- lastly, govern the processes of knowledge transfer from the individual directly involved at the local level to the 'ignorant' central structure.

If these are the areas of similarity that could facilitate an experienced organisation in alliances for international development and vice versa, it is worth noting that an alliance remains an anomalous mode of organisation compared to internalised solutions. From an organisational perspective, an alliance presents a problem both in general rules of the organisational game and in more specific aspects of human resource management. From the first perspective, an alliance poses a challenge to the general boundaries of the organisation as it:

- calls into question the organisational boundaries;
- requires a revision of the ways of organising work (especially in cases where it involves rationalisation processes);
- demands original investment in coordination, communication, and integration procedures and schemes, regardless of the usual levers of hierarchical control and authority;
- expects a shift in past behavioural models towards a more collaborative orientation.

At the same time, it represents a human resource management problem because it:

- absorbs human resources at various levels, both directly and indirectly (opportunity cost vs. saturation);
- covers different development perspectives for individuals between internal and external contexts;
- requires the identification of new categories for position evaluation, performance assessment, and potential (Lyles, 1987);
- involves a greater effort to provide clarity in identifying career paths, training, and rewards;
- leads to a new sensitivity towards individual needs for identity, stability, and growth;
- demands a management of people outside the usual bureaucratic and hierarchical frameworks.

The combination of all these critical points highlights the need for an original interpretation of the alliance as an organisational solution.

At the same time, however, the quality of the international alliance depends on the availability of general competencies within the organisation. From the considerations emerged in the previous paragraphs, it is clear that the modes of international expansion are strongly influenced by the balanced interaction of internal conditions within the company (subjective complexity of a host country) and external constraints (country risk). The subjective complexity is, in turn, subordinate to the degree of coherence between the competencies required to address a specific host country and the competencies available internally within the company. For a more detailed breakdown, competencies can be disaggregated into:

- general competencies, skills, and knowledge of international management;
- specific competencies, skills, and knowledge of the host country system;
- in the specific case of alliances considered, a third group of specific competencies is added, necessary to manage cooperative relationships.

The competencies of the first type have been extensively discussed in the literature, seeking answers to questions such as: What should be the professional and personal profile of an international manager? What are the best human resource management criteria on an international level? Which organisational structure is better able to balance the centre and the periphery? These are questions to which the literature and the daily behaviour of companies have provided numerous answers, often differing from case to case, reflecting the impact of specific national and corporate cultures in determining the relationship with the foreign world beyond their own borders. The identification of general competencies in international management can arise from a reflection on the main problems that companies engaged in these operations face:

I. Problems related to the management of production abroad.
II. Problems related to legal aspects of the process.
III. Problems related to administrative and financial issues.
IV. Problems related to commercial issues. Goldenberg (1988) considers the case of China.
V. Problems with information gathering.
VI. Problems related to knowledge transfer and joint development.
VII. Problems with managerial training.

I. *Problems related to the management of production abroad.*

Company A formed an alliance with Company B located in Country 1 to produce a large quantity of semi-finished leather products. However, after a year, the production rate was significantly lower than the expected productivity levels. The main problems were related to maintaining a steady flow of supplies. This was due to difficulties in integrating the joint venture into the complex centralised planning process and the slow transportation of raw materials caused by the scarcity of reliable means and routes. Additionally, it was observed within Company A that the local management seemed to lack sufficient entrepreneurial drive to address production exceptions. Moreover, due to political reasons, remuneration criteria, and limited availability of technical resources to be transferred, it was not possible to allocate Italian technicians to the joint venture.

One year after signing a production agreement with a local operator in a post-Soviet Eastern European country, Company K, operating in the white goods industry, experienced an unexplained increase in unit production costs. A quick investigation revealed that Company K had limited options for sourcing spare parts, components, and ancillary items for the production process, such as pallets and cranes, from the local market. This compelled the company to either produce everything internally or rely on supplies from abroad, resulting in a considerable increase in costs.

II. *Problems related to legal aspects of the process* (see paragraph 4.4).
III. *Problems related to administrative and financial issues*

The convertibility of currencies, their instability (high inflation, sudden devaluations, etc.), are the problems faced by Company B in dealing with Developing Countries (PVS).

This requires the search for innovative solutions of a certain managerial complexity, such as countertrade [...] *In an Argentine experience dating back to the mid-1980s, we found ourselves in a system of triangulations that exchanged: telecommunications systems, pleasure boats, and food products. Since we operate in the first of the three sectors, this entailed a significant effort in evaluating the trading system [...] Administrative and financial issues then encompass a substantial area, including: assessment of contributions, depreciation, taxation, profit transfer, divestment, general accounting, etc.*

The manager of a US company recounts the experience of a joint venture in Argentina:

[...] As the joint venture shares were traded on the Buenos Aires Stock Exchange, we became shareholders of a company controlled by a French company in serious economic difficulties, both in France and Argentina, and it did not pay dividends to the shareholders. The only source of income for us, a technical assistance fee, ran out at the end of the 5-year assistance contract [...]

Twenty-five years later, the French company expressed its intention to acquire our shares. The share price, traded on the local stock exchange, was more or less equivalent to the original investment, so 25 years after investing in a joint venture in Argentina, we were able to recover the original investment. Twenty-five years during which that investment had not generated any income.

IV. *Problems related to commercial issues.*

Goldenberg (1988) considers the case of China: *"Western managers who believe that merchandising is merchandising anywhere in the universe quickly realize that China is not part of this galaxy. For the Chinese, the American practice of testing consumer needs and preferences through surveys and then designing consistent products is an alien concept [...] A second aspect of this problem is what Western managers define as 'phantom borders' between provinces, determined by centuries of local competition. This rivalry threatens sales even when the primitive Chinese transport and distribution systems manage to function. At the same time, overcoming these issues through advertising is difficult since [...] the Cultural Revolution banned wall advertising as a capitalist expression"* (p.199).

Although China's evolution is now regaining a heritage of typically Western commercial communication, the distance between the two models is still enormous. Apart from the argument put forward by Goldenberg, there are additional commercial issues that companies may encounter when engaging in joint ventures or business activities in China. These issues arise due to the unique business environment and market conditions in the country. Some of the key commercial challenges are:

- Complex Regulatory Environment. China's regulatory landscape can be intricate and subject to frequent changes. Navigating through various permits, licenses, and compliance requirements can be time-consuming and challenging for foreign companies.
- Intellectual Property Protection. Protecting intellectual property (IP) rights in China has been a longstanding concern for international companies. Cases of IP infringement and counterfeiting have been reported, making it essential for companies to implement robust strategies for safeguarding their innovations and proprietary information.
- Local Partner Selection. Finding the right local partner for a joint venture is crucial. Language barriers, cultural differences, and varying business practices can affect the alliance's success. Thorough due diligence and understanding of the potential partner's capabilities are essential to establish a strong and harmonious alliance.
- Market Access Barriers. Despite China's significant market opportunities, certain sectors remain heavily restricted for foreign participation. Companies may face limitations on foreign ownership or face bureaucratic hurdles in certain industries, affecting market access and expansion plans.
- Price and Cost Dynamics. Fluctuations in raw material costs, labour wages, and other production expenses can affect the profitability of operations in China. Maintaining cost competitiveness and managing price volatility become critical for sustaining business success.

- Market Competition. China's market is highly competitive, with both domestic and international players vying for market share. Understanding local consumer preferences and effectively positioning products or services in a crowded market becomes essential for capturing demand.
- Supply Chain Disruptions. Companies operating in China need to consider potential supply chain disruptions, especially during geopolitical tensions or global crises. Developing contingency plans and diversifying sourcing strategies can help mitigate risks.
- Currency and Exchange Rate Fluctuations. Dealing with foreign currency transactions and managing exchange rate risks can affect financial performance, especially for companies with significant exposure to China's currency, the Yuan (CNY/RMB).
- Brand Perception. Building a positive brand image in China requires a deep understanding of local culture and consumer behaviour. Companies need to tailor their marketing and branding strategies to resonate with Chinese consumers effectively.
- Government Relations. Building strong relationships with local and central government authorities is essential for successful operations in China. Engaging in constructive dialogues and understanding government policies and priorities can facilitate smoother business operations.

V. *Problems with information gathering.*

The CEO of Company C explains: as impossible as it may seem, information gathering about a country is not a central problem for us in our process of international expansion. In part, and primarily, this is because our approach prioritises the partner over the host country where we operate. This means that finding the right counterpart is more important than the host country; their selection is based on genuine expressions of interest and technical competence, relying on word-of-mouth from mutual acquaintances. Secondly, and equally in part, the criterion guiding our process follows this rule: as the physical distance between us and the country increases, the strategic importance of the operation decreases. Hence, the need for strict control over the partner's behaviour diminishes, as does the level of involvement we impose on ourselves. Therefore, in reality, as our knowledge of a certain country decreases, the need for complete information also decreases.

VI. *Problems related to knowledge transfer and joint development.*

If cooperative action serves, among other things, to reduce the risk of entering conditions of low familiarity with the destination country of the investment (Roberts and Berry, 1985), or to increase cognitive transparency about that national system, the central element for the success of an alliance is the ability to transit knowledge between partner companies. Doz and Prahalad (1986) emphasise that, in this regard, there are three critical factors:

- the pressure that each partner exerts to transmit and receive such knowledge, where both literature and managerial practice agree that the second of the two activities (reception) is by far the most challenging for Western companies, also due to the conditions of 'not invented here syndrome' (Harrigan, 1985; Lyles, 1987);
- the ease of information flow between partners, in reference to establishing roles for facilitating communication, appropriateness of skills and knowledge, and prepared communication models;

- the receptiveness of the organisation, exacerbated by the difficulty of transmitting certain categories of resources, such as technical and managerial know-how (Teece, 2014).

  VII. *Problems with managerial training.*

The head of resource development at Company H comments on the experience of their company in a series of joint ventures:

"We have had about fifty international joint ventures, all characterized by human resource issues, sometimes small and sometimes enormous. Most of the time, these issues are related to technical specialists who are also given managerial responsibilities. At first, I believed it was due to a lack of genuine motivation to work abroad, compensated by substantial economic incentives. Then we realized that many people were not mature enough to handle the dual challenge of management and human relations. From a managerial standpoint, these individuals often found themselves, for the first time, as the frontline of the company facing external partners, especially abroad. In other words, they were overwhelmed by their own responsibilities. Then there was a human problem: on one hand, estrangement from the parent company, perceived threats to their career, and disruptions to social relationships at work; on the other hand, tension on the family front. It is worth noting that in the beginning, our programs oscillated between being stingy and excessively generous towards expatriates. Today, we guarantee family relocation and offer top-notch infrastructural support (housing, schools, etc.). Secondly, we provide more managerial training and support to individuals, although our people remain essentially technicians".

The combination of these problems defines a repertoire of competencies required to address a generic internationalisation process. It involves the ability to anticipate problems and prepare appropriate responses. It is evident that this requires developing a set of resources within the company capable of facing the internationalisation process, especially in terms of widespread and generic sensitivity towards 'the other'. It prefigures an overall willingness to work in unfamiliar contexts, with partners and international interlocutors.

The actualisation of this sensitivity, these competencies, and skills in specific national contexts represents the second component of the know-how required for internationalisation. They represent specific assets for transactions with each individual country. They also form the basis for building a general international competence, but it is clear that in the absence of homogeneous international conditions, their transferability to other country systems can be significantly reduced. Examples of such competencies can be deduced, by contrast, from the 'natural' difficulties outlined in section 3, as well as from 'general' problems of international expansion that fall under the broad umbrella of cross-cultural management, as evidenced by numerous cases of unsuccessful export and exchange processes in relatively unknown or limitedly appreciated markets ex ante. Beyond theoretical evaluations, the list of difficulties in this regard is quite extensive. Many companies have faced difficulties related to the marketing mix. Ohmae cites (1986) the case of Mattel's Barbie in Japan regarding the physical image of the product. Other unfortunate incidents of internationalising products include GM with the NOVA model (NOVA = 'doesn't go' in Spanish), Mitsubishi with the PAJERO model in Spanish-speaking countries, and Volkswagen with the JETTA model in Italy. Other natural commercial obstacles include distribution barriers, local product standards (whether the product is marketable based on consumer morphological characteristics in the pharmaceutical sector, environmental safety in detergents and chemicals, public regulations in the automotive sector, etc.), and consumer loyalty to national images. The sales manager of a major jeans manufacturer comments on the initial phase of entering Japan:

Today, jeans are popular in Japan, but at first, any approach we adopted resulted in failure. This, among other reasons, was because the parent company could not understand that the Asian model produced in Hong Kong was not at all in line with the physique of the Japanese.

Integration into the commercial culture of the host country is just one relevant aspect. Managerial literature and business experience highlight numerous difficulties of cultural adaptation (Laurent, 1986; Pettigrew, 1979). Differences in national cultures can affect fundamental intentions related to:

- attitudes towards work;
- interaction between individuals and organisations (Ouchi, 1981);
- relationships between superiors and subordinates (Bhawuck and Brislin, 1992);
- reward and punishment systems (Etzioni, 1968; Terpstra, 1978);
- time and space orientation (Lawler and Hall, 1976; Peterson and Shimada, 1978; Zimmerman, 1984);
- references derived from philosophical and religious systems (Terpstra, 1985; Hofstede, 1985);
- the significance of the family system (Davis and Stern, 1988).

Moreover, the implications of a national cultural model on the modus operandi of those who operate within it are highly significant: the importance given to completeness and correctness of formal contracts, a sense of belonging to institutions and organisations (Peterson and Shimada, 1978; Sakakibara, 1997), ritual negotiation methods (Clegg and Wilson, 1990), time and ethical management. Whilst the aforementioned issues are common to any international initiative, regardless of the characteristics of the adopted ownership structure, an additional set of competencies is determined by the specific nature of alliances when used to support the international development process. These alliances show several general conditions of instability, extensively documented in the literature.

An additional effort to analyse the sources of difficulty in managing an alliance is conducted by Turati (1990), who groups recurring problems into three main areas:

- factors of inter-company distance, which encompass the challenges arising from differences in corporate culture and organisational structure between partners.
- Factors of structural inadequacy. These are related to the lack of coherence between cooperative objectives and the available cooperation resources within the company (dedicated structures and/or resources, operational mechanisms aware of the alliance's functioning conditions, suitable managerial roles, etc.). In addition, factors related to competence in designing the organisational structure for cooperation (i.e., the ability to develop organisational solutions that foster integration between distant systems).
- Counter-effect factors, which refer to the consequences of initiating and operating the alliance on other parts of the parent company's organisational system. These consequences can be either positive or negative, acting as either support or obstacles to other unrelated actions of the company.

The combination of these elements highlights the competencies required to manage an alliance:

- organisational analysis skills (understanding inter-company distance and translating it into necessary differentiation and compatibility analysis);
- negotiation and mediation abilities (managing the alliance formation process and building trust);
- coordination skills between the alliance objectives and other internal activities, core business, available resources, etc.;
- organisational design capabilities (identifying areas of necessary integration, consistent coordination tools, adopting organisational logics coherent with the alliance objectives, etc.).

Furthermore, the competencies and management abilities required for an alliance converge with general international competencies at the national level to form the necessary knowledge base for effectively governing an international development process. This convergence is illustrated by De Bari (1990), who identifies critical steps in the international expansion process towards PVS:

- defining customer needs, which cannot be done without knowledge of the country and its requirements;
- partner selection;
- operational design of the international initiative, including transactional organisation and managerial management;
- evaluation of the initiative's costs;
- formulating a formal proposal for the initiative.

All the considerations presented above define the minimum set of competencies and capabilities necessary to address an international development process through alliances, summarised as:

- general analysis and evaluation of country systems (market, consumer preferences, infrastructure, etc.);
- identification and contact of potential partners;
- evaluation of potential partners;
- negotiation;
- contractual construction;
- needs identification (alliance costs);
- organisational design;
- managerial and technical cooperative management.

This is by no means a minimal repertoire, nor is it easy to acquire. Internal shortcomings within an organisation can manifest at different levels of the competency system described in section 6. Furthermore, these shortcomings can be derived and amplified by the problems that will be dealt with in Chapter 5. They may lead to a lack of success in international operations or a radical redefinition of preferences in this area, even resulting in paralysis of such initiatives. The enumeration of recurring problems in international alliances generates a need for effective corporate responses. These responses can be organised into three main areas:

- the need to dynamically revise the alliance by correctly defining its phases to build a favourable relationship between partners;

- the need to analyse the alliance as a comparable organisational alternative to other business development strategies, through a more satisfactory analysis and interpretation of the implications of collaborative actions (resource commitment, changes in organisational roles, structural modifications, etc.).
- The need to place greater emphasis on some indirect benefits of the alliance, such as indirect learning, potential evaluation, and opening up alternative career paths, etc.

The following paragraphs will focus on these aspects.

4.6. The Alliance as a Process: Alliance Building

In this perspective, the alliance is primarily the process of building a alliance, namely a trusting relationship between the partners. In it, the two relevant analysis parameters are:

a. time, both understood as the timeframe needed to construct a shared set of rules of the game, and as the intensity of managerial time dedicated to supporting the alliance, an expression of
b. cooperative intention, meaning the *mental and organisational* predisposition to maintain a positive attitude towards the partner and the alliance.

The cooperative relationship is a set of parallel processes, and within each of them, operations or phases are aimed at achieving performance objectives that are satisfactory for each of the involved parties (Wankmüller and Reiner, 2020). In this perspective, the fallibility of alliances often stems from a fallibility in the relationship between the parties within the system. The more an alliance involves the exchange of information or critical resources among partners, the greater the need for relational trust. Therefore, the cooperative relationship can also be observed as a process of building trust, which includes a sequence of activities that reduce the sense of competitiveness and lead to the formation of an almost unstable social system composed of members from parent organisations (Mazzarol et al., 2018). The usefulness of adopting a process perspective in the study of alliance phenomena derives from two general considerations:

a. conceptually, companies do not possess the complete ability to accurately and pre-determine their needs, due to their imperfect capacity to define their objectives ex ante; rather, they result from a progressive adjustment through paths of convergence/divergence among actors operating within the common organisational reality (Reid and Yang, 2018). The application of a temporal model accepts the principle of mistrust among partners as natural but reducible with the prolongation of the relationship, depending on the parties' ability to construct a stable social model.
b. In operational terms, the disaggregation of the alliance's life into phases of an integrated process can help in selecting the set of skills and preparing responses that are more suitable phase by phase. This means that the correct approach to each phase becomes a reason for advancing in building a positive relationship between the partners. Secondly, the adoption of a dynamic approach allows us to grasp the evolution of the cooperative relationship over time through different stages and cycles, each characterised by distinct attitudes and reactions.

Operationally, the alliance is marked by a sequence of interconnected but distinguishable operations on a logical level. The extensive literature in this field focuses on at least six phases:

I. identification of cooperative needs;
II. search and selection of potential partners;
III. negotiation;
IV. agreement design;
V. operational management and potential adjustments to the preliminary agreement;
VI. dissolution.

Grouping the six phases by homogeneous content, Kohtamäki et al. (2023) suggest some general conditions that favour a positive development for each of them.

I. Initiation and Design Phase

This phase encompasses the initial moments of alliance building work (development plans, partner search and selection, negotiation, defining the framework within which the partners will collaborate). Difficulties in this phase arise from a lack of judgment due to the inability to foresee the full range of internal and external events, zones of behavioural opportunism in the negotiation process, perceptual distortions in partner judgment, and a weak predisposition to organisational design.

Conditions that can favour a favourable outcome in this phase include, but are not limited to, the following:

a. *The degree of transparency regarding each partner's objectives.* An alliance often has external implications beyond the focal objectives declared by the partners, which are frequently as significant as the explicit reasons for forming the alliance. These external implications represent the hidden agenda of the partners and are not openly stated. They arise from parallel actions in which the explicit objectives may compete for strategic direction, resource allocation with other internal centres of the partners, and, especially in cases where these actions involve other components of the external network, for poor compatibility with other stakeholders.

The moment when these hidden objectives emerge is not during the initiation phase but rather in the subsequent implementation and, above all, in the review phase when partners are asked to increase their commitment to the alliance's purpose. Although there is a certain time interval between these two moments, during the negotiation and design phase, it is possible to attempt to limit the influence of hidden agendas. This can be achieved at four levels:

i. through a more careful evaluation of the alliance's interdependence with other initiatives, especially external ones, of the partner (in addition to their own);
ii. through the verification of potential alternative interests within the partner;
iii. through the construction of the agreement structure that facilitates the acceleration of verification moments;

iv. through the division of the agreement into multiple modules of increasing strategic importance, so that each allows greater control of the real level of involvement of the counterpart and managerial and organisational compatibility.

b. The existence of sufficient levels of mutual knowledge. If relational trust is the foundation of good alliances, direct mutual experience is, *coeteris paribus*, the best guarantee of a successful alliance. Mutual knowledge operates on multiple levels: reputation for reliability, interpersonal networks, and familiarity with each other's organisational practices. Prior mutual knowledge, therefore, reduces both the cost of verifying compatibility and the cost of building trust. Once again, the logic of gradualism emerges as an ingredient to initiate positive cooperative relationships.

c. Affinity or compatibility of management styles. Strategic convergence, the interpenetration of strengths and weaknesses of the partners, undoubtedly play a significant role in determining the formation of an alliance (Mitsuhashi and Greve, 2008). However, the choice of a partner also depends on the suitability of their respective management styles. Compatibility does not imply equality: systems designed to govern different competitive environments are naturally diverse, and different national cultures and corporate traditions naturally influence how a company organises itself. Compatibility rather means the possibility that the two systems establish a process of intelligible communication, whilst inter-company differences should be the pivot for designing integration. For this reason, the negotiation process must seek to highlight areas of affinity, compatibility, and distance, avoiding the trap of 'we cannot work together because we are different',, but also the trap of 'it does not matter how different we are, we will still be able to build a harmonious situation'. Instead, attention should be drawn to potential areas of distance. First and foremost, the soft areas of managerial ethics and underlying culture, but also the more measurable hard areas:

- The management systems in terms of:
    - risk orientation
    - innovation orientation (research and development as a percentage of revenue, % of revenue by product age, training as a percentage of revenue, etc.);
    - temporal orientation (ability to wait);
    - general strategic orientation (adaptive, reactive, proactive, etc.);
    - profit orientation (desired profit levels);
    - people orientation (Theory X vs. Theory Y, McGregor, 1960);
    - quality orientation;
    - market orientation;
    - delegation orientation.
- Organisational structures (number of levels, degree of lateralisation, integration tools, degree of centralisation/decentralisation, etc.);
- Marketing and distribution strategies (customer service policies, distribution methods, marketing mix, etc.);
    - Production (procurement policies, level of vertical integration, facilities and their obsolescence, degree of automation, just-in-time orientation, etc.);
    - Financial policies (debt structure, dividend and reinvestment policies, debt/equity ratio, other financial indicators, etc.);

- Ownership (public or private, concentrated or fragmented, etc.);
- Industrial relations (internal marketing, labour relations, etc.);
- Integration capabilities, in terms of:
- Ease of intra-organisational integration (intensity of integration tools, length of the hierarchical chain, etc.)
- Ease of inter-organisational interaction (reputation, exposure to cooperation agreements)
- Ease of inter-organisational integration (reputation, structure of past agreements).

For this point, as for the previous ones, the caution to adopt negotiation and design strategies aimed at gradual progress applies: starting from areas where it is easier to minimise inter-company differences, creating conditions of trust and awareness of the disparities that make the subsequent integration process smoother.

d. *The common propensity for co-design*. Co-design refers to the shared inclination among individuals or entities to actively participate and collaborate in the process of designing or shaping a particular project, product, or solution (Castañer et al., 2020). It signifies a willingness to engage in collective brainstorming, problem-solving, and decision-making, fostering a collaborative environment where diverse perspectives and expertise converge. Emphasising inclusivity and open communication, co-design encourages stakeholders to contribute their unique insights and creative inputs, ultimately leading to more innovative and effective outcomes (Nusir et al., 2021). By embracing this collaborative approach, organisations and communities can harness the power of collective intelligence, leveraging the diverse strengths and talents of their members to achieve common goals and address complex challenges with a unified vision (Durall et al, 2020). The common propensity for co-design not only enhances the quality and relevance of the final results but also promotes a sense of ownership and empowerment among participants, fostering stronger relationships and meaningful engagement in the pursuit of shared objectives (Hodson et al., 2023).

It is natural that this type of impasse can only be resolved to the extent that the partners give up their own established perspective on reading the problems and designing the solutions

II. Implementation Phase. This phase encompasses all the operations that allow the alliance to evolve from task definition to its implementation, laying the groundwork for result distribution. It is the natural outcome of what the partners have been able to produce during the previous phase, the effort to understand the inter-organisational distance, and the preparation of appropriate integration programmes and tools.

Factors that increase the likelihood of successful action in this phase are:

a. *Limited propensity for organisational replication*. The alliance is atypical compared to its originating partners. Typically, it has smaller dimensions and a more pressing need to innovate, be flexible, and demonstrate flexibility. At the same time, from the design phase, the partners (either due to an exaggerated desire for control or a pronounced difficulty in recognising organisational functioning patterns different from their own) tend to operate in a way that reduces the organisational differentiation of the alliance structure compared to the dominant internal organisational model. This is particularly evident in the case of alliances between large companies where the partners tend to burden the alliance with organisational redundancies (duplicating roles, aligning roles with internal ones, etc.) and operating rules (procedures, accounting criteria, etc.). By this way they create decision-making processes that are incongruent (in terms of timing and flexibility) with the needs for which the alliance was formed and its specific reference environment.

Although the desire behind these decisions is often to reduce the cost of integration with partners, it results in allocating resources to the alliance for activities that are not closely related to the objectives of cooperation but rather serve to maintain substantial uniformity in language with the procedures used by their respective parent companies.

At the same time, it is essential to highlight that the alliances, especially more structured ones (e.g., consortia, joint projects, joint ventures), must acquire a level of almost-autonomous organisational dignity. This is imperative for their future effective functioning. They must possess:

- *Self-reference,* Self-reference, meaning the possession of a psychological and cultural identity that allows them to learn (Golubickis and Macrae, 2022).

The term 'self-reference' in the context of alliances refers to the alliance's ability to develop and maintain its distinct identity, separate from the individual partner organisations. This identity includes the alliance's unique vision, mission, values, and culture, which collectively form its psychological and cultural identity. When an alliance possesses a strong sense of self-reference, it can effectively learn from its experiences, adapt to changing environments, and continuously improve its performance.

By having a clear identity, the alliance can better understand its strengths, weaknesses, opportunities, and threats (SWOT analysis) and use this knowledge to make informed decisions and strategic choices. Self-reference also enables the alliance to learn from both its successes and failures, fostering a culture of continuous improvement and innovation.

In practical terms, self-reference involves establishing effective communication channels, shared norms and values, and mechanisms for knowledge-sharing and collaboration among alliance members. It also requires the cultivation of a collaborative and learning-oriented mindset among alliance participants, encouraging them to actively contribute their insights and experiences to the collective learning process.

When alliances actively embrace self-reference and invest in developing their unique identity, they can become more resilient, adaptable, and successful in achieving their objectives (Durall et al., 2020). This self-referential capacity enhances their ability to navigate complexities, build trust among partners, and foster a cohesive and cooperative working environment. Furthermore, it empowers the alliance to identify opportunities for improvement and innovation, contributing to its long-term viability and competitiveness in a dynamic business landscape.

- *Autonomy,* meaning the ability to control sufficient resources and to act and react independently. This includes the capacity to dynamically define their own operational and organisational contents and boundaries. In the context of alliances, autonomy is a critical factor that enables the alliance to function effectively as a separate entity, distinct from its partner organisations. It refers to the alliance's capability to make independent decisions, allocate resources, and take actions aligned with its strategic objectives (De Man and Luvison, 2019). Autonomy is not about isolation or detachment from the partners, but rather about having the flexibility and authority to pursue its defined goals without being overly constrained by the individual interests of the partner organisations.

To achieve autonomy, alliances must establish clear governance structures, decision-making processes, and resource allocation mechanisms that allow them to operate independently whilst still maintaining effective collaboration with the partners. This includes defining the roles and responsibilities of each partner within the alliance and setting boundaries for decision-making authority. Autonomy also implies the ability to adapt and respond to changing circumstances and market conditions, allowing the alliance to seize opportunities and address challenges proactively (Kale and Singh, 2009).

By having autonomy, alliances can leverage their unique strengths and capabilities, unlocking the full potential of collaboration and co-creation. This independent agency empowers the alliance to pursue innovative strategies, explore new markets, and drive value for all participating partners (Kamalaldin et al., 2020). Moreover, autonomy enhances the alliance's ability to negotiate with external stakeholders, fostering credibility and trust in the market (Hodson et al., 2023).

- *Redundancy,* meaning the availability of resources exceeding the operational needs at an efficient steady-state (Buch, 2020). A redundant system can achieve greater dynamic efficiency since it has resources that can be diverted from day-to-day operations and directed towards learning (including knowledge transfer) and innovation (Durall et al., 2020). In the context of organisations and alliances, redundancy refers to having surplus resources beyond what is strictly required for regular operations. These surplus resources serve as a buffer, allowing the organisation or alliance to respond to unexpected challenges, changes in the environment, and opportunities for growth and innovation. By having redundancy, organisations can be more agile and resilient, as they have the capacity to adapt and learn from experiences without jeopardising their core operations.

Redundancy also plays a crucial role in facilitating learning and knowledge transfer within an alliance. The availability of surplus resources allows partners to dedicate time and effort to exploring new ideas, conducting research, and sharing knowledge with one another. This learning process fosters a culture of continuous improvement and innovation, enhancing the alliance's competitiveness and capacity to deliver value to its stakeholders.

However, it is essential to strike a balance in maintaining redundancy, as excessive redundancy can lead to inefficiencies and waste of resources. Organisations and alliances must carefully assess their actual needs and ensure that surplus resources are appropriately set for learning and innovation initiatives (Gehrisch and Süß, 2023).

b. *The limited inertial propensity of partners.* Every alliance has sponsors and opponents. Although a part of the negotiation process may have been dedicated to bringing the opponents to light (deal killers), rarely are all the inertias and resistances clearly visible during the initiation and design phase. An alliance is often an integral part of an internal power game within each individual partner: it shifts activities and budget allocations to the external context, creates phase competitors (as in the case of joint research and development laboratories/activities), fuels conflicts, and generates new evaluation parameters. All these factors can cause a kind of silent resistance to the smooth functioning of the joint initiative. To some extent, the inertial and resistance phenomenon is connected to what we have called negative collateral factors and is indirectly reinforced by the organisational replication propensity mentioned in the preceding paragraph. The study conducted by Killing demonstrates that the restraining force of the inertial propensity can be reduced by decreasing the degree of dependence of the operational units involved in the alliance on the rest of the organisation. By increasing their level of self-sufficiency, elevating the level of actual delegation, and enabling a better focus on their managers, for example, by operating with similar logics as those used in project-based activities.

c. *The long-term cooperative intention.* The keyword in developing alliances is commitment or cooperative intent (Buch, 2020). The cooperative intent aims to express the quality and quantity of collaboration that each partner is willing to offer. From a normative perspective, 'for cooperation to be considered efficient, it must contain as much cooperative intent from the participants as the amount of coordination required between the parties to achieve the expected outcome'. A joint venture created to develop a new technology through combined know-how needs more coordination and cooperation than one formed for collusive or process rationalisation purposes (Teece, 2014). The commitment assessment can happen at two levels: commitment to internationalisation and commitment to cooperation. The assessment and measurement of commitment can occur at two distinct levels:

- the level of commitment to internationalisation;
- the level of commitment to cooperation.

The commitment of the first type can be detected through usual indicators of international integration (Ohmae, 1987):

- Foreign direct investments (for localisation)
- Internationalised phases of the value chain (for localisation)
- Third-country managers (for localisation)/total management
- Host-country managers (for localisation)/total management
- Adaptation of products.

The commitment to cooperation, in turn, can be understood at three distinct levels:

- the level of attention to the cooperative instrument;
- the level of attention to the alliance task;
- the level of attention to the partner.

In a long-term perspective, however, the mutual commitment of the partners depends not only on the agreement itself. The outcome of a single initiative cannot disregard the search for support from the partners, considering how they navigate other tables and scenarios. An alliance has higher chances of success when integrated into a long-term development plan, where it interacts with other parallel initiatives.

d. *The minimisation of reliance on contracts as a control mechanism* is a key aspect. Regarding the level of detail in a good cooperation contract, there is no unanimous agreement. There might be echoes here of general principles about human behaviour and how individuals pursue their interests. Regardless of these, organisational common sense leads us to believe that the impossibility of forecasting conditions leads to prefer a more formalised forms of collaboration over simple market exchanges (Lumineau, 2017).

In recent literature, scholars have emphasised the importance of balancing formal contracts with relational governance mechanisms in alliances and collaborations. Whilst formal contracts are necessary to specify legal obligations and safeguard interests, they might not capture the complex interdependencies and uncertainties inherent in cooperative endeavours. Relational governance mechanisms, such as trust-building activities, regular communication, and shared values, play a crucial role in maintaining cooperative relationships and ensuring the commitment of partners beyond what can be explicitly stated in contracts.

Furthermore, overly detailed contracts might restrict the flexibility needed to adapt to changing circumstances and emergent opportunities. Collaborative ventures often involve dynamic and evolving environments, making it challenging to anticipate all possible contingencies and outcomes upfront.

Emphasising trust and cooperation in conjunction with formal contracts can foster a more robust and adaptive alliance framework (Galvin et al., 2021).

Preference for more formalised forms of collaboration over simple market exchanges would lead to preferring contracts aimed at establishing common frames of reference, deferring the choice of optimal conditions for their management to each specific event. At the same time, many joint venture managers emphasise the importance of having a detailed contract in place. This does not mean working solely based on the contract (a kind of 'cooperation strike'), but rather equipping themselves with a meticulous protective network, even though it might be eventually set aside, whilst indicating to the partner the possibility of sanctions for any evasive behaviour regarding the commitment made. Indeed, a cooperative relationship is based on the assumption of decisions and actions by the parties involved, far beyond what is established during the contractual phase, and an overly restrictive reliance on the contract signals an attitude distant from the desire for joint construction of results.

III. Redefinition phase. Due to the impossibility of exhaustively defining the contracts that bind the partners, those involved in alliances engage in an almost daily review of their own modus operandi and collaboration structure. Alongside this ongoing process of change, there are moments of profound transformation within the alliance. In addition to the institutional verification moments typically provided for in the contract, various factors may lead to these transformations, including:

- changes in the development trajectories of the partners.
- variations in strategies.
- changes in commitment.

These changes can arise from new threats/opportunities that emerge as the alliance evolves (new markets, new competitors, shifts in demand, etc.). The shifting objectives naturally have repercussions on the structures, operational mechanisms, and human resources engaged in the alliance, particularly in terms of:

- variations in the net workload of human resources.
- changes in the professional profiles of individuals.
- alterations in roles.
- adjustments in the contribution balances of the partners.
- variations in the configurations of governing bodies.
- changes in the responsibilities and composition of governing bodies.
- modifications in roles and connection methods.

In dynamic and ever-changing environments, alliances must adapt to new circumstances and evolving goals, necessitating constant assessment and adjustments to ensure continued success and effectiveness.

These variations can occur without threatening the survival of the alliance if certain conditions come into play:

- The existence of long-term reciprocal commitments or interests. Having time-bound constraints or commitments between partners, parallel to the one being considered, reduces the evasive inclination of the parties and raises its cost. Partners, therefore, have an incentive to invest in a network of joint initiatives, each of which can be seen as an almost-binding pledge for all the others.

- Organisational congruence. Even in the presence of strategic convergence, the likelihood of the parties going through the redefinition phase of the agreement is linked to their ability to align from an organisational perspective. Since the inter-organisational distance, i.e., the organisational languages of the partners, has been emphasised as an obstacle to success, the successful outcome of the change process presupposes that the preceding implementation phase has allowed the identification of effective integration models or, at the very least, a growing sensitivity to diversity.
- The presence of a dyadic view of specific manoeuvres. The probability of an alliance successfully navigating the redefinition phase depends on the partners' ability to view it as part of a larger framework, with an awareness of the collateral effects it has on the entire system of relationships between them, within each partner, and finally, in relation to other systems of inter-organisational relationships external to the focal one.
- The ability to leverage personal networking elements is crucial in forming successful alliances (Gulati, 1998). An alliance is not solely a contractual arrangement but is built on strong interpersonal relationships among the partnering individuals or entities (Kogut, 1990). A significant body of literature in the field has underscored the importance of ensuring coherence between the human profiles, that is, the individuals involved, and the professional profiles required for the cooperative relationship to thrive. This alignment between personal and professional attributes enhances communication, trust, and collaboration, ultimately contributing to the overall success of the alliance. Perrone (1990) observes:

"When dealing with informal agreements based on shared values and trusting relationships, there is a risk of attributing capabilities to the company as a whole that it does not inherently possess, but rather, can be induced in the actual actors of the relationship: the managers or employees who define the contents and manage the operations (p. 30)".

The significance of interpersonal relationships should govern a wide range of human resource management actions, both within the cooperative structure (as in the case of joint ventures) and within each partner company. In relationships between large and small companies, for instance, excessive personnel mobility from the larger company to interact with actors from the smaller company can destabilise the built-up relational trust. In every personnel manoeuvre within cooperative actions, there must be a consideration of the trade-off between internal interests (e.g., individual development and career) and the need for external trust.

Research, evaluation, negotiation, building, and maintaining trust are the stages of a complex process defining and sustaining inter-company alliances. It follows a temporal logic that progresses from adversarial to ally conditions, as the parties move towards convergence. This evolution is marked by the maturation of perceptual statuses that increasingly approach the state of relational trust. The possible interpretive frameworks also evolve: from a hostage system to a market exchange, the alliance transforms into a negotiating arena, culminating in a territory of free exchange between partners and a relatively stable social system within it.

4.7. The Alliance as an Organisational Alternative

It has been emphasised that alongside the numerous advantages it offers, an alliance is not without costs for the internal structure from which it draws material resources and knowledge and of which it absorbs, directly or indirectly, human resources and managerial time. Assessing the organisational cost of an alliance systematically is quite critical. On the one hand, many burdens are indirectly absorbed by the structure; on the other hand, a systematic budget of commitments should take into account items that are, to use the term, esoteric. For instance, costs related to reducing passive resistance within the line towards collaboration or governing manifestations of organisational xenophobia, costs that originate from the cultural origins of each company. To tackle the problem, a first approximation can be suggested by schematising the process of alliance implementation in terms of cost items generated, i.e., the type of resources absorbed along the phases that define the alliance process, identified as:

a. ideation and delineation of the alliance's implementation scheme;
b. alliance design and its internalisation within the partners;
c. governance and integration.

Each phase involves some categories of explicit cost, represented by the types of human/time resources absorbed. The first phase absorbs ideation resources, research resources, and negotiation resources.

The second phase includes design resources and legitimisation resources.

The third phase encompasses the absorption of performance, coordination, control, and interface resources.

There is no precise correlation between resource types and organisational positions, although it is plausible to expect that moving from the first to the third phase results in an increased involvement of the line in the alliance and, therefore, an increase in complexity in delivering these resources. Whilst the activities of the first two phases are part of the functions of strategic top management or central staff, and although they may also require a contribution from the line, they respond to explicit and unambiguous expectations towards those positions. In contrast, the third phase imposes an additional workload on the line beyond its usual objectives. This exceptional nature constitutes an even greater cost, as it conflicts with established expectations of efficiency and effectiveness towards the line from the higher levels of the organisation. It is evident that this condition of schizophrenic tension generates a zone of latent conflict towards cooperation, which can lead to the rejection of synergies, especially those that require learning efforts, or to refusal or resistance to providing the quantum required by the common structure.

To complete the conceptual schema of the organisational costs of an alliance, it is appropriate to consider three recurring sources of tension throughout the alliance building process: external-internal tensions towards the partner and the common structure, top-down and bottom-up tensions within the parent company, and tensions of organisational behaviour. The combination of these tensions accompanies the process, imposing an additional integration cost borne by the company's top management. The cost items can facilitate a more serene comparison between the organisation undertaking a alliance and the common structure when it begins to operate, reducing the cost and risk of rejection or, worse, passive and hidden resistance. Each cost category can be direct or indirect.

Directly absorbed resources are those allocated to the alliance on a full-time or part-time basis, such as individuals who pass completely or partially under the direct dependence of the alliance.

Indirect resources are those that, whilst consumed by the alliance, remain permanently at the partner's disposal. Indirect performance resources refer to all the services provided by the parent company to the alliance. In many cases, to avoid burdening the structure of the new organisation, some service areas are directly acquired from the partner. For these activities, the alliance pays the providing partner a share equivalent to the amount of time consumed, just as it would pay an external supplier.

Secondly, it is plausible that the alliance seeks to draw not only on the partner's direct delivery time but also on their expertise in the form of contacts with the outside world (consultants, banks, public and social organisations, etc.). Similarly to the previous resources, these are considered indirect performance resources since they absorb managerial time for mediation, building social relationships, and, above all, because they force parent companies to spend part of their credits with their stakeholders or accumulate social debts with them.

Within the alliance, coordination resources are also consumed, i.e., integration resources between the courses of action of the partners and those of the alliance, or between partners themselves. These resources can concern both the direct transaction between the parts of the system and the routing of information directed at the partner's internal structure to facilitate their interaction with the outside. For example, preparing reports for top management or critical functional directions, acquiring relevant information within the company, participating in boards, or other formal moments with the partner or joint venture general manager (JVGM).

The commitment of coordination required from the parent company is naturally increasing with the interdependence between the parts of the system, inter-company distance, and the level of differentiation useful for maximising partner contributions to the common structure. Although it is generally sorted by strategic top management or dedicated bodies within the structure, it is also true that the coordination effort permeates the line at all levels, to the extent that the relationship between the alliance and the parent company is mainly lateral (request for resources, solutions, consensus, etc.).

This implies that the volume of coordination resources absorbed by an alliance is typically very high and, at the same time, poorly predictable. Only partially, in fact, the intensity of optimal exchanges between the parts of the system can be predicted: environmental dynamism, desire for control, management of exceptions, and demand for extraordinary resources, all factors that influence the number and intensity of relationships between the common structure and parent companies, hence areas that provoke the consumption of coordination resources. To the extent that the action of the alliance draws physical or informative resources from the partner or vice versa, it also absorbs interface resources, expressed by the amount of time required to govern the transfer processes. Interface resources are properly indirect and concern the phases of negotiation and exchange of necessary information, for example, adjusting specifications or operational standards or reporting between the parties. They act as intermediaries both in transactions with the partner and with the alliance, serving as privileged interlocutors.

The last group of resources absorbed by the alliance is control resources. Control relationships occupy a significant space in the alliance system. They refer to both the partner and the alliance and can take direct and indirect forms. They are mostly direct concerning the alliance, acting as dedicated insiders. However, control resources are mostly absorbed indirectly: visits by company managers to the alliance, examples of auditing, time spent verifying the partner's reputation, and so on.

The combination of these resources constitutes a manifestation of the cost that the company must bear to fuel the alliance system. When a company frequently resorts to this tool, the indirect burden it bears can be extremely high, although mostly hidden. It is plausible to believe that the greater the indirect exposure of an organisation, the greater its resistance to the interference of the action resulting from the alliance with its current activity. On the other hand, prolonged exposure produces a learning effect to avoid its dispersion. To maintain this, the company must focus on rationalisation goals of the process and seek ways to maximise the benefits of collaboration. This once again confirms the importance of adopting appropriate structures and measures to support maintaining correct tension towards the cooperation area.

4.8 The Alliance as a Learning Potential

4.8.1 Some Insights on Learning. Every organisation learns from its mistakes and successes, deriving more suitable action models. A successful company stands out from a mediocre one because it uses its mistakes as a basis for correcting its future course of action (Hitt et al., 2013). Even in the case of alliances, the ability to learn from one's mistakes is an extremely important factor for the organisational success of the joint structure. However, the acquisition of knowledge, learning, is not free, and in the case of alliances, identifying mistakes and diagnosing solutions is made even more challenging by the multitude of factors that contribute to determining their performance (Heimeriks and Duysters, 2007). The alliance may fail due to incompatibility with the partner, the disappearance of an apparently favourable market, changing competitive conditions among and between partners, inadequate organisational design of the alliance, and the lack of understanding or incomplete comprehension of the benefits derived from it, and so on.

That said, learning organisations could develop both targeted programmes and suitable management systems. When an organisation repeatedly encounters a situation (such as an alliance), it generates methodologies to govern the most repetitive decisions, thus preventing wastage of managerial time resources (Hitt et al., 2013). Learning organisations also know that past models do not have perpetual validity (Senge, 1990). As Drucker observed: "*Part of learning consists in unlearning, that is, in reformulating those past behaviours that are no longer appropriate for the present*" (1987, p. 79). The author emphasised the importance of continuous learning and adaptability in the face of changing circumstances. The concept of 'unlearning' involves letting go of outdated knowledge or habits to make room for new and more relevant insights or behaviours. The correction of past behavioural patterns naturally requires that these patterns exist, that is, they are embedded within the organisation. It also requires that the organisation is prepared to perceive signals of change, meaning its members are incentivised to renew their reference models. Lastly, it necessitates the organisation to facilitate the learning of the new, both at the level of operational mechanisms (e.g., widespread information systems and involvement in decision-making processes) and at the structural level, by establishing change sensors that act as receivers and transmitters of stimuli for the more stable components of the system (Aldrich and Herker, 1977). Alongside experiential learning and learning based on successful past models (lower-level learning) (Lyles, 1988), the organisation is thus exposed to developmental processes that must relinquish experience and successful models (higher-level learning).

This second level of organisational learning operates through the construction of new paradigms, new values, and new skills (Starbuck, 1983). It necessarily entails both:

(a) unlearning past models;
(b) innovating and experimenting with new behavioural models.

Businesses that are capable of unlearning, that is, letting go of successful past models, are also better equipped to withstand the impact of environmental changes, adapt to them, and survive (Starbuck, 1983). The same applies when an organisation develops a history composed of countless unique episodes or those with sufficient traits of originality, where the past does not serve as a valid reference for the future. The ability to innovate and experiment is closely related to an organisation's willingness to unlearn: it leads to the development of new models of organisational behaviour that can cope with the evolution of the environment in which the business operates. There is also another learning approach that involves adopting new models of organisational behaviour through imitation. It is quite plausible that an organisation reproduces its behavioural models by stimulating newcomers to imitate veterans, as traditionally practiced in on-the-job learning. Naturally, this process can also be applied in inter-organisational encounters.

4.8.2 Areas of Learning for an Alliance. Every alliance encompasses mixed objectives: on one hand, creating synergies, and on the other, learning. The alliance between General Motors and Toyota at the California plant (NUMMI) aimed to achieve a certain output and facilitated GM's learning in producing small cars and taught Toyota how to manage a plant in the United States with American personnel and unique labour relations for a Japanese company. Since every alliance requires not only the application of production capabilities but also managerial methods, it is quite reasonable for each partner to seek to derive maximum learning from the other through shared experience. The maximisation of alliance benefits stems from an organisation's ability to be receptive to the knowledge generated by the joint venture and its skill in transforming it into its own benefit in product, process, and managerial improvements.

Learning curves in the management of inter-organisational alliances also develop on two other fronts. The first involves raising awareness within the stable component of the company of the additional workload required by the activation of an alliance and the direct and indirect benefits that can result from it. In many companies, resistance to collaboration arises because they feel deprived of resources without seeing a return. When this happens, resistance to external innovation (the 'not invented here' syndrome) undermines the deeper advantages of collaboration.

The second, of a more technical nature, concerns the maturation of specific interaction skills with the other parts of the system: partners and the alliance itself. It seems reasonable that a company with good experience in cooperation strategies will be better equipped to effectively and efficiently manage new relationships (Harrigan, 1985). Part of this process is individual, as the individuals directly involved in the alliance will develop superior expertise and greater sensitivity to interaction problems. Naturally, the more the organisation utilises these individuals, the higher the benefit it can derive from their past experiences. On the other hand, these same individuals must also be called upon to 'seed' their particular familiarity with the tool and the process, transferring methodologies to others and fostering the institutionalisation of useful rules and patterns. In this sense, learning becomes over time an asset of the entire organisation (Allinson, 1988). The learning plans within an inter-company alliance are diverse. Particularly, they involve: (a) learning the method of cooperation itself; (b) learning partner knowledge; and (c) learning receptivity towards novelty and external factors (Allinson, 1988). A company with stronger learning capabilities can derive greater overall benefits from alliances by:

a. reducing inter-organisational frictions, increasing partner information exchange, and potential knowledge implementation;
b. decreasing intra-organisational tensions and resistance, enhancing awareness of agreement benefits, and willingness to allocate resources and competencies;
c. enhancing sensitivity to novelty stimuli, reducing aversion to assimilating knowledge gained from the alliance.

From this concise learning agenda, it is evident that organisational learning is not without purpose. Resistance to learning is also resistance to collaborative efforts, and the lack of support for alliances from the stable component of the structure is influenced by inadequate endorsement from the organisation's leadership, additional costs incurred by the line, and a vague perception of potential advantages. The company's adaptation to cooperative tools, thus, necessitates:

- raising the organisation's awareness of the burdens arising from the alliance,
- legitimising its functions, full organisational involvement concerning structural articulation, operational mechanisms, and
- implementing measures to prevent resistance to cooperation, and fostering a widespread attitude toward learning.

4.8.3 The Feedback Factors. The transfer of technologies or managerial competencies generates, for the exposed company, a complex system of reverberation and feedback interactions, even on those parts of the organisation that are not immediately exposed to such transfer actions (Agarwal and Helfat, 2009). These feedback and reverberation elements affect the structure of the transferring company, its strategy, its identity, as well as the ways in which its daily operations are carried out. These elements can be summarised under the concise expression of feedback factors. These factors concern eight areas:

a. organisational flexibility;
b. formalisation of knowledge;
c. business scope;
d. renewal of the company's image;
e. technological scope
f. diversification of managerial practices;
g. development of new managerial systems and decentralised decision-making processes;
h. renewal of thc company's identity (Agarwal and Helfat, 2009).

a. Organisational flexibility. It is a crucial aspect that companies must consider when engaging in joint ventures. Joint ventures often bring about new collaborative projects and initiatives, which can lead to an additional workload for the involved organisations. Whilst this increased workload may be temporary, it poses challenges for the participating companies in terms of resource allocation and management. In such cases, the traditional approach of expanding the organisational structure to accommodate the increased workload is not suitable. Creating new departments or hiring additional staff could lead to unnecessary fixed costs, especially when the demand is expected to be transient. Therefore, organisations are compelled to seek alternative strategies that enable them to adapt efficiently to the changing circumstances without burdening the company with long-term expenses.

To address these challenges, companies are encouraged to adopt solutions that prioritise flexibility in the application of resources. One effective approach is to enhance the capacity of existing support functions within the organisation. By empowering these support functions and providing them with the necessary skills and training, companies can leverage their potential to handle the additional workload effectively.

Furthermore, widening the skillset of support functions not only enables them to contribute more substantially to the joint venture but also fosters adaptability in handling diverse tasks. This multifunctional approach ensures that resources can be efficiently allocated and redirected as needed, depending on the demands of the joint venture projects.

b. The formalisation of knowledge. The formalisation of knowledge is another critical factor in the context of alliances and joint ventures. Although the knowledge involved in these collaborative endeavours is often associated with team efforts (Teece, 2014), it tends to be concentrated in the hands of a select few individuals within the organisation. This concentration of knowledge, commonly referred to as 'know-how', can present challenges for the sharing and dissemination of vital expertise across the alliance. One of the key characteristics of know-how is its limited degree of codification. Unlike explicit knowledge, which can be easily articulated and documented, know-how is often tacit and deeply rooted in the experience and intuition of those possessing it. Consequently, the transfer of such knowledge becomes a complex task, as it requires not only effective communication channels but also a deep understanding of the context and nuances that surround the expertise.

The standardisation of know-how is also a significant challenge in collaborative ventures. Given its tacit nature, know-how may not have well-defined and uniform procedures for application. Instead, it relies heavily on the unique experiences and approaches of individuals. Consequently, attempts to standardise know-how can encounter resistance and may be met with scepticism, particularly if the standardisation process overlooks the value of individual contributions and experience-based learning.

Moreover, the diffusion of knowledge within the alliance often follows irregular and voluntary patterns. Whilst some elements of know-how may naturally spread through informal networks and interactions, there might not be a structured approach to ensure widespread dissemination. This lack of systematic knowledge-sharing can hinder the efficient transfer of critical expertise, leading to suboptimal outcomes for the joint venture.

Another aspect that deserves attention is the continuous updating of knowledge. Since know-how is often based on practical experience, it may lack systematic criteria for regular updates and improvements. This absence of a structured approach to keeping the knowledge relevant and up-to-date can lead to missed opportunities and hinder the growth potential of the alliance.

However, recognising the primary nature of alliances as vehicles for knowledge transfer, proactive efforts towards better systematisation of know-how can have profound positive impacts on the involved companies. By investing in ways to organise internal knowledge and make it more explicit, companies can enhance their ability to leverage their own expertise effectively. Furthermore, such efforts also facilitate the systematisation, standardisation, and dissemination of knowledge, not only within the alliance but also throughout the entire organisation. Therefore, the formalisation of knowledge, especially in the context of alliances and joint ventures, is a complex undertaking. The inherently tacit nature of know-how requires innovative approaches to facilitate effective communication and transfer. Emphasising systematic efforts for standardisation, diffusion, and continuous updating of knowledge can significantly contribute to the success of collaborative ventures and strengthen the capacity of participating companies to harness and leverage their collective expertise.

c. *The broadening of the company's scope of action.* It is a significant outcome resulting from its exposure to alliances and joint ventures. Collaborative ventures bring together diverse expertise, resources, and perspectives, which can lead to transformative changes in the company's products and market reach.

One noticeable impact of alliances on products is the potential for product improvements and innovations. Through collaborative efforts, companies can exchange valuable knowledge and best practices, leading to the optimisation of product packaging. Packaging plays a crucial role in attracting consumers and differentiating products from competitors. By leveraging the expertise of alliance partners, companies can design more appealing and customer-centric packaging, enhancing the overall value proposition of their products.

Furthermore, the technical documentation related to products can also undergo refinements and adaptations as a result of collaborations. Companies can learn from their partners' experiences and adopt more efficient and effective approaches to convey technical information to customers and end-users. Clear and comprehensive technical documentation can boost customer satisfaction and lead to increased loyalty and trust in the company's products.

The collaborative environment of alliances encourages the exploration of new commercial philosophies and strategies. Companies can learn from the marketing and sales practices of their partners and adopt successful techniques to expand their customer base and increase market share. The exposure to different markets and customer segments through the alliance can inspire fresh approaches to marketing and sales, ultimately enhancing the company's competitiveness in the industry.

Additionally, alliances often result in the expansion of certain functional areas, particularly the technical ones. Companies can enhance their technical capabilities by leveraging the expertise of their alliance partners. For example, access to specialised technical knowledge and resources can accelerate product development cycles, leading to the introduction of new and innovative products to the market. This expansion of technical capabilities can open up opportunities to target new customer needs and demands.

The broadening of the company's scope of action not only pertains to product-related improvements but also extends to market expansion. Collaborative ventures enable companies to access new markets and customer segments through their alliance partners. Establishing stable and reliable relationships with these partners facilitates market penetration in regions or industries where the company may have had limited presence previously. This strategic alliance-driven market expansion can lead to increased market share, revenue growth, and overall business success.

Therefore, the exposure of a company to alliances and joint ventures leads to a multifaceted broadening of its scope of action. It stimulates product improvements, refines technical documentation, fosters the adoption of innovative commercial philosophies, and strengthens technical capabilities. Moreover, the establishment of stable alliances enables companies to explore new markets and seize growth opportunities that may have been otherwise challenging to access. Overall, embracing collaborative ventures strategically enhances the company's competitiveness, market reach, and potential for sustained success in a dynamic and ever-evolving business landscape.

d. The renewal of the company's image. Alliances are frequently utilised to breathe new life into the image of a company, both within its domestic market and on an international scale. By engaging in strategic alliances, a company displays its capacity to embrace cooperation, its willingness to engage in negotiation and compromise, and its commitment to transferring its valuable knowledge and expertise.

An alliance serves as a testament to the company's adaptability and openness to collaboration, portraying it as a forward-thinking and innovative player in its industry. This positive image can resonate with customers, investors, and other stakeholders, enhancing the company's reputation and creating new opportunities for growth and market expansion.

Furthermore, the association with reputable and successful partners through alliances can significantly boost the company's credibility and trustworthiness. Collaborating with established and respected organisations reflects positively on the company's capabilities and can attract potential customers and investors who may have been hesitant to engage with the company independently.

The renewal of the company's image through alliances is not limited to the external perception alone; it can also have a profound impact on the company's internal culture and employee morale. Successful collaborations instil a sense of pride and accomplishment among employees, fostering a culture of innovation, collaboration, and continuous improvement. This, in turn, can attract and retain top talent, further contributing to the company's long-term success.

The expansion of the technology's scope of action. When alliances involve the transfer of technology, significant benefits can be expected, in terms of both the company's implementation capabilities and advancements in the core technology being transferred. The collaborative exchange of knowledge between partners can lead to a synergistic effect, where each partner gains access to valuable insights, resources, and expertise that accelerate their technological progress.

In cases where knowledge sharing is mutual and the alliance aims to develop a technological symbiosis, the potential for substantial advancements is even greater. Through mutual learning and joint development efforts, the partners can create novel solutions, products, or services that leverage the strengths of each party, resulting in a shared technological growth that benefits all involved.

Moreover, alliances can lead to opportunities for technology adaptation and customisation. When applying one's technology to address the specific needs expressed by the partners, the company may need to adapt its original technology to suit the context of the collaborative project fully. This process of adaptation often stimulates innovative thinking and problem solving, encouraging the company to explore new possibilities and expand the potential applications of its technology.

Overall, the expansion of the technology's scope of action through alliances contributes to the company's competitive edge and long-term sustainability. By engaging in strategic alliances and technology transfers, companies can tap into new markets, enhance their product offerings, and stay at the forefront of innovation in their industry. Embracing collaborative ventures becomes a strategic imperative for companies seeking to thrive in a rapidly evolving technological landscape.

e. The diversification of management systems. In numerous instances, the engagement in inter-company cooperation agreements has led to an immediate increase in awareness and attentiveness towards risk analysis. The collaborative nature of such alliances necessitates a thorough understanding of potential risks and uncertainties that may arise during joint endeavours. As a result, companies involved in these alliances tend to develop a more comprehensive and proactive approach to risk management, which can enhance their ability to navigate challenges and seize opportunities effectively.

Moreover, the exposure to diverse management practices and organisational approaches through alliances presents an opportunity for companies to explore innovative strategies for personnel management, work organisation, and organisational structure. Collaborating with partners from different cultural backgrounds, industries, or operational models can offer valuable insights and fresh perspectives that challenge conventional management norms. This exposure encourages companies to embrace adaptability and creativity in devising customised management approaches that align with the unique needs and goals of the joint projects.

The exchange of management methodologies with alliance partners serves as a valuable source of benchmarking and evaluation. When companies compare their own management systems with those of their partners, they gain a deeper understanding of their own strengths, weaknesses, and potential areas for improvement. This constructive comparison fosters a continuous learning process, prompting companies to reassess their existing practices and adapt them to best practices identified within the collaborative venture.

Furthermore, the exposure to diverse management systems encourages a shift from reliance solely on experiential knowledge to a more evidence-based and analytical decision-making approach. By witnessing the methodologies implemented by their alliance partners, companies can evaluate the effectiveness and efficiency of various management practices. This evidence-based evaluation can lead to a more thoughtful and data-driven adoption of management strategies, reducing the reliance on outdated or unexamined practices.

Additionally, the experience of collaborating with partners with different management systems can foster a culture of openness and receptiveness to change within the company. As employees interact with diverse teams, they become more adaptable and open to new ideas and approaches. This cultural transformation can result in a more dynamic and agile organisation, capable of navigating complex business landscapes with resilience and innovation.

Therefore, the diversification of management systems through inter-company cooperation agreements offers numerous advantages for companies. Beyond enhancing risk analysis capabilities, it paves the way for innovative management philosophies and practices. By embracing diversity and learning from their partners, companies can create a more agile, evidence-based, and open organisational culture that can respond effectively to challenges and drive sustained success in today's ever-changing business environment.

f. The contribution to new organisational and decision-making solutions. The contribution to new organisational and decision-making solutions. Exposure to alliances not only brings about collaboration between different companies but also triggers the need for innovative organisational and decision-making approaches within each participating organisation. The nature of joint ventures requires a level of crosscutting and lateral integration that may be uncommon in traditional organisational structures.

Firstly, within the alliance, resources from various functional areas must be brought together to function as an autonomous and cohesive unit. This integration of diverse expertise, skills, and perspectives can be challenging, as individuals from different backgrounds and departments must align their efforts towards a common, yet often uncertain, goal. The pressure to deliver results and meet shared objectives is typically higher in the context of alliances, as the success of the collaborative project depends on effective coordination and cooperation between the partner organisations.

Secondly, the expertise and knowledge required for the successful execution of the cooperative project may not be centralised within a single department or team. Instead, critical insights and competencies may be distributed across different parts of the organisation. As a result, effective communication and knowledge sharing become essential to ensure that the collective knowledge of the organisation is leveraged optimally. Moreover, in a joint venturing scenario, there is often a greater need for decentralisation of decision-making. The strategic leadership may choose to empower teams and individuals involved in the alliance to make timely and informed decisions independently. This decentralisation allows for faster responses to challenges and opportunities, without being overwhelmed by excessive bureaucracy and top-down approvals. However, it also requires a robust communication framework to ensure alignment with the overall strategic direction and objectives of the company.

Furthermore, joint venturing brings together individuals with different perspectives, interests, and goals. This diversity can lead to divergent opinions and pressures within the collaborative project. As a result, effective coordination mechanisms and conflict resolution strategies are crucial to managing differences and maintaining a positive working relationship between the partner organisations.

To address these complexities and ensure successful outcomes, companies engaged in alliances must invest in building effective coordination mechanisms. This involves establishing clear communication channels, defining roles and responsibilities, and fostering a culture of mutual respect and trust. Emphasising the importance of teamwork, flexibility, and adaptability within the organisation becomes essential to navigate the challenges and seize the opportunities presented by the alliance.

Therefore, exposure to alliances creates a unique set of organisational and decision-making challenges for the participating companies. Embracing cross-cutting, lateral integration, and decentralisation becomes critical to enable effective collaboration and knowledge sharing within the alliance. By investing in robust coordination mechanisms and fostering a collaborative culture, companies can unlock the full potential of joint venturing, driving innovation, and achieving collective success in the dynamic and competitive business landscape.

g. The renewal of the company's identity. Although an alliance is operationally managed by middle management, it requires support from the top leadership to legitimise the stable structure and have an impact on the company's culture. This impact is mainly manifested by integrating the culture of cooperation within the organisation's existing culture. Additionally, the successes or failures of cooperative actions become part of the company's history, influencing its future behaviour.

Rarely are people in the company indifferent to the lessons from past experiences that permeate and shape current and future choices. They can alter the desire for control, amplify or diminish unwarranted fear of opportunistic behaviour, and modify the trade-off between the desire for cooperation and competition. This is particularly evident in the collaborative experiences of companies. For example, Truck waited almost ten years before embarking on its second cooperative venture after having learned from several missteps in its first attempt. The financial setback due to the partner's lack of interest and the complete failure of the alliance's fundamental strategy led to an unavoidable orientation towards control – expressed through majority shareholding and key position control – and substantial scepticism towards any additional requests for know-how or financial and managerial support within the common structure.

Secondly, exposure to alliances brings about a change in the company's attitude towards cultural differences, fostering greater tolerance for diversity. Finally, it contributes to enriching people's willingness in terms of mobility and dynamism, acceptance of risk, and a preference for lateral and social relationships over hierarchical and formal ones.

Because of these changes, the company's identity evolves, adapting to new cooperative and collaborative approaches, and becoming more open to embracing diverse perspectives and attitudes. This transformation enhances the company's adaptability, resilience, and ability to seize opportunities in an increasingly interconnected and global business environment. The lessons learned from previous alliance experiences become an essential part of the company's learning and growth process, shaping its strategic decisions and cultural orientation for the future.

The set of feedback factors positively influences the company exposed to agreements. It represents an additional value compared to the benefits encoded in the definition of the alliance's pay-offs. Although this may seem challenging, or even unnecessary, quantifying these factors is a useful process to strengthen the collaborative inclination of people within the company. At the same time, one must not overlook that alongside the hidden benefits, an alliance may also entail disadvantages (negative counter-effects) and a series of indirect costs, often overlooked by decision-makers and negotiators. Difficult, potentially conflicting, costly, and at high risk of rejection: international alliances appear to the observer as a crucible of interconnected and difficult-to-solve problems. At the same time, the judgment cannot be dissimilar when considering go-it-alone strategies: difficult, costly, at high risk of internal rejection and rejection by the host country. The comparison between the two classes of international development strategies highlights that it remains a process not devoid of obstacles. However, at the same time, a company must choose the most convenient solution without preconceptions, considering multiple aspects:

- speed of entry into the target country;
- overcoming institutional and structural barriers to entry;
- minimising the necessary structure costs for entry;
- maximising the return on results following entry and accelerating their achievement;
- minimising the risks of country system rejection;
- maximising learning, both related to the target country and international phenomena in general.

The pros and cons of an international cooperation strategy have been analysed in this work with the aim of highlighting both the feasibility of the approach and the need not to overestimate its potential and underestimate its costs and difficulties. In particular, the less obvious implications (in terms of cost and advantage) of the cooperative approach have been emphasised, with the goal of providing a more precise and operational basis for comparison between alternative strategies of international development.

4.9 Alliance Strategies vis-à-vis Digitalisation and Industry 4.0

In today's rapidly evolving business landscape, characterised by the ongoing digital transformation and the advent of Industry 4.0, strategic alliances have gained paramount importance as a means for companies to adapt, innovate, and stay competitive in the global market. The emergence of digital technologies has disrupted traditional business models, necessitating a profound shift in how organisations approach their strategies. As companies strive to leverage the opportunities presented by digitalisation and Industry 4.0, alliances have proven to be a crucial vehicle for unlocking new growth avenues, sharing knowledge and expertise, and enhancing overall competitiveness. One of the key reasons why alliances are sought in the context of digitalisation and Industry 4.0 is the need for complementary capabilities. Digital technologies have permeated every aspect of business operations, from data analytics and artificial intelligence to the Internet of Things (IoT) and blockchain. However, companies may not possess all the necessary skills and resources in-house to fully exploit the potential of these technologies. Collaborating with other companies, each specialising in different aspects of digitalisation, allows them to pool their expertise, access cutting-edge technologies, and jointly develop innovative solutions that would be challenging to achieve alone (Bleeke and Ernst, 1995). Additionally, digitalisation and Industry 4.0 have expanded the scope of value chains, driving companies to explore new markets and territories. Strategic alliances enable businesses to establish a global footprint by partnering with companies already established in foreign markets. These alliances provide local market knowledge, distribution channels, and customer insights, facilitating swift market entry and reducing the risks associated with international expansion (Lehmann-Ortega and Schoettl, 2005).

Furthermore, the accelerated pace of technological change necessitates rapid adaptation and learning. In the face of disruptive technologies, alliances allow companies to enhance their learning agility by sharing best practices, conducting joint research and development, and staying at the forefront of industry trends. Collaborating with partners enables companies to mitigate the risks associated with experimentation and early-stage technology adoption, as well as fosters a culture of continuous innovation (Sambharya and Musteen, 2014). However, whilst strategic alliances offer significant benefits in the digital era, they also present challenges that need to be carefully addressed. Chief among these is ensuring data security and protection. As digital technologies heavily rely on data exchange, partnering companies must establish robust data governance frameworks, adhere to stringent privacy regulations, and establish trust to safeguard sensitive information (Haksar et al., 2021). Moreover, maintaining alignment among partners' digital strategies and goals is critical for the success of alliances. Divergent objectives or misaligned technological trajectories can lead to conflicts and hinder progress. Effective communication and a clear understanding of each partner's contribution and expected outcomes are crucial to overcome such hurdles.

In addition to the opportunities and challenges mentioned earlier, strategic alliances in the context of digitalisation and Industry 4.0 also provide a means for companies to share the financial burden of investing in expensive technologies and research. Implementing digital transformation and adopting cutting-edge technologies can be capital-intensive endeavours. By forming alliances, companies can pool financial resources and share the costs of technology acquisition, infrastructure development, and research initiatives (Amin and Boamah, 2023). This collaborative approach not only reduces individual financial risks but also accelerates the pace of technological adoption, enabling companies to gain a competitive edge faster.

Moreover, strategic alliances facilitate access to a diverse talent pool and foster a culture of collaboration and learning. In the digital age, talent with specialised digital skills, such as data scientists, AI experts, and cyber security professionals, is in high demand. By partnering with other companies, companies can tap into a broader range of expertise and attract top digital talent, thus enhancing their ability to innovate and stay ahead in the digital race.

In certain industries, the rapid convergence of technologies has blurred traditional sector boundaries, leading to the emergence of new business models and ecosystems. In response to this trend, companies are increasingly forming cross-industry alliances to create innovative solutions that transcend their traditional domains. For instance, the automotive and technology industries are collaborating to develop autonomous vehicles, bringing together expertise in mobility and artificial intelligence (Song et al., 2003). These cross-industry alliances allow companies to capitalise on new market opportunities, access untapped customer segments, and pioneer novel product offerings. Nevertheless, successful digital alliances require effective management and governance structures. To ensure alignment and coordination among partners, clear roles, responsibilities, and decision-making processes must be established. Frequent communication and monitoring mechanisms are essential to address emerging challenges and maintain flexibility in an ever-changing digital landscape.

It is also worth noting that the emergence of digital technologies has led to the rise of platform ecosystems, which create new possibilities for collaborative innovation. Companies can now participate in platform-based alliances where they share data, APIs, and resources to co-create value and access a broader ecosystem of customers and partners. These digital platform alliances enable companies to foster network effects, scale their operations rapidly, and tap into new revenue streams.

In conclusion, the digital era has revolutionised the way companies approach strategic alliances by bringing opportunities and challenges for businesses worldwide. Leveraging on digitalisation and Industry 4.0 technologies, strategic alliances have emerged as a potent tool to navigate this rapidly changing landscape by fostering collaboration, sharing resources, and leveraging complementary capabilities. Alliances offer a range of benefits, including complementary capabilities, global market access, enhanced learning agility, cost-sharing, access to talent, and the ability to explore cross-industry collaborations. By forming alliances, companies can access the expertise and technologies necessary to capitalise on digital opportunities, expand their global presence, and foster a culture of innovation. However, forming and achieving successful alliances in the digital era requires a careful attention and approach to address challenges related to data security, goal alignment, financial burden sharing, talent acquisition, governance and effective communication. By embracing alliances as part of their digitalisation strategies, companies can position themselves at the forefront of innovation, competitive advantage and secure sustainable growth in the digital age.

REFERENCES

Agarwal, R., & Helfat, C. E. (2009). Strategic Renewal of Organisations. *Organization Science*, *20*(2), 281–293. https://www.jstor.org/stable/25614656. doi:10.1287/orsc.1090.0423

Aiyar, S., Chen, J., Ebeke, C. H., Garcia-Saltos, R., Gudmundsson, T., Ilyina, A., Kangur, A., Kunaratskul, T., Rodriguez, S. L., Ruta, M., Schulze, T., Soderberg, G., & Trevino, J. P. (2023). *Geoeconomic Fragmentation and the Future of Multilateralism*. International Monetary Fund. doi:10.5089/9798400229046.006

Aldrich, H., & Herker, D. (1977). Boundary Spanning Roles and Organisation Structure. *Academy of Management Review*, *2*(2), 217–230. doi:10.2307/257905

Aldrich, H. E. (1979). *Organisations and Environment*. Prentice Hall.

Allinson, G. D. (1988). Imitation and Innovation: The Transfer of Western Organisational Patterns to Meiji Japan. *Business History Review, 62*(4), 745+. https://link.gale.com/apps/doc/A8190667/AONE?u=googlescholar&sid=bookmark-AONE&xid=6219e073

Amin, G. A., & Boamah, M. I. (2023). Modeling business partnerships: A data envelopment analysis approach. *European Journal of Operational Research*, *305*(1), 329–337. doi:10.1016/j.ejor.2022.05.036

Anderson, E., & Gatignon, H. (1986). Modes of Foreign Entry: A Transaction Cost Analysis and Propositions. *Journal of International Business Studies*, *17*(3), 1–26. doi:10.1057/palgrave.jibs.8490432

Balcet, G. (1989). *Economia dell'impresa multinazionale*. Giappichelli.

Barkema, H. G., Chen, X. P., George, G., Luo, Y., & Tsui, A. S. (2015). West Meets East: New Concepts and Theories. (2015). *Academy of Management Journal*, *58*(2), 460–479. doi:10.5465/amj.2015.4021

Bartlett, C., & Ghoshal, S. (1990). The multinational corporation as an interorganisational network. *Academy of Management Review*, *15*(4), 603–625. doi:10.2307/258684

Beamish, P. (1988). *Multinational joint ventures in developing countries*. Routledge.

Bhawuk, D., & Brislin, R. (1992). The Measurement of Intercultural Sensitivity Using the Concept of Individualism and Collectivism. *International Journal of Intercultural Relations*, *16*(4), 413–436. doi:10.1016/0147-1767(92)90031-O

Bleeke, J. A., & Ernst, D. (1995). Is Your Strategic Alliance Really a Sale. *Harvard Business Review*, *13*, 97–105.

Castañer, X., & Oliveira, N. (2020). Collaboration, Coordination, and Cooperation Among Organisations: Establishing the Distinctive Meanings of These Terms Through a Systematic Literature Review. *Journal of Management*, *46*(6), 965–1001. doi:10.1177/0149206320901565

Clegg, S., & Wilson, F. (1990). Power, Technology and Flexibility in Organisations. *The Sociological Review, 38*(1, suppl), 223–273. doi:10.1111/j.1467-954X.1990.tb03354.x

Cohen, M. D., March, J. C., & Olsen, J. P. (1976). *Ambiguity and Choice in Organisations*. Universitet Forlaget.

Contractor, F. J., & Lorange, P. (1988). *Cooperative Strategies in International Business*. Lexington Books.

Cuervo-Cazurra, A., & Genc, M. (2008). Article. *Journal of International Business Studies, 39*(6), 957-979.

Davis, P., & Stern, D. (1988). Adaptation, Survival, and Growth of the Family Business: An Integrated Systems Perspective. *Family Business Review, 1*(1), 69–84. doi:10.1111/j.1741-6248.1988.00069.x

De Bari, F. (1990). Counter trade & offset: un approccio efficace ai paesi dell'est e PVS. *Economia e Management,* 15.

de Man, A. P., & Luvison, D. (2019). Collaborative business models: Aligning and operationalizing alliances. *Business Horizons, 62*(4), 473–482. doi:10.1016/j.bushor.2019.02.004

Decastri, M. (1984). *Organizzazione e cultura dell'innovazione in impresa*. Giuffrè.

Decastri, M., Buonocore, F., Battini, S., & Gagliarducci, F. (2020). *Organisational Development in Public Administration: The ltalian Way*. Palgrave Mc Millan.

Doz, Y., & Prahalad, C. K. (1986). Controlled Variety: A Challenge for Human Resource Management in the MNC. *Human Resource Management, 25*(1), 55–71. doi:10.1002/hrm.3930250105

Drucker, P. (1974). *Management Tasks, Responsibilities and Practices*. Harper & Row.

Durall, E., Bauters, M., Hietala, I., Leinonen, T., & Kapros, E. (2020). Co-creation and co-design in technology- enhanced learning: Innovating science learning outside the classroom. *Interaction Design and Architecture(s)*. . doi:10.55612/s-5002-042-010

Dyer, J. H., & Singh, H. (1998). The Relational View: Cooperative Strategy and Sources of Interorganisational Competitive Advantage. *Academy of Management Review, 23*(4), 660–679. doi:10.2307/259056

Dymsza, W. A. (1988). Successes and failures of joint ventures in developing countries: Lessons from experience. In F. J. Contractor & P. Lorange (Eds.), *Cooperative strategies in international business*. Lexington Books.

Eisenhardt, K. M. (1989). Building Theories from Case Study Research. *Academy of Management Review, 14*(4), 532–550. doi:10.2307/258557

Eriksson, K., Johanson, J., Majkgård, A., & Sharma, D.D. (2015). Experiential Knowledge and Cost in the Internationalization Process. In Knowledge, Networks and Power. Palgrave Macmillan. doi:10.1057/9781137508829_2

Etzioni, A. (1968). Social Analysis and Social Action. *The American Behavioral Scientist, 12*(1), 31–33. doi:10.1177/000276426801200107

Galvin, P., Tywoniak, S., & Sutherland, J. (2021). Collaboration and opportunism in megaproject alliance contracts: The interplay between governance, trust and culture. *International Journal of Project Management, 39*(4), 394–405. doi:10.1016/j.ijproman.2021.02.007

Gammeltoft, P., & Cuervo-Cazurra, A. (2021). Enriching internationalization process theory: Insights from the study of emerging market multinationals. *Journal of International Management, 27*(3), 100884. Advance online publication. doi:10.1016/j.intman.2021.100884

Gehrisch, M. G., & Süß, S. (2023). Organisational behaviour in international strategic alliances and the relation to performance–a literature review and avenues for future research. *Management Review Quarterly, 73*(3), 1045–1107. doi:10.1007/s11301-022-00268-7

Geringer, J., & Hebert, L. (1989). Control and Performance of International Joint Ventures. *Journal of International Business Studies, 20*(2), 235–254. doi:10.1057/palgrave.jibs.8490359

Goldenberg, S. (1988). *Hands across the Ocean: Managing Joint Ventures with a Spotlight on China and Japan*. Harvard Business School Press.

Golubickis, M., & Macrae, C. N. (2022). Sticky me: Self-relevance slows reinforcement learning. *Cognition, 227*, 105207. Advance online publication. doi:10.1016/j.cognition.2022.105207 PMID:35752015

Gomes-Casseres, B. (1990). Firm Ownership Preferences and Host Government Restrictions: An Integrated Approach. *Journal of International Business Studies, 21*(1), 1–22. doi:10.1057/palgrave.jibs.8490324

Gorbis, M. & Yorke, K. (1986). Strategic Partnerships: A New Corporate Response. *Business Intelligence Program, 73.*

Gorbis, M., & Yorke, K. (1986). *Strategic Partnership: A New Corporate Response*. SRI International.

Gulati, R., Wohlgezogen, F., & Zhelyazkov, P. (2012). The Two Facets of Collaboration: Cooperation and Coordination in Strategic Alliances. *The Academy of Management Annals, 6*(1), 1–53. doi:10.5465/19416520.2012.691646

Guth, W. D., & MacMillan, I. C. (1986). Strategy Implementation Versus Middle Management Self-Interest. *Strategic Management Journal, 7*(4), 313–327. doi:10.1002/smj.4250070403

Haksar, V., Carrière-Swallow, Y., Giddings, A., Islam, E., Kao, K., Kopp, E., & Quirós-Romero, G. (2021). *Toward a Global Approach to Data in the Digital Age, Staff Discussion Note, SDN/2021/005*. International Monetary Fund.

Harrigan, K. R. (1985). *Strategies for joint ventures*. Lexington Books.

Harris, P., & Moran, R. (1979). *Managing Cultural! Differences*. Gulf Publishing Company.

Hedlund, H. (1984). Organisation In-Between: The Evolution of the Mother-Daughter Structure of Managing Foreign Subsidiaries in Swedish mncs. *Journal of International Business Studies, 15*(2), 109–123. doi:10.1057/palgrave.jibs.8490485

Heenan, D. A., & Perlmutter, H. W. (1979). *Multinational Organisation Development*. Addison-Wesley.

Heimeriks, K. H., & Duysters, G. (2007). Alliance Capability as a Mediator between Experience and Alliance Performance: An Empirical Investigation into the Alliance Capability Development Process. *Journal of Management Studies*, *44*(1), 25–49. doi:10.1111/j.1467-6486.2006.00639.x

Hennart, F. (1988). A transaction costs theory of equity joint ventures. *Strategic Management Journal*, *9*(4), 361–374. doi:10.1002/smj.4250090406

Hodson, E., Svanda, A., & Dadashi, N. (2023). Whom do we include and when? participatory design with vulnerable groups. *CoDesign*, *19*(4), 269–286. doi:10.1080/15710882.2022.2160464

Hofstede, G. (1985). The Interaction between National and Organisational Value Systems. *Journal of Management Studies*, *22*(4), 347–357. doi:10.1111/j.1467-6486.1985.tb00001.x

Hutzschenreuter, T., Matt, T., & Kleindienst, I. (2020). Going subnational: A literature review and research agenda. *Journal of World Business, 55*. DOI:. . doi:101076

Javaid, M., Haleem, A., Pratap Singh, R., Suman, R., & Santibañez Gonzalez, E. (2022). Understanding the adoption of Industry 4.0 technologies in improving environmental sustainability. *Sustainable Operations and Computers*, *3*, 203–217. doi:10.1016/j.susoc.2022.01.008

JETRO. (1989). *A Survey on successful cases of Foreign-affiliated Companies in Japan*. Japan External Trade Organisation.

Kale, P., & Singh, H. (2009). Managing Strategic Alliances: What Do We Know Now, and Where Do We Go from Here? *The Academy of Management Perspectives*, *23*(3), 45–62. doi:10.5465/amp.2009.43479263

Kamalaldin, A., Linde, L., Sjödin, D., & Parida, V. (2020). Transforming provider-customer relationships in digital servitization: A relational view on digitalisation. *Industrial Marketing Management*, *89*, 306–325. doi:10.1016/j.indmarman.2020.02.004

Kano, L., Tsang, E. W. K., & Yeung, H. W. (2020). Global value chains: A review of the multi-disciplinary literature. *Journal of International Business Studies*, *51*(4), 577–622. doi:10.1057/s41267-020-00304-2

Kijek, A., & Kijek, T. (2019). Knowledge Spillovers: An Evidence from The European Regions. *Journal of Open Innovation*, *5*(3), 68. doi:10.3390/joitmc5030068

Killing, J. P. (1983). *Strategies for joint venture success*. Praeger.

Killing, J. P. (1988). Understanding Alliances: The Role of Task and Organisational Complexity. In F. J. Contractor & R. Lorange (Eds.), *Cooperative Strategies in International Business. Lexington* (pp. 55–68). Lexington Books.

Kogut, B. (1990). International Sequential Advantages and Network Flexibility. In: *Managing the Global Firm*. In C. Bartlett, Y. Doz, & G. Hedlund (Eds.), *Managing the Global Firm* (pp. 47–68). Routledge.

Kohtamäki, M., Rabetino, R., & Huikkola, T. (2023). Learning in strategic alliances: Reviewing the literature streams and crafting the agenda for future research. *Industrial Marketing Management*, *110*, 68–84. doi:10.1016/j.indmarman.2023.02.011

Laurent, A. (1986). The Cross-Cultural Puzzle of International Human Resource Management. *Human Resource Management*, *25*(1), 91–101. doi:10.1002/hrm.3930250107

Lawler, E., & Hall, D. (1970). Relationships of job characteristics to job involvement, satisfaction and intrinsic motivation. *The Journal of Applied Psychology, 54*(4), 305–312. doi:10.1037/h0029692

Leach, M., MacGregor, H., Scoones, I., & Wilkinson, A. (2021). Post-pandemic transformations: How and why COVID-19 requires us to rethink development. *World Development, 138*, 105233. doi:10.1016/j.worlddev.2020.105233 PMID:33100478

Lehmann-Ortega, L., & Schoettl, J. M. (2005). From buzzword to managerial tool: The role of business model in strategic innovation. CLADEA, Santiago de Chile.

Li, R., Fu, L., & Liu, Z. (2020). Does openness to innovation matter? The moderating role of open innovation between Organisational Ambidexterity and Innovation Performance. *Asian Journal of Technology Innovation, 28*(2), 251–271. doi:10.1080/19761597.2020.1734037

Link, A. N. (2021). *Collaborative R&D and the National Research Joint Venture Database: A Statistical Analysis.* Emerald Publishing Limited., doi:10.1108/9781839095740

Lorange, P. (1976). A Framework for Strategic Planning in Multinational Corporations. *Long Range Planning, 9*(3), 30–37. doi:10.1016/S0024-6301(76)80005-2

Lumineau, F. (2017). How Contracts Influence Trust and Distrust. *Journal of Management, 43*(5), 1553–1577. doi:10.1177/0149206314556656

Luo, Y., & Peng, M. W. (1999). Learning to Compete in a Transition Economy: Experience, Environment, and Performance. *Journal of International Business Studies, 30*(2), 269–295. https://www.jstor.org/stable/155313. doi:10.1057/palgrave.jibs.8490070

Luo, Y., & Shenkar, O. (2006). The multinational corporation as a multilingual community: Language and organisation in a global context. *Journal of International Business Studies, 37*(3), 321–339. doi:10.1057/palgrave.jibs.8400197

Luo, Y., & Tung, R. L. (2018). A general theory of springboard MNEs. *Journal of International Business Studies, 49*(2), 129–152. doi:10.1057/s41267-017-0114-8

Luu, D. T. (2023). Internationalisation, knowledge intensity, adaptive culture and absorptive capacity: A strategic entrepreneurship enabling logic for export firms. *Journal of Small Business and Enterprise Development, 30*(2), 390–418. doi:10.1108/JSBED-06-2022-0288

Lyles, M. (1987). Learning among joint venture-sophisticate firms. In F. J. Contractor & P. Lorange (Eds.), *Cooperative strategies in international business* (pp. 301–316). Lexington Books.

March, J. C. (1978). Bounded Rationality, Ambiguity and the Engineering of Choice. *The Bell Journal of Economics, 9*(2), 587–608. doi:10.2307/3003600

Mariani, L., Trivellato, B., Martini, M., & Marafioti, E. (2022). Achieving Sustainable Development Goals Through Collaborative Innovation: Evidence from Four European Initiatives. *Journal of Business Ethics, 180*(4), 1075–1095. doi:10.1007/s10551-022-05193-z PMID:35855697

Mazzarol, T., Clark, D., Reboud, S., & Limnios, E. (2018). Developing a conceptual framework for the co-operative and mutual enterprise business model. *Journal of Management & Organization*, *24*(4), 1–31. doi:10.1017/jmo.2018.29

McGregor, D. (1960). *The Human Side of Enterprise*. McGraw-Hill Book Co.

Meyer, K. E. (2018). Catch-Up and Leapfrogging: Emerging Economy Multinational Enterprises on the Global Stage. *International Journal of the Economics of Business*, *25*(1), 19–30. doi:10.1080/13571516.2017.1374624

Milgrom, P., & Roberts, J. (1992). *Economics, Organisation & Management*. Prentice Hall.

Miller, E. L., & Cheng, J. L. C. (1978). A Closer Look at the Decision to Accept an Overseas Position. *Management International Review*, *18*(3), 25–33.

Mitsuhashi, H., & Greve, H. (2008). A Matching Theory of Alliance Formation and Organisational Success: Complementarity and Compatibility. *Academy of Management Journal*, *52*(5), 975–995. Advance online publication. doi:10.5465/amj.2009.44634482

Nambisan, S., Shaker, Z., & Luo, Y. (2019). Global platforms and ecosystems: Implications for international business theories. *Journal of International Business Studies*, *50*(9), 1464–1486. Advance online publication. doi:10.1057/s41267-019-00262-4

North, D. C. (1990). *Institutions, Institutional Change and Economic Performance*. Cambridge University Press. doi:10.1017/CBO9780511808678

Nusir, M., Tariq, U., & Ahanger, T. (2021). Engaging Diverse Stakeholders in Interdisciplinary Co-Design Project for Better Service Design. *Journal of Cases on Information Technology*, *23*(4), 1–29. doi:10.4018/JCIT.296253

Ohmae, K. (1985). *Triad power: The coming shape of global competition*. Free Press.

Ouchi, W., & Boulton, M. N. (1988). The logic of joint research and development. *California Management Review*, *30*(3), 9–33. doi:10.2307/41166512

Ouchi, W. G. (1981). *Theory Z: How American Business Can Meet the Japanese Challenge.* Addison Wesley. 10.1016/0007-6813(81)90031-8

Pauwels, C., Clarysse, B., Wright, M., & Van Hove, J. (2016). Understanding a new generation incubation model: The accelerator. *Technovation*, *50–51*, 13–24. doi:10.1016/j.technovation.2015.09.003

Peterson, R. B., & Shimada, J. Y. (1978). Sources of Management Problems in Japanese/American Joint Ventures. *Academy of Management Review*, *3*(4), 796–804. doi:10.2307/257934

Pettigrew, A. M. (1979). On Studying Organisational Cultures. *Administrative Science Quarterly*, *24*(4), 570–581. doi:10.2307/2392363

Porter, M. E., Takeuchi, H., & Sakakibara, M. (2000). Can Japan Compete? Basic Books.

Priyono, A., & Hidayat, A. (2024). Fostering innovation through learning from digital business ecosystem: A dynamic capability perspective. *Journal of Open Innovation, 10*(1), 100196. Advance online publication. doi:10.1016/j.joitmc.2023.100196

Pucik, V. (1983). Management practices in Japan and their impact on business strategy. In R. B. Lamb (Ed.), *Advances in strategic management* (pp. 103–131). JAI Press Greenwich.

Pucik, V., & Katz, J. H. (1986). Information, control human resource management in multinational firms. *Human Resource Management, 25*(1), 121–132. doi:10.1002/hrm.3930250109

Pushpananthan, G., & Elmquist, M. (2022). Joining forces to create value: The emergence of an innovation ecosystem. *Technovation, 115*, 102453. Advance online publication. doi:10.1016/j.technovation.2021.102453

Reid, M. F., & Yang, S. (2018). Organisational Institutionalism. In A. Farazmand (Ed.), *Global Encyclopedia of Public Administration, Public Policy, and Governance*. Springer., doi:10.1007/978-3-319-20928-9_91

Roberts, E., & Berry, C. (1985). Entering new businesses: Selecting strategies for success. *Sloan Management Review, 27*, 3–17.

Rodríguez-Espíndola, O., Chowdhury, S., Dey, P. K., Albores, P., & Emrouznejad, A. (2022). Analysis of the adoption of emergent technologies for risk management in the era of digital manufacturing. *Technological Forecasting and Social Change, 178*, 121562. Advance online publication. doi:10.1016/j.techfore.2022.121562

Sakakibara, M. (1997). Evaluating government sponsored R&D consortia in Japan: Who benefits and how. *Research Policy, 26*(4-5), 447–473. doi:10.1016/S0048-7333(97)00018-8

Sambharya, R., & Musteen, M. (2014). Institutional environment and entrepreneurship: An empirical study across countries. *Journal of International Entrepreneurship, 12*, 314–330. doi:10.1007/s10843-014-0137-1

Santos, F. M., & Eisenhardt, K. M. (2005). Organisational Boundaries and Theories of Organisation. *Organization Science, 16*(5), 491–508. doi:10.1287/orsc.1050.0152

Sarpong, D., Boakye, D., Ofosu, G., & Botchie, D. (2023). The three pointers of research and development (R&D) for growth-boosting sustainable innovation system. *Technovation, 122*, 102581. Advance online publication. doi:10.1016/j.technovation.2022.102581

Schaan, J. L., & Beamish, P. W. (1988). Joint venture general managers in LCD's. In F. Contractor & P. Lorange (Eds.), Cooperative strategies in international business (pp. 279–299). Academic Press.

Scott-Kennel, J., & Enderwick, P. (2004). Inter-firm alliance and network relationships and the eclectic paradigm of international production: An exploratory analysis of quasi-internalisation at the subsidiary level. *International Business Review, 13*(4), 425–445. doi:10.1016/j.ibusrev.2004.03.004

Scott-Kennel, J., & Saittakari, I. (2019). Sourcing or sharing in MNE networks? National headquarters and foreign subsidiaries as knowledge conduits in SMOPECs. *International Business Review, 29*(1), 101622. Advance online publication. doi:10.1016/j.ibusrev.2019.101622

Senge, P. M. (1990). *The Fifth Discipline*. The Art & Practice of The Learning Organisation.

Smale, A., & Suutari, V. (2011). Expatriate perspectives on knowledge transfers into Central and Eastern Europe. In S. Mariano, M. Mohamed, & Q. Mohiuddin (Eds.), *The role of expatriates in MNCs knowledge mobilization* (pp. 63–90). Emerald Group Publishing Limited. doi:10.1108/S1876-066X(2011)0000027007

Smith, K.G., & Grimm, C.M. (1987). *Environmental variation, strategic change and firm performance: A study of railroad deregulation*. . doi:10.1002/smj.4250080406

Song, J., Almeida, P., & Wu, G. (2003). Learning-by-Hiring: When Is Mobility More Likely to Facilitate Interfirm Knowledge Transfer? *Management Science*, *49*(4), 351–365. doi:10.1287/mnsc.49.4.351.14429

Starbuck, W. H. (1985). Acting first and thinking later: Theory versus reality in strategic change. In J. M. Pennings (Ed.), *Organisational Strategy and Change* (pp. 336–372). Jossey Bass.

Teece, D. (2014). A dynamic capabilities-based entrepreneurial theory of the multinational enterprise. *Journal of International Business Studies*, *45*(1), 8–37. doi:10.1057/jibs.2013.54

Terpstra, V. (1985). *The Cultural Environment of International Business* (2nd ed.). South Western.

Trompenaars, F., & Hampden-Turner, C. (1997). *Riding the Waves of Culture: Understanding Diversity in Global Business*. McGraw-Hill.

Turati, C. (1990). *Economia e organizzazione delle joint venture*. Egea.

Uckamr, V. (2005). *Global Business*. Etas Libri.

VakulchukR.OverlandI.ScholtenD. (2020). Renewable Energy and Geopolitics: A Review. *Renewable and Sustainable Energy Reviews, 122,* 109547. https://ssrn.com/abstract=3565990

Wankmüller, C., & Reiner, G. (2020). Coordination, cooperation and collaboration in relief supply chain management. *Journal of Business Economics*, *90*(2), 239–276. doi:10.1007/s11573-019-00945-2

Weick, K. E. (1969). *The Social Psychology of Organizing*. Addison-Wesley.

Williamson, O. E. W. (1975). *Market and Hierarchies*. The Free Press.

Williamson, O. E. W. (1981). The Economics of Organisations: The Transaction Cost Approach. *American Journal of Sociology*, *87*(3), 548–577. doi:10.1086/227496

Williamson, P. J. (2016a). Building and Leveraging Dynamic Capabilities: Insights from Accelerated Innovation in China. *Global Strategy Journal*, *6*(3), 197–210. doi:10.1002/gsj.1124

Williamson, P. J. (2016b). Chinese acquisitions in Europe: Absorptive capability and impacts on competitive advantage. *International Relations*, *13*(49), 61–83.

Wilson, D. (1990). A Dynamic Approach to Strategic Alliances. efmd Research Conference, Barcelona.

Xu, K., Hitt, M. A., Brock, D., Pisano, V., & Huang, L. S. R. (2021). Country institutional environments and international strategy: A review and analysis of the research. *Journal of International Management*, *27*(1), 100811. Advance online publication. doi:10.1016/j.intman.2020.100811

Zaheer, S. (1995). Overcoming the Liability of Foreignness. *Academy of Management Journal, 38*(2), 341–363. doi:10.2307/256683

Zeng, M., & Williamson, P. J. (2007). *Dragons At Your Door: How Chinese Cost Innovation Is Disrupting Global Competition.* Harvard Business School Press.

Zhao, S. (1999). Joint Ventures for Entry Deterrence. *MDE. Managerial and Decision Economics, 20*(1), 25–35. doi:10.1002/(SICI)1099-1468(199902)20:1<25::AID-MDE915>3.0.CO;2-4

Zimmerman, M. (1985). *How to do Business with the Japanese.* Randon House.

Section 2

National Culture, Corporate Culture, and Governance of Internationality

Chapter 5
National Culture, Corporate Culture, and Governance of Internationality:
The Challenge of Cultural Differences

ABSTRACT

This chapter addresses the challenges posed by cultural differences in a global context. It examines the multifaceted dimensions of cultural differences and their impact on international business environments. It also discusses individual factors affecting the process of adaptation whilst emphasising the role of socialisation. Moreover, it examines the adaptation process through the lens of the position profile, offering insights into the specific challenges and requisites for successful integration. It further analyses the dynamic relationship between national and corporate cultures whilst explaining how these intertwined forces shape organisational strategies, operations, and interactions on the international stage. By exploring the advantages and disadvantages of cultural differences, strategic approaches to mitigate conflicts are suggested. Ultimately, the chapter equips readers with practical insights, tools, and frameworks that are crucial for devising adaptive internationalisation strategies in an increasingly interconnected global environment.

5. THE CHALLENGE OF CULTURAL DIFFERENCES

The challenge of cultural differences is a complex and ever-evolving aspect of human interactions in our globalised world. As societies become more interconnected and diverse, individuals and organisations frequently find themselves navigating a rich tapestry of cultures, each with its unique beliefs, norms, values, and communication styles. Whilst cultural diversity can offer numerous benefits, such as fostering creativity and expanding perspectives, it also presents significant hurdles that require careful consideration and sensitivity. One of the central challenges is the way cultural backgrounds influence how people

DOI: 10.4018/979-8-3693-3482-9.ch005

perceive and interpret the world. Each individual's lived experience, shaped by their upbringing and exposure to diverse customs and traditions, constructs a lens through which they view the world. This mental framework, often operating unconsciously, influences how people respond to various situations and interact with others. Misunderstandings, misinterpretations, and communication breakdowns can easily arise when individuals from different cultures attempt to communicate or collaborate without a thorough understanding of each other's cultural perspectives. Another pressing issue in today's multi-cultural world is the concept of culture shock. When individuals move or work in a foreign country or organisation, they may experience varying degrees of culture shock, a phenomenon characterised by feelings of disorientation, discomfort, and even frustration due to the stark contrasts between their own cultural norms and those of the new environment. Such an experience can be particularly challenging for expatriates and international employees, as they grapple with adapting to new customs, language barriers, and social norms (Smale and Suutari, 2011). As businesses and institutions increasingly encourage cross-border collaborations, addressing culture shock and providing adequate support to individuals undergoing cultural transitions becomes imperative for fostering successful international relationships.

Moreover, cultural differences can deeply affect the dynamics within organisations and teams. In multinational corporations or diverse workplaces, intercultural interactions can influence decision-making processes, conflict resolution approaches, and leadership styles. Understanding and managing cultural diversity within the organisational context are essential for building inclusive work environments that harness the collective strengths of a diverse workforce. Additionally, certain deeply rooted cultural values and beliefs may at times be in conflict with the requirements of cross-cultural cooperation. This challenge becomes particularly significant when confronting ethical dilemmas, as diverse perspectives on what constitutes right and wrong may vary significantly across cultures. Developing strategies to address ethical differences and ensuring alignment with organisational values becomes vital for maintaining ethical standards and mutual respect in international collaborations. Addressing the challenge of cultural differences requires a multi-faceted approach that includes cultural sensitivity training, cross-cultural communication workshops, and ongoing support for individuals experiencing culture shock. Encouraging open dialogue and active listening among team members can foster mutual understanding and pave the way for effective collaboration despite cultural disparities. Emphasising a culture of respect for diversity and cultural competence within organisations helps create an inclusive environment that embraces the richness of cultural differences and turns them into assets for innovation and growth.

Giving continuity and meaning to existence: driven by these primordial needs, human beings structure a significant part of their lived experience. Every passing minute, every human interaction, every event in the external world is interpreted and deciphered in that inner world that each of us has constructed within ourselves. Aspiration for logic, rationality, and certainties compels us to systematise the facets of life in a way that forges an internally coherent and homogeneous puzzle. In this delicate process of decoding external events, the human mind relies on interpretive frameworks, partly shaped by past personal experiences and partly influenced by the culture in which it is immersed and breathes.

Individual experiences and cultural background serve as the starting point for attempting to understand how the experience of moving abroad can be interpreted and internalised. What lies behind the widespread concept of culture shock and the conditions under which an expatriate can adapt to a multicultural reality will be explored. Reference will be made to cross-cultural studies, and significant attention will be given to national culture due to its profound influence on individual personality and corporate culture, making it one of the foundations of the cognitive map through which individuals filter their own experiences.

Certain core values are so deeply ingrained in our minds that they operate at an unconscious level and condition behaviour in an almost automatic manner. At times, these values crystallise into an unchanging fixity, rendering them resistant to modification even when external circumstances may demand it.

Hence, the feeling of disorientation and estrangement induced by contact with a culture different from one's own; each nation has indeed developed its own ways of thinking, living, and behaving in relation to the variety of environmental events it has witnessed. Therefore, it is inevitable that this diversity in the way different ethnic groups exist leads to misunderstandings and communication difficulties.

It is in this observation that we can find the reasons why recently, management sciences have directed their attention to the theme of national cultures, once a privileged field of analysis in cultural anthropology. Cross-cultural management studies focus on analysing the behaviour of individuals from different cultural contexts who operate within the same organisation. Adler (1983) put forward a clear definition of it:

"Cross-cultural management deals with traditional themes of organisational behaviour such as motivation, leadership, decision-making processes, and group dynamics, which are typically addressed at the micro level, i.e., within organisational systems. It encompasses both international and intra-national studies and examines the impact of cultural differences within and across national borders. It describes the behaviour of individuals from different cultures operating within the same organisation and compares the behaviours of individuals belonging to organisations located in two or more different cultures. Cross-cultural management thus studies organisational behaviour while incorporating the multicultural dimension. Moreover, it complements international management studies - which tend to focus on the macro and structural level of multinational companies - by adding the behavioural dimension" (Adler, 1983a; p.227).

Cross-cultural management studies, therefore, attempt to provide answers to questions such as: 'What is the influence of culture on people's behaviour within an organisation?'; 'To what extent should management styles be modified when directed towards people from different cultures?'; 'In what aspects does cross-cultural interaction management differ from managing interactions within culturally homogenous groups?'.

Before examining the various positions taken by researchers on these issues (which will be the subject of subsequent chapters), it is important to preface some considerations about the concept of culture. Defining culture in a universally acceptable way is difficult; the abstract, complex, and multidimensional nature of this concept makes it challenging to find a comprehensive definition. Some useful insights can be drawn from the following definitions:

"In our daily tasks, it is too easy to forget what is less rational and instrumental, the social fabric around us that gives meaning to the tasks; [...] the continuous sense of what is reality [...] Culture is the system of publicly and collectively accepted meanings that operates in a given group at a given time: [...] culture as the source of a family of concepts: symbols, language, ideology, beliefs, rituals, and myths" (Pettigrew, 1986; 172).

"Culture consists of those patterns of behaviour and products of human action that can be inherited, transmitted from generation to generation independently of genetic data" (Parsons, 1937; p.9).

"We believe that culture is a product, that it is historical, that it includes ideas, patterns, values; that it is selective, that it is learned, that it is based on symbols; and that it is an abstraction from behaviour and the products of behaviour. The essential core of culture consists of traditional ideas and especially the values attributed to them; cultural systems can be considered both products of action and conditioning elements of future action" (Kluckhohn and Kroeber, 1952; p.12).

"I define the concept of culture as collective mental programming that distinguishes one group from another" (Hofstede, 1980; 15).

Finally, an important definition was put forward by Kluckhohn and Kroeber (1952). They identified a limited number of 'universal' human problems that can be solved in different ways; the peculiarity of each culture lies in how it approaches these problems compared to other cultures. The basic assumptions that allow for the comparability of cultures are as follows:

1. There is a limited number of common human problems for which every population in every period must find a solution: for example, every society must decide how to dress, nourish, communicate, govern, etc.
2. There is a limited number of alternatives available to address these problems.
3. All alternatives are present in any society at any given time, but some are preferred over others.
4. Each society has a dominant profile or orientation towards values, and in addition, it has numerous variations or alternative profiles.
5. Both in the dominant profile and in the variations, there exists a scale of preference among the alternatives.
6. In societies undergoing profound changes, the order of preference may not be well-defined.

In the assumptions of Kluckhohn and Kroeber, two elements of great importance can be found. First, the existence of a limited number of common human problems allows for the classification of cultures according to their preferences in solving these problems, which can be summarised into five categories (Schein, 1985):

a. Human relationships with nature, which influences the organisation's relationship with its environment, such as dominance, submission, adaptation, etc.
b. Nature of reality and truth, including fundamental conceptions related to space and time and the principles by which a phenomenon is considered true or false.
c. Nature of human beings, referring to the conception of human beings in moral and existential terms.
d. Nature of human activity, which relates to the meaning of work and the attitude (passive or active) towards life.
e. Nature of human relationships, including prevalent conceptions related to power, authority, collaboration, and competition.

Second, it is essential to recognise that culture has a normative characteristic, understood statistically, meaning that it should be considered as the average value of a group of people concerning a specific dimension. Consequently, it is incorrect to deduce the cultural characteristics of an individual from the cultural stereotype of a group to which they belong.

Culture can thus be defined as the set of values, norms, traditions, symbols, beliefs, myths, and rituals related to a group, a social aggregate, or a category of individuals, transmitted through social learning mechanisms (also influenced by history), which serves to reduce uncertainty and guide behaviour. Specifically within organisations, culture can be seen as the 'historical personality' of a nation or organisational system that suggests to individuals the behaviours deemed right and good.

In what some call the 'planetary era', culture assumes a crucial role as an indispensable variable in the formulation of strategies for international companies, as it can be both a source of opportunities and significant challenges. Embracing a multicultural approach offers numerous opportunities for companies. Amongst those, there is an increased open-mindedness through continuous exposure to diversity, the ability to attract qualified personnel from around the world, developing resilience in facing environmental changes and responding to them innovatively and creatively, improved understanding of markets through culturally empathetic lenses, and the capacity to explore a broader perspective on potential development opportunities in the environmental context. However, managing multicultural groups also comes with complexity and challenges. Coordinating management policies and techniques and integrating individuals from different cultures can be particularly challenging (Adler, 1983).

The key lies in knowledge as a prelude to understanding and, consequently, more mindful multicultural management. Both companies and individuals engaging with new countries must embrace a mindset open to accepting diversity, which goes beyond their natural tendency to stabilise familiar reference frameworks, making them blind to events that may shake the foundations.

This is due to the innate human tendency to judge and consider the behaviour of others with ourselves as the central reference point, assuming that others employ our same cognitive maps. Such an attitude can sometimes hide a sense of superiority towards perceived differences, leading to rigidity and close-mindedness, and in some cases, even rejection of the other. Often, facing the complexity and quantity of information received in foreign countries leads individuals to rely on stereotyped images, labelling the entire population they encounter with predetermined characteristics, attitudes, and behaviours, disregarding individual specificity (Knotts, 1989). Whilst this may simplify the impact of encountering a different culture and alleviate the shock, it perpetuates generalised assumptions. The winning strategy to minimise cultural shock is knowledge and awareness of oneself and others, their reference structures, habits, and beliefs —basically, their 'cultural environment'. An effective approach to gaining such knowledge is to analyse the elements that compose a given culture. This understanding allows one to distinguish information about reality from judgments and evaluations that our cognitive maps may naturally provide. Separating information from evaluation is the key to successful communication between cultures and adapting to foreign environments and countries.

Understanding a culture involves focusing on a multitude of diverse factors, which can be roughly grouped into three levels. The first encompasses fundamental principles developed to explain the essence of human nature, its relationship with nature and the divine. The second level derives from the first and encompasses values and attitudes, explaining the reasons behind most human behaviours. The third level, an emanation of the previous ones, reveals the tangible environment of culture, visible patterns of behaviour, and material products like artistic manifestations or technological creations (Schein, 1984).

a. *The fundamental assumptions.* What is the characteristic of human nature? What is the relationship between humans and nature? What are the relationships between individuals?

The different types of responses to these timeless questions have evolved over the centuries and not only influenced the way individuals exist and live, but also, in turn, conditioned the actions of businesses. Some practical examples can help better understand this situation.

If a country's culture strongly emphasises the concept of humans as 'social animals' and places enormous importance on the group or family, a company operating in this country will tend to hire personnel from within the family or the group of its employees. In contrast, in an Anglo-Saxon culture, a company may choose to select candidates based on their skills and professional qualifications without hesitation. Furthermore, if the relationship between humans and nature is perceived through a fatalistic lens, where human destiny is subject to the 'will of Allah' or any other transcendent being, why invest so much energy in strategic planning and long-term forecasting if the future cannot be altered?

Moreover, is it preferable to 'be' or to 'do'? Those who lean towards the first alternative may work to live; whereas those who choose the latter will live to work and be highly motivated towards success, prestige, and personal fulfilment in practical life. Similarly, those who prioritise 'being' will be incentivised by close collaboration with colleagues rather than material rewards or promotions, in contrast to those who focus on 'doing'.

b. *Values and attitudes*. As Milton Rokeach (1968a, 1968b, 1969, 1973) argued, stating that a person has values means that they have a deep certainty within themselves that a specific way of life is personally or socially preferable to others. Thus, in every culture, there exists a scale of priorities upon which individuals base their behaviour; greater importance may be given to personal prestige and success, social interactions among individuals, material possessions rather than spiritual growth. It is not surprising, therefore, if an Egyptian executive does not bother to inform in advance that they will not be punctual for a meeting scheduled months ago to attend a family member's funeral: work interests will still come after those of their family.

Furthermore, there are significant divergences in the attitudes of nations towards time. Some cultures focus on the past, like African and Oceanian cultures, whilst others are future-oriented, like Western cultures. In more strictly organisational terms, this can influence the different time orientation that characterises the goals of businesses, in the sense that some companies may be inclined to maintain the same objectives as in the past, whilst others project their goals within the context of anticipated evolutionary trends (Gaffney, 1989). The underlying philosophy of the notion of time also changes considerably among different nations. In those cultures where the traditional conception predominates, time is perceived as a circle, and therefore, there is always a possibility to return to the same point: 'if today's time has been spent on unproductive activities, no problem, as it will return tomorrow!' There is a profound contrast between this view and the modern conception of time: it is perceived as a straight line, mathematically divided into hours and minutes, oriented towards the future; today is seen and considered in relation to tomorrow. Activism, dynamism, and a progressive mindset are logical corollaries of this view of time (Knotts, 1989). The most evident manifestation of this diversity is observed in the importance given by nations to punctuality: whilst in the United States, it is normal to arrive at an appointment 5 minutes early, in Latin America, the meeting takes place from 30 to 60 minutes after the agreed-upon time.

Another relevant aspect of a foreign culture is the informal rules that underlie the concept of space, such as the distance that should be maintained during a conversation with another individual. It will be much easier for a Westerner to engage in a conversation with an Arab or an African, once they understand that in their culture, it is considered appropriate to speak to another individual from a very close distance.

c. *Symbols and Artefacts.* The symbolic level of culture is particularly relevant in the context of communication processes. No social organisation, be it a company, family, or nation, can disregard the construction of that 'system of vocal signs used by individuals to communicate', which we generically define as language (Gauthey et al., 1988). Together with the so-called nonverbal communication systems (gestures, facial expressions, etc.), it represents the cornerstone of information and thought exchange between individuals. As such, it stimulates the development of human civilisations and, in a more strictly economic context, constitutes the lifeblood for the functioning of organisations.

In the international context as well, it represents a strategic resource to the extent that it is a tool for smoothing differences, shedding light on misunderstandings, and translating the irreducible complexity of a relationship between individuals of different nationalities into terms more understandable to the parties. However, communication processes between individuals, rather than clarifying potential problems in the light of human logic and rationality, often become sources of misunderstandings and mutual tensions, conveying frustrations and resulting in considerable inefficiency (Mead, 1990).

Human beings are creatures who naturally use symbols to convey messages to others; thus, an object, a gesture, a sound takes on a particular, unique meaning generally shared by members of a group. As a product of human mental elaboration, the symbolic meaning of elements has a relative value over time as well as in space (Gaffney, 1989). Each human being is then endowed with an almost inexhaustible versatility in inventing new and articulate means of communication; research in this regard has shown that only 10% of communications are made through the usual grammatical and lexical forms: languages are also intonations, expressions, gestures, in a word, the varied set of human behaviours. However, each individual lives, thinks, and therefore communicates within their own frame of reference, that is, the world mentally reconstructed by our perception mechanisms and which constitutes a sort of 'psychological environment' for us. Since the communication process involves a complex network of projections of ourselves onto others, it will also reflect our entire perceived world with its accompanying values, expectations, ideals, systems of needs, and motivations (Ronen, 1986). This observation lies at the heart of the problem of intercultural communication: that perceived world, to which each individual implicitly refers, represents not only the product of their life experience but also, and perhaps above all, a faithful mirror of the culture in which they have been socialised.

The influence of cultural assumptions in communication processes involves both their content, determining which topics are most important, extraordinary, and worthy of being transmitted to others, and the specific mode of their transmission. Thus, culture can determine grammatical structures or the appropriate vocabulary in certain situations and inappropriate in others. It can alter the episodic structure of a conversation, establishing, for example, that in an economic negotiation, it is not suitable to address the heart of the problem immediately and it is preferable instead to engage first in insignificant topics. Culture can then assign different importance and meaning to nonverbal communication means, preferring silence to open speech and body language to the more decipherable language of words.

For instance, Spanish contains many comparatives and superlatives, which are suitable means for expressing emotions. The languages of countries where Aristotelian deductive reasoning predominates have a very logical structure. The low tolerance for ambiguity typical of North Americans is expressed in the precision with which they present their thoughts; in Japan, where harmony and concord among individuals are cardinal values, a certain ambiguity in speech is deliberately used to allow the interlocutor a wider range of responses (Mead, 1990; Ronen, 1986). Communicating with a foreigner, therefore, not only means memorising a sequence of words or sounds but also immersing oneself in the cultural experience of that individual. Conversely, persisting in interpreting the words of the other based on our limited experience and the relative map of reality, we attribute to them a meaning that probably does not coincide with the intentions of the interlocutor. Misunderstandings, intolerance phenomena, and declines in efficiency are logical consequences of this.

5.1 The Process of Adaptation to a New Territory

In a country, there is not only arid geographical space with defined characteristics of structure and size, environment, and climate. In it, another type of spatiality, deeper and hidden, is intermingled: it is the lived space, the way an individual thinks of and perceives oneself in a specific place, the manner in which they relate to it and project a part of themselves into the things that surround them. Therefore, the house is not just a dwelling but also a critical reference point in the construction of one's identity, a vehicle to satisfy the need for belonging and recognition, the cornerstone of one's psychological balance. To fully understand the subjective significance of inner equilibrium and security provided by the environment in which an individual's life unfolds, it also means looking at the phenomenon of work mobility with a magnifying glass. It means not only focusing on the objective aspects of the transfer but also addressing questions regarding the ways of perceiving, feeling, and experiencing of the protagonists (Song et al., 2003).

The exact sciences have sought effects and causes of problems induced by geographical mobility, identifying the causes in the lack of technical skills in expatriates or in the scarcity of economic incentives and support, and the effects in decreased work performance or early repatriation. The objective is to place the issues of international transfer in a broader perspective that encompasses all aspects of an individual's existence and goes beyond what is visible. Alongside mobility, a series of complex phenomena come into play that not only concern the individual's social and work role, their relationships with the environment but also touch upon the private and lived sphere. Mobility calls into question the very life of a person, their history, their cultural background, and severely tests their ability to adapt to new situations, their personal security, and the preservation of their core values. Among the multiple facets of the phenomenon of international mobility, we have chosen, as the privileged field of investigation, the realm of managerial mobility.

Despite the undeniable privileged condition in which this 'elite migration' finds itself (compared, for example, to the category of emigrants), it has still aroused growing attention from many scholars in recent decades. The figures speak quite clearly: the costs of an expatriate's premature return range from $50,000 to $150,000; about 30% of overseas transfers made by numerous American multinational companies are considered mistakes. Not to mention the decline in productivity in the managerial performance, the immediate impact on their self-esteem and confidence in their abilities, and the even more indirect repercussions on the tranquillity of their family life. If communicative skills, mental flexibility, social adaptability, and tolerance for frustration are the new watchwords for today's successful manager abroad, the aim here is to trace back all the determining or simply influential factors that lie at its origin.

In this perspective, the analysis will be conducted having two systems of variables as schematic reference points: the first will encompass all the objective factors that characterise the life of the expatriate at the time of transfer (such as family composition, type of work, standard of living, spouse's occupation, etc.). The second will include variables that are more individual in nature – age, personality, attitude towards work, scale of priorities in the expatriate's motivations. Equal attention has been given to both groups of variables unlike many scholars who have focused their analysis only on the first. It is believed that only by looking at their complex interaction is it possible to understand how an individual perceives the situations they are involved in the extent to which they judge them critical, and the strength with which they are able to confront them. What changes occur in the mind of an individual immersed in an organisational territory that is foreign to them? What psychic processes are triggered by the impact of the new, the different? What stages does the gradual path of adaptation to a new territory go through? How can the company reduce the difficulties of the process and improve the results?

In everyday life, in all those events that make up our daily existence, a large part of the behaviours put into action to meet the demands of the external world do not require the intervention of conscious thinking mechanisms. Of the countless aspects that compose our existence, many of them are dominated by habit, repetitiveness, and the teachings of past experiences. Deciding which behaviours to adopt in response to external stimuli is a mental operation that is carried out almost automatically, based on a series of behavioural patterns internalised by the individual and considered correct.

The learning processes that lead to the definition of scripts that shape part of our lives are initiated when entering a new environment, whether it is familiar, work-related, or social. Being part of an organisation means not only knowing how to do one's job but also identifying, understanding, and internalising these interpretative patterns; they reflect the 'personality' of an organisation and hide the keys to understanding the sequences of events and their connections to outcomes. As long as expectations are not disappointed by reality and behaviours lead to the expected results, there is no stimulus for the individual to dedicate mental energy to searching for deep reasons. In case events occur that go beyond these behavioural patterns, those who are part of an organisation have two paths to take: firstly, the history of the organisation, its experiences, and past events can provide fertile ground for analogical interpretations; secondly, contacts with other 'experts' can offer opportunities for constructive comparison of their perceptions and interpretations of reality. There are sources of knowledge available that allow individuals to feel at ease and not let the level of anxiety grow too much.

What happens when an individual enters an organisation, a territory that is unknown to them for the first time? What does a manager experience in their first, abrupt impact with the new world? Everything that happens inside and around them seems to be marked by change and diversity; it is both objective, a new job, often a promotion, different responsibilities, different ways of interacting with colleagues, and subjective, meaning the new way in which a situation is characterised and interpreted by the individual. Whilst objective changes are generally easily understandable, the implicit and symbolic characteristics that depend strictly on the individual's previous experiences are much more elusive and vague: it is the differences and not the similarities that strike the mind of an individual in the transition from one context to another.

Before facing such an involving experience as a transfer abroad or, more generally, entering a new territory, it is inevitable that, in a more or less conscious way, an individual forms expectations both about the characteristics of the new job and about their abilities and capabilities to cope with it. However, often the newcomer, once they enter the new environment, confronts the evidence of facts: many of the expectations they had previously formulated must be revised in light of a different reality. There are numerous possible forms in which this surprise (Louis, 1980), or this mismatch between expectations and reality, materialises.

The first of these surprises occurs when the expectations about the characteristics of the new job are not confirmed. Excessive expectations in this regard are probably the origin of the dissatisfaction expressed by many managers transferred abroad towards their work, which they judge as less interesting and with fewer development opportunities compared to the work done by stable managers (Brett, 1982).

A second type of surprise arises when one realises they have overestimated their abilities. The majority of managers selected for international transfers have had to face performance standards much lower than those encountered in their home country and accept the relativity of their skills and abilities.

Another type of surprise concerns the emotional reactions that an individual experiences when faced with a new situation and the levels of anxiety that follow.

The last type of surprise stems from the realisation that the cultural map developed by the individual in previous environments no longer fulfils its role as an operative guide to behaviours, and that it is therefore necessary to start from scratch and reconstruct a socially acceptable behavioural pattern. This last form of surprise will be even more intense if the transfer is made to countries with very marked cultural peculiarities.

The combination of these factors leads the newcomer to experience what has been defined as a 'reality shock' (Hughes, 1958), a state of general disorientation in which it becomes particularly difficult to interpret the signals coming from the outside, to select those to which to respond, and the most appropriate way to do so. Often, one does not even become aware of the diversity of the new situation and interprets actions and events by applying aprioristic dictionaries of meaning learned in other contexts.

The failure of this attempt and the impossibility of relying on the support of colleagues (developing deep social relationships takes a long time) create a state of psychological tension in the individual. A person cannot tolerate living in a situation of which they do not know the rules of the game for long, and it is at this point that conscious thought plays a determining role. A mental process is triggered whose primary focus is to understand the meanings of events and then select the most appropriate response behaviours based on these. The way in which this gradual process of adaptation takes shape is significantly influenced by some variables. On one hand, the comparison with the perceptions of colleagues and the existence of specific interpretative schemes within the organisation, as we have already mentioned in previous pages. On the other hand, the individual' s personal characteristics and the specific reason that led them to enter the new organisation. The individual's past experiences and how they reacted to critical situations in the past also become important. From this diagnostic investigation activity, the correct interpretation of events according to the new social context and the internalisation of the new dictionaries of meaning can emerge.

5.2 Role Shock: Modes, Timing, and Degree of Adaptation to a New Role

The continuum of existence breaks. Points of reference, interpretative patterns, and maps of meaning disappear: a transfer involves the entirety of a human being, affecting their way of life and altering the filters through which they view the world. In analysing the role that an individual plays within a society and the environment they live in, one realises how the experience of mobility can potentially undermine a person's sense of security. Setting aside, for now, the phenomenon of identity crisis (caused by the dissolution of the foundations of the Self) and culture shock (due to transplantation into an unfamiliar socio-cultural environment), particular attention will be given to the intermediate level of existence, connected to the role assumed by the individual in the work context. A sudden encounter with a new role or a familiar role performed in a different manner or environment can give rise to a phenomenon known as role shock (Minkler and Biller, 1979). The 'role shock' is a syndrome that originates from the sudden awareness of both the substantial differences in how a professional role is performed in one's home country compared to abroad and the discrepancy between the anticipated nature of the role and its actual reality. It is the perception of discontinuity in the face of an expectation of continuity that triggers the shock. Consequently, tensions and stress emerge, surpassing the individual's threshold for adaptive response to changes, thereby requiring a 'restructuring' of oneself, the role, or both. A comprehensive understanding of the difficulties of adapting to a new role is more complete when moving away from a narrow view of work as mere tasks requiring certain skills or as a means of survival. Work can satisfy a person's desire to control and manipulate nature, to test in reality what they think of themselves in terms of personal abilities. It can provide a temporal structure to the day, week, or entire life. Work is the theatre in which a significant portion of an individual's interpersonal relationships takes place, greatly influencing their social value (prestige, power, status), and it serves as a source for transmitting social norms and values.

The dynamic evolution of an individual's personality, encompassing internalised values, general behavioural tendencies, patterns, and emotional responses, is influenced and, in turn, affects the work sphere. Within this broader perspective, it becomes easier to understand the critical nature of the entry phase into a new job and a new territory. This phase represents the moment when an individual must clarify what is expected of them, assess the organisation's demands, and identify the paths to follow within it. The entry phase is potentially a source of conflict when the individual's objectives diverge from those of the organisation, inevitably becoming a ground for confrontation. The individual is required to express their identity and actively deploy their skills and competencies, with the risk of seeing their expectations and self-evaluations collapse. Being in an unfamiliar region justifies the difficulties encountered in giving clear direction to one's choices and actively engaging in resolving contingent problems of daily life. The encounter/clash with the unusual and different arouses, in the newcomer, the primary concern of forging a new identity by assuming the new role and understanding others' expectations to guide their behaviour. This requires adequate cognitive restructuring, meaning the definition of new scripts based on which to shape their actions.

The process through which an individual reaches a new perception of the self/role relationship, a different evaluation of their scope of action, a cognitive reorganisation and/or modification of self-images may entail some negative consequences. If the individual has difficulty adapting to a new role, defensive mechanisms of their inner stability may be triggered. These can range from stubbornly and blindly repeating the action patterns and schemas used in their home territory to, at the opposite extreme, an excessive receptivity and willingness to passively accept rules and procedures proposed in the new work environment.

Regardless of how this adaptation process concludes, it subjects the individual to a considerable accumulation of stress. According to Jacques (1970), stress is not caused by difficulties, complexity, or the weight of the task an individual is called to perform; rather, it is more likely that situations where the individual operates under inadequate conditions are stressful. Such conditions may consist of:

1. Being responsible for tasks that are unachievable due to insufficient resources or organisational inconsistencies, or excessively easy due to an excess of resources.
2. Being responsible for tasks that are too difficult because the level of work is beyond one's abilities or too easy because the level of work is below one's abilities (Jacques, 1970).

In the more specific context of managerial mobility, these conditions translate into deficiencies in the operational mechanisms governing international transfers, insufficient support provided to the expatriate by the parent company, and assigning managers solely based on technical skills without any, albeit imperfect, measurement of their generic cross-cultural adaptability.

On the other hand, personality characteristics (such as tension levels, aggressiveness, ambition, preference for competitive activities, a tendency to surpass one's limits and increase one's professional productivity, a high perception of the urgency to achieve results) help distinguish individuals 'at risk' of stress.

A typical psychological manifestation of a situation of discomfort and stress is alienation with its dual nature. Alienation is:

- Personal: resulting from the perception of a discrepancy between one's daily behaviour and one's self-image
- Social: meaning the feeling of not having a mental structure similar to that of others and on which to base interaction with them (Korman et al., 1981).

A form of personal alienation may affect those managers induced to leave more by societal pressures than by autonomous choice, leading to a consequent feeling of losing personal control.

Social alienation, on the other hand, seems almost inevitable when encountering a country, culture, or world different from one's own. The desire for personal contacts is particularly frustrated in the case of a foreign experience because a significant amount of time must be dedicated to learning about the new work territory.

Thus far, we have considered various manifestations of role shock that characterise an individual's adaptation process to a new work experience: stress, alienation, anxiety, and ego defence mechanisms.

However, many questions still remain unanswered. How do individuals adapt to a new role, and how much time and to what degree is this adaptation achieved over time?

To answer the first question, it is particularly useful to revisit the outlines of Nigel Nicholson's (1984) theory on role transitions. According to this theory, an individual can choose a combination of two fundamental adaptation strategies. One is focused on personal development, and the other on role development. Opting for the former implies modifying oneself, one's abilities, and mental patterns to conform to the new role and absorb the change internally. Opting for the latter involves taking an active role in shaping the characteristics of the role to make it more suitable for oneself by changing its goals, methods, and procedures.

Considering these two relevant variables together, a model emerges that schematically proposes four distinct modes of adaptation to a new role.

The 'replication' mode of adaptation is likely to be observed in all role transitions that do not entail substantial modifications between the previous work experience and the current one. Therefore, it requires minimal personal adaptation to the role's demands. This strategy tends toward maintaining the status quo and performing tasks in ways and forms previously experienced. Role transitions that involve high personal development and limited role development fall into the 'absorption' mode. This strategy is commonly employed when facing an environment and social context entirely new compared to previous ones. All energies are directed towards learning new skills, abilities, and reference patterns useful for making sense of and contenting with the new situation. When the role assumption results in a radical change in the position's characteristics, which become configured almost in the image and likeness of the individual, we are facing the 'determination' mode. Generally, this mode features individuals with exceptional abilities who can shape the activities they perform according to their identity.

The last, most complex, and innovative adaptation strategy is that of 'exploration'. In this mode, both the individual and the role they are called to fill undergo a simultaneous change. This adaptation strategy appears particularly suitable for understanding experiences related to international mobility. Expatriate managers are required to capitalise on their previous experiences and apply them to a new context, thus leading to a mutual modification of both the role and the individual. The role and the person will be shaped, each in its specific characteristics, in such a way as to mutually adapt to one another.

Despite appearances, it is not necessarily the case that adopting an adaptation strategy based on the objective needs of the situation (replication in the case of similar role transitions, absorption in the case of completely different contexts) is the best alternative from the perspective of the subject's psychological and emotional well-being. All the indicated modes present both positive and negative aspects.

Replication can lead to feelings of stability and security, as well as frustration and powerlessness. Absorption can stimulate the desire to learn new knowledge but may also lead to the realisation of having overestimated one's capabilities or the lack of reference patterns to anchor oneself to. Exploration offers a wide range of opportunities for satisfying all higher-order human needs but often comes with high levels of anxiety and tension. This emphasises that there is no single path to follow when adapting to a new role. There is no one best way, and it is not possible to establish a priori precise laws that relate certain objective role characteristics to specific adaptation modes. The ways, forms, and content through which an individual fills their adaptation process are the result of a kaleidoscopic configuration of multiple interacting factors. Among others, of particular relevance are factors related to:

- individual's specific personality (such as motivational scale, competencies, and abilities);
- factors related to the organisational system (such as the nature and configuration of insertion and socialisation policies or the objective characteristics of the new position);
- context-related factors (such as the cultural distance between the host and home country or the family's readiness to adapt to the new world.

The same reasoning applies to the examination of the time required for an individual to adapt to the new role (and the new way of being) or the various degrees commonly experienced in an adaptation process. Conducting an analysis without considering the evolving configuration of all these factors is likely to lead to a dead-end. Certainly, generalisations such as the morale curve can be of valuable assistance. However, an analysis conducted solely based on these schemes may be reductive and not allow a real understanding of the phenomenon. The adaptation of a manager following a transfer still leaves unresolved the thorny question of why the curve has that shape and what factors determine its profile and design.

In the following paragraphs, the themes of modes, times, and phases of adaptation to an international role will be presented, aiming to grasp the underlying structures of this phenomenon. Particular attention will be given to factors that have not been addressed previously (as was done for individual competencies and abilities) or that, due to their particular relevance, require specific treatment.

5.3 The Process of Adaptation: Individual Factors

Randomness, disorder and unexpected events constitute the main challenge for today's managers. Besides the managerial skills, which are required to master the art of one's work, there are the so-called 'negative capabilities' which have come into play. The latter are aimed at dealing with the emotional aspects connected with decision-making in complex situations. Among these, the ability to tolerate anxiety, to live with uncertainty, to think in a relativistic way, rejecting any sort of sterile dogmatism. At the international level, the consideration of the individual becomes even more critical, as well as the integration between cognition and emotion. For example, as previously observed, one of the causes of failure in overseas transfers lies precisely in the excessive emphasis placed on technical skills as a selection criterion, neglecting other equally important components for the success of a foreign experience, such as mental flexibility or the ability to withstand high levels of anxiety. One should aim to adapt the individual to the task and vice versa, giving at least as much emphasis to promoting the match between the psychological demands of the job and the individual's psychological structure as is dedicated to finding the suitable knowledge and technical skills in the latter. Since people also change over time, the process of adaptation must be viewed from a dynamic perspective. Humans tend to maintain a homeostatic balance with the environment by reducing dissonance between their relatively stable cognitive maps and the demands for change originating from external stimuli. They also deal with a stimulus that disrupts homeostasis through a global reaction that activates the cognitive, affective, and motivational components underlying personality dynamics. The analysis that follows will be conducted with this perspective as a reference.

Overcoming the sterile dichotomy between subjective and objective approaches in psychology, the trends of recent decades have increasingly leaned towards an integrated and dynamic approach: subjective activity and behaviour are two dimensions of one unit, the human personality. The personality is not perceived as a simple agglomeration of distinct parts, but rather as a functional integration of inherited and acquired factors, subjective and objective aspects, endogenous and exogenous motivations, biological, psychological, and environmental characteristics. Consequently, it becomes impossible to study a human being apart from the situation in which they are embedded, and it is essential to examine the influences derived from it based on how they are subjectively experienced. From a psychological point of view, the environment is not what is external to the individual but what comes from the outside and is perceived and internalised. The increasing integration of subjective and objective aspects has led to the development of concepts that oscillate between these two poles, intrinsic and extrinsic, of the human personality. Concepts closely related to subjective activity, such as perception, memory, and thought, and those connected to behaviour, such as reaction and response, have been joined by others like opinions, beliefs, attitudes, and attribution mechanisms. All these aspects of being contribute to the continuity of the human personality and give meaning to their actions. Understanding the underlying causes of human behaviour cannot be separated from the influence exerted by attitudes, which are the general orientations of the individual evident in their interests, inclinations, acceptance of things, and rejections.

Similarly, one cannot comprehend an individual's actions without first analysing their values and beliefs, their cultural background (the result of a lifetime of experience), and the cognitive map with which they interpret the world (Decastri, 2020). Moreover, an individual's behaviour must be placed within the framework of their attribution mechanisms, or the mental processes through which they clarify the causes of the events around them. This is because humans do not act based on raw data from the external world but according to their re-elaborations of reality, re-elaborations in which the subjective determination of causality plays a role as crucial as that of knowledge storage, transformation, and recall processes. The reality with which we measure ourselves is, therefore, a reality mentally reconstructed based on the material provided by the environment and the meaning attributed to that material. A dominant factor in attribution processes is the defence of the self, in the dual form of maintaining high self-esteem and defending one's public image. Hence, the natural tendency to attribute success to oneself and failure to external causes.

The attribution process is also influenced by the information available following the individual's selection. Such selection and subsequent elaboration are largely influenced by the value systems, beliefs, representations, and symbols related to the characteristics of the context and the person. Different causality schemes are identified in relation to both the type of event and the personal dispositions of the observer-actor. Given that an individual's personality (in a broad sense) plays such a significant role in determining their modes of interaction with the environment, it is possible to outline the profile of the 'ideal person' for an overseas transfer. What are their attitudes and motivations, the traits of their personality, what and how does the mobile manager think? In connection with the arguments presented on the topic of selection, can the profile outlined by empirical research be confirmed?

Firstly, the mere fact of living in a complex and ambiguous situation such as an overseas transfer requires relinquishing certainty, logical and linear thinking, and embracing uncertainty and divergent thinking, oriented towards the new and the probable. The manager may be required to bear the burden of being unable to decide, leaving problems open and resisting the temptation to conclude prematurely.

The significance of emotional and affective components of a manager who must live with uncertainty can only lead to the addition of symbolic, mythological, and magical thinking to empirical, technical, and rational thinking. The problem becomes even more complex when the loss of reference points and the security of being 'similar among one's peers' are associated with the complexity and uncertainty of the task. In addition to flexibility, open-mindedness, tolerance for frustrations, and communication skills, the mobile manager also needs the singular quality of being chameleonic, capable of adapting their mental attire when interacting with individuals from different cultures. Based on the data from a study conducted by Indrei Ratiu (1983) on a sample of 250 young executives, it is possible to delve more deeply into what 'thinking internationally' consists of – that is, the mental processes of individuals who are suitable for living an overseas experience. The indicators used to identify this sort of inclination towards internationality are attributed by the Author to four fundamental dimensions:

1. the way of experiencing the transfer and understanding what it means to be international;
2. assumptions upon which the consideration of the world and oneself is based;
3. the approach to coping with stress;
4. the mental processes triggered by the need to attribute meanings to the situations one experiences.

For the truly international manager, living abroad translates into an invigorating experience of personal growth. Listening skills, observation, risk-taking, and an active and engaged involvement are the main entry points into the new world. Possessing inherent qualities such as patience, empathy, flexibility, and mental openness is of little value if one does not learn to adapt to specific situations and their unique characteristics. The essence of the new reality can only be absorbed through living it, enjoying continuous contact with people, and learning in ways that are essentially empirical, intuitive, and immediate.

Relativism, subjectivism, and dynamism are the pillars around which all assumptions internalised by the most international individuals revolve, concerning the world and themselves. As faithful followers of Heraclitus, they observe reality in its constant becoming, avoiding categorisations and dogmatism, always reflecting.

Another distinctive characteristic of the international manager is the extreme ease and promptness with which he recalls the tensions and stresses induced by cultural shock. Recognising and understanding the most emotional part of oneself and as well as the effects that the experience of relocation has, it is essential to start from 'how to get tolerant' in order to bear or overcome the anxieties and tensions induced by mobility (Song et al., 2003).

The last typical characteristic of the international manager lies in the particular way through which he gives meaning to the surrounding reality. Since the whole world is enveloped in a spiral of change and stable reference points cannot be identified, every impression, consideration, and evaluation must be constantly measured with the yardstick of reality and rechecked through trial and error procedures. Rather than explaining phenomena and seeking the truth, it is preferable to engage in activities of description and interpretation, relying on one's own perceptions and feelings. Based on these considerations, it is possible to summarise as follows the diversity of approaches that distinguish managers particularly suited to international positions from others (Ratiu, 1983).

The traditional international manager adopts an objective macro-strategy. He adapts to society and macro-culture, must possess particular qualities such as patience, empathy, and flexibility, considers stable aspects of the world as objective data, as ascertainable facts, searches for the ultimate causes of his experience, considers facts as relevant information, compares and evaluates cultures, confirms his own stereotypes, is socially rather isolated, and judgmental. In contrast to this traditional profile, we find the more international manager who adopts a subjective micro-strategy. He/she adapts to the individual and micro-culture. He/she does not need specific qualities because the success of the adaptation process depends on the specific characteristics of different situations. He/she considers stable aspects of the world as subjective data, searches for the description, interpretation, and meaning of experiences, considers feelings and impressions as relevant information, qualitatively differentiates them without evaluating them, modifies his own stereotypes, is socially engaged, flexible, and open.

Given the substantial diversity with which these two approaches to reality are configured, one wonders what factors influence such a decisive dichotomy. These factors can be attributed to the two different aspects of the learning cycle through which individuals filter their experience to give it meaning. This cycle is composed of two closed circuits, which Ratiu identifies with the names of the blue loop and the red loop.

The first is used whenever one is interested in knowing what happened in a specific experience, in a mainly descriptive logic, and mainly using intuition and subjective impressions.

The second is used whenever stable assumptions about the environment are formulated, and the reasons for the phenomena are sought to place them in a stable, objectively valid framework of explanations.

The use of the blue loop has as its corollary the conception of a constantly changing world and inevitably places the individual in continuous tension, leading him to suspend any judgment or evaluation. On the other hand, the red loop feeds the sense of security, familiarity, and individual stability, as it induces the subject to find confirmation of past experiences. The focal point of the analysis is that there is no best way. It is not advisable for the international manager to be induced to use only the blue loop and relegate the harmful red loop; adapting to a foreign environment requires learning processes that are related to both circuits, given that their use must occur in appropriate ways and times.

Resorting to the macro-strategy is essential, for example, to develop a sense of psychological security and inner stability without which some individuals cannot live in an unfamiliar environment; on the other hand, developing an active and invigorating social relationship with others requires a micro strategy.

From these considerations, it is evident how limiting the common understanding of learning as a process through which skills and knowledge are acquired for work performance can be; moving abroad also means learning to be with others, to build zones of stability, and to make conscious use of the most intuitive and immediate learning circuit.

Personality should be understood as a structure with two poles - the self and the world - a structure in which the social dimension is closely integrated (so much so that it cannot be separated) with the biophysical individuality. The set of interactions between the two poles is the primary and most significant datum of personality, and motivations must be seen in the context of these interactions. However, the study of motivations is particularly complex due to the following circumstances. First, human motivations differ from one culture to another and, within the same culture, from person to person. For the same behaviour, multiple motivations may contribute, and conversely, different motivations may be the origin of the same behaviour; not to mention the unconscious motives that act, often masked, outside our and others' awareness.

The impossibility of taking all these factors into account leads to an inevitable degree of arbitrariness in the attempts to classify motivations made by different authors. To be more simple, we will adopt a classification, however broad, of possible motivations related to work. According to this classification, these motivations can be divided into:

- motivations related to individual economic interests,
- motivations related to social relationships,
- motivations related to the meaning of work and self-realisation.

Regarding the first group of motivations, their satisfaction is almost always ensured in the case of international transfers, given the substantial amount of economic incentives and benefits generally granted to managers, and even if not, it is still a problem of easy solution, except for the greater burden on the company. On the other hand, the satisfaction of needs related to social relationships is much more critical. This is the most critical aspect of every transfer: individuals with a strong drive for affiliation and affective integration prefer environments where appreciation for their attitude prevails over attention to efficiency and results. The perceived human warmth, the frequency and intensity of social contacts, the number and direction of signals coming from reference groups deeply mark their energy production capacity and, in the case of negative situations, prevent any possibility of success in the foreign assignment. In other words, they are 'at risk' individuals.

As for motivations related to the meaning of work and self-realisation, the evaluation is not univocal: whilst it is true that the international location increases complexity, the position itself is not always stimulating the manager's potential. In the case of complex positions, the manager motivated by the intrinsic content of the work can only find further satisfaction from the international multiplier; success in performing such a task will fuel his desire for self-realisation and lead him to seek even higher standards of performance. However, a high motivation for self-realisation often associates with a high desire for control and feedback; when given a difficult task, an individual with a strong drive for self-realisation may demand to know if his actions are successful: he prefers activities that provide immediate and precise information about his performance. He works with greater commitment if he is told exactly what is going well and what is not, rather than a generic appreciation, even if positive.

The concepts of the desire for feedback and the desire for control are particularly significant in connection with the already seen Nicholson's schema (1984); these concepts are identified as the motivational categories that can influence the choice of modes of adaptation to a new role more than others can. Therefore, if the desire for both control and feedback is low, the replication mode (which implies few changes in the person and the role) is the most suitable. Similarly, a high desire for feedback and control requires a particularly complex mode of role assumption (exploration).

Changes in an individual's personality can also occur if the objective characteristics of the work situation require the adoption of an adaptation mode different from that, which is consistent with the subject's motivational orientations. If, for example, the role's needs require the absorption mode and the individual has a motivational structure characterised by a high desire for control and a low desire for feedback, different types of reactions can occur. The individual may submit to the demands of the situation and modify his motivational orientation or, alternatively, alter the characteristics of the role; or he may passively suffer from this discrepancy and its negative psychological consequences. Hence, once again, the importance of carefully selecting the person and taking great care of the insertion and adaptation process.

5.4 The Adaptation Process: Socialisation

"The individual understands that they share the world with others. They realise that the environment includes not only themselves but also others, and that they have a relationship with the surrounding environment similar to that of their peers [...]. Common actions and the need for collaboration require this relationship of intelligibility and structural transparency" [...] (Asch, 1955; p. 17).

During the entry into an unfamiliar environment, the socio-emotional support from reference groups becomes significant in facilitating the newcomer's adaptation. This support removes uncertainty, alleviates anxiety, and interprets ambiguity. The group provides physical, emotional, or simply symbolic contributions that increase the reserve of emotional energy to cope with new situations, facilitate change, and reduce the time of adaptation (Pinder and Schroeder, 1989).

The mental process through which an individual gives meaning to the reality surrounding them is guided and directed by cues from others. Generally, when faced with an unstable and unstructured situation, the individual establishes a range of judgment variation and within it, a norm or a reference point. This range and norm are specific to each individual and may differ to varying degrees from those developed by others. In the case of group situations, however, individuals tend to structure the field by converging judgments toward a common and shared norm capable of explaining reality. The norm and interpretation are also formulated based on personal coordinates, but they primarily consider the group they are in relation with.

Hence, the utility of external support in the case of relocating abroad: advice, opinions, and information from insiders become essential for understanding local expectations and culture, the tricks of the trade, mistakes to avoid, symbols, and common interpretations. Any feedback becomes a valuable ally in reducing role ambiguity and a valid ground for assessing one's capabilities.

Based on these principles, socialisation tactics are founded, and organisational practices aimed at facilitating the newcomer's integration into the new environment should be defined. Formalised techniques of social support can constitute a valid counterbalance to the difficulties inherent in the objective characteristics of the new role, reducing uncertainty, and mediating adaptation.

The process by which individuals acquire knowledge, attitudes, skills, and values in line with those of the group they are part of, in order to live their social experience satisfactorily, is defined as the socialisation process. The success or failure of this process has relevant effects on individual and social destiny: for the individual, it may represent an opportunity to maintain or redefine their identity beyond blindly submitting to the demands of the situation and the group; for the group, it can mean having active members who, in a coordinated manner, cooperate to achieve collective goals.

It is a complex interactive process that takes place based on different purposes, needs, and resources possessed by the two poles of interaction. That is the individual and the group. This interaction involves the individual as a whole and can alternately be a moment pushing for passive adoption of behaviours required by the context or, conversely, a favourable opportunity for the expansion of the individual and their identity in relation to the people and things that are part of the work environment. Entry into an unfamiliar environment forces the individual to a complex and dynamic redefinition of their interpretive schemes of reality and the construction of space-time maps that allow them to choose the right path to learn both the most appropriate ways of performing the new role and the cultural assumptions that define the 'personality' of the new organisation (Decastri, 2016).

The protagonist and undisputed director of the script designed for the new reality, however, is not the individual, as the organisation itself, defining the setting, is capable of shaping the outcome of the representation in various ways. It can mould the newcomer's response by defining tasks, control methods, cultural maps, reward systems, etc. In particular, the way role orientation is configured can be influenced by the type of socialisation practices used. This influence is particularly vivid and intense in the phases immediately before and after entry into the organisation when the individual experiences the highest level of disorientation and uncertainty and requires greater external support and guidance. Van Maanen and Schein (1979) proposed a classification of socialisation techniques used in companies, differentiating them based on the reference scope (group or individual), informational content (more or less rich), and the social aspects involved. Each of these techniques is designed to induce a subject going through the process of assuming a new role to develop, depending on the case and needs, either an innovative orientation or a passive adaptation to pre-existing models. Below are the key characteristics of these various socialisation techniques, their respective consequences on roles, and the difficulties due to the different configurations of individual personalities.

- Group Techniques. The distinctive feature of group techniques lies in the particular context in which information is conveyed. The individual goes through the learning process of the new reality together with other newcomers, following common stages designed by the company to facilitate the internalisation of standardised and homogeneous behaviours. The use of these methods allows the organisation to exploit the phenomenon of emulation (Barney et al., 1985): the intellectual capacities of the individual tend to weaken, opinions conform to those expressed by the group, ultimately creating a kind of mental unity. The power of the group is utilised to reinforce the learning of organisational and cultural models deemed effective by the company.
- Individual Techniques. These techniques involve the subject experiencing the learning process in isolation. This offers a wider margin of manoeuvre and more opportunities for personalised and heterogeneous responses.

From what has been said, it can be argued that group socialisation techniques can be used if the aim is to develop in the individual a role orientation aimed at maintaining the status quo, whilst individual techniques are more suitable for stimulating more innovative attitudes.

The classification of socialisation modalities based on their informational content presents a continuum with highly structured and analytical information on the sequence of experiences that the newcomer will go through and the respective ways and timing in which this will happen at one end. On the other hand, techniques where providing specific information is not considered useful and the individual is required to cope with a high degree of uncertainty. Providing generalisations about the role orientation produced by different levels of information structuring presents some difficulties due to the considerable diversity in individuals' personalities. For example, if an individual has low self-esteem, socialisation techniques with poor informational content may induce them to reduce uncertainty by adopting adaptive and emulative behaviours, acquiescing to existing models in the organisational context. On the other hand, for individuals with considerable self-confidence, open methods stimulate innovative and creative behaviours.

The final classification concerns the social or interpersonal aspects of the socialisation process and opposes techniques where newcomers have the opportunity to interact intensely with members of the reference group and acquire information about the expected role profile. It goes from the role models operating in the organisation (thus obtaining positive social support that fuels their self-esteem and reassures them) to methods where individuals are forced to develop the most appropriate role model themselves (with few points of reference), risking conflicts and negative reactions from the group. The specific characteristics of the individual's personality are also decisive in the outcome of the role assumption process.

Techniques of the first type, by fostering inner security and individuals' self-esteem can stimulate both innovative behaviours and passive behaviour.

Innovative behaviour occur if individuals find in the group's emotional support a stimulus to employ their creative abilities and potential in a later phase.

Passive adaptation behaviours happen if the approval of others and constant confirmation of their capabilities and skills serve as an easy opportunity and further push for immobility and passivity).

It is conceivable that group techniques, rich in detailed information and able to provide ample social support, are negatively correlated with the level of conflict, role ambiguity, and the propensity to leave the company, whilst positively correlated with satisfaction and the energy expended (Jones, 1986). However, this consideration must be formulated in relative terms and must absolutely take into account individual characteristics.

Once again, it is clear that the process of socialisation cannot ignore the two involved parties together: individuals with their needs for certain references, as well as autonomous appropriation of social reality, on one hand, and the organisational context often unconsciously pressing to shape people in the image and likeness of their dominant models, on the other.

5.5 The Adaptation Process: The Profile of the Position

Whilst the behaviours required at the headquarters are often of a predominantly executive and conservative nature (in terms of rules, procedures, established practices, and routines in general), abroad, the predominant values, connected to the 'frontier role', are opposite:

- innovating rules or their application methods in line with company objectives,
- negotiating methodologies and resources both within and outside the organisation,
- managing changes and unexpected events whilst coping with the anxiety that comes with it.

From this brief description of the main features of a foreign assignment, it can be easily inferred that, regardless of the degree of difficulty, its execution will impose on the manager a higher level of complexity and challenges compared to those experienced at home. The expatriate finds themselves in the delicate position of having to guard a borderline that separates two different worlds and must be able to reconcile the needs and requirements of both. The local personnel perceives them as a 'coloniser', whilst in the eyes of the headquarters, they represent the 'local man'. In a certain way, the expatriate is part of both worlds and, at the same time, does not belong to either of them.

Their role is ambiguous, subject to sudden changes, and lacking models to refer to. It is highly innovative, often involving tasks never done before, not only for the individual but for the entire company. As if that were not enough, it is a role filled with responsibilities, autonomy, and extensive decision-making powers.

The international manager finds themselves at the centre of a complex network of relationships that more or less indirectly link various social actors with different characteristics and needs. In addition, if this 'intrigue' of relationships were not complex enough, it should be noted that the direction of the pressures converging on the expatriate is almost never univocal. This exposes them to experience considerable role conflict, accompanied by anxiety and frustration.

As seen earlier, the expatriate must identify appropriate solutions to reconcile the incongruities between the ideologies, legal systems, commercial policies, tariff regulations, etc., of the host country compared to their home country and obtain all necessary permissions and authorisations from the local government for financial transfers, investments, employment policies, waste disposal, etc. (Yun, 1973).

The foreign assignment makes them the pivot of connections between the headquarters and the foreign subsidiary, as well as a vehicle or even a living embodiment of the business policies and philosophies promoted by the central offices. Their main task is to translate these policies into operational practices, overcoming the obstacles resulting from any potential incompatibilities with the way the local community operates. The motivation of collaborators requires leadership styles suitable for the culture and values expressed by the context they are guests in whilst remaining consistent with the guidelines given by the headquarters. The centre-periphery relationship overlaps with the normal hierarchical relationship, creating greater complexity but also conditions for high flexibility in determining the role boundaries. The headquarters, to meet their flexibility needs, know they must accept flexible frontier positions capable of interacting with an often distant and unstable environment.

The effectiveness with which the manager manages the cross-interaction between centre/periphery and superior/subordinate can be compromised by the inadequacy of support from communication and information systems. Deficiencies in communication mechanisms are the main source of the headquarters' inability to understand the needs and requirements of subsidiaries, leading to further uncertainty and frustration for the international manager. Having established that ambiguity, novelty, uncertainty, and role conflict seem to be inseparable travel companions for an expatriate, it is important to consider how the consequences of these characteristics can be minimised or at least prevented.

One of the factors highlighted by numerous studies in this regard is the level of role ambiguity (Black, 1988; Minkler and Biller, 1979). The greater difficulties in adapting to a position with unstructured and ambiguous characteristics stem from the need that every individual feels, to a greater or lesser extent, to know in advance the consequences of their actions and the connections between means and ends. Role ambiguity concerns nothing more than the clarity of cause-and-effect relationships (Lawrence and Lorsch, 1967). From it arises the difficulty and often the futility of using in the new context the behaviours learned in the past, which are no longer suitable for meeting present demands. In Pearce's model (1981), ambiguity is traced back to some triggering factors:

- entering an unfamiliar environment and consequently modifying one's expectations about the connections between work behaviours and results;
- having to work interdependently with others and calibrate one's behaviours based on the meanings attributed to the behaviours of others and vice versa;
- the delay or absence of feedback and information on the achieved results.

All these factors are present in the case of an overseas experience and deeply impact the level of tension and stress experienced by the expatriate (although differently depending on their personality) (Black, 1988).

From the numerous studies conducted, a particularly strong link has been identified between the difficulties of adaptation and the discretion of the role, i.e., the degree to which a subject has the possibility to modify the objectives of their work, the means to achieve them, and the relationships between resources and results. Adaptation becomes less critical in the case of high discretion because it allows the individual to shape the role characteristics in a way that makes them more suitable for themselves and their abilities.

Another possible source of role shock and, therefore, difficulties in adaptation, is the change in the nature of the role, from predominantly active to passive or vice versa. Many American professionals sent abroad to work as consultants report their dissatisfaction when transitioning to a role with a predominantly passive nature, such as that of a consultant, compared to the managerial tasks performed at home.

5.6 Influence of Culture in Organisations

Culture is always a collective phenomenon because it is shared, at least, by the people who live or have lived within the same social groups where it was learnt. Culture consists of the unwritten rules of social interaction. It makes distinction between members of a group or social category that are different from all others. Culture is learnt, not innate: it comes from one's environment more than from one's genes.

It should be distinguished from the concept of human nature on one hand and individual personality on the other, although the exact boundary between nature and culture, and between culture and personality, remains a subject of controversy among scholars. Presiding over an activity abroad demands a delicate balance of navigating diverse and sometimes conflicting needs. It entails adeptly managing the expectations of various social stakeholders whilst remaining aligned with one's own mission, sphere of autonomy, and the directives provided by the central headquarters of the parent company. This complex role requires the expatriate to mould their behaviour and decision-making to suit the unique characteristics and cultural nuances of the host country. However, this adaptation process can prove challenging as the expatriate may encounter obstacles when trying to apply their learned and familiar management style from their home country. The exercise of usual leadership functions becomes a multifaceted endeavour abroad, as the management techniques and approaches that served well domestically might not be directly applicable or effective in the foreign environment. The expatriate may face significant difficulties when they fail to acknowledge or embrace the variations in managerial practices that exist among different countries.

To be a successful leader in a foreign setting, it is crucial for the expatriate to be aware and sensitive to the local context, customs, and business practices. Rigidly adhering to one's previous managerial approach, without considering the unique challenges and opportunities presented by the new setting, can lead to less-than-optimal outcomes. Instead, a flexible and adaptive leadership style is essential, one that embraces the art of understanding and embracing cultural differences, whilst also capitalising on common ground.

Navigating these complexities requires a keen ability to listen, learn, and communicate effectively. The expatriate must be open to new ideas, willing to integrate local insights and perspectives, and capable of building strong relationships with the diverse workforce and stakeholders. Furthermore, an appreciation for the fluidity of cross-cultural communication, and the ability to bridge language and cultural gaps, will foster a more harmonious and productive working environment.

By approaching the international role with an open mind and a willingness to embrace change, the expatriate can cultivate a leadership style that successfully adapts to the unique demands of the foreign context.

If you want to act globally, think locally, and remember that even in today's more or less globalised world, we are rich in contrasts between individuals, groups, organisations, and nations that think, feel, and act in different ways. Cultural intelligence (Hofstede 2001; 2002; 2005) is part of the set of soft skills that help us realise the reference values that guide, inspire, and influence the behaviours of 'others' - opening up dimensions of great relevance both for understanding the world we live in and, in particular, in the fields of management and international business development.

This blend of flexibility, cultural competence, and a willingness to learn from the experience will not only improve the expatriate's own effectiveness but also positively affect the entire organisation's operations in the foreign market. Through this process of constant adjustment and refinement, the expatriate can transform the challenges posed by managing activities abroad into opportunities for personal growth, professional development, and the flourishing success of the organisation on the global stage.

Researchers and practitioners have identified various traits and skills that contribute to the success of individuals working in international assignments. Here are some common characteristics of the ideal expatriate based on the available literature:

1. *adaptability and flexibility*. The ability to adapt to new environments, cultures, and work practices is crucial for expatriates. They should be open-minded and flexible in dealing with unfamiliar situations and be able to adjust their behaviour and communication style accordingly.
2. *Cultural awareness and sensitivity*. Successful expatriates possess a high level of cultural intelligence. They are sensitive to cultural differences, have a deep understanding of local customs, norms, and values, and can navigate intercultural interactions with ease.
3. *Communication skills*. Effective communication is essential in any international assignment. Ideal expatriates are proficient in cross-cultural communication, including verbal and non-verbal cues, and can bridge language barriers to foster collaboration and understanding.
4. *Emotional resilience*. International assignments can be challenging, and expatriates may encounter stress, isolation, and homesickness. The ideal expatriate exhibits emotional resilience and can cope with the difficulties of living and working in a foreign country.
5. *Global mindset*. Expatriates with a global mindset demonstrate a deep interest in international affairs, possess a global perspective, and are open to learning from diverse experiences and cultures.
6. *Problem-solving skills*. The ability to tackle complex challenges and solve problems in unfamiliar settings is highly valued in expatriates. They should be resourceful and able to think critically to address unique situations.
7. *Interpersonal skills*. Building positive relationships with local colleagues, clients, and stakeholders is crucial for expatriates' success. Ideal expatriates are approachable, respectful, and skilled at building rapport.
8. *Cross-cultural training and experience*. Prior exposure to different cultures and experiences in multicultural settings can enhance an expatriate's ability to function effectively in international assignments.

9. *Job competence.* Along with cross-cultural skills, the ideal expatriate possesses the necessary technical expertise and job-specific competencies to excel in their assigned role.
10. *Motivation and commitment.* Successful expatriates are motivated and committed to achieving their objectives in the foreign assignment. They demonstrate a strong work ethic and a willingness to invest time and effort into their role.

It is essential to note that the characteristics of the ideal expatriate may vary depending on the nature of the international assignment, the host country's culture, the industry, and the specific organisational context. Additionally, the importance of certain traits may differ for different types of international assignments, such as short-term vs. long-term assignments or developmental vs. strategic assignments. Research in this area continues to evolve, and organisations often tailor their selection criteria based on their unique needs and the specific demands of the international assignments they offer.

The above characteristics are in line with the results of a study conducted by Zeira and Harari (1977, 1979) on a sample of 77 multinational companies operating in Great Britain, the Netherlands, Belgium, and Germany. Although very dated, this study anticipated the characteristics that are found in recent literature about the ideal expatriate: he/she should demonstrate trust in their collaborators, delegate tasks, avoid distant attitudes, show respect for local cultural traditions, and listen to advice on the characteristics of the host country. A proper management of the superior-subordinate relationship is obviously critical in determining the effectiveness of any type of international operation. It is therefore vital to identify the variables that influence a specific model of management style in order to derive the factors for success. Among these variables, we can mention the environmental characteristics that constitute the framework within which the company operates (such as the sector size, the level of industrial concentration, etc.) and, in general, all the so-called contextual factors; the internal characteristics of the company (strategies, financial structure, organisational structure, and operational systems); certain traits of the individual manager's personality, among others. However, this diverse set of elements cannot be deciphered without considering the dimension in which they are immersed and from which they draw nourishment: the national culture. The next chapter will focus on the examination of this complex dimension, its relationships with organisational culture, and its impact on the world of international operations.

REFERENCES

Adler, N. J. (1983a). Cross-cultural Management Research: The Ostrich and the Trend. *Academy of Management Review*, *8*(20), 226–232. doi:10.5465/amr.1983.4284725

Adler, N. J. (1983b). Cross-cultural Management: Issues To Be Faced. *International Studies of Management & Organization*, *13*(1-2), 7–45. doi:10.1080/00208825.1983.11656357

Adler, N. J., & Devillafranca, J. (1983). Epistemological Foundations of a Symposium Process: A Framework for Understanding Culturally Diverse Organisations. *International Studies of Management & Organization*, *12*(4), 7–22. doi:10.1080/00208825.1982.11656350

Asch, S. E. (1956). Studies of independence and conformity: I. A minority of one against a unanimous majority. *Psychological Monographs*, *70*(9), 1–70. doi:10.1037/h0093718

Barney, B. J., & Ouchi, W. G. (1985). Costi delle informazioni e strutture economiche di governo delle transazioni. In R. C. D. Nacamulli & A. Rugiadini (Eds.), *Organizzazioni e Mercato*. Il Mulino.

Black, J. S. (1988). Work Role Transitions: A Study of American Expatriate Managers in Japan. *Journal of International Business Studies*, *19*(2), 277–294. doi:10.1057/palgrave.jibs.8490383

Brett, J. M. (1982). Job transfer and well-being. *The Journal of Applied Psychology*, *67*(4), 450–463. doi:10.1037/0021-9010.67.4.450

Decastri, M. (2016). *Indagine sulle trasformazioni indotte nel processo produttivo dalle nuove tecnologie e dall'innovazione in generale*. Editoriale Scientifica.

Decastri, M., Buonocore, F., Battini, S., & Gagliarducci, F. (2020). *Organisational Development in Public Administration: The ltalian Way*. Palgrave McMillan.

Gaffney, S. (1989). *Cultures, Business and Communications*. Institute of International Business Stockholm School of Economics.

Gauthey, F., Ratiu, I., Rodgers, I., & Xardel, D. (1988). *Leaders sans frontiéres. Le dèfi des difference*. McGraw-Hill.

Hofstede, G. (1980). *Culture's consequences: International differences in work-related values*. Sage.

Hofstede, G. (1985). The Interaction between National and Organisational Value Systems. *Journal of Management Studies*, *22*(4), 347–357. doi:10.1111/j.1467-6486.1985.tb00001.x

Hofstede, G. (2001). *Culture's Consequences: Comparing Values, Behaviors, Institutions, and Organisations across Nations*. Sage.

Hofstede, G. (2002). Dimensions Do Not Exist: A Reply to Brendan McSweeney. *Journal of Technological Advancements*, *55*(11), 1355–1361. doi:10.1177/0018726702055011921

Hofstede, G., & Hofstede, G. J. (2005). *Culture and Organisations. Software of the Mind*. McGrawHill.

Hughes, E. C. (1958). *Men and Their Work*. Free Press.

Jacques, E. (1970). *Work, Creativity and Social Justice*. Heinemann Educational Books.

Jones, G. R. (1986). Socialization Tactics, Self-efficacy, and Newcomers Adjustment to Organisations. *Academy of Management Journal*, *29*(2), 262–279. doi:10.2307/256188

Knotts, R. (1989). Cross-cultural management: transformations and adaptations. *Business Horizons, 32*(1), 29+. link.gale.com/apps/doc/A7393085/AONE?u=googlescholar&sid=bookmark-AONE&xid=6f37bdd2

Korman, A. K., Berman, U. W., & Lang, D. (1981). Career success and personal failure: Alienation in professionals and managers. *The Academy of Management Journal*, 342-360. . doi:10.5465/255846

Kroeber, A. L., & Kluckhohn, C. (1952). *Culture. A Critical Review of Concepts and Definitions*. Peabody Museum Press.

Lawrence, P. R., & Lorsch, J. W. (1967). Differentiation and Integration in Complex Organisations. *Administrative Science Quarterly, 12*(1), 1–47. doi:10.2307/2391211

Lawrence, P. R., & Lorsch, J. W. (1967). *Organisation and Environment, Managing Differentiation and Integration*. Harvard Business School.

Louis, M. R. (1980). Surprise and Sense Making: What Newcomers Experiences in Entering Unfamiliar Organisational Settings. *Administrative Science Quarterly, 25*(2), 226–251. doi:10.2307/2392453 PMID:10247029

Mead, R. (1990). *Cross-Cultural Management Communication*. John Wiley & Sons.

Minkler, M., & Biller, R. (1979). Role Shock: A Tool for Conceptualizing Stresses Accompanying Disruptive Role Transitions. *Human Relations, 32*(2), 125–140. Advance online publication. doi:10.1177/001872677903200203

Nicholson, N. (1984). A theory of work role transitions. *Administrative Science Quarterly, 29*(2), 172–191. doi:10.2307/2393172

Parsons, T. (1937). *The Structure of Social Action*. The Free Press.

Pearce, J. (1981). Bringing Some Clarity to Role Ambiguity Research. *Academy of Management Review, 6*(4), 665. Advance online publication. doi:10.2307/257646

Pettigrew, T. F. (1986). The intergroup contact hypothesis reconsidered. In M. Hewstone & R. Brown (Eds.), *Contact and conflict in intergroup encounters* (pp. 169–195). Basil Blackwell.

Pinder, C. C., & Schroeder, K. G. (1987). Time to Proficiency following Job Transfers. *Academy of Management Journal, 30*(2), 336–353. doi:10.2307/256278

Ratiu, I. (1983). Thinking Internationally: A Comparison of How International Executives Learn. *International Studies of Management & Organization, 13*(1-2), 139–153. doi:10.1080/00208825.1983.11656362

Rokeach, M. (1968a). A Theory of Organisation and Change Within Value-Attitude Systems. *The Journal of Social Issues, 24*(1), 13–33. doi:10.1111/j.1540-4560.1968.tb01466.x

Rokeach, M. (1968b). *Beliefs, Attitudes, and Values*. Jossey Bass.

Rokeach, M. (1969). The role of values in public opinion research. *Public Opinion Quarterly, 32*(4), 547–559. doi:10.1086/267645

Rokeach, M. (1973). *The Nature of Human Values*. The Free Press.

Ronen, S. (1986). *Comparative and Multinational Management*. John Wiley & Sons.

Schein, E. H. (1984). Coming to a New Awareness of Organisational Culture. *Sloan Management Review, 25*, 3–16.

Smale, A., & Suutari, V. (2011). Expatriate Perspectives on Knowledge Transfers into Central and Eastern Europe. In S. Mariano, M. Mohamed, & Q. Mohiuddin (Eds.), *The Role of Expatriates in MNCs Knowledge Mobilization. International Business and Management, 27* (pp. 63–90). Emerald Group Publishing Limited. doi:10.1108/S1876-066X(2011)0000027007

Song, J., Almeida, P., & Wu, G. (2003). Learning-by-Hiring: When Is Mobility More Likely to Facilitate Interfirm Knowledge Transfer? *Management Science*, *49*(4), 351–365. doi:10.1287/mnsc.49.4.351.14429

Yun, C. K. (1973). Role Conflicts of Expatriate Managers: A Construct. *Management International Review*, *13*(3). Advance online publication. doi:10.1177/239700229901300302

Zeira, Y., & Harari, E. (1977). Managing third-country nationals in multinational companys. *Business Horizons*, *20*(5), 83–88. doi:10.1016/0007-6813(77)90062-3

Zeira, Y., & Harari, E. (1979). Host-Country Organisations and Expatriate Managers in Europe. *California Management Review*, *21*(3), 40–50. doi:10.2307/41165306

Chapter 6
National Culture and Organization Theory:
Different Methodological Approaches

ABSTRACT

The relationship between national culture and organisational theory has been a subject of deep interest within academic research. This chapter explores the diverse methodological approaches employed in studying such a critical connection, which contribute to understanding how national cultural values affect organisational behaviour, structures, and practices. These perspectives provide information about different cultural aspects, capturing subjective experiences and contextual nuances through ethnographic studies or interviews. Acknowledging the significance of different methodological perspectives is crucial for developing a holistic understanding of how national culture influences organisational theories and practices. By embracing this diversity, practitioners have a more holistic understanding of the interplay between national culture and organisational phenomena.

6. NATIONAL CULTURE AND ORGANISATION THEORY. DIFFERENT METHODOLOGICAL APPROACHES

Cultural differences play a crucial role in the realm of management, especially in the context of international operations. When organisations expand their activities across borders, they encounter diverse cultural norms, values, and practices that can significantly affect their managerial approach and overall effectiveness. Understanding and navigating these cultural variations are essential for successful cross-border operations. One of the most apparent areas where cultural differences come into play is in communication styles and interpersonal interactions. Different cultures have unique communication patterns, ranging from direct and explicit to indirect and implicit. Misinterpretations and misunderstandings can arise when individuals from different cultural backgrounds interact, potentially leading to conflicts or misalignment of objectives. Managers must develop cross-cultural communication skills to foster effective collaboration and promote a harmonious work environment. Cultural norms also influence

DOI: 10.4018/979-8-3693-3482-9.ch006

leadership styles and decision-making processes. For instance, some cultures place a strong emphasis on hierarchical structures, where authority is highly respected and decisions are made by top management. In contrast, others prefer participative and democratic leadership, where decisions are made collectively with input from team members. Managers working in diverse cultural settings must adapt their leadership approach to align with local preferences and expectations. Moreover, the concept of time and punctuality can vary significantly across cultures. In some cultures, strict adherence to schedules and deadlines is paramount, while in others, a more flexible approach is accepted. These differences can impact project planning, meeting arrangements, and overall organisational efficiency. Managers need to be mindful of these cultural attitudes toward time to avoid potential conflicts and ensure smooth operations. Cultural values and attitudes towards risk-taking, innovation, and change also diverge between societies. Some cultures embrace risk and innovation as catalysts for growth and progress, while others prioritize stability and tradition, being more risk-averse. Such variations can shape how organisations approach strategic decisions, product development, and adaptation to market changes. Managers must be attuned to cultural preferences and design strategies that resonate with the values of the local workforce and consumers. Embracing cultural diversity and fostering an inclusive work environment is vital for organisations aiming to leverage the strengths of their multicultural teams. A diverse workforce can bring fresh perspectives, creativity, and problem-solving capabilities. However, without effective cross-cultural management, cultural diversity can become a source of tension and hinder collaboration. Managers should encourage intercultural awareness and sensitivity, promoting open dialogue and mutual respect among team members.

The theme of cultural differences in management began to emerge simultaneously with the international expansion of large American companies. At that time, the almost uncontested American hegemony allowed its scholars and managers to view the phenomenon merely as a problem of managing foreign subordinates, without challenging the underlying assumption of the implicit superiority of the American model, except in some theories of leadership and motivation. Subsequently, new management philosophies emerged that, through an original reinterpretation of overseas theories, presented new organisational configurations and, therefore, new design criteria. If, as it seems, the success of new industrial powers is also due to the peculiar characteristics of their management, organisational theory can no longer limit itself to highlighting the need to adapt some management practices to the cultural specificities of foreign subsidiaries. It must question its own basic assumptions to explain the reasons for this success and, conversely, the factors contributing to American decline.

The challenge to the dominant American paradigm actually came mainly from European scholars: Crozier and Friedberg from France, the English Aldrich, and the school of the Swede Weick. While the spread of attention to cultural issues found a receptive ground in Europe and Asia for innovative perspectives in organisational analysis, the American discipline of cross-cultural management is more a result imposed by historical conditions that questioned the validity and universality of established theories.

Despite the general recognition by scholars, consultants, and managers of the importance of the intercultural approach, an analysis conducted by Nancy Adler on management studies conducted in the United States in the 1960s and 1970s shows that business activities internationalized more quickly than the production of articles in American management journals. In fact, most of the organisation and management articles published in American journals during that period focused on the domestic context and did not refer to cultural issues in any way. Even articles on international organisational behaviour that considered cultural issues mostly studied a single country other than the United States or analysed comparative organisational practices of two countries. Even rarer are articles concerning the interaction between different cultures within a single organisational context (Adler, 1983).

6.1 Different Methodological Perspectives

The positive evolution of attitudes toward cross-cultural studies has led to a significant number of contributions that stand out for the originality and quality of their proposals. To provide the reader with a useful reading path of these contributions, two modalities of classification of methodologies have been suggested to address the theme of intercultural management (Adler and Ghadar, 1990). The first important classification of studies focusing on the relationship between national culture, organisational culture, and organisation is suggested by Bodega (1996) which has been later borrowed by Denison and Mishra (1995). Bodega proposes an interpretative scheme articulated along two dimensions. On the one hand, it considers the distinction between research oriented towards the study of similarities and those oriented towards the study of differences in culture. On the other hand, it focuses the analysis on the micro or macro organisational dimension. The first distinction refers to the dichotomy of scientific investigation between a) *idiographic* methods and b) *nomothetic* methods.

a) *Idiographic* literally means "seeking the particular" (as opposed to the general) and contrasts with the concept of "nomothetic," which, on the contrary, denotes the search for universal laws. The distinction between these two approaches dates back to Windelband, who identified the idiographic style as characteristic of historical disciplines and the nomothetic style as typical of natural sciences. A similar distinction is proposed by anthropologist Pike (1954, 1967, 182, 1988, 1990, 1998), who defines "emic" as those who highlight unique aspects within a culture, and "etic" as those who research common elements in order to compare them (Hofstede and Bollinger, 1989). In anthropology, the idiographic orientation has been conceptually conceptualized rigorously by the nineteenth-century scholar Boas (one of the fathers of ethnological method), who strongly emphasized the need for a focused but in-depth study of individual social aspects, rejecting any attempt to subject the analysis to laws or general explanations.

"In the idiographic approach, it is assumed that the relationships between organisations and their contexts form configurations that remain specific to a defined unit of space and time....In other words, it is hypothesized that if certain contingent and economic factors (in hypothetical country A and at a given historical moment) can be associated with organisational variables according to a particular configuration, in country B (in the same period or at any other time) those same factors and variables will give rise to a different organisational configuration" (Child and Tayeb, 1983; p. 25).

There are two epistemological reasons to support the validity of an idiographic approach to the study of organisations: firstly, because science does not always seek regularities but can find justification in the in-depth understanding, even if not reproducible and generalizable, of the uniqueness of a phenomenon. Secondly, the search for particularities is also consistent with a nomothetic approach.

b) *Nomothetic* implements Popper's (1972) "principle of falsification," according to which, in essence, the validity of an empirical law can never be definitively accompanied by verified regularities but can only be subject to attempts to find exceptions that question it. In defining the scientific character of a law, Popper states, among other things, that "A law that cannot be refuted by any conceivable event is not (as is often believed) an advantage, but a defect; any genuine test of a law is an attempt to falsify or refute it" (Lammers and Hickson, 1979; p. 3).

Clearly, in this light, the idiographic approach becomes a complementary mode of analysis, rather than antithetical, to the nomothetic one, which can thus avoid to describe a social phenomenon by resorting to an explanation that leaves no room for the control of unconsidered variables.

Based on the two dimensions of analysis level (micro and macro) and research focus (similarities and differences), Bodega (1996) constructs a taxonomy capable of clarifying the framework of the main research strategies of organisational culture followed so far.

Along this perspective there is the argument advanced by Kerr, Dunlop, Harbison, and Myers (1960). The authors argue that a logic of industrialism exists that generates imperatives of an economic and technological nature. It strongly influences the development of industrial societies according to a common model. Regardless of the diverse political, ideological, and cultural origins of these societies, institutional models converge under the influence of a common industrial logic.

Later, these positions have been developed with particular regard to organisational structures and management issues by Harbison and Myers (1960). The two authors argue that industrialization inevitably involves increasing specialization of functions within economic organisations, greater internal complexity, and a drastic increase in company size. On the one hand, specialization and complexity accentuate the problems of coordination and integration within the organisation; on the other hand, specialization and size make it difficult to maintain decision-making power exclusively centralized at the highest level of organisational hierarchies.

The industrial logic prevails regardless of the cultural context, although it is recognized that cultural factors may clash with this process and slow it down. The strengthening of this logic is a binding condition for achieving institutional results. It is, thus, asserted that stable relationships exist between structural characteristics of organisations (formalizations, functional specialization, and authority centralization) and context variables of different countries.

These hypotheses imply that such relationships will be constant in direction where they are fundamentally linear, as in the companies investigated by Hickson et al. (1974), they should also be constant in terms of magnitude, regardless of differences in structures or contexts characterizing different social realms. Hickson (1974) summarizes the concept that the relationship between the structural characteristics of organisations and context variables will be stable across societies. In fact, the position is not as rigid as it appears. It admits the possibility that the relationships between organisational structure and context, while essentially stable as stated above, may be influenced to some extent by the cultural variable.

It is recognized that cultural models in a society can influence the structures and organisational processes mainly in three ways (Lammers and Hickson, 1983).

a. The values of a society inspire the norms and rules that make up its legal and political system: organisations must comply with the provisions of institutions and constantly verify that their rules are consistent or otherwise compatible with the values of their significant public.
b. The culture of a society, considered in its broadest sense, includes the economic and organisational theories that those responsible for defining the structure and operating mechanisms of a company can use.
c. The values and norms of society influence the assumption and performance of roles within the organisation: the patterns of action and interaction acquired before entering the organisation (in the family, in the community, at school, in peer groups, etc.) constitute what is commonly called informal organisation.

Among the main scholars in favour of idiographic orientation, it is important to mention Child and Kieser (1979), who suggest that cultural factors can mediate the relationships between the role system and organisational behaviour. They offer a different interpretation of the context-structure variable relationship, which is central to the argument of the culture-free thesis. The starting point is the observation that some structural characteristics of companies operating in different countries can be traced back to general organisational principles and models. This could mean that the similarity in structural solutions is the result of both the diffusion of the same organisational theories in different countries and a planned and conscious response to objective contingent factors.

Another piece of scholar research emphasized the role of culture as a cohesive force for subsystems that may or should be different due to the differentiation needs perceived by the collective entity to which it refers (Lawrence and Lorsch, 1967). If different tasks in terms of complexity, uncertainty, and predictability require equally different modes of operation, creating articulation and fragmentation in the social system, culture can be interpreted as a possible integration mechanism. According to these studies, culture is a factor that represents the common denominator of different subsystems (Van Maanen and Barley, 1984).

Lastly, studies focusing on inter-company and international dimensions and their explanatory laws are enable to distinguish and identify the cultural profile of social systems by emphasizing differences. The researchers referring to this quadrant strive to identify conceptual frameworks and categories of analysis that prioritize differences. Adler (1984) proposes the second important distinction between methodological approaches used in intercultural research on management, identifying six of them:

1. parochial research,
2. ethnocentric research,
3. polycentric research,
4. geocentric research,
5. synergistic research,
6. comparative research.

The first line of studies concerns and includes research projects conceived and carried out within a culture by scholars from the same culture. Paradoxically, this extreme relativity is rarely recognized, so much so that, in the absence of contrary indications, it is assumed that the conclusions of such studies enjoy universality; alternatively, with the same effects, a certain similarity between the cultures of industrialized countries is postulated. Culture is excluded, both as an independent variable and as a dependent variable. Culture is implicitly considered a constant.

A similar attitude is proposed by Triandis (1983), who justifies it by arguing that organisational scholars spontaneously develop theories that concern the world they know and understand. As a result, many of these theories are inappropriate and inadequate when applied to other cultures. We create organisations that work well for us and people like us. However, these organisations often fail for people with different perspectives. In short, it is evident that this category is subject to all the limits of relativity and anachronism in which many of the studies whose validity is not verified at the international level fall today. This closed-minded attitude towards everything that happens abroad, a consequence of the vastness of the domestic market and the national education system, has been typical of North American culture. It has become the target of harsh criticism by intellectuals, politicians, and managers, who blame this provincialism for many of the faults of the US economic decline (Vaccà and Zanfei, 1989; Adler, 1986). It is worth noting, in this regard, the metaphor cited by Adler (1986) regarding American indifference to everything that happens beyond national borders: *"[...] our approach is similar to that of someone who, when asked what bothers him more between ignorance and apathy, answers: 'I don't know, and I don't care".* (p.20).

In addition to provincialism, another attitude stigmatized by anthropologists is *ethnocentrism*, which is the attitude of considering one's own culture as the most valid in absolute terms compared to any other existing in the past and present. It is distinguished from the spontaneous attitude of preferential attachment to the culture in which we have been raised, which is an essential element of social cohesion present in all known peoples, because it is "theorized" and thus takes on the guise of an ideology. In the organisational field, *ethnocentric* research generally consists of replicating studies originally conducted within the researchers' own culture in a new cultural context; the objective is to test the possibility of transferring managerial theories developed in one country to another. From this perspective, culture can add various dimensions to the research, as it becomes possible to experimentally analyse the impact of different environmental conditions on the organisation. Historically, the first ethnocentric studies in the modern sense date back to the Second World War, on the famous research commissioned by the American Ministry of Defence to anthropologists such as Ruth Benedict or Margaret Mead, in order to understand and predict the behaviours of military enemies and allies. In the economic field, this approach was adopted by American scholars following the initial organisational failures in foreign subsidiaries. Its main problem is that it tends to explain foreign culture in terms of variance from one's own culture, thereby inhibiting a comprehensive and in-depth understanding.

In the *polycentric* approach, research is designed to describe social and managerial practices within specific cultures, without any reference to the existence of general laws or at least similarities with characteristics found in other national contexts. In their most extreme form, these studies fall within the ideographic approach: institutions are fully understandable only within their culture (Bodega, 1988). From this perspective, any attempt to resort to general laws to explain organisational behaviour would be methodologically incorrect and misleading. Incorrect because it is not verifiable a priori that institutions of the same kind in different countries respond to the same logics; but such a comparison would also be misleading because it would unduly separate the organisation from its context and its history, thus making many of the profound reasons that inspire the behaviour of its actors "invisible".

Geocentric research focuses on understanding the functioning of companies, without particular reference to cultural issues: implicitly, it is assumed that there are organisation and management approaches that are universally effective. Studies in international strategy generally focus on the geographic dispersion aspect of multinational companies. They concentrate on the fact that multinational companies operate in many places but do not dwell on the cultural differences between these countries. In many studies, culture is completely ignored; thus, geocentric research often assumes the hypothesis of intercultural universality without questioning its validity (Adler, 1984). It is also worth noting some phenomena that favour the geocentric perspective.

Firstly, as already seen, it is possible to observe greater homogeneity of configurations at the macrostructural level compared to the microstructural level (where cultural factors have greater influence), and therefore some degree of generalization is legitimate, at least for macro phenomena.

Secondly, it is worth highlighting the most recent interpretations of the global or transnational company, which is increasingly seen as an entity attentive to the "changes and incremental adjustments that the company must make to its conduct to meet the demands of the host country, the country where its subsidiaries and operational units of other multinational companies operate" (Valdani, 1990).

Directly connected and complementary to the geocentric approach is the *synergistic* research. It concerns of the interaction between people from different cultures in a single work environment: synergistic research focuses on the behaviour of (1) people within international organisations; (2) people assigned to international assignments for organisations from their own country; (3) people in organisations from their own country that have employees, suppliers, or customers of different nationalities (Adler, 1984). The key questions that this line of study seeks to answer refer to three categories.

1. When to use a "pluralistic" management approach? In other words, when is it necessary to adapt to specific managerial practices in the national context where one operates?
2. When to use a geocentric approach? Or, when to subject all situations to homogeneous management standards?
3. When to exploit synergies resulting from attempting to create an efficient and innovative interaction between the peculiar aspects of the cultures involved and the strategic and organisational directions expressed according to a geocentric logic?

This approach obviously shifts the focus of analysis from descriptive research to research aimed at identifying normative models and aimed at identifying what should be rather than what is. Dealing with different cultures means highlighting and questioning, often for the first time, one's own system of values: hence the impulse to assume a psychological attitude of defence, which often leads to not objectively considering the behaviours of the counterpart that do not fit into our mental schemes (Hendon and Heldon, 1989). However, the ability to effectively dialogue with a different world cannot derive from analytical and, above all, "scientific" models: each people has its range of beliefs, values, habits, and ceremonies that cannot be summarized or formalized in a manual. Precisely the tacit, difficult-to-communicate, complex, and distinct nature of this kind of knowledge prevents achieving a definitive modelling and instead requires a long process of learning in the field, through direct experience, interaction as well as considerable relational skills.

The only way to overcome these distortions is to become aware of the structure of one's psychological system when interacting with people who do not share the same system (McCall and Warrington, 1988). Paradoxically, knowledge of other cultures and learning intercultural competencies are formed through a process of understanding oneself and one's tacit assumptions.

Another significant problem that the *synergistic approach* focuses on is the dilemma between local managers and expatriate managers heading foreign subsidiaries: the problem can essentially be related to organisational design choices inspired by the concepts of differentiation and integration (Lawrence and Lorsch, 1967). If, for an assignment to lead a foreign subsidiary, a local manager is chosen, one can certainly rely on their insider quality (thus reducing many risks of cultural inadequacy). However, the costs of a probable lesser integration with the international strategies of the parent company must also be considered; the opposite problems will obviously arise when installing a manager from the parent company in the subsidiary. In general, in the past, the central problem has been about how to minimize the impact of culture on the organisation and how to adopt a single, universal approach to manage the global operations of an international company. In stark contrast, the central issue of some new models of international companies seems to be: *"How can the company recognize and respect the specific behavioural patterns of different nations and cultures and coordinate them in order to increase the effectiveness of the entire company?"* (Adler, 1983b).

In this second case, the reference is to the ideal possibility of creating an integrated organisational culture based on the best aspects of individual national cultures: this benefit can be called "cultural synergy" (Adler, 1983b). New technologies and the nature of globalization processes have, indeed, led to an emphasis on the specific learning paths of each culture. Finally, as already seen, both the transnational company of Bartlett and Ghoshal and the heterarchy of Hedlund have "cultural synergy" as one of the most distinctive characteristics.

The last research approach to consider is the *comparative* one, which is designed to identify similarities and differences between two or more cultures. Using intercultural similarities, *comparative studie*s seek to identify emerging universals. In ethnocentric studies, "universal" theories belonging to one culture are imposed on another culture. In polycentric studies, the possibility of universality is denied through the attempt to define emerging patterns from all the cultures studied. In this way, comparative studies seek both similarities and divergences. They define emerging similarity as universality and emerging difference as cultural specificity (Adler, 1984). In comparative studies, therefore, the coexistence of universal aspects and particular aspects is not just a starting hypothesis but an authentic research objective. This chapter has provided a thorough analysis of various methodological approaches used in intercultural management research. It emphasizes the importance of cultural context in understanding organisational behaviour and highlights the need for a nuanced and open-minded approach to studying cross-cultural phenomena. The insights from these approaches can help organisations navigate the complexities of managing in an increasingly globalized world.

REFERENCES

Adler, N. J. (1980). Cultural synergy: the management of cross-cultural organisations. In W. W. Burke & L. D. Goodstein (Eds.), *Trends and Issues in OD: Current Theory and Practice* (pp. 163–184). University Associates.

Adler, N. J. (1983a). Cross-cultural Management Research: The Ostrich and the Trend. *Academy of Management Review*, *8*(2), 226. Advance online publication. doi:10.2307/257749

Adler, N. J. (1983b). Cross-cultural Management: Issues to Be Faced. *International Studies of Management & Organization*, *12*(1-2), 7–45. Advance online publication. doi:10.1080/00208825.1983.11656357

Adler, N. J. (1984). Expecting International Success: Female Managers Overseas. *The Columbia Journal of World Business*, *19*(3), 79–85. https://www.journals.elsevier.com/journal-of-world-business

Adler, N. J. (1984). Understanding the ways of understanding: Cross-cultural management reviewed. In R. N. Farmer (Ed.), *Advances in international comparative management* (Vol. 1, pp. 31–67). JAI Press.

Adler, N. J. (1986). *International Dimensions of Organisational Behaviour*. Kent Publishing Company.

Adler, N.J, & Ghadar, F. (1990). Strategic HRM: A global perspective. *HRM in International Comparison*, 235-260. . doi:10.1515/9783110869101.235

Adler, N. J., & Jelinek, M. (1986). Is organisation culture "Culture Bound? *Human Resource Management*, *25*(2), 73–90. doi:10.1002/hrm.3930250106

Bodega, D. (1988). L'organizzazione si proietta in se stessa. *Sviluppo & Organizzazione,* 110.

Bodega, D. (1996). *Organizzazione e cultura. Teoria e metodo della prospettiva culturale nell'organizzazione d'azienda*. Guerini e Associati.

Child, C., & Tayeb, M. (1983). Theoretical Perspectives in Cross-National Organisation Research. *International Studies of Management & Organization*, *12*(4), 23–70. doi:10.1080/00208825.1982.11656351

Child, J., & Keiser, A. (1979). Organisations and managerial roles in British and West German companies: An examination of the culture-free thesis. In C. J. Lammers & D. J. Hickson (Eds.), *Organisations alike and unalike: International and interinstitutional studies in the sociology of organisations* (pp. 251-272). Routledge Kegan Paul, London.

Denison, D. R., & Mishra, A. K. (1995). Toward a Theory of Organisational Culture and Effectiveness. *Organization Science*, *6*(2), 204–223. doi:10.1287/orsc.6.2.204

Harbison, F., & Myers, C. A. (1959). *Management in the Industrial World*. McGraw Hill.

Heldon, D. W., & Hendon, R. A. (1989). *How to Negotiate Worldwide: a Practical Handbook*. Gower.

Hickson, D., Hinings, C., Mcmillan, C., & Schwitter, J. (1974). The Culture-Free Context of Organisation Structure: A Tri-National Comparison. *Sociology*, *8*(1), 59–80. doi:10.1177/003803857400800104

Hickson, D. J., McMillan, C. J., Azumi, K., & Horvath, D. (1979). Grounds for comparative organisation theory: quicksand or hard core? In C. J. Lammers & D. J. Hickson (Eds.), *Organisations Alike and Unlike: International and Inter-Institutional Studies in the Sociology of Organisation* (pp. 25–41). Routledge & Kegan Paul.

Hofstede, G., & Bollinger, D. (1989). *Inter Nazionalità*. Guerini e Associati.

Kerr, C., Dunlop, J., Harbison, P., & Myers, G. (1960). *Industrialism and Industrial Man*. Harvard University Press.

Lamiell, J. T. (1998). Nomothetic and idiographic: Contrasting Windelband's understanding with contemporary usage. *Theory & Psychology*, *8*(1), 23–38. doi:10.1177/0959354398081002

Lammers, C. J., & Hickson, D. J. (1979). *Organisations Alike and Unlike*. Routledge and Kegan.

Lawrence, P. R., & Lorsch, J. W. (1967). Differentiation and Integration in Complex Organisations. *Administrative Science Quarterly*, *12*(1), 1–47. doi:10.2307/2391211

McCall, J. B., & Warrington, M. B. (1988). *Marketing by Agreement. A Cross-Cultural Approach to Business Negotiations*. John Wiley & Sons.

Pike, K. L. (1954). Language in relation to a unified theory of the structure of human behaviour. Part I. The Summer Institute of Linguistics. doi:10.1515/9783111657158

Pike, K. L. (1967). *Language in relation to a unified theory of the structure of human behaviour* (2nd ed.). Mouton. doi:10.1515/9783111657158

Pike, K. L. (1982). *Linguistic concepts: an introduction to tagmemics*. University of Nebraska Press.

Pike, K. L. (1988). Cultural relativism in relation to constraints on world view — An emic perspective. *Bulletin of the Institute of History and Philology*, *59*, 385–399.

Pike, K. L. (1990). Pike's Reply to Harris. In T. N. Headland, K. L. Pike, & M. Harris (Eds.), *Emics and etics: The insider/outsider debate* (pp. 62–74). Sage.

Pike, K. L. (1998). A linguistic pilgrimage. In E. F. K. Koerner (Ed.), *First person singular III: Autobiographies by North American scholars in the language sciences* (pp. 145–158). John Benjamins. doi:10.1075/sihols.88.09pik

Popper, K. R. (1972). *Objective knowledge: an evolutionary approach.* Oxford University Press.

Triandis, H. C. (1983). Dimensions of Cultural Variations Parameters of Organisational Thrones-. *International Studies of Management & Organization, 11*(4), 285–302. doi:10.1002/1520-6629(198310)11:4<285:AID-JCOP2290110403>3.0.CO;2-8

Vaccà, S., & Zanfei, A. (1989). L'impresa globale come "sistema aperto" a rapporti di cooperazione. *Economia e Politica Industriale*, 64.

Valdani, E. (1991). *Marketing globale*. Egea.

Van Maanen, J., & Schein, E. H. (1978). Toward a theory of organisation socialization. *Research in Organizational Behavior, 1*, 209–226.

Windelband, W. (1998). History and natural science. *Theory & Psychology, 8*(1), 5–22. doi:10.1177/0959354398081001

Chapter 7
Culture and Management: From Method to Content

ABSTRACT

This chapter deals with the topic of dynamic relationship between culture and management, exploring varying perspectives from the culture-free thesis to the culture-bound outlook. It goes through the studies of Laurent and his Western management styles, Hofstede, and Trompenaars' multifaceted cultural dimensions. Additionally, it examines the GLOBE Study, which synthesized cross-cultural theories, and acknowledges contributions by Triandis, Schneider, Boisot, and Sorge. The chapter addresses the issue of freedom and limitations within cultural action, contemplating the implications in management practices. This comprehensive review not only addresses the methodological aspects but also encompasses the substantive content of culture in the realm of management, offering a multifaceted understanding of its impact, significance, and application within organisational frameworks.

7. CULTURE AND MANAGEMENT: FROM METHOD TO CONTENT

Culture and management have emerged as integral components in the study of organisational behaviour and effectiveness. Initially, the focus was on the methodological approaches used to explore the relationship between national culture, organisational culture, and management practices. Scholars like Bodega and Adler proposed classification systems, distinguishing between idiographic and nomothetic methods, emphasizing the search for particularities and universal laws, respectively. Over time, the emphasis has shifted from method to content, delving into the impact of culture on management practices and vice versa. Researchers now recognize that culture plays a crucial role in shaping managerial philosophies, decision-making processes, and organisational structures. It is no longer just about understanding cultural differences, but also about leveraging cultural synergies to create integrated and effective organisational cultures that transcend national boundaries. This shift in focus has led to a deeper understanding of the complexities of culture and management, fostering the development of more comprehensive and inclusive approaches in the field. Some important classifications refer not only to the research method but also to the content of research works. Therefore, the theses considered most accurate regarding the role of culture

DOI: 10.4018/979-8-3693-3482-9.ch007

in international managerial choices. In general, these classifications are quite similar and tend to assess the contribution that culture can offer to the interpretation of business and market phenomena. The joint analysis of the classifications proposed in the literature (Ajiferuke and Boddewyn, 1970; Miller, 1984; Child, 1981) allows us to identify two extreme poles on a continuum: on one side, the culture-free perspectives, and on the other, the culture-bound approaches. In the former case, a substantial homogeneity of managerial practices is emphasized, even in different national and cultural contexts. In the latter case, there is a strong emphasis on national culture as the determining variable in the design and governance of organisational systems. Within this second line of thought, different approaches are distinguished based on the conception given to the term "culture". From the ideationalist perspective, it takes the form of values and preferences of organisational actors. From the institutionalist strand, culture is the result of a historical process of social learning and adaptation that gives rise to specific institutional models (political, educational, legal, economic, etc.) which continually interact with organisational behaviours.

However, it is universally accepted that culture plays an important and indispensable role in the construction of supranational organisational theories and models. The issue is not whether to consider or not the cultural influence on managerial practices but rather to understand if it is genuinely impossible to identify stable relationships between variables in different cultural contexts (culture-bound approach) or if, on the contrary, such relationships exist but differ from country to country depending on the intensity with which they manifest (culture-free approach). For instance, in the first case, the degree of formalization of organisational structure may not be linked to the company's size and may vary depending on the national culture in which the company operates. In contrast, in the second case, formalization and size are correlated worldwide, but with varying intensity and impact depending on the specific context being studied.

7.1 Culture-Free Thesis

The culture-free thesis is a perspective within cross-cultural management research that emphasizes the universality of managerial practices and organisational behaviour across different national and cultural contexts. According to this thesis, cultural factors are considered to have minimal or no impact on managerial decision-making and organisational processes. Instead, it posits that there are fundamental principles and management practices that can be applied universally, regardless of the cultural context. Advocates of the culture-free thesis argue that managerial practices are primarily influenced by economic and technological factors rather than cultural ones. They contend that in an increasingly globalized world, businesses operate under similar market conditions and face comparable challenges, leading to convergence in managerial practices. The roots of the culture-free thesis can be traced back to research conducted in the mid-20th century, particularly during the early stages of multinational business expansion. Scholars observed that certain organisational structures and management practices appeared to be consistent across different countries, leading to the belief that cultural variations played a limited role in shaping managerial behaviour.

However, the culture-free thesis has faced criticism and challenges from various quarters. Critics argue that it oversimplifies the complexity of cultural influences on managerial decision-making. They contend that culture permeates every aspect of organisational life and plays a crucial role in shaping values, communication styles, leadership approaches, and employee behaviour. Moreover, cross-cultural studies have demonstrated that cultural differences can significantly affect the effectiveness of management practices. What may be successful in one cultural context might not work as effectively in another, necessitating adjustments and adaptations to accommodate local norms and values.

Nevertheless, scholars have recognized the significance of incorporating cultural sensitivity and adaptability in managerial practices when dealing with diverse international markets and workforces. As a result, many researchers now emphasize the importance of adopting a more culture-conscious approach to management, acknowledging and understanding the ways in which cultural nuances can influence organisational dynamics and success in the global arena. The thesis supported by this research perspective refers to the fundamental principle that the relationships between contextual variables (typically environment, strategy, and technology) and the organisational dimensions of business configurations are similar across different national cultures. There are significant analogies between this hypothesis and that of convergence, according to which companies worldwide, due to the processes of industrialization and globalization, are and will be compelled to participate in a game governed by the same rules for everyone. If competition operates in the same way worldwide, then there must exist a more effective organisational configuration independent of national culture. The latter can only play a disturbing role, preventing the company from quickly adopting the most effective organisational logic. For example, Farmer and Richman (1965) state that once the general similarity of people worldwide is recognized and managerial and technological needs push all cultures of every type towards a common path, nations become increasingly similar everywhere.

Hence, comparative management studies will become obsolete. Instead of differences, we will find similarities, as the logic of technology and management will lead everyone to the same general position. If this thesis is accepted, the level of industrial development becomes the determining variable for the characteristic organisational and managerial profile of a nation. This leads to a corollary of the culture-free approach, suggesting that if companies from two countries characterized by a similar level of industrialization operate under similar contextual factors, then they should not show significant differences in organisational structure and management (Child, 1981). Similarly, contingency theories, although not recommending a universal model of the company, tend to identify stable relationships between causal variables and organisational structure, irrespective of national culture, without elaborating on the universality of the distribution of contingencies worldwide. This relationship is based on three conceptual pillars (Child, 1981; Child and Tayeb, 1983):

a. technological imperative;
b. stability in context-structure relationships;
c. the role of strategic evolution.

This third factor operates similarly to what was previously discussed regarding industrial growth: different stages of strategic development should lead to correlated organisational structures, highlighting the classic “strategy-structure” relationship that excludes any influence of variables unrelated to the typical economic combination of the company. The role of technology has been emphasized, especially by the research of Woodward (1965), Perrow (1967, 1970, 1976), and Thompson (1967). In the field of comparative management, their theories can be reinterpreted by stating that the adoption of a given technology will have the same consequences on the design of the organisational structure, the type of employees to be hired, and the work relationships in any country worldwide (Child, 1981).

Later research (Gallie, 1978; Maurice et al., 1980) has questioned the imperative nature of technological prescriptions, noting significant organisational differences between companies with the same technology but of different nationalities, suggesting a possible cultural influence. To these empirical discrepancies, we must add the theoretical objections of Crozier and Friedberg (1978), who accuse this perspective of technological determinism: in seeking universal laws of organisational behaviour, the social and non-natural nature of organisations is forgotten. However, the main foundation of contingency theory is the hypothesis of stability in the relationships between contextual features and organisational configuration; it is summarized in the assumption that companies respond similarly to external stimuli and similar internal constraints: in other words, a given competitive and technological environment will give rise to predictable behaviours (Boisot, 1986).

Once applied to businesses of different nationalities, this assumption becomes the central pivot of the culture-free perspective: it would be possible to construct an organisational theory that is valid regardless of national or corporate cultural specificities. However, the contingency theories have developed without verification of their validity at the international level: all the most important studies originated from comparative research within a single context, either the North American one (for example, the models of Lawrence and Lorsch, 1967; Galbraith, 1973; Mintzberg 1980, 1983) or the British one (the Aston model – Pugh et al., 1976). Only the latter school has attempted to conduct similar research at the international level, ensuring comparability with traditional organisational theories by adopting a nearly identical methodology of investigation (Hickson et al., 1974). In some ways, the propositions put forward by culture-free studies resemble an international translation of the indications developed by the contingency school at the national level. The culture-free approach aims to demonstrate that the relationships between contextual variables and organisational features are universal and valid for all companies, regardless of their national culture. However, this perspective has received criticism for its lack of consideration of cultural and social influences, and the need for more rigorous and in-depth verification of the validity of theories at the international level.

The context variables used refer to size, technology, dependence on other organisations, and the degree of environmental variability. The organisational variables involved are formalization, specialization, and centralization. In summary, the identified relationships can be summarized as follows (Hickson et al., 1979):

- in all countries, large organisations will be more formalized and specialized.
- in all countries, organisations integrated into a large group will be more specialized and formalized.
- in all countries, organisations dependent on others will make centralized decisions and have less autonomy.

This result allows us to assert that the consistency of the relationships between contextual and organisational variables supports the "strong" hypothesis that these relationships are valid for companies worldwide (both in direction and intensity), regardless of the economic and social context in which they operate.

Many studies have been inspired by this pioneering research. Negandhi (1982), following a seven-year study in six developing countries, identified two main types of organisations: modern ones (modelled after the American example) and traditional ones (characterized by low levels of specialization and formalization and high degrees of centralization and hierarchical control). However, except for some differences in interpersonal relationships and the organisational climate (linked to cultural factors), the most significant variances (especially those concerning planning and control systems) were found to be associated with constraints imposed by the market or technology. Furthermore, the differences observed in management styles do not seem to be related to subordinates' cultural preferences for a more or less autocratic leader (as would be interpreted, for example, by Hofstede). It is essential to distinguish between what subordinates prefer and what they are compelled to accept: lower-level subordinates accept authoritarian leaders simply because it is the only way to keep their jobs, while in conditions of lesser necessity (typical of developed countries), they would demand more participation and equality.

The conclusion is that aspects usually interpreted, as results of cultural values must actually be reinterpreted from a more objective perspective. Further confirmation of the culture-free perspective comes from a study conducted by Miller (1987), based on a meta-analysis of comparative management. Miller statistically re-examined the conclusions reached by the main empirical studies on the subject to verify the relative uniformity of a mass of data that would be difficult to obtain with a single field study. Such analysis had to deal primarily with the differences in methodologies used in the various examined studies, aiming to understand whether the causes of discrepancies between the results of different studies were due to methodological errors or real cultural differences.

The investigation's results pay particular attention to the relationships between size and organisational variables: a considerable stability in the relationships between size, specialization, and formalization emerges, regardless of nationality; however, the degree of centralization is not correlated with either size or national culture. This confirms Hickson's hypothesis regarding the relationship between size on one hand and formalization and specialization on the other, while explanations are provided for variations in the degree of centralization. However, beyond the method, Miller's results do not reveal much new information: Sorge had already emphasized years before (1983) that the universalist approach had identified size as the only variable capable of giving rise to significantly valid relationships. Certainly, size alone is not sufficient to explain any supranational organisational configuration; moreover, the universality of all other contextual variables remains an ambiguous and yet-to-be-proven fact. In general, the unsatisfactory degree of explanation offered by comparative research conducted according to the Aston methodology is, according to many scholars, due to the abstractness and generality of the dimensions considered (for example, Crozier and Friedberg, 1978; Lammers and Hickson, 1979). In fact, the universality claimed by the Hickson group seems more a product of the methodology used than of empirical findings. The organisational dimensions adopted by universalists (formalization, centralization, specialization, etc.), as well as the relationships between these dimensions and contextual variables (size, technology, dependence on other organisations, etc.), are based on general concepts (and indicators) that they automatically deserve the status of universals, thereby preventing the possibility of verifying the presence of national (or cultural) influence (Lammers and Hickson, 1979).

The methodology used by the researchers at Aston to construct a culture-free theory tends to become a self-fulfilling prophecy: in order to verify the resistance of a national cultural effect, they identify and employ concepts and indicators that preclude the possibility of highlighting any exposure of the organisation to social influences. Roberts and Boyacigiller (1993) question the robustness of Hickson's theses, finding it somewhat subjective to conclude that, although there are indeed differences between organisations of different nationalities that are not due to contextual factors, aspects of similarity tend to prevail. Such a statement appears rather generic, and, above all, the ambiguity of many of the identified relationships could lead the researchers at Aston, quite legitimately, to opposite conclusions and validate the culture-bound thesis. Despite the conclusions reached by the research having their foundations on a certain number of stable relationships in terms of direction and magnitude, there are also sufficient discrepancies that suggest at least a need for further investigation, if not even the possibility of an actual cultural influence on organisational arrangements. Similar conclusions are also reached by Lammers and

Hickson (1979), who acknowledge that the research from 1974 fails to identify certain relationships. In particular, decentralization and size are correlated for the United States, Great Britain, and Germany, but not for Sweden and Japan, while in Canada, the direction of the correlation is inverted. Why such differences exist, only God knows, especially as long as the authors themselves feel unable to address the problem.

In summary, it can be argued that research in this area is still in a very embryonic stage: the use of only the theoretical model from Aston and its related instrumentation does not allow for reaching highly relevant conclusions. The exclusive focus on a single framework, in fact, while on the one hand, enables the direct comparison of empirical findings from different studies, on the other hand, leaves two sets of problems open.

Firstly, it has been highlighted that the Aston model leads to mostly generic and ambiguous conclusions, as its validity and explanatory power have been doubted even within a single national context (Child, 1981). In the international context, despite the "tendentiously" generic nature of its concepts and indicators (Lammers and Hickson, 1979), the approach failed to conceal a series of variations that are most likely attributable to socio-cultural factors. The only contextual variable with a universal influence was found to be size (Miller, 1987). There is always a lack of precise and systematic reference to the conditions of pressure on the results, making it difficult to highlight the degree of constraint expressed by contingencies. The absence of this factor, therefore, produces two consequences: first, it gives rise to a variance in the context-organisation relationships, presumably greater than in a normative approach where the environment creates greater urgency for adaptation and hence greater uniformity of response.

Secondly, and consequently, it does not allow us to understand the actual ability of organisational actors to follow their cultural preferences. As an example, let us consider Negandhi's (1982) distinction between what is accepted and what is preferred by employees; it is certainly true that in organisations in certain countries, the subordinate's situation of necessity forces them to accept a leadership style that is quite different from what they desire. However, it then becomes natural to ask whether in this case, an approach is appropriate that:

1. highlights when employees can follow their preferences and when they are forced to follow a different orientation;
2. brings to light, beforehand, the preferences of employees in order to distinguish whether a certain behaviour is attributable to cultural influence or to a constraint determined by the situation.

It is evident that the first objection refers to the need to include the variable of pressure on results, while the second refers to Child's (1981) prescription to a priori highlight cultural hypotheses: the validity of the approach followed in this thesis is thus confirmed.

In general, it is probably legitimate to question why the international comparison of contingent models was carried out with exclusive reference to a single theory and why the verification of the international applicability of a much more developed approach. The latter being the one based on the concept of organisation as an information processing system, has always been avoided, especially in the general version proposed by Galbraith (Decastri, 1984), in which situational factors are related to informational needs and pressure on results. What is needed for the construction of a supranational theory, in other words, is to have a combination of situational theoretical approaches that allows for a three-dimensional view of organisational functioning and is less constrained by the limitations of each perspective.

From the analysis of the different contributions in the literature, two fundamental factors influencing the effectiveness of an organisational configuration emerge: uncertainty and pressure on results.

Both factors have given rise to a series of criticisms and clarifications, which, although formulated with purposes other than demonstrating the cultural relativity of the theories, allow for a better qualification of the scope of applicability of contingent models.

Firstly, we need to reflect on the concept of pressure on results, introduced in a comprehensive way by Galbraith, which essentially sheds light on an aspect too often implicit in contingent models: the relationship between the environment and the organisation they identify only holds in hypotheses of efficiency.

From this perspective, the situational approach hypothesizes (often implicitly) a situation of perfect competitive rivalry according to the neoclassical framework. This holds in two situations. Firstly, it means that with contingent models, we find ourselves in a situation of "ineluctably strained economy" (Hirschman, 1985), a situation where no trial-and-error experimentation or power strategy as intended by Crozier is allowed.

Secondly, a process of ex-post experimentation and learning is not even considered necessary because it is assumed that the organisational designer can decide according to patterns of substantive rationality, meaning a decision-making process similar to that of the economic man in neoclassical theory.

In other words, the uncertainty mentioned by contingency theorists refers only to the state of bounded rationality of the organisational members subject to design, while the designer still acts according to absolute rationality capable of optimizing the result of the company. This hidden neoclassical nature of contingent models has two important consequences for our purposes.

The first consequence relates to the concept of pressure on results. This clarifies that when situational theories identify a relationship between the environment and the organisation, most of the time they provide not a descriptive but a normative indication. In other words, they indicate how the organisation should be rather than how it actually is. Unfortunately, this design nature is not always explicit, and there are indeed models that can be defined as contingent because they identify a stable relationship between contextual variables and organisation but do not present a clear definition of the conditions of pressure on results in which the relationships were found. The Aston model is one of these; competitive pressure is only mentioned, so we face a theoretical corpus that, due to its descriptive nature, cannot be compared to other contingent models, which are inherently normative. The fact that major cross-cultural comparative studies have been conducted with the Aston model's data and methodologies, as their main reference, explains why an acceptable international translation of contingent models has not yet been achieved. The reason is simple: until now, contingent studies conducted within a single cultural context and those developed at an international level are not comparable because they refer to different conditions of pressure on results; or, in other words, the former are normative, while the latter are descriptive. This point is fundamental and will be addressed further in the following pages.

It is important to recall the attempt made by Lawrence and Dyer (cited in Decastri, 1984) to arrive at a descriptive classification of organisational configurations based on the two dimensions mentioned: uncertainty and resource scarcity (a concept somewhat similar to that of pressure on results). In this model, an acceptable integration is achieved between the prescriptions of traditional organisational theory (e.g., the differentiation/integration duality of Lawrence and Lorsch) and descriptions of alternative configurations such as Mintzberg's professional bureaucracy or Cohen, March, and Olsen's loosely coupled system. However, its limitation is that it remains tied to a national context, the North American one, without providing indications of its applicability at the international level; Adler (1984) would classify this research as part of the American theoretical provincialism.

The second consequence arises from the "orthodoxy" of the premises of the situational approach: given the prevailing optimizing logic in the decisions of the organisational designer, no other preferences can be hypothesized outside those related to profit maximization unless we return to the microeconomic foundations and question the postulates of utility functions. This would require introducing new values into the utility curves, which would immediately take the theory beyond the neoclassical paradigm. From this perspective, a theory like that of the contingent-transactional paradigm, which, in contrast to the orthodox approach, introduced the concept of "organisational transaction" (Boisot, 1986), ends up falling within the classical microeconomic rationality conception.

A comparative reflection, then, allows us to reveal some implicit assumptions of traditional organisational theory, supporting the arguments of those who, like Negandhi (1982) or Smelser (1982), see comparative research as the normal mode of progress in the social sciences. In this way, in addition to objections concerning the nature of the rationality underlying design choices and the scope of application of contingent theories, other ambiguities and perplexities have arisen, among which we must mention the three epistemological considerations with which Sorge (1983) criticizes the traditional theory's lack of consideration for culture. These considerations refer to the concepts of universality, causality, and the means-ends relationship.

a. *Universality.* This category obviously refers to the repeatedly mentioned claims of the general applicability of organisational theories regardless of the nation. According to Sorge, the only acceptable general relationship is the pervasive influence of size, which, as it increases, generates structural differentiation but at a decreasing rate. From all other points of view, organisational studies have led to contradictory results, both due to methodological differences and the actual inability of universalistic theory to explain the observed variance.
b. *Causality.* In contingent models, causal influences in the form of "if...then" tend to be unidirectional, originating from external variables that affect internal ones through a process similar to the following: Environment - Context - Organisational Boundaries - Structure - Roles - Behaviour. However, the causal chain does not always have the same direction: authors like Aldrich (1979), Child, or Weick (cited by Grandori, 1984) have shown that the direction can be inverted, meaning that actors can choose certain constraints, and past choices can constrain future ones.
c. *Means-ends relationship.* In this category, Sorge draws on the literature regarding the structure of the goals of the company, from Pfeffer and Salancik to Crozier and the "technology of foolishness" of March and Olsen, emphasizing the empirical nature (learning from trial and error) of organisational design and the coexistence of multiple preferences within it, which differ from the goal of profit maximization.

Sorge's conclusion is that the three epistemological considerations show the need for a less one-sided and more interactive view of the relationship between the company and the environment, as well as a shift towards a much more subjective notion of the environment (the "enacted environment" by Weick), increasingly based on the meaning attributed to it by organisational actors. This shift towards radical subjectivism constitutes the fundamental premise of a culturalist approach, the symbolist approach, which attributes to culture a role not only as contingent but as the very foundation of the organisation's meaning.

The symbolist objections to contingent theory represent such a departure from tradition that they unequivocally lead to a new research paradigm, which is also unrelated to this thesis. This line of research will be mentioned in the next chapter. For now, it is enough to highlight that it emphasizes once again that the criticisms raised against contingent theory open up the theoretical possibility for greater consideration of cultural issues; in other words, they have paved the way for the development of the culturalist orientation that will now be discussed.

7.2 The Culture-Bound Perspective

The culture-bound perspective refers to an approach in social sciences and research that emphasizes the influence of culture on various aspects of human behaviour, beliefs, values, and practices. In this context, "culture-bound" means that certain theories, concepts, and findings are specific to a particular culture or social context and may not be universally applicable across different cultures. In contrast to the culture-free perspective, which seeks to develop theories and models that are presumed to be universally valid and applicable across cultures, the culture-bound perspective recognizes that cultural differences can significantly shape individuals, groups, and organisations' behaviour and practices. It suggests that cultural norms, values, and beliefs can influence how people perceive the world, make decisions, and interact with others. Researchers adopting a culture-bound perspective often explore the unique characteristics of specific cultures and attempt to understand how these cultural factors influence behaviour and organisational dynamics.

This approach acknowledges the importance of cultural context in shaping human experiences and seeks to avoid making generalizations that may not hold true in diverse cultural settings. By taking a culture-bound perspective, researchers can gain insights into the complexities of human behaviour and organisational dynamics, recognizing that different cultural contexts may require tailored approaches and solutions. It also helps in avoiding ethnocentrism, which is the tendency to view one's own culture as superior and to interpret other cultures through the lens of one's own cultural norms and values.

The thesis advocated by this research perspective refers to the fundamental principle that the relationships between variables and organisational dimensions are influenced by cultural factors. In this sense, each organisational configuration is unique as it is determined by the joint interplay of national culture and organisational culture. Within this context, it is possible to distinguish between theories that treat culture as an adaptive or institutional system and those that consider it as an ideationalist system.

Ideationalist theories view cultures as sets of shared ideas, values, symbols, and meanings, while the institutionalist tradition focuses on the ways of life through which communities have survived and adapted to their environmental contexts, placing particular emphasis on the social modes of transmitting patterns of behaviour. In this sense, Schein's (1985) definition can certainly be attributed to the institutionalist school, while Hofstede's (1980) "collective mental programming" is closer to the ideationalist view.

This contrast between the two notions of culture also gives rise to different approaches to intercultural research. The ideationalist perspective adopts the distinction made by Kroeber and Parsons (1958) between the social system and the cultural system. The two authors suggest that the concept of culture should be confined to the patterns of values transmitted and created, ideas, and other symbolic systems endowed with meaning as factors capable of guiding human behaviour. This is true because the term "social system" should be used to indicate a specifically relational system of interaction between individuals and collectives. In other words, the cultural system is exclusively focused on systems of meaning, while the social system is a way of organizing human behaviour by linking meanings to the conditions of concrete behaviour in a given context (Child, 1981). The distinction between the social system and the cultural system does not so much indicate two different objects but rather two alternative approaches to the study of the same phenomenon:

[...]Culture will be represented by the set of behaviour patterns that guide humans in dealing with the reality of nature and their peers within the total social phenomenon, while society will be constituted, still within the same phenomenon, by those human behaviours that are motivated by the cultural patterns governing the organisation of social relationships. The latter take the form of social forces, institutions, and social practices in general, in which such relationships materialize. This means that the distinction between culture and society is not a distinction between "things" but between perspectives for analysing a single reality, that of the total social phenomenon [...] (Tullio-Altan, 1996; p. 309).

The *institutionalist approach*, considering the distinction between the social and cultural system as impossible or at least artificial, has instead sought to verify the extent and manner in which organisations reflect the institutional patterns of the countries in which they operate. For this purpose, its relatively few studies have focused on formalized and structural aspects such as division of labour and operational systems.

The following pages will be dedicated to the analysis of the main contributions within these two strands, with the obvious caveat that they represent only the two poles of a continuum along which different positions are situated.

7.2.1 The Institutional Approach. The institutional approach in sociology and organisational studies is a significant perspective that deals with the influential role of institutions in shaping human behaviour, organisational dynamics, and societal structures. Institutions, encompassing formal rules, norms, and cultural values, serve as the fundamental building blocks of societies and organisations. This approach emphasizes the powerful impact of culture, historical context, and external pressures on individuals and groups, leading to the convergence of practices and behaviours among organisations within the same environment. By examining the interplay between formal and informal institutions, the institutional approach provides valuable insights into understanding the mechanisms that drive societal and organisational change.

This orientation *"focuses on institutions as tangible manifestations of cultural characteristics, [...] in the sense that they reflect the choices that have been made among different structural arrangements"* (Child and Tayeb, 1983; p. 39). It draws on positions expressed in the post-war period by scholars such as Polany (1959) and Dalton (1960), who criticized the formalism of economic science and instead advocated for the "immersion" of a nation's economic development in its historical and social peculiarities (Tullio-Altan, 1996).

Many institutionalist studies seek in a country's history the hidden reasons behind a particular cultural model and recommend a historical approach to isolate with greater reliability the cultural characteristics of a people. Child (1981) argues that a synchronic statistical investigation, no matter how meticulous, always runs the risk of isolating values linked to transient historical contingencies. The example Child uses to illustrate his position refers to the attitude towards immigrants observed in Britain in the 1970s. *"A recent trend has generated expressions of intolerance that represent an exception compared to the historically verified tradition of the country. It would be very wrong to conclude that British culture is intolerant towards immigrants. In attempting to isolate what is inherently cultural, it is necessary to judge which values and norms are historically implicated in the social and institutional development of a country"*. (Child, 1976; p. 11).

Authors such as Barrington Moore (1967) and Dahrendorf (1968), both cited in Child (1981), try to reconstruct the reasons behind the cultural peculiarities of France and the United States in the former's case, and Germany in the latter's case, through the analysis of historical development processes. Dahrendorf, in particular, focuses on how the process of German industrialization occurred to answer what he himself calls "the German question," namely, the nation's inability to achieve levels of economic and ideological liberalism equal to other European countries. Dahrendorf's attention to the industrialization process also proposes a situation where cultures of different advanced nations are compared. If it is true that in each country a blend of cultural traditions emerge which reflect on the level of industrialisation, then the hypothesis of comparing different countries based on the ways they have reached the stage of advanced economy becomes plausible.

An institutionalist attempt that is more directly connected to the organisational sphere is the one undertaken by Crozier (1969) in his study on the French bureaucracy. In this study, he links the functioning of the organisation to the cultural characteristics of the French people, which are, in turn, shaped and reinforced by the country's institutions. Particularly, the educational system in France, polarized between two subsystems, seems to play a central role in creating a selection of future leaders from an early age. Inspired by Crozier's approach there is the research conducted by the group of Maurice, Sorge, Brossard and Warner. In a comparative study carried out in France, Germany, and Great Britain, Brossard and Maurice (1974), Sorge and Warner (1980) highlighted how, under conditions of similar transnational environments and shared objectives, companies of different nationalities differ in the way they achieve their goals. These differences must be explained by factors other than those of traditional theory. This finding confirms Kluckhohn and Strodtbeck's (1961) view that cultures must fulfil the same needs but can choose different paths to realize them. In particular, significant differences are identified in the processes of recruitment and training, the extent of control, and the degree of specialization in managerial roles. According to Brossard and Maurice (1974), these differences must be "explained not only in terms of internal structural factors of the company but also with reference to external factors peculiar to the social context in which they operate". This refers to the differences existing in their respective institutional contexts, especially in prevalent educational systems and mechanisms of social mobility.

Lammers and Hickson also propose an approach (called "organisations within societies") aimed at identifying the so-called "social effect" on the organisational structure. Such a position represents a clear departure from universalistic approaches, as it hypothesizes that the organisational structures of companies in a given country reflect its specific national/institutional context.

The "social effect" approach postulates not the convergence of societies but their discontinuity (historical and cultural) and believes that the objective of organisational theories is essentially to investigate the social conditions of the formation and development of companies.

Only a comparison of the relationships between social structure and organisations and the processes through which they manifest in each national situation can lead to the development of a theory of organisations that integrates the specificities and discontinuities of each national experience into a universal model (Lammers and Hickson, 1979).

7.2.2 The Ideationalist Approach. This approach is another significant perspective in social sciences as it places a strong emphasis on the role of ideas, beliefs, and ideologies in shaping human behaviour, societal structures, and political systems. It seeks to understand how ideas and ideologies influence decision-making processes, social interactions, and the formation of institutions. By examining the impact of ideas on various aspects of society, the ideationalist approach provides valuable insights into the complexities of human behaviour and the dynamics of social change. Let us explore the key features and applications of this approach to gain a deeper understanding of its significance in the study of human societies and political systems. The ideationalist approach is based on the belief that systems of shared ideas and meanings persist over time and heavily influence people's behaviours and motivations.

Passed down through generations via socialization, these ideas have a profound impact on individuals. However, this approach generally overlooks the influence exerted by a country's institutions or, at the very least, considers institutions themselves as outcomes of the same fundamental principles determining behaviour within organisations.

The ideationalist approach can be traced back to what Schollhammer (1969) referred to as the "behavioural orientation" and focuses on the values and related behaviours of managers and employees in companies operating within different cultural contexts. It has seen more rapid development compared to the institutionalist approach, leading to a plethora of studies. However, these studies often lack cohesiveness and fail to form an integrated theoretical framework like that found in institutionalism.

One of the pioneering works in this field is the research by Haire, Ghiselli, and Porter (1966), which identified significant differences in management styles between German and English managers. Another comparative study on management styles was conducted by England (1978) over a decade, revealing considerable variations in personal values held by managers of different nationalities. Tannenbaum's study (1958, 1974) attempted to compare organisations to determine whether the elimination of private ownership leads to a reduction in certain undesirable effects of hierarchy. The conclusion was that "differences between the two systems (Marxist and capitalist) are not consistent in all aspects: there are differences within the systems as much as between the two systems," and some significant variations can be attributed to cultural values of each country.

Two other research works by Gallie (1978) and Lachman et. al., (1994) yielded more precise results. Gallie observed differences in work organisation between English and French refineries that were not due to contingent factors but rather related to 1) different management styles and objectives, 2) distinct power distributions, and 3) the ideology and organisation of unions in the two countries.

Lachman et. al., on the other hand, directly compare the United States and Great Britain on organisational variables and managerial attitudes, finding significant correspondences between the two cultures and their respective structural and ideological characteristics of the companies. The differences touch upon various aspects (formalization, control techniques, management styles); however, the conclusions fail to demonstrate the preponderance of cultural factors over economic ones.

Through a questionnaire distributed to managers of different nationalities during a managerial training course, Laurent (1983) identifies a surprising discrepancy of opinions regarding the ideal characteristics of an organisation. It emerges that each manager carries their own organisational theory, and this ideal vision is heavily influenced by their nationality. The first sign of this phenomenon appeared when Laurent encountered mental resistance from some French managers to the idea of a matrix structure: "An organisation that involved two bosses for one person was considered an absurdity to the point of appearing a futile, impossible theoretical exercise" (Laurent, 1983). This initial finding, confirmed by comparing the responses of French managers with those of other nationalities, led to the assertion that *"the management process can be considered as an implementation process through which managers translate into behaviour some of their fundamental, implicit beliefs about the most effective way an organisation should function"*. (p.76). From the statistical analysis of the data obtained, Laurent identified four "theoretical visions" of structure.

a. Organisation as a political system; this dimension groups three items: the political role played by managers in society, their perception of motivation provided by power, and the extent to which organisational structures are clearly defined in the minds of those involved. France and Italy showed high scores in the first two dimensions and a low value in the third, whereas England recorded the opposite result.

b. Organisations as systems of authority; in this case, the items considered are the conception of the hierarchical structure as a realm of power relations, the perception of the strength of authority in organisations, and the image of the manager as a negotiator. Latin managers have a more personal conception of authority and organisational relations, while Anglo-Saxon managers seem to refer to a more rational, instrumental, and abstract view of hierarchy and structure.
c. Organisations as systems of role formalization; the three items grouped under this dimension all focus on the relative importance of defining and specifying the functions and roles of personnel (using tools such as job descriptions). Latin countries tend to have higher scores compared to Anglo-Saxon countries.
d. Organisations as systems of hierarchical relationships; this dimension groups four questions that refer to the possibility of resolving conflicts by enhancing hierarchical relationships and the role of the leader.

Such an index can provide some indications about the feasibility of a matrix structure (where conflicts of interest are considered physiological) and, as already mentioned, shows a tendency of French managers and, in general, Latin managers to have an aversion to loosely defined structures.

In a later study, Laurent (1983) examines the effect of national origin in a potentially homogeneous context, such as that of a single corporate culture. The result is surprising: not only was a homogenizing effect not detected, but managers from the same company and different national cultures show an even more marked difference in their conception of the organisation. These results seem to indicate the limited reliability of hypotheses about the convergence and universality of managerial practices and the need for a phenomenological approach capable of reconstructing the collective mental maps of managers regarding the organisation.

Even if the structure of different organisations may appear the same in some objective dimensions, its meaning for individuals can be very different, and this difference can be important in influencing their behaviour (Laurentand Inzerilli, 1983).

Moreover, the influence of nationality is not limited to managerial practices but also seems to extend to research programs in the organisational field. It is no coincidence that while the English school of Aston conducted its rational analysis on the structural characteristics of organisations, French sociologists described them as sets of power strategies: these representations closely match those expressed by managers of the respective nationalities. In this way, cultural differences can influence not only the implicit concepts of managers but also the explicit concepts of researchers (Laurent, 1983).

7.3 Laurent's Study on Differences in Western Management Styles

French professor André Laurent conceived the idea of a study on cultural differences in the business context when he observed them personally through the diverse reactions of an international audience attending his lectures during a managerial training course. The pivotal point was a questionnaire distributed to managers of various nationalities, through which Laurent discovered a surprising discrepancy of opinions regarding the ideal characteristics of an organisation. It emerged that each manager carries his or her own organisational theory, and this ideal vision is heavily influenced by nationality.

The first sign of this phenomenon appeared when Laurent encountered mental resistance from some French managers to the idea of a matrix structure: "An organisation that proposed two bosses for one person was considered an absurdity to the point of appearing a futile, impossible theoretical exercise" (Laurent, 1983). This initial finding, confirmed by comparing responses of French managers with those from other nationalities, led to the assertion that "the management process can be considered as an implementation process through which managers transfer into behaviour some of their fundamental, implicit beliefs about the most effective way an organisation should function."

This initial restricted investigation, simply conducted by comparing the results obtained from 40 French managers with those of 20 from other European countries, supported Laurent's idea about the existence of cross-cultural differences. The study was later significantly expanded, also influenced by the comprehensive research Hofstede was conducting during the same years. Hofstede initially interviewed a sample of 817 Western managers, all participants in training courses at INSEAD, and later a representative sample of managers of Asian origin from Japan, Indonesia, and China (Adler, Campbell, and Laurent, 1989). However, the discussed results here exclusively refer to the European research (Laurent, 1983), as this subsequent expansion showed numerous signs of potential distortion due to techniques too tied to Western cognitive patterns. An error that Hofstede also partially committed, to the extent that his initial four-dimensional model was expanded to better fit the peculiar characteristics of Eastern cultures.

The study was conducted by subjecting managers from various European nationalities to a questionnaire in which they were asked to provide judgments on a series of statements related to business management and organisation. The obtained responses made it possible to consistently group a series of questions, suggesting dimensions of analysis that reasonably differentiate managerial interpretations from different cultures.

The resulting study (Laurent, 1983) aims to demonstrate that the nationality of managers significantly influences their interpretations of the functions and styles of the business management process. According to Laurent, the managerial and organisational behaviour of each manager is determined by a personal conception of business activity, a mental structure that is heavily dependent on the culture of the country of origin.

Thus, four theoretical visions of organisational structure emerged, serving as indicators capable of capturing differences among countries in the structure of collective managerial ideologies:

- organisation as a political system;
- organisation as a system of authority;
- organisation as a system of role formalization;
- organisation as a system of hierarchical relationships.

The first dimension evaluates the organisation as a political system, considering both internal and external perspectives of business analysis to grasp the social aspects of managerial responsibilities. The roles of managers in society, their motivational factors (tending toward power attainment rather than goal achievement), and the degree to which the structure is defined in the minds of those involved were considered. Results indicate that certain countries, especially Italy and France, but also the United States to a lesser extent, possess a vague notion of organisational structure. Motivational drive for managers primarily stems from their needs for social achievement, and managers are attributed an important political role. This is widely confirmed by the contemporary political scene of the mentioned countries.

In contrast, Danish and British managers view the company as the source of motivation and reason for power, with a strong awareness of the role of organisational structure.

The effects of these cultural differences on the directions of organisational theory are intriguing. At the time Laurent was writing, while Britain focused on rational analyses of structural characteristics of organisations, French sociologists described organisations as sets of power strategies meant to blur role boundaries to generate more power through ambiguity. Thus, cultural differences can influence not only managers' implicit concepts but also explicit ones held by researchers.

The second dimension interprets the organisation as a system of authority, evaluating whether hierarchies constitute a power structure, whether a crisis of authority is forming within organisations, and whether the manager has the function of a negotiator. Results show that managers of French, Belgian, and Italian origin strongly agree with such a view, indicating a personal and social concept of authority binding individuals within the organisation. In contrast, the United States, Switzerland, and Germany present a more rational and instrumental interpretation of hierarchy, considering authority as an intrinsic attribute of the role or function.

The third dimension of analysis views the organisation as a system of role formalization. Parameters measuring the importance of role and function definitions and specifications are used, including the importance of job descriptions in resolving conflicts, determining responsibilities within a department, and attributing high specification of roles to managers. Countries that markedly express such a need are Germany, Switzerland, and Italy. In contrast, the definition of roles does not seem fundamental for Swedish, British, and American managers.

Lastly, the organisation is analysed as a system of hierarchical relationships. This indicator measures the degree of acceptance towards various forms of managing organisational tensions and provides an important discriminatory basis for the cross-cultural application of complex and potentially conflicting organisational structures, such as the matrix structure. A high level of tolerance towards company conflicts is shown by the Swedish and American managers, while a greater need for security and hierarchical structure is manifested by Italy.

The study's results allow for the identification of two clusters of countries, distinguishing between Latin and Nordic cultures (including the United States), as they exhibited rather homogeneous trends across the four dimensions assessed. Particularly, the highest values of perception, social relevance, and formalization of hierarchical structures are observed in Latin countries.

Laurent's conclusion is that there is empirical evidence that a specific interpretation of hierarchical structure, whether personal or instrumental, legitimizes and determines organisational behaviours within companies. The culture of origin imposes interaction patterns on individuals that are transposed into the structuring of roles within a formal hierarchy (Laurent and Inzerrilli, 1983).

However, the same author acknowledges the limitations of the proposed model. One limitation of Laurent's findings lies in the fact that the number of countries included in the sample is too limited and that the sample itself poorly represents the managerial reality, as it only consists of managers participating in the INSEAD training course. The survey also reflects the limitations of a questionnaire prepared based on a specific cultural model, the French one, which may have influenced the results or at least resulted in such a clear separation between Latin countries (France, Belgium, and Italy) and Nordic countries (United States and Northern Europe). A later study conducted in China (Adler, Campbell, and Laurent, 1989) seems to support this hypothesis. The same questionnaire generated bipolar results for over half of the questions suggesting inconsistency due to the mismatch between Western and Eastern managerial styles: "We fear that our observations and interpretations may be too tied to our culture to significantly increase our understanding" of Chinese culture (Adler, Campbell, and Laurent, 1989, p. 72).

In this regard, it is interesting to deal with one of the questionnaire questions: *"It is important for superiors to have precise answers to key questions that subordinates may raise about their work?"*.

The agreement percentages shown by Western managers vary from 10% in Sweden to 66% in Italy. The Asian values in the test, on the other hand, are higher: 73% for Indonesia, 74% for China, and 78% for Japan. Among the countries with the highest scores, the reasons for managers' responses change profoundly based on their cultural background: while Italians and French managers responded affirmatively because they believe managers should be knowledgeable, the reasons for their Japanese counterparts lie in the fact that they "could never ask a superior a question they might not know the answer to." Rather than demonstrating intelligence, a Japanese subordinate in this case would display insensitivity and rudeness, as they would be responsible for the superior's loss of credibility.

In a subsequent study, Laurent (1983) examines the effect of national origin in a potentially homogeneous context, such as that of a single corporate culture. The result is surprising: not only is a homogenizing effect not observed, but also managers from the same company and different national cultures show an even more pronounced difference in their conception of the organisation. These findings seem to indicate the low reliability of hypotheses about the convergence and universality of managerial practices and the need for a phenomenological approach capable of reconstructing the collective mental maps of managers regarding the organisation. Even if the structure of different organisations may appear the same based on certain objective dimensions, its meaning for people can be very different, and this difference can be important in influencing their behaviour (Laurent and Inzerilli, 1983).

7.4 The Hofstede's Research

Hofstede's research is a pioneering and influential contribution in the field of cross-cultural psychology and organisational behaviour. Conducted by Dutch social psychologist Geert Hofstede, this extensive research explores the impact of culture on individual attitudes, behaviours, and organisational practices across different countries and regions. Hofstede's work has had a profound impact on our understanding of cultural dimensions and their effects on various aspects of society, ranging from management and leadership styles to communication patterns and decision-making processes. By analysing cultural differences and similarities through a comprehensive framework, Hofstede's research provides valuable insights for individuals and organisations operating in a globalized world. In this introduction, we will delve into the key concepts and findings of Hofstede's research, highlighting its significance in fostering cross-cultural understanding and effective intercultural interactions.

Hofstede (1980) and Hofstede and Bollinger (1989) arrives at a similar conclusion in an attempt to demonstrate that managerial techniques "have been widely exported worldwide as absolute norms, without any concern for adapting them according to cultures". Hofstede does not spare accusations of ethnocentrism for anyone. He asserts that all theoretical production in the organisational and managerial field has developed models and norms without considering their scope of applicability, forgetting that there are no universal laws in the social realm. This is due to the fact that every phenomenon must be related to the cultural context in which it is applied, just as every theory or scientific law is the result of its author's culture.

The data on which Hofstede's work is based comes from research conducted in two successive rounds between 1967 and 1973, later expanded at the end of the century, through a questionnaire distributed in over forty countries (totalling over 116,000 processed questionnaires). The questionnaires were drafted in about 20 different languages, and the questions, following a factorial analysis, were gradually reduced from 180 to a core of sixty mandatory questions and around ninety optional ones. They sought information about values (the enduring element of mental programming) and referred to four categories: job satisfaction, perceptions, personal preferences, and demographic data. After eliminating some potential distortions, Hofstede identifies the five cultural dimensions that constitute the "core" of the research through the iterative use of factor analysis, meaning by identifying clusters of variables characterized by similar trends. The complexity of the analysis is determined not only by the considerable breadth of the processed data but also by the lack of determinacy of the object considered. Hofstede recalls that nations cannot be analysed based on theoretical structures constructed for individuals. Nations are sociological aggregates, which stand to humans as a forest stands to a tree, and therefore they not only have larger dimensions but also significant complexity due to the relationships between individuals, institutions, and resources.

The empirically identified dimensions, namely power distance, uncertainty avoidance, masculinity, and individualism, serve Hofstede to establish whether, and to what extent, an individual's national culture component influences their behaviour, work, and underlying values. This result confirms the hypothesis of a strong influence of national culture on organisational life and seems to undermine the cornerstone on which many management theories rested: the belief that there were universal principles of sound administration.

In 2001, Hoftede published a new updated version of "Culture's Consequences," including a review of the applications and critiques of his work conducted by other researchers, which appeared from 1980 onwards. Initially based on four cultural dimensions, two more were added, with the final dimension added in 2010. Therefore, Hofstede's theory of six cultural dimensions suggests that each dimension exists on a continuum from low to high. In other words, each country exhibits various degrees of multiple traits: power distance, inequality, masculinity, femininity, uncertainty avoidance, social integration, and openness to change.

It will be possible to examine the meanings of the six cultural dimensions in the following paragraphs.

7.4.1 Power Distance. This dimension reflects how a society reacts to existing biological and capability differences among individuals and, in particular, indicates whether this diversity is shielded and translated into material differences, status, and power, or whether, on the contrary, equal opportunities are sought for everyone. Inequality, expressed as an unequal distribution of power, is considered by Hofstede as an essential and not replaceable element for the survival of organisations, which counteract the tendency towards disorder caused by the principle of entropy through it. However, this universal tendency takes on profoundly different forms based on different cultural preferences, particularly concerning the need for dependency expressed by each individual. Power distance is measured based on the subordinate's perception of their superior's power, as the mental representation of the authority enjoyed by the superior will determine their behaviour. Power distance is precisely the perception of the degree of power disparity between those who hold this power and those who are subordinate to it (Hofstede and Bollinger, 1989).

In societies with high power distance, inequality is considered a completely natural condition that requires no justification. This belief legitimizes the establishment of formalized hierarchies, makes individuals more willing to accept unconditional orders, and instils even a need for dependency in "inferior" individuals.

Conversely, in countries with a low degree of power distance, efforts are made to mitigate inequalities (or at least demand a justification), and the relationships between individuals are more governed by a commitment to collaborate rather than power play.

The results, showing significant variance in responses among cultures, suggest important organisational consequences. For example, a high score in power distance, as seen in France, hypothesizes tendencies towards centralization, a sharp pyramid-like structure, a preference for coercive and referent authority, and strong status distinctions between "white-collar" and "blue-collar" workers. On the other hand, companies in nations with low scores, such as the United States, would exhibit the opposite characteristics.

Gauthey and Xardel cite the example of an Indian manager responsible for a group composed of Europeans and Americans, who recounted his difficulties as follows: "*My subordinates reproached me for constantly being on their backs, treating them like teenagers. This was due to my natural tendency to closely follow them (high power distance) rather than letting them operate within established parameters. My personal difficulty was amplified by the fact that when trying to adapt my style to theirs (low power distance), I felt I was not fulfilling my responsibilities as a manager*" (p.62).

7.4.2 Uncertainty Avoidance. Time flows inexorably in one direction, carrying with it the timeless uncertainty of the future. Although every individual is fully aware that "there is no certainty about tomorrow," there are different ways to react to the anxiety produced by this absolute truth. In some societies, tolerance for ambiguity and uncertainty is learnt, accepting each day as it comes, fostering a spirit of openness towards anything new or different, and considering change as an integral and desirable part of life. In contrast, in other societies, the obsession with uncertainty is overcome by trying to control it: religions that preach absolute and incontrovertible truths spread, legal systems capable of providing unequivocal guidelines for behaviour are created, and scientific traditions that guarantee control over uncertainty may emerge. In such countries, reliance on institutions that oversee stability and preservation of the status quo is more pronounced, and pre-established rules, norms, and codes are sought after. A conformist and less tolerant mentality towards deviance (seen as a threat to the established order) develops. The anxiety to "frame" time also induces strong aggression and emotionality in individuals, feelings that continuously seek an external outlet. Moreover, in countries with high uncertainty avoidance, personal fulfilment is more tied to acquiring security rather than success resulting from personal initiatives, thereby discourage individuals from taking risks on their own.

Following a tradition in organisational theory, which interprets the development of formalized management tools as a protective response to uncertainty (March and Simon, 1966), Hofstede argues that nations scoring high on this dimension (e.g., France) tend to increase organisational rituals. Amongst the latter are meetings, training programs, reminders and reports, certain aspects of the accounting system, planning systems, control systems, and the appointment of experts. To these instruments, which lose much of their functional nature and take on a symbolic form, the following characteristics should be added:

- a low career ambition and a clear preference for hierarchically senior and specialized managers.
- a tendency to avoid competition among employees and prefer collectively made decisions over individual ones.
- resistance to being managed by a foreign boss.
- resistance to change.
- a pessimistic view of the reasons motivating the company to take action, even though employees express great loyalty (Hofstede-Bollinger, 1989).

Gauthey and Xardel also provide a useful anecdote: when the executive team of a new French subsidiary (with high power distance and high uncertainty avoidance) of a powerful British group was asked for marketing proposals, they reacted by stating: *"It's a trap! How is it possible that they have no idea about the topic? What do they want us to respond? Couldn't they be more direct? Why don't they tell us where they want to go and stop playing hide and seek!"* (p. 37).

In contrast, the reaction of the London executive team (with low power distance and low uncertainty avoidance) was: *"They want us to tell them everything! They were invited to submit their proposals to feel involved, empowered, and autonomous in their market. But what they expect are instructions that we are not able to provide!"* (p. 40).

7.4.3 Individualism Versus Collectivism. Individualism and collectivism are two fundamental cultural dimensions that play a pivotal role in shaping the behaviours, attitudes, and societal structures across different cultures and societies. These contrasting ideologies represent varying approaches to how individuals relate to their social groups, prioritize their personal goals, and interact with others in their communities. The dichotomy between individualism and collectivism serves as a cornerstone in the field of cross-cultural psychology, providing invaluable insights into the complexities of human behaviour and societal dynamics. In this section, we will explore the characteristics and implications of individualism and collectivism, shedding light on their significance in understanding cultural diversity and fostering effective intercultural communication and cooperation. When we think of ourselves, do we perceive ourselves as distinct individuals or as members of a group? When making decisions about our actions, do we consider our exclusive interests and those of our close family members, or do we prioritize the interests of the entire community to which we belong? Individualism defines the mode of relationships that each individual maintains with other members of society.

In general terms, it can be said that communal societies value the time spent for the group, while individualistic societies prioritize the time that each individual uses for their personal existence (Hofstede and Bollinger, 1989).

The phenomenon of individualism is closely linked in a very linear way to the economic development of a country, so much so that it can be presumed that the "industrial man" tends to be much more selfish compared to the "rural man," who is immersed in a network of communal personal relationships. However, this tendency, which could represent confirmation of the convergence hypothesis, is attenuated in the results obtained from traditionally collectivist countries such as Japan and Korea, which maintain considerably lower values compared to nations characterized by an equal level of development, such as European and American ones. In some societies that Hofstede defines as individualistic, members are taught to consider personal interest, success, self-fulfilment, and autonomy as core values in their lives. Generally, these individuals are emotionally independent, aspire to achieve prominent positions, and pay particular attention to their own convenience in social relationships.

Conversely, in collectivist societies, where the individual is first and foremost part of a group, morally bound by reciprocal obligations, and actively seeking the group's interests and fulfilment, loyalty to the group is considered essential and sometimes even superior to efficiency. Interference from the group or organisation in the private lives of its members and in the choice of friendships is also allowed.

At the organisational level, an individualistic culture tends to endorse a sense of detachment between the individual and the company, so that the employment relationship is maintained on the terms of an exchange contract. The values underlying this relationship are then professionalism, freedom, and universalism, where decisions are made in an identical manner for everyone, not based on the personal relationships of those in charge. More individualistic countries (such as the United States) do not fear the emergence of conflict; in fact, they may even theorize its necessity. On the other hand, many collectivist countries seek to maintain harmony among people so that no one risks "losing face".

7.4.4 Masculinity versus Femininity. Masculinity and femininity are two contrasting cultural dimensions that profoundly influence gender roles, behaviours, and societal expectations across different cultures and societies. These dimensions represent varying approaches to the expression of gender identity and the roles that individuals are expected to fulfil within their communities. The dichotomy between masculinity and femininity is a critical aspect of cross-cultural research, shedding light on the complexities of gender dynamics and societal norms. In this section, we will explore the characteristics and implications of masculinity and femininity, examining how these cultural constructs shape individuals' self-perception, interpersonal relationships, and societal structures. Understanding the interplay between masculinity and femininity is crucial for fostering gender equality, challenging stereotypes, and promoting inclusive and respectful cultural exchanges in a globalized world.

This dimension refers to the extent to which societies exaggerate the social differences between the two genders. In what Hofstede defines as masculine societies, the differentiation between genders is very pronounced, and typically masculine orientations, such as striving for success, material achievement, and the display of strength and heroism, prevail in determining the salient characteristics of society. Competitiveness among individuals is positively evaluated, work occupies the vast majority of time, and rationality and the absence of emotions are highly valued.

On the contrary, in feminine societies, the focus is on reducing role differentiation, prioritizing harmony in relationships with others over personal success, modesty over ambition, and a better quality of life over financial gain. Competitive spirit is set aside to make room for cooperation.

In the organisational context, employees from highly masculine nations (such as the United States) tend to emphasize ambition, conflicts, and tension, while more feminine nations (such as France) prefer less charged, less conflictual situations characterized by a greater balance between men and women. These differences carry significant weight in the structure of incentives: in masculine countries, greater motivation is achieved by promising opportunities for self-realization (and, indeed, all American theories of motivation revolve around the concept of achievement), while in more feminine nations, the focus is on improving the quality of working conditions. After analysing the individual dimensions, Hofstede proposes an overview of them by constructing cultural maps.

7.4.5 Long-Term versus Short-Term Mental Patterns. The final element of Hofstede's analysis was added to the initial model (1980) through a subsequent study (2001) conducted with the aim of better capturing the cultural characteristics of Asian countries. The addition of this dimension stems from the growing attention that scholars of the 1970s and 1980s have paid to differences in future orientation, a cultural dimension that emerged with the disruptive rise of the Japanese economy and other Asian tigers. Initially, Hofstede (1980) and later Bond (2001) developed a measure of "Confucian dynamism," analysing the tenets of Confucianism, such as the importance and verticality of relationships, civic and moral duty to live a healthy life in a healthy society, and their positive correlation with a country's economic growth rate. A subsequent interpretation of the measurement designed for Confucian dynamism revealed that the index did not actually capture all the ethical values of Confucianism, but rather reflected society's orientation towards the future. This led to the definition of the cultural dimension known as "long-term orientation" (House et al., 2004). This dimension thus reflects the cognitive patterns of a culture regarding its vision of the future: short-term orientation, characteristic of Western cultures, emphasizes valuing the present or at most the past, while long-term orientation, typically Oriental, entails a strong focus on the future, hence the valuation of frugality, savings, patience, and persistence.

The implications for business organisations are also very evident in this case. Long-term cognitive patterns are reflected in structured corporate planning programs, solid partnership relationships with suppliers and customers, and high percentages of income set aside to tackle potential future difficulties. Future orientation also leads to substantial investments in training and development and favours long and gradual growth paths as well as long-term contractual forms. Overall management is thus oriented towards consolidating market position rather than achieving short-term results reflected in the bottom line. Unlike what was just mentioned, short-term orientation implies the rejection of long-term planning and excessive structural rigidity, including personnel management practices: attention is directed towards current issues, perhaps myopically ignoring long-term trends.

7.4.6 Indulgence versus Restraint. This dimension of culture focuses on how different cultures approach the gratification of human desires and impulses. Cultures that lean towards indulgence place value on enjoying life, seeking pleasure, and fulfilling individual desires. They tend to have a more relaxed attitude towards social norms and are more accepting of unconventional behaviours and lifestyles. People in indulgent cultures prioritize personal happiness, self-expression, and spontaneous enjoyment, valuing leisure time and seeking immediate gratification. Such societies may exhibit a higher level of tolerance towards diverse lifestyles, recreational activities, and diverse forms of self-expression. On the other hand, cultures with a preference for restraint emphasize self-control, strict adherence to societal norms, and the suppression of gratification for the sake of long-term goals or societal harmony. Individuals in restrained cultures prioritize the collective well-being over individual desires and often exercise discipline in their behaviour. Social norms and traditions are highly regarded, and there is an emphasis on maintaining self-discipline and adhering to established rules and regulations. Delayed gratification and a focus on long-term planning are valued virtues in restrained societies, where self-restraint is seen as a path to achieving societal order and stability.

Understanding the indulgence versus restraint dimension is crucial for comprehending cultural differences in attitudes towards leisure, pleasure, and self-control. It sheds light on the varying levels of acceptance towards individual freedoms and unconventional behaviours across societies. Recognizing these cultural variations can help facilitate effective cross-cultural communication and cooperation, as well as inform the design of marketing strategies and business practices in different regions. Moreover, acknowledging and appreciating these cultural variations fosters mutual respect and cultural sensitivity, leading to a more harmonious and interconnected global community.

The dimensions of Hofstede's cultural framework are not mutually exclusive but rather interconnected, and societies often display patterns of cultural values that align with specific combinations of dimensions. The relationships between these dimensions contribute to shaping the overall cultural fabric of a society, influencing various aspects of social behaviour, communication styles, decision-making processes, and organisational structures. For instance, cultures with high power distance, which signifies a significant gap in authority and status between individuals, tend to exhibit collectivist tendencies. In such societies, there is a strong emphasis on group harmony, loyalty, and adherence to social norms and hierarchies. This collectivist orientation reinforces the hierarchical structure, making it more acceptable for individuals to defer to authority figures and maintain the status quo. Additionally, the high power distance might also lead to a higher level of uncertainty avoidance. The desire for structured and well-defined rules and regulations serves to mitigate the discomfort caused by ambiguous or unpredictable situations.

On the other hand, cultures with low power distance may lean more towards individualism. In such societies, individuals are encouraged to express their opinions freely, and there is a reduced emphasis on rigid hierarchical structures. The lower power distance allows for more egalitarian communication and collaboration across different levels of society. Moreover, societies that are more individualistic may also be more open to risk-taking and change, as they are less bound by traditional norms and collective expectations. This characteristic aligns with a lower level of uncertainty avoidance.

The combination of long-term orientation and indulgence versus restraint also provides valuable insights into the cultural dynamics of societies. Cultures that prioritize long-term orientation, with a focus on future rewards and perseverance, might exhibit more restrained behaviours, emphasizing self-discipline and suppression of immediate desires for the sake of long-term goals. On the other hand, short-term oriented cultures, which prioritize immediate gratification and enjoyment, might lean more towards indulgence and a greater acceptance of diverse lifestyles and recreational activities. Understanding these interconnected relationships between cultural dimensions provides a comprehensive view of cultural variations and enables individuals and organisations to navigate cross-cultural interactions more effectively and respectfully. It helps in identifying potential challenges and opportunities for collaboration, communication, and cooperation across diverse cultural contexts. By recognizing how cultural values intertwine and influence each other, individuals can develop cultural intelligence and adapt their approaches to foster positive and productive cross-cultural relationships. This awareness is particularly essential in today's globalized world, where intercultural interactions are becoming increasingly common in business, education, and various aspects of everyday life.

Considering all six dimensions, it can be argued that these have produced significant implications on business. From the perspective of leadership and management style, the concept of power distance plays a relevant role. The degree to which a society allows an unequal distribution of power directly correlates with the extent to which centralized (rather than decentralized) decision-making tendencies develop within organisations and the use of an autocratic (rather than participative) leadership style (Hofstede, 1980).

In a high power distance country, where individuals believe that hierarchy reflects a natural inequality of roles, it is more effective to adopt a leadership style with a rigidly vertical flow of decision-making and limited room for deviation from given directives (House et al., 2004). The exercise of authority generally does not generate frustration in such societies, and it is even facilitated by the latent need for dependence instilled in the minds of subordinates during the acculturation process (Oyserman et al., 2002). The management style largely depends on the cultural conditioning of subordinates, meaning their level of submission and dependence.

This is why managing personnel becomes difficult when a manager is transferred to a country with a different power distance; this is particularly true if the power distance is much lower than in the manager's home country: it is generally easier to adopt a more authoritarian approach rather than having to learn to seek consensus. The degree of power distance also determines the ease with which a subordinate can express dissatisfaction or communicate grievances to higher levels. If it is relatively low, companies typically have established channels through which subordinates can voice their complaints without facing negative repercussions; conversely, in organisations with high power distance, questioning decisions made by the established authority is strictly forbidden (House et al., 2004). A strong need to control the unknown leads organisations to take few risks, fear failure, and hinder change; individuals expect clear and detailed instructions from their superiors (towards whom they naturally feel loyalty) and prefer job security and stability over rapid career advancements (especially if these involve international transfers or moves to other companies) (Oyserman et al., 2002). Anxiety about the future induces individuals to have a strong emotional need for order and stability, which is fulfilled through the use of written and unwritten rules to guide their behaviour. While all groups have norms or social codes to ensure orderly living, in societies with a high uncertainty avoidance, these norms almost take on the character of sacred truths, while in others, they are simply tools to enable group functioning (Oddou et al., 2009).

In companies, this need for order translates into a preference for greater formalization of the structure, standardization of procedures, and ritualization of behaviours. If a manager operates with collaborators who have a high uncertainty avoidance, they must be more precise and comprehensive in their instructions and adhere to schedules (Hofstede and Bollinger, 1989).

By linking power distance and uncertainty avoidance, it is possible to determine the implicit models of organisation that best fit different cultural types (Hofstede, 1980). Two fundamental questions that a specific social structure must address are "who decides what?" (power distance) and "how to make outcomes predictable?" (uncertainty avoidance) (Hofstede, 1980). Based on these foundations, Hofstede identified four implicit models of organisation, known as "pyramid of people," "market-village," "extended family," and "well-oiled machine" (Hofstede, 1980).

The "pyramid of people" model closely approximates the ideal of bureaucracy, where relationships between individuals, task characteristics, evaluation, and reward procedures are rigidly established by meticulous rules. Individuals accept an unequal distribution of power and the rights of superiors to reinforce rules and exercise strict control, resulting in a centralized and formalized structure (Hofstede, 1980). At the opposite end of the spectrum lies the "market-village" structure, which is neither formalized nor centralized. Here, relationships between individuals and work procedures often exhibit flexibility and improvisation. People emphasize social connections more than their hierarchical position (Hofstede, 1980). The "well-oiled machine" structure is formalized but decentralized. It ensures exact task execution to avoid uncertainty but does not regulate interpersonal relationships (Hofstede, 1980).

The final organisational model is that of the "extended family" (centralized but not formalized). In this setting, group life typically revolves around a charismatic leader who controls activities through direct supervision, holding polarized authority. However, since role characteristics are not explicitly specified, subordinates implicitly deduce their roles by closely observing the leader's needs (Hofstede, 1980). The substantial diversity of values that separates individualistic societies from collectivist ones (the former oriented towards personal success and achievement, the latter towards the vitality and interests of the group) significantly affects the nature of the relationship between individuals and organisations (House et al., 2004).

Desires for autonomy, clear separation between private and professional spheres, and a strong sense of competitiveness often accompany individualism. Relationships among individuals are driven by reciprocity and entail a calculation of convenience. On the other hand, collectivist organisations are characterized by loyalty, the pursuit of harmony, decision-making based on consultation, and a strong focus on the preferences of the collective. In this case, organisational effectiveness is closely tied to the sense of belongingness shared by all members of the group. Social relationships take precedence over business, and anyone seeking to engage in economic negotiations must consider these differences in priorities.

Gauthey and Xardel offer some suggestions to the Western manager sent to a collectivist country like Japan:

"The manager will find it beneficial to use intermediaries to avoid major blunders caused by both frankness and the tendency to highlight the individual rather than the company. With a primary concern for employee motivation, the manager should focus on maintaining harmony within the group. Publicly criticizing a collaborator should be avoided at all costs, as the collaborator's main concern will likely be to save face in front of peers" (p.53).

Masculinity versus Femininity is likely the dimension in which the effects are less visible in the governance of companies. Its influence is primarily exerted on the individual sphere of motivations, as it leads to the enhancement of the need to stand out and assert oneself rather than the need to socialize. The consequences can be seen in the way the so-called labour reform has been understood, a topic that many countries have been promoting for some time: while everyone agrees on the need to make work more humane, not everyone agrees on the meaning to attribute to the term "humane." In masculine cultures, such work is one that allows for career advancements, challenging opportunities, and personal fulfilment. On the contrary, in feminine cultures, there is a greater emphasis on genuine collaboration among people and a pleasant work atmosphere. The second difference concerns the methods of resolving labour conflicts, more assertive and direct in high masculinity countries, softer and mediated in high femininity ones.

Frugality, perseverance, and balanced development are the main characteristics of societies characterized by a strong future orientation. Primarily family-owned companies favour improvement and learning, but also the establishment of a stable and harmonious hierarchy, as the predefined order allows the preservation of the predetermined social and organisational structure over time. Investment choices prioritize creating a strong market position, ensuring a prosperous future even at the cost of sacrificing immediate results. Conversely, short-term results constitute the primary objective of companies in low future-oriented contexts, and for this reason, management judgment parameters are built around the annual value of the company's success, making extensive use of internal control systems. However, in such circumstances, the need for stability and constant individual regularity discourages risk propensity, initiative, and flexibility towards change – all essential for the success of entrepreneurial operations. Excessive respect for traditions therefore risks diminishing the innovative potential of different entities in our economies, while a significant portion of the success of Asian tigers is precisely due to their cultural ease in effortlessly and surprisingly quickly adopting Western technologies.

The extensive empirical investigation conducted on employees of a major multinational company led Hofstede to supplement the results obtained regarding the differences that national culture determines in individuals with a cross-organisational inquiry into the specificities of corporate cultures and their ability to take root globally, without suffering from the anthropological and sociological superstructures of the reference context. It emerged that at the intra-organisational level, there is a reversal of the roles of values and cultural practices compared to what happens at the national level, leading the latter to prevail over the former. The effect is that the comparative study of similar individuals in different organisational contexts showed great heterogeneity in behaviours associated, however, with considerable similarity in values, demonstrating how organisational culture is essentially constituted by shared perceptions about daily practices. This explains how Hofstede's initial research, much like Laurent's, highlighted differences in values linked to national culture but did not provide any direct information about the organisational culture of the multinational to which all the interviewees belonged (Hofstede and Hofstede, 2005).

From a theoretical standpoint, Hofstede's study demonstrates that it is possible to construct an anthropological typology of cultural differences in management, capable of identifying analytically sound categories with a high degree of universality (the six dimensions). The breadth of the sample and methodological rigor make Hofstede's research an extremely significant contribution to the field of cultural management.

From our perspective, it is worth noting that Hofstede does not outright reject, as idiosyncratic researchers do, any attempts at theory exportation. On the contrary, with a pragmatic approach, he provides parameters for assessing the likelihood of success in such an operation, as well as for identifying the direction for potential adaptation of general theory to local specificities.

7.5 Trompenaars' Different Cultural Dimensions

An innovative echo of Hofstede's work is the study developed by Trompenaars (1993) on cultural differences. However, rather than focusing on the identification of universal categories, his approach aims to analyse national cultures based on specific values that influence the process and forms of business management in a multinational context. The two studies are thus quite different, also because Trompenaars considers individual countries as the main discriminating factor for the different connections between values and behaviours, while Hofstede takes a step further by seeking general correlations between cultural dimensions and psychological structures that allow for a determination of behaviours beyond country specificity. Trompenaars believes that there are three specific areas of cultural differentiation among countries, which are relationships with other individuals, perception of the passage of time, and the placement of individuals in their environment. Based on this, dominant cultural values are identified, including:

- universalism versus particularism
- collectivism versus individualism
- affective versus neutral relationships
- diffuse versus specific relationships
- achievement versus ascription
- sequential versus synchronic time
- internal versus external locus of control

The first five dimensions relate to the social sphere of interpersonal relationships, while the last two relate to time and the environment.

1. Universalism refers to principles governing interpersonal relationships that are considered universal and thus binding in all situations, or rather, they allow for differentiated interpretations depending on circumstances. In universalistic countries like Switzerland, Germany, or the United States, great importance is given to respecting agreements, which are more significant than personal relationships. In particularistic cultures, like the majority of those in the East, a reliable person is not someone who adheres to agreements, but someone who allows mutual adaptation of the agreement and seeks to address all objections that may arise in a dispute. This is why negotiations between countries with different perceptions of the absoluteness of rules, whether they are common sense, custom, or law, tend to be particularly lengthy and often result in contractual disputes. At the organisational level, universalistic companies rely heavily on procedures to ensure consistency and fairness, while particularistic ones attach greater importance to informal networks, accept adaptive changes to activities, and pursue fairness by considering the specifics of each individual case. The headquarters of a universalistic international company tends to be more oriented towards standardization and globalization, while in particularistic contexts, subsidiaries gain more independence in response to adaptation needs.

2. The distinction between individualism and collectivism refers to the recognition of the individual rather than the group as the basic social unit, and the resulting conflict between the needs of the individual and those of the collective. A collectivistic culture places great importance on an individual's social role, and this is reflected in various aspects of business practices: representation delegations are always quite numerous, as the absence of an accompanied person symbolizes a lack of status. Even decision-making processes involve numerous individuals, which is why they usually take a long time to conclude. The motivational aspects of personnel management systems require the greatest conformity with this dimension's cultural characteristics for their fragile effectiveness. Individualism entails strong competitiveness and a focus on economic compensation and personal achievement, whereas in collectivistic cultures, belonging and group esteem are considered more important.
3. Culture also determine a greater or lesser inclination to display one's feelings, depending on whether interactions are managed in a detached manner or whether emotional expression is allowed. This distinction is made between neutral and affective cultures. The effect of this dimension is evident in communication styles, both in verbal communication forms, such as the speed of interaction or the tone and melody of expression, and in non-verbal language forms, such as eye contact or physical contact. In affective cultures, like the Italian or Spanish culture, it is important to show empathy towards the feelings expressed by others and to avoid cold or unfriendly attitudes. In this case, when interacting with more neutral cultures, such as the Japanese or Austrian cultures, it is necessary not to attribute a negative meaning to the absence of emotional expressions. In these situations, written communication should be favoured over direct confrontation, and work-related behaviours should be "depersonalized," achieving a high level of objectivity, clarity, and both formal and substantial simplicity.
4. A distinction closely related to this is that between specific cultures and diffuse cultures, which indicates the degree to which involvement with other individuals is confined to certain areas of interaction and limited levels of engagement, akin to the social effects resulting from a given level of power distance à la Hofstede. This leads to the potential overlap of different levels of experience regarding the context of authority and corporate hierarchy: "*Monsieur le Directeur, being able to manage the company, is generally considered more qualified even in matters of haute cuisine.*" The impact on negotiation styles is very clear. In diffuse cultures, such as Chinese culture, it is not possible to separate work-related matters from private ones, resulting in a need for particular caution and consequently, slowness in reaching agreements. Moreover, tools of performance evaluation typical of specific cultures, such as the United States or the United Kingdom, like the management by objectives, would be difficult to apply, as productivity is primarily determined by the personal relationship between superior and subordinate. The emotional involvement typical of these relationships also requires special attention when using open criticism, as it might be interpreted as a personal offense.
5. Another difference can be observed in how a person's status is determined, essentially investigating the aprioristic causes of power distance. In some cultures, social rank is the result of one's achievements, and thus, it is attainable based on merit. In other cultures, it derives from attributes such as social class, level of education, age, or gender, and is therefore passively attributed to the individual. This results in cultures of ascription, such as the Japanese or Italian cultures, making extensive use of status symbols and titles, both educational and hierarchical, as well as social rank, which are used less in achievement-oriented cultural contexts (among others, the United States,

Sweden, Denmark). At the corporate level, in cultures that value personal achievement, initiative is appreciated and common, hierarchy is respected only when it reflects individuals' real capabilities, and delegation tools are widespread and fully utilized. In ascription contexts, on the other hand, those in the top positions of the organisational chart must always be involved in the major aspects of activities, regardless of their actual competencies, and must receive the attention and consideration befitting their hierarchical level. Naturally, different motivational mechanisms arise, which should favour, based on the cultural context, rewards and recognition for excellent performance rather than the attribution of status symbols.

6. Regarding the orientation towards the passage of time, cultures can be distinguished between sequential and synchronous, based on whether the sequence of events is considered random and independent, or whether a causal connection is identified in it. There are differences not only in the weight attributed to the past, present, and future but also in the perception of the passage of time, which can be linear or circular and, therefore, predetermined and unchangeable. This dimension is rooted in the ethics of Confucianism, as is Hofstede's (2001), but the values obtained by the two studies are different for many countries and underlie a different formulation of the index related to the temporal dimension. Trompenaars considers the temporal horizon and measures it as the average perception of past, present, and future. On the other hand, Hofstede's orientation towards the future indicates a predisposition to consider the effects of our actions on the future, regardless of analysing the value of the past and present and regardless of quantitatively determining the "long term," which may not necessarily be "long."
7. An orientation towards sequentiality, characteristic of British and Scandinavian cultures, determines a mental order that requires performing one task at a time. Synchronous cultures, such as the Italian one, on the other hand, lead individuals to carry out multiple actions of various processes simultaneously, often in a disorderly manner. In companies, depending on the dominant orientation, there may be a clear separation of tasks or rather an overlap of roles or responsibilities. Sequentiality is often also associated with the concept of achievement and the use of meritocratic career mechanisms. Within cultures that interpret the passage of time in a circular manner, the personal relationship with a superior is the primary way to achieve promotion, as its evolution over time allows for an assessment of individual learning and capabilities. It should also be noted that in cultures oriented towards the past, like African cultures, managing corporate change is particularly delicate and successful only when members are certain of preserving cultural and experiential heritage.

Lastly, there are differences in the way individuals relate to the environment. A distinction is made between a logic of adaptation (outer locus of control), typical of Eastern cultures, which emphasizes harmony with the environment and with other individuals, and a logic of control (inner locus of control), found, for example, in the United States, which instead determines a strong orientation towards seeking success and dominance. In the latter case, determination and aggressiveness are considered positive values, reflecting in the corporate environment a climate of intense internal competition and the appreciation of individuality. Any discussions and conflicts are accepted as a means to identify the best solution for achieving shared objectives. Cultural effects are particularly evident in the attribution of meaning to the organisational structure. In control-oriented contexts, it is conceived and realized to achieve specific results from a mechanistic perspective. While in adaptive-oriented contexts, the organisation is an intrinsic prerequisite of business activities, unchangeable as it is derived from nature and necessary representation of things and people.

These are the dimensions, and their main consequences, that Trompenaars identifies as constitutive of the cultural peculiarities of different countries. In practical business dealings, the main problems of cultural clashes between an organisation and a new partner generally arise based on a dominant dimension, or at most, two. The way international managers resolve such conflicts constitutes the true essence of their work.

This cross-cultural analysis and the resulting interpretation of the organisation as a "subjective construct" have led Trompenaars, as was the case with Hofstede before, to use cultural dimensions to identify different models of organisational culture. Indeed, a relationship has been observed between the geographic distribution of individuals' cognitive structures and that of associated corporate values, demonstrating that employees attribute meanings to their environment derived from their "cultural programming." Using explanatory metaphorical images, organisational cultures have been distinguished as Family, Eiffel Tower, Guided Missile, and Incubator.

The Family is an organisation in which the personal dimension, represented by close and affectionate relationships among members, coexists with hierarchical authority associated with the figure of the *pater familias*. The organisation features a very steep hierarchical structure, where power generally derives from allocation. As a result, the leader acts benevolently: they are accepted precisely because it is believed that they work for the common good. Work relationships are long-term and interpreted as a mutual growth partnership. The culture is generally diffuse, effectiveness is prioritized over efficiency, and the main motivational lever is the need for group belonging. The Family culture is found in Eastern countries such as China and Japan, as well as in France and Spain.

On the other hand, the Eiffel Tower represents a highly bureaucratic organisation with well-defined roles and responsibilities along a hierarchy with a strong vertical connotation. The culture is stable and strong, resulting in a low propensity for change. The leader is only incidentally an individual, as they assume authority based on their role. Relationships are specific, emotional displays are very limited, and conflicts are avoided as they are interpreted as anomalies in the system. Motivation primarily stems from the desire for promotion to more prestigious roles. This type of organisational culture is prevalent in Germany and, to a lesser extent, in Denmark and the Netherlands. The Guided Missile differs from the models just described as it is based on equality rather than the verticalization of personal relationships, although like the Eiffel Tower, it is impersonal and task-oriented. It is a culture typical of the United States and, to a lesser extent, of England and Canada, finding solidity through shared objectives, which are then specified to determine the tasks of each member. Personal relationships are neutral and specific, authority derives from achievement, and the main motivational lever is the monetary recognition of work performed.

Finally, the image of the Incubator defines an organisational culture based on the idea that hierarchies are secondary to individual fulfilment: it is egalitarian and personal, diffuse and affectionate. There is no formalization or hierarchy, only a strong commitment to common goals, making managing change particularly straightforward. Here too, power and prestige stem from personal achievement, but motivational mechanisms are primarily linked to a sense of participation (even referred to as "management by enthusiasm"). The goal is to seek and stabilize, through the exploitation of organisational culture, a delicate balance between flexibility and effectiveness. The complexity of its full realization limits its spread: manifestations of this culture can be partially observed in Sweden.

7.5.1 The Reconciliation of Cultural Differences as a Value Creation Process. An interesting aspect of the study is that for each of the opposing categories and resulting potential cultural conflicts, managerial solutions are proposed for their reconciliation. The notion that the two extremes of a cultural determination can coexist within the same individual led Trompenaars to define cross-cultural competencies as the ability to navigate cultural differences in a way that conflicts generated by them do not limit the analytical and action capabilities of companies, but rather enrich them. Taking it a step further, cultural differences are regarded as simple modifications in the allocation of relative importance to different individual values, thus assuming that the resulting heterogeneities are nothing but the "inverted reflection in the mirror" of another culture's socio-cultural characteristics (Trompenaars et al., 2004). For example, regarding differences between universalism and particularism, applying universal rules and procedures promotes internal consistency, but to prevent it from deteriorating into rigidity and bureaucracy, flexibility and personal initiative need to be encouraged. This includes paying due attention to achieving the end goal through the application of the aforementioned rules and procedures. By revisiting various cultural dimensions, the establishment of universal guidelines is necessary for equitable, efficient, and structured adaptation to contingencies. It is important to set group goals that also require personal initiative to achieve. Controlling emotions to facilitate goal attainment is useful, but it should not suppress their natural expression. Leveraging the quality of human relationships as a tool to achieve the best possible outcome reconciles a personal view of work with an objective and task-oriented approach. It is crucial to respect individuals' status, even when it has attributed based on non-shared criteria, and to contextualize emotional expressions (or their absence) relative to the prevailing culture rather than forming a personal judgment. Lastly, to implement an interconnected system of interdependent parts, a precise temporal sequence and clear causal chain for each activity are important, and opportunities offered by the environment should be seized to generate advantage through innovative use of available organisational resources.

The reconciliation patterns proposed here are seen as actual tools available to international businesses to implement an effective value creation process from various perspectives. Externally, a company that can align internal reconciliation processes with those involving external customers inherently possesses the ability to satisfy multiple parties simultaneously and thrive over time. Regarding the internal organisation of the company, creativity, innovation, and improvement are more easily attainable within an environment that allows continuous comparison between best and worst practices. Thus, the advantage of reconciliation lies in preserving and enhancing the diversity of the foreign, which can represent a genuine added value.

This interpretation of management processes defines a new responsibility for international leaders: the ability to merge opposites into an effective action plan, rather than choosing one extreme at the expense of the other. This adds a new element to the traditional attributes of leadership: cross-cultural competence, the ability to reconcile conflicts (Trompenaars and Wolliams, 2003).

7.6 The GLOBE Study: Original Synthesis of Cross-Cultural Theories

The GLOBE research (Global Leadership and Organisational Behaviour Effectiveness Research Program) (House et al., 2004) presents a new and comprehensive study on the consequences of cultural differences in international business practice. The results are derived from analysing responses from 17,000 middle managers belonging to 951 different organisations, through a questionnaire distributed across 62 countries. These countries were selected to include at least three from each major geographical region, ensuring statistical consistency and making this study the most ambitious in terms of data collection. Hofstede analysed a much larger number of individuals, but did not construct such a well-balanced analytical foundation argued West and Graham (2004). The independent variables of the model were defined based on the mathematical reprocessing of available data, thereby avoiding predefined structures that could have biased the direction of research. These variables define nine cultural attributes, dimensions that create a comprehensive analytical matrix of differentiating elements among cultures. This matrix is built with clear reference to numerous prior theoretical contributions in cross-cultural studies.

The empirical robustness of the study has allowed for a deeper analysis of leadership issues. Six culturally embedded implicit theories of leadership were identified, which represent potential managerial behaviours and styles associated with the concept of leadership. The main goal of the research is to create an empirically grounded theory of leadership and organisational differences among cultures. This is based on the assumption that acceptance and effectiveness of authority ultimately depend on culture. The GLOBE Study combines theories of implicit leadership (Lord and Maher, 1991) and value-belief theories (Hofstede, 1980; Triandis, 1995 and 2004). It constructs a theoretical framework where leadership acceptance is derived not only from the individual attributes and behaviours of the leader, but also from culturally valid leadership values within the context. Leadership effectiveness, on the other hand, primarily arises from organisational and strategic contingencies, which are influenced by cultural specifics as well as the leader's personal characteristics. This approach challenges traditional leadership theories based on American, European, or Canadian cultural models, and therefore on individualism, democracy, rationality, and the hedonic motivational logic characteristic of these societies.

7.6.1 Cultural Dimensions. The dimensions considered in the GLOBE Study are as follows:

1. uncertainty avoidance
2. power distance
3. institutional collectivism
4. in-group collectivism
5. gender egalitarianism
6. assertiveness
7. future orientation
8. performance orientation
9. humane orientation

1. As previously noted by Hofstede (1980), individuals perceive uncertainty in a different manner and respond variably to the sensations generated by this inherent attribute of human existence. Individuals with high uncertainty avoidance actively attempt to reduce the likelihood that future events negatively affect activities and behaviours. In social relations, this leads to tendencies to formalize interactions among individuals, extensive use of documentation in negotiations, and the adoption of rules and customs to establish greater reliability. Organisational practices also reflect this: business practices focus on increasing mutual trust and engagement in work, roles are structured with greater formalization, and low-risk personnel selection tools are employed.

2. Power distance, identified by numerous studies including Hofstede's, was universally accepted following his work. The GLOBE Study results show widespread presence of social practices associated with high power distance, although considerable national differences exist, particularly between traditional Eastern hierarchies and Western democratic equality. A notable duality exists that links this result with the diffusion of cultural values associated with power distance, identifying a global aspiration to reduce social hierarchies. In terms of business, organisations generally reflect the power distance values present in their societies as a tool for legitimization and functioning assurance.

3. Individualism and collectivism, dimensions well-established in cross-cultural literature, received an innovative interpretation within the GLOBE Study. Through a factor analysis aimed at measuring individualism in a general sense, two distinct dimensions emerged: in-group collectivism and institutional collectivism.

4. In-group collectivism reflects the extent to which individuals are proud of and value their families and organisations, while the institutional collectivism, introduced for the first time in this study, is manifested in laws, social programs, or institutional practices that encourage the development of a sense of community. Group collectivism is robustly and negatively correlated with Hofstede's proposed individualism dimension. Interestingly, the presence of in-group collectivism is not correlated with institutional collectivism.

5. Gender egalitarianism is defined as the degree to which an organisation or society minimizes role differences based on the distinction between male and female. Cultures with strong gender egalitarianism do not attribute roles in family, society, and business based on biological sex but value individual capabilities instead. This cultural dimension was derived from Hofstede's masculinity dimension, but it represents a significant revision. The GLOBE Study employs two distinct dimensions, gender egalitarianism and assertiveness, to capture different cultural nuances observed by Hofstede through a single indicator. Gender egalitarianism is constructed based on the idea that gender-related stereotypes and ideologies influence specific behavioural manifestations, leading to either equality or discrimination.

6. Assertiveness is defined in the GLOBE Study as the extent to which individuals are assertive, persistent, dominant, and aggressive in social relations, virtually placing assertiveness in the centre of a continuum between non-assertive and aggressive. Assertive attitudes are common in Western business (using Hofstede's model, assertiveness is present in cultures he defines as masculine) and often carry a positive connotation. In assertive cultures (such as Albanian, German, Austrian), competition is valued, strong and charismatic individuals are esteemed, communications are direct, feelings are expressed openly, and disagreements are voiced. Less emphasis on aggressiveness and determination, found in cultures like Swedish or New Zealand, is associated with sympathizing with the weak, associating competition with defeat, valuing cooperation, and utilizing indirect and implicit communication. Assertiveness values in organisations are reflected in attention to and remuneration of performance, setting challenging goals, and attributing individual value through achievement logic.

7. Taking inspiration from Kluckhohn and Strodtbeck's work (1961), where orientation toward the past, present, and future was first considered a cultural attribute, future orientation in this study is defined as the extent to which members of a society or organisation believe that current actions can influence their future. Hence, greater value on tomorrow is placed as well as on planning activities and actions investing in the future and based on long-term effects. The temporal perspective allows individuals to organize personal and social experiences into well-defined categories (past, present, future) and give them coherence and meaning. Cultures with low future orientation (like Polish, Argentinean, Russian) value experiences when lived, do not experience anxieties related to the past or uncertainty of the future, and tend to neglect planning activities and consider warning signals of impending dangers. Cultures with strong future orientation (like Swiss, South African) demonstrate strong predictive and planning capabilities but may devalue personal relationships and current moments.

8. The collective focus on innovation, continuous improvement, and raising existing quality standards contributes to defining performance orientation. The robust presence of this dimension implies an endogenous interpretation of external world changes and a proactive and innovative view of individual responsibilities within the group. Performance orientation in organisational behaviour is reflected in

prioritizing results over people, consistent investment in development and training, creating career paths and motivating remuneration schemes.

9. Humane orientation is a new dimension introduced by the GLOBE Study, inspired by Kluckhohn and Strodtbeck's "Good Human Nature" and "Bad Human Nature." It indicates the extent to which individuals in societies or organisations encourage and reward values such as altruism, loyalty, friendship, charity, and generosity. Cultures with high humane orientation values place significant attention on the needs of others, which leads to strong family and friendship bonds, as well as respect for strangers. Human orientation seems to arise from the real needs of a population within a specific cultural context. Societies with strong human orientation are characterized by informal relationships and control based on shared values and norms. In societies with less emphasis on others, control relies on bureaucratic practices, often resulting in formal and standardized relationships.

The study's results led to the identification of ten distinct cultural clusters, unsurprisingly aligned with geographical regions. These clusters are: Anglo Saxon, Latin Europe, Germanic Europe, Eastern Europe, Northern Europe, Sub-Saharan, Middle East, Confucian Asia, South Asian, and Latin America.

7.6.2 The Perspective of Culturally Contingent Leadership. The new dimensions identified by the empirical investigation were used to modify the context of validity for implicit theories of leadership. Instead of focusing on the individual-level differences in leadership perception, the authors used cultural diversities as a discriminating factor and investigated the contexts of validity of behaviours at both national and organisational levels. The international investigation allowed a shift from an individual effectiveness perspective to a cultural effectiveness perspective, aiming to identify the attributes that make leadership effective within a particular context. The definition of culturally endorsed implicit theories of leadership is based on the idea that the structure and content of classic elements, proposed by implicit leadership theory, are shared by individuals within the same cultural context rather than stemming from an individual's personal processing of behaviours, attitudes, and relationships. The GLOBE Study identified six distinct leadership attributes, some already present in previous literature and others newly introduced, and examined the relative importance assigned to each attribute in the different cultural groups identified by the research. The order among these attributes is heterogeneous and dependent on the presence of certain cultural characteristics in the populations. In other words, the acceptance and effectiveness of leadership are determined by the attributes and behaviours of the leader, which in turn derive from the characteristics of the organisation and the national context. The culturally endorsed implicit leadership theories that emerged from the study are as follows:

- charismatic-visionary leadership. An extensive definition reflecting a leader's ability to inspire, motivate, and cultivate expectations for high performance through strong moral firmness and solidity.
- Team-oriented leadership is reflected in attitudes that support team building and the dissemination of a common goal among all participants.
- Participative leadership refers to the extent to which managers involve other workers in the decision-making process and subsequent implementation of adopted solutions.
- Humane-oriented leadership is characterized by compassionate spirit and generosity that do not undermine the leader's authority.
- Autonomous leadership is established through the leader's independence and autonomy.
- Self-protective leadership is manifested in the pursuit of individual security and protection, strengthening one's status and avoiding association with negative events (face saving).

The leadership attributes that demonstrated greater cross-cultural prevalence are charismatic-visionary leadership and team-oriented leadership, as they are perceived as positive in all ten clusters identified by the authors. Their universality stems from the fact that the main traits characterizing them represent universally rooted determinants of leadership: integrity, visionary charisma, inspirational charisma, and team-building skills. However, not all elements of the culturally endorsed implicit leadership theories are universal. The ten cultural clusters identified in the study were used as a framework for analysing leadership heterogeneities. This approach allowed the identification of an ideal leader profile for each of the different cultural contexts, defining a specific configuration of attributes that vary in perceived importance based on variations in the nine dimensions. For example, individualistic leadership is considered an ineffective leadership attribute in all contexts except for countries with high levels of individualism. Similarly, displaying a propensity for risk is negatively perceived in a context of uncertainty avoidance.

The importance of collaboration and follower empowerment is evident in the lesser influence attributed to autonomous leadership, which is inversely correlated with institutional collectivism. Self-protective leadership, often seen as inhibiting effectiveness, is prevalent in Eastern cultures characterized by high power distance and uncertainty avoidance. Participative leadership, while accepted in all clusters, is particularly linked to Northern European countries and less prevalent in Eastern countries due to its association with result orientation and gender equality. Result orientation is also connected to charismatic leadership, and as expected, humane-oriented leadership is linked to the cultural dimension defined as humane orientation. Group collectivism and uncertainty avoidance are, finally, correlated with team-oriented leadership.

7.7 The Contributions by Triandis, Schneider, Boisot, and Sorge

The contributions of scholars Triandis, Schneider, Boisot, and Sorge have been instrumental in advancing our understanding of cultural differences and their profound impact on business, organisations, and management practices. Through their ground-breaking research and theoretical frameworks, these scholars have shed light on the complexities of cross-cultural interactions, providing valuable insights for managers, leaders, and researchers alike. Each of these scholars has delved into different aspects of cultural dimensions, organisational climate, information management, and human resource practices, contributing significantly to the field of cultural management studies. In this overview, we will explore the key contributions of Triandis, Schneider, Boisot, and Sorge, highlighting the enduring relevance of their work in today's globalized and culturally diverse business environment. The contributions of the above mentioned authors refer to their respective research and theories on cultural differences in the context of business and organisations. These scholars have provided significant insights and theoretical models to analyse how cultures influence management practices and organisational dynamics.

Triandis developed the theoretical model of individualism-collectivism, focusing on the differences between societies where individualism is predominant and those where collectivism prevails. This model examines how people in these different cultures perceive the self, social bonds, and the role of individuals within the group (Triandis, 1989).

Schneider contributed with his model of organisational climate, which explores how the cultural characteristics of an organisation influence employee behaviour and attitudes. The organisational climate model helps to understand how collective norms, values, and expectations in corporate cultures are reflected in interactions and the goals of organisation members (Schneider, 1988 and 1989).

Boisot provided an information theory-based approach to analyse cultural differences in the organisation of knowledge. His model explores how corporate cultures may differ in managing, sharing, and interpreting information, and how this may influence innovation and organisational learning (Boisot, 1998).

On the other hand, Sorge contributed to understanding the differences between national cultures and their impact on human resource management practices. His work focuses on the human resource management strategies adopted by different corporate cultures and how they influence organisational dynamics, leadership and employee engagement (Sorge, 2003). Moving on to contributions of a more distinctly theoretical nature, Triandis (1983) identifies a series of hypotheses correlating cultural dimensions with organisational functioning. Through an analysis of cultural categories derived from major anthropological and organisational studies, Triandis integrates and classifies the literature, categorizing the resulting twenty dimensions into three sets.

a. Perceptual differences:
   - emphasis on what the other person does rather than on what the other person is;
   - definition of who belongs to a group, be it familial, professional, national, etc.;
   - group size dimension;
   - ease of entry into the group;
   - emphasis on age, gender, social class;
   - self-concept in terms of self-esteem, power, and activity.
b. Utilization and evaluation of information:
   - ideology versus pragmatism;
   - associative versus abstract communications;
   - good or bad human nature;
   - dominance over nature versus subordination to nature;
   - emphasis on the past, present, or future;
   - emphasis on doing, being, or becoming;
   - individualism versus collectivism;
   - control of uncertainty;
   - masculinity versus femininity of goals.
c. Action models:
   - contact versus non-contact (Dionysus versus Apollo).

After analysing the meaning of these dichotomies and specifying their geographical scope, Triandis then hypothesizes their consequences on the organisation, distinguishing between managerial functions (goal-setting, planning, selection, training, personnel control, and motivation) and behaviours (productivity, job satisfaction, leadership style). Triandis' model is highly commendable for its effort towards precision and orderly schematization, making it a useful tool (a sort of dashboard) for setting up and interpreting any empirical research. However, it should be emphasized that there is a significant number of dimensions involved, which could make the schema somewhat scattered.

A similar approach to Triandis' is proposed by Schneider (1989) for studying the impact of national culture on the processes of strategy formulation. After identifying five stages in this process (analysis, selection, interpretation, validation, and priority setting), Schneider adopts Schein's (1984) distinction between external adaptation issues (i.e., relationships with the environment) and internal integration issues (i.e., interpersonal relationships within the organisational boundaries). According to Schneider, this distinction perfectly overlaps with the two managerial aspects involved in the planning process: the analytical moment and the implementation moment. Thus, it becomes straightforward to correlate the cultural dimensions related to external adaptation and internal integration with the five stages of the strategic formulation process, hypothesizing that, in each case, some dimensions may influence the choice of how a particular phase is managed more than others. As for the external adaptation, Schneider identifies six indicators:

- uncertainty and ambiguity: tolerated or avoided, reduced or amplified.
- control over the environment: managed or endured.
- proactivity versus reactivity: doing or being, fatalism.
- truth and reality: empirical evidence or philosophical, induction or deduction.
- time orientation: past, present, or future.
- change: positive or destructive.

On the other hand, internal integration issues are influenced by the following three dilemmas:

1. hierarchy: power and status or competence.
2. individualism or collectivism.
3. task orientation or people orientation.

Schneider's model is particularly commendable for the precision with which it defines the interaction between strategic formulation and national culture. Furthermore, it highlights the need for an approach that not only focuses on the more strictly organisational aspects, i.e., internal integration, but also investigates how the company interacts with the external environment.

Two fundamental management models emerge. One is oriented towards control and the other one is towards adaptation, precisely as indicated by some contributions from organisational theory.

Schneider's novelty lies in the possibility that national culture directs this choice as it influences the nature of the organisation's relations with its environment as much as the relationships between people within it. It is then hypothesized that the environmental management model prevails in cultures where uncertainty is controlled through its reduction, while a more adaptive attitude is found in cultures where uncertainty is perceived as an immutable fact.

Another fascinating theoretical contribution comes from Boisot (1986), who reinterprets in cultural terms the rationality underlying Organisation and Market models and contingency models. Boisot develops a matrix, called cultural space, in which economic transactions are classified based on the degree of codification and dissemination of knowledge related to them.

The same matrix also configures the dynamic process by which knowledge of the transaction follows a circular path starting from a stage of low codification and dissemination and moves towards the opposite conditions through individual and social learning processes.

This interpretation allows placing national cultures within the matrix space. Thus, for example, a culture that places great emphasis on transparency in economic relations (like the American one) seeks to bring transactions to a level of codification that allows them to be subjected to precise rules. Conversely, a social-oriented culture (like the Japanese one) aims for a high diffusion of non-formalized rules: the prevalence of classic or market structures (Barney and Ouchi, 1985). Furthermore, a country like China tends to create organisations where the flow of information is very limited (low diffusion) and linked to bureaucratic rules and norms (high codification). Lastly, France may sit somewhere between the United States and China, characterized by a preference for impersonal and meticulously formalized transactions.

Boisot's scheme also provides interesting insights into the so-called convergence hypothesis: the hypothesis that rational forces prevail over cultural ones in the long term can be rephrased by stating that global management knowledge moves towards the quadrant of high codification and high diffusion. However, this shift is only "half of the story" because it is conceivable that the process continues in a circular manner and leads to a stage of significant divergence.

Boisot's model is certainly very original; its main limitation lies in the difficulty of operationalizing the variables: it is not very clear, for example, how to translate a culture's preferences for a certain degree of codification and dissemination of knowledge into empirical terms, unless it is deduced ex post from the characteristics of the organisations studied. However, this would create a self-fulfilling prophecy and preclude the verification of other influences, contradicting Popper's principle of falsification (Popper, 1972).

A theoretical but also empirical approach that takes the ideationalist view to the extreme is the symbolist perspective, which, starting from the hyper-subjective conception of reality, suggests an interpretation of the company as an entity not influenced but literally created by culture.

In this view, culture becomes the primary driver shaping the identity and behaviour of the organisation, from its values and symbols to its routines and decision-making processes (Eisenhardt and Martin, 2000). The symbolist approach emphasizes the significance of shared meanings and symbols in organisational life. It suggests that the very existence and functioning of the organisation are deeply embedded in cultural codes and interpretations. As a result, the organisation's structure, practices, and strategies are shaped by the prevailing cultural values and norms, which are often taken for granted and unconsciously accepted by its members (Smircich, 1983). By understanding the influence of culture at such a fundamental level, the symbolist perspective offers valuable insights into how organisations can develop a distinct identity and cultivate a coherent culture. However, just like the ideationalist approach, it may face challenges in empirical research, as measuring and operationalizing cultural symbols and their effects can be complex and subjective.

In conclusion, both Boisot's model and the symbolist perspective contribute to the richness of cultural studies in organisational management. While Boisot's model offers a structured framework to understand the relationship between national culture and strategic formulation, the symbolist perspective highlights the profound impact of culture on organisational identity and behaviour. Integrating these perspectives with other theoretical approaches can lead to a comprehensive understanding of the complex interplay between culture and management practices in organisations.

These studies do not typically consider culture as an additional contingency factor, as something that the organisation has, along with other things, but as something that the organisation is. Bodega (1996) argues that "the inclusion of the cultural dimension in the study of organisations can occur at two levels: culture can be an external factor that simply influences the structural and behavioural arrangement of a company, or it can be the true inspiring principle, the ethical pillar of this arrangement. It can be an important independent variable, interacting with other independent variables in the overall functioning of a company, or it can be the vital breath that creates and distinguishes that very company in all its manifestations. In this second case, culture stands to the company as personality stands to an individual". Undoubtedly, this approach tends to shift the terms of the interaction between culture and transnational environment to a different level. In this conception, companies are considered cultures and research, rather than identifying laws, aims to identify meanings. The significant contribution of this perspective lies in emphasizing the historical nature of each company, a nature that makes it a unique and unrepeatable entity in both time and space, enabling it to resist the tendencies of forced homogenization imposed by the industrialization process.

The earlier contribution by Sorge (1983) seems to shed more light on the complementary aspects of ideationalist and institutionalist approaches. Sorge builds on the epistemological contributions of Popper proposing an interpretation of contingency theory as an attempt to shift organisational and managerial knowledge from a state of craft to one of science, from predominantly empirical and informal knowledge to one codified in the form of demonstrable scientific theory. Such an effort would be justified only if organisations followed coherent laws and exhibited a certain regularity in the relationships between variables. This, in turn, is only possible if resistance to rational behaviour is assumed on the part of the decision-maker. However, this phenomenon does not always occur. Decision-makers may follow a process of post hoc rationalization, and within the organisation, the rationalities of multiple actors interact along with their intuitive faculties.

This line of reasoning leads Sorge to embrace the approach of Crozier and Friedberg (1978), which interprets the organisation as a system of interactions between free actors and sanctioning rules without making strong assumptions about the nature of the involved rationality. The impossibility of interpreting the organisation as the result of rational design leads to a rediscovery of culture as a system of patterns consolidated by a collective to respond to specific contingencies. These patterns function as mechanisms, selected through an evolutionary process, guiding decision-makers' perception of problems and compensating for their limited rationality, following a scheme that has proven to be a suitable response to the organisation's reference context. In this perspective, the deterministic model of the institutionalist approach, where educational and political systems represent the most influential variable, must be revisited by considering institutions themselves as a response to certain cultural values expressed by a specific population through a historical process of collective learning. It becomes evident that it is not possible to trace one-way causal chains between different variables (culture, institutions, transnational environment, organisation) because the focus of the analysis, that is the organisational actor, is a psychosocial entity. The latter expresses within itself and through its behaviour an inseparable synthesis of shared values and attitudes (ideationalist perspective) on the one hand, and their institutional manifestations (institutionalist perspective) on the other (Child and Tayeb, 1983).

Sorge summarizes his position by stating that, according to this approach, there is no culture-free organisational context because even if organisational solutions or contexts are similar, they are always constructed according to a cultural schema and are imperfectly interpreted as a reaction to certain constraints. An important element emerges from this perspective (Child and Tayeb, 1983); it asserts that decision-makers always formulate policies and seek solutions within their cultural perspectives, attributing almost limitless power to this cultural process. Thus, Sorge tends to attribute to the decision-making process considerable intuitive value, as well as an almost absolute freedom to reinterpret the situation in a manner consistent with the cultural preferences of the decision-maker. From the perspective of the intuitive and non-rational nature of strategic decisions, Sorge's position finds partial support in the contributions of Mintzberg et al. (2000), but especially in the garbage can model by Cohen, March and Olsen. However, the latter specifies the underlying peculiarities of its analysis, making it applicable only under conditions of maximum uncertainty. Sorge's position is more radical and emphasizes the one-way nature of the non-rational decision-making process.

Child and Tayeb (1983) argue that there is a clear difference between the thesis that the not entirely rational nature of organisational action produces certain distinctive characteristics related to cultural phenomena. As well as the thesis that decision-makers make no rational attempt to calculate the consequences of failure to adapt to the situation. "Strictly speaking, it is certainly true that situational factors most often do not constitute imperatives giving rise to organisations with characteristics independent of decision-makers' inclinations". What raises doubts, however, is the assumption that decision-makers never take into account the specificities of the situation, attributing the differences between organisational forms to cultural preferences. This leads to a point of fundamental relevance: the problem is no longer to understand whether national culture influences the functioning of companies, but rather it becomes crucial to understand which elements of the organisational arrangement are conditioned by cultural factors.

7.8 Freedom and Limits of Cultural Action

Freedom and limits of cultural action focuses on the intricate relationship between culture and human behaviour, exploring the extent to which cultural norms, beliefs, and values shape individual and collective actions. Culture plays a fundamental role in shaping societies, influencing their social structures, traditions, and ways of life. It acts as a powerful force that guides people's perceptions, decisions, and interactions with others. However, this influence is not absolute, and individuals and groups often navigate within certain boundaries, experiencing both freedom and limitations in the expression of their cultural identity. This exploration raises intriguing questions about the dynamic interplay between culture and human agency. To what extent do individuals have the autonomy to act outside cultural norms and challenge established traditions? Conversely, how much do cultural norms restrict behaviour and hinder the acceptance of diverse perspectives? Understanding the delicate balance between cultural freedom and constraints is essential to comprehend the complexities of human societies and their ongoing evolution. Throughout history, cultural practices have shaped civilizations, laying the groundwork for traditions, governance systems, and societal norms. These cultural pillars have offered stability, continuity, and a sense of belonging to communities. However, as societies progress and interact with global influences, the dynamics of cultural action become increasingly complex. The advent of modern communication technologies and mass media has facilitated the exchange of ideas and beliefs across borders, leading to a richer tapestry of cultural diversity but also sparking tensions between global homogenization and the preservation of local customs.

This topic invites us to explore the nuances of cultural autonomy and the potential for cultural clashes in an interconnected world. It raises questions about the impact of cultural freedom on personal identity, creativity, and innovation. Additionally, it challenges us to consider the ethical dimensions of cultural expression, such as when cultural practices clash with universal human rights principles.

In the previous paragraph, the question posed so far is whether cultural influences determine organisational differences. The question now is if national culture affects the selection of organisational aspects. This has been a subject of extensive research. Already in 1979, Child and Kieser have attempted to answer this important question through a comparative analysis of 133 companies in Great Britain and Germany.

The results of the investigation showed that, although the logic of industrialization was evident, organisational differences persisted and were congruent with national cultural characteristics. In particular, Child and Kieser identified different patterns and differences of decentralization and managerial behaviour that could not be attributed to the contingent factors considered by the Aston model and that align with the unique cultural characteristics of each nation. Surprisingly, such variations could not be fully attributed to the contingent factors typically considered by conventional organisational models like the Aston model.

The research by Child and Kieser highlights how cultural dimensions, deeply ingrained in the social fabric of a nation, interact with organisational systems, shaping their design and functioning. Cultural values, norms, and beliefs significantly influence the preferences and priorities of both individuals and groups within an organisation. These cultural factors can manifest themselves in various ways, such as decision-making processes, communication styles, hierarchical structures, and approaches to conflict resolution.

The data collected led the two researchers to important considerations:

- firstly, the technological and environmental contingencies of traditional theory have a greater influence on the design of the macrostructure, while different cultural models are more likely to manifest in micro-organisational processes, such as role adoption and managerial behaviours.
- Secondly, the possibility that certain contingencies do not necessarily lead to the adoption of organisational configurations predicted by contingency theory can give rise to two consequences: if contingency theory were truly universal, one would expect to observe inefficiency resulting from a lack of adaptation. On the other hand, if this is not the case, it would mean that organisational practices have managed to find configurations adapted to local cultural expectations that work better than standardized prescriptions of contingency theory. This would provide evidence of the normative (and not just descriptive) limitations of traditional precepts. The adoption of a configuration different from the "rational" one may also be permitted by a permissive competitive situation, which, while still yielding positive results, may not highlight any potential low level of efficiency.

Child and Kieser's conclusion is that at every point in the causal chain developed by universalist contingency theory, other influences (most of which are of cultural origin) have the possibility of intervening. Thus, culture can be interpreted as a factor of distortion that allows soft variables to adapt to local specificities.

A comparable study to that of Child and Kieser is the one conducted by Aiken and Bacharach in 1979. The findings seem to confirm the greater exposure of micro-structural aspects to cultural influence. Specifically, based on research conducted in two public bureaucracies located in two regions of Belgium (the first in Flanders, which has cultural proximity to Anglo-Saxon culture, and the second in the Walloon region, similar to the French-speaking area), it was asserted that the effect of culture on organisations becomes more apparent in behavioural processes rather than in structural solutions.

Compared to Child and Kieser's study, the research conducted by Aiken and Bacharach provides more precise specifications regarding which relationships are free from cultural conditioning and, conversely, on which organisational variables the contingent factors have a limited ability to exert their influence universally. In particular, culture has not demonstrated a decisive influence on:

- Macrostructure;
- distribution of power and influence;
- communication processes.

On the other hand, a strong cultural influence is observed on the following internal processes:

- social control
- work practices

- criteria for promotion and remuneration
- innovation processes

In a more general sense, culture appears to have a significant impact on the dimension of formalization, emphasizing the informal aspects of organisational processes. In light of the studies by Aiken and Bacharach, as well as Child and Kieser, Maurice's critique of Aston's methodology becomes evident: by focusing exclusively on macro-structural aspects, it practically hindered the identification of cultural influences from the outset. The researches examined so far all constitute valuable contributions towards a synthesis between universalist and culturalist approaches.

However, the scholar who has come closest to developing a truly "general" theory is Child. The study proposed by Child (1981) and Child and Tayeb (1983) is probably the most comprehensive attempt to integrate different research perspectives into a unified and pragmatic framework.

Child starts from Roberts' (1970) metaphor of the elephant to lament the persistent lack of communication between different comparative management approaches, mainly due to the absence of a theory capable of integrating the concept of culture into the economic functioning of a company. Child argues that, in reality, the various models are not necessarily incompatible but represent different ways of looking at a single, complex reality.

Unlike previous orientations, Child does not merely acknowledge the coexistence of influences of different nature but seeks common ground among the various approaches. This effort of synthesis leads him to recognize both correctness and limitations in each of the approaches considered so far. According to Child, the dichotomy between the approaches arises from the apparent contradiction existing between the causal chain identified by the contingency theory (independent variables - structure - behavioural models) and the culturalist perspective (culture - preferences - organisational structure). It disappears, however, when the following two assumptions are accepted:

- the decision to adopt a structural configuration is not rigidly determined by contextual factors; moreover, these factors themselves are subject to some degree of manipulation: it is not difficult to refer to the concept of an "acted" or "enacted" environment.
- culture itself can be considered as an additional contingent factor, as seen through the analyses of Child and Kieser (1979). An author like Sorge (1983) would probably reject such a hypothesis, arguing that culture acts more upstream and deeply than other contextual variables: being rooted in people's minds, culture is deemed more powerful than the objective factors identifying the situation and can lead to different behaviour

Continuing along this path, Sekaran and Snodgrass (1986) argue that culture directs organisational design along lines that may be in contrast to those indicated by structural contingencies. To the extent that the cultural preferences of designers align with the environmental and strategic situation, culture becomes a factor of competitive advantage compared to companies characterized by different "mental programming".

Conversely, achieving effective alignment between the divergent indications given by culture and context can be challenging and costly, with evident repercussions on organisational efficiency (Decastri, 1989).

For instance, a nation characterized by high hierarchical distance will give rise to "mechanistic" structures suited for stable environments; if a stable sector suddenly becomes dynamic, companies with a "static national culture" may struggle compared to companies from more flexible cultures. National culture thus becomes a "constraint on alternative choices," in the sense that it guides and channels organisational design efforts towards a set of possible solutions that are acceptable, within which the company's arrangement must be chosen. In some ways, the organisational system fails to imagine solutions far from the package proposed by national culture, leading to a considerable loss of efficiency due to the lack of coherence between contingent factors and culture. The extent to which this phenomenon can be felt depends on the competitiveness of the sector in which the company operates. If the environment allows the survival of even less efficient actors, cultural factors conflicting with the demands expressed by the environmental and strategic situation continue to influence the life of the company without endangering its survival (Hannan and Freeman, 1977). On the contrary, if the pressure for results is significant, the room for manoeuvre is much narrower, and market mechanisms tend to select companies with "rational" organisational arrangements. A non-favourable national culture becomes a source of inefficiencies that leads to the disappearance of the company and must, therefore, be considered a siren to avoid being ensnared by.

National culture acts as a subtle yet powerful force, influencing not only the formal aspects of an organisation, such as its policies and procedures, but also the informal aspects, such as organisational climate and employee behaviour. For instance, a culture that places high emphasis on individualism may encourage a more competitive and autonomous work environment, whereas a collectivist culture might foster collaboration and harmony within the organisation.

Moreover, the impact of cultural factors on organisational aspects extends beyond the internal functioning of a company. Cultural values can also affect the organisation's relationships with external stakeholders, including customers, suppliers, and government entities. Understanding and accommodating cultural nuances become crucial in building effective relationships and navigating business practices in diverse cultural contexts. Overall, the research by Child and Kieser emphasizes the complex interplay between national culture and organisational dynamics. It underscores the importance of recognizing cultural influences as a key determinant in shaping the structure, behaviour, and practices of organisations within a specific country. By acknowledging and understanding these cultural influences, leaders and managers can better navigate the challenges and opportunities that arise in a diverse global business landscape, ultimately contributing to the success and sustainability of their organisations.

7.9 Conclusions

In light of the considerations made so far, it is possible to draw some conclusions that are certainly not definitive but probably useful for reducing the high level of ambiguity on the subject. A first aspect concerns the rationalization of positions in the field. Supporters of the convergence thesis argue that:

- the growth of business schools and consulting companies contributes to spreading a common language and methodology;
- the diffusion of technology (production, transportation, communication) suggests a process of standardization;
- globalization, more generally, has led to an increased circulation of resources and information, making national traditions less important and making the world as a "global village".

Conversely, defenders of the thesis of the persistence of cultural factors even at advanced levels of industrialization rely on the following considerations:

- the diversity of each country's history and, above all, the uniqueness of the processes of industrialization have created deeply rooted legacies in institutional structures and development paths, resulting in different trajectories for each nation.
- If we accept the previously discussed approach of Boisot (1986), according to which culture follows circular processes of convergence and divergence, then the possibility of managerial practices of different nations becoming closer depends on the position of their culture along the cycle of knowledge diffusion relative to the positions of other nations.
- Different nations seem to exhibit very distinct populations of companies; convergence, even if it were to occur, is a phenomenon achievable only in the long term. Moreover, data collected by Hofstede at different times even indicate an increase in cultural differentiation.

A second relevant aspect concerns the areas of influence of national culture: it is now universally accepted that culture tends to act more on certain aspects than on others. From the perspective of levels of analysis, it exerts greater influence on microstructural processes (especially informal organisation) and to a lesser extent on macro-structural ones. From a functional point of view, it can be stated that boundary units are more exposed to culture compared to the technical core (Thompson, 1967).

Finally, it is quite evident that compatibility between cultural and contingency theories becomes achievable when cultural factors are considered as an additional category of independent variables, characteristic of the situation, and on which the optimal organisational arrangement should be designed. The relevance of culture is also a function of performance pressure: as this pressure increases, cultural preferences incongruent with the requirements imposed by the environment should progressively give way to rational design, and vice versa. In summary, two concepts have emerged from the analysis conducted so far. The first is that human nature conceals under its surface an irreducible diversity of forms of expression. This diversity is partly attributable to the influence of culture; the second refers to the belief that none of us can claim to live in the "best of all possible worlds" and consider ourselves, for some mysterious reason, superior to others: everything that originates and develops within a group of individuals has a validity that is entirely relative.

This dual premise leads us to reflect on the modes of governance of these new complexities:

a. how can an organisation that intends to operate abroad overcome the barriers of cultural diversity,
b. how can individuals who, due to their work, find themselves balancing between two worlds reconcile their different nature?

a. Organisations find themselves having to decide whether to change others or themselves. That is, whether to impose their own way of being and functioning rather than accepting a sort of compromise in diversity. In the context of a globalized world with diverse cultures, organisations often face a critical dilemma: should they strive to change and impose their own established practices and norms on others, or should they adapt and compromise with the inherent diversity of different cultural contexts? This decision is at the heart of cultural integration and presents complex challenges for businesses operating internationally.

On one hand, organisations may be tempted to promote and enforce their existing organisational models and management styles in new environments. This approach assumes that their methods have proven successful and that replicating them will lead to desired outcomes. However, imposing a one-size-fits-all approach risks alienating local employees and stakeholders, leading to resistance, inefficiencies, and ultimately, failure. On the other hand, embracing cultural diversity and seeking a compromise may be a more inclusive and sustainable path. By being open to learning from and adapting to the local culture, organisations can create harmonious and productive relationships with employees, customers, and partners. This approach fosters a deeper understanding of the local market and enables organisations to tailor their strategies and practices to meet specific needs and expectations. Navigating these choices requires a delicate balance between preserving core values and flexibility in adopting new practices.

Organisations must recognize that a blanket application of their home-grown practices may not fit the cultural nuances and preferences of other regions. Instead, they need to cultivate a culture of inclusivity, mutual respect, and continuous learning. This mindset empowers employees to contribute their diverse perspectives, enables cross-cultural collaboration, and fosters innovation and adaptability. Moreover, organisations can leverage cultural diversity as a strategic advantage by fostering creativity, agility, and resilience in the face of dynamic global challenges. In conclusion, the decision to change others or oneself encapsulates the essence of cultural intelligence and adaptability for organisations operating in diverse cultural settings. Embracing diversity and finding a middle ground that respects both the organisation's values and the cultural context it operates in can lead to more sustainable and successful outcomes in today's interconnected world.

b. As far as the modes that individuals have to reconcile their culture with that of the organisation, according to Adler, organisations can adopt one of three conceptual models when dealing with the challenge of cultural integration: the *Dominance Cultural Model (I), the Cultural Compromise Model (II) and the Cultural Synergy Model (III)* (Adler, 1989).

(I). In the *Dominance Cultural Model*, organisations tend to extend the influence of their management practices based on a belief in their absolute superiority. This ethnocentric approach closes the door to any interference from different cultures and ways of doing things. The interaction between organisations from different cultures results in the dominant culture of the parent company being imposed on the weaker subsidiary. However, this model hampers any coordination between the interests and resources of different nations, as everything is subordinated to the objectives of the parent company. The interaction between cultures leads to a cultural convergence, almost identical to that of the parent company (Adler, 1989). The strength of this cultural model lies in its simplicity of application and coherence. No extensive cultural analysis is needed, as the world is flattened to a single level governed by the same principles and techniques. However, these benefits are overshadowed by weaknesses, such as resistance from subsidiary personnel to being imposed with a foreign identity and a minimal level of cross-cultural learning. Instead of valuing cultural diversity as a learning tool, this model deliberately ignores it, depriving the organisation of the potential knowledge derived from every culture.

(II) The *Cultural Compromise Model*, on the other hand, acknowledges the indelible differences between cultures worldwide. It seeks to construct a corporate culture based solely on areas of similarity among different countries. This approach involves comparing management models, structures, and operational mechanisms in use in various nations to identify similarities and differences. Based on these evaluations, managerial practices are inspired by the attitudes and behaviours of multiple cultures without an a priori preference. The main advantage of adopting this model in managing international organisations is the lack of resistance from subsidiaries, as each is allowed to maintain its specific identity. However, the limited range of options and the complexity and cost of analysing cultural differences/similarities between countries make this model less applicable to complex companies.

(III) In the third model, the *Cultural Synergy Model*, existing similarities and divergences between cultures are evaluated and valued. The aim is to create a strong corporate culture that incorporates the best aspects of individual national cultures while transcending them. The main objective of organisations in this case is to design organisational structures and implement operational mechanisms that reflect the best aspects of all cultures they interact with without violating any norms.

The underlying theoretical assumptions of the Cultural Synergy Model stem from the belief that there are multiple ways of looking at a situation and interpreting objectives. Local situations can be perceived differently abroad, and management practices successful in the home country may prove ineffective overseas. Managers must, therefore, adopt a mindset open to cultural diversity and aware of the relativity of ideas, beliefs, and perceptions of reality.

The core of this conceptual model revolves around an accurate and precise analysis of one's own and others' culture. Adler suggests a logical approach to achieving this cultural synergy.

The first step is to describe the situation as objectively and clearly as possible, considering the perspectives of all involved cultures. Recognizing the problem's resistance may hide significant differences in interpretation. Once aware of the conflicting situation, the delicate phase of cultural analysis begins, identifying the values and norms that shape group behaviour.

Putting oneself in someone else's shoes becomes a critical tool to understand the reasons behind the problem and correctly assess the points of contact and conflict between different cultures. The next step is to devise a solution that is acceptable to all parties, compatible with their respective cultures, and, at the same time, innovative and capable of transcending them. Below there is an example in which this cultural synergy is concretely achieved (Adler, 1989: p.51):

"In a large specialized hospital in California, a Uruguayan doctor became concerned when he realized that a machine was not being used correctly in the treatment of a patient. He explained the correct procedure to the Filipino nurse and asked if she understood. She replied "yes". Two hours later, the patient's condition worsened because the treatment had been performed incorrectly. The doctor questioned the nurse again, and she once more claimed to have understood the procedure. What had gone wrong? Analysing the situation, the doctor came to understand that many Filipinos do not like to contradict people of higher rank. For the Filipino nurse, the doctor's position was clearly superior to hers. He was a man, she was a woman; he was older, she was younger. According to her cultural beliefs, she couldn't say that she didn't understand without losing face. The doctor, on the other hand, expected open communication and considered it incompetent to take responsibility for a patient's care without a full understanding of the treatment methods. After analysing the situation, a solution was suggested. After giving his initial instructions, the doctor had to ask the nurse to describe the procedure she would follow. While listening, the doctor could verify the accuracy of the nurse's understanding and identify the points that needed to be explained again. The nurse, who was never directly asked if she understood, would not be forced to respond "no" to a superior. The problem was resolved without violating the assumptions of both cultures".

At this point, all that remains is to carefully plan the implementation of the adopted solution, observe its impact from all perspectives, and potentially modify the chosen strategy. This approach, of course, is highly resource-intensive and extremely complex, but it seems to be the only one offering a wide range of management tools and techniques capable of effectively functioning in a complex international organisation.

Among the main critical areas identified by a group of experts in a research conducted by Adler (1989) concerning the relationship between international companies and their reference environment, many can find answers through the application of the Cultural Synergy model. These include the need to determine:

- the applicability of the headquarters' structures and strategies to various foreign operations (an area deemed critical by 83.3% of respondents);
- coordinating the values and ethical norms that inspire management across different cultures (75%);
- paying more attention to the socio-cultural aspects of the company (70.8%);
- determining the focus of control between the headquarter and foreign subsidiaries (66.7%).

If the organisation takes on the responsibility of addressing these problems before any foreign operation, it will undoubtedly make the mission of managers abroad much easier. A better mutual understanding is a key prerequisite in managing diverse organisations since it establishes the purpose of the group, a shared language understood by all, clarity on everything necessary and appropriate to do, and awareness of the advantages that cultural diversity brings. On this basis, it will be easier to implement operational mechanisms for managing international personnel capable of creating true "leaders without borders". For these individuals, the key to adaptation lies in acquiring and developing appropriate integration skills with different cultural worlds. One possible strategy to reduce the impact of cultural shock is to invest time and resources in the ten areas indicated by Gaffney (1989):

- deeply understanding the culture of the new country;
- learning the complexity of verbal and non-verbal communication systems;
- actively integrating with foreigners by immersing oneself in their way of life;
- being creative and experimental: taking risks to gain and attempting to learn;
- being culturally sensitive: avoiding stereotypes, ethnocentric attitudes, and acknowledging that one is not "the best";
- recognizing the complexity of foreign cultures: avoiding simplistic evaluations and generalizations;
- recognizing oneself as a product of one's own culture;
- being patient, understanding, and accepting oneself and others from different cultures;
- being more realistic in expectations;
- embracing the challenge of intercultural experiences: being ready to modify oneself and one's way of life.

The examination of culture-free and culture-bound theories offers valuable insights into the complexities of managing organisations in a globalized world. The culture-free approach, aiming for universal principles and management practices, assumes that certain organisational structures and strategies are applicable across cultures. However, this perspective overlooks the profound impact of cultural diversity on management processes, leading to potential misunderstandings, inefficiencies, and resistance.

On the other hand, the culture-bound approach emphasizes the significance of culture in shaping management practices. It recognizes that different cultures have unique values, norms, and ways of operating, which can significantly influence organisational dynamics. While this perspective fosters an appreciation for cultural nuances, it risks falling into essentialism, generalizations, and stereotyping, limiting the potential for cross-cultural collaboration and adaptability. Amid these two distinct approaches, a synthesis is necessary to navigate the challenges posed by cultural differences while embracing the opportunities they offer. The concept of "cultural synergy" emerges as a compelling approach, emphasizing the importance of understanding, respecting, and integrating cultural diversity within the organisational fabric. Cultural synergy encourages organisations to seek the best aspects of various cultures and combine them in a way that transcends individual national identities, leading to a more flexible and effective organisational structure.

Cultural synergy necessitates a profound analysis of each culture's values, norms, and communication styles to identify areas of compatibility and conflict. It demands open-mindedness, empathy, and a willingness to learn and adapt, fostering a culture of continuous learning within the organisation. Managers must adopt a more flexible and integrative mindset, promoting communication and collaboration across cultures to build trust and cohesion among diverse teams. Implementing cultural synergy is a challenging yet essential process. It requires considerable effort, resources, and a willingness to embrace cultural differences while maintaining a shared vision and purpose. By prioritizing cultural synergy, organisations can create an environment where diverse perspectives are valued, leading to increased creativity, innovation, and resilience in the face of change.

In conclusion of this review of culture-free and culture-bound theories, it is useful to propose a logic of synthesis that allows appreciating the positive aspects of both approaches. The key concept of this synthesis is "pressure on results" (Galbraith, 1975), which refers to the external and internal forces that impact the company and drive it, to a greater or lesser extent, to achieve particularly positive performances. The decision tree identifies two basic paths based on the level of pressure on results. In the case of low pressure, the company tends to adapt to cultural preferences first and only later takes into account "rational and objective" rules of organisational design. The opposite occurs when there is high pressure on results, where cultural preferences are used to fine-tune and refine organisational arrangement in its marginal aspects, assuming the fundamental profile has been identified based on "rational and objective" rules of organisational design. The awareness of the role played by culture and the related suggestions undoubtedly have validity in facilitating an individual's adaptation to an unfamiliar environment. However, their effect will be nullified if the individual in question is not the "right person". It is vital for organisations to be able to identify the most suitable person for a mission abroad, and therefore, it is critical that they have effective personnel selection and development mechanisms. This will be the topic of the next chapter.

REFERENCES

Adler, N., Campbell, N., & Laurent, A. (1989). In Search of Appropriate Methodology: From Outside The People's Republic of China Looking In. *Journal of International Business Studies*, *20*(1), 61–74. doi:10.1057/palgrave.jibs.8490351

Ajiferuke, M., & Boddewyn, J. (1970). Culture and Other Explanatory Variables in Comparative Management Studies. *Academy of Management Journal*, *13*(2), 153–163. doi:10.2307/255102

Barney, J. B., & Ouchi, W. G. (1986). Organisational Economics. *Organization Studies*, *9*(1). Advance online publication. doi:10.1177/017084068800900120

Barrington, M. (1967). *Social origins of dictatorship and democracy: lord and peasant in the making of the modern world*. Beacon Press.

Boisot, M. (1986). Markets and Hierarchies in a Cultural Perspective. *Organization Studies*, *7*(2), 135–158. doi:10.1177/017084068600700204

Boisot, M. H. (1998). *Knowledge Assets*. Oxford University Press.

Bond, M. H. (2002). Reclaiming the individual from Hofstede's ecological analysis—A 20-year odyssey: Comment on Oyserman et al. (2002). *Psychological Bulletin*, *128*(1), 73–77. doi:10.1037/0033-2909.128.1.73 PMID:11843548

Brossard, M., & Maurice, M. (1976). Is There a Universal Model of Organisation Structure. *International Studies of Management & Organization*, *6*(3), 11–45. doi:10.1080/00208825.1976.11656204

Child, C., & Tayeb, M. (1983). Theoretical Perspectives in Cross-National Organisation Research. *International Studies of Management & Organization*, *12*(4), 23–70. doi:10.1080/00208825.1982.11656351

Child, J. (1976). Organisational Structures: Extensions and Replications. Westmead.

Child, J. (1981). Culture, contingency and capitalism in the cross-national study of organisations. In L. L. Cummings & B. M. Staw (Eds.), *Research in organisational behaviour* (Vol. 3, pp. 303–356). JAI Press.

Child, J., & Kieser, A. (1979). *Organisational and Managerial Roles in British And West German Companies: An Examination of The Culture-Free Thesis. Organisations Alike and Unlike*. Routledge.

Cohen, M. D., March, J. C., & Olsen, J. P. (1976). *Ambiguity and Choice in Organisations*. Universitet Forlaget.

Crozier, M., & Friedberg, E. (1978). *Attore sociale e sistema*. Etas Libri.

Dahrendorf, R. (1968). *Essays in the theory of society*. Stanford University Press.

Dalton, G. (1960). A Note of Clarification on Economic Surplus. *American Anthropologist*, *62*(3), 483–490. doi:10.1525/aa.1960.62.3.02a00070

Decastri, M. (1984). *Organizzazione e cultura dell'innovazione in impresa*. Giuffrè.

Decastri, M. (1989). L'organizzazione per l'intemazionalizzazione. *Sviluppo & Organizzazione*, 11.

Eisenhardt, K. M., & Martin, J. A. (2000). Dynamic Capabilities: What Are They? *Strategic Management Journal*, *21*(10/11), 1105–1121. doi:10.1002/1097-0266(200010/11)21:10/11<1105::AID-SMJ133>3.0.CO;2-E

England, G. W. (1978). Managers and their value systems: A five country comparative study. *The Columbia Journal of World Business*, *13*(2), 33–44.

Farmer, R., & Richman, B. M. (1965). *Comparative Management and Economic Progress*. Irwin.

Galbraith, J. R. (1973). *Designing Complex Organisation*. Addison Wesley.

Galbraith, R. C. (1975). On the independence of attributes of memory. *Journal of Experimental Psychology. Human Learning and Memory*, *1*(1), 23–30. doi:10.1037/0278-7393.1.1.23

Gallie, D. (1978). *In Search of the New Working Class: Automation and Social Integration within the Capitalist Enterprise*. Cambridge University Press.

Gauthey, F., & Xardel, D. (1990). *Le management interculturel. Collection Que Sais-Je?* Presses universitaires de France.

Grandori, A. (1984). A prescriptive contingency view of organisational decision-making. *Administrative Science Quarterly*, *29*(2), 192–209. doi:10.2307/2393173

Haire, M., Ghiselli, E. E., & Porter, L. W. (1966). *Managerial Thinking: an International Study*. John Wiley.

Hannan, M. H., & Freeman, J. (1977). The Population Ecology of Organisations. *American Journal of Sociology*, *82*(5), 929–964. doi:10.1086/226424

Hickson, D., Hinings, C., Mcmillan, C., & Schwitter, J. (1974). The Culture-Free Context of Organisation Structure: A Tri-National Comparison. *Sociology*, *8*(1), 59–80. doi:10.1177/003803857400800104

Hickson, D. J., McMillan, C. J., Azumi, K., & Horvath, D. (1979). Grounds for comparative organisation theory: quicksand or hard core? In C. J. Lammers & D. J. Hickson (Eds.), *Organisations Alike and Unlike: International and Inter-Institutional Studies in the Sociology of Organisation* (pp. 25–41). Routledge & Kegan Paul.

Hofstede, G. (1980). Culture' S Consequences: National Differences. In *Thinking and Organizing*. Sage.

Hofstede, G. (2001). *Culture's Consequences: Comparing Values, Behaviours, Institutions, and Organisations Across Nations* (2nd ed.). Sage., doi:10.1016/S0005-7967(02)00184-5

Hofstede, G., & Hofstede, G. J. (2005). *Culture and Organisations. Software of the Mind: Intercultural Cooperation and its Importance for Survival* (2nd ed.). McGraw Hill.

House, R. J., Hanges, P. J., Javidan, M., Dorfman, P. W., & Gupta, V. (2004). *Culture, Leadership and Organisations. The GLOBE Study of 62 Societies*. Sage.

Inzerilli, G., & Laurent, A. (1983). Managerial Views of Organisation Structure in France and the USA. *International Studies of Management & Organization*, *13*(1/2), 97–118. doi:10.1080/00208825.1983.11656360

Kluckhohn, F. R., & Strodtbeck, F. L. (1961). *Variations in value orientations*. Row, Peterson.

Kroeber, A. L., & Parsons, T. (1858). The Concepts of Culture and of Social System. *American Sociological Review*, *23*, 582–583.

Lachman, M. E., Lewkowicz, C., Marcus, A., & Peng, Y. (1994). Images of midlife development among young, middle-aged, and older adults. *Journal of Adult Development*, *1*(4), 201–211. doi:10.1007/BF02277581

Laurent, A. (1978). *Ma*trix Organisations and Latin Cultures. *Working paper 78*(28). The European Institute for Advanced Studies in Management.

Laurent, A. (1983). The Cultural Diversity of Western Conceptions of Management. *International Studies of Management & Organization*, *13*(1-2), 75–96. doi:10.1080/00208825.1983.11656359

Lawrence, P. R., & Lorsch, J. W. (1967). Differentiation and Integration in Complex Organisations. *Administrative Science Quarterly, 12*(1), 1–47. doi:10.2307/2391211

Lord, R., & Maher, K. J. (1991). *Leadership and Information Processing: Linking Perceptions and Performance*. Unwin-Everyman.

March, J. G., & Olsen, J. P. (1984). The New Institutionalism: Organisational Factors in Political Life. *The American Political Science Review, 78*(3), 734–749. doi:10.2307/1961840

March, J. G., & Simon, H. A. (1966). *Teoria dell'organizzazione*. Edizioni di Comunità.

Maurice, M., Sorge, A., & Warner, M. (1980). Societal Differences in Organizing Manufacturing Units: A Comparison of France, West Germany, and Great Britain. *International Studies of Management & Organization, 10*(4), 74–100. doi:10.1080/00208825.1980.11656303

Maurice, M., Sorge, A., & Warner, M. (1980). Societal Differences in Organizing Manufacturing Units: A Comparison of France, West Germany, and Great Britain. *Organization Studies, 1*(1), 59–86. Advance online publication. doi:10.1177/017084068000100105

Miller, E. L. (1984). Comparative management conceptualization: An assessment. In R. Farmer (Ed.), *Advances in international comparative management, 1* (pp. 69–82). JAI Press.

Miller, G. A. (1987). Meta-Analysis and the Culture-Free Hypothesis. *Organization Studies, 8*(4), 309–326. Advance online publication. doi:10.1177/017084068700800402

Mintzberg, H. (1980). *The Nature of Managerial Work*. Prentice Hall.

Mintzberg, H. (1983). *Structuring in Fives: Designing Effective Organisations*. Prentice Hall.

Mintzberg, H., McCarthy, D. J., & Markides, C. (2000). View from the Top: Henry Mintzberg on Strategy and Management [and Commentary]. *The Academy of Management Executive, 14*(3), 31–42. https://www.jstor.org/stable/4165656

Negandhi, A. R. (1982). *Functioning of the mnc; a Global Comparative Study*. Pergamon Press.

Oddou, G., Osland, J. S., & Blakeney, R. N. (2009). Repatriating Knowledge: Variables Influencing the "Transfer" Process. *Journal of International Business Studies, 40*(2), 181–199. doi:10.1057/palgrave.jibs.8400402

Oyserman, D., Coon, H. M., & Kemmelmeier, M. (2002). Rethinking individualism and collectivism: Evaluation of theoretical assumptions and meta-analyses. *Psychological Bulletin, 128*(1), 3–72. doi:10.1037/0033-2909.128.1.3 PMID:11843547

Perrow, C. (1967). A Framework for the Comparative Analysis of Organisations. *American Sociological Review, 32*(2), 194–208. doi:10.2307/2091811

Perrow, C. (1970). *Organisational Analysis*. Tavistock.

Perrow, C. (1976). [Review of *Organisations and Beyond: Selected Essays of James D. Thompson*, by J. D. Thompson, W. A. Rushing, & M. N. Zald. *Administrative Science Quarterly, 21*(4), 718–721. doi:10.2307/2391729

Pfeffer, J., & Salancik, G. (1978). *The External Control of Organisations: A Resource Dependence Perspective*. Harper & Row.

Polanyi, K. (1959). Anthropology and economic theory. In Readings in anthropology II. Morton H. Fried.

Popper, K. (1972). *Objective knowledge: an evolutionary approach*. Oxford University Press.

Pugh, D. S., & Hickson, J. D. (1976). *Organisational structure in its context: The Aston programme I*. Westmead.

Roberts, K. H., & Boyacigiller, N. (1993). Cross-national organisational research. The grasp of the blind men. In T.D. Weinshall (Eds.), Societal Culture and Management (pp. 50-69). DeGruyter.

Schneider, S. (1988). National vs Corporate Culture: Implications for Human Resource Management. *Human Resource Management, 27*(2), 231–246. doi:10.1002/hrm.3930270207

Schneider, S. C. (1989). Strategy Formulation: The Impact of National Culture. *Organization Studies, 10*(2), 157–176. doi:10.1177/017084068901000202

Schollhammer, H. (1969). The Comparative Management Theory Jungle. *Academy of Management Journal, 12*(1), 81–97. doi:10.2307/254675

Sekaran, U., & Snodgrass, C. R. (1986). A Model for Examining Organisational Effectiveness Cross-Culturally. *Advances in International Comparative Management, 2*, 211–232. doi:10.2139/ssrn.2159716

Smelser, N. J. (1982). *La comparazione nelle scienze sociali*. Il Mulino.

Smircich, L. (1983). Concepts of Culture and Organisational Analysis. *Administrative Science Quarterly, 28*(3), 339–358. doi:10.2307/2392246

Sorge, A. (1983). Cultured organisation. *International Studies of Management & Organization, 12*(4), 106–138. doi:10.1080/00208825.1982.11656353

Sorge, A., & Warner, M. (1981). Culture, Management & Manufacturing Organisation: A Study of British and German Firms. *Management International Review, 21*(1), 35–48. https://www.jstor.org/stable/40227575

Tannenbaum, A. S., & Cooke, R. A. (1979). Organisational control: a review of studies employing the control graph method. In C. J. Lammers & D. J. Hickson (Eds.), *Organisations Alike and Unlike*. Routledge & Kegan Paul.

Tannenbaum, R., & Schmidt, W.H. (1958). How to choose a leadership pattern. *Harvard Business Review, 36*(2), 162–80.

Thompson, J. D. (1967). *Organisation in Action*. McGraw-Hill.

Triandis, H. C. (1995). *Individualism and Collectivism*. Westview Press.

Triandis, H. C. (2004). The Many Dimensions of Culture. *The Academy of Management Perspectives, 18*(1), 88–93. doi:10.5465/ame.2004.12689599

Trompenaars, F., & Hampden-Turner, C. (2004). *Managing people across Cultures*. Capstone Publishing Ltd.

Trompenaars, F., & Wolliams, P. (2003). *Business across Cultures*. Capstone Publishing Ltd.

Tullio-Altan, C. (1996). Un percorso di pensiero. *Belfagor*, *51*(3), 303–319. https://www.jstor.org/stable/26147782

Weick, K. E. (1969). *The Social Psychology of Organizing*. Addison-Wesley.

West, J., & Graham, J. L. (2004). A Linguistic-based Measure of Cultural Distance and Its Relationship to Managerial Values. *MIR. Management International Review*, *44*(3), 239–260. https://www.jstor.org/stable/40835991

Woodward, J. (1965). *Industrial organisation: Theory and Practice*. Oxford University Press.

Section 3
Human Resource Management

Chapter 8
Human Resource Management:
Governance Policies of International Human Resources Management

ABSTRACT

This chapter explores the multifaceted landscape of governance policies within international human resources (HR). It suggests six pivotal dimensions that shape effective governance strategies in multinational corporations. Firstly, it examines the dynamics of inter-company relationships in knowledge creation and dissemination, emphasising collaborative mechanisms. Secondly, it analyses international assignment policies, evaluating their impact on talent retention and global mobility. Thirdly, it addresses the challenges stemming from cultural backgrounds of staff, highlighting strategies to navigate diverse cultural landscapes. Fourthly, it studies the management of international assignments and the criteria for selecting adept global managers. Fifthly, it investigates local staff reactions, emphasising the phenomenon of opposite ethnocentrism and strategies to mitigate its effects. Finally, it assesses the design of HR management systems tailored for global contexts.

8. GOVERNANCE POLICIES OF INTERNATIONAL HUMAN RESOURCES MANAGEMENT

Governance policies of international human resources play a pivotal role in shaping the dynamics of the modern global workforce. In an era marked by unprecedented interconnectedness and cross-border collaborations, multinational companies face a multitude of challenges in managing their diverse talent pool across different regions and cultures. These governance policies are essential for establishing a cohesive and standardised approach to HR practices, ensuring fairness, equity, and compliance with local labour laws and regulations. One of the key aspects of international HR governance is recruitment and talent acquisition. Companies operating on a global scale must devise strategies to attract and retain the best talent from various countries, whilst also respecting the unique cultural backgrounds and individual differences of their employees. Adapting recruitment methods to suit local contexts and leveraging global talent networks are critical to building a diverse and high-performing workforce. Moreover, effective

DOI: 10.4018/979-8-3693-3482-9.ch008

governance policies in international HR encompass training and development programmes that cater to the diverse needs of employees across different regions. By providing training opportunities that address skill gaps and encourage professional growth, organisations can foster an empowered workforce capable of navigating the complexities of global markets competently. Compensation and benefits also form an integral part of international HR governance. Companies must navigate diverse labour markets with varying cost-of-living standards, local employment laws, and currency fluctuations. Developing equitable compensation structures that account for these variations is essential for attracting and retaining talent whilst promoting a sense of fairness and transparency within the organisation.

In recent years, there has been a growing emphasis on the importance of employee rights and well-being in international HR governance. Companies are increasingly recognising the significance of adhering to internationally recognised labour standards and ethical business practices. Ensuring a safe and supportive work environment, providing work-life balance initiatives, and respecting employees' rights to freedom of association are becoming fundamental pillars of responsible HR governance. Whilst some governance policies may be set at the corporate level, successful implementation often requires collaboration with local HR teams and understanding the intricacies of each region's employment landscape. Striking the right balance between global consistency and local adaptability is crucial to building a cohesive corporate culture which respects diversity whilst promoting organisational unity. Furthermore, advancements in technology and the increasing use of remote work have added new dimensions to international HR governance. Policymakers must address challenges related to virtual team management, data privacy, and cybersecurity, whilst also creating an inclusive digital work environment that enables effective communication and collaboration across borders.

Before dealing with more technical and methodological aspects of international personnel management, it is useful to consider the possible governance policies for this population, employing a cultural perspective that allows for the identification of the company's underlying attitudes upon which individual management systems are then built. It is helpful to revisit a fundamental classification already illustrated earlier, a classification elaborated by Perlmutter (1969), which also refers to the policies for assigning managers:

a. *Ethnocentric company.* Key positions in international units are assigned to parent country nationals (PCNs), which means expatriates. The fundamental motivation for this choice is the assurance of greater reliability that such an origin provides. The organisational structure is usually centralised, authority is concentrated in the headquarters, communications primarily take the form of orders and suggestions from the centre, and the standards and objectives of programming and evaluation systems are developed in the central functions. In companies that adopt this policy, both at the headquarters and at the subsidiary, the top management is the bearer of a single set of values (corporate culture and national culture of the home country) that is exported and radiated internationally.
b. *Polycentric company.* It uses host country nationals (HCNs) in foreign positions, meaning managers who come from the host country where the subsidiary is located. Based on the awareness of the difficulty of understanding the local culture, the parent company deems it more effective to have direct involvement of local individuals. This policy presupposes a more widespread power, strong autonomy of subsidiaries, two-way and limited frequency communications between the centre and the periphery, evaluation and control systems mainly developed locally and autonomously. A particular version of polycentrism is region-centrism, which means the tendency to consider not a single country but rather a larger geographic area with shared history, traditions, and lifestyles

as a homogeneous cultural domain. In such areas, regional headquarters are located, led by 'local' managers (where 'local' refers to individuals from one of the countries included in the region).

c. *Geocentric company.* Tends to employ a mix of PCNs, HCNs, and third country nationals (TCNs) in top positions of responsibility, meaning people recruited from the entire international system regardless of ethnicity and nationality. This results in a global approach to international assignment, an integrated system, close cooperation between the centre and periphery, and a high volume of communications.

Based on this classification, Robinson (1978) suggests a synopsis of the basic characteristics of each policy that can also be interpreted in terms of the evolution of international human resources management policies and organisational structure.

Typically, any entrepreneurial activity begins at the national level, and international expansion usually occurs gradually. Initially, foreign business is only marginal, especially when there is a substantial domestic market. Internationalisation often relies on monopolistic advantages that can be fully exploited by expanding business boundaries across borders (see Dunning's (1988) theory of foreign direct investment based on company-specific advantage). These advantages, such as technological know-how, are utilised through a slow and gradual process, leading the company to move concentrically away from the domestic market and invest in more demanding forms, transitioning from exporting to foreign countries to establishing production facilities. In this early 'exploratory' stage, the company (including its foreign units) is led by parent country individuals who own in-depth knowledge of the company, they know its objectives, and the correct methods to achieve them. The role of subsidiaries is operational, and strategies are formulated centrally.

Therefore, the interdependence between the centre and the periphery is sequential: products, know-how, and financial resources for investments follow a unidirectional flow from the centre to the periphery, whilst the novelty and high uncertainty of foreign operations favour the use of hierarchy rather than the market or other federative solutions (Williamson, 1975).

Over time, international activities can become significant, and subsidiaries take on more responsibilities, becoming more autonomous. Management begins to adopt a host country-oriented approach, leading to the emergence of a host country nationals (HCN) component. The company evolves into an assembly of semi-independent units, with lower personnel turnover and, to some extent, less internalisation compared to ethnocentric policies. The competitive strength is now based not only on technological ownership but also on access to distribution channels, brand reputation, and international experience.

Control from the headquarters becomes quantitative, focusing on financial and profit results rather than influencing behaviours or the quality of key decisions. There is a progressive shift away from the hierarchy (typical of ethnocentrism) towards market solutions. For instance, market-based transfer pricing and increased supplier selection freedom are introduced. The consequential transition from polycentrism to geo-centrism is often perceived by host country nationals as a return to strong control by the parent company, influenced by management philosophies of the home country.

This stage represents global competition, where a company faces the same rivals in multiple markets, and actions taken by a subsidiary in country A influence those of a subsidiary in country B. Competition is no longer limited to a single national market but is widespread throughout the international economic system. Exploiting all the advantages of the corporate system at a global level becomes an essential imperative.

The international strategy is increasingly guided by considerations of competitors' and current or potential partners' behaviour, rather than solely focusing on exploiting company-specific advantages as in ethnocentric companies or the attractiveness of individual markets as in polycentric ones

We have seen how a distinctive trait of a company's geo-centricity is the use of third-country nationals (TCNs) in management. This typically leads to an increase in personnel turnover and a return to normative and hierarchical controls for international coordination. Subsidiaries must implement strategies based on a global logic, be able to act swiftly in line with competitive conditions, and be encouraged to maintain a broad analytical perspective at all times.

The interdependence among the units of the company becomes reciprocal: products, know-how, financial and human resources move according to increasingly complex patterns, and not, as in the ethnocentric policy, from the centre to the periphery. This leads to the concept of an integrated network.

The extreme concept of geo-centrism is the disappearance of the international dimension of business, and the relevant competitive arena becomes something similar to a large and unified home market: the world as one big national market. However, the concept of geocentrism, although relevant at a conceptual level as an analytical category, sometimes appears distant from the reality of many multinational companies. The principles inherent in market globalisation clash with some negative observations:

a. despite the proclaimed increased homogenisation of demand, strong differences still exist among countries and regions of the world. Furthermore, the disappearance of protectionism is still far off, and the loyalty of employees and customers is still primarily towards their own country rather than towards the company or brand.
b. Cultural differences and management styles cast doubt on the universal validity of control systems and managerial practices.
c. The dimensions themselves can be a serious obstacle to coordinating international operations; the complexity and variability of environmental circumstances increase the breadth of management control, and the response time may prove too long to keep up with market changes.
d. Global strategies guided by the centre with a view of the world as a single market can lead to neglecting the opportunity to exploit the existing differences between various nations.

As previously seen, the departure from geocentrism has led to the development of innovative models for international companies; in particular, reference has been made to the concepts of the transnational company and heterarchy. Both differ from the standard geocentric approach in terms of both strategy and structure. The central strategy involves actively seeking and leveraging competitive advantages that originate within the globally dispersed system. In extreme form, this may even make it impossible to classify the company within a particular industry: any opportunity that arises in any geographic location where the company operates can form the basis for expanding the range of products and services offered. On a more limited scale, the concept of leveraging internationality as such can also be applicable in relatively restricted business areas. In fact, information about competition, technological trends, advances in related sectors, and the peculiarities of different national environments can lead to opportunities practically denied to companies operating at the local level, to polycentric or even global companies but 'contaminated' by ethnocentrism.

The difference becomes even more evident when considering organisational structure; in both the heterarchical and transnational company, the structure determines the strategy: before identifying the characteristics of the sector in which to compete and thus defining its own structure, the company establishes its structural arrangement and then analyses the strategic options derived from it. This results in an extremely broad and indeterminate strategic choice, which can be highly useful, for example, for companies operating in sectors where achieving global integration and local differentiation are essential (e.g., to adapt to the requirements of the host government). However, managing this dichotomy requires particular structural solutions and management practices.

1. Heterarchical and transnational companies have multiple centres; one could speak of polyarchy instead of monarchy if it were not for the lack of integration implicit in the former term. The bases of competitive advantage no longer reside in a single country but in many countries simultaneously: new ideas can emerge anywhere and subsequently be exploited on a global scale. Thus, a network of geographically dispersed competencies is formed, each node having specific abilities. These specific abilities may represent existing geographical or cultural diversities or simply reflect the spatial distribution of talents within the company. The immediate implication is that one cannot think of an organisation with a 'mind' (e.g., the headquarters in the ethnocentric model) and a 'body' that implements actions. The notions of 'headquarters', 'centre', 'home country', and 'corporate level' disappear, and strategic actions are decided, formulated, and put into practice in different nodes of a geographically dispersed network. (Source citation not provided as I don't have access to external sources).
2. Heterarchical or transnational companies involve a multiple organisational structure in which a mix of organisational dimensions (functions, products, geographic areas, customer types) operates, reflecting the need to coordinate activities according to multiple priorities without any dimension being superior to others. This creates great flexibility and adaptability to different operating realities.
3. The links between organisational units are very loose and allow for a high degree of local autonomy: joint ventures and other types of cooperation are more easily implementable, unlike what may occur in a globally controlled multinational.
4. Integration is mainly achieved through non-native-social control, and only secondarily through quantitative parameters or bureaucratic mechanisms. Therefore, organisational culture and management style become critical. Bureaucratic control would fail due to informational overload, and quantitative control, which may work well in a polycentric multinational, would not establish the necessary climate of mutual trust, willingness to sacrifice local interests for global interests, and short-term for long-term goals. This also necessitates disseminating information throughout all levels of the company: everyone must be aware of all aspects of operations, or at least there needs to be widespread awareness and sharing of fundamental objectives, corporate strategies, and critical interdependencies among the company's units.
5. Both heterarchy and transnational companies revolve around individuals with extensive company experience; each employee is part of the company's communication system, and knowledge of the history of the system of interpersonal relations can become a strategic resource. This concept can be compared to the functioning of clan mechanisms studied by Ouchi and adhocracy structures by Mintzberg (Ouchi & Wilkins, 1985; Mintzberg, 1985). This communicative network is not easily imitated by other companies, nor can a part of it be effectively used by others; an employee may be valuable to competitors as an information source, but once 'squeezed', they are of little use since the idiosyncrasy of the relationship with the company is very high. This idiosyncratic trait leads to an intense use of the internal labour market, understood in terms of more exhaustive and long-term employment contracts, or widespread involvement in company ownership. Many activities

in the heterarchical company also require extreme flexibility, especially regarding personnel: joint ventures or other forms of cooperation (based, for example, on specific projects) involve continuous entry and exit of people from the system. It would, therefore, be more accurate to speak of a dual career system, where there are limited groups of people tied to the company for most of their working lives and a substantial number of employees whose relationship with the company is more transient. This system should provide a good combination of flexibility and stability: the core provides the memory and informational infrastructure necessary to seize global opportunities and maintain an identity over time, whilst ties with 'transient' employees allow for openness to new ideas and prevent rigidity.

With these general and sometimes almost generic considerations in mind, it is currently not possible to pinpoint precise characteristics of the personnel management systems of transnational and heterarchical companies; these models are still largely being defined, and the consolidation of technicalities is still far off.

International Human Resource Management is one of the critical activities for the success of international strategies, regardless of the specific phase of the internationalisation process undertaken by the company. In particular, the issues related to the selection of international managers represent a challenging process of analysis and evaluation. Consider, in this regard, the management of assignments at various foreign locations (international assignments), the difficulties in the adaptation process of expatriates, cultural diversities, and social and ethical differences among executives at various levels – all factors that international companies must grapple with. This discussion focuses on some aspects of managing international managers by the top management in transnational companies, where a continuous process of alignment and collaboration between the headquarters and peripheral units is implemented to respond more effectively to local contexts. The following points are addressed:

- the role of interaction among individuals from different countries and cultures in the creation and dissemination of knowledge within globalised companies and international networks of businesses, with a particular focus on the transfer of human resource management methodologies.
- The management of international assignments by top management, considering the factors that influence the selection of expatriates, such as managerial expectations, culture, and motivations that lead managers to accept international assignments.
- Some aspects of the adaptation process for international executives and their relationships with local managers.
- The issue of managerial ethics in the internationalisation process of companies and in the management of human resources.

8.1 Inter-Company Relationships in the Creation and Dissemination of Knowledge

In a competitive environment characterised by increased levels of complexity (Ray et al., 2003), operating internationally represents a sometimes necessary condition for the development, or even the survival, of many companies. It has been verified that certain economic and social elements of the international context profoundly influence corporate policies. One primary element concerns the opposing trends of the globalisation phenomenon. On the one hand, there is a process of homogenisation of consumer behaviours and needs, working conditions, technologies, and offered products. On the other hand, there is a growing differentiation of markets and corporate strategies to respond more effectively to persistent economic, social, and cultural heterogeneity that characterises countries. It has been highlighted that complete homogenisation of international markets cannot be achieved; instead, there exist cross-sectional market segments at the international level derived from the aggregation of specific sub-national segments with characteristics of homogeneity. Another factor relates to the impossibility of universally implementing a 'global-local' combination (Bartlett and Ghoshal, 1989). Companies continually modify their strategies by managing a trade-off between a worldwide and a nation/region-wide perspective, based on business needs and changes in the specific external competitive environment.

This leads to the belief that the process of interaction in international contexts depends on the 'sensitivity' and interest with which companies approach different countries and regions. The mode of internationalisation is also relevant, and it does not seem solely determined by a strategic plan to expand the internal dimension of the company on an international scale, as many internationalisation processes are based on the awareness of the advantages achievable through forms of cooperation. In fact, the experience of many companies shows that relationships today do not solely develop based on hierarchical structures but also through networks, both infra-organisational among organisational members and inter-company with various types of stakeholders. The networks among managers of different international units involve individuals from various cultures, giving rise to relationships that are independent of geographical boundaries and nationalities (Manev and Stevenson, 2001). This allows for the development of organisational learning (Doz and Prahalad, 1991), resulting from synergistic 'cumulative' relationships where each company, participating in one or more international networks, can benefit from a 'pool of knowledge' accumulated by other members of the system, contributing in turn to enriching its own assets and value.

The company can no longer be considered as a separate entity that implements its strategies with a more or less global orientation. Instead, it must be analysed and understood as part of a system of international networks. In this sense, the capacity and degree of internationalisation depend on the type and intensity of relationships that a company can establish and manage at the international level (Buckley and Ghaury, 1999).

However, despite the transnational company being considered as a network, it does not imply that the transfer of know-how, skills, and management innovations happens entirely spontaneously (Nonaka and 1999), especially when it comes to transferring personnel management methodologies. Indeed, the transfer of Human Resource Management policies and practices from the headquarters to subsidiaries does not simply involve duplication; the key element of this transfer is the ability of various organisational units to internalise the acquired knowledge. One factor that can facilitate or limit the transfer of knowledge between units of a transnational organisation is 'absorptive capacity', defined as the ability of the company or individual business unit to recognise the value of information, assimilate it, and apply it for business purposes.

Bringing corporate culture to a foreign country poses a challenge for the company, as the orientations of the core strategy cannot entirely determine the policies of peripheral units, nor can managerial systems be fully defined by national contexts (Geppert, Matten and Williams, 2001). In this regard, several scholars (Bartlett and Ghoshal, 1987; Bird, Taylor and Beechler, 1998) have emphasised the problematic aspects of international human resource management in the relationship between the parent company and subsidiaries.

One aspect to highlight is the tendency to use the same human resource management policies and practices by the corporate management in subsidiaries. Empirical evidence has shown that top management tends to choose and transfer personnel management methodologies that are already known and proven effective in the home country. It should be noted that this form of 'management imprinting' will be stronger the more the employed methodologies represent a distinctive competence for the company (Barney, 1991).

In practice, however, the transfer of policies and management practices from the parent company to subsidiaries occurs through an evolving process, based on the degree of collaboration and coordination among the various units involved (Rosenzweig and Nohria, 1994). Finally, interesting are the origins and direction of innovations applied to human resource management. Some studies have indicated that the diffusion and sharing of such innovations tend to occur along unidirectional terms, from the centre to peripheral units, and rarely from affiliates to the centre or other subsidiaries. The management of 'human assets' becomes even more critical, especially in the case of subsidiaries located in countries considered key areas for international development or characterised by rapidly evolving and changing economies.

However, the sharing of knowledge and procedures in the field of personnel management between the headquarters and peripheral units does not follow the same modalities for all companies. The type of company, target market, cultural and social environment, and individual characteristics of international managers are factors that not only influence the sharing process but also the individuals' ability to promote and absorb innovative elements beneficial for improving corporate performance. The heterogeneity of situations and the diversity of contexts also influence the system of interpersonal relationships, both at the infra-organisational and inter-company levels, sometimes resulting in conflicts and divergences within the sharing process within the same organisation.

8.2 The Policies of International Assignments

The development of international relationships urges companies to pay greater attention to the selection and training of management capable of handling relationships with stakeholders operating in diverse contexts. Specifically, the choice of managers from different countries and the assignment of international roles at the strategic or subsidiary level are driven by the need to coordinate international business activities, stimulate intra- and inter-organisational learning, and respond more swiftly to changes in national contexts. The key professional trait required of international managers is the ability to analyse, develop, and manage relationships within the 'network' of actors involved in the internationalisation process, aiming to leverage the differences inherent in specific local cultures. The objective, therefore, is to foster global organisational learning, promoting innovation and the circulation of ideas irrespective of geographical boundaries, to achieve consistent improvement in company performance. International assignments represent a concrete opportunity for managers to establish interpersonal networks on an international level and enhance their managerial skills. Indeed, international assignments are considered the most impactful experience for developing the competencies of a global leader. Based on the fundamental approaches previously identified (ethnocentrism, polycentrism, geocentrism), the topic of criteria for assigning managers to international positions can be addressed. In each of the three types of international human resource management policies mentioned above, the choice between expatriates, host country nationals (HCN), or third-country nationals (TCN) must be considered, along with more technical issues such as the duration of the foreign assignment, compensation levels, and skill development for replacements (Edstrom and Galbraith, 1977). There are essentially three motivations that lead to personnel transfers abroad:

1. *Filling vacant positions.* The most direct reason for transferring a manager is to fill a vacant position due to a lack of qualified or trusted local personnel. This situation often arises during significant organisational changes (such as the start of new operations or decisions on expansion and/or production rationalisation) that require managerial capabilities not readily available on-site. Therefore, it becomes necessary to resort to personnel transfers from the headquarters. These situations are usually not planned or foreseeable and are dealt with individually as they occur.
2. *Management development.* The second important reason is the personal and professional development of managers through an international transfer. This development encompasses both technical-managerial skills and orientations and relational capabilities. Such transfers may address the need to gain an overall view of the group's activities and its key administrative, technical, and economic systems. For example, a transfer to a central office provides an opportunity to gain in-depth knowledge of procurement mechanisms, financial control, and the direction of international policies. Similarly, an international transfer can develop an individual's ability to act independently and autonomously. An assignment in a small subsidiary may require making decisions and assuming responsibilities, something not feasible within the bureaucratic structure of a central office. Moreover, training abroad fosters tolerance towards diversity and adaptability to change.
3. *Organisational structure development.* A third objective is to use transfers to develop the international potential of the organisational structure. This involves strategically deploying personnel to strengthen and expand the company's international presence. Through these transfers, the organisation can build a globally competent workforce, enhance its ability to respond to diverse market demands, and foster effective communication and collaboration across different locations.

For this to happen, it is necessary not only for the individual to be able to modify their behaviour but also for this to have an impact on the organisation, following a pattern like: *transfer - behaviour - individual organisational behaviour.*

Through international transfers, individuals acquire information about the company's policies (which they can later influence if holding an appropriate position) and develop a strong identification with the organisation. In this sense, the company can govern changes in its international policy through career paths. International assignments allow for the evaluation of international potential, the assessment of the real value and personal qualities of the expatriate, and a rigorous selection process for advancement to top positions within the company. International transfers and careers can also be used to build a solid informal network based on strong socialisation. Mobility is no longer limited to transfers between the headquarters and foreign subsidiaries but also extends to transfers between different subsidiaries (Song et al., 2003).

Influencing organisational communication patterns requires a certain volume of transfers, especially if intense communication is desired. On the other hand, having a critical mass of managers with international experiences serves as an excellent guarantee for achieving effective integration between local units and the centre, as well as between different local units, enabling the development of coherent thinking patterns within the management group.

Having defined the main reasons leading to international transfers, it is possible to link them to the three previously identified human resource management policies. An ethnocentric approach implies international transfers to fill vacant positions: there is no need for individual development processes. Managers are transferred from the headquarters to assume key positions in peripheral units to ensure complete control and implementation of the policies of the parent company and facilitate communications from the centre to the subsidiary. Managerial skills development takes place at the centre of the system, and foreign assignments are perceived exclusively as a means of control and implementation of strategies defined at the parent company level. If a polycentric orientation predominates, international transfers are necessary for managerial development in two directions:

a. from the periphery to the centre – host country managers are called upon to fill positions at the headquarters to learn managerial techniques used there and, less explicitly, to be indoctrinated according to its organisational culture norms and values;
b. from the centre to the periphery – headquarters managers are transferred to subsidiaries to facilitate the flow of communications, although the intensity of this flow is limited.

Lastly, in the case of a geocentric approach, a profound process of acculturation and socialisation becomes essential for transfers to be oriented towards both organisational and management development objectives. This is because the geocentric approach involves the formation of a diverse managerial group in terms of origin, experience, culture requiring a high level of cooperation and interaction between subsidiaries and the headquarters. Mobility must, thus, be intense in terms of volume and levels involved, involving exchanges between the headquarters and subsidiaries and among multiple subsidiaries (Song et al., 2003).

8.3 Difficulties Related to the Cultural Background of Staff

The cultural background of personnel introduces a range of challenges in today's multicultural workplaces. One of the primary difficulties is communication. Different cultural norms, language barriers, and communication styles can lead to misunderstandings and misinterpretations among team members. Additionally, varying approaches to decision-making and problem-solving can create conflicts and hinder the smooth functioning of teams. Cultural differences can also affect the perception of authority and hierarchy, affecting how employees interact with their superiors and colleagues. Furthermore, cultural norms regarding work-life balance, punctuality, and attitudes towards authority can differ significantly, leading to potential friction within the workforce. To overcome these challenges, organisations must promote cultural sensitivity and awareness, provide intercultural training, and encourage an inclusive environment where diverse perspectives are valued and integrated to foster collaboration and synergy among employees from different cultural backgrounds. The implications of each of the illustrated human resource management policies have been the subject of various empirical research. Firstly, a study by Tung (1982) on a substantial number of US, European, and Japanese multinational companies provides some important quantitative insights into the use of Parent-Country Nationals (PCNs), Host-Country Nationals (HCNs), and Third-Country Nationals (TCNs).

In European and US companies, HCNs are more commonly employed in economically advanced regions, whereas Japanese companies use a significantly higher number of PCNs and do not employ any TCNs. Notable differences emerge when comparing the American approach to the European and Japanese approaches in subsidiaries operating in developing countries. For example, in Latin America, 44% of senior positions in North American companies are filled by PCNs, compared to 79% in European companies and 83% in Japanese companies; in the Middle East, the percentages are 42%, 86%, and 67%, respectively; in Africa, they are 36%, 75%, and 50%.

The use of expatriates as a tool for organisational control in foreign subsidiaries of multinational companys is widely discussed by Egelhoff (1984), who examines it in comparison with another possible mechanism: the system of reporting on economic results. The examination is carried out using a conceptual model that distinguishes behaviour control and output control. The reporting system, through which the subsidiary provides a complete set of data to the headquarters, constitutes a means of achieving output control, whilst the assignment of parent company managers to key positions in the foreign subsidiary falls conceptually under behaviour control. Egelhoff's research (conducted on 50 companies - 24 American and 26 European) has shown that the nationality of a foreign company influences the type of organisational control it chooses. American companies prefer output control, mainly relying on the examination of information and data provided by foreign units (managed by local managers), whilst European and Japanese companies prefer to implement behavioural control through the use of personnel from the home country. For the American sample, the most important reasons for employing HCN staff are:

- familiarity with the local culture;
- language proficiency;
- their ability to maintain good public relations;
- cost reduction (as the cost of an expatriate is very high).

On the other hand, European companies identify the main reasons for using PCNs as follows:

- the desire of the parent company to develop executives with international orientation for central offices (thus, international transfer as a technique for professional and individual development);
- greater experience and technical capability;
- needs for control during the start-up phase of the foreign unit.

Kobrin (1988), in light of the significant reduction in the use of expatriates by American multinational companies and the generally positive assessments that accompany this policy in terms of internationalisation, environmental competence of host country nationals, fairness, and costs of maintaining managers abroad, observes how this process has taken worrying dimensions. He believes that the prevalence of a polycentric assignment policy in American companies, to a greater extent than in European and Japanese competitors, is actually due to the difficulties faced by American managers in adapting to a foreign context and the consequent high failure rate recorded in international assignments. The pros and cons of each of the policies (ethnocentric, polycentric, geocentric) are also documented in the empirical research conducted by Zeira et al., (1975), Zeira (1976), Edstrom and Galbraith (1977), Zeira and Harari (1979). It is necessary at this point to summarise the main conclusions of these studies.

8.3.1 The Use of Parent Country Nationals (PCNs). The human resource policy in an ethnocentric company, which aims to fill managerial positions in subsidiaries with Parent Country Nationals (PCNs), is often considered the most suitable for achieving identification and integration with the policies of the parent company. However, despite these advantages, such a policy presents a long series of problems primarily related to the resistance of local staff to the expatriates and the tense atmosphere that can arise. Below are analysed the main causes of these difficulties.

a. *Blocked promotions and careers*. One of the major grievances regarding an ethnocentric human resource policy is that it limits the promotion and advancement opportunities for local staff. Additionally, excellent performance by a Host Country National (HCN) is not equally appreciated if achieved by a PCN. In such cases, reactions are essentially of two types: the first is characteristic of young, ambitious, and competent individuals who, after gaining sufficient experience within the subsidiary, seek similar employment in the same sector (usually in a local company where career blockage is not an issue). They are often absorbed by competitors who are also interested in acquiring their know-how. The second form of negative reaction is more typical of staff with greater seniority, for whom it is more challenging to seek new employment due to age, close social ties within the subsidiary, lack of formal education, and so on. The reaction, therefore, is not to leave but rather to become detached and dissatisfied, leading to decreased productivity and limited identification with the company's objectives.

b. *Imposed managerial styles and models*. Another expression of an ethnocentric policy is the frequent tendency of PCNs to impose cultural and managerial models from the parent company and home country on subordinates at peripheral units. Even though the parent company claims to be aware of the need to adapt management models to local demands and expectations, expatriates often tend to apply traditional and already proven models. This may be because they believe it will improve their identification and integration with central policies or because they think that a personal approach that has proven successful at the parent company will guarantee success in the international assignment.

c. *Difficult adaptation*. The adaptation of PCNs to the demands, customs, and conditions of the new country is usually a relatively lengthy process, primarily due to their lack of preparation to deal with a completely different cultural context. As a result, they may make serious mistakes and make rather poor decisions during the initial period of their stay abroad. The causes mainly lie in their unpreparedness to face different cultural contexts and their reluctance to seek information and advice from subordinates from the host country, who have a deep understanding of the local culture. Such behaviour has very negative effects on the morale of the subsidiary's employees and leads to a relationship based on mutual mistrust. Additionally, this negative perception may not easily disappear. Instead, with each change in top positions at the subsidiary, resulting from the rotation policy and limited duration of international assignments, the negative cycle usually renews itself, leading to further decreased organisational effectiveness and a decline in morale among HCNs.

d. *Short-term objectives*. The rotation characteristic of international assignments leads to another problem associated with ethnocentrism: the lack of commitment to long-term commitments and projects by expatriates. They tend to focus on short-term programmes with quickly achievable and measurable results and avoid engaging in initiatives that have returns only beyond the duration of their assignment, which would necessitate questioning the existing managerial styles.

e. *Discrimination in reward systems*. Taking up a foreign assignment often means a drastic change in status for the individual, a significant promotion, and inclusion in the higher social class of the host country (as a representative of a powerful foreign institution). Moreover, fringe benefits such as insurance, housing, and education for children allow for a considerably higher standard of living than that of local peers or what PCNs can expect upon returning to the parent company. HCNs under their direct supervision believe that this elevated status reduces the sensitivity of expatriates towards the problems and needs of the subsidiary. Even the remuneration system, an integral part of the rotation policy, is often perceived as unjustified discrimination against local managers, contrary to the principle of equal pay for equal work. The recognition of such high rewards is usually justified by the need to compensate for the discomfort of relocation and foreign assignment, as well as by the conditions of the domestic labour market where expatriates are typically scarce due to a limited pool of available individuals and a shortage of international expertise.

8.3.2 The Use of Host Country Nationals (HCNs). HCNs are individuals who belong to the country where the subsidiary operates, and their employment in key positions offers several advantages. Firstly, HCNs possess in-depth knowledge of the local culture, language, and business practices, allowing them to navigate complex market dynamics with ease. Their presence helps to bridge the cultural gap between the parent company and the subsidiary, leading to smoother operations and enhanced communication. Moreover, employing HCNs in leadership positions demonstrates a commitment to the local workforce and contributes to building a positive image within the host community. By tapping into their talents and insights, multinational companies can gain a competitive edge by tailoring their strategies to suit local preferences and needs. However, it is essential for companies to strike a balance between employing HCNs and ensuring effective communication and alignment with the parent company's goals and policies to create a successful global company. The massive (or prevalent) use of Host Country Nationals (HCNs) in key positions of subsidiaries, on the one hand, allows for a better understanding of the different culture and local environment, providing adequate means to deal with them. On the other hand, it implies problems such as:

- the risk of isolation of subsidiaries and their personalised management by HCNs, especially if they occupy all executive positions, including the general management;
- dissatisfaction of HCNs heading local operating units due to the preclusion of positions at the headquarters.

8.3.3 The Use of Third Country Nationals (TCNs). TCNs are individuals who originate from a country different from both the parent company and the subsidiary's host country. Opting for a policy that employs TCNs can lead to a more cosmopolitan and globally-oriented corporate culture. These individuals bring a wealth of cross-cultural experiences, enabling them to navigate complex international markets with adaptability and creativity. TCNs can act as effective intermediaries, bridging the gap between the parent company's practices and the local context, fostering better communication and collaboration. Moreover, TCNs can serve as talent reservoirs, offering a pool of skills and competencies that might not be readily available in the host country. However, companies must carefully manage the challenges associated with TCN employment, such as providing adequate support for their integration, addressing potential concerns related to job security and career progression, and ensuring a harmonious blending of diverse perspectives within the organisation. When leveraged strategically, the use of TCNs can enhance a multinational company's capacity to thrive in the global market and drive innovation through cultural diversity.

On the other hand, aiming for a policy based on the employment of TCNs (though not very common, gradually increasing) does provide the company with a more international character (with all the advantages that may arise from this). However, it also entails dysfunctions and significant problems:

- blocked promotions due to the tendency to reserve higher positions at the headquarters for Parent Country Nationals (PCNs);

- anxiety and concern about future transfers due to uncertainty regarding the period and country of the next transfer, the position to be occupied, and the level of autonomy implied in the future assignment;
- continuous difficulty in adapting to new environments;
- insufficient authority delegated by central bodies, resulting in partial inefficiency and/or frustration among TCNs;
- lack of commitment and loyalty to the company;
- Inappropriate management styles and failure to implement long-term projects (for the same reasons analysed in the case of PCNs).

8.4 The Management of International Assignments and the Selection of International Managers

The development of an international network of relationships pushes companies to pay greater attention to the selection and training of management capable of handling relationships with stakeholders operating in diverse contexts. Particularly, the choice of managers from different countries and the assignment of international roles at the strategic or subsidiary level respond to the need to coordinate international business activities, stimulate intra-organisational and inter-company learning, and respond more quickly to changes in national contexts. The key professional characteristic required of international managers is the ability to analyse, develop, and manage relationships within the 'network' of actors involved in the internationalisation process, in order to leverage the differences in specific local cultures.

The goal is thus to develop global organisational learning, promoting innovation and the circulation of ideas regardless of geographical boundaries to achieve continuous improvement in corporate performance. International assignments represent a concrete opportunity for managers to create international networks of interpersonal relationships and, in this way, improve their managerial capabilities. In fact, international assignments are considered the most impactful experience for developing global leadership skills. However, despite the strategic significance that top management of transnational companies attaches to international assignments, it does not always result in an improvement in managerial performance upon the completion of the assignment. The issue can be attributed to the discrepancy between the transnational companies' decision to 'internationalise' their personnel across various units (by deploying managers from different countries and utilising international assignments) and the actual implementation of international human resource management policies. Two relevant reasons can be identified as the basis for this incongruence.

Firstly, the majority of HR executives still seem to be primarily focused on responding to short-term tactical needs, based on activities such as recruitment, selection, training, and performance measurement, without adequately considering the strategic implications and long-term objectives of Human Resource Management for achieving organisational goals in the long-run. In this regard, HR planning should instead be seen as a 'systematic process of integrating decisions into a coherent framework', to enable a proper evaluation of constraints and opportunities, and the appropriate selection of tools and policies in the short and medium term.

The second reason lies in the fact that companies often underestimate the role of international HR management. It has been shown that one of the main reasons for the failure of international strategies is the lack of understanding of the diversities that characterise individuals in different international contexts. Therefore, it becomes crucial for companies to engage in recruiting activities to identify and attract managers who can meet organisational needs and implement company policies effectively. The recruitment of international managers represents a key element in human resource management and depends on the conditions of the international labour market, the organisational characteristics of the company, the available economic and financial resources, the level of internationalisation achieved, and the type of products and/or services offered (Schuler and Jackson, 1996). In this part of the study, the focus is on the selection factors related to subjective characteristics of managers, such as the expectations they express (Cooke and Rousseau, 1988; Hales and Tamangani, 1996), the cultural background (Hofstede, 1980; Schwartz, 1994), and the motivations that lead them to become expatriates (Tung, 1998; Black et al., 1999).

8.5 The Reactions of Local Staff: The Opposite Ethnocentrism

Expatriate managers leading foreign subsidiaries interact with a wide range of institutions in the host country. As a result of such interaction, they must face, among other things, three problematic aspects:

a. understanding the expectations placed upon them;
b. determining the degree of compatibility of these expectations with company policies and their own behavioural models;
c. adapting their behavioural models to the demands coming from the environment.

These issues cannot be addressed without a good understanding of all the pressures arising from the external context, including the economic, socio-cultural, financial, political, and labour systems of the host country. Such analysis allows the multinational company and its HR management to select and train expatriates in a way that promotes a *culture of differences*. It is common, however, to observe situations of deep isolation and complete detachment of expatriates who, in top positions, govern the foreign subsidiary. These situations are not only due to the foreign personnel's limited propensity to adapt to multinational companies but also to the defensive and 'national pride' attitudes of the host country.

The results of an extensive study conducted on 111 local organisations in Great Britain, the Netherlands, Belgium, France, and Germany in contact with foreign subsidiaries of multinational companies show a high degree of opposite ethnocentrism, indicating a contrast between the local culture and the ethnocentric policies of the multinational company (Zeira et al., 1979; Zeira and Banai, 1981). A local institution or company is considered ethnocentric if its representatives require host country nationals (HCNs) to lead the foreign subsidiary and express the following expectations towards potential parent country nationals (PCNs):

- all PCNs should be from Western Europe.
- they should have a deep understanding of the host country's culture.
- they should adapt to local managerial models.
- they should have a perfect knowledge of the host country's language and history.
- they should have a thorough understanding of local social characteristics.

Based on these requirements, most local organisations were found to be strongly ethnocentric towards their foreign subsidiaries. The responses to the survey were unanimous (ranging from 63% to 100% in the average data). However, the importance of the subsidiary's top management having real influence in decision-making processes at the headquarters is recognised, and it is understood that this condition is achieved especially when managerial responsibility is entrusted to a parent country manager (PCN). In partial correction of this, the local managers interviewed indicate two positions that should always be assigned to host country nationals (HCNs): Marketing Director and HR Director. Additionally, regarding expatriates, they introduce an additional condition: these managers should hold medium to high-level positions in the headquarters' hierarchy. On one hand, host country organisations expect these counterparts to have sufficient autonomy so that the agreements made with them have real value. On the other hand, an expatriate in a too high position may become less sensitive to the needs and demands addressed to them by local counterparts.

Given that adopting ethnocentric positions, both on the part of international companies and host country organisations, still generates a conflicting situation, there are some tools that can attenuate its intensity (Harari and Zeira, 1979). In particular, the following are highlighted:

a. Facilitate the adaptation of PCN behaviours to the expectations that emerge in the local context through appropriate training programmes and evaluation procedures that take into account the results achieved by managers in this direction.
b. Appoint HCNs as assistants to expatriates, thus enabling the formation of a team that combines familiarity and knowledge of local customs with influence towards the headquarters. In the face of all the problems that have been presented as a consequence of adopting an ethnocentric assignment policy, it seems that the best alternative for the international organisation is to adopt a polycentric or geocentric model. Regardless of the fact that some categories of multinational companies cannot assign host country managers to key positions in foreign subsidiaries, polycentric or geocentric alternatives are not without dysfunctions or disadvantages (Harari and Zeira, 1979; Kobrin, 1988).

Indeed, whilst recognising the validity of the reasons given for replacing expatriates, it is essential to consider that it has significant negative implications for the management of international personnel.

1. Identification with local objectives rather than those of the company as a whole: Although conflicts between foreign units and the parent company are often unavoidable, managers leading foreign subsidiaries need to be able to identify with the overall objectives pursued by the multinational company (this is more likely to happen with parent country managers).
2. Understanding the company system: Replacing expatriates with local managers increases the difficulties of establishing an informal relationship system capable of overcoming organisational conflicts and cultural and linguistic differences. It is often the expatriate executives, not fully integrated into the foreign units, who create a group of international managers bound by personal ties extending worldwide (Bartlett, 1982).
3. Subsidiary control: As already noted, control over subsidiaries is particularly challenging in an international company due to geographical and cultural distances, differences in legal and political systems, and their general tendency towards increasing autonomy. One of the most effective control mechanisms is to have parent country managers in key positions in subsidiaries.
4. Acquisition of international managerial competencies: Most American executives report acquiring international competence (cross-cultural flexibility, language skills, familiarity with social, political, and cultural systems of other countries) through business travel and foreign assignments.

In conclusion, multinational companies need to be aware that none of the three policies (ethnocentric, polycentric, and geocentric) is immune to dysfunctions, and instead of seeking an approach that can eliminate every disadvantage, they should work to reduce the negative effects that each mode of personnel management presents. This brings forth the crucial issues of selection, training, mobility, and repatriation that will be addressed in the following.

8.6 The Design of Human Resources Management Systems

A fundamental aspect, often overlooked and poorly analysed in internationalisation processes, is the management of human resources and the related issues. The HR function must take into account and adapt to the socio-economic context that is constantly evolving, with changes that strongly affect the needs of organisations, the composition of the workforce, its characteristics, and needs. Organisations are facing a labour market that is experiencing and will continue to experience profound changes. When a multinational operates in different countries, the factors for gaining a competitive advantage are: strategy, organisational structure, and technological innovation. However, the most critical factor remains the management of human resources because none of the factors mentioned above can be activated without the involvement of people (Black et al., 1999). Hence, the design of HR management systems is a crucial aspect for any organisation aiming to effectively manage its workforce. It involves creating a comprehensive and well-structured framework that encompasses various HR functions, such as recruitment, training and development, performance management, compensation, and employee relations. A well designed HR management system should align with the organisation's overall strategic goals and values, ensuring that the right talent is recruited, nurtured and retained. The system should also incorporate modern HR technologies and data-driven approaches to optimise decisionmaking processes. Given these premises, it has to be argued that much work remains to be done to make Human resources management systems truly effective. International companies that have introduced selection, training, and development mechanisms tailored to the specific needs of international managers are the exception rather than the rule. Most companies seem to rely on rather rigid and simplistic management systems that do not take into account the multidimensionality of an overseas experience.

As mentioned earlier, the manager is not only required to perform well in their role but also to live in close contact with a different world where they must re-establish their roots and find new points of reference.

8.6.1 The Role and Function of International HRM. Human resource management (HRM) refers to all activities involved in managing the organisational structure of personnel, from the recruitment and selection phase to the training, development, and subsequent evaluation of internal resources. This function can perform various roles and assume different responsibilities depending on the size of the company, the characteristics of the personnel, and the sector in which the company operates. In recent years, personnel management has undergone significant transformations, primarily due to the changes in the market, which has become increasingly fast-paced and competitive. Consequently, human resource management is now considered necessary and fundamental for achieving company objectives. It is no longer seen as a cost but as a source of added value. The amount of time dedicated by the HR function to traditional activities is decreasing, whilst its role as a strategic partner, change agent, and employee advocate is becoming increasingly important.

In particular, the so called 'resource-based view' emphasises how assets, competencies, and activities have strategic value, as they can be an important source of competitive advantage if they are valuable, rare, difficult to imitate, and replace (Prandstraller and Quacquarelli, 2011). Among these competencies, the ability of a company to coordinate the activities of independent actors to create value from the combination of existing resources can be included. Globalisation has opened up new markets, which, in turn, have brought new opportunities and challenges. Technological innovations have contributed to eliminating barriers between private life and work, making people constantly connected through increasingly pervasive mobile technology. Work has become more flexible, and many people have found themselves working within global teams. In this context, international human resource management (IHRM) is widely recognised as one of the determinants of the success or failure of international business (Schuler et al., 2002).

The role of IHRM practices becomes crucial because other production factors such as capital, technology, or raw materials can be obtained and imitated, but human resources create a competitive advantage as they ensure control over other resources. HR must actively participate in such changes, helping the company achieve its goals by formulating precise strategies suitable for a constantly changing environment and actively participating in the implementation of these strategies (Briscoe and Schuler, 2004).

In particular, in an international scenario, training for international human resources helps understand the needs of the subsidiary company and relate them to the objectives of the multinational company. This enables not only the knowledge of the political, economic, and cultural environment of other countries but also increases the managers' ability to interact more effectively on a global level. IHRM, therefore, allows the creation of a fundamental network of relationships between companies, leveraging interdependencies whilst also valuing the differences among people from different countries and cultures that belong to the same corporate network and thus share common strategic objectives. Globalisation has progressively changed the tasks of the human resources function in international companies. In particular, it is essential to focus on some key points, such as the shift of multinational interests to geographically distant countries, especially in terms of culture, and the social change in the concept of career that initiates a rethinking of recruitment and personnel management policies in multinational companies. These developments necessitate the creation of an integration network among the various countries and the involved companies. Specifically, the main tasks of Human Resource Management (HRM) in a dynamic environment like the international one are:

- developing individuals who, having grown up in a specific cultural environment, can effectively interact with people from different cultures;
- implementing policies and practices that are effective in each of the environments in which people operate;
- Integrating and coordinating activities that take place in different environments with people from different cultural backgrounds.

At this point, it becomes evident how the IHRM function differs from traditional HRM, as it is responsible for a greater number of activities and requires a broader perspective. It must deal with a greater number of external influences and consider increasing complexity in decision making processes (Prandstraller and Quacquarelli, 2011). To enhance the competitive advantage of global companies, the HR function needs to focus on developing its international competencies. IHRM must shift from a purely administrative orientation to one that prioritises the internationalisation processes that involve the company.

Firstly, IHRM must learn the fundamentals of global business. It cannot adopt a global perspective if it does not thoroughly understand the principles of international strategies. Then, a solid knowledge of strategy must be complemented by a globalisation of individual skills. Finally, there should be a deep understanding and analysis of key competitors and how rival companies have planned their global strategies and used methods and tools to build a global competency network. When referring to international human resources, it is not just about expatriates but a diverse variety of individuals working within the organisation, identifiable as international managers:

- managers based in their own country with a focus on international markets;
- members of multicultural teams working on a range of international project;
- people in specialised non-managerial roles that involve international activities or knowledge transfer;
- managers who move internationally with visits to foreign locations;
- expatriates who bring the organisational culture of the parent company and hold long-term positions in which they represent the company in foreign countries;
- transnational managers who move across borders but are relatively independent from the parent company.

Managing international human resources means coordinating this diverse workforce, contributing to the achievement of company goals, seeking coherence whilst allowing flexibility, and overcoming various complex barriers such as legal, political, and cultural barriers. It involves addressing global issues that aim to engage people from different cultures in the company's strategy, building strategic competencies that differentiate the company and determine its competitive advantage. Another important aspect is promoting initiatives for talent development and building the company's brand, so that individuals can identify with the company's image and reputation, fostering ideas that people spread across the world can recognise and actively support the brand. The management of international human resources tends to be highly complex because it involves different countries and nationalities. The key to internationalisation lies in personnel management, not only in terms of expatriate management but also in coordinating and controlling between local subsidiaries and the parent company, managing knowledge, and developing global talents.

In this regard, the research conducted by Baker and Ivancevich (1971) on a sample of 326 international human resource managers and 300 expatriates from the top 500 largest US multinational companies is highly significant. According to this research, findings demonstrated that many decisions on who, how, and where to send staff abroad were based on the assumption that about 60% of foreign managerial positions were currently filled internally without considering the possibility of hiring local managers. According to many of the interviewees, management was considered a scientific activity, and as such, anyone who had exercised it proficiently in New York might do so just as effectively in Hong Kong. According to the research abovementioned, as far as criteria for selecting expatriates are concerned, four critical factors emerged:

- the manager's ability to achieve results with scarce resources;
- integrity;
- sincerity;
- sense of fairness;

- technical competence;
- ability to handle tasks with greater responsibilities.

It has to be argued, however, that it is necessary to combine the indispensable criterion of technical competence with that of relational ability (that is the aptitude to easily deal with 'distant' individuals) as well as leveraging on the peculiar traits of personality in determining the success or failure of foreign operations. Below, the argument of a manager, extracted from the research conducted by Baker and Ivancevich (1971).

"Americans, by their nature, are often disdainful when they have to coexist with a foreign culture. The degree to which this offensive (towards others) sense of superiority is present varies among individuals. The task of selectors is, therefore, to also explore the candidates' personality traits to identify and eliminate this innate malignity [...]. Our company will be able to present a better image of itself as a result" (p. 41).

The same research has also demonstrated that the inadequacy of selection procedures is accompanied by a low effectiveness of pre-departure training programmes, which are mechanisms aimed at providing information and guidance to facilitate knowledge and, consequently, adaptation to a foreign country. Out of the 124 multinational companies included in the study, approximately 65% did not have formal training programmes internally. Despite some managers recognising their importance in reducing the phenomenon of cultural shock, the lack of time between candidate selection and actual departure, as well as the preconceived belief in the manager's technical skills as a panacea to solve all adaptation issues, were considered sufficient reasons not to invest time and resources in training. This clearly disadvantaged the expatriates' adaptation process to the new way of life.

"Some executives at the parent company are convinced that there is no substitute for the experience that comes from on-the-job learning. This may be true regarding the technical aspects of my work abroad. I was adequately trained to handle this aspect of the job. One area where I lacked experience was in dealing with others. It is essential that American managers who are transferred abroad have information about the customs, traditions, and attitudes of the new people before the airplane takes off. One possible solution is an intense training program in these vital areas" (Baker and Ivancevich, 1971; p.42).

Further significant research was conducted by Tung (1984) through a comparative study of international human resource management systems used by European, Japanese, and American companies, with particular reference to the policies that follow. The extent to which vacant positions in foreign subsidiaries are filled with local personnel, the criteria and procedures used to select candidates, training programmes, failure rates, and reasons given for failures. Of particular interest is the discovery that selection criteria adopted by multinational companies vary depending on the type of task assigned and, specifically, the level of interaction required with the foreign community and the length of stay abroad.

For the American sample, candidates performing high responsibility tasks, such as leading an entire operation abroad, are required to have qualities of adaptability to the new foreign environment and communication skills, whereas requests for more operational roles are focused on technical competencies.

In Europe and Japan, on the other hand, great importance is given to adaptability and flexibility to new environments for both levels. Whilst these are the preferences 'on paper', the reality reveals that, especially in the case of American multinational companies, they have not been able to translate these theoretical principles into operational reality.

As for the role played by the candidate's family, American and European companies appear to be moving towards greater awareness of its relevance, as demonstrated by the fact that about half of the companies involve the partner in the process. The picture of the situation regarding training programmes in American companies is not encouraging: as many as 68% of them do not offer any type of pre-departure training programme. The reasons given to justify this unjustifiable lack are the temporary nature of these transfers, the questionable effectiveness of training, and the lack of time. The situation is different in Europe and Japan: 69% in Europe and 57% in Japan are the percentages of companies that have formal training programmes for foreign assignments. The last group of questions in the research aimed to determine the main causes of unsatisfactory foreign performance. In summary, the results, in order of importance, are as follows:

United States:

1. the inability of the manager's partner to adapt to the different physical and cultural environment.
2. The inability of the manager to adapt to the different physical and cultural environment.
3. Other family-related problems.
4. The personality and emotional maturity of the manager.
5. The manager's inability to handle the increased responsibilities of the foreign assignment.
6. Lack of technical competence.
7. Lack of motivation for a foreign assignment.

Western Europe:

The inability of the partner to adapt to the different physical and cultural environment.

Japan:

1. The manager's inability to handle the increased responsibilities of the foreign assignment.
2. The manager's inability to adapt to the different physical and cultural environment.
3. The personality and emotional maturity of the manager.
4. Lack of technical competence.
5. The partner's inability to adapt.
6. Lack of motivation for a foreign assignment.
7. Other family-related problems.

One last, highly significant piece of data from Tung's research remains to be reported: the failure and early return rates of foreign assignments for the examined companies. Among American companies, 7% of them report failure rates between 20% and 40%; 69% report rates between 10% and 20%; and the remaining 24% report rates below 10%.

In European companies, 59% report rates below 5%; 38% report rates between 6% and 10%; and only 3% report rates between 11% and 15%.

In Japanese companies, a remarkable 76% report failure rates below 5%; 10% report rates between 6% and 10%; and 14% report rates between 11% and 19%.

The disparity in situations is evident; the problem is understanding the winning strategies of European and Japanese companies that attribute to the lower failure rates of foreign assignments and transfers.

A common trait among companies in these two geographical areas is the less pressing temporal orientation that informs their human resource management systems.

One significant consequence can be observed in the performance evaluation approach. Whilst in the United States, the short-term orientation exerts continuous pressure on the expatriate for an immediate return on investments, generating frustrations and quickly branding the initial lack of profit as a mistake, in Japan and Europe, there is a tendency to 'turn a blind eye' during the initial assignment period, allowing them more serenity in the adaptation process. The medium-term orientation is also accompanied by longer assignment durations: an average of 5 years in Japan and Europe compared to 2-3 years in the United States. Additional advantages for Japanese and European companies come from careful planning of the repatriation of expatriates to their home country. The reluctance observed in many American managers to accept a foreign assignment is often due to the fear of not finding their place once they return. The negative consequences of a short-term foreign assignment are significant: a manager sent abroad for 18 months takes on average the first 6 months to adapt and the last 6 to plan their return home.

Another factor that may account for the success of Japanese and European companies is the level of sophistication of pre-departure training programmes. Out of the 80 American multinational companies analysed by Tung, only 32% had training programmes for future expatriates. On the other hand, more attention is paid to training programmes in Europe and Japan, as a logical consequence of their future-oriented approach to personnel planning. Many European companies resort to cross-cultural training programmes. In Japanese companies, the training programmes are even more rigorous due to the philosophy of lifetime employment that characterises their human resource management systems. Many of them send a manager abroad for a year just to allow them to experience the transfer first hand, with their only task being to observe and learn. It is also common practice to send 10-20 potential expatriates to the best international business schools every year to expand their knowledge of Western management practices. However, all outcomes regarding the inclusion of the manager's spouse and, if applicable, children in the training programmes have been unsuccessful, despite the wife's difficulty in adapting to the new environment being highlighted as the primary cause of failure in foreign assignments.

Another strength of European and Japanese companies lies in the validity and accuracy of the support systems provided by the parent company. The primary purpose of these mechanisms is to maintain a continuous direct line of communication between expatriates and the headquarters, to assess the progress of the foreign operation at any time, and, above all, to reassure the manager that distance does not mean forgetfulness. Among these support systems, particular effectiveness appears to be achieved through:

- the practice of pairing each expatriate with a colleague back home who keeps them constantly informed about 'home affairs' and ensures them a job upon their return.
- the creation of organisational units specifically dedicated to monitoring and supervising the well-being and careers of expatriates;
- the presence, within foreign subsidiaries, of managers with the responsibility of guiding the newcomer to the 'new world', advising and instructing them.

One last success factor is related to Japanese companies only: it concerns the criteria for personnel selection.

Many American and European selection managers still primarily use technical and managerial excellence as the main criterion for determining the international potential of candidates. In contrast, in Japan, the selection process looks at the overall candidate, evaluating their personality and technical skills comprehensively, and the three formal selection procedures are replaced, with equal effectiveness, by the knowledge of candidates that comes from their long tenure in the company, which is typical of large Japanese companies. In summary, the cited research suggests a series of basic elements that should be considered in the development of international human resource management policies.

a. *Develop a longer-term perspective* refers to extending the length of foreign assignments to allow managers to achieve full efficiency. It also consider evaluation of their performance with reference not only to short-term but also to medium-term objectives. This perspective pays greater attention to forecasting personnel demands from subsidiaries, so as to have sufficient time to plan the selection and training of expatriates. It takes into account the nurturing of certain individuals from their entry into the company and plan their careers in a way that makes them excellent 'potential expatriates', thus, creating a pool of 'foreign-minded' managers to draw upon in case of unforeseen needs (Gibbs, 2006; Maznevski and Chudoba, 2000).
b. *Develop centralised and formalised support systems* to closely monitor the professional and geographical journey of foreign personnel.
c. *Develop evaluation mechanisms in which economic and financial indicators* such as ROI, market share, and cash flow constantly refer to critical environmental factors such as currency devaluation and inflation, political stability, geographic portfolio, social equilibrium, learning mechanisms, and the economic structure of the host country.
d. *Consider the 'family factor'* in all phases of the transfer management process, given its decisive role in determining the success of foreign operations.
e. *Develop tailored selection and training mechanisms.*

However, all of this is not sufficient to guarantee international success; it is essential to add that any HR management system, no matter how sophisticated and carefully designed, holds little value if not embedded within a contingent approach (Tung, 1981). This is true because there are no magic formulas for success abroad. Anyone who demonstrates above-average performance standards at home can be considered a valid candidate for overseas assignments. There are no universal magic formulas for managing a specific assignment in Peru versus Japan; possessing innate relational skills, communication abilities, and cooperative spirit may be critical in Sweden (highest score in terms of 'femininity'), just as possessing charismatic and leadership qualities may be of great importance in India or the Philippines (high 'power distance').

Therefore, to design HR management systems, it is necessary to conduct a preliminary analysis of three key factors:

- the characteristics of the foreign position;
- the corporate culture (in terms of leadership style, control methods, reward and evaluation systems, etc.);
- the host country's culture (especially in terms of distance from the culture of the home country and those aspects that could hinder the manager's and their family's adaptation).

REFERENCES

Baker, J. C., & Ivancevich, J. M. (1971). The Assignment of American Executives Abroad: Systematic, Haphazard or Chaotic? *California Management Review, 13*(3), 39–44. doi:10.2307/41164292

Barney, J. (1991). Firm Resources and Sustained Competitive Advantage. *Journal of Management, 17*(1), 99–120. doi:10.1177/014920639101700108

Bartlett, C. A. (1982). How Multinational Organisations Evolve. *The Journal of Business Strategy, 3*(1), 20–32. doi:10.1108/eb038953

Bartlett, C. A., & Ghoshal, S. (1987). Managing Across Borders: New Organisational Responses. *MIT Sloan Management Review, 29*(1), 43–54.

Bartlett, C. A., & Ghoshal, S. (1989). *Management Globale. La soluzione transnazionale per la direzione d'impresa*. Etas Libri.

Bird, A., Taylor, S., & Beechler, S. (1998). A typology of international human resource management in Japanese multinational corporations: *Organisational implications. Human Resource Management, 37*(2), 159–172. doi:10.1002/(SICI)1099-050X(199822)37:2<159::AID-HRM6>3.0.CO;2-V

Black, J. S., Gregerson, H. B., Mendenhall, M. E., & Stroh, L. K. (1999). *Globalizing people through international assignments*. Addison Wesley Longman.

Buckley, P. J., & Ghauri, P. N. (2004). Globalisation, Economic Geography and the Strategy of Multinational Enterprises. *Journal of International Business Studies, 35*(2), 81–98. doi:10.1057/palgrave.jibs.8400076

Cooke, R. A., & Rousseau, D. M. (1988). Behavioral norms and expectations: A quantitative approach to the assessment of organisational culture. *Group & Organization Studies, 13*(3), 245–273. doi:10.1177/105960118801300302

Doz, Y. L., & Prahalad, C. K. (1999). Managing DMNCs: A search for a new paradigm. *Strategic Management Journal, 12*(S1), 145–164. doi:10.1002/smj.4250120911

Dunning, J. H. (1988). The Eclectic Paradigm of International Production: A Restatement and Some Possible. *Journal of International Business Studies, 19*(1), 1–31. doi:10.1057/palgrave.jibs.8490372

Edström, A., & Galbraith, J. R. (1977). Transfer of Managers as a Coordination and Control Strategy in Multinational Organisations. *Administrative Science Quarterly, 22*(2), 248–263. doi:10.2307/2391959

Egelhoff, W. (1984). Patterns of Control in U.S., UK and European Multinational Corporations. *Journal of International Business Studies, 15*(2), 73–83. doi:10.1057/palgrave.jibs.8490866

Geppert, M., Matten, D., & Williams, K. (2003). Change Management in MNCs: How Global Convergence Intertwines with National Diversities. *Human Relations, 56*(7), 807–838. doi:10.1177/00187267030567003

Gibbs, R. W. Jr. (2006). *Embodiment and cognitive science*. Cambridge University Press.

Hales, C., & Tamangani, Z. (1996). An Investigation of The Relationship Between Organisational Structure, Managerial Role Expectations and Managers' Work Activities. *Journal of Management Studies*, *33*(6), 731–756. doi:10.1111/j.1467-6486.1996.tb00170.x

Hofstede, G. (1980). Culture' S Consequences: National Differences. In *Thinking and Organizing*. Sage.

Kobrin, S. (1988). Expatriate Reduction and Strategic Control in American Multinational Corporations. *Human Resource Management*, *27*(1), 63–75. doi:10.1002/hrm.3930270104

Manev, I. M., & Stevenson, W. B. (2001). Balancing Ties: Boundary Spanning and Influence in the Organisation's Extended Network of Communication. *The Journal of Business Communication, 38*(2), 183-205. . doi:10.1177/002194360103800203

Maznevski, M. L., & Chudoba, K. M. (2000). Bridging space over time: Global virtual team dynamics and effectiveness. *Organization Science*, *11*(5), 473–492. doi:10.1287/orsc.11.5.473.15200

Mintzberg, H. (1985). The organisation as political arena. *Journal of Management Studies*, *22*(2), 133–154. doi:10.1111/j.1467-6486.1985.tb00069.x

Nonaka, I., & Takeuchi, H. (1995). *The Knowledge creating company*. Oxford University Press. doi:10.1093/oso/9780195092691.001.0001

Ouchi, W. G., & Wilkins, A. L. (1985). Organisational culture. *Annual Review of Sociology*, *11*(1), 457–483. doi:10.1146/annurev.so.11.080185.002325

Perlmutter, F. (1969). A Theoretical Model of Social Agency Development. *Social Casework*, *50*(8), 467–473. doi:10.1177/104438946905000804

Prandstraller, F., & Quacquarelli, B. (2011). *Risorse umane internazionali. Cultura, competenze, strategia*. Apogeo Education.

Ray, G., Wu, D., & Konana, P. (2009). Competitive Environment and the Relationship Between IT and Vertical Integration. *Information Systems Research*, *20*(4), 585–603. doi:10.1287/isre.1080.0202

Rosenzweig, P. M., & Nohria, N. (1994). Influences on Human Resource Management Practices in Multinational Corporations. *Journal of International Business Studies*, *25*(2), 229–251. doi:10.1057/palgrave.jibs.8490199

Schuler, R., Budhwar, P., & Florkowski, G. (2002). International Human Resource Management: Review and Critique. *International Journal of Management Reviews*, *4*(1), 41–70. Advance online publication. doi:10.1111/1468-2370.00076

Schuler, R. S., & Jackson, S. E. (1996). *Human Resource Management: Positioning for the 21st Century* (6th ed.). West Publishing Company.

Schwartz, S. H. (1994). Are there universal aspects in the structure and contents of human values? *The Journal of Social Issues*, *50*(4), 19–45. doi:10.1111/j.1540-4560.1994.tb01196.x

Song, J., Almeida, P., & Geraldine, W. (2003). Learning-by-Hiring: When Is Mobility More Likely to Facilitate Interfirm Knowledge Transfer? *Management Science*, *49*(4), 351–365. doi:10.1287/mnsc.49.4.351.14429

Tung, R. L. (1998). A contingency framework of selection and training of expatriates revisited. *Human Resource Management Review*, *8*(1), 23–37. doi:10.1016/S1053-4822(99)80038-2

Williamson, O. E. (1975). *Markets and Hierarchies: Analysis and Antitrust Implications*. Free Press.

Zeira, Y. (1976). Management Development in Ethnocentric Multinational Corporations. *California Management Review*, *18*(4), 34–42. doi:10.2307/41164666

Zeira, Y., & Banai, M. (1985). Selection of Expatriate Managers in MNCs: The Host-Environment Point of View. *International Studies of Management & Organization*, *15*(1), 33–51. doi:10.1080/00208825.1985.11656402

Zeira, Y., & Harari, E. (1979). Host-Country Organisations and Expatriate Managers in Europe. *California Management Review*, *21*(3), 40–50. doi:10.2307/41165306

Zeira, Y., Harari, E., & Nundi, D. I. (1975). Some Structural and Cultural Factors in Ethnocentric MNCs and Employees Morale. *Journal of Management Studies*, *12*(1-2), 66–82. doi:10.1111/j.1467-6486.1975.tb00887.x

Chapter 9
International Human Resource Management Systems

ABSTRACT

This chapter examines the core components of international human resource management (IHRM) systems, specifically focusing on the selection process and training initiatives. Firstly, it examines the complexities of the selection process in the context of global talent acquisition, exploring methods to identify and recruit individuals best suited for international assignments. It discusses the criteria and frameworks used to assess cross-cultural adaptability and competencies crucial for success in diverse settings. Secondly, it investigates training programs tailored for global assignments, emphasizing the development of intercultural competence, language proficiency, and job-specific skills necessary for diverse work environments. This comprehensive analysis provides a strategic roadmap for organisations aiming to optimize their IHRM systems, ensuring the selection and training processes align with global business objectives while nurturing a skilled and culturally adept workforce capable of thriving in an interconnected world.

9. INTERNATIONAL HUMAN RESOURCE MANAGEMENT SYSTEMS

Many of the problems that emerged while analysing different personnel policies are due to technical deficiencies in the selection, training, and support during international assignments, as well as in defining career paths. The systems of international human resource management are multifaceted and complex. To address the challenges of managing a diverse global workforce effectively, companies must carefully design and implement policies and practices that account for cultural differences, provide adequate support to expatriates, consider long-term perspectives, and incorporate broader environmental factors into evaluations. An effective IHRM system not only enhances the success of international assignments but also contributes to the overall competitive advantage and success of multinational corporations in the global marketplace. A useful starting point for analysing international human resource management techniques is the examination of expatriate failure rates in their foreign assignments (Dowling et al., 1996; Forster, 2000). In addition to explicit costs, there are other less visible costs: the effectiveness of foreign

DOI: 10.4018/979-8-3693-3482-9.ch009

operations can be significantly reduced; the company's reputation and image may be damaged; and the individual expatriate may feel demoralized and face negative reactions from colleagues. The causes of these high failure rates have traditionally been attributed to selection criteria that rely solely on technical competence and good domestic performance of candidates. More recent research has highlighted the criticality of another variable in international transfers, identified as the difficulty of the expatriate's family in adapting to the new physical and cultural environment and the resulting pressure experienced by them due to family stress (Hays, 1974; Harvey, 1985; Caligiuri et al., 1998; Forster, 2000).

Another reason for failure can be traced to the lack of attention dedicated to the introduction of more refined human resource management methods. This poor structuring is often justified by the temporary nature of the assignment, the long time required to conduct an effective training, or the urgency to fill a vacant position. However, this does not excuse neglecting the crucial aspects of international assignments, namely selection, training, transfer policies, and repatriation, which should be approached more scientifically.

It is evident that a comprehensive approach to international human resource management is essential for the success of expatriate assignments. Selecting candidates based not only on technical skills but also on their adaptability to new environments and cultures, providing adequate training and support for both the expatriate and their family, and implementing more sophisticated human resource management techniques will lead to a reduction in expatriate failure rates and contribute to the overall success of international operations.

9.1 The Selection Process

The approach to the selection of managers destined for positions abroad has historically been a mere listing of factors deemed crucial for the success of the assignment. However, the process of adapting to an international role as an expatriate follows a complex multidimensional path that goes far beyond a sophisticated "laundry list". This multidimensionality is a direct consequence of the considerations outlined in the previous chapter: the overseas transfer primarily requires an individual who can adapt to the sociocultural environment surrounding them and effectively embody and implement the cultural policies and principles of the representing company. An illustrative example of the traditional approach to selection is provided by Gertsen (1990), which presents a series of factors considered crucial for identifying a high-potential candidate and links the success of the foreign assignment to the presence of the following factors:

- technical skills;
- empathy in social relationships;
- managerial competencies and abilities.

He proposes a list of qualities that a successful executive should possess. It is all too easy to observe that this creates a profile of an all-powerful and flawless individual that hardly aligns with daily reality. While providing detailed lists of indispensable requirements for success represents a step forward in the selection process (moving away from purely qualitative criteria based mainly on the candidate's past domestic performance), this approach has a fundamental limitation that makes it only partially valid. It has not led to the definition of a model capable of rationalizing and systematizing the selection process. It is, indeed, important to identify the crucial variables for the success or failure of the overseas assignment, but it is equally essential to identify the existing relationships between these variables and assign different weights to each of them based on the environmental context. It is not considered useful, therefore, to identify a universal model of an ideal expatriate, suitable for every moment and place; instead, it is believed that adapting the selection and training process to the type of assignment and the country to which the transfer is directed is more crucial. In previous year, a model proposed by Hays (1974) and subsequently developed by Tung (1981) proves useful in defining a "selection benchmark" and grouping the fundamental skills that should be considered in international selection, making them operational.

The scheme starts by grouping the selection criteria most frequently proposed in the literature and business practices and identifies four main variables:

- technical competence;
- personality traits and relational skills;
- environment;
- family.

Although the importance of considering these factors together is recognized, the design and implementation of selection processes in actual businesses are almost exclusively based on the first factor, technical competence. It is surprising that a large majority of the companies included in the study do not evaluate the candidates' relational skills, despite recognizing, and research has shown, that such skills are important and crucial for overseas positions (Tung, 1981). There appear to be two possible reasons for the prevalence of technical skills in the selection criteria: their easier evaluation compared to, for example, relational abilities, and the fact that they are a necessary condition to avoid immediate failure, especially in a situation with strong pressure on results. Besides the greater ease and speed of verification, the explanation for this attitude can also be found elsewhere, as evidenced by a study conducted by Miller (1972). This study highlights how home-country managers believe that selections for international transfers entail a certain degree of risk and personal cost. For the selection manager, a decision that turns out to be mediocre or even incorrect can lead to unpleasant consequences. The poor performance of the selected candidate can damage their reputation in the eyes of their superiors and their career; it may require continuous intervention to support the expatriate; and it can entail high costs for the entire company in case of resignations. The selector, therefore, tries to limit the level of personal risk by favouring extremely qualified individuals and basing the decision on parameters that are as certain and objective as possible. The greater the pressure on the selector, the higher the likelihood of using such parameters. While this strategy may be optimal for the individual decision-maker as it reduces the risk of error, it is suboptimal in terms of effective utilization of human resources and the managerial development of the candidates. On one hand, selecting highly qualified personnel for a certain position may carry the risk that the position is overestimated and thus prevents the appointee from achieving any developmental and professional growth objectives (objectives that may have motivated the transfer in the first place). On the other hand, a focus on executives whose performance is well-known and reliable may excessively limit the pool of potential candidates available within the company.

One last finding from the study concerns the observation that, in practice, little importance is attributed to selection criteria such as the ability to understand a foreign culture and adapt to a new context.

"There is a considerable discrepancy between what has been written about the necessary qualities to operate abroad and what is considered crucial by corporate decision-makers for candidate selection.

Apparently, these managers have not read the literature, do not agree with the importance of cultural empathy aspects, or select candidates based on other criteria. One wonders if there is indeed a good deal of mythology surrounding the area of international selection" (Miller, 1972; p. 52).

This is not to deny the importance of technical skills, provided that they refer to the necessary capabilities to perform the position. It is, in fact, essential to emphasize that they are one of the most critical elements in gaining acceptance and respect from the local management and in dealing with the cultural shock of the transfer more smoothly (Naeem et al., 2015). The essential point is not to make the "profession" the sole factor of choice. A second methodological observation regarding the selection process concerns the variation of criteria based on different categories of overseas assignments. The proposed typology of positions is as follows (Hays, 1974):

a. *Development of structures*. The assignment is to create a structure in the foreign subsidiary similar to those already existing in other parts of the company.
b. *Trouble-shooter*. The task involves analysing and solving specific operational problems.
c. *Operational role*. The task consists of providing a specific performance within an existing operational structure.
d. *Chief executive officer*. The assignment involves supervising and directing the entire foreign operation.

Certain types of tasks require individuals to operate within an existing structure, while others involve creating a new structure: excellent performance in the established setting of the parent company does not guarantee good capabilities for developing new initiatives. Some positions require much more significant interaction with the local culture initially compared to others: the introduction of a new marketing mix or the coordination action of the general manager greatly depends on the individual's ability to effectively interact with the local environment, whereas in a purely technical-specialist or trouble-shooter position, such ability is of less importance. Certain tasks entail an exceptionally high capacity to tolerate ambiguity, while others require operating in close alignment with rules and procedures issued by the headquarters.

In summary, it is not possible to think of a single criterion or a rigid list of factors on which to base the selection process.

Different selection criteria have been used to define the best candidates for the four identified types of assignments. According to this approach, each assignment must be evaluated individually: identifying the ideal candidate can only occur after careful consideration of:

- the task - in terms of duration and intensity of interaction with the local community;
- the environment - for local peculiarities and differences compared to the home environment;
- the individual's personality - with reference to their and their family's ability to adapt to a new social and cultural context.

A first selection model based on this perspective according to which the process starts with the attempt to resort to local personnel in case of negative outcomes.

The first step is aimed at evaluating the degree of interaction with the local community necessary for achieving success. Limited interaction leads to a definitive choice focused on the position and the personal characteristics required for it. The opposite situation identifies the differences between the political, legal, social, economic, and cultural systems of the home and host countries. Strong similarities imply a selection based on criteria related to the position, while significant differences require high attention to relational skills, the ability to tolerate diverse, distant, uncertain situations, and family circumstances.

In this approach, the family is considered only at the final stage.

A second selection model, however, places the evaluation of adaptability to the foreign cultural context at the centre of attention (Kierner, 2015). This evaluation aims to verify the candidate's and their family's ability to cope with life abroad. Typically, the indicators considered include: (1) effectiveness in handling domestic transfers and (2) reactions manifested during a meeting (organized by the company) where the couple examines the consequences of the transfer, expresses any possible disagreements, and analyses hidden anxieties and concerns.

An appropriately trained psychologist or personnel manager conducts the interview with both spouses, attempting to establish a two-way communication through a series of open-ended questions. The discussion aims to make the couple aware of the problems and anxieties that arise when dealing with a different culture, to uncover their real motivations for going abroad, and to provide an opportunity for the wife (or the candidate) to reject the assignment before being transferred. During the discussion, attention is given to evaluating the existence and potential severity of family problems related to the stability of the couple rather than the needs of the children or elderly parents. The intensity of the bond between the family and the local community is assessed and to what extent it is part of their identity. These considerations may seem trivial, but it is precisely these small difficulties that can create an extremely strong cultural shock and make its overcoming more challenging. For example, a factor that may appear unscientific but requires extreme attention and can turn the foreign assignment into a personal disaster is family stability. Experience seems to demonstrate that a strong marriage can become even stronger during an international transfer, while if it is already wavering, it can end more easily and traumatically. Psychologists suggest that pre-existing marital conflicts intensify under conditions of higher tension and uncertainty.

Once the adaptability evaluation phase is completed, a careful analysis of the "internationality potential" of the family is necessary. This examination is based on the assumption that individuals may have characteristics that make them more or less adaptable to environmental changes, and each country requires a different mix of these characteristics, which should receive more attention during the selection phase. This evaluation can be conducted by using an analysis that is made explicit and quantifiable. Each factor is weighted and evaluated based on its relevance and criticality in the specific country to which the assignment is destined. Then, the candidate is evaluated on a scale of 1 to 5 for each factor.

The total score calculated represents the candidate's international potential. This score is compared with that of the ideal candidate defined for the specific assignment decision and with the scores of other candidates. An element that cannot be underestimated in this process is the interviewer. They must have a deep understanding of the company's policies regarding international assignments and the career paths open to expatriates, in addition to possessing excellent interviewing skills and techniques.

The systematic application of this procedure not only reduces expatriate turnover but also contributes to the continuous refinement of the selection process and techniques.

An interesting example of the key points around which to structure an interview for an international assignment was proposed by Noer (1975) and revolves around the following work sheet, expressly designed for this purpose:

a. motivation
b. health

c. language skills
d. considerations regarding the family
e. personal balance and initiative
f. adaptability
g. career planning
h. financial aspects.

Another selection technique, less widespread due to its complexity and cost, is the classic assessment centre. In short, these centres involve conducting individual and group exercises, individual interviews with managers and psychologists, and tests related to personality and intellectual abilities over the course of three to four days. Group exercises can be either competitive (for example, a group discussion without a leader) or cooperative (for example, a group management simulation). Individual exercises may involve simulations of problems that a manager should be able to solve or may include a conversation in which the candidate introduces themselves (Caligiuri, 2000). The exercises that create specific situations are obviously different from those normally used to select and evaluate domestic managers, as they replicate realities typical of the culture to which the transfer is destined.

9.2 Training

Training activities aimed at international human resources, similar to initiatives for general management, are considered extremely relevant. However, they do not receive much attention when it comes to the operational phase due to their high cost and the difficulty in quantifying and measuring their benefits. "The dominant note" for success abroad: this is how training activities have been defined by Blue and Haynes (1977). Despite this, many companies remain deaf to this call and continue to ignore that training can be vital in reducing the cultural shock that is especially encountered during the initial stages of the transfer. Adequate preparation before departure serves to attenuate the feeling of stepping into the unknown, particularly for the partner of the expatriate who is more exposed to the harmful effects of cultural distance. Research data on training in international assignments indicate that a variable percentage, ranging from thirty to fifty percent, of international companies do not provide any kind of cultural orientation or support before the transfer. Among the companies that offer training programs, around 50% do not involve the partners and children of the expatriates (Harris and Moran, 1979). In particular, little attention is given to cultural orientation programs, which are intended to help individuals learn to interact effectively with the host culture in an attempt to minimize misunderstandings.

The logical process for designing training programs is not much different from that used in selection: each international assignment has specific needs and issues that require unique training interventions (Bichi, 1996). The choice of training methods, program duration, depth, and level of sophistication is the result of various factors, including the characteristics of the host country, the characteristics of the assignment, and the individual's personality traits and managerial skills (Ronen, 1986). Regarding this last point, Mendenhall and Oddou (1985) group individual factors influencing the international adaptation process into three key dimensions:

a. a self-oriented dimension, which includes all qualities related to an individual's mental and psychological balance (such as stress tolerance and the ability to cope with isolation);

b. a second other-oriented dimension, which includes all the skills and attitudes necessary for effective interaction with individuals from different cultures (such as relational abilities, communication readiness, and attention to nonverbal language);
c. a perception-oriented dimension, which relates to an individual's ability to understand the motivations, values, and cultural assumptions underlying others' behaviour. This dimension translates into the ability to make correct attributions, effective listening, open-mindedness, and judgment flexibility.

All these dimensions influence the outcome of the adaptation process, and training should focus on the specific needs of the international assignment, addressing these dimensions accordingly. Different training interventions can be identified, encompassing six different modalities (Tung, 1981; Blue and Haynes, 1977):

1. Language training. This is the basic program as it refers to acquiring proficiency in the main means of communication and interaction with the host country and its culture. Knowing the language is essential not only to minimize interpretation errors but, above all, to understand the cultural background that shapes the current social structure of a community.
2. Field experience. Sending candidates to the future host country or similar cultures allows them to experience situations that generate similar stress to what they will encounter during their assignment, resulting from interactions with individuals with different values. Every trip abroad, even for short periods, is a significant learning opportunity that contributes to the personal and professional growth of the potential expatriate.
3. Management courses in foreign institutions. Participating in study periods abroad offers the opportunity to meet colleagues from around the world, learn about different cases and methodologies belonging to various cultures. Being in a minority position in a study environment should encourage a quicker understanding and higher tolerance of foreign economic and management cultures. This immersion in international studies is one of the best preparations for an international manager and is valuable whether they are assigned abroad or remain at the headquarters supporting international management.
4. Cultural briefing. This provides information about cultural institutions, value systems, socio-economic systems, history, education, religion, and geography of the host country (Blue and Haynes, 1977).
5. Sensitivity training. These initiatives are designed to develop attitudes of openness towards unfamiliar behaviour patterns and value systems. They consist of approximately five-day courses in which films, group discussions, and interventions from journalists, business people, and expatriates from the host country are employed.
6. Culture assimilator. This method, particularly suitable for short-term assignments requiring rapid support, uses critical episodes of cross-cultural encounters that frequently occur in the host country and have a high probability of occurring during the assignment. These intercultural experiences involve experts and managers with international experience or even the expatriate and their family, aiming for direct understanding (although in a "protected" laboratory setting) of the mechanisms and issues related to cross-cultural interactions.

The recommendation accompanying all six training modalities is to involve the expatriate's partner in at least the most complex activities so that they are also engaged in the internationalization process and develop a good understanding of their partner's work. The effectiveness of these various training methods has been subject to various investigations, among which the study conducted by Earley (1987) stands out. This empirical study examined the documentary method and the interpersonal method. The documentary method uses written material concerning general aspects of the cultural area where the assignment will take place and contains more detailed information about daily social interactions (critical incidents). The interpersonal method employs exercises and simulations designed to develop self-assessment skills, understanding of other cultures, and openness to behaviours and values different from one's own. The research results demonstrate the importance of both types of training interventions. Although no significant difference in effectiveness was found between interpersonal training and documentary training, participants clearly preferred the interpersonal training methodology.

Tung proposes differentiating training interventions, just as selection criteria are differentiated, based on the characteristics of the task and the environmental context of the assignment:

- if the position requires a high level of interaction with the local community and significant cultural differences, candidates should undergo all six types of training programs with a particular emphasis on methods 2 and 5.
- if contact with the local community is minimal, and cultural differences are limited, cultural briefings should be sufficient. There is a continuum of situations between these two extremes, which requires different levels of interaction with the local culture and involves varying levels of cultural distance (Tung, 1981).

Mendenhall and Oddou (1986) established a correlation between the training methodology and the duration of the training and two characteristics of the international assignment: the degree of interaction of the manager with the foreign community and the duration of the assignment.

The training theme also occupies significant space in the studies conducted by Zeira and Harari (1979) on the organisational aspects of international expansion processes. Their analysis suggests considering some particularly relevant personal behavioural models when designing appropriate training interventions.

The guiding idea of the study conducted in this context supports that the content of each training intervention must be designed based on a thorough analysis of the attitudes directed towards expatriates by the host country organisation and the subsidiary staff. Emphasis is placed on five expectations that are generally overlooked in the design of training programs, as follows:

a. *Change.* It is not realistic to expect the host country nationals to change their attitudes towards expatriates. Instead, it is the expatriates' responsibility to adapt their behaviour to meet the expectations of the local environment.
b. *Suspicion.* Local people often resent the lack of trust displayed by expatriates towards them. Therefore, it is essential to sensitize expatriate managers to this issue and train them to avoid such behaviours.
c. *Overruling.* This refers to situations where expatriates, following an unfavourable decision by a representative of the host country with whom they interact, resort to higher authorities. Expatriates should be adequately informed about the negative consequences of frequent overruling.
d. *Confidentiality.* This concerns the decision of whether or not to involve local personnel in organisational and personnel management issues that arise between the local unit and the headquarters. There is no universal position on this matter: some consider this practice negative as it tarnishes

the image of both the manager and the company, while others view the confidential transmission of information from subsidiary management as beneficial. This situation is particularly complex for expatriates and should be addressed comprehensively in their training, including consideration and simulation of possible solutions.

e. *Subordinate.* The judgment of host country political and economic organisations regarding the subsidiary is strongly influenced by how its managers behave towards local employees. Therefore, the training program should help managers recognize and analyse the requests of local staff.

Once the basic principle that training must be designed with the expectations of the host country in mind is established, the fact that these expectations may change over time makes it necessary for the international company to continuously monitor and update the training program. Furthermore, training interventions can be differentiated into:

a. Pre-departure training (in the parent country).
b. Post-departure training (in the host country).

a. Pre-departure training can be conducted either at the company's headquarters or at external training institutes. In the former case, the training will address topics such as the relationship between the parent company and subsidiaries, the structure and problems of local units, and interactions between them and their environment. In the latter case, topics covered will include the host country's history, cultural and social aspects, economic aspects, legal system, and industrial relations.

b. Post-departure training essentially consists of an acculturation program carried out using the following methods:

- participation in training programs for expatriates available in the host country;
- developing work contacts with local counterparts;
- shadowing the manager being replaced;
- familiarization with the organisational environment of the local unit (Harari and Zeira, 1978).

Regarding the organisation and management of training interventions, Harvey (1983) proposes the establishment of cooperatives (Trans-cultural Training Cooperative) to which various multinational companies can join. The main objective of these cooperatives is to provide their members with highly specialized, high-quality training services at affordable costs. In addition to more traditional programs (such as sessions providing information about historical, cultural, social, and economic aspects of the host country and those focusing on language learning and developing openness to unfamiliar behaviour patterns and cultures), the TTC should be involved in evaluating potential expatriates based on their problem-solving style and cultural compatibility with the international contexts they are destined for.

Another area that deserves attention in training interventions is the study conducted by Pazy and Zeira (1983). Based on research conducted in various American industrial sectors, they identified a growing trend of a particular training intervention aimed at professionals and conducted at a company in the host country. This initiative involves two organisations operating in culturally diverse contexts and employing professionals in the same field. The most common scenario involves a group of professionals temporarily leaving their company, which may be less advanced in a specific technological field, to join a foreign company for training purposes. During this period, they work full-time at the host country company, which evaluates and compensates them according to its standards. The professionals are not mere observers but fully integrated into the workforce of the host company (even if temporarily). This training method closely resembles action learning and is characterized by being both on-the-job and off-the-job. It is on-the-job because participants become an integral part of the host company's workforce. It is off-the-job because they are away from the organisational unit they are accustomed to and live in a "protected" environment.

This method offers several exclusive advantages for both the parent company and the host company, but it also presents some dysfunctions. It is clear that this particular type of training takes place within the context of a genuine international joint venture, where representatives from both parties agree in advance on the most relevant aspects of the agreement, such as program duration, compensation, tasks the trainer will perform, conditions of stay, criteria for selection and evaluation.

REFERENCES

Bichi, R. (1996). Globalizzazione E Management: I Dirigenti Espatriati. *Studi di Sociologia*, *34*(2), 157–172. https://www.jstor.org/stable/23004378

Blue, J. L., & Haynes, U. Jr. (1977). Preparation for the overseas assignment. *Business Horizons*, *20*(3), 61–67. doi:10.1016/0007-6813(77)90072-6

Caligiuri, P. M. (1997). Assessing expatriate success: Beyond just "being there". In Z. Aycan (Ed.), *New approaches to employee management, Expatriate management: Theory and Research* (Vol. 4, pp. 117–140). JAI.

Caligiuri, P. M. (2000). The Big Five personality characteristics as predictors of expatriates' desire to terminate the assignment and supervisor-rated performance. *Personnel Psychology*, *53*(1), 67–88. doi:10.1111/j.1744-6570.2000.tb00194.x

Caligiuri, P. M., Hyland, M. M., Joshi, A., & Bross, A. S. (1998). Testing a theoretical model for examining the relationship between family adjustment and expatriates' work adjustment. *The Journal of Applied Psychology*, *83*(4), 598–614. doi:10.1037/0021-9010.83.4.598 PMID:9729928

Dowling, P. J., Schuler, R. S., & Welch, D. E. (1996). *International dimensions of human resource management*. Wadsworth Publishing Company.

Forster, N. (2000). *Managing Staff on International Assignments: A Strategic Guide*. Pearson Educational/ Financial Times Publications.

Gertsen, M. C. (1990). Intercultural competence and expatriates. *International Journal of Human Resource Management*, *1*(3), 341–362. doi:10.1080/09585199000000054

Harris, M., & Moran, R. (1979). *Managing Culture Differences*. Gulf.

Harvey, M. C. (1982). The Other Side of Foreign Assignments: Dealing with the Repatriation Dilemma. *The Columbia Journal of World Business*, *17*(1), 53–59.

Harvey, M. G. (1983). The multinational corporation's expatriate problem: An application of Murphy's law. *Business Horizon*, 71-78.

Harvey, M. G. (1985). The executive family: An overlooked variable in international assignments. *The Columbia Journal of World Business, 20*, 84–92.

Harvey, M. G. (1989). Repatriation of Corporate Executives: An Empirical Study. *Journal of International Business Studies, 20*(1), 131–144. doi:10.1057/palgrave.jibs.8490355

Hays, R. (1974). Expatriate Selection: Insuring Success and Avoiding Failure. *Journal of International Business Studies, 5*(1), 25–37. doi:10.1057/palgrave.jibs.8490810

Hays, R. D. (1972). Minimizing behavioural porblmes problems. *Business Horizons, 15*(3), 87–93. doi:10.1016/S0007-6813(72)80011-9

Kierner, A. (2015). Dual-income and dual-career couples in international context. In L. Mäkelä & V. Suutari (Eds.), Work and family interface in the international career context (pp. 95–116). Springer International Publishing/Springer Nature. doi:10.1007/978-3-319-17647-5_6

Mendenhall, M., Dunbar, E., & Oddou, G. (1987). Expatriate Selection, Training and Career-Pathing: A Review and Critique. *Human Resource Management, 26*(3), 331–345. doi:10.1002/hrm.3930260303

Mendenhall, M., & Oddou, G. (1985). The Dimensions of Expatriate Acculturation: A Review. *Academy of Management Review, 10*(1), 39–47. doi:10.5465/amr.1985.4277340

Mendenhall, M., & Oddou, G. (1986). Acculturation Profiles of Expatriate Managers: Implications for Cross-Cultural Training Programs. *Columbia Journal off World Business, 21*(4), 73-79.

Miller, E. L. (1972). The Selection Decision for an International Assignment: A Study of the Decision Maker's Behaviour. *Journal of International Business Studies, 3*(2), 49–65. doi:10.1057/palgrave.jibs.8490746

Miller, E. L. (1973). The International Selection Decision: A Study of Some Dimensions of Managerial Behavior in the Selection Decision Process. *Academy of Management Journal, 16*(2), 239–252. doi:10.2307/255325

Miller, G. A. (1987). Meta-Analysis and the Culture-Free Hypothesis. *Organization Studies, 8*(4), 309–326. Advance online publication. doi:10.1177/017084068700800402

Naeem, A., Nadeem, A. B., & Khan, I. (2015). Culture Shock and Its effects on Expatriates. *Global Advanced Research Journal of Management and Business Studies, 4*, 2315–5086.

Noer, D. M. (1975). *MNC People Management; A Guide far Organisation and Employees*. Bureau of National Affairs.

Pazy, A., & Zeira, Y. (1983). Training Parent-Country Professions in Host-Country Organisations. *Academy of Management Review, 8*(2), 262. Advance online publication. doi:10.2307/257754

Ronen, S. (1986). Equity perception in multiple comparisons: A field study. *Human Relations, 39*(4), 333–346. doi:10.1177/001872678603900403

Tung, R. (1984). Human Resource Planning in Japanese Multinationals: A Model for U.S. Firms? *Journal of International Business Studies, 15*(2), 139–149. doi:10.1057/palgrave.jibs.8490487

Tung, R. (1987). Expatriate assignments: Enhancing success and minimizing failure. *The Academy of Management Executive*, *1*, 117–126.

Tung, R. L. (1981). Selection and Training of Personnel for Overseas Assignments. *The Columbia Journal of World Business*, *16*(1), 68–78.

Tung, R. L. (1982). Selection and Training Procedures of US, European and Japanese MNCs. *California Management Review*, *25*(1), 57–71. doi:10.2307/41164993

Tung, R. L. (1984). Strategic Management of Human Resources in the Multinational Enterprises. *Human Resource Management*, *23*(2), 129–143. doi:10.1002/hrm.3930230204

Tung, R. L. (1988). *The New Expatriate*. Ballinger Publishing Company.

Chapter 10
The Process of Adaptation of Expatriates to the Local Context

ABSTRACT

This chapter addresses the multifaceted process of expatriate adaptation to new environments, addressing pivotal aspects shaping their assignments. Firstly, it analyses the pivotal role of family dynamics in an expatriate's relocation, highlighting the challenges and discomfort often faced during this transition. Secondly, it explores the complexities of repatriation, illuminating the intricacies of returning to familiar yet transformed environments. Additionally, the chapter focuses on the competencies and inclinations of expatriate managers, shedding light on essential traits and skills crucial for successful adaptation. It further investigates the issue of anxiety management in an unfamiliar setting, emphasizing strategies to mitigate apprehensions and uncertainties. Ethical considerations in cross-cultural engagements and the imperative need for personalised work relationships are addressed to promote ethical and sustainable practices within diverse contexts.

10. THE PROCESS OF ADAPTATION OF EXPATRIATES TO THE LOCAL CONTEXT

Cultural aspects significantly influence the adaptation process of expatriate managers, who must face the challenges brought about by changes in the operational and relational environment (Black, Mendenhall and Oddou, 1991). Some studies have shown that the integration of expatriate managers in foreign countries is influenced by the context and opportunities existing outside the work environment as well (Black and Porter, 1989). One factor that facilitates the adaptation process to the new environment is undoubtedly the quality of social relationships that the expatriate manager can establish with colleagues and also with individuals outside the organisation (Black, Mendenhall and Oddou, 1991). In this regard, Albrecht and Adelman (1984) argue that social ties can help individuals cope with change, and such relationships are even more critical in an international environment, as they provide information about the unfamiliar context (Black and Gregersen, 1991). Two critical aspects can be identified in interpersonal relationships.

DOI: 10.4018/979-8-3693-3482-9.ch010

- Executives tend to establish and maintain strong "expressive" bonds (i.e., relationships established outside the workplace) with colleagues from similar cultures, while strong "instrumental" ties (related to the work environment) seem to characterize relationships between managers from different cultural backgrounds (Manev and Stevenson, 2001). Furthermore, even in conflict situations, belonging to the same nationality allows expatriates to interact with fellow country managers directly, regardless of hierarchical positions. This creates systems of informal relationships that are more flexible but also less identifiable and controllable.
- Another critical in interpersonal relationships concerns the communication and interaction styles of managers with their colleagues and subordinates. In particular, one-way and top-down approaches tend to create miscommunication, increasing the gap and distance between individuals from already diverse contexts (Adler, 1997). This condition occurs more frequently in the case of executives from subsidiaries located in industrialized countries, who operate in units located in developing countries where individuals have different behavioural and social characteristics. These diversities also influence the subjects' initiative capacity and propensity to assume positions within decision-making processes. Moreover, cultural differences can also affect the perception of "power distance" - the hierarchical distance perceived by individuals between managerial and subordinate roles - influencing relationships among colleagues, superiors, and subordinates.

Regarding "power distance," an interesting study conducted by Harrison, McKinno, Wu, Chow (2000) highlights the importance of cultural aspects in influencing the degree of adaptation of individuals within workgroups and temporary teams. The empirical investigation showed that managers from Taiwan, characterized by a "collectivist" culture and high "power distance," face more adaptation challenges within temporary teams, especially in cases of personnel, role, or function changes within the group. The reason lies in the fact that managers from Eastern countries perceive the end of teamwork as the disruption of a system of authority and leadership, and transitioning to another group means disobeying ethical and moral principles, leading to a sense of insecurity and crisis. In contrast, managers from Australia, who strongly reflect the Anglo-Saxon culture (with highly individualistic social traits and limited "power distance"), establish relationships with individuals operating at different hierarchical levels. These managers demonstrate greater adaptability and flexibility, perceiving change as a natural aspect of temporary teams.

As mentioned, relationships among individuals within the same organisation can also be conflictual, leading to situations of uncertainty and discomfort that slow down the adaptation process of expatriate managers to the new work and environmental context (Alabi and Sarkiunaite, 2022).

Ultimately, the "expatriate community" represents a relevant phenomenon characterized by specific issues. The company's ability to select, manage, and motivate its international staff allows, under certain conditions, influencing the adaptation and improvement process of managerial qualities, thus generating an organisationa environment that respects professional and personal specificities.

10.1 The Family and the Discomfort of Relocation

One aspect that has always been neglected (perhaps because it was considered trivial) is related to the difficulties that the expatriate and their family encounter in international relocation. Only recently has it been given due consideration in the analysis of successes and failures in foreign assignments. It is indeed possible to identify a vicious circle that hypothesizes a direct relationship between professional performance and family tranquility, with the expatriate bearing the pressure resulting from the negative impact that the transfer can have on the family, hindering them from working with serenity and concentration. Therefore, at least two aspects are of considerable importance:

1. the effects of an international transfer on the expatriate and their family;
2. the company's possibilities to minimize the risk of strong pressures on the expatriate and subsequent negative performance or early returns.

The first theme arises from considerations about the cultural shock that the relocated family faces. This can be referred to as the trauma stemming from the discovery of their inadequacy in the new context and the need to learn to deal with attitudes and expectations very different from those they are accustomed to:

"Cultural shock is created by the anxiety resulting from the loss of all the signs and symbols used in social relationships that we are familiar with. These signs or cues include the thousand and one ways in which we navigate everyday life situations: how to give orders, how to make purchases, when and if to respond. Now, these symbols such as words, gestures, facial expressions, traditions, or norms are acquired by all of us during our growth; they are part of our culture, just like the language we speak or the beliefs we accept. We all rely on hundreds of these signs for our serenity and mental efficiency, many of which we are not consciously aware of [...] It is a work malady experienced by people who are suddenly transferred abroad" (Harris and Moran, 1979; p. 22).

Some disconcerting aspects of mobility are found among the pages of studies on the physical and psychological distress it originates. Among the physical issues, there is a higher percentage of heart diseases, respiratory disorders, and cases of insomnia. Among the psychological issues, there is a slow progression towards more or less severe forms of depression. Initially, a sense of discomfort emerges due to the difficulty of reproducing one's reference models, ethnic, family, and interpersonal ties in the new country. Later, a conflict between old and new values arises, leading to the difficult experience of identity crisis, the collapse of the coordinates of self-security. Hence, the uncertainty, distrust, doubt about one's abilities, and fear of vulnerability; hence the extreme cases of self-fracturing and manifest psychological distress. It is mainly the partner of the expatriate (wife or husband) who suffers from this trauma due to the lack of specific commitments or formal roles.

In the process of adaptation, the "victim" may experience irritation, confusion, disorientation, hostility towards the foreign community where they reside, or even paranoia. The effects of culture shock are amplified when viewed from the perspective of the family. Children have to start new schools (with programs often radically different from their usual ones), leave behind old friendships and have to build new ones, experience anxiety about their parents' new social relationships, and clearly perceive any difficulties in the couple's relationship. On the other hand, they may not understand the reasons for the transfer: incentives such as the father's career advancement or the improvement of the family's economic conditions have an abstract and difficult-to-accept meaning. The problems that have the most negative impact on the expatriate's performance and productivity are related to the partner's situation: in most cases, this plays a crucial role in determining whether the mission will turn out to be a nightmare or a pleasant and productive experience. Research seems to indicate that the wife, in particular, bears the highest price for the family's transfer, experiences the most stress, and deserves much of the recognition when the transfer is successfully accomplished.

With no prior orientation or language preparation before departure, it is her who faces the foreign culture in the most immediate and daily problems (shopping, the children's school, the bank, eating habits as well as high probability of finding herself in a culture where there are many limitations on women).

Numerous theoretical studies and, unfortunately, few empirical researches have clashed on the delicate ground of the effects of work mobility on the emotional and professional lives of expatriates' wives: however, the results and reflections conducted in these studies do not lead to a clear direction.

Empirical evidence, based on the data reported in Jeanne Brett's study (1982), does not fully support these theoretical hypotheses, showing that there are no strong correlations between an individual's physical and psychological well-being and the degree of mobility they undergo (referring here to the narrower context of managerial mobility). This is so, except from a decreased sense of security experienced by the wife and a general dissatisfaction in the realm of extra-work social relationships. However, it seems undeniable that the wife is subjected to a considerable degree of emotional tension for multiple reasons: the complex demands imposed by a transfer often require her to sacrifice a significant part of her own interests to fully dedicate herself to the role of supporting family stability and balance. The fact that it is common practice for international companies not to include the expatriate's family in their training programs, along with the lack of attention given to notice periods and information regarding the transfer, further fuels the wife's frustration and creates the bitter feeling of being treated as a mere "package".

While the husband and children may rely on interpersonal networks in their respective work and school environments, the wife is left to cope with a radical change in her social life. Seidenberg (1973) also emphasizes that, unlike the husband who is sent abroad based on (hopefully!) proven skills and competencies, the wife who desires to work in the assigned country must first find employment and then demonstrate her abilities. She must rebuild an entire social fabric in search of a new acceptable identity.

The successful outcome of this challenging experience can be partly attributed to factors related to the wife's personality and age and partly to situational factors. Among the former are a natural attraction to novelty and challenging experiences, a high degree of tolerance for loneliness and uncertainty, and generally being of a younger age. Among the latter are a motivational scale that prioritizes her career less, a strong pre-existing marital bond, societal support to ensure the education of children, home acquisition, and involvement in certain organized activities such as clubs and meeting places.

The crisis of many marriages following a transfer is not so much due to tensions generated by this experience but, rather, to the unfortunate combination of three contingent circumstances. The unexpected request for transfer arriving when the manager was already approaching the twilight of their career, a certain degree of pre-existing discord between spouses, and finally, the forced relinquishment of a job to which they were particularly attached (Pinder, 1989).

Beyond these cases, wives often seem to embrace this "adventure in a foreign land" with enthusiasm. Taking their needs and contingent situations into account when planning transfers can represent a valid step forward for companies to prevent problems and failures in international adaptation processes.

Similar problems arise for the children of expatriate families. The desire to maintain continuity in the educational process sometimes leads spouses to remain geographically separated until a delicate schooling phase is completed, and the aim to preserve the quality of education may influence the choice of location.

Age appears to have the highest correlation with the serenity and well-being of children forced to relocate. Some studies indicate two age groups particularly susceptible to the stress and strains of moving: those between 3 and 5 years old and the adolescence period. In the first case, this age group is when children learn to socialize with their first friends, and terms like "career advancement" or "improvement of the family's economic well-being" have a meaning too abstract for them to understand (some younger children have shown emotional disturbances and an unnatural attachment to anything that could provide stability, primarily the mother). In the second case, it is the period when peer groups play a significant role in fostering a sense of security for adolescents and it becomes particularly challenging to recreate these bonds in a new environment (adolescents tend to form closed circles and may hinder the integration of newcomers). Empirical evidence supports these considerations, as Brett's study reveals that the children of mobile managers are less socially integrated, less involved in extracurricular activities, and less adept at forming new friendships. Social relationships hold particular relevance in the life of the transferred family. Membership in exclusive clubs, a high standard of living, and privileges stemming from position do not compensate for the void left by the absence of friends and relatives.

Every life experience, every change in existence, is always lived in relation to others: the problem is that "others" in the case of overseas transfer are strangers. Phenomenological studies attach great importance, in terms of psychological balance, to the feeling of being-in-the-world-with-others. The transfer brings individuals into a world different from what they are familiar with, a world where being with others is not easy because these others are not easily recognizable as "kin", given the many linguistic, cultural, and social differences. The manager and, indirectly, the entire family depart with the idea of being-for-work and rarely manage to be-with-others. Hence the integration issues and difficulties in rebuilding the complex web of informal relationships that each individual needs; hence, also, one of the sources of profound dissatisfaction. This is one of the few aspects where theoretical studies, empirical research, and testimonies all unanimously agree: the tensions arising from the dissolution of their social contacts and the difficulty of reestablishing them seem to be one of the main causes of failure in international transfers.

Considering that the parents' happiness and, consequently, their "productivity," are linked to the serenity of their children, it becomes clear how important all efforts are to make their relocation as least traumatic as possible. This can be possible by providing them with all the nevessary information and support, describing the difficulties and tensions they will face, involving them gradually in social and cultural activities in the new country, and equipping them with useful tools to face the new situation without excessive anxiety (Hsu, 2012; Nery-Kjerfve and McLean, 2012). All of this cannot be solved merely by placing the family in a luxurious neighborhood and enrolling the children in the best available schools. The communication and discussion of these problems put the expatriate in a very difficult position due to the choice they must make between dedicating all available time to the struggling family rather than to work. This can lead to a significant decrease in productivity or, alternatively, an increasingly likely early return to their home country. Interestingly, negative reactions to the new situation typically emerge in the very early stages of the transfer. Harris and Moran (1979) have developed a model that illustrates the various phases experienced by a family transferred abroad, resulting in a "family experience curve" that synthesizes the adaptation (or non-adaptation) cycle and its consequences.

When individuals enter a new culture, they are sometimes treated with kid gloves. They are welcomed at the airport, a company limousine takes them to the hotel and work, and invitations to lunch and dinner are frequent. The attention given to customs delays, delays in the shipment of personal belongings, and other possible inconveniences is remarkable. They are put on a pedestal. This enthusiasm can last from a few hours to a few weeks or even months. However, eventually, the harsh reality of living in a new country comes to the surface. The honeymoon phase is over. They enter the second phase called "the party is over" (Harris and Moran, 1979).

At this stage, the family starts complaining more frequently about life in the new country. There is also a desire to meet other fellow nationals. It is a critical phase, and the family should be cautious about the type of compatriots they befriend or connect with. Americans who are having negative experiences in a specific country seem to show missionary zeal towards newcomers from home, involving them in gossip about the boredom and difficulties of life in that country and the joys belonging to their home country.

This kind of unhealthy conversation can distort the foreign experience. Families should try to bond with people who are having a positive experience.

The third phase is the turning point. Will the family be able to stop complaining and continue the experience of living and working abroad? Alternatively, will they continue to create problems and protest? A good sign is when humor returns. Can they laugh at themselves and the kind of experience they are having, or is everything deadly serious? Once a family begins to get to know local people and their traditions and habits, things no longer seem so strange and bothersome. The final phase is "healthy recovery". For example, an American family may accept the new lifestyle as just another style. Local people are not strange or wrong. They have their way of life, just as Americans have theirs (Harris and Moran, 1979). Once again, many of the problems related to the expatriate and their family discussed above could be substantially reduced through the use of more effective selection criteria. In addition to the phases identified by Harris and Moran, it is essential to consider the launch period of the transfer. Often, a few weeks elapse between the request for transfer and its operational start. Such a short notice does not allow for timely resolution of practical problems related to relocation, such as the potential sale of the house or all the bureaucratic formalities required to transfer children to other schools. These and other possible contingent concerns (such as the desire for children to complete a delicate school phase before being "uprooted") force the family into a temporary separation. In addition to the manager's exhausting trips and already demanding work responsibilities, there is a constant concern about the effects of their absence on the family. In these first weeks, several issues may undermine the tranquility of the family unit. From the excessive burden placed on the wife (being both a mother and father at the same time), fewer opportunities for leisure and social gatherings (half a couple is not a socially accepted unit), and the insecurities of younger children who do not easily understand the idea of having a father only on weekends.

These discomforts may dissipate after a few months when the plan to reunite the family is realised, and the benefits of the overseas assignment (limousine, invitations, etc.) start to be appreciated. Certainly, a perfect family composed of flexible individuals with broad intellectual horizons, cultural empathy, always courteous, patient, and cautious, with impeccable academic and professional credentials, all in robust health and full of creativity cannot exist (Heller, 1980, 1988). More realistically, considering the different categories of international assignments and the contribution of various factors to the success of the transfer, a truly comprehensive selection paradigm must encompass this complex of variables and allow for their systematic analysis. The training system must be able to address psychological and professional conditions that reduce the ambiguity and anxiety that naturally surround the transfer.

10.2 The Return

Abroad, the expatriate is normally in a position characterized by a rather high level of autonomy. Foreign positions are generally very challenging, and the manager can behave almost like an entrepreneur. Instead of being a leader, the repatriate becomes just another member of the organisation and must be very careful about every action they take. They have experienced the feeling of being like Patton and roaming freely through the desert, and now they find themselves as a staff member of Eisenhower, where every move must be carefully evaluated step by step. Two or three years have passed, the international assignment has been successfully completed, and there is a strong belief in having acquired managerial skills, the ability to make decisions in ambiguous situations, and aptitudes for management and communication. The expatriate returns and expects to re-establish the old bond with the past, which is kept in the internalized images of their memory, and to "overlay" it with the baggage of knowledge and experiences gathered abroad. However, time has changed things. Then one discovers that the search for lost time is in vain and that the geographical place is quite different from the place of the soul: the former is transformed by the passage of time, while the latter is petrified in memory. There is a gap between the two, which is not only temporal but also lived space. The readjustment upon returning is so much like the readjustment due to the impact with the country to which one had been transferred, to the extent that it is called reverse culture shock (Ronen, 1986). The intensity of this unexpected reverse culture shock naturally varies, depending on multiple factors.The individual's personal characteristics, the features of the assignment country and in which aspects it may be considered "better" than the home country, the ease with which the family has managed to reestablish their roots abroad, the expatriate's success at work, the duration of the transfer, etc. For simplicity, it is necessary to consider the case of a "lucky" expatriate who has been sent abroad for 2-3 years, to an economically advanced country with all the necessary services, where the adjustment has been facilitated by the valid support mechanisms provided by the company. Despite this "luck," it is typical that no one has prepared a program to plan the repatriation of the expatriate, and, indeed, the need for it is often not even recognized. Hence, a series of problems arises that affect both the manager and their family.

The family's problems range from disappointment arising from the comparison between the blurred memories of their territory and the actual reality they find, to the difficulty of reestablishing relationships with old friends. From concern about disrupting the children's continuity in education (foreign schools are often of high quality, and maintaining the same standard in the home country is not always possible) to the difficulty for the wife to find a new job (Harvey, 1990). Additionally, there are significant financial pressures that the entire family faces: while abroad, the compensation was generously inflated with substantial allowances and various benefits, allowing for a particularly high standard of living; upon returning, however, the available income undergoes a sudden compression. If we consider the difficulties of the wife finding employment and the probable need to purchase a house and a car, the financial pressures can deeply affect the family's well-being (Ronen, 1986; Harvey, 1990). The re-entry shock can indeed produce consequences that organisations pay a high price for: beyond the psychological discomfort of the manager and the resulting reduction in performance levels, we must add that their negative experience will serve as a strong deterrent for colleagues to accept international assignments.

So far, we have discussed problems related to the family and the cultural and psychological re-adaptation. Frustration levels increase significantly when the manager realizes that their colleagues at work have been promoted and, consequently, received substantial salary increases during their time abroad, or worse still, that there is no intention to manage their reintegration into the company.

Issues such as housing, readjusting to the national culture and environment, and the reduced family budget due to the loss of incentives (both material and financial) enjoyed abroad may be of short duration and resolved relatively easily. However, the disorientation towards company procedures and readjustment to the central organisation mostly stems from the ambiguity that often surrounds the executive after repatriation. This reintegration often does not allow the manager to fully capitalize on the skills acquired during their foreign experience: their expectations may be frustrated, decision-making powers limited, and autonomy reduced compared to the past. Further loss of motivation can come from realizing they are now "out of the game" in the race for top positions: upon their return, the expatriate often discovers that their colleagues who remained at the headquarters have become their superiors; during the international assignment, the expatriate is not considered for promotions within the parent company. This raises the question of whether an international assignment can genuinely lead to top positions (Harvey, 1982).

Reintegration is particularly critical when the international assignment was conceived within a professional and managerial development project. Finding the right position at the right time to fully leverage the expertise acquired can be challenging (Edstrom and Galbraith, 1977). It should be noted that very frequently, the experience gained at the international level becomes a considerable attraction for other companies that are eager to offer highly lucrative remuneration to secure the services of the repatriated manager; the resulting resignations can be attributed to both motivational and economic reasons (Shepherd and Patzelt, 2018). The complexity of the repatriation problem naturally varies from company to company and from individual to individual. Factors such as the number of years spent abroad, the purpose and position of the assignment, the employee's age, family situation, etc., can make a difference. However, the problems commonly complained about by expatriates upon their return revolve around some themes (Harvey, 1982):

- *International assignments as a one-way street.* Too often, the transfer aims to hastily fill a suddenly vacant position. Once trained and sent abroad with the family, the company considers the problem solved, and the employee becomes part of the "out of sight, out of mind" category; they are not taken into consideration until the terms of the assignment expire. In other words, there is no planning for the repatriation and the placement of the foreign assignment in the individual's career path.
- *The isolation of exile.* Many times, the expatriate feels personally and professionally isolated due to the lack of communication between the headquarters and the peripheral unit (often unaware of the company's general policies). This not only causes problems while operating abroad but also makes readjustment to company practices very difficult, especially if significant changes have occurred in the meantime.
- *Lack of defined career paths.* Assuming an international assignment without knowing where it will lead causes great anxiety both before and during the foreign stay (and leads to the belief that the transfer is a dead-end road).
- *Returning to the central organisation without a specific placement.* If there is no planning regarding the repatriation of personnel from abroad, the company must place the individual in the structure without a suitable position, leading to feelings of frustration and disappointment.
- *Loss of autonomy.* Finally, there is the issue related to the reduction of discretionary spaces: in the foreign assignment, the position held tends to be a professional challenge, with the expatriate acting almost like an entrepreneur; upon their return, they often become just another member of the organisation and must now cautiously measure their decisions.

There are two main reasons why an international company should be concerned about resolving the repatriation problem. Firstly, if an individual leaves the company due to lack of recognition for their work or motivation, the company loses a valuable person in whom they have invested time and money, and whose experiences and skills, developed also through the international assignment, could be effectively utilized. Secondly, if future expatriates become aware of the difficulties faced by their colleagues who preceded them and the lack of support from the company, there is a high likelihood of strong resistance to new transfer proposals. To adequately prepare managers for reintegration into the parent company, the issue of repatriation must be addressed from its roots, taking it into account from the early stages of the transfer. It is useful to identify four reference moments:

1. relocation planning,
2. pre- relocation,
3. during the relocation,
4. repatriation.

This approach allows for identifying the main objectives of each phase and enabling the individual's optimal reintegration into the organisation.

Relocation planning implies:

- the *assignment of international assignments* considering career paths and professional development;
- *developing procedures for evaluating the different contexts* characterizing each assignment: geographic isolation, level of economic development, length of time the company has been present in the country, cultural diversity, political-economic stability, legal restrictions. This way, the company can have an idea of the challenges the expatriate will face and, above all, assess the intensity of the need for readjustment at the end of the assignment;
- *defining the duration of the assignment.* The longer the expatriate stays in the host country, the greater the likelihood of problems upon repatriation; therefore, an early assessment is needed to estimate the impact of the time variable on the reintegration process into the headquarters.

2. Pre-relocation requires:

- Describing and communicating the organisationa and personal objectives to be achieved during the international assignment, so that the candidate fully understands the purpose of their transfer. The expatriate's primary concern in this phase is usually their career path, and much of this concern can be alleviated by informing them about how the assignment will impact their future in the organisation. One possible alternative solution is a "repatriation agreement"; before the person accepts the international assignment, the company provides a general promise regarding its duration and the type of position the expatriate may hold upon their return. This type of agreement has very positive psychological effects; however, it can create rigidity within the company: it must be clarified that the agreement does not represent a written guarantee and that the expatriate must be open to some flexibility. In this sense, it can be useful to constantly review the agreement during the assignment, thus giving both the company and the expatriate the opportunity to modify their expectations.
- Defining consensus criteria for evaluating the international assignment. The position's objectives and performance evaluation criteria must be determined in advance to provide the candidate with sufficiently certain reference points.
- A high level of information and awareness about repatriation issues. The most important aspect of the pre-departure phase is to provide as comprehensive education as possible about potential repatriation problems: professional, personal, and family difficulties should be analysed in detail, with the perspective that greater awareness leads to easier problem prevention or a more serene acceptance of them.

3. During relocation. To continue the planning and preparation work for repatriation, it is necessary to:

- Establish and maintain open communication channels with the expatriate: Transmitting data and information about domestic activities and the importance of international assignments allows the expatriate to still feel part of the company.
- Systematically and periodically analyse the assignment and performance of the expatriate. This is the ideal way to review career paths and, if necessary, renegotiate the assignment's objectives. This can be done through a Repatriation Evaluation Committee tasked with monitoring the activities of foreign managers. Concrete examples can be observed in some Japanese companies; one of the most well-known and effective examples is the Overseas Section of Nissan Motors, whose sole responsibility is to diligently monitor the situation of executives and technicians engaged in overseas assignments and provide them with organisationa and psychological support (Tung, 1984)
- Occasionally allow the expatriate to spend some time in the headquarters and directly experience the changes that occur: This provides an opportunity to stay informed about job opportunities upon repatriation and potential alignment with the expected career path.

4. Repatriation. The psychological pressure of repatriation reaches its peak when the manager and their family return to their home country. The lack of orientation, both within the organisationa system of the headquarters and in the economic and social environment, increases stress in intolerable ways, with serious repercussions on the company's performance and the life of the repatriate (Harvey, 1982). To make this period less challenging, the following measures are necessary:

- *Intensive updating of the repatriate* on organisationa and environmental changes that have occurred in the meantime; this program should provide comprehensive information about the modifications made in policies and procedures, realignments in the company's strategy, newly hired personnel, and, above all, a detailed description of the new position that the repatriate will be taking on.
- A period of *professional orientation* (lasting about a month) during which the individual serves as a mere observer of meetings, roles, and tasks within the organisation before fully assuming the new position.
- An economic and financial counseling program to facilitate reintegration, financial counseling services or even financial aid should be made available to the manager and their family, considering that the end of the overseas assignment inevitably leads to a drastic reduction in income.

10.3 Expatriate Managers: Competences and Inclinations

Expatriate managers play a critical role in today's globalized business environment, where multinational companies operate across borders and cultural boundaries. These individuals are chosen to lead and represent their organisations in foreign countries, facing the complex challenges of adapting to new cultures, business practices, and environments. The success of an expatriate manager depends not only on their technical competencies but also on their inclinations and personal qualities.

- Firstly, expatriate managers need to possess a diverse set of competencies to navigate the complexities of international assignments. *Strong cross-cultural communication skills are essential* as they interact with diverse stakeholders, including local employees, customers, suppliers, and government officials. Language proficiency is a significant advantage, allowing them to break down barriers and build rapport with local communities.
- *Adaptability* is another crucial competency, as expatriate managers must be open-minded and willing to embrace new perspectives and ways of doing things. They need to demonstrate flexibility in decision-making and problem-solving, especially in situations where standard business practices may not apply. The ability to adjust to different cultural norms and workstyles is crucial for building trust and effective collaboration with local teams.
- They must possess *strong leadership and management skills* to lead multinational teams successfully. They need to be *strategic thinkers*, capable of aligning global business objectives with local priorities, and effectively coordinate cross-border operations. Building and sustaining a cohesive team in a culturally diverse setting requires inclusive leadership, where differences are embraced and leveraged for collective success.
- *Cultural intelligence is an invaluable competency* for expatriate managers, enabling them to navigate cultural differences sensitively and avoid misunderstandings. This skill involves cultural awareness, empathy, and the capacity to adapt behaviour according to cultural contexts. Cultivating cultural intelligence ensures that expatriate managers can bridge gaps and foster mutual understanding, fostering strong intercultural relationships.

In addition to technical competencies, expatriate managers must have certain inclinations and personal qualities to thrive in international assignments. They need to exhibit:

- *resilience and emotional intelligence* to cope with the challenges and stressors associated with living and working in foreign environments. Being far away from home, family, and friends can be emotionally taxing, requiring a high level of emotional maturity and coping mechanisms.
- A *global mindset* is a distinguishing inclination among successful expatriate managers. They possess a genuine curiosity about different cultures and a willingness to embrace diversity. A global mindset enables them to see opportunities in international assignments and approach challenges with a positive and open perspective.
- They should be *self-motivated and proactive* in their professional development. The ability to take initiative and continuously learn about the host culture and market dynamics is instrumental in making well-informed decisions and capitalizing on emerging opportunities. Their eagerness to learn and adapt fosters a culture of continuous improvement within their teams and organisations.
- They should own strong interpersonal skills, as building and maintaining relationships with diverse stakeholders is critical for achieving organisationa goals. Cultural sensitivity, active listening, and effective communication are key to establishing trust and fostering collaborations with local partners, employees, and customers.

Expatriate managers, in addition to their technical competencies and personal inclinations, also face unique challenges related to the dynamics of international assignments.

a. One crucial aspect is the need for cross-cultural training and preparation before embarking on their overseas mission. Organisations must invest in comprehensive pre-departure training programs that equip expatriate managers with a deeper understanding of the host country's culture, business practices, and societal norms. This preparation helps reduce culture shock and increases the likelihood of successful adaptation.
b. Furthermore, successful expatriate managers are those who actively seek to integrate themselves into the local community. They recognize the importance of cultural immersion and engage in activities that facilitate deeper connections with locals, such as participating in community events, learning the local language, and embracing local customs and traditions. By demonstrating respect for the host culture and genuinely immersing themselves in it, expatriate managers can foster goodwill and build strong relationships with stakeholders.
c. Another aspect that sets exceptional expatriate managers apart is their ability to strike a balance between maintaining the organisation's global strategy and being sensitive to local needs. They act as cultural intermediaries, translating the organisation's vision and values into actions that resonate with the local workforce and customers. This requires a high level of cultural agility and adaptability to tailor their leadership approach while staying aligned with the overall corporate mission.
d. Moreover, expatriate managers should possess a strong awareness of the potential cultural biases and assumptions they might bring with them from their home country. They actively work to overcome these biases, fostering a more inclusive and diverse work environment that embraces the strengths of all team members, regardless of their cultural backgrounds.
e. The support and mentoring provided by the organisation to expatriate managers also play a significant role in their success. Regular check-ins with HR or senior leadership, peer support networks, and access to resources that aid in cultural integration and personal well-being all contribute to a positive expatriate experience. Organisations that prioritize their expatriate managers' well-being demonstrate a commitment to their success and foster loyalty and dedication in return.
f. Finally, expatriate managers should possess strong conflict resolution skills. Working across cultures and navigating differences can lead to potential conflicts and misunderstandings. Effective conflict resolution involves active listening, empathy, and a willingness to find mutually beneficial solutions. By addressing conflicts proactively and constructively, expatriate managers can enhance team dynamics and build a more harmonious work environment.

10.4 An Unknown World: Anxiety and Its Management

An unknown world: anxiety and its management have been subjects of great interest and research in recent years (Hsu, 2012). As individuals step into new cultures or undertake international assignments, they often encounter various challenges that trigger feelings of uncertainty and apprehension. The process of adaptation to unfamiliar environments can be overwhelming, and expatriates may experience a range of emotions, including fear, stress, and disorientation. These feelings are especially pronounced during the initial phases of expatriation when individuals are faced with cultural differences, language barriers, and the need to adjust to new work and social norms (Nery-Kjerfve and McLean, 2012).

One of the critical aspects of managing anxiety in an unfamiliar environment is *the support provided by the organisation and the expatriate's social network* (Gehrisch and Süß, 2023). Companies that invest in comprehensive pre-departure training, cultural orientation, and ongoing assistance during the international assignment tend to have better outcomes in terms of expatriate satisfaction and performanc. By providing resources and guidance, organisations can help expatriates develop coping mechanisms, foster resilience, and navigate the challenges they face in the host country. Moreover, the role of interpersonal relationships cannot be underestimated in mitigating anxiety during international assignments. Establishing a support system that includes colleagues, friends, and other expatriates can significantly contribute to a smoother adaptation process (Chen, 2019). Social networks provide opportunities for information exchange, emotional support, and a sense of belonging, which are crucial for expatriates to feel more at ease and confident in their new surroundings.

The process of managing anxiety during an international assignment is not limited to the pre-departure and initial adaptation phases; it is an ongoing endeavor throughout the entire assignment duration. Cultural training and support need to be complemented with regular check-ins and feedback sessions to address any emerging issues and offer timely guidance. Encouraging open communication channels and creating a positive work environment where expatriates feel comfortable expressing their concerns can make a significant difference in anxiety management. Furthermore, organisations can proactively help expatriates cope with anxiety by providing opportunities for cross-cultural interactions and promoting cultural curiosity (Ilie, 2019). This can be achieved through events, workshops, and training sessions that encourage knowledge exchange and mutual understanding among employees from diverse backgrounds. Beyond organisationa support, self-awareness and self-care play a vital role in managing anxiety during international assignments. Expatriates often find themselves in unfamiliar environments, far from their familiar support systems, which can lead to feelings of isolation and vulnerability. Hence, they should be encouraged to reflect on their feelings and emotions and seek appropriate resources or assistance when needed. Cultivating self-awareness allows expatriates to recognize and acknowledge their emotions, thoughts, and reactions to the challenges they encounter (O'Brien et al., 2005). A developed introspective skills, such as a sense of emotional intelligence and mindfulness may enhance an expatriate's ability to navigate stressful situations and adapt to new cultural contexts (Ilie, 2019) and enable to gain a deeper understanding of stress triggers and coping mechanisms, making it easier to navigate the complexities of living and working abroad. Practicing self-care is equally crucial in the process of anxiety management. Expatriates should be encouraged to prioritize their physical and mental well-being, especially during periods of high stress.

Engaging in activities that promote relaxation, such as exercise, meditation, or spending time in nature, can help alleviate anxiety and improve overall resilience (Mikhaylov et al., 2014). Adequate rest, nutrition, and the establishment of healthy routines contribute to maintaining a balanced state of mind, which is particularly valuable when facing the uncertainties of a foreign environment. Furthermore, emotional intelligence plays a significant role in managing anxiety during international assignments. Expatriates who develop emotional intelligence can effectively identify and manage their emotions, as well as empathize with others' feelings (Gehrisch and Süß, 2023). This skill enables them to communicate effectively, build meaningful relationships, and navigate cultural differences with greater sensitivity and understanding. Emotional intelligence also facilitates conflict resolution and helps expatriates adapt to new social norms and expectations, fostering a sense of belonging in their host country (Huang et al., 2022).

Mindfulness, another valuable aspect of anxiety management, involves being fully present in the moment without judgment. By practicing mindfulness, expatriates can reduce anxiety related to past regrets or future uncertainties and focus on the opportunities and challenges presented to them in their new environment. Mindfulness techniques, such as deep breathing exercises or meditation, can serve as valuable tools in moments of stress, allowing expatriates to regain composure and approach challenges with a calmer mindset (O'Brien et al., 2005). Moreover, addressing the challenges faced by expatriates' families is equally important in anxiety management. Organisations can offer support to spouses and children through family-oriented programs that address their specific needs and concerns (Buch, 2020). By ensuring the well-being and integration of the entire expatriate family, organisations can enhance the overall success and satisfaction of the international assignment.

In conclusion, the management of anxiety in the context of expatriation is a complex and multifaceted process that requires attention from both individuals and organisations. Understanding the factors that contribute to anxiety and implementing effective support systems can lead to more successful international assignments and better overall expatriate experiences. By acknowledging the challenges and uncertainties associated with expatriation, organisations can create strategies to assist their employees in navigating the unknown world and facilitate a smoother transition into the global landscape. With the right support and resources, expatriates can embrace the opportunities of living and working in a foreign culture, grow personally and professionally, and ultimately contribute to the success of their organisations in an increasingly interconnected world.

10.5 The Need to Address Role Ambiguity, Role Conflict, and Emotional Reactions

The adaptation process for expatriate workers is profoundly influenced by factors such as role ambiguity, role conflict, and emotional reactions, each contributing to the intricate psychological landscape of adjustment.

Role ambiguity, stemming from unclear job expectations and responsibilities, can evoke feelings of uncertainty and disorientation, hindering effective integration into the new work environment.

Role ambiguity, for instance, not only blurs professional boundaries but also triggers existential questions about one's purpose and contribution within the organization. This can lead to a sense of identity crisis and erode confidence, particularly if the expatriate feels adrift without clear objectives or benchmarks for success.

Similarly, role conflict, arising from conflicting demands or expectations from different sources, can generate internal tension and frustration, impeding the expatriate's ability to perform optimally and navigate interpersonal relationships. Moreover, role conflict not only disrupts workflow but also fractures the expatriate's sense of cohesion and belonging within the team. Juggling conflicting demands from various stakeholders may evoke feelings of being torn between loyalty to one's home organization and the pressures of adapting to local practices, exacerbating feelings of isolation and alienation.

Emotional reactions play a pivotal role, as expatriates grapple with a myriad of feelings ranging from excitement and curiosity to anxiety and homesickness. Overestimating one's abilities may lead to unrealistic expectations, exacerbating stress and potentially leading to burnout or disillusionment. Moreover, emotional reactions to new situations, such as culture shock or language barriers, can trigger feelings of inadequacy or incompetence, challenging the expatriate's sense of self-efficacy and resilience. Understanding these complex psychological and emotional dynamics is crucial for organizations and individuals alike, as it sheds light on the multifaceted challenges inherent in international mobility and underscores the importance of providing adequate support and resources for expatriates to thrive in their new environments. Emotional reactions serve as the linchpin of expatriate adjustment, coloring perceptions and shaping behavioral responses to new challenges. The initial euphoria of embarking on a foreign assignment may quickly give way to the stark reality of cultural differences and logistical hurdles. This transition can evoke a range of emotions, from exhilaration and curiosity to anxiety and homesickness. Expatriates may grapple with a profound sense of loss — be it the comfort of familiar surroundings, the support of social networks, or the ease of communication in their native language. These emotional upheavals not only impede adaptation but also underscore the deeply human aspect of the expatriate experience, transcending mere logistical challenges to encompass a profound journey of self-discovery and resilience.

Exploring deeper into the psychological and emotional aspects of expatriate adaptation unveils a spectrum of nuanced experiences and potential consequences. The latter regarding overestimation of the worker's abilities cannot be overlooked. Expatriates may enter their assignments with inflated expectations of their own adaptability or cultural competence, only to encounter unforeseen obstacles that puncture their confidence. This mismatch between expectation and reality can precipitate a crisis of confidence, leading to feelings of inadequacy or imposter syndrome. Furthermore, emotional reactions to new situations may exacerbate these feelings, as expatriates grapple with the dissonance between their idealized self-image and the challenges they face on the ground.

Studying the intricate terrain of expatriate adaptation requires a holistic approach that encompasses not only logistical support but also emotional and psychological well-being. Organizations must recognize the importance of providing comprehensive resources and support networks to facilitate expatriate adjustment, from cultural training and language immersion programs to mentorship and counseling services. By acknowledging the multifaceted nature of expatriate challenges and fostering a culture of empathy and support, organizations can empower expatriates to navigate the complexities of international mobility with resilience and success.

10.6 The Need to Address Ethical Issues

The ethical influences on social and economic activities are now much more relevant, as they stem from the increased awareness of the impact that organisations have on the surrounding environment (Vogel, 1991). In particular, the growing interest in "business ethics" and "ethics within the company" represents an appropriate response to the current needs of individuals (MacIntyre, 1989). There is a need for guiding principles capable of restoring a common sense of order and control in a confused and uncertain social context, where changes—often driven by technology, new organisationa forms, and modes of work management, occur rapidly. Metanational companys are starting to recognize the necessity, but also the opportunity, to find a common interpretation of what should be considered "ethical behaviour". The need to establish a "corporate ethical code" arises from the process of integration that characterizes competitive environments (Dobson, 2003). This integration, among other things, results from numerous interferences between organisations, connections between different markets, and communication networks that have developed due to the disappearance of traditional geographical boundaries. The process of globalization has multiplied the number of ethical dilemmas: for a transnational company, it becomes challenging to reconcile its own "ethical standards" with those prevailing in other countries, as it is impossible to define a "global business ethics". For instance, many practices considered unethical (or even illegal) in certain countries are allowed in others. The difficulty in determining a singular and universally accepted meaning of "ethics" is also induced by the fact that ethical principles not only vary from one society to another but also within the same social reality, both temporally and historically (Donaldson, 1989). However, it is possible to identify some guidelines that provide a basis for regulating specific contexts. In this regard, the term "international business ethics" (Deresky, 2000) refers to the ethical conduct of businesses in their relations with individuals and societies at a global level. Such behaviour is based on systems of cultural values, which are influenced by various elements such as history, religion, legal systems, etc. (Quintanilla et al., 2021). An interesting study has highlighted that managers from countries with socialist political tendencies are less likely to justify unethical behaviours, while managers from capitalist countries seem to tolerate, within the limits of business ethics, unethical attitudes in a general sense (Ralston et al., 1997). Certainly, the issue of "ethics" is also an important influencing factor in human resources management (Donaldson and Dunfee, 1994) and becomes particularly critical when it comes to managing human recources at an international level, given the greater cultural and ethical differences that managers face (Ralston et al., 1997; Wang & Houston, 2011). These diversities also influence the selection of expatriate managers, as the behaviours of individuals within the transnational organisation must conform to the moral and ethical standards implicit in the "corporate heritage". Business ethics is, in fact, formalized through the establishment and implementation of a "corporate code of ethics" (Weaver, 1993), which gains weight and relevance when policies and behaviours adhere to ethical rules created and shared by individuals within the organisation and by external stakeholders with whom the organisation interacts. In this way, the formulation of the company's mission and strategy can also be expressed through a system of organisationa values, communicated and bureaucratically reinforced by a corporate code of ethics (Buch, 2020). This can preserve and extend the social legitimacy of the organisation in the external environment, creating a corporate image that differentiates the company from its competitors (Rispoli, 1993). However, it should be noted that, although the sharing of ethical principles at the intra-organisationa level can represent an element of "identity" for the company, such sharing presents some crucial aspects in the interaction between managers at the inter-company international level. In this regard, it has been observed that expatriate managers have a dual identity, due to the constant need to share the values and objectives of the strategic headquarters while adapting to the specificities of the local unit (Ambos et al, 2020).

It emerges the need for top management and Human Resources directors to evaluate the moral norms and ethical behaviours of managers when they diverge from those of peripheral units. The meaning of "ethics" becomes difficult to interpret in this case, and various aspects need to be addressed:

- the ethical behaviour that executives in subsidiaries should adopt;
- the degree of adaptation to the ethical standards of the host country;
- the ways in which ethics influence company objectives;
- the managers' need to reconcile their responsibilities towards different types of stakeholders with ethical behaviours that are recognized and universally accepted.

The role of expatriate managers thus becomes much more complex; they must interact with superiors, colleagues, and subordinates while respecting the ethical standards of the parent company. At the same time, they must also assess the interference of behaviours that are not consistent with those standards, as there is no universally valid "ethical manual" (Primeaux, 1992). This leads to a reconsideration of the moral authority of management: instead of institutionalizing ethical standards derived from cultural particularities, the task of management becomes to identify elements of cultural homogeneity capable of generating consensus among individuals and forming the core of ethical principles for the entire organisation (Sinclair, 1993).

From this perspective, ethics no longer stems from an imposition of authority but becomes the result of an agreement among individuals who share values and behavioural rules. This interaction can still take place within a system of democratic and transparent relationships. Ultimately, a fundamental open issue is this: which entities define the specific ethical standards within the company operationally? How do power relationships within the organisation influence the creation of ethical values? These questions require further research and can be developed through a dedicated empirical investigation.

10.6 The Need to Address Personalization in Work Relationships

In today's rapidly evolving work landscape, there is an increasing need to address the demand for personalization in work relationships. Traditional organisationa structures and rigid employment practices are giving way to more flexible and employee-centered approaches, driven by the desire for greater autonomy, purpose, and work-life integration among employees. The spread of communicative technologies create a situation where workers justify the needs (what are recently more explicit demands) for self-managed personal development, self-realization, and personal exploration of the meaning of their own experiences. One of the key drivers behind the demand for personalization in work relationships is the recognition that each individual brings unique talents, skills, and aspirations to the workplace. Employees no longer want to be treated as mere cogs in a machine, but rather as individuals with distinct needs and goals. They seek a work environment that values their uniqueness and allows them to align their personal values and passions with their professional endeavors. At least for individuals endowed with significant psychosocial resources, the expectation of self-realization supports the request for greater discretion in autonomously pursuing personally meaningful tasks that satisfy not only material needs but also higher-order needs for personal growth, altruism, and collective well-being. In this direction, interventions that promote voluntary psychological contracts (known as I-deals or idiosyncratic agreements) between workers and companies, mutually beneficial, concerning non-standard work conditions, personalized working hours, and self-organized work activities (Lyu et al, 2022), are gaining ground.

Personalization in work relationships also plays a crucial role in employee engagement and satisfaction. When individuals feel seen, heard, and understood by their employers, they are more likely to be motivated, committed, and loyal to the organisation. It fosters a sense of belonging and emotional attachment to the workplace, leading to increased productivity and overall well-being.

Interventions facilitating this type of agreement overturn the traditional model of instrumental flexibility, introducing an "employee-oriented" flexibility as a humanistic management practice with reduced authoritarian controls, which can have a strong impact on the relational climate within the company.

Psychological interventions aimed at promoting job-crafting (Dubbelt, Demerouti and Rispens, 2019) also correspond to the aforementioned demands for autonomy, discretion, and personalization of work. In this case, the goal is to incentivize and value the modification of work activities, which are redesigned and self-organized by the workers themselves (and not formally authorized) to make the work "tailored to themselves," aligning with their expectations and passions. These proactive contributions to improving work "from the bottom" can also lead to generalizable innovations for organisationa design and change.

Facilitating these two modes of self-regulation, renegotiation, and self-management of work enhances its profitability not only economically but also socially, as it contributes to making its meaning more fulfilling (the meanings and purposes attributed to work), to enhancing emotional involvement (attachment to one's work, group, or organisation), and to improving work-life balance (positive interactions between professional and private life). These interventions ultimately foster a healthier work environment where employees feel more fulfilled, engaged, and motivated, benefiting both the individual and the organisation as a whole. Addressing the need for personalization in work relationships also aligns with the changing expectations of the modern workforce, particularly among younger generations. Millennials and Gen Z employees, in particular, place a high value on work that is meaningful, socially responsible, and aligned with their personal values. They are more likely to seek employers who offer opportunities for personal growth, a sense of purpose, and a positive impact on society. To meet these demands, organisations need to adopt a more human-centric and agile approach to talent management. This includes leveraging technology to personalize learning and development opportunities, creating mentorship programs, and fostering open communication channels where employees can express their needs and aspirations.

10.7 The Need to Address Sustainability Issues

This refers to a broad area of emerging questions that are already embraced by psychology and transformed into socially relevant responses. Indeed, there is an expansion of the notion of sustainable social development with the inclusion of personal well-being and social justice in the conception of economic prosperity and environmental protection. In this conceptual enrichment, psychology and its applications play a significant role (Di Fabio, 2017). Firstly, they can act as “repair tools” for recurring social ruptures caused by intolerable exploitation of environmental resources, through immediate psychosocial assistance. In addition to this, programs are developed to enhance the mediation skills and resilience of individuals and social groups in situations of ethnic conflicts, economic challenges, or cases of forced migration, and to support extreme poverty (think of emergency psychology). Secondly, even in the most advanced societies, they become “indicators of the quality of development” for a specific community or its shortcomings, helping to recognize the deficits in its institutions and organisations that can be quantified by considering, for example:

- an increase in stress-related disorders (such as depression, anxiety, chronic insomnia);
- the rise in accidents and injuries related to work environments (and urban settings)
- unsafe and unsustainable modes of operation in the long term.

By this perspective, the value of psychology can be recognized as a means to help build more sustainable organisations and ways of working. In this light, Di Fabio and Svicher (2021) propose design proposals that consider sustainable development as the main objective of primary preventive actions aimed at promoting efficient and healthy organisations, thereby avoiding negative impacts on individuals both immediately (fatigue and strain) and in the long term (concerns about future insecurity, job positions, wages, and loss of autonomy). Moreover, the authors suggest the explicit adoption of a “psychology of sustainability” in the workplace as a conceptual framework for interventions. It will be capable of not only preventing work-related risks but also promoting engagement and facilitating the success and satisfaction of individuals without falling into the risks of self-exploitation or exploitation by others, as often associated with prevailing neo-liberal orientations in our society.

This can be achieved through the development of psychological devices and strategies aimed at enhancing individuals’ psychosocial resources, their personal strengths, their self-reflective capacities, and their potential for intra-organisationa and external social protagonism. It is plausible that by also intervening on environmental conditions to align them with individuals’ talents, high performance, safety, and well-being can be achieved, leading to the creation of sustainable employment opportunities for vulnerable social groups. In general, the goal is to obtain dignified, meaningful, and socially inclusive work for everyone.

10.8 Coping With the Challenges of International Mobility and Cross-Cultural Management: Some Final Raccomandations

The considerations given in the previous chapters and paragraphs, set the premises for providing more practical and actionable recommendations for individuals and organizations to effectively cope with challenges of international mobility and cross-cultural management. While awareness of these challenges is crucial, practical strategies are essential to equip individuals with the tools and resources they need to thrive in diverse environments. The issues such as role ambiguity, role conflict, and emotional reactions that have been addressed in this chapter require specific guidance tailored to the unique dynamics of cross-cultural interactions. Moreover, developing adaptive leadership styles and fostering inclusive, innovative, and growth-oriented environments are imperative for organizations seeking to leverage the full potential of their global workforce. By offering concrete strategies and actionable steps, individuals and organizations can enhance their ability to navigate the complexities of international mobility with confidence, agility, and success. It is worth mentioninf some practical recommendations for both individuals and organizations to enable them to cope with the challenges of international mobility and cross-cultural management in an effective manner. At the individual level, it woul be necessary to enahance strategies of:

- self-awareness: to engage single workers in introspection activities to understand personal strengths, weaknesses, and cultural biases;
- cultural competence development: meaning that workers shoule invest time in learning about the culture, customs, and communication styles of the host country (such as participating to cultural training programs, language classes);
- flexibility and adaptability: workers should be prompt to embrace ambiguity and uncertainty as inherent aspects of cross-cultural interactions in order to develop a flexible mindset that can pivot in response to changing circumstances and cultural nuances;
- support networks: means connect with other expatriates, locals, and support groups to share experiences, seek advice, and build a sense of community;
- manage emotional reactions through practising mindfulness techniques to regulate emotions and maintain perspective during stressful situations.

At the level of the Organizatoins, instead, it is important to consider the following strategies and raccommandations:

- prrovide comprehensive pre-departure training and orientation programs that address cultural, logistical, and psychological aspects of international assignments. Equip expatriates with the skills and resources they need to succeed in diverse environments;
- clarify job expectations, responsibilities, and performance metrics to minimize role ambiguity and conflict while fostering open communication channels between expatriates, local teams, and headquarters to ensure alignment and transparency;
- invest in leadership development programs that emphasize cultural intelligence, empathy, and adaptive leadership styles. It would be effective to equip workers with the skills to cope with diverse teams, bridge cultural divides, and foster inclusive environments.

- establish robust support systems, such as employee assistance programs, counseling services, and expatriate networks, to address the emotional and psychological needs of expatriates. This can be effectivel achieved after providing access to resources for language training, cultural adaptation, and community integration;
- encourage a culture of continuous learning and feedback, where expatriates can share insights, challenges, and best practices with colleagues across the organization. It is pivotal, at this stage, to foster a growth mindset that values diversity, innovation, and collaboration as drivers of success in the global marketplace.

REFERENCES

Adler, E. (1997). Seizing the Middle Ground: Constructivism in World Politics. *European Journal of International Relations*, *3*(3), 319–363. doi:10.1177/1354066197003003003

Alabi, B., & Sarkiunaite, I. (2022). The Impact of Workplace Environment on Expatriates' Adaptation to New Workplace. *Vilnius University Open Series,* 5-13. DOI:. doi:10.15388/ISC.2022.1

Albrecht, T. L., & Adelman, M. B. (1984). Social support and life stress: New directions for communication research. *Human Communication Research*, *11*(1), 3–32. doi:10.1111/j.1468-2958.1984.tb00036.x

Ambos, T. C., Fuchs, S. H., & Zimmermann, A. (2020). Managing interrelated tensions in headquarters–subsidiary relationships: The case of a multinational hybrid organisation. *Journal of International Business Studies*, *51*(6), 906–932. doi:10.1057/s41267-020-00307-z

Bhaskar, A., & Gupta, V. (2020). Expatriate Adjustment and Performance: A Meta-Analysis. *Journal of International Business Studies*, *51*(4), 497–517. doi:10.1057/s41267-020-00344-8

Black, J. S., & Gregersen, H. B. (1991). Antecedents to cross-cultural adjustment for expatriates in Pacific Rim assignments. *Human Relations*, *44*(5), 497–515. doi:10.1177/001872679104400505

Black, J. S., Mendenhall, M., & Oddou, G. (1991). Toward a Comprehensive Model of International Adjustment: An Integration of Multiple Theoretical Perspectives. *Academy of Management Review*, *16*(2), 291–317. doi:10.2307/258863

Black, J. S., & Porter, L. W. (1989). Managerial Behaviours and Job Performance: A Successful Manager in Los Angeles May Not Succeed in Hong Kong. *Journal of International Business Studies*, *22*(1), 99–113. doi:10.1057/palgrave.jibs.8490294

Brett, J. M. (1982). Job transfer and well-being. *The Journal of Applied Psychology*, *67*(4), 450–463. doi:10.1037/0021-9010.67.4.450

Chen, M. (2019). The Impact of Expatriates' Cross-Cultural Adjustment on Work Stress and Job Involvement in the High-Tech Industry. *Frontiers in Psychology*, *10*, 2228. doi:10.3389/fpsyg.2019.02228 PMID:31649581

Deresky, H. (2000). *International Management* (3rd ed.). Prentice Hall.

Di Fabio, A. (2017). Positive healthy organisations: promoting well-being, meaningfulness, and sustainability in organisations. *Front. Psychol.,* 8(1938). . doi:10.3389/fpsyg.2017.01938

Di Fabio, A., & Svicher, A. (2021). The Psychology of Sustainability and Sustainable Development: Advancing Decent Work, Inclusivity, and Positive Strength-Based Primary Preventive Interventions for Vulnerable Workers. *Frontiers in Psychology*, *12*(718354), 1–8. doi:10.3389/fpsyg.2021.718354 PMID:34385966

Dobson, J. (2003). Why Ethics Codes Don't Work. *Financial Analysts Journal*, *59*(6), 29–34. doi:10.2469/faj.v59.n6.2572

Donaldson, T., & Dunfee, T. W. (1994). Toward a Unified Conception of Business Ethics: Integrative Social Contracts Theory. *Academy of Management Review*, *19*(2), 252–284. doi:10.2307/258705

Dubbelt, L., Demerouti, E., & Rispens, S. (2019). Job crafting and employee well-being: A systematic review of longitudinal studies. *Journal of Occupational Health Psychology*, *24*(4), 498–513.

Dubbelt, L., Demerouti, E., & Rispens, S. (2019). The value of job crafting for work engagement, task performance, and career satisfaction: Longitudinal and quasi-experimental evidence. *European Journal of Work and Organizational Psychology*, *28*(3), 300–314. doi:10.1080/1359432X.2019.1576632

Earley, P. C., & Ang, S. (2003). *Cultural Intelligence: Individual Interactions Across Cultures*. Stanford University Press. doi:10.1515/9780804766005

Edström, A., & Galbraith, J. R. (1977). Transfer of Managers as a Coordination and Control Strategy in Multinational Organisations. *Administrative Science Quarterly*, *22*(2), 248–263. doi:10.2307/2391959

Gehrisch, M. G., & Süß, S. (2023). Organisationa behavior in international strategic alliances and the relation to performance – a literature review and avenues for future research. *Management Review Quarterly*, *73*(3), 1045–1107. doi:10.1007/s11301-022-00268-7

Gregersen, H. B., & Stroh, L. K. (2019). *Expatriate Management: New Ideas for International Business*. Routledge.

Harris, M., & Moran, R. (1979). *Managing Culture Differences*. Gulf.

Harrison, G., McKinnon, J., Wu, A., & Chow, C. (2000). Cultural Influences on Adaptation To Fluid Workgroups And Teams. *Journal of International Business Studies*, *31*(3), 489–505. doi:10.1057/palgrave.jibs.8490918

Harvey, D. (1982). *The Limits to Capital*. Blackwell.

Harvey, D. (1990). Between Space and Time: Reflections on the Geographical Imagination. *Annals of the Association of American Geographers*, *80*(3), 418–434. doi:10.1111/j.1467-8306.1990.tb00305.x

Heller, F. A. (1988). Cost benefits of multinational research on organisations. *Journal of Anthropological Research*, *51*(3), 247–261.

Heller, J. E. (1980). Criteria for selecting an international manager. *Personnel*, *57*(3), 47–55.

Hsu, Y. (2012). The impact of expatriate support on expatriate adjustment and performance: A study of Taiwanese expatriates in China. *International Journal of Human Resource Management*, *23*(2), 333–349.

Hsu, Y. S. (2012). *Knowledge transfer between expatriates and host country nationals: a social capital perspective. UWM. Digital Commons*. University of Wisconsin. doi:10.1037/e518332013-315

Huang, H., Gao, L., Deng, X., & Fu, H. (2022). The Relationship Between Emotional Intelligence and Expatriate Performance in International Construction Projects. *Psychology Research and Behavior Management*, *22*(15), 3825–3843. doi:10.2147/PRBM.S387287 PMID:36578282

Ilie, O. (2019). The Intercultural Competence. Developing Effective Intercultural Communication Skills. *Knowledge-Based Organisation, 25*(2) 264-268. 10.2478/kbo-2019-0092

Lyu, B., Liao, X., & Yang, Y. (2022). Relationships between temporal leadership, transactive memory systems and Team Innovation Performance. *Psychology Research and Behavior Management*, *51*, 2543–2559. doi:10.2147/PRBM.S380989 PMID:36124335

MacIntyre, P. D., & Gardner, R. C. (1989). Anxiety and Second Language Learning: Toward a Theoretical Clarification. *Language Learning*, *39*(2), 251–275. doi:10.1111/j.1467-1770.1989.tb00423.x

Manev, I., & Stevenson, W. (2001). Nationality, Cultural Distance, and Expatriate Status: Effects on the Managerial Network in a Multinational Enterprise. *Journal of International Business Studies*, *32*(2), 285–303. doi:10.1057/palgrave.jibs.8490953

Mendenhall, M. E., & Oddou, G. R. (2016). *Readings and Cases in International Human Resource Management*. Routledge.

Mikhaylov, F., Kolesnikova, J., & Eldar, S. (2014). Current Tendencies of the Development of Service of Human Resources Management. *Procedia: Social and Behavioral Sciences*, *150*, 330–335. doi:10.1016/j.sbspro.2014.09.072

Nery-Kjerfve, T., & McLean, G. N. (2012). Repatriation of expatriate employees, knowledge transfer, and organisationa learning: What do we know? *European Journal of Training and Development*, *36*(6), 614–629. doi:10.1108/03090591211245512

O'Brien, M., Hanton, S., & Mellalieu, S. D. (2005). Intensity and direction of competitive anxiety as a function of goal attainment expectation and competition goal generation. *Journal of Science and Medicine in Sport*, *8*(4), 423–432. doi:10.1016/S1440-2440(05)80057-X PMID:16602170

Pinder, C. (1989). The Dark Side of Executive Relocation. *Organizational Dynamics*, *17*(4), 48–58. doi:10.1016/S0090-2616(89)80026-9

Primeaux, P. (1992). Experiential Ethics: A Blueprint for Personal and Corporate Ethics. *Journal of Business Ethics*, *11*(10), 779–788. doi:10.1007/BF00872310

Quintanilla, L., Giménez-Dasí, M., Sarmento-Henrique, R., & Lucas-Molina, B. (2021). Longitudinal evidence for an emotion-action lag on desire: The role of emotional understanding. *Cognitive Development*, *59*(101096), 101096. Advance online publication. doi:10.1016/j.cogdev.2021.101096

Ralston, D., Holt, D., Terpstra, R., & Kai-Cheng, Y. (1997). The Impact of Natural Culture and Economic Ideology on Managerial Work Values: A Study of the United States, Russia, Japan, and China. *Journal of International Business Studies*, *28*(1), 177–207. doi:10.1057/palgrave.jibs.8490097

Seidenberg, R. (1973). *Marriage between equals: Studies from life and literature*. Anchor Press.

Shaffer, M. A., Harrison, D. A., & Gilley, K. M. (2019). *Expatriate Adaptation and Effectiveness: Current Directions and Future Challenges*. Routledge.

Shepherd, D. A., & Patzelt, H. (2018). Motivation and Entrepreneurial Cognition. In *Entrepreneurial Cognition*. Palgrave Macmillan., doi:10.1007/978-3-319-71782-1_3

Sinclair, A. (1993). Approaches to organisational culture and ethics. *Journal of Business Ethics*, *12*(1), 63–73. doi:10.1007/BF01845788

Vogel, D. (1991). Business Ethics: New Perspectives on Old Problems. *California Management Review*, *33*(4), 101–117. doi:10.2307/41166675

Wang, J., & Houston, V. (2011). Expatriate Selection: The Key to International Success. *The International Business & Economics Research Journal*, *1*(11). Advance online publication. doi:10.19030/iber.v1i11.3999

Weaver, G. R. (1993). Corporate Codes of Ethics: Purpose, Process and Content Issues. *Business & Society*, *32*(1), 44–58. doi:10.1177/000765039303200106

Compilation of References

Adler, N.J, & Ghadar, F. (1990). Strategic HRM: A global perspective. *HRM in International Comparison*, 235-260. . doi:10.1515/9783110869101.235

Adler, E. (1997). Seizing the Middle Ground: Constructivism in World Politics. *European Journal of International Relations*, *3*(3), 319–363. doi:10.1177/1354066197003003003

Adler, N. J. (1980). Cultural synergy: the management of cross-cultural organisations. In W. W. Burke & L. D. Goodstein (Eds.), *Trends and Issues in OD: Current Theory and Practice* (pp. 163–184). University Associates.

Adler, N. J. (1983a). Cross-cultural Management Research: The Ostrich and the Trend. *Academy of Management Review*, *8*(20), 226–232. doi:10.5465/amr.1983.4284725

Adler, N. J. (1983b). Cross cultural Management: Issues To Be Faced. *International Studies of Management & Organization*, *13*(1-2), 7–45. doi:10.1080/00208825.1983.11656357

Adler, N. J. (1984). Expecting International Success: Female Managers Overseas. *The Columbia Journal of World Business*, *19*(3), 79–85. https://www.journals.elsevier.com/journal-of-world-business

Adler, N. J. (1984). Understanding the ways of understanding: Cross-cultural management reviewed. In R. N. Farmer (Ed.), *Advances in international comparative management* (Vol. 1, pp. 31–67). JAI Press.

Adler, N. J. (1986). *International Dimensions of Organisational Behaviour*. Kent Publishing Company.

Adler, N. J., & Devillafranca, J. (1983). Epistemological Foundations of a Symposium Process: A Framework for Understanding Culturally Diverse Organisations. *International Studies of Management & Organization*, *12*(4), 7–22. doi: 10.1080/00208825.1982.11656350

Adler, N. J., & Jelinek, M. (1986). Is organisation culture "Culture Bound? *Human Resource Management*, *25*(2), 73–90. doi:10.1002/hrm.3930250106

Adler, N., Campbell, N., & Laurent, A. (1989). In Search of Appropriate Methodology: From Outside The People's Republic of China Looking In. *Journal of International Business Studies*, *20*(1), 61–74. doi:10.1057/palgrave.jibs.8490351

Agarwal, R., & Helfat, C. E. (2009). Strategic Renewal of Organisations. *Organization Science*, *20*(2), 281–293. https://www.jstor.org/stable/25614656. doi:10.1287/orsc.1090.0423

Agliati, M., & Beretta, S. (1990). *I sistemi amministrativi nei gruppi di imprese*. Egea.

Airoldi, G. (1980). *I sistemi operativi*. Giuffrè.

Airoldi, G., Brunetti, G., & Coda, V. (1989). *Lezioni di economia aziendale*. Il Mulino.

Airoldi, G., & Decastri, M. (1983). *Le funzioni di organizzazione in impresa*. Giuffrè.

Aiyar, S., Chen, J., Ebeke, C. H., Garcia-Saltos, R., Gudmundsson, T., Ilyina, A., Kangur, A., Kunaratskul, T., Rodriguez, S. L., Ruta, M., Schulze, T., Soderberg, G., & Trevino, J. P. (2023). *Geoeconomic Fragmentation and the Future of Multilateralism*. International Monetary Fund. doi:10.5089/9798400229046.006

Ajiferuke, M., & Boddewyn, J. (1970). Culture and Other Explanatory Variables in Comparative Management Studies. *Academy of Management Journal, 13*(2), 153–163. doi:10.2307/255102

Aksoy, C. (2023). Digital Business Ecosystems: An Environment of Collaboration, Innovation, and Value Creation in the Digital Age. *Journal of Business and Trade, 4*(2), 156–180. doi:10.58767/joinbat.1358560

Alabi, B., & Sarkiunaite, I. (2022). The Impact of Workplace Environment on Expatriates' Adaptation to New Workplace. *Vilnius University Open Series,* 5-13. DOI:. doi:10.15388/ISC.2022.1

Albrecht, T. L., & Adelman, M. B. (1984). Social support and life stress: New directions for communication research. *Human Communication Research, 11*(1), 3–32. doi:10.1111/j.1468-2958.1984.tb00036.x

Aldrich, H. E. (1979). *Organisations and Environment*. Prentice Hall.

Aldrich, H., & Herker, D. (1977). Boundary Spanning Roles and Organisation Structure. *Academy of Management Review, 2*(2), 217–230. doi:10.2307/257905

Allegretti, S., Seidenstricker, S., Fischer, H., & Arslan, S. (2021). Executing a business model change: Identifying key characteristics to succeed in volatile markets. *Leadership, Education, Personality. An Interdisciplinary Journal, 3*(1), 1–13. doi:10.1365/s42681-021-00020-x

Allinson, G. D. (1988). Imitation and Innovation: The Transfer of Western Organisational Patterns to Meiji Japan. *Business History Review, 62*(4), 745+. https://link.gale.com/apps/doc/A8190667/AONE?u=googlescholar&sid=bookmark-AONE&xid=6219e073

Altman, S., & Bastian, C. (2021). *DHL Global Connectedness Index 2021 Update. Globalization Shock and Recovery in the Covid-19 Crisis*. NYU Stern School of Business Centre for the Future of Management. DHL Initiative on Globalization.

Ambos, T. C., Fuchs, S. H., & Zimmermann, A. (2020). Managing interrelated tensions in headquarters–subsidiary relationships: The case of a multinational hybrid organisation. *Journal of International Business Studies, 51*(6), 906–932. doi:10.1057/s41267-020-00307-z

Amin, G. A., & Boamah, M. I. (2023). Modeling business partnerships: A data envelopment analysis approach. *European Journal of Operational Research, 305*(1), 329–337. doi:10.1016/j.ejor.2022.05.036

Anderson, E., & Gatignon, H. (1986). Modes of Foreign Entry: A Transaction Cost Analysis and Propositions. *Journal of International Business Studies, 17*(3), 1–26. doi:10.1057/palgrave.jibs.8490432

Andersson, U., Gaur, A., Mudambi, R., & Persson, M. (2015). Unpacking inter unit knowledge transfer in multinational enterprises. *Global Strategy Journal, 5*(3), 241–245. doi:10.1002/gsj.1100

Andreassen, T. W., Lervik-Olsen, L., Snyder, H., Van Riel, A. C., Sweeney, J. C., & Van Vaerenbergh, Y. (2018). Business model innovation and value-creation: The triadic way. *Journal of Service Management, 29*(5), 883–906. doi:10.1108/JOSM-05-2018-0125

Ariño, A., de la Torre, J., & Ring, P. (2005). Relational quality and inter-personal trust in strategic alliances. *European Management Review, 2*(1), 15–27. doi:10.1057/palgrave.emr.1500026

Arrow, K. J. (1974). *The Limits of Organisations*. W.W. Norton.

Asch, S. E. (1956). Studies of independence and conformity: I. A minority of one against a unanimous majority. *Psychological Monographs, 70*(9), 1–70. doi:10.1037/h0093718

Attila, B., & Gherardi, S. (2007). *Studiare le pratiche lavorative.* Il mulino.

Austin, G., Dávila, C., & Jones, G. (2017). Emerging Markets and the future of Business History. *Working Paper*, 18-012, Harvard Business School.

Autio, E., Mudambi, R., & Yoo, Y. (2021). Digitalization and globalization in a turbulent world: Centrifugal and centripetal forces. *Global Strategy Journal, 11*(1), 3–16. doi:10.1002/gsj.1396

Awais, M., Ali, A., Khattak, M. S., Arfeen, M. I., Chaudhary, M. A. I., & Syed, A. (2023). Strategic Flexibility and Organisational Performance: Mediating Role of Innovation. *SAGE Open, 13*(2). Advance online publication. doi:10.1177/21582440231181432

Aylmer, R. J. (1970). Who Makes Marketing Decisions in the Multinational Finn? *Journal of Marketing, 34*(4), 25–30. doi:10.1177/002224297003400405

Baker, J. C., & Ivancevich, J. M. (1971). The Assignment of American Executives Abroad: Systematic, Haphazard or Chaotic? *California Management Review, 13*(3), 39–44. doi:10.2307/41164292

Balcet, G. (1989). *Economia dell'impresa multinazionale.* Giappichelli.

Barkema, H. G., Chen, X. P., George, G., Luo, Y., & Tsui, A. S. (2015). West Meets East: New Concepts and Theories. (2015). *Academy of Management Journal, 58*(2), 460–479. https://ink.library.smu.edu.sg/lkcsb_research/4750. doi:10.5465/amj.2015.4021

Barney, B. J., & Ouchi, W. G. (1985). Costi delle informazioni e strutture economiche di governo delle transazioni. In R. C. D. Nacamulli & A. Rugiadini (Eds.), *Organizzazioni e Mercato.* Il Mulino.

Barney, J. (1991). Firm Resources and Sustained Competitive Advantage. *Journal of Management, 17*(1), 99–120. doi:10.1177/014920639101700108

Barney, J. B., & Ouchi, W. G. (1986). Organisational Economics. *Organization Studies, 9*(1). Advance online publication. doi:10.1177/017084068800900120

Barrington, M. (1967). *Social origins of dictatorship and democracy: lord and peasant in the making of the modern world.* Beacon Press.

Bartlett, C. A. (1982). How Multinational Organisations Evolve. *The Journal of Business Strategy, 3*(1), 20–32. doi:10.1108/eb038953

Bartlett, C. A. (1982). National Culture-Business Relations: United States and Japan Contrasted. *Management International Review*, 4–12.

Bartlett, C. A., Doz, Y., & Hedlund, G. (1990). *Managing the Global Company.* Routledge.

Bartlett, C. A., & Ghoshal, S. (1986). Tap your subsidiaries for global reach. *Harvard Business Review, 64*(6), 87–94. doi:10.5465/amr.1990.4310825

Bartlett, C. A., & Ghoshal, S. (1987). Managing Across Borders: New Organisational Responses. *MIT Sloan Management Review, 29*(1), 43–54.

Bartlett, C. A., & Ghoshal, S. (1988). *International Transfer of Manager in Multinational Corporation.* Acta Universitatis Upsaliensis, Studia Oeconomiae Negotiorum. Lars Engwall and Jan Johanson.

Bartlett, C. A., & Ghoshal, S. (1989). *Management Globale. La soluzione transnazionale per la direzione d'impresa*. Etas Libri.

Bartlett, C. A., & Ghoshal, S. (1989). *Managing Across Borders: The Transnational Solution*. Harvard Business School Press.

Bartlett, C., & Ghoshal, S. (1990). The multinational corporation as an interorganisational network. *Academy of Management Review*, *15*(4), 603–625. doi:10.2307/258684

Battilana, J. (2018). Cracking the organisational challenge of pursuing joint social and financial goals: Social enterprise as a laboratory to understand hybrid organizing. *M@n@gement*, *21*(4), 1278–1305. doi:10.3917/mana.214.1278

Beamish, P. (1988). *Multinational joint ventures in developing countries*. Routledge.

Becker, M. C. (2004). Organisational routines: A review of the literature. *Industrial and Corporate Change*, *13*(4), 643–678. doi:10.1093/icc/dth026

Behrman, J. N., & Fisher, W. A. (1980). *Overseas R&D Activities of Transnational Companies*. Oelgeschlager. doi:10.1002/tie.5060220309

Beverly, S. Y. T., & Vinh, V. T. (2015). Global knowledge hubs: Introducing a new conceptual model. *International Journal of Knowledge-Based Development. Inderscience Enterprises Ltd*, *6*(2), 131–151. doi:10.1504/IJKBD.2015.071471

Bhaskar, A., & Gupta, V. (2020). Expatriate Adjustment and Performance: A Meta-Analysis. *Journal of International Business Studies*, *51*(4), 497–517. doi:10.1057/s41267-020-00344-8

Bhawuk, D., & Brislin, R. (1992). The Measurement of Intercultural Sensitivity Using the Concept of Individualism and Collectivism. *International Journal of Intercultural Relations*, *16*(4), 413–436. doi:10.1016/0147-1767(92)90031-O

Bichi, R. (1996). Globalizzazione E Management: I Dirigenti Espatriati. *Studi di Sociologia*, *34*(2), 157–172. https://www.jstor.org/stable/23004378

Bird, A., Taylor, S., & Beechler, S. (1998). A typology of international human resource management in Japanese multinational corporations: *Organisational implications. Human Resource Management*, *37*(2), 159–172. doi:10.1002/(SICI)1099-050X(199822)37:2<159::AID-HRM6>3.0.CO;2-V

Birkinshaw, J. (1996). How Multinational Subsidiary Mandates Are Gained and Lost. *Journal of International Business Studies*, *27*(3), 467–495. doi:10.1057/palgrave.jibs.8490845

Birkinshaw, J. (2022). Move fast and break things: Reassessing IB research in the light of the digital revolution. *Global Strategy Journal*, *12*(4), 619–631. doi:10.1002/gsj.1427

Birkinshaw, J. M., & Morrison, A. J. (1996). Configurations of strategy and structure in multinational subsidiaries. *Journal of International Business Studies*, *26*(4), 729–794. doi:10.1057/palgrave.jibs.8490818

Black, J. S. (1988). Work Role Transitions: A Study of American Expatriate Managers in Japan. *Journal of International Business Studies*, *19*(2), 277–294. doi:10.1057/palgrave.jibs.8490383

Black, J. S., & Gregersen, H. B. (1991). Antecedents to cross-cultural adjustment for expatriates in Pacific Rim assignments. *Human Relations*, *44*(5), 497–515. doi:10.1177/001872679104400505

Black, J. S., Gregerson, H. B., Mendenhall, M. E., & Stroh, L. K. (1999). *Globalizing people through international assignments*. Addison Wesley Longman.

Black, J. S., Mendenhall, M., & Oddou, G. (1991). Toward a Comprehensive Model of International Adjustment: An Integration of Multiple Theoretical Perspectives. *Academy of Management Review*, *16*(2), 291–317. doi:10.2307/258863

Black, J. S., & Porter, L. W. (1989). Managerial Behaviours and Job Performance: A Successful Manager in Los Angeles May Not Succeed in Hong Kong. *Journal of International Business Studies*, *22*(1), 99–113. doi:10.1057/palgrave.jibs.8490294

Blake, P. H., & Walters, P. S. (1976). *The Politics of Global Economic Relations*. Prentice Hall. doi:10.1002/tie.5060180211

Bleeke, J. A., & Ernst, D. (1995). Is Your Strategic Alliance Really a Sale. *Harvard Business Review*, *13*, 97–105.

Blue, J. L., & Haynes, U. Jr. (1977). Preparation for the overseas assignment. *Business Horizons*, *20*(3), 61–67. doi:10.1016/0007-6813(77)90072-6

Bodega, D. (1988). L'organizzazione si proietta in se stessa. *Sviluppo & Organizzazione,* 110.

Bodega, D. (1988). L'organizzazione si proietta in se stessa. *Sviluppo and Organizzazione,* 110.

Bodega, D. (1991). *Cultura and Organizzazione*. Este.

Bodega, D. (1996). *Organizzazione e cultura. Teoria e metodo della prospettiva culturale nell'organizzazione d'azienda*. Guerini e Associati.

Bodega, D. (1996). *Organizzazione e cultura. Teoria e metodo della prospettiva culturale nell'organizzazione di azienda*. Guerini e Associati.

Bodega, D., Decastri, M., & Prina, G. (1992). *Innovazione, apprendimento e formazione: un'indagine empirica*. Franco Angeli.

Boisot, M. (1986). Markets and Hierarchies in a Cultural Perspective. *Organization Studies*, *7*(2), 135–158. doi:10.1177/017084068600700204

Boisot, M. H. (1998). *Knowledge Assets*. Oxford University Press.

Bond, M. H. (2002). Reclaiming the individual from Hofstede's ecological analysis A 20 year odyssey: Comment on Oyserman et al. (2002). *Psychological Bulletin*, *128*(1), 73–77. doi:10.1037/0033-2909.128.1.73 PMID:11843548

Brett, J. M. (1982). Job transfer and well-being. *The Journal of Applied Psychology*, *67*(4), 450–463. doi:10.1037/0021-9010.67.4.450

Brossard, M., & Maurice, M. (1976). Is There a Universal Model of Organisation Structure. *International Studies of Management & Organization*, *6*(3), 11–45. doi:10.1080/00208825.1976.11656204

Brumana, M., Decastri, M., Scarozza, D., & Za, S. (2014). A bibliometric study of the literature on technological innovation: an analysis of 60 international academic journals. In Management, Organisation and Control: Smart Practices and Effects (pp. 141-152). Springer International Publishing. doi:10.1007/978-3-319-07905-9_9

Buch, A. (2020). People and practices in organisational learning. *Forskning or Forandring*, *3*(1), 70–88. doi:10.23865/fof.v3.2103

Buckley, P. J., & Ghauri, P. N. (2004). Globalisation, Economic Geography and the Strategy of Multinational Enterprises. *Journal of International Business Studies*, *35*(2), 81–98. doi:10.1057/palgrave.jibs.8400076

Buckley, P., & Casson, M. (1976). *The future of the multinational enterprise*. Macmillan. doi:10.1007/978-1-349-02899-3

Butera, F. (2008). *Knowledge Working. Lavoro, lavoratori, società della conoscenza*. Mondadori Università.

Caligiuri, P. M. (1997). Assessing expatriate success: Beyond just "being there". In Z. Aycan (Ed.), *New approaches to employee management, Expatriate management: Theory and Research* (Vol. 4, pp. 117–140). JAI.

Caligiuri, P. M. (2000). The Big Five personality characteristics as predictors of expatriates' desire to terminate the assignment and supervisor-rated performance. *Personnel Psychology, 53*(1), 67–88. doi:10.1111/j.1744-6570.2000.tb00194.x

Caligiuri, P. M., Hyland, M. M., Joshi, A., & Bross, A. S. (1998). Testing a theoretical model for examining the relationship between family adjustment and expatriates' work adjustment. *The Journal of Applied Psychology, 83*(4), 598–614. doi:10.1037/0021-9010.83.4.598 PMID:9729928

Castañer, X., & Oliveira, N. (2020). Collaboration, Coordination, and Cooperation Among Organisations: Establishing the Distinctive Meanings of These Terms Through a Systematic Literature Review. *Journal of Management, 46*(6), 965–1001. doi:10.1177/0149206320901565

Chen, M. (2019). The Impact of Expatriates' Cross-Cultural Adjustment on Work Stress and Job Involvement in the High-Tech Industry. *Frontiers in Psychology, 10*, 2228. doi:10.3389/fpsyg.2019.02228 PMID:31649581

Chesbrough, H. (2003). *Open Innovation: The New Imperative for Creating and Profiting from Technology.* Harvard Business Press.

Chesbrough, H., Vanhaverbeke, W., & West, J. (2006). *Open Innovation: Researching a New Paradigm.* Oxford University Press. doi:10.1093/oso/9780199290727.001.0001

Child, J. (1976). Organisational Structures: Extensions and Replications. Westmead.

Child, J., & Keiser, A. (1979). Organisations and managerial roles in British and West German companies: An examination of the culture-free thesis. In C. J. Lammers & D. J. Hickson (Eds.), *Organisations alike and unalike: International and interinstitutional studies in the sociology of organisations* (pp. 251-272). Routledge Kegan Paul, London.

Child, J., & Kieser, A. (1979). *Organisational and Managerial Roles in British And West German Companies: An Examination of The Culture-Free Thesis. Organisations Alike and Unlike.* Routledge.

Child, C., & Tayeb, M. (1983). Theoretical Perspectives in Cross-National Organisation Research. *International Studies of Management & Organization, 12*(4), 23–70. doi:10.1080/00208825.1982.11656351

Child, J. (1981). Culture, contingency and capitalism in the cross-national study of organisations. In L. L. Cummings & B. M. Staw (Eds.), *Research in organisational behaviour* (Vol. 3, pp. 303–356). JAI Press.

Chui, M., Manyika, J., & Miremadi, M. (2018). What Ceos Are. Mckinsey and Company.

Clegg, S., & Wilson, F. (1990). Power, Technology and Flexibility in Organisations. *The Sociological Review, 38*(1, suppl), 223–273. doi:10.1111/j.1467-954X.1990.tb03354.x

Coda, V. (1965). *Le coordinazioni produttive. Introduzione al sistema delle rilevazioni d'impresa.* Giuffrè.

Cohen, M. D., March, J. C., & Olsen, J. P. (1976). *Ambiguity and Choice in Organisations.* Universitet Forlaget.

Contractor, F. J., & Lorange, P. (1988). *Cooperative Strategies in International Business.* Lexington Books.

Cooke, R. A., & Rousseau, D. M. (1988). Behavioral norms and expectations: A quantitative approach to the assessment of organisational culture. *Group & Organization Studies, 13*(3), 245–273. doi:10.1177/105960118801300302

Cristelli, M., Gabrielli, A., Tacchella, A., Caldarelli, G., & Pietronero, L. (2013). Measuring the Intangibles: A Metrics for the Economic Complexity of Countries and Products. *PLoS One, 8*(8), e70726. doi:10.1371/journal.pone.0070726 PMID:23940633

Crookell, H. H. (1986). Specialization and International Competitiveness. In H. Etemad & L. S. Dulude (Eds.), *Managing the Multinational Subsidiary* (pp. 102–111). Croom Helm.

Crozier, M., & Friedberg, E. (1978). *Attore sociale e sistema*. Etas Libri.

Cuervo-Cazurra, A., & Genc, M. (2008). Article. *Journal of International Business Studies, 39*(6), 957-979.

Cuervo-Cazurra, A., & Genc, M. (2008). Transforming disadvantages into advantages: developing country MNEs in the least developed MNEs. *Journal of International Business Studies, 39*(6), 957-979. https://www.jstor.org/stable/25483316

Cuervo-Cazurra, A., Ciravegna, L., Melgarejo, M., & Lopez, L. (2018). Home country uncertainty and the internationalization-performance relationship: Building an uncertainty management capability. *Journal of World Business, 53*(2), 209–221. doi:10.1016/j.jwb.2017.11.002

Dahrendorf, R. (1968). *Essays in the theory of society*. Stanford University Press.

Dalton, G. (1960). A Note of Clarification on Economic Surplus. *American Anthropologist, 62*(3), 483–490. doi:10.1525/aa.1960.62.3.02a00070

Daniels, J. L., & Frost, N. C. (1991). The Global Frontier. Harper and Row.

Davis, P., & Stern, D. (1988). Adaptation, Survival, and Growth of the Family Business: An Integrated Systems Perspective. *Family Business Review, 1*(1), 69–84. doi:10.1111/j.1741-6248.1988.00069.x

Davis, S. M. (1971). *Comparative Management, Organisational and Cultural Perspective*. Prentice Hall.

De Bari, F. (1990). Counter trade & offset: un approccio efficace ai paesi dell'est e PVS. *Economia e Management,* 15.

de Man, A. P., & Luvison, D. (2019). Collaborative business models: Aligning and operationalizing alliances. *Business Horizons, 62*(4), 473–482. doi:10.1016/j.bushor.2019.02.004

Decastri, M. (1989). L'organizzazione per l'intemazionalizzazione. *Sviluppo & Organizzazione*, 11.

Decastri, M., Tomasi, D., & Scravaglieri, S. (2012). Performance Management Systems as Driver of Public Administration Improvement: a Dream? In A. D'Atri & D. Saccà (Eds.), Designing Organisational Systems. An interdisciplinary discourse (pp.245-267). Physica-Verlag, Springer.

Decastri, M. (1984). *Organizzazione e cultura dell'innovazione in impresa*. Giuffrè.

Decastri, M. (2016). *Indagine sulle trasformazioni indotte nel processo produttivo dalle nuove tecnologie e dall'innovazione in generale*. Editoriale Scientifica.

Decastri, M., Buonocore, F., Battini, S., & Gagliarducci, F. (2020). *Organisational Development in Public Administration: The ltalian Way*. Palgrave Mc Millan.

Decastri, M., Scravaglieri, S., Trotta, M., & Yamak, S. (2011). The value of work: an antidote against the neo-bureaucratic drift of public administration. In E. Borgonovi & R. Mussari (Eds.), *Collaborare e competere per un mercato responsabile e solidale*. Il Mulino.

Demir, R., & Angwin, D. (2021). Multidexterity: Combining Competing Business Models in Transforming Economies. *Management and Organization Review, 17*(2), 282–313. doi:10.1017/mor.2020.56

Denison, D. R., & Mishra, A. K. (1995). Toward a Theory of Organisational Culture and Effectiveness. *Organization Science, 6*(2), 204–223. doi:10.1287/orsc.6.2.204

Denning, S. (2019). *Agile innovation: The revolutionary approach to accelerate success, inspire engagement, and ignite creativity*. John Wiley and Sons.

Deresky, H. (2000). *International Management* (3rd ed.). Prentice Hall.

Di Fabio, A. (2017). Positive healthy organisations: promoting well-being, meaningfulness, and sustainability in organisations. *Front. Psychol., 8*(1938). . doi:10.3389/fpsyg.2017.01938

Di Fabio, A., & Svicher, A. (2021). The Psychology of Sustainability and Sustainable Development: Advancing Decent Work, Inclusivity, and Positive Strength-Based Primary Preventive Interventions for Vulnerable Workers. *Frontiers in Psychology, 12*(718354), 1–8. doi:10.3389/fpsyg.2021.718354 PMID:34385966

Dobson, J. (2003). Why Ethics Codes Don't Work. *Financial Analysts Journal, 59*(6), 29–34. doi:10.2469/faj.v59.n6.2572

Donaldson, T., & Dunfee, T. W. (1994). Toward a Unified Conception of Business Ethics: Integrative Social Contracts Theory. *Academy of Management Review, 19*(2), 252–284. doi:10.2307/258705

Dowling, P. J., Schuler, R. S., & Welch, D. E. (1996). *International dimensions of human resource management*. Wadsworth Publishing Company.

Doz, Y. M., & Prahalad, C. K. (1984). Patterns of Strategic Control within Multinational Corporation. *Journal of International Business Studies, 15*(2), 55-72.

Doz, Y., & Kosonen, M. (2010). Embedding Strategic Agility: A Leadership Agenda for Accelerating Business Model Renewal. *Long Range Planning, 43*(2–3), 370–382. . doi:10.1016/j.lrp.2009.07.006

Doz, Y. (1986). *Strategie Management in Multinational Company*. Pergamon Press.

Doz, Y. (1987). Technology Partnerships between Larger and Smaller Companies: Some Critical Issues. *International Studies of Management & Organization, 17*(4), 31–57. doi:10.1080/00208825.1987.11656466

Doz, Y. (2006). *Harnessing Global Knowledge for Metanational Innovation. Special Interview. Rieti Report, 066- 25*. Research Institute of Economy, Trade and Industry.

Doz, Y. (2011). Qualitative research for international business. *Journal of International Business Studies, 42*(5), 582–590. https://www.jstor.org/stable/29789446. doi:10.1057/jibs.2011.18

Doz, Y. L., & Prahalad, C. K. (1999). Managing DMNCs: A search for a new paradigm. *Strategic Management Journal, 12*(S1), 145–164. doi:10.1002/smj.4250120911

Doz, Y., & Prahalad, C. K. (1981). An Approach to Strategic Control in MNCs. *Sloan Management Review, 22*(4), 5.

Doz, Y., & Prahalad, C. K. (1986). Controlled Variety: A Challenge for Human Resource Management in the mnc. *Human Resource Management, 25*(1), 55–71. doi:10.1002/hrm.3930250105

Doz, Y., & Prahalad, C. K. (1987). *The Multinational Mission. Balancing Local Demands and Global Vision*. The Free Press.

Doz, Y., Santos, J., & Williamson, P. (2001). From Global to Metanational How Companies Win in the Knowledge Economy. *Ubiquity, 2001*(December), 2. Advance online publication. doi:10.1145/503351.503119

Doz, Y., Santos, J., & Williamson, P. (2004). Is Your Innovation Process Global? *MIT Sloan Management Review, 45*(4), 31–37.

Drogendijk, R., & Slangen, A. (2006). Hofstede, Schwartz, Or Managerial Perceptions? The Effects of Different Cultural Distance Measures on Establishment Mode Choices by Multinational Enterprises. *International Business Review*, *15*(4), 361–380. doi:10.1016/j.ibusrev.2006.05.003

Drucker, P. F. (1974). *Management Tasks, Responsibilities and Practices*. Harper & Row.

Drucker, P. F. (1996). The shape of things to come. *Leader to Leader*, *1996*(1), 12–18. doi:10.1002/ltl.40619960306

Dubbelt, L., Demerouti, E., & Rispens, S. (2019). Job crafting and employee well-being: A systematic review of longitudinal studies. *Journal of Occupational Health Psychology*, *24*(4), 498–513.

Dubbelt, L., Demerouti, E., & Rispens, S. (2019). The value of job crafting for work engagement, task performance, and career satisfaction: Longitudinal and quasi-experimental evidence. *European Journal of Work and Organizational Psychology*, *28*(3), 300–314. doi:10.1080/1359432X.2019.1576632

Dunning, J. H. (1980). Toward an Eclectic Theory of International Production: Some Empirical Tests. *Journal of International Business Studies*, *11*(1), 9–31. doi:10.1057/palgrave.jibs.8490593

Dunning, J. H. (1981). *International Production and the Multinational Enterprises*. George Allen and Unwin.

Dunning, J. H. (1988). The Eclectic Paradigm of International Production: A Restatement and Some Possible Extensions. *Journal of International Business Studies*, *19*(1), 1–31. doi:10.1057/palgrave.jibs.8490372

Durall, E., Bauters, M., Hietala, I., Leinonen, T., & Kapros, E. (2020). Co-creation and co-design in technology- enhanced learning: Innovating science learning outside the classroom. *Interaction Design and Architecture(s)*. . doi:10.55612/s-5002-042-010

Durand, R., & Ioannou, I. (2023). *How Leaders Can Create a Purpose-Driven Culture*. Harward Business Review.

Durmuş-Özdemir, E., & Mecikoglu, S. (2016). A Case Study on Performance Implications of Hybrid Strategy in Automotive Supplier Industry. *International Business Research*, *9*(6), 31. doi:10.5539/ibr.v9n6p31

Dyer, J. H., & Singh, H. (1998). The Relational View: Cooperative Strategy and Sources of Interorganisational Competitive Advantage. *Academy of Management Review*, *23*(4), 660–679. doi:10.2307/259056

Dymsza, W. A. (1988). Successes and failures of joint ventures in developing countries: Lessons from experience. In F. J. Contractor & P. Lorange (Eds.), *Cooperative strategies in international business*. Lexington Books.

Earley, P. C., & Ang, S. (2003). *Cultural Intelligence: Individual Interactions Across Cultures*. Stanford University Press. doi:10.1515/9780804766005

EdenL. (2018). The Fourth Industrial Revolution: Seven Lessons from the Past. In R. van Tulder, A. Verbeke & L. Piscitello (Eds.), *International Business in the Information and Digital Age, Progress in International Business Research, 13*. Emerald. https://ssrn.com/abstract=3244096

Edmondson, A. (2019). *The fearless organisation: Creating psychological safety in the workplace for learning, innovation, and growth*. John Wiley and Sons.

Edström, A., & Galbraith, J. R. (1977). Transfer of Managers as a Coordination and Control Strategy in Multinational Organisations. *Administrative Science Quarterly*, *22*(2), 248–263. doi:10.2307/2391959

Egelhoff, W. (1984). Patterns of Control in U.S., UK and European Multinational Corporations. *Journal of International Business Studies*, *15*(2), 73–83. doi:10.1057/palgrave.jibs.8490866

Eisenhardt, K. M. (1989). Building Theories from Case Study Research. *Academy of Management Review, 14*(4), 532–550. doi:10.2307/258557

Eisenhardt, K. M., & Martin, J. A. (2000). Dynamic capabilities: What are they? *Strategic Management Journal, 21*(10/11), 1105–1121. doi:10.1002/1097-0266(200010/11)21:10/11<1105::AID-SMJ133>3.0.CO;2-E

England, G. W. (1978). Managers and their value systems: A five country comparative study. *The Columbia Journal of World Business, 13*(2), 33–44.

Eriksson, K., Johanson, J., Majkgård, A., & Sharma, D.D. (2015). Experiential Knowledge and Cost in the Internationalization Process. In Knowledge, Networks and Power. Palgrave Macmillan. doi:10.1057/9781137508829_2

Etzioni, A. (1968). Social Analysis and Social Action. *The American Behavioral Scientist, 12*(1), 31–33. doi:10.1177/000276426801200107

Etzioni, A. (1968). *The Active Society.* The Free Press.

Evans, P., Doz, Y., & Laurent, A. (1990). *Human Resource Management in International Companies. St.* Martin Press.

Fabris, A., & Garbellano, S. (1991). Modelli di internazionalizzazione delle imprese. *Sviluppo and Organizzazione, 124.*

Farmer, R., & Richman, B. M. (1965). *Comparative Management and Economic Progress.* Irwin.

Forster, N. (2000). *Managing Staff on International Assignments: A Strategic Guide.* Pearson Educational/ Financial Times Publications.

Franko, L. G. (1976). *The European Multinational.* Greylock.

Gabriel, P. (1977). mncs in the Third World: Is Conflict Unavoidable? *Harvard Business Review, 56,* 83–93.

Gaffney, S. (1989). *Cultures, Business and Communications.* Institute of International Business Stockholm School of Economics.

Gagliardi, P. (1986). *Le imprese come cultura.* Isedi.

Galbraith, J.R. (1975). La progettazione organizzativa: un'analisi dal punto di vista del trattamento delle informazioni. *Problemi di gestione,* 9.

Galbraith, J. R. (1897). *Designing Complex Organisation.* Addison Wesley.

Galbraith, J. R., & Kazanjian, R. K. (1986). Organizing to Implement Strategies of Diversity and Globalization: The Role of Matrix Design. *Human Resource Management, 25*(1), 37–54. Advance online publication. doi:10.1002/hrm.3930250104

Galbraith, R. C. (1975). On the independence of attributes of memory. *Journal of Experimental Psychology. Human Learning and Memory, 1*(1), 23–30. doi:10.1037/0278-7393.1.1.23

Gallie, D. (1978). *In Search of the New Working Class: Automation and Social Integration within the Capitalist Enterprise.* Cambridge University Press.

Galvin, P., Tywoniak, S., & Sutherland, J. (2021). Collaboration and opportunism in megaproject alliance contracts: The interplay between governance, trust and culture. *International Journal of Project Management, 39*(4), 394–405. doi:10.1016/j.ijproman.2021.02.007

Gammeltoft, P., & Cuervo-Cazurra, A. (2021). Enriching internationalization process theory: Insights from the study of emerging market multinationals. *Journal of International Management, 27*(3), 100884. Advance online publication. doi:10.1016/j.intman.2021.100884

Garro-Abarca, V., Palos-Sanchez, P., & Aguayo-Camacho, M. (2021). Virtual teams in times of pandemic: Factors that influence performance. *Frontiers in Psychology, 12*, 624637. Advance online publication. doi:10.3389/fpsyg.2021.624637 PMID:33679543

Gauthey, F., Ratiu, I., Rodgers, I., & Xardel, D. (1988). *Leaders sans frontiéres. Le dèfi des difference*. McGraw-Hill.

Gauthey, F., & Xardel, D. (1990). *Le management interculturel. Collection Que Sais-Je?* Presses universitaires de France.

Gehrisch, M. G., & Süß, S. (2023). Organisational behaviour in international strategic alliances and the relation to performance–a literature review and avenues for future research. *Management Review Quarterly, 73*(3), 1045–1107. doi:10.1007/s11301-022-00268-7

Geppert, M., Matten, D., & Williams, K. (2003). Change Management in MNCs: How Global Convergence Intertwines with National Diversities. *Human Relations, 56*(7), 807–838. doi:10.1177/00187267030567003

Geringer, J., & Hebert, L. (1989). Control and Performance of International Joint Ventures. *Journal of International Business Studies, 20*(2), 235–254. doi:10.1057/palgrave.jibs.8490359

Gertsen, M. C. (1990). Intercultural competence and expatriates. *International Journal of Human Resource Management, 1*(3), 341–362. doi:10.1080/09585199000000054

Gibbs, R. W. Jr. (2006). *Embodiment and cognitive science*. Cambridge University Press.

Godiwalla, H. Y. (2018). Global Organisational Innovation Strategy. *International Journal of Social Science Studies, 6*(8), 45–53. doi:10.11114/ijsss.v6i8.3477

Godiwalla, Y. (2018). Strategic Management for Global Companies: A Conceptual Discussion. *International Journal of Social Science Studies, 6*(40), 40. Advance online publication. doi:10.11114/ijsss.v6i11.3695

Goldenberg, S. (1988). *Hands across the Ocean: Managing Joint Ventures with a Spotlight on China and Japan*. Harvard Business School Press.

Golubickis, M., & Macrae, C. N. (2022). Sticky me: Self-relevance slows reinforcement learning. *Cognition, 227*, 105207. Advance online publication. doi:10.1016/j.cognition.2022.105207 PMID:35752015

Gomes-Casseres, B. (1990). Firm Ownership Preferences and Host Government Restrictions: An Integrated Approach. *Journal of International Business Studies, 21*(1), 1–22. doi:10.1057/palgrave.jibs.8490324

Gooderham, P. N., Pedersen, T., Madsen Sandvik, A., Dasí, A., Elter, F., & Hildrum, J. (2022). Contextualizing AMO Explanations of Knowledge Sharing in MNEs: The Role of Organisational and National Culture. *MIR. Management International Review, 62*(6), 859–884. doi:10.1007/s11575-022-00483-0

Goold, M., & Campbell, A. (2003). Making Matrix Structures Work. Creating Clarity on Unit Roles and Responsibility. *European Management Journal, 21*(3), 351–363. doi:10.1016/S0263-2373(03)00048-3

Gorbis, M. & Yorke, K. (1986). Strategic Partnerships: A New Corporate Response. *Business Intelligence Program, 73.*

Gorbis, M., & Yorke, K. (1986). *Strategic Partnership: A New Corporate Response*. SRI International.

Grandori, A. (1984). A prescriptive contingency view of organisational decision-making. *Administrative Science Quarterly, 29*(2), 192–209. doi:10.2307/2393173

Gregersen, H. B., & Stroh, L. K. (2019). *Expatriate Management: New Ideas for International Business*. Routledge.

Gulati, R., Wohlgezogen, F., & Zhelyazkov, P. (2012). The Two Facets of Collaboration: Cooperation and Coordination in Strategic Alliances. *The Academy of Management Annals, 6*(1), 1–53. doi:10.5465/19416520.2012.691646

Gupta, A., & Govindarajah, G. (1990). Knowledge Flows and the Structure of Control Within Multinational Corporations. *Academy of Management Review*, *16*(4), 768–792. doi:10.2307/258980

Guth, W. D., & MacMillan, I. C. (1986). Strategy Implementation Versus Middle Management Self-Interest. *Strategic Management Journal*, *7*(4), 313–327. doi:10.1002/smj.4250070403

GuttermanA. (2023). *Human Resources Management*. doi:10.2139/ssrn.4549619

Hagstrom, P. (1990). New information systems and the changing structure of MNCs. In C. A. Bartlett, Y. Doz, & G. Hedlund (Eds.), *Managing the Global Company* (pp. 164–185). Routledge.

Haire, M., Ghiselli, E. E., & Porter, L. W. (1966). *Managerial Thinking: an International Study*. John Wiley.

Haksar, V., Carrière-Swallow, Y., Giddings, A., Islam, E., Kao, K., Kopp, E., & Quirós-Romero, G. (2021). *Toward a Global Approach to Data in the Digital Age, Staff Discussion Note, SDN/2021/005*. International Monetary Fund.

Hales, C., & Tamangani, Z. (1996). An Investigation of The Relationship Between Organisational Structure, Managerial Role Expectations and Managers' Work Activities. *Journal of Management Studies*, *33*(6), 731–756. doi:10.1111/j.1467-6486.1996.tb00170.x

Hannan, M. H., & Freeman, J. (1977). The Population Ecology of Organisations. *American Journal of Sociology*, *82*(5), 929–964. doi:10.1086/226424

Hanush, M. (2012). *Jobless Growth? Okun's Law in East Asia*. World Bank. doi:10.1596/1813-9450-6156

Harbison, F., & Myers, C. A. (1959). *Management in the Industrial World*. McGraw Hill.

Harrigan, K. R. (1985). *Strategies for joint ventures*. Lexington Books.

Harris, M., & Moran, R. (1979). *Managing Culture Differences*. Gulf.

Harrison, G., McKinnon, J., Wu, A., & Chow, C. (2000). Cultural Influences on Adaptation To Fluid Workgroups And Teams. *Journal of International Business Studies*, *31*(3), 489–505. doi:10.1057/palgrave.jibs.8490918

Harris, P., & Moran, R. (1979). *Managing Cultural! Differences*. Gulf Publishing Company.

Harvey, M. G. (1983). The multinational corporation's expatriate problem: An application of Murphy's law. *Business Horizon*, 71-78.

Harvey, D. (1982). *The Limits to Capital*. Blackwell.

Harvey, D. (1990). Between Space and Time: Reflections on the Geographical Imagination. *Annals of the Association of American Geographers*, *80*(3), 418–434. doi:10.1111/j.1467-8306.1990.tb00305.x

Harvey, M. C. (1982). The Other Side of Foreign Assignments: Dealing with the Repatriation Dilemma. *The Columbia Journal of World Business*, *17*(1), 53–59.

Harvey, M. G. (1985). The executive family: An overlooked variable in international assignments. *The Columbia Journal of World Business*, *20*, 84–92.

Harvey, M. G. (1989). Repatriation of Corporate Executives: An Empirical Study. *Journal of International Business Studies*, *20*(1), 131–144. doi:10.1057/palgrave.jibs.8490355

Hays, R. (1974). Expatriate Selection: Insuring Success and Avoiding Failure. *Journal of International Business Studies*, *5*(1), 25–37. doi:10.1057/palgrave.jibs.8490810

Hays, R. D. (1972). Minimizing behavioural porblmes problems. *Business Horizons*, *15*(3), 87–93. doi:10.1016/S0007-6813(72)80011-9

Hedlund, G. (1986). The Hypermodem MNC - A Heterarchy? *Human Resource Management*, *25*(1), 9–35. doi:10.1002/hrm.3930250103

Hedlund, G., & Rolander, D. (1990). Actions in heterarchies: new approaches to managing the MN. In C. A. Bartlett, Y. Doz, & G. Hedlund (Eds.), *Managing the Global Company*. Routledge.

Hedlund, H. (1984). Organisation In-Between: The Evolution of the Mother-Daughter Structure of Managing Foreign Subsidiaries in Swedish mncs. *Journal of International Business Studies*, *15*(2), 109–123. doi:10.1057/palgrave.jibs.8490485

Heenan, D. A., & Perlmutter, H. W. (1979). *Multinational Organisation Development*. Addison-Wesley.

Heimeriks, K. H., & Duysters, G. (2007). Alliance Capability as a Mediator between Experience and Alliance Performance: An Empirical Investigation into the Alliance Capability Development Process. *Journal of Management Studies*, *44*(1), 25–49. doi:10.1111/j.1467-6486.2006.00639.x

Heldon, D. W., & Hendon, R. A. (1989). *How to Negotiate Worldwide: a Practical Handbook*. Gower.

Heller, F. A. (1988). Cost benefits of multinational research on organisations. *Journal of Anthropological Research*, *51*(3), 247–261.

Heller, J. E. (1980). Criteria for selecting an international manager. *Personnel*, *57*(3), 47–55.

Hennart, F. (1988). A transaction costs theory of equity joint ventures. *Strategic Management Journal*, *9*(4), 361–374. doi:10.1002/smj.4250090406

Hickson, D. J., McMillan, C. J., Azumi, K., & Horvath, D. (1979). Grounds for comparative organisation theory: quicksand or hard core? In C. J. Lammers & D. J. Hickson (Eds.), *Organisations Alike and Unlike: International and Inter-Institutional Studies in the Sociology of Organisation* (pp. 25–41). Routledge & Kegan Paul.

Hickson, D., Hinings, C., Mcmillan, C., & Schwitter, J. (1974). The Culture-Free Context of Organisation Structure: A Tri-National Comparison. *Sociology*, *8*(1), 59–80. doi:10.1177/003803857400800104

Hidalgo, C. A., Hausmann, R., & Dasgupta, P. S. (2009). The Building Blocks of Economic Complexity. *Proceedings of the National Academy of Sciences of the United States of America*, *106*(26), 10570–10575. doi:10.1073/pnas.0900943106 PMID:19549871

Hitt, M., Ireland, R., & Hoskisson, R. (2013). *Strategic Management: Competitiveness and Globalization* (10th ed.). Cengage Southwestern Publishing Co.

Hodson, E., Svanda, A., & Dadashi, N. (2023). Whom do we include and when? participatory design with vulnerable groups. *CoDesign*, *19*(4), 269–286. doi:10.1080/15710882.2022.2160464

Hofstede, G. (1980). Culture' S Consequences: National Differences. In *Thinking and Organizing*. Sage.

Hofstede, G. (1980). *Culture's Consequences: International Differences in Work Related Values*. Sage.London.

Hofstede, G. (1980). *Culture's consequences: International differences in work-related values*. Sage.

Hofstede, G. (1980). Motivation, Leadership, and Organisations: Do American Theories Apply Abroad? *Organizational Dynamics*, *9*(1), 42–63. doi:10.1016/0090-2616(80)90013-3

Hofstede, G. (1985). The Interaction between National and Organisational Value Systems. *Journal of Management Studies*, *22*(4), 347–357. doi:10.1111/j.1467-6486.1985.tb00001.x

Hofstede, G. (2001). *Culture's Consequences: Comparing Values, Behaviors, Institutions, and Organisations across Nations*. Sage.

Hofstede, G. (2001). *Culture's Consequences: Comparing Values, Behaviours, Institutions, and Organisations Across Nations* (2nd ed.). Sage., doi:10.1016/S0005-7967(02)00184-5

Hofstede, G. (2002). Dimensions Do Not Exist: A Reply to Brendan McSweeney. *Journal of Technological Advancements, 55*(11), 1355–1361. doi:10.1177/0018726702055011921

Hofstede, G., & Bollinger, D. (1989). *Inter Nazionalità*. Guerini e Associati.

Hofstede, G., & Hofstede, G. J. (2005). *Culture and Organisations. Software of the Mind*. McGrawHill.

Hofstede, G., & Hofstede, G. J. (2005). *Culture and Organisations. Software of the Mind: Intercultural Cooperation and its Importance for Survival* (2nd ed.). McGraw Hill.

Hoskisson, R. E., Eden, L., Lau, C. M., & Wright, M. (2000). Strategy in emerging economies. *Academy of Management Journal, 43*(3), 249–267. doi:10.2307/1556394

House, R. J., Hanges, P. J., Javidan, M., Dorfman, P. W., & Gupta, V. (2004). *Culture, Leadership and Organisations. The GLOBE Study of 62 Societies*. Sage.

Hsu, Y. (2012). The impact of expatriate support on expatriate adjustment and performance: A study of Taiwanese expatriates in China. *International Journal of Human Resource Management, 23*(2), 333–349.

Hsu, Y. S. (2012). *Knowledge transfer between expatriates and host country nationals: a social capital perspective. UWM. Digital Commons*. University of Wisconsin. doi:10.1037/e518332013-315

Huang, H., Gao, L., Deng, X., & Fu, H. (2022). The Relationship Between Emotional Intelligence and Expatriate Performance in International Construction Projects. *Psychology Research and Behavior Management, 22*(15), 3825–3843. doi:10.2147/PRBM.S387287 PMID:36578282

Hughes, E. C. (1958). *Men and Their Work*. Free Press.

Hutzschenreuter, T., Matt, T., & Kleindienst, I. (2020). Going subnational: A literature review and research agenda. *Journal of World Business, 55*. DOI:. . doi:101076

Hymer, S. (1970). The Efficiency (Contradictions) of Multinational Corporations. *The American Economic Review, 60*(2), 441–448.

Iansiti, M., & Lakhani, K. R. (2020). *Competing in the Age of AI: Strategy and Leadership When Algorithms and Networks Run the World*. Harvard Business Review Press.

Ilie, O. (2019). The Intercultural Competence. Developing Effective Intercultural Communication Skills. *Knowledge-Based Organisation, 25*(2) 264-268. 10.2478/kbo-2019-0092

Imandin, L., Bisschoff, C., & Botha, C. (2014). A model to measure employee engagement. *Problems and Perspectives in Management, 12*, 520–532.

Inzerilli, G., & Laurent, A. (1983). Managerial Views of Organisation Structure in France and the USA. *International Studies of Management & Organization, 13*(1/2), 97–118. doi:10.1080/00208825.1983.11656360

Ismail, M., Sobri, S. S., Zulkifly, N. A., Hamzah, S. R., & Yamato, E. (2016). Knowledge transfer between expatriates and host country nationals: Contribution of individual and social capital factors. *Organizations and Markets in Emerging Economies, 7*(2), 65–87. doi:10.15388/omee.2016.7.2.14208

Jacoby, N. H. (1984). The multinational corporation. In P. D. Grub, F. Ghadar, & D. Khambata (Eds.), *The multinational corporation in transition*. Darwin Press.

Jacques, E. (1970). *Work, Creativity and Social Justice*. Heinemann Educational Books.

Javaid, M., Haleem, A., Pratap Singh, R., Suman, R., & Santibañez Gonzalez, E. (2022). Understanding the adoption of Industry 4.0 technologies in improving environmental sustainability. *Sustainable Operations and Computers*, *3*, 203–217. doi:10.1016/j.susoc.2022.01.008

JerabD. A.MabroukT. (2023). *The Role of Leadership in Changing Organisational Culture*. doi:10.2139/ssrn.4574324

Jessop, B. (2005). Critical Realism and the Strategic-Relational Approach. *New Formations*, *2005*(56). https://api.semanticscholar.org/CorpusID:142627525

JETRO. (1989). *A Survey on successful cases of Foreign-affiliated Companies in Japan*. Japan External Trade Organisation.

Jones, G. R. (1983). Psychological Orientation and the Process of Organisational Socialization: An Interactionist Perspective. *Academy of Management Review*, *8*(3), 464–474. doi:10.2307/257835

Jones, G. R. (1986). Socialization Tactics, Self-efficacy, and Newcomers Adjustment to Organisations. *Academy of Management Journal*, *29*(2), 262–279. doi:10.2307/256188

Jones, R. A., Jimmieson, N. L., & Griffiths, A. (2005). The impact of organisational culture and reshaping capabilities on change implementation success: The mediating role of readiness for change. *Journal of Management Studies*, *42*(2), 361–386. doi:10.1111/j.1467-6486.2005.00500.x

Jong, J., & Faerman, S. R. (2021). Centralization and Decentralization: Balancing Organisational and Employee Expectations. In A. Farazmand (Eds), Global Encyclopedia of Public Administration, Public Policy, and Governance. Springer. doi:10.1007/978-3-319-31816-5_4179-1

Kale, P., & Singh, H. (2009). Managing Strategic Alliances: What Do We Know Now, and Where Do We Go from Here? *The Academy of Management Perspectives*, *23*(3), 45–62. doi:10.5465/amp.2009.43479263

Kamalaldin, A., Linde, L., Sjödin, D., & Parida, V. (2020). Transforming provider-customer relationships in digital servitization: A relational view on digitalisation. *Industrial Marketing Management*, *89*, 306–325. doi:10.1016/j.indmarman.2020.02.004

Kano, L., Tsang, E. W. K., & Yeung, H. W. (2020). Global value chains: A review of the multi-disciplinary literature. *Journal of International Business Studies*, *51*(4), 577–622. doi:10.1057/s41267-020-00304-2

Kenworthy, T. (2008). Multidivisional vs Metanational Governance of The Multinational Enterprise. *Journal of International Business Studies*, *39*(6), 940–956. doi:10.1057/palgrave.jibs.8400344

Kerr, C., Dunlop, J., Harbison, P., & Myers, G. (1960). *Industrialism and Industrial Man*. Harvard University Press.

Kierner, A. (2015). Dual-income and dual-career couples in international context. In L. Mäkelä & V. Suutari (Eds.), Work and family interface in the international career context (pp. 95–116). Springer International Publishing/Springer Nature. doi:10.1007/978-3-319-17647-5_6

Kijek, A., & Kijek, T. (2019). Knowledge Spillovers: An Evidence from The European Regions. *Journal of Open Innovation*, *5*(3), 68. doi:10.3390/joitmc5030068

Killing, J. P. (1983). *Strategies for joint venture success*. Praeger.

Killing, J. P. (1988). Understanding Alliances: The Role of Task and Organisational Complexity. In F. J. Contractor & R. Lorange (Eds.), *Cooperative Strategies in International Business. Lexington* (pp. 55–68). Lexington Books.

Kindleberg, C. (1969). *American Business Abroad, Six Lectures on Direct Investments*. Yale University Press.

Kluckhohn, F. R., & Strodtbeck, F. L. (1961). *Variations in value orientations*. Row, Peterson.

Knotts, R. (1989). Cross-cultural management: transformations and adaptations. *Business Horizons, 32*(1), 29+. link.gale.com/apps/doc/A7393085/AONE?u=googlescholar&sid=bookmark-AONE&xid=6f37bdd2

Kobrin, S. (1988). Expatriate Reduction and Strategic Control in American Multinational Corporations. *Human Resource Management, 27*(1), 63–75. doi:10.1002/hrm.3930270104

Kogut, B. (1990). International Sequential Advantages and Network Flexibility. In: *Managing the Global Company*. In C. Bartlett, Y. Doz, & G. Hedlund (Eds.), *Managing the Global Company* (pp. 47–68). Routledge.

Kogut, B. (1990). International Sequential Advantages and Network Flexibility. In: *Managing the Global Firm*. In C. Bartlett, Y. Doz, & G. Hedlund (Eds.), *Managing the Global Firm* (pp. 47–68). Routledge.

Kohtamäki, M., Rabetino, R., & Huikkola, T. (2023). Learning in strategic alliances: Reviewing the literature streams and crafting the agenda for future research. *Industrial Marketing Management, 110*, 68–84. doi:10.1016/j.indmarman.2023.02.011

Korman, A. K., Berman, U. W., & Lang, D. (1981). Career success and personal failure: Alienation in professionals and managers. *The Academy of Management Journal*, 342-360. . doi:10.5465/255846

Kostova, T., & Zaheer, S. (1999). Organisational Legitimacy under Conditions of Complexity: The Case of the Multinational Enterprise. *Academy of Management Review, 24*(1), 64–81. doi:10.2307/259037

Kroeber, A. L., & Kluckhohn, C. (1952). *Culture. A Critical Review of Concepts and Definitions*. Peabody Museum Press.

Kroeber, A. L., & Parsons, T. (1858). The Concepts of Culture and of Social System. *American Sociological Review, 23*, 582–583.

Kumar, V., & Mukherjee, S. (2018). Holacracy – the future of organizing? The case of Zappos. *Human Resource Management International Digest, 26*(7), 12–15. Advance online publication. doi:10.1108/HRMID-08-2018-0161

Lachman, M. E., Lewkowicz, C., Marcus, A., & Peng, Y. (1994). Images of midlife development among young, middle-aged, and older adults. *Journal of Adult Development, 1*(4), 201–211. doi:10.1007/BF02277581

Lamiell, J. T. (1998). Nomothetic and idiographic: Contrasting Windelband's understanding with contemporary usage. *Theory & Psychology, 8*(1), 23–38. doi:10.1177/0959354398081002

Lammers, C. J., & Hickson, D. J. (1979). *Organisations Alike and Unlike*. Routledge and Kegan.

Laurent, A. (1978). *Ma*trix Organisations and Latin Cultures. *Working paper 78*(28). The European Institute for Advanced Studies in Management.

Laurent, A. (1983). The Cultural Diversity of Western Conceptions of Management. *International Studies of Management & Organization, 13*(1-2), 75–96. doi:10.1080/00208825.1983.11656359

Laurent, A. (1986). The Cross-Cultural Puzzle of International Human Resource Management. *Human Resource Management, 25*(1), 91–101. doi:10.1002/hrm.3930250107

Lawler, E., & Hall, D. (1970). Relationships of job characteristics to job involvement, satisfaction and intrinsic motivation. *The Journal of Applied Psychology, 54*(4), 305–312. doi:10.1037/h0029692

Lawrence, P. R., & Lorsch, J. W. (1967). Differentiation and Integration in Complex Organisations. *Administrative Science Quarterly*, *12*(1), 1–47. doi:10.2307/2391211

Lawrence, P. R., & Lorsch, J. W. (1967). *Organisation and Environment, Managing Differentiation and Integration.* Harvard Business School.

Leach, M., MacGregor, H., Scoones, I., & Wilkinson, A. (2021). Post-pandemic transformations: How and why COVID-19 requires us to rethink development. *World Development*, *138*, 105233. doi:10.1016/j.worlddev.2020.105233 PMID:33100478

Lehmann-Ortega, L., & Schoettl, J. M. (2005). From buzzword to managerial tool: The role of business model in strategic innovation. CLADEA, Santiago de Chile.

Leoni, R. (2013). Organisation of Work Practices and Productivity. In A. Grandori (Ed.), *Handbook of Economic Organisation.* Edward Elgar.

Liang, F., & Cao, L. (2021). Linking Employee Resilience with Organisational Resilience: The Roles of Coping Mechanism and Managerial Resilience. *Psychology Research and Behavior Management*, *14*, 1063–1075. doi:10.2147/PRBM.S318632 PMID:34321935

Link, A. N. (2021). *Collaborative R&D and the National Research Joint Venture Database: A Statistical Analysis.* Emerald Publishing Limited., doi:10.1108/9781839095740

Lioukas, C. S., & Reuer, J. J. (2015). Isolating trust outcomes from exchange relationships: Social exchange and learning benefits of prior ties in alliances. *Academy of Management Journal*, *58*(6), 1826–1847. doi:10.5465/amj.2011.0934

Li, R., Fu, L., & Liu, Z. (2020). Does openness to innovation matter? The moderating role of open innovation between Organisational Ambidexterity and Innovation Performance. *Asian Journal of Technology Innovation*, *28*(2), 251–271. doi:10.1080/19761597.2020.1734037

Lorange, P. (1976). A Framework for Strategic Planning in Multinational Corporations. *Long Range Planning*, *9*(3), 30–37. doi:10.1016/S0024-6301(76)80005-2

Lord, R., & Maher, K. J. (1991). *Leadership and Information Processing: Linking Perceptions and Performance.* Unwin-Everyman.

Louis, M. R. (1980). Surprise and Sense Making: What Newcomers Experiences in Entering Unfamiliar Organisational Settings. *Administrative Science Quarterly*, *25*(2), 226–251. doi:10.2307/2392453 PMID:10247029

Lumineau, F. (2017). How Contracts Influence Trust and Distrust. *Journal of Management*, *43*(5), 1553–1577. doi:10.1177/0149206314556656

Luo, Y. (2022). New connectivity in the fragmented world. *Journal of International Business Studies*, *53*(5), 962–980. doi:10.1057/s41267-022-00530-w PMID:35634198

Luo, Y., & Peng, M. W. (1999). Learning to Compete in a Transition Economy: Experience, Environment, and Performance. *Journal of International Business Studies*, *30*(2), 269–295. https://www.jstor.org/stable/155313. doi:10.1057/palgrave.jibs.8490070

Luo, Y., & Shenkar, O. (2006). The multinational corporation as a multilingual community: Language and organisation in a global context. *Journal of International Business Studies*, *37*(3), 321–339. doi:10.1057/palgrave.jibs.8400197

Luo, Y., & Tung, R. L. (2007). International expansion of emerging market enterprises: A springboard perspective. *Journal of International Business Studies*, *38*(4), 481–498. doi:10.1057/palgrave.jibs.8400275

Luo, Y., & Tung, R. L. (2018). A general theory of springboard MNEs. *Journal of International Business Studies*, *49*(2), 129–152. doi:10.1057/s41267-017-0114-8

Luu, D. T. (2023). Internationalisation, knowledge intensity, adaptive culture and absorptive capacity: A strategic entrepreneurship enabling logic for export companies. *Journal of Small Business and Enterprise Development*, *30*(2), 390–418. doi:10.1108/JSBED-06-2022-0288

Lyles, M. (1987). Learning among joint venture-sophisticate firms. In F. J. Contractor & P. Lorange (Eds.), *Cooperative strategies in international business* (pp. 301–316). Lexington Books.

Lyu, B., Liao, X., & Yang, Y. (2022). Relationships between temporal leadership, transactive memory systems and Team Innovation Performance. *Psychology Research and Behavior Management*, *51*, 2543–2559. doi:10.2147/PRBM.S380989 PMID:36124335

MacIntyre, P. D., & Gardner, R. C. (1989). Anxiety and Second Language Learning: Toward a Theoretical Clarification. *Language Learning*, *39*(2), 251–275. doi:10.1111/j.1467-1770.1989.tb00423.x

Manev, I. M., & Stevenson, W. B. (2001). Balancing Ties: Boundary Spanning and Influence in the Organisation's Extended Network of Communication. *The Journal of Business Communication*, *38*(2), 183-205. . doi:10.1177/002194360103800203

Manev, I., & Stevenson, W. (2001). Nationality, Cultural Distance, and Expatriate Status: Effects on the Managerial Network in a Multinational Enterprise. *Journal of International Business Studies*, *32*(2), 285–303. doi:10.1057/palgrave.jibs.8490953

Manzi, C., Coen, S., Regalia, C., Yévenes, A. M., Giuliani, C., & Vignoles, V. L. (2018). Being in the Social: A cross-cultural and cross-generational study on identity processes related to Facebook use. *Computers in Human Behavior*, *80*, 81–87. doi:10.1016/j.chb.2017.10.046

March, J. C. (1978). Bounded Rationality, Ambiguity and the Engineering of Choice. *The Bell Journal of Economics*, *9*(2), 587–608. doi:10.2307/3003600

March, J. G., & Olsen, J. P. (1984). The New Institutionalism: Organisational Factors in Political Life. *The American Political Science Review*, *78*(3), 734–749. doi:10.2307/1961840

March, J. G., & Simon, H. A. (1966). *Teoria dell'organizzazione*. Edizioni di Comunità.

Mariani, L., Trivellato, B., Martini, M., & Marafioti, E. (2022). Achieving Sustainable Development Goals Through Collaborative Innovation: Evidence from Four European Initiatives. *Journal of Business Ethics*, *180*(4), 1075–1095. doi:10.1007/s10551-022-05193-z PMID:35855697

Martínez-Peláez, R., Ochoa-Brust, A., Rivera, S., Félix, V. G., Ostos, R., Brito, H., Félix, R. A., & Mena, L. J. (2023). Role of Digital Transformation for Achieving Sustainability: Mediated Role of Stakeholders, Key Capabilities, and Technology. *Sustainability (Basel)*, *15*(14), 11221. doi:10.3390/su151411221

Masini, C. (1970). *Lavoro e risparmio*. Utet.

Maurice, M., Sorge, A., & Warner, M. (1980). Societal Differences in Organizing Manufacturing Units: A Comparison of France, West Germany, and Great Britain. *International Studies of Management & Organization*, *10*(4), 74–100. doi:10.1080/00208825.1980.11656303

Maurice, M., Sorge, A., & Warner, M. (1980). Societal Differences in Organizing Manufacturing Units: A Comparison of France, West Germany, and Great Britain. *Organization Studies*, *1*(1), 59–86. Advance online publication. doi:10.1177/017084068000100105

Maznevski, M. L., & Chudoba, K. M. (2000). Bridging space over time: Global virtual team dynamics and effectiveness. *Organization Science*, *11*(5), 473–492. doi:10.1287/orsc.11.5.473.15200

Mazzarol, T., Clark, D., Reboud, S., & Limnios, E. (2018). Developing a conceptual framework for the co-operative and mutual enterprise business model. *Journal of Management & Organization*, *24*(4), 1–31. doi:10.1017/jmo.2018.29

McCall, J. B., & Warrington, M. B. (1988). *Marketing by Agreement. A Cross-Cultural Approach to Business Negotiations*. John Wiley & Sons.

McGregor, D. (1960). *The Human Side of Enterprise*. McGraw-Hill Book Co.

Mead, R. (1990). *Cross-Cultural Management Communication*. John Wiley & Sons.

Mendenhall, M., & Oddou, G. (1986). Acculturation Profiles of Expatriate Managers: Implications for Cross-Cultural Training Programs. *Columbia Journal off World Business, 21*(4), 73-79.

Mendenhall, M. E., & Oddou, G. R. (2016). *Readings and Cases in International Human Resource Management*. Routledge.

Mendenhall, M., Dunbar, E., & Oddou, G. (1987). Expatriate Selection, Training and Career-Pathing: A Review and Critique. *Human Resource Management*, *26*(3), 331–345. doi:10.1002/hrm.3930260303

Mendenhall, M., & Oddou, G. (1985). The Dimensions of Expatriate Acculturation: A Review. *Academy of Management Review*, *10*(1), 39–47. doi:10.5465/amr.1985.4277340

Meyer, K. E., & Grosse, R. (2019). Introduction to Managing in Emerging Markets. In Oxford Handbook of Management in Emerging Markets. Oxford University Press.

Meyer, K. E. (2018). Catch-Up and Leapfrogging: Emerging Economy Multinational Enterprises on the Global Stage. *International Journal of the Economics of Business*, *25*(1), 19–30. doi:10.1080/13571516.2017.1374624

Mikhaylov, F., Kolesnikova, J., & Eldar, S. (2014). Current Tendencies of the Development of Service of Human Resources Management. *Procedia: Social and Behavioral Sciences*, *150*, 330–335. doi:10.1016/j.sbspro.2014.09.072

Milgrom, P., & Roberts, J. (1992). *Economics, Organisation & Management*. Prentice Hall.

Miller, E. L. (1972). The Selection Decision for an International Assignment: A Study of the Decision Maker's Behaviour. *Journal of International Business Studies*, *3*(2), 49–65. doi:10.1057/palgrave.jibs.8490746

Miller, E. L. (1973). The International Selection Decision: A Study of Some Dimensions of Managerial Behavior in the Selection Decision Process. *Academy of Management Journal*, *16*(2), 239–252. doi:10.2307/255325

Miller, E. L. (1984). Comparative management conceptualization: An assessment. In R. Farmer (Ed.), *Advances in international comparative management, 1* (pp. 69–82). JAI Press.

Miller, E. L., & Cheng, J. L. C. (1978). A Closer Look at the Decision to Accept an Overseas Position. *Management International Review*, *18*(3), 25–33.

Miller, G. A. (1987). Meta-Analysis and the Culture-Free Hypothesis. *Organization Studies*, *8*(4), 309–326. Advance online publication. doi:10.1177/017084068700800402

Minkler, M., & Biller, R. (1979). Role Shock: A Tool for Conceptualizing Stresses Accompanying Disruptive Role Transitions. *Human Relations*, *32*(2), 125–140. Advance online publication. doi:10.1177/001872677903200203

Mintzberg, H., McCarthy, D. J., & Markides, C. (2000). View from the Top: Henry Mintzberg on Strategy and Management [and Commentary]. *The Academy of Management Executive, 14*(3), 31–42. https://www.jstor.org/stable/4165656

Mintzberg, H. (1980). *The Nature of Managerial Work*. Prentice Hall.

Mintzberg, H. (1983). *Structuring in Fives: Designing Effective Organisations*. Prentice Hall.

Mintzberg, H. (1985). The organisation as political arena. *Journal of Management Studies*, *22*(2), 133–154. doi:10.1111/j.1467-6486.1985.tb00069.x

Mitsuhashi, H., & Greve, H. (2008). A Matching Theory of Alliance Formation and Organisational Success: Complementarity and Compatibility. *Academy of Management Journal*, *52*(5), 975–995. Advance online publication. doi:10.5465/amj.2009.44634482

Monaghan, S., Tippmann, E., & Coviello, N. (2020). Born digitals: Thoughts on their internationalization and a research agenda. *Journal of International Business Studies*, *51*(1), 11–22. doi:10.1057/s41267-019-00290-0

Naeem, A., Nadeem, A. B., & Khan, I. (2015). Culture Shock and Its effects on Expatriates. *Global Advanced Research Journal of Management and Business Studies*, *4*, 2315–5086.

Nambisan, S., Shaker, Z., & Luo, Y. (2019). Global platforms and ecosystems: Implications for international business theories. *Journal of International Business Studies*, *50*(9), 1464–1486. Advance online publication. doi:10.1057/s41267-019-00262-4

Narula, R., Verbeke, A., & Yuan, W. (2021). The theory of international business strategy. In K. Mellahi, K. Meyer, R. Narula, I. Surdu, & A. Verbeke (Eds.), The Oxford Handbook of International Business Strategy (pp. 11-36). Oxford University Press. doi:10.1093/oxfordhb/9780198868378.013.1

Negandhi, A. R. (1982). *Functioning of the mnc; a Global Comparative Study*. Pergamon Press.

Nelson, R., & Winter, S. (1982). *An Evolutionary Theory of Economic Change*. Beiknap Press.

Nery-Kjerfve, T., & McLean, G. N. (2012). Repatriation of expatriate employees, knowledge transfer, and organisationa learning: What do we know? *European Journal of Training and Development*, *36*(6), 614–629. doi:10.1108/03090591211245512

Nicholson, N. (1984). A theory of work role transitions. *Administrative Science Quarterly*, *29*(2), 172–191. doi:10.2307/2393172

Nicolini, D., Pyrko, I., Omidvar, O., & Spanellis, A. (2022). Understanding Communities of Practice: Taking Stock and Moving Forward. *The Academy of Management Annals*. Advance online publication. 16

Noer, D. M. (1975). *MNC People Management; A Guide far Organisation and Employees*. Bureau of National Affairs.

Nonaka, I., & Takeuchi, H. (1995). *The Knowledge creating company*. Oxford University Press. doi:10.1093/oso/9780195092691.001.0001

North, D. C. (1990). *Institutions, Institutional Change and Economic Performance*. Cambridge University Press. doi:10.1017/CBO9780511808678

Nusir, M., Tariq, U., & Ahanger, T. (2021). Engaging Diverse Stakeholders in Interdisciplinary Co-Design Project for Better Service Design. *Journal of Cases on Information Technology*, *23*(4), 1–29. doi:10.4018/JCIT.296253

O'Brien, M., Hanton, S., & Mellalieu, S. D. (2005). Intensity and direction of competitive anxiety as a function of goal attainment expectation and competition goal generation. *Journal of Science and Medicine in Sport*, *8*(4), 423–432. doi:10.1016/S1440-2440(05)80057-X PMID:16602170

Öberg, C., & Lundberg, H. (2022). Mechanisms of knowledge development in a knowledge ecosystem. *Journal of Knowledge Management*, *26*(11), 293–307. doi:10.1108/JKM-11-2021-0814

Obholzer, A., & Roberts, V. Z. (Eds.). (2019). The unconscious at work: A Tavistock approach to making sense of organisational life (2nd ed.). Routledge/Taylor & Francis Group. doi:10.4324/9781351104166

Oddou, G., Osland, J. S., & Blakeney, R. N. (2009). Repatriating Knowledge: Variables Influencing the "Transfer" Process. *Journal of International Business Studies*, *40*(2), 181–199. doi:10.1057/palgrave.jibs.8400402

Ohmae, K. (1985). *Triad power: The coming shape of global competition*. Free Press.

Ohmae, K. (1986). Becoming a Triad Power: The New Global Corporation. *International Marketing Review*, *3*(3), 7–20. doi:10.1108/eb008307

Ostrom, A. L., Parasuraman, A., Bowen, D. E., Patrício, L., Voss, C. A., & Lemon, K. N. (2021). Service research priorities in a rapidly changing world. *Journal of Service Research*, *24*(2), 129–145. doi:10.1177/1094670515576315

Ouchi, W. G. (1981). *Theory Z: How American Business Can Meet the Japanese Challenge*. Addison Wesley. 10.1016/0007-6813(81)90031-8

Ouchi, W. G., & Wilkins, A. L. (1985). Organisational culture. *Annual Review of Sociology*, *11*(1), 457–483. doi:10.1146/annurev.so.11.080185.002325

Ouchi, W., & Boulton, M. N. (1988). The logic of joint research and development. *California Management Review*, *30*(3), 9–33. doi:10.2307/41166512

Øyna, S., & Alon, I. (2018). A Review of Born globals. *International Studies of Management & Organization*, *48*(2), 157–180. doi:10.1080/00208825.2018.1443737

Oyserman, D., Coon, H. M., & Kemmelmeier, M. (2002). Rethinking individualism and collectivism: Evaluation of theoretical assumptions and meta-analyses. *Psychological Bulletin*, *128*(1), 3–72. doi:10.1037/0033-2909.128.1.3 PMID:11843547

Pan, Y., Verbeke, A., & Wenlong, Y. (2021). CEO Transformational Leadership and Corporate Entrepreneurship in China. *Management and Organization Review*, *17*(1), 1–32. doi:10.1017/mor.2020.59

Parmigiani, A., & Howard-Grenville, J. (2011). Routines revisited: Exploring the capabilities and practice perspectives. *The Academy of Management Annals*, *5*(1), 413–453. doi:10.5465/19416520.2011.589143

Parsons, T. (1937). *The Structure of Social Action*. The Free Press.

Pascale, R. T., & Athos, A. G. (1981). *The Art of Japanese Management: Applications for American Executives*. Wamer Books. doi:10.1016/0007-6813(81)90032-X

Pauwels, C., Clarysse, B., Wright, M., & Van Hove, J. (2016). Understanding a new generation incubation model: The accelerator. *Technovation*, *50–51*, 13–24. doi:10.1016/j.technovation.2015.09.003

Pazy, A., & Zeira, Y. (1983). Training Parent-Country Professions in Host-Country Organisations. *Academy of Management Review*, *8*(2), 262. Advance online publication. doi:10.2307/257754

Pearce, J. (1981). Bringing Some Clarity to Role Ambiguity Research. *Academy of Management Review*, *6*(4), 665. Advance online publication. doi:10.2307/257646

Pennington, M. W. (2002). The coming metanational era. *Strategy and Leadership*, *30*(4). Advance online publication. doi:10.1108/sl.2002.26130dae.003

Pentland, B. T., & Feldman, M. S. (2008). 13 issues in empirical field studies of organisational routines. In M. Becker (Ed.), *Handbook of organisational routines* (pp. 281–300). Edward Elgar. doi:10.4337/9781848442702.00021

Perlmutter, F. (1969). A Theoretical Model of Social Agency Development. *Social Casework, 50*(8), 467–473. doi:10.1177/104438946905000804

Perlmutter, H. V. (1972). The Multinational Firm and the Future. *The Annals of the American Academy of Political and Social Science, 404*(1), 139–152. Advance online publication. doi:10.1177/000271627240300113

Perlmutter, H. V., & Heenan, D. (1974). How Multinational Should Your Top Managers Be? *Harvard Business Review, 52*(6), 121–132.

Perrone, V. (1990). *Le strutture organizzative d'impresa. Criteri e modelli di progettazione*. Egea.

Perrow, C. (1967). A Framework for the Comparative Analysis of Organisations. *American Sociological Review, 32*(2), 194–208. doi:10.2307/2091811

Perrow, C. (1970). *Organisational Analysis*. Tavistock.

Perrow, C. (1976). [Review of *Organisations and Beyond: Selected Essays of James D. Thompson*, by J. D. Thompson, W. A. Rushing, & M. N. Zald. *Administrative Science Quarterly, 21*(4), 718–721. doi:10.2307/2391729

Peterson, R. B., & Shimada, J. Y. (1978). Sources of Management Problems in Japanese/American Joint Ventures. *Academy of Management Review, 3*(4), 796–804. doi:10.2307/257934

Pettigrew, A. M. (1979). On Studying Organisational Cultures. *Administrative Science Quarterly, 24*(4), 570–581. doi:10.2307/2392363

Pettigrew, T. F. (1986). The intergroup contact hypothesis reconsidered. In M. Hewstone & R. Brown (Eds.), *Contact and conflict in intergroup encounters* (pp. 169–195). Basil Blackwell.

Pfeffer, J., & Salancik, G. (1978). *The External Control of Organisations: A Resource Dependence Perspective*. Harper & Row.

Pike, K. L. (1954). Language in relation to a unified theory of the structure of human behaviour. Part I. The Summer Institute of Linguistics. doi:10.1515/9783111657158

Pike, K. L. (1982). *Linguistic concepts: an introduction to tagmemics*. University of Nebraska Press.

Pike, K. L. (1988). Cultural relativism in relation to constraints on world view — An emic perspective. *Bulletin of the Institute of History and Philology, 59*, 385–399.

Pike, K. L. (1990). Pike's Reply to Harris. In T. N. Headland, K. L. Pike, & M. Harris (Eds.), *Emics and etics: The insider/outsider debate* (pp. 62–74). Sage.

Pike, K. L. (1998). A linguistic pilgrimage. In E. F. K. Koerner (Ed.), *First person singular III: Autobiographies by North American scholars in the language sciences* (pp. 145–158). John Benjamins. doi:10.1075/sihols.88.09pik

Pinder, C. (1989). The Dark Side of Executive Relocation. *Organizational Dynamics, 17*(4), 48–58. doi:10.1016/S0090-2616(89)80026-9

Pinder, C. C., & Schroeder, K. G. (1987). Time to Proficiency following Job Transfers. *Academy of Management Journal, 30*(2), 336–353. doi:10.2307/256278

Plekhanov, D., Franke, H., & Netland, T. H. (2022). Digital transformation: A review and research agenda. *European Management Journal*. Advance online publication. doi:10.1016/j.emj.2022.09.007

Polanyi, K. (1959). Anthropology and economic theory. In Readings in anthropology II. Morton H. Fried.

Popper, K. R. (1972). *Objective knowledge: an evolutionary approach.* Oxford University Press.

Porter, M. E. (1990). The Competitive Advantage of Nations. Macmillan. doi:10.1007/978-1-349-11336-1

Porter, M. E., Takeuchi, H., & Sakakibara, M. (2000). Can Japan Compete? Basic Books.

Porter, M. E. (1987). *Competition in Global Industries.* Harvard Business School Press.

Prabhu, J., & Jain, S. (2015). Innovation and entrepreneurship in India: Understanding Jugaad. *Asia Pacific Journal of Management, 32*(4), 843–868. doi:10.1007/s10490-015-9445-9

Prahalad, C. K., & Doz, Y. (1981). Headquarter's Influence and Strategic Control in Multinational Corporation. *Sloan Management Review, 23*(1), 15–29. http://search.epnet.com/login.aspx?direct=trueanddb=buhandan=4014035

Prahalad, C. K., & Doz, Y. (1987). *The Multinational Mission.* The Free Press.

Prahalad, C. K., & Ramaswamy, V. (2004). Co-Creation Experiences: The Next Practice in Value Creation. *Journal of Interactive Marketing, 18*(3), 5–14. doi:10.1002/dir.20015

Prandstraller, F., & Quacquarelli, B. (2011). *Risorse umane internazionali. Cultura, competenze, strategia.* Apogeo Education.

Primeaux, P. (1992). Experiential Ethics: A Blueprint for Personal and Corporate Ethics. *Journal of Business Ethics, 11*(10), 779–788. doi:10.1007/BF00872310

Priyono, A., & Hidayat, A. (2024). Fostering innovation through learning from digital business ecosystem: A dynamic capability perspective. *Journal of Open Innovation, 10*(1), 100196. Advance online publication. doi:10.1016/j.joitmc.2023.100196

Pucik, V. (1983). Management practices in Japan and their impact on business strategy. In R. B. Lamb (Ed.), *Advances in strategic management* (pp. 103–131). JAI Press Greenwich.

Pucik, V., & Katz, J. H. (1986). Information, control human resource management in multinational firms. *Human Resource Management, 25*(1), 121–132. doi:10.1002/hrm.3930250109

Pugh, D. S., & Hickson, J. D. (1976). *Organisational structure in its context: The Aston programme I.* Westmead.

Pushpananthan, G., & Elmquist, M. (2022). Joining forces to create value: The emergence of an innovation ecosystem. *Technovation, 115*, 102453. Advance online publication. doi:10.1016/j.technovation.2021.102453

Quintanilla, L., Giménez-Dasí, M., Sarmento-Henrique, R., & Lucas-Molina, B. (2021). Longitudinal evidence for an emotion-action lag on desire: The role of emotional understanding. *Cognitive Development, 59*(101096), 101096. Advance online publication. doi:10.1016/j.cogdev.2021.101096

Ralston, D., Holt, D., Terpstra, R., & Kai-Cheng, Y. (1997). The Impact of Natural Culture and Economic Ideology on Managerial Work Values: A Study of the United States, Russia, Japan, and China. *Journal of International Business Studies, 28*(1), 177–207. doi:10.1057/palgrave.jibs.8490097

Ramamurti, R., & Singh, J. V. (2009). *Emerging multinationals in emerging markets.* Cambridge University Press. doi:10.1017/CBO9780511576485

Ramamurti, R., & Williamson, P. J. (2019). Rivalry between emerging-market MNEs and developed-country MNEs: Capability holes and the race to the future. *Business Horizons, 62*(2), 157–169. doi:10.1016/j.bushor.2018.11.001

Rammal, H. G., Rose, E. L., & Ferreira, J. J. (2023). Managing cross-border knowledge transfer for innovation: An introduction to the special issue. *International Business Review, 32*(2), 102098. Advance online publication. doi:10.1016/j.ibusrev.2022.102098

Ratiu, I. (1983). Thinking Internationally: A Comparison of How International Executives Learn. *International Studies of Management & Organization, 13*(1-2), 139–153. doi:10.1080/00208825.1983.11656362

Ray, G., Wu, D., & Konana, P. (2009). Competitive Environment and the Relationship Between IT and Vertical Integration. *Information Systems Research, 20*(4), 585–603. doi:10.1287/isre.1080.0202

Redding, G. (2005). The Thick Description and Comparison of Societal Systems of Capitalism. *Journal of International Business Studies, 36*(2), 123–155. doi:10.1057/palgrave.jibs.8400129

Reid, M. F., & Yang, S. (2018). Organisational Institutionalism. In A. Farazmand (Ed.), *Global Encyclopedia of Public Administration, Public Policy, and Governance*. Springer., doi:10.1007/978-3-319-20928-9_91

Ribeiro, M. T., Wu, T., Guestrin, C., & Singh, S. (2020). Beyond Accuracy: Behavioral Testing of NLP Models with CheckList. In D. Jurafsky, J. Chai, N. Schluter, & J. Tetreault (Eds.), *Proceedings of the 58th Annual Meeting of the Association for Computational Linguistics*, (pp. 4902–4912). Association for Computational Linguistics. 10.18653/v1/2020.acl-main.442

Riemer, K., & Vehring, N. (2012). Virtual or vague? A literature review exposing conceptual differences in defining virtual organisations in IS research. *Electronic Markets, 22*(4), 267–282. doi:10.1007/s12525-012-0094-2

Rios, C. M., Erhardt, N. L., & Manev, I. M. (2022). Interfirm collaboration for knowledge resources interaction among small innovative companies. *Journal of Business Research, 153*, 206–215. doi:10.1016/j.jbusres.2022.08.024

Robert, G., Locock, L., Williams, O., Cornwell, J., Donetto, S., & Goodrich, J. (2022). *Co-Producing and Co-Designing*. Cambridge University Press., doi:10.1017/9781009237024

Roberts, K. H., & Boyacigiller, N. (1993). Cross-national organisational research. The grasp of the blind men. In T.D. Weinshall (Eds.), Societal Culture and Management (pp. 50-69). DeGruyter.

Roberts, E., & Berry, C. (1985). Entering new businesses: Selecting strategies for success. *Sloan Management Review, 27*, 3–17.

Robertson, B. (2015). *Holacracy: The Revolutionary Management System that Abolishes Hierarchy*. Portfolio Penguin. Penguin Random House.

Robock, S. H. (1974). The Case of Home Country Controls over Multinational Firms. *The Columbia Journal of World Business, 9*, 75–79.

Robock, S. H., Simmons, K., & Zwick, J. (1977). *International business and multinational enterprise*. Irwin.

Rodríguez-Espíndola, O., Chowdhury, S., Dey, P. K., Albores, P., & Emrouznejad, A. (2022). Analysis of the adoption of emergent technologies for risk management in the era of digital manufacturing. *Technological Forecasting and Social Change, 178*, 121562. Advance online publication. doi:10.1016/j.techfore.2022.121562

Rokeach, M. (1968a). A Theory of Organisation and Change Within Value-Attitude Systems. *The Journal of Social Issues, 24*(1), 13–33. doi:10.1111/j.1540-4560.1968.tb01466.x

Rokeach, M. (1968b). *Beliefs, Attitudes, and Values*. Jossey Bass.

Rokeach, M. (1969). The role of values in public opinion research. *Public Opinion Quarterly, 32*(4), 547–559. doi:10.1086/267645

Rokeach, M. (1973). *The Nature of Human Values*. The Free Press.

Ronen, S. (1986). *Comparative and Multinational Management*. John Wiley & Sons.

Ronen, S. (1986). Equity perception in multiple comparisons: A field study. *Human Relations*, *39*(4), 333–346. doi:10.1177/001872678603900403

Rosenzweig, P. M., & Nohria, N. (1994). Influences on Human Resource Management Practices in Multinational Corporations. *Journal of International Business Studies*, *25*(2), 229–251. doi:10.1057/palgrave.jibs.8490199

Rugiardini, A. (1979). *Organizzazione d'impresa*. Giuffrè.

Rugman, A. M., & Verbeke, A. (2008). A New Perspective on the Regional and Global Strategies of Multinational Services Firms. *MIR. Management International Review*, *48*(4), 397–411. https://www.jstor.org/stable/40658272. doi:10.1007/s11575-008-0023-y

Sakakibara, M. (1997). Evaluating government sponsored R&D consortia in Japan: Who benefits and how. *Research Policy*, *26*(4-5), 447–473. doi:10.1016/S0048-7333(97)00018-8

Salomon, R. (2016). *Global Vision. How Companies Can Overcome the Pitfalls of Globalization*. Palgrave Macmillan.

Sambharya, R., & Musteen, M. (2014). Institutional environment and entrepreneurship: An empirical study across countries. *Journal of International Entrepreneurship, 12,* 314-330. doi:10.1007/s10843-014-0137-1

Santistevan, D., & Josserand, E. (2019). Meta-Teams: Getting Global Work Done in MNEs. *Journal of Management*, *45*(2), 510–539. doi:10.1177/0149206318793184

Santos, F. P., & Williamson, P. J. (2022). Discovering Strategy: Dealing With Uncertainty By Harnessing Serendipity. *Working Paper, 2*(22). Cambridge Judge Business School.

Santos, F., & Eisenhardt, K. (2005). Organisational Boundaries and Theories of Organisation. *Organization Science*, *16*(5), 491–508. doi:10.1287/orsc.1050.0152

Santos, J. (2007). Strategy lessons from left field. *Harvard Business Review*, *85*(4), 20–21.

Santos, J. F., & Williamson, P. J. (2015). The new mission for multinationals. *MIT Sloan Management Review*, *6*(4), 45–55.

Sarfraz, M., He, B., & Shah, S. (2020). Elucidating the effectiveness of cognitive CEO on corporate environmental performance: The mediating role of corporate innovation. *Environmental Science and Pollution Research International*, *27*(36), 45938–45948. Advance online publication. doi:10.1007/s11356-020-10496-7 PMID:32808125

Sarpong, D., Boakye, D., Ofosu, G., & Botchie, D. (2023). The three pointers of research and development (R&D) for growth-boosting sustainable innovation system. *Technovation*, *122*, 102581. Advance online publication. doi:10.1016/j.technovation.2022.102581

Schaan, J. L., & Beamish, P. W. (1988). Joint venture general managers in LCD's. In F. Contractor & P. Lorange (Eds.), Cooperative strategies in international business (pp. 279–299). Academic Press.

Schein, E. H. (1984). Coming to a New Awareness of Organisational Culture. *Sloan Management Review*, *25*, 3–16.

Schein, E. H. (1985). *Organisation Culture and Leadership*. Jossey-Bass.

Schein, E. H. (1986). International Human Resource Management: New Directions, Perpetual Issues and Missing Opportunities. *Human Resource Management*, *25*(1), 169–176. doi:10.1002/hrm.3930250112

Schneider, S. (1988). National vs Corporate Culture: Implications for Human Resource Management. *Human Resource Management*, *27*(2), 231–246. doi:10.1002/hrm.3930270207

Schneider, S. C. (1989). Strategy Formulation: The Impact of National Culture. *Organization Studies*, *10*(2), 157–176. doi:10.1177/017084068901000202

Schollhammer, H. (1969). The Comparative Management Theory Jungle. *Academy of Management Journal*, *12*(1), 81–97. doi:10.2307/254675

Schotter, A. P. J., Mudambi, R., Doz, Y. L., & Gaur, A. (2017). Boundary spanning in global organisations. *Journal of Management Studies*, *54*(4), 403–421. doi:10.1111/joms.12256

Schuler, R. S., & Jackson, S. E. (1996). *Human Resource Management: Positioning for the 21st Century* (6th ed.). West Publishing Company.

Schuler, R., Budhwar, P., & Florkowski, G. (2002). International Human Resource Management: Review and Critique. *International Journal of Management Reviews*, *4*(1), 41–70. Advance online publication. doi:10.1111/1468-2370.00076

Schwartz, S. H. (1994). Are there universal aspects in the structure and contents of human values? *The Journal of Social Issues*, *50*(4), 19–45. doi:10.1111/j.1540-4560.1994.tb01196.x

Scott-Kennel, J., & Enderwick, P. (2004). Inter-firm alliance and network relationships and the eclectic paradigm of international production: An exploratory analysis of quasi-internalisation at the subsidiary level. *International Business Review*, *13*(4), 425–445. doi:10.1016/j.ibusrev.2004.03.004

Scott-Kennel, J., & Saittakari, I. (2019). Sourcing or sharing in MNE networks? National headquarters and foreign subsidiaries as knowledge conduits in SMOPECs. *International Business Review*, *29*(1), 101622. Advance online publication. doi:10.1016/j.ibusrev.2019.101622

Seidenberg, R. (1973). *Marriage between equals: Studies from life and literature*. Anchor Press.

Sekaran, U., & Snodgrass, C. R. (1986). A Model for Examining Organisational Effectiveness Cross-Culturally. *Advances in Intemational Comparative Management*, *2*, 211–232. doi:10.2139/ssrn.2159716

Senge, P. M. (1990). *The Fifth Discipline*. The Art & Practice of The Learning Organisation.

Shaffer, M. A., Harrison, D. A., & Gilley, K. M. (2019). *Expatriate Adaptation and Effectiveness: Current Directions and Future Challenges*. Routledge.

Shepherd, D. A., & Patzelt, H. (2018). Motivation and Entrepreneurial Cognition. In *Entrepreneurial Cognition*. Palgrave Macmillan., doi:10.1007/978-3-319-71782-1_3

Sinclair, A. (1993). Approaches to organisational culture and ethics. *Journal of Business Ethics*, *12*(1), 63–73. doi:10.1007/BF01845788

Smale, A., & Suutari, V. (2011). Expatriate perspectives on knowledge transfers into Central and Eastern Europe. In S. Mariano, M. Mohamed, & Q. Mohiuddin (Eds.), *The role of expatriates in MNCs knowledge mobilization* (pp. 63–90). Emerald Group Publishing Limited. doi:10.1108/S1876-066X(2011)0000027007

Smelser, N. J. (1982). *La comparazione nelle scienze sociali*. Il Mulino.

Smircich, L. (1983). Concepts of Culture and Organisational Analysis. *Administrative Science Quarterly*, *28*(3), 339–358. doi:10.2307/2392246

Smith, K.G., & Grimm, C.M. (1987). *Environmental variation, strategic change and firm performance: A study of railroad deregulation.* . doi:10.1002/smj.4250080406

Song, J., Almeida, P., & Wu, G. (2003). Learning-by-Hiring: When Is Mobility More Likely to Facilitate Interfirm Knowledge Transfer? *Management Science, 49*(4), 351–365. doi:10.1287/mnsc.49.4.351.14429

Sorge, A. (1983). Cultured organisation. *International Studies of Management & Organization, 12*(4), 106–138. doi:10.1080/00208825.1982.11656353

Sorge, A., & Warner, M. (1981). Culture, Management & Manufacturing Organisation: A Study of British and German Firms. *Management International Review, 21*(1), 35–48. https://www.jstor.org/stable/40227575

Stallkamp, M., Chen, L., & Li, S. (2023). Boots on the ground: Foreign direct investment by born digital firms. *Global Strategy Journal, 13*(4), 1–25. doi:10.1002/gsj.1474

Stallkamp, M., & Schotter, A. P. (2021). Platforms without borders? The international strategies of digital platform firms. *Global Strategy Journal, 11*(1), 58–80. doi:10.1002/gsj.1336

Starbuck, W. H. (1985). Acting first and thinking later: Theory versus reality in strategic change. In J. M. Pennings (Ed.), *Organisational Strategy and Change* (pp. 336–372). Jossey Bass.

Stopford, J. M., & Wells, L. T. (1972). *Managing the Multinational Enterprise.* Basic Books.

Swaminathan, V., & Moorman, C. (2009). Marketing Alliances, Firm Networks, and Firm Value Creation. *Journal of Marketing, 73*(5), 52–69. doi:10.1509/jmkg.73.5.52

Syed, J., & Tariq, M. (2017). Global Diversity Management. In Oxford research Encyclopedia of business and management. Oxford University Press. https://doi.org/ doi:10.1093/acrefore/9780190224851.013.62

Tannenbaum, R., & Schmidt, W.H. (1958). How to choose a leadership pattern. *Harvard Business Review, 36*(2), 162–80.

Tannenbaum, A. S., & Cooke, R. A. (1979). Organisational control: a review of studies employing the control graph method. In C. J. Lammers & D. J. Hickson (Eds.), *Organisations Alike and Unlike.* Routledge & Kegan Paul.

Teece, D. J. (2006). Reflections on the Hymer thesis and the multinational enterprise. *International Business Review, 15*(2), 124–139. doi:10.1016/j.ibusrev.2005.11.003

Teece, D. (2014). A dynamic capabilities-based entrepreneurial theory of the multinational enterprise. *Journal of International Business Studies, 45*(1), 8–37. doi:10.1057/jibs.2013.54

Teece, D. J., Pisano, G., & Shuen, A. (1997). Dynamic capabilities and strategic management. *Strategic Management Journal, 18*(7), 509–533. doi:10.1002/(SICI)1097-0266(199708)18:7<509::AID-SMJ882>3.0.CO;2-Z

Terpstra, V. (1985). *The Cultural Environment of International Business* (2nd ed.). South Western.

Thompson, J. D. (1967). *Organisation in Action.* McGraw-Hill.

Tondolo, V., & Bitencourt, C. (2014). Understanding Dynamic Capabilities from Its Antecedents, Processes and Outcomes. *Brazilian Business Review, 11*(5), 122–144. doi:10.15728/bbr.2014.11.5.6

Triandis, H. C. (1983). Dimensions of Cultural Variations Parameters of Organisational Thrones-. *International Studies of Management & Organization, 11*(4), 285–302. doi:10.1002/1520-6629(198310)11:4<285:AID-JCOP2290110403>3.0.CO;2-8

Triandis, H. C. (1995). *Individualism and Collectivism.* Westview Press.

Triandis, H. C. (2004). The Many Dimensions of Culture. *The Academy of Management Perspectives*, *18*(1), 88–93. doi:10.5465/ame.2004.12689599

Trompenaars, F., & Hampden-Turner, C. (1997). *Riding the Waves of Culture: Understanding Diversity in Global Business*. McGraw-Hill.

Trompenaars, F., & Hampden-Turner, C. (2004). *Managing people across Cultures*. Capstone Publishing Ltd.

Trompenaars, F., & Wolliams, P. (2003). *Business across Cultures*. Capstone Publishing Ltd.

Tullio-Altan, C. (1996). Un percorso di pensiero. *Belfagor*, *51*(3), 303–319. https://www.jstor.org/stable/26147782

Tung, R. (1984). Human Resource Planning in Japanese Multinationals: A Model for U.S. Firms? *Journal of International Business Studies*, *15*(2), 139–149. doi:10.1057/palgrave.jibs.8490487

Tung, R. (1987). Expatriate assignments: Enhancing success and minimizing failure. *The Academy of Management Executive*, *1*, 117–126.

Tung, R. L. (1981). Selection and Training of Personnel for Overseas Assignments. *The Columbia Journal of World Business*, *16*(1), 68–78.

Tung, R. L. (1982). Selection and Training Procedures of US, European and Japanese MNCs. *California Management Review*, *25*(1), 57–71. doi:10.2307/41164993

Tung, R. L. (1984). Strategic Management of Human Resources in the Multinational Enterprises. *Human Resource Management*, *23*(2), 129–143. doi:10.1002/hrm.3930230204

Tung, R. L. (1988). *The New Expatriate*. Ballinger Publishing Company.

Tung, R. L. (1998). A contingency framework of selection and training of expatriates revisited. *Human Resource Management Review*, *8*(1), 23–37. doi:10.1016/S1053-4822(99)80038-2

Turati, C. (1990). Economia ed organizzazione delle joint venture. EGEA.

Turati, C. (1990). *Economia e organizzazione delle joint venture*. Egea.

Uckamr, V. (2005). *Global Business*. Etas Libri.

Vaccà, S., & Zanfei, A. (1989). L'impresa globale come "sistema aperto" a rapporti di cooperazione. *Economia e Politica Industriale*, 64.

Vaccà, S., & Zanfei, A. (1989). L'impresa globale come sistema aperto a rapporti di cooperazione. *Economia e Politica Industriale*, *64*, 47–89.

VakulchukR.OverlandI.ScholtenD. (2020). Renewable Energy and Geopolitics: A Review. *Renewable and Sustainable Energy Reviews*, *122*, 109547. https://ssrn.com/abstract=3565990

Valdani, E. (1991). *Marketing globale*. Egea.

Van Maanen, J., & Schein, E. H. (1978). Toward a theory of organisation socialization. *Research in Organizational Behavior*, *1*, 209–226.

Verbeke, A., Coeurderoy, R., & Matt, T. (2018). The future of international business research on corporate globalization that never was. *Journal of International Business Studies*, *49*(9), 1101–1112. doi:10.1057/s41267-018-0192-2

Vernon, R. (1966). International Trade and International Investment in the Product Cycle. *The Quarterly Journal of Economics*, *80*(2), 190–207. doi:10.2307/1880689

Vicari. (1991). *L'impresa vivente*. Franco Angeli.

Vieira, E. S. (2023). The influence of research collaboration on citation impact: The countries in the European Innovation Scoreboard. *Scientometrics*, *128*(6), 3555–3579. doi:10.1007/s11192-023-04715-4

Vogel, D. (1991). Business Ethics: New Perspectives on Old Problems. *California Management Review*, *33*(4), 101–117. doi:10.2307/41166675

Von Borell, D., & Franco, M. (2017). Trust-Building Mechanisms in a Coopetition Relationship: A Case Study Design. *The International Journal of Organizational Analysis*, *25*(3), 378–394. Advance online publication. doi:10.1108/IJOA-04-2016-1012

Vuchkovski, D., Zalaznik, M., Mitręga, M., & Pfajfar, G. (2023). A look at the future of work: The digital transformation of teams from conventional to virtual. *Journal of Business Research*, *163*, 113912. Advance online publication. doi:10.1016/j.jbusres.2023.113912

Wadhwa, V., Aggarwal, R., & Holly, K. (2018). *The Immigrant Exodus: Why America Is Losing the Global Race to Capture Entrepreneurial Talent*. Wharton Digital Press.

Wan, F., Williamson, P., & Yin, E. (2015). Antecedents and implications of disruptive innovation: Evidence from China. *Technovation*, *39-40*, 94–104. doi:10.1016/j.technovation.2014.05.012

Wang, J., & Houston, V. (2011). Expatriate Selection: The Key to International Success. *The International Business & Economics Research Journal*, *1*(11). Advance online publication. doi:10.19030/iber.v1i11.3999

Wankmüller, C., & Reiner, G. (2020). Coordination, cooperation and collaboration in relief supply chain management. *Journal of Business Economics*, *90*(2), 239–276. doi:10.1007/s11573-019-00945-2

Weaver, G. R. (1993). Corporate Codes of Ethics: Purpose, Process and Content Issues. *Business & Society*, *32*(1), 44–58. doi:10.1177/000765039303200106

Weber, Y., & Tarba, S. Y. (2014). Strategic Agility: A State of the Art: Introduction to the Special Section on Strategic Agility. *California Management Review*, *56*(3), 5–12. doi:10.1525/cmr.2014.56.3.5

Weick, K. E. (1969). Social psychology in an era of social change. *The American Psychologist*, *24*(11), 990–998. doi:10.1037/h0028881

Weick, K. E. (1969). *The Social Psychology of Organizing*. Addison-Wesley.

Wells, L. T. (2016). Third World Multinationals: A Retrospective. In Progress in International Business Research. Emerald Group Publishing. doi:10.1108/S1745-886220160000011003

West, D. M. (2020). *Digital governance: New technologies for improving public service and participation*. Brookings Institution Press.

West, J., & Graham, J. L. (2004). A Linguistic-based Measure of Cultural Distance and Its Relationship to Managerial Values. *MIR. Management International Review*, *44*(3), 239–260. https://www.jstor.org/stable/40835991

Williamson, P. J., & Santos, J. F. P. (2021). Emerging Economies: The Impact of Context on Global Strategic Management. In I.M. Duhaime, M.A. Hitt, & Lyles, M. A. (Eds.), Strategic management: State of the field and its future (pp. 319-335). Oxford University Press.

Williamson, O. E. (1975). *Markets and Hierarchies: Analysis and Antitrust Implications*. Free Press.

Williamson, O. E. W. (1975). *Market and Hierarchies*. The Free Press.

Williamson, O. E. W. (1981). The Economics of Organisations: The Transaction Cost Approach. *American Journal of Sociology*, *87*(3), 548–577. doi:10.1086/227496

Williamson, P. J. (2015). The Competitive Advantages of Emerging Market Multinationals: A Re-assessment. *Critical Perspectives on International Business*, *11*(3/4), 216–235. doi:10.1108/cpoib-02-2014-0008

Williamson, P. J. (2016a). Building and Leveraging Dynamic Capabilities: Insights from Accelerated Innovation in China. *Global Strategy Journal*, *6*(3), 197–210. doi:10.1002/gsj.1124

Williamson, P. J. (2016b). Chinese acquisitions in Europe: Absorptive capability and impacts on competitive advantage. *International Relations*, *13*(49), 61–83.

Wilson, D. (1990). A Dynamic Approach to Strategic Alliances. efmd Research Conference, Barcelona.

Windelband, W. (1998). History and natural science. *Theory & Psychology*, *8*(1), 5–22. doi:10.1177/0959354398081001

Wind, Y., Douglas, S. P., & Perlmutter, H. V. (1973). Guidelines for Developing International Marketing Strategies. *Journal of Marketing*. *Journal of Marketing*, *37*(2), 14–23. doi:10.1177/002224297303700205

Woodward, J. (1965). *Industrial organisation: Theory and Practice*. Oxford University Press.

Xu, K., Hitt, M. A., Brock, D., Pisano, V., & Huang, L. S. R. (2021). Country institutional environments and international strategy: A review and analysis of the research. *Journal of International Management*, *27*(1), 100811. Advance online publication. doi:10.1016/j.intman.2020.100811

Yun, C. K. (1973). Role Conflicts of Expatriate Managers: A Construct. *Management International Review*, *13*(3). Advance online publication. doi:10.1177/239700229901300302

Zaheer, S. (1995). Overcoming the Liability of Foreignness. *Academy of Management Journal*, *38*(2), 341–363. doi:10.2307/256683

Zamenopoulos, T., & Alexiou, K. (2018). Co-Design as Collaborative Research. *Open Research Online*. Connected Communities Foundation Series. University of Bristol/AHRC.

Zeira, Y. (1976). Management Development in Ethnocentric Multinational Corporations. *California Management Review*, *18*(4), 34–42. doi:10.2307/41164666

Zeira, Y., & Banai, M. (1985). Selection of Expatriate Managers in MNCs: The Host-Environment Point of View. *International Studies of Management & Organization*, *15*(1), 33–51. doi:10.1080/00208825.1985.11656402

Zeira, Y., & Harari, E. (1977). Managing third-country nationals in multinational companys. *Business Horizons*, *20*(5), 83–88. doi:10.1016/0007-6813(77)90062-3

Zeira, Y., & Harari, E. (1979). Host-Country Organisations and Expatriate Managers in Europe. *California Management Review*, *21*(3), 40–50. doi:10.2307/41165306

Zeira, Y., Harari, E., & Nundi, D. I. (1975). Some Structural and Cultural Factors in Ethnocentric MNCs and Employees Morale. *Journal of Management Studies*, *12*(1-2), 66–82. doi:10.1111/j.1467-6486.1975.tb00887.x

Zeng, M., & Williamson, P. J. (2007). *Dragons At Your Door: How Chinese Cost Innovation Is Disrupting Global Competition*. Harvard Business School Press.

Zhao, S. (1999). Joint Ventures for Entry Deterrence. *MDE. Managerial and Decision Economics*, *20*(1), 25–35. doi:10.1002/(SICI)1099-1468(199902)20:1<25::AID-MDE915>3.0.CO;2-4

Zimmerman, M. (1985). *How to do Business with the Japanese*. Randon House.

About the Authors

Alessandra Ricciardelli holds a Master of ScIence in Development Studies at the University of Oxford in 2004. She obtained her Phd in Economics and Management of Natural Resources at LUM University where she is lecturer of Organizational Behaviour. She also teaches a complementary course in Economics and Management of Smart Cities. She also works in the LUM School of Management as a Scientific Coordinator of several post-graduate Master courses related to Public Administration issues. From 2018 she also carries out professional activity as an EY Advisory consultant for local development. In 2019 she was appointed as a Researcher of Management at National School of Administration. In the same year, she has been Visiting Scholar at MIT Media Lab. Her research interests are: organizational power relations, organizational aesthetics, organizational culture, leadership,relationships, work climate and job crafting.

Maurizio Decastri, PhD, is a Full Professor of Organizational Management at the University of Rome Tor Vergata since 2001 where is has also served as Vice Rector for Personnel and Organization. He teaches courses on Organizational Management, Cross-Cultural Management, and Organizational and Human Resource Management that are also his main research interests. He is also member of companies' board of Directors in Italy.

Index

www.ingramcontent.com/pod-product-compliance
Lightning Source LLC
LaVergne TN
LVHW060418300926
849162LV00006B/1460